The Private Life of
Thomas Cromwell

The Private Life of Thomas Cromwell

Caroline Angus

PEN & SWORD
HISTORY

First published in Great Britain in 2022 by
Pen & Sword History
An imprint of
Pen & Sword Books Ltd
Yorkshire – Philadelphia

ISBN 978 1 39909 581 5

A CIP catalogue record for this book is
available from the British Library.

Typeset by Mac Style
Printed and bound in the UK by CPI Group (UK) Ltd,
Croydon, CR0 4YY.

FSC
www.fsc.org

MIX
Paper from
responsible sources
FSC® C013604

Pen & Sword Books Limited incorporates the imprints of Atlas,
Archaeology, Aviation, Discovery, Family History, Fiction, History,
Maritime, Military, Military Classics, Politics, Select, Transport,
True Crime, Air World, Frontline Publishing, Leo Cooper, Remember
When, Seaforth Publishing, The Praetorian Press, Wharncliffe
Local History, Wharncliffe Transport, Wharncliffe True Crime
and White Owl.

For a complete list of Pen & Sword titles please contact

PEN & SWORD BOOKS LIMITED
47 Church Street, Barnsley, South Yorkshire, S70 2AS, England
E-mail: enquiries@pen-and-sword.co.uk
Website: www.pen-and-sword.co.uk

Or

PEN AND SWORD BOOKS
1950 Lawrence Rd, Havertown, PA 19083, USA
E-mail: Uspen-and-sword@casematepublishers.com
Website: www.penandswordbooks.com

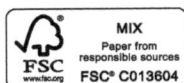

For Grayson, Torben, Espen
and Lachlan
You have my eternal love, appreciation,
adoration and devotion

Contents

Thomas Cromwell

John Cromwell — Margaret Smyth

John Cromwell — Joan Smyth

Walter Cromwell — Katherine Meverell

Margaret Cromwell — William Michell (unknown niece)

Ellen Michell — Ralph Sadler

Thomas Sadler and six others

Thomas Cromwell — Elizabeth Wyckes

Katherine Cromwell — Morgan Williams

Elizabeth Cromwell — William Wellyfed

Gregory Cromwell — Elizabeth Seymour

Anne Cromwell

Grace Cromwell

Jane Cromwell — William Hough

Alice Hough

Sir John Williams — Frances Murfyn

Richard Cromwell — Frances Murfyn
Gregory Williams
Walter Cromwell

Henry Cromwell
Francis Cromwell

Christopher Wellyfed
William Wellyfed
Alice Wellyfed — 1 Thomas Rotherham / 2 Ralph Astney

George Rotherham
two daughters

Richard Cromwell
Oliver Cromwell

Joan Cromwell
Anne Cromwell
son unknown

Thomas Cromwell
Katherine Cromwell

Frances Cromwell — John Williamson

Joan Williamson

Joan Wyckes — 1 Henry Wyckes / 2 Sir John Prior

Mercy unknown

Henry Cromwell
Edward Cromwell

Cromwell Family Tree

Acknowledgements

As always, my deepest appreciation goes to my four children, Grayson, Torben, Espen, and Lachlan, for listening to my constant discussion about Cromwell over the last decade. You probably know more than you ever wished.

After publishing a book on Thomas Cromwell's letters, it is obvious that Cromwell appears not in his own words, but in the words of others. He went to great lengths to keep himself quiet, and so it is the authors, the scholars, the letter-writers, and the clerks who have filled in the gaps left by England's only Vicegerent. It took a year for Cromwell's belongings to be gathered and catalogued after his death, by which time most paperwork was destroyed, and so those of us who love Cromwell have relied on the talents of early biographers like Ralph Morice, George Cavendish, Edward Lord Herbert of Chirbury, John Foxe, Alexander Alesius, Edward Hall, and Thomas Fuller. The bulk of surviving Cromwell documents are now in the National Archives and the British Library, both sets from a singular collection ripped open in the seventeenth and nineteenth centuries.

Because Cromwell's story lies not in what he left behind, but in the dark spaces where his presence is hidden, two online resources are invaluable and hold a deep place in my heart. Firstly, State Papers Online, 1509–1714, by Cengage/Gale in through the National Archives and the British Library. Without these thousands of documents available, historians like me could not complete our work, and so remain forever in my debt. Secondly, Letters and Papers Foreign and Domestic, Henry VIII through British History Online, is a vast achievement in Victorian academic research, giving us insight to the inner workings of the lives of the Tudor period for anyone willing to listen. This resource is available for anyone to use, and so I tend to use it as a point of reference where possible, so that readers can quickly access notes on primary sources at their own leisure.

There are so many authors to thank, it is almost impossible to list everyone. Above all, thank you to Diarmaid MacCulloch, whose work on Thomas Cromwell is incomparable. To couple this, MacCulloch's work on Thomas Cranmer is unrivaled. Thank you to Nick Holder, whose work on Austin Friars is unmatched, and to Lauren Mackay, whose work on Thomas Boleyn and Eustace Chapuys is boundless. Many other authors have provided inspiration: Melita Thomas and her illuminating work on the Grey dynasty; Owen Emmerson's adoration of Anne Boleyn; Janet Wertman and her studious research on the Seymour family; Heather Darsie's revelations about Anna of Cleves; Adrienne Dillard's accuracy on Jane Boleyn; Thomas Penn's invaluable discoveries on the Frescobaldi smuggling trade; Terri FitzGerald's tireless work on Richard Cromwell; Amy Licence's faithful illumination of Katherine of Aragon; Natalie Grueninger's commitment to Tudor architecture; Heidi Malagisi's continuous support; and Sylvia Barbara Soberton's limitless knowledge of Tudor women.

My sincerest thanks go to all those who helped me at Pen & Sword – Claire Hopkins, Laura Hirst, Lucy May, Eleri Pipien, and Sarah-Beth Watkins. My undying and grateful thanks go to Grayson Angus-Baker for being my proofreader and constant sounding board. I deeply appreciate the support. As support comes in so many forms, I have so many people on Twitter who listen to my constant complaints about writing, whether it is the writers and readers of history, or the eclectic group of New Zealanders on kiwi twitter. The online support during the times we live in is invaluable. Finally, thank you to Thomas Cromwell, for going on such an adventure that created a life so diverse of all those around him, paving the way for a new world.

Introduction

No one expects a pawn to take the queen.

The men and women who dared to defy Thomas Cromwell rarely noticed when he laid in wait to destroy them. A charming, ruthless, and scrupulous man from Putney became the right man, at the right place, at the right time to upset an entire country. Someone needed to be the one to pull England from the medieval period into the light of renaissance and reformation, and it fell on the shoulders of an unassuming merchant turned lawyer, who had no desire to rule.

After languishing in archives for centuries, Thomas Cromwell, or Crumwell, as he was known, is now notorious and well-assumed to be the man behind King Henry VIII. Cromwell has become popular in fiction and non-fiction alike, yet many tropes remain. The man who killed Anne Boleyn. The man who destroyed the monasteries. A dull, overweight man who plodded the royal halls destroying lives, who got what he deserved in July 1540. But how much is true, and how much makes for a convenient scapegoat in history, or an easy villain in novels?

A man whose formal education, in the weakest form of the expression, comprised of basic reading and writing became the shrewdest, most formidable man in the kingdom and entirely reformed English government. Cromwell grew up in a household that understood the importance of honest labour, and yet also knew how to leave international diplomats hanging on his words. His father was a yeoman, his mother from a simple but respected family, and yet Cromwell learned to speak the languages of European kings and queens, popes and emperors. The disparity could not be more astonishing. But King Henry liked men from less auspicious backgrounds; common men had no supporters, and this brief window of opportunity gave Thomas Cromwell an elevation he never sought.

To go from the family home of selling beer and fulling cloth, to a clerk in Florence, and then a certified lawyer and merchant in the Italian community of London was a grand elevation. How was it done? With a personality that drew in friends, and a community of people who valued one another. While the nobility jostled for power, living on what they believed they were owed, the commoners carved out their own lives. There, in the merchant streets of east London, Thomas Cromwell and his family developed everything they wanted. Only when Thomas Cromwell's master, Cardinal Wolsey, was betrayed and ruined did Cromwell dare poke his head into the royal court to help a man in need. This uncharacteristic move led to ten years of English reformation, both in religion and governance, and the creation or destruction of four queens.

When a man was pulled from his life at his king's command, thrust into a world not his own, he needed friends and supporters. Cromwell's rise at court is often described as startling, unforeseen, rapid, yet Cromwell was a man well-placed for such a position. Nothing happened by surprise, and no successes came by luck. Thomas Cromwell was no quiet loner, but a man surrounded by family and friends, giving him a private life filled with the support that could propel him to public revolution.

Chapter 1

1485–1504: Adventure

'nothing as so hard with which wit and industry he could not compass'

On the day Henry Tudor, Earl of Richmond, battled King Richard III at the Battle of Bosworth in 1485, the men who would control the royal court one generation later were taking their first steps in splendid and well-appointed nurseries. Thomas Howard was learning to walk around Kenninghall Manor. Charles Brandon was blissfully unaware his father would not return home from battle. Thomas More was attending class at St Anthony's School outside London. But men, both noble and common, fought for the future of England, men like farrier Walter Cromwell shoeing horses for Henry Tudor's army.[1] His infant son Thomas was at home in Putney, none of the family under any impression the boy would one day control England beside the future king's son.

The origins of the Cromwell family suffer the fate of anyone born beneath the noble class, with their births, deaths and marriages not recorded. In the absence of evidence, a mixture of half-truths, guesses and fabrications have filled the vacuum over the past 500 years.

The nineteenth-century theory has been told many times, a mixture of guesswork and poor assumptions. The story begins with Robert, Lord Cromwell of Coleton, who died in the devastating Battle of Towton in 1461 while aiding Edward IV.[2] While the Cromwell family estate was in Norwell, Nottinghamshire, his son William Cromwell had been granted land in Wandsworth in 1452 by Archbishop John Kemp. William Cromwell gave up much of his family land in Palacehall in Norwell and he and his wife Margaret Smyth relocated south to Putney in the heart of the Wandsworth and Wimbledon areas.[3] This long-accepted tale of the Cromwell family was thrown into doubt, when, a century later, Sir George Paulet, charged by his king to quell rebellion in Ireland, let down his guard and told slanderous stories of England's Lord Privy Seal.

While speaking poorly of Thomas Lord Cromwell's treatment of the rebellious FitzGeralds, arguing Cromwell had been too lenient, Paulet said, 'the lord Cromwell was so affectionate unto the same land because his ancestors were born there and had been the cause of the King wasting his treasure in suppressing the Geraldines'.[4] The FitzGerald family ruled the huge county of Kildare, west of Dublin, for almost 100 years before King Henry VIII gave the country to Thomas Cromwell, expecting it to be ruled from London. While Paulet's comments could have simply been a mistake, the information came from eyewitness accounts. It is entirely possible a young Walter Cromwell came over from Ireland with his parents and bore little or no relation to the Norwell Cromwell family at all. On the other hand, Paulet was also heard to say, 'a pelican would fly out of Ireland to England to do marvellous things', such as predict the future. Each theory about the Cromwell family seems as obscure as the other.

But what is certain, is that the land in Putney, leased from Archbishop Kemp, gave William Cromwell approximately sixty acres and a fuller mill,[5] a building on the edge of the Thames with a watermill for making fabric. William and Margaret Cromwell had two sons, William and John, with John soon taking over as the patriarch, claiming the mill and lands,[6] describing himself as the 'fuller of Wandsworth'. John Cromwell married his cousin Joan Smyth in the early 1460s and together they had three surviving children: Walter, John, and Margaret.[7]

The Cromwell and Smyth families could not claim to be much in society. A man could call only himself a yeoman if he owned the land he worked. John and Joan's daughter Margaret Cromwell married William Michell, and they appear to have moved to Sussex to raise their children.[8] John Cromwell described himself as a beer-brewer and possibly gained himself a part-time job as a cook for the new archbishop at nearby Mortlake Manor, five miles upstream from Putney.[9] The Wandsworth farmlands went to son Walter around the time of his marriage in 1474, a man whose character has taken multiple turns throughout history.

Walter Cromwell, like most people of the period, is difficult to track. He appears to have been born earlier than his siblings and is likely to have been a blacksmith's apprentice, as he took his mother's maiden name of Smyth at times.[10] It would have been a straightforward way for young Walter to be put to work with his relatives. With his father John being a cloth-fuller, this meant Walter could grow up with knowledge of multiple trades. Putney sat on the edge of the Thames, a collection of timber houses with whitewashed walls to hide the tar sealing the homes from the weather. These buildings afforded a basic life, all one-room homes where animals were brought inside in the winter to generate heat. Chimneys began to replace open hearths, but only for those who could afford them. The floor of a Putney home would be covered in rushes and herbs to mask the smell of the muddy lanes and the people who had only basic bathing and laundry facilities. The streets around Putney were not safe, and while London, six miles downstream, was written about with great generosity for its fine walls, cathedrals and bridges, Putney would have felt a thousand miles away from the wealthy city.

Another theory of how the Cromwell family gained land in Putney is a claim Walter and his brother John were granted ownership of the leased land as a reward for fighting for Henry VII at Bosworth.[11] It is likely Walter's brother John turned the main Putney home into an alehouse alongside Walter's cloth-making business in the mid-1470s, though as owner, Walter was summoned to court forty-eight times for breaking the assizes of ale over the next twenty-six years.[12] The Brewers Company regularly attempted to regulate beer-brewing, leaving already struggling families like the Cromwells at the mercy of the courts. These constant charges have long been assumed to be a result of Walter Cromwell watering down ale, but this is another half-truth made into fact. Beer needed to be checked by ale-testers before being sold, and the regulations changed dramatically over this period, turning what was a basic industry into a heavy-regulated money-spinner for local government in a short period. There is nothing to suggest anything was amiss with Cromwell ale, rather that changes to centuries-old habits were hard on small producers.

In 1477, Walter was again in the courts, after assaulting Thomas Michell, his brother-in-law's brother, and was fined twenty pence, or roughly two days' wages.[13] Between working as a blacksmith, a fuller, and running an alehouse, it was little wonder Walter's cattle often strayed off their pasture, with Walter also in court multiple times for allowing his cattle to graze on public pasture. All was not bad though, as by 1500, Walter had amassed 240 acres of land around Wandsworth and straightened himself out, working as a constable in Putney, and serving as a juryman.[14] He was likely a man of his time; a hard man forged in a hard life, a world where a man worked or starved, and with little entertainment or diversion other than ale.

The Cromwell alehouse was aptly named the Anchor,[15] on tiny Brewhouse Lane on the shore of the Thames where barges and ferries would cross the river (where Putney Bridge stands today). Beer brewing was predominately the work of women until around the early sixteenth century when government regulations handed the work to men.[16] Walter's wife was likely one such brewster or alewife, helping to run their business interests. In the late 1470s, Walter married Katherine Meverell, a daughter of Thomas Meverell of Throwley in Derbyshire,[17] and one of the many daughters (legitimate or illegitimate) of Sir John Babington.[18] How Katherine and Walter met remains a mystery. Katherine had been working for lawyer John Walbeck, likely put into his household at a young age, which could help explain how she managed to travel 140 miles from her parents' home in Derbyshire.

Sadly, the family connections of Katherine Meverell cannot be accurately traced, not even her first name. It is only through cousins such as Arthur and Francis Meverell[19] and John Babington[20] that her surname appears, and a mention she had a sister who married a Glossop in Derbyshire.[21] Even her age is in doubt thanks to an off-hand comment made by her son decades later. Katherine Meverell had daughters Katherine and Elizabeth in the early 1480s, followed by a son, Thomas, in approximately 1485. Baby Thomas would one day grow up to tell Imperial ambassador Eustace Chapuys his mother was fifty-two years old when she had her son,[22] though this may have been a lie Cromwell told while defending Queen Katherine years later. Walter Cromwell would have married a woman thirty years his senior for this to be true, but then he was not the first man to marry in such a manner, particularly if she came from a family of minor gentry with a dowry. It is also claimed Walter was not the actual father of Katherine, Elizabeth, or Thomas, as their mother married multiple times, and yet there is also no evidence of this occurring either. When John Foxe wrote of Thomas Cromwell's mother marrying several times, he may have simply confused Cromwell's mother with his mother-in-law.[23]

Life at the Anchor cannot have been peaceful or pleasant. The rushes on the floor would have to cover the smell of brewing ale and the customers who drank it while wearing shoes covered in foul pathway mud, not to mention the fishery on Brewhouse Lane. Thomas and his family would have slept on straw mattresses on the floor, perfect for attracting rats and lice, and in summer, the plague drifted upstream from London. Families such as the Cromwells may have had partitions in their open living space, and all bathroom and laundry facilities were outside the house.[24] Many of the foods available in London were probably also available in Putney, with the barges going back and forth with goods for the city. Fish was abundant, along with oysters collected on the Thames shore. Beef, mutton, rabbit, deer, and swan were all also available for a price, and the Cromwells had plenty of land to raise cattle and sheep.[25] A child such as Thomas would have been sent away as an apprentice in another household by the age of about seven.[26] Whether Thomas received any basic education or entered a seven-year apprenticeship is unknown. Thomas may have opted to work fulling cloth for the family, being the only son and unable to be spared. By the time future King Henry VIII was born in 1491, Thomas' childhood would have been over, put to work in the harsh landscape of Putney.

A possible way to alleviate the manner of living would be to work in a wealthy household. With Thomas' uncle John just upstream in the kitchens at Mortlake Manor, it could have been advantageous to hope for a position in Cardinal Morton's country home on the rare occasion he stayed at Mortlake. Yet it seems Thomas did not try to gain favour at Mortlake. Thomas was 'comfortable with humble beginnings',[27] and never sought to hide or lie about his early life in Putney. He told Eustace Chapuys he had spent time in prison as a teen, the reason or length of the stint unmentioned.[28] There is no way to know what happened, nor any record in Wimbledon of a Thomas Cromwell being in jail. Some have claimed a Thomas Smyth imprisoned in Putney is Thomas Cromwell using another surname. Thomas Smyth was a common name, so common there was one either on trial, or on a jury, every year. Sentences for imprisonment varied at the time, and even young people, essentially children, could be in prison for crimes or debts. Fathers could also have their sons imprisoned without cause 'for correction', and this theory could hold weight if Walter Cromwell was the brute some narratives suggest. Commentators have laid the claim Thomas and his father were on offensive terms, or that Walter Cromwell was violent, but these also have only a theoretical base. There is no reason for Thomas to have lied to Chapuys about his time in prison, nor for Chapuys to lie, so we can only assume Thomas spent at least a quick spell in prison for unknown reasons. Many crimes were settled with fines, and acts of theft, fraud, deception, and assault would generally carry short penalties, measured in days or weeks. Only serious and violent crimes would receive a full year. Thomas was no innocent babe; by his own admission he was a ruffian,[29] a bully or thug in his Putney days.

Around the turn of the century, the Cromwell family was on the move. Paperwork shows Walter and Katherine living in Wandsworth rather than Putney in 1501.[30] Husbands were found for daughters Katherine and Elizabeth. Katherine married well in the new century, to an aspiring lawyer named Morgan Williams, a Welsh gentleman well-known and respected in the area.[31] This became a lifelong link between the Cromwell family and Wales, particularly the Llanishen region outside Cardiff. The Williams and Cromwell families would be ever more intertwined, the marriage excellent for Katherine. Katherine and Morgan soon moved to Wales where their sons were born, before returning to England a little over a decade later.

Elizabeth Cromwell married William Wellyfed, son of a sheep farming family, after the Cromwell family shifted to Wandsworth.[32] While this marriage brought no advantages, it appeared to be a happy match for Elizabeth, and Wellyfed worked for the archbishop in his kitchens, mostly in Lambeth Palace in London, but likely started in the kitchens at Mortlake. Wellyfed would be a close member of the Cromwell household, providing loyal service for the rest of his days.

With the changes going on in the Cromwell household, it is entirely plausible Thomas decided he needed something new, especially after his sister Katherine went to Wales. He demonstrated throughout his life a desire to educate himself, being self-taught in every area of his knowledge.[33] At around fifteen, it was time to leave Putney behind. Despite his long absence from home, there are names that originate in Putney that never left Thomas' life, such as Thomas Megges, the nephew of Archbishop Morton, a boy the same age as Thomas.[34] Likewise, another local Putney boy, Thomas Mundy who became a monk at Wandsworth monastery, and Henry Polstead and Thomas Avery, both Putney men who Thomas never forgot as he rose in notoriety. Another boy close to young Thomas

Cromwell was Anthony St Leger, nephew to Archbishop Warham, who labelled himself a favourite of Walter Cromwell and remained very close to Thomas for the rest of his life.[35] Every important person close to Thomas as a boy would keep strong connections with him later.

The true reason for Thomas' departure from Putney is unknown. While the ever exaggerating and whimsical novelist Matteo Bandello wrote Thomas 'fled from his father',[36] the tale woven by Bandello is littered with errors to add flair. Thomas may have simply wished to explore, to travel, to educate himself instead of settling for making cloth or pouring ale. With the family moving, it was the perfect time for Cromwell to shrug off the poor behaviour of his past and try something adventurous.

Leaving England would not have been such a struggle; merchant ships left regularly from London and Dover, primarily carrying wool and fabrics to Calais and Antwerp. Money for such a sea voyage may not have been necessary as ships needed crew, some requiring hundreds of people. Ships were floating villages in need of people to care for every facet of life. It would not have been hard to find someone travelling through Putney, and a cheeky boy with charm could get a tip about finding work in London and beyond. As John Foxe wrote of young Thomas Cromwell, a boy ready to make his fortune, 'nothing as so hard with which wit and industry he could not compass'.[37]

Sadly, we shall never be able to track where the young Cromwell travelled to when he left England but following Bandello's dramatic tale of the boy he called Tommaso Cremonello,[38] Cromwell went to France and joined the army. Perhaps the wages of a paid soldier in a temporary militia was the only option available, the promise of a place to eat and sleep too irresistible to a boy living in a foreign country. His father and uncle had done well after the Battle of Bosworth, and perhaps young Thomas thought battle could do the same for him.

France was a few years into Louis XII's reign, and deep in the Italian Wars. The Italian states formed the League of Venice, or Holy League, to repel the French from Italy.[39] Spain had a claim to the vast kingdom of Naples, as did the French, leaving Italians exposed and endangered on multiple fronts. The French had regularly used foreigners or mercenaries in their temporary militias and needed many to fill the ranks, most coming from Switzerland.[40] An Englishman could join these militias; some in the Low Countries had joined in the past and had men from

French-allied kingdoms such as Burgundy. Cromwell may have even landed in these northern countries from England and made his way to the French army from there, alongside other foreigners looking for glory. Most of the French militias were gathered from men in southern France, but some groups were moved from northern quarters of the country as Louis XII signed peace treaties, leaving much of France otherwise safe from any northern invaders.[41] It would be plausible to assume Cromwell travelled south with these northern French militias.

The French army had been supported by multiple Italian rulers, among them Ludovico II del Vasto, Marquis of Saluzzo, who had aided France to take Milan. France wanted the jewel of the kingdom of Naples, and after multiple wins on behalf of the French, Ludovico prepared to take Naples for the French.[42] France and Spain signed the Treaty of Granada, splitting Naples in 1500, but the peace would not last. By 1502, French and Spanish peace had broken down, and King Louis XII wanted the entire kingdom of Naples for himself,[43] sending in extra troops to repel the Spanish.

The only mention of Thomas Cromwell is in a single battle in Italy, the Battle of Garigliano, 75 kilometres north of Naples city. As Bandello wrote, Cromwell claimed to have carried a pike for a foot soldier,[44] part of an army of 15,000.[45] Given that Cromwell eventually marched north to Florence after the battle, it is possible he was a foot soldier or a noncombatant page under an Italian-led *lances fournies*. One such Florentine fighting for the French was Piero de' Medici, the man who had lost Florence in 1494. Medici had been in exile in Venice but supported the French in their battle in Naples.

What poor Cromwell walked into was more a slaughter than a battle. The French and Spanish were separated by the Garigliano river in late December 1503, a seemingly safe position for the French in the river-side town of Traetta. But the French were suffering from severe illness. On the night of 28 December, the Spanish built a pontoon bridge, allowing 6,000 Spanish troops to flood onto the French side of the river.[46] The French were ill and under-prepared for the attack, and ordered a retreat to Gaeta, leaving the sick men behind with their cannons to await their fate. A resilient band of French men stayed with the sick and fought for the town of Traetta and its nearby bridge over the Garigliano.[47] These men held off the Spanish troops long enough for the rest of the French army to escape, though Piero de' Medici drowned in the Garigliano river.[48] But even the men who retreated to Gaeta were not safe, as the Spanish laid siege to the port and the French finally surrendered, leaving Naples in Spain's hands.[49]

Cromwell, only eighteen at the time, had borne witness to a bloody, demoralising, and decisive battle that ended France's claim to Italy. The French had 4,000 dead to bury on the battlefield, almost five times the losses of the Spanish. Little did Cromwell know that fighting at Garigliano with Piero de' Medici, seeing what happened, and of Medici's burial at Monte Cassino, would come in extremely helpful for him more than a decade later. With the war over, there is no record of Cromwell's march north to Florence, how long it took, who he travelled with or why Florence was his destination. It may simply have been a place to stop and lick his wounds on the 1,900-kilometre journey back to Putney, as Rome was closed off with its own battles.

The Republic of Florence was under the rule of Piero di Tommaso Soderini, a favourite of Piero de' Medici, who had been voted in as Gonfaloniere in 1500.[50] Soderini was sympathetic to the French, so soldiers marching from battle could cross through Florentine lands in 1504. Florence too was changing their army, with Secretary of War Niccolò Machiavelli setting up a new system of militia, no longer hiring foreign mercenaries, citing their questionable loyalty.[51] It is again Matteo Bandello who fills in the gaps of Cromwell's story, as he wrote that Francesco Frescobaldi, a wealthy merchant's son was at home in Florence when 'a poor man presented himself before him and craved his charity for the love of God. Frescobaldi, seeing him so ill accoutered and noting signs of gentle breeding in his countenance, was moved to pity, more by token he knew him to be English'.[52]

Bandello paints the image of Frescobaldi finding the English man begging on the streets, likely, given Cromwell's state after the battle. But the battle cannot have taken his ability to charm, as Bandello wrote the Frescobaldi family soon took Cromwell into the household, where he remained for almost a decade. While there is proof that Cromwell knew the Frescobaldi family well, and Francesco Frescobaldi was close to Cromwell, he was still young when he found Cromwell begging in the streets. Francesco's father, merchant Girolamo Frescobaldi, a wealthy banker and merchant based out of Florence, Antwerp, and London, took in the Englishman, and Cromwell grew close to Girolamo's sons Francesco and Leonardo. Cromwell had found his new home and family.

Cromwell, an uneducated Putney boy, likely humbled out of his childish bully behaviour by a stint in the army, found himself living at the heart of the Renaissance. Florence sat at the centre of all artistic, scientific, humanist, and technological changes going on throughout Europe. The boy who could have looked forward to a lifetime of pouring ale or scouring and carding wool suddenly sat at the centre of the rediscovery of classical texts. The quality and quantity of literature greatly increased, as did the innovations in medicine, architecture, mathematics, arts, and engineering, all within Cromwell's grasp. The political and financial development in Florence had also had a tremendous overhaul, leaving copious opportunities for Cromwell to aspire to and emulate. The Renaissance humanist beliefs brought science and the arts together for the first time, allowing the pair to be appreciated for their importance. Cromwell, working for the pro-English Frescobaldi family, would learn how to conquer languages, become a lawyer, a merchant, and investor. All these things were suddenly possible in a new world.

In 1504, Michelangelo unveiled his statue of David in Palazzo Vecchio, a symbol of civil liberties, something Cromwell would have walked past on his daily tasks in the civic centre of the city.[53] Notions of freedom of thought, of speech and ideas, were something the young man could embrace, his passion of being self-taught allowed open season on a variety of subjects. It is likely the literature of the era, with the rediscovery of the classics, is where Cromwell taught himself his Latin and Greek skills, and the works he collected would end up pride of place in his Austin Friars library later in life. This environment would have undoubtedly changed Thomas Cromwell's outlook. The freedom, the artistic explosion, the propulsion of new ideas all would have been a feast for a quick, intelligent, and charming young man. While Florence was a city of haves and have-nots, like any city of the period, Florence offered hope for Cromwell. England had never given him such possibility.

While Cromwell could not know that he would take on politics in later life, one inescapable influence was Niccolò Machiavelli. While Soderini ruled over Florence, it was Secretary Machiavelli that had a profound impact on the city during his reign, and the timeless influence of Machiavelli's literary works did not escape Cromwell. He possessed published works by Machiavelli, and likely also handwritten, popular works such as *The Prince* and *Discourses on Livy*, both of which would not be printed until 1532. Machiavelli's blazing new style of government can be directly seen in Cromwell's later work. Before Machiavelli, political science was almost an alien concept, with rulers only placed into prominent positions by birthright. Machiavelli set out to show how power could be effectively used, crafted by a mind not encumbered with old school thought processes. Men like Machiavelli paved a way for men like Cromwell, showing that a man can be serious and rule effectively while also turning their intellect to more joyous avenues. Machiavelli worked in government but also freely wrote poetry and plays.[54] He overhauled the Florentine army and worked on diplomatic relations while creating music and literature. Machiavelli showed men like Cromwell how to balance cunning and manipulation with morality and principle. While he likely did not realise it, Thomas Cromwell was standing at the precipice of limitless knowledge. As Thomas Cromwell would one day do himself, Machiavelli sat as a private mind behind the public ruler, establishing new foundations in Florence at a time of immense change in power, thought, art, science, war, and control. Machiavelli did not play by the rules – he rewrote the rules of what a kingdom could or could not do. He did not see issues through traditional means; he saw it as a game of chess, where situations could be manipulated to achieve a new outcome. Machiavelli could remove morality from a situation when a difficult situation arose, and while this may have appeared distasteful or even downright cruel, Machiavelli learned how to stomach these trials.[55] Cromwell would one day rule in the same manner. But for now, Cromwell was about to find himself at the heart of a clandestine project to help King Henry VII.

Chapter 2

1505–1512: Duplicity

'more by token he knew him to be English'

It took a quick mind to survive in Florence. The dialect spoken by Cromwell's master in the army would have been different to those Florentines in the regiment who fought in Naples. Hundreds of variants of languages would have crossed Cromwell's path as he trekked through France and Italy into Naples and then north to a new life in Florence. Now in the household of the Frescobaldi, communication again would be vital. There is no way to fully ascertain which variants of Italian and French Cromwell had already gathered, though letters in his hand show a traditional form of French understood today, and his Italian correspondence was close to the Florentine variation of the early Renaissance.[1]

Cromwell's role in the Frescobaldi house was as a clerk, encompassing a wide number of administrative tasks. Given there were less than ten years between Cromwell and Francesco Frescobaldi, Girolamo Frescobaldi likely recruited Cromwell to work for his sons. With Cromwell's knowledge and experience later shown in law, trading and banking shown in the Low Countries and then England, Cromwell likely worked with these heads of the family to learn from their long-practised skills. One of Cromwell's many personal talents, shown throughout his years at the royal court, was his impressive ability to pick up and retain information, a great help when looking to rise through the ranks of trusted men in Frescobaldi administration. Also, while it was considered proper to follow a family's rules and protocols, Cromwell always had his clever scheme of befriending those lower in rank in any household, something that continued to appear throughout his social climbing in later years. Cromwell seemingly made no distinction when giving out his friendship and loyalty.

The Frescobaldi had numerous buildings in the city of Florence, the main being the Frescobaldi Palace on via Santo Spirito, which stretched for blocks through Florence to their San Jacopo Palace.[2] Niccolò Machiavelli lived in the same area, his home on the same street front as Frescobaldi Palace. Cromwell's life would have been like that of a servant or agent in any fine household of the period, with a bedroom on the third floor of the family's home, rising at 6.00 am for prayer and breakfast, before beginning the day's work by 7.30 am.[3] While women ran the household, men worked in the family's business, primarily wool and fine wine exports alongside banking.

As wool merchants, the Frescobaldi would oversee everything from the raw materials to the export of products, primarily to the Low Countries. Frescobaldi wine routinely made its way to England, some of the finest available of the period, serving the table of the English king. As a clerk organising the exported wine, Cromwell would see all aspects, from grape harvest right through to the logistics of the ships carrying the products into England. The wool business, a position Cromwell knew from the very bottom, taught him how to prepare and send wool materials to be finished in the Low Countries and sold for profit. He could meet those involved in the trade, knew who to trust, who was unscrupulous, and where the best prices could be sought. It meant a man who started as someone destined for a life of manual labour could see all sides of a business, an insight that would eventually distinguish him from those around him in England. It also gave Cromwell something the English lacked – an understanding of different people and nationalities at all ranks, their struggles, their joys, their insights, and their friendships. While nobles sneered at Cromwell as a member of the peasantry, he did not attempt to hide this side of himself and valued the work and relationships with those considered common.

A day in a typical Italian household would see dinner served at 6.00 pm, with office work done after dinner before bed at 10.00 pm,[4] though Cromwell showed in later years that sleep was something he rarely required. The long hours Cromwell pulled throughout his life both benefitted him with success and took a serious toll on his wellbeing. The Frescobaldi home gave opportunities that life in Putney could not provide Cromwell, and with Francesco Frescobaldi still at an age to receive education, Cromwell's passion for knowledge was easily indulged. Unlike England, both boys and girls of a respectable rank such as the Frescobaldi would expect a fine education. Cromwell would have the opportunity to read and write in Italian, Latin, and Greek. Boys and girls were educated and included in chess, hunting, card games, falconry, lute playing, archery, croquet, backgammon and given lessons on many popular Italian dances used at court.[5] While the prevailing image of Thomas Cromwell is of a plump old man, he would have once been youthful, energetic, and offered the privileges and entertainment of those young and spirited in Florence. Cromwell only had one vice, that of gambling on cards and dice, and remained spectacularly bad at it throughout his life. Cromwell's position meant he could be at home at Frescobaldi Palace, teaching himself business, languages or indulging in classical literature, but also out in the Florentine nightlife to gamble.

While evening activities provided entertainment, during the day Cromwell gained the chance to enhance his spirited mind in finance. An agent in a merchant household would hold two account books, one for cash, and another detailing transactions and tasks undertaken.[6] Working for Girolamo Frescobaldi may also be where Cromwell picked up his habit of keeping a third book, his remembrance lists. These books would have accompanied Cromwell everywhere on business, while attired in the basics for a young clerk, with a white shirt, black doublet and hose, and a short tunic for the cooler months, as the longer cloaks were reserved for older wealthy men.[7] A lower-level agent for a wealthy family would be afforded much in the way of respect, giving the impression of a young Cromwell, head down, going about his business within the city. The Frescobaldi bank's head office in Florence, with accompanying offices in Rome, Bruges, Antwerp, and London, regularly financed English kings.[8] Not only was Cromwell learning how to make money, but he was also watching how the nobility made political moves through finance, especially King Henry VII of England.

The Frescobaldi bank was a *banchi grossi*, one of the great banks, and filled the vacuum left when the Medici family collapsed. Great banks relied on trade and merchandise as their primary form of business,[9] and watched markets and saw where profit was made and lost, further enriching the Frescobaldi coffers. Working as a Frescobaldi clerk was no invisible position, for it was the agents of these grand families that could make connections and friendships. While banks such as the Frescobaldi were the top-ranked style in the period, Florence had three other types of banks, and being a clerk in a *banchi grossi* would afford Cromwell the chance to learn the less scrupulous and risker styles of making money, two of which came in helpful for the young Englishmen. The *banchi di pegno*, the pawnshops, were small money lenders charging up to 20% interest,[10] something Cromwell mastered when he returned to England. The *banchi a minuto*, the small banks, could be as simple as a one-man operation, trading in currency conversion and using gold and jewels to transfer funds,[11] another useful skill Cromwell used much later in Henry VIII's Jewel House.

Exactly how much of the Frescobaldi business Cromwell knew can never be known, but with a decade spent in their company, it would be reasonable to assume Cromwell eventually worked his way up to be an integral part of the family business. The community itself was close-knit, so when Cromwell went back to England, he already had an Italian 'family' awaiting him. Cromwell had fallen in with one of the finest families of the Republic.

The Frescobaldi had held the papal monopoly on wine since 1330 to export their luxury product to England. Wool, however, was the ultimate product in the international trade, the item everyone, rich or poor, required, and this mix of luxury and necessity gave Cromwell insight into international relations with England, the Low Countries, Lübeck and Germany, and the international trade fairs held in Antwerp and Brussels. But the French Valois were natural enemies of the Hapsburg empire, and the Frescobaldi supported the Hapsburgs and ignored the French. Even from this early period, Cromwell seemingly had no business in France, and would later have no affinity for the country, despite the never-ending diplomacy he was forced to entertain. But the Frescobaldi had a new product to make a swift profit and make good use of the family's love for England.

While the Frescobaldi were highly respected, well-known, and established in their markets, they were not above working against powers for profit. As a clerk for the family, Cromwell would have undoubtedly known of the illegal alum smuggling business the Frescobaldi created with King Henry VII of England. King Henry had trusted the Frescobaldi bank before, using Girolamo Frescobaldi's Burges bank headquarters to transfer £100,000 from England to Emperor Maximilian in 1502 when no other bank would oversee such a large transfer,[12] and now Henry was ready to make serious money with the Italian family. Henry VII wanted to be a big player in European politics without war, and money was the ultimate solution.

Alum had many uses for fabrics, medicine, and cosmetics, though at the beginning of the sixteenth century was most valuable for dyeing wool. Pope Julius II had a monopoly on the import and use of alum in Europe, resulting in high taxes on each purchase. The sole source of alum in Europe was Tolfa outside Rome, and to use alum from elsewhere was business with the 'infidels,' resulting in financial and religious penalties. In 1504, just one year into Julius' reign, he increased the high taxes on alum, overseen by banker Agostino Chigi, who operated cartels to enforce costs and usage. As a result, a black-market smuggling ring flourished against this monopoly. Early in Henry VII's reign, a ship pirated in English waters by Italian merchants had become an international scandal, with King Henry opting to keep his hands free of the drama.[13] But the idea had been lodged; smuggling alum and avoiding papal tax would greatly help Henry VII enrich his kingdom. By 1504, a plan formed where England would 'acquire' alum without paying anything to the Apostolic treasury. King Henry went into business with the Frescobaldi family, with the English financing two triple-masted ships, the *Sovereign*, and the *Regent*. These ships were loaded with alum in Phocaea in the Gulf of Smyrna, Anatolia (now Foça, in the Gulf of İzmir, Turkey), and from Thrace (Thracian lands now spread between Turkey, Greece and Bulgaria).[14] These Frescobaldi-run vessels would attempt the passage from these lands to Spain or England without being stopped by papal agents. Italian merchant Ludovico della Fava, former head of the Medici bank in London, worked with Sir Edmund Dudley and Sir Richard Empson, Henry VII's notorious revenue collectors, negotiating deals for the alum with Low Countries merchants. Both King Henry and the Frescobaldi bank got a share of the large tax-free profits.[15] Alum was measured in quintals, one quintal being 100lbs. The papal tax usually took 13s 2d per quintal, and now this money went to the king, with a cut sent to the Frescobaldi bank. Frescobaldi ships bringing untaxed alum to England could easily net the project four-figure sums in profits, the largest shipment making 15,166l 13s 4d (or £ 1,100,000 today).[16] As a clerk in the Frescobaldi office, it would have been impossible for Cromwell to miss these payments moving between his homeland and new masters, as this was a major financial gain for the Frescobaldi and created vast sums of money for England at a desperately needed time.

The venture was not without its risks; Pope Julius released a papal bull in 1507 calling for the capture of the *Sovereign* and her cargo,[17] and when caught, Girolamo Frescobaldi was charged with smuggling alum to Philip of Castile. It appears no punishment was handed to the Frescobaldi family, who had King James IV of Scotland on their side. James wrote to Pope Julius on 12 February 1508, telling Julius that the Frescobaldi ship had been forced to hand over the alum, and it was (the conveniently recently dead) Philip of Castile who would take the blame for the smuggling operation.[18] King James also wrote to King Louis XII in France and asked him to petition for a pardon for Girolamo Frescobaldi,[19] so it is easy to assume Scotland had been enjoying the fruits of the Frescobaldi smuggling operation.

During this scheme, an Italian named Giovanni Cavalcanti worked as a Frescobaldi clerk in Rome before becoming a broker's agent in England. Cavalcanti would become one of Cromwell's closest friends on his return to London. The two men would live as neighbours in London's Italian quarter, which stretched from Lombard Street to Austin Friars on Broad Street. These two men had similar roles for the family in different cities, so secretive correspondence between the men on issues such as the alum is highly likely. Cavalcanti was a fine patron of Renaissance art, an influence that immediately rubbed off on young Cromwell. Cavalcanti personally unearthed a 1,500-year-old Roman statue in 1506 and favoured artists Michelangelo and Torrigiano. Torrigiano, famous for being the Borgia mercenary who destroyed Michelangelo's nose, went to London on Cavalcanti's advice to bring Italian art and skill to the English court, which would continue for several decades, giving Cromwell a friendly connection when looking for favour in the future.[20] Cromwell's friend Cavalcanti introduced him to Pier Francesco Portinari, a merchant who had been overseeing Henry VII's desire for a new hospital and to add finishing touches to Westminster Abbey.[21] Cromwell's friends Portinari and Cavalcanti worked out of Frescobaldi manor on Botolph Lane in the Italian quarter in London, meaning when the time came, Cromwell did not need to find work, for the Frescobaldi manor and all its friendships guaranteed him support.

While the Frescobaldi side of the alum operation was largely successful, so too was King Henry VII's plan to increase the royal coffers. Thanks to easy access to all products needed in the wool trade, England increased its productivity by 61% in the final six years of Henry VII's reign. Henry also prosecuted Englishmen smuggling alum that did not come from the Frescobaldi ships, both making money and appeasing the Pope by 'attempting' to crack down on the smuggling trade.[22] When Henry VIII rose to power in 1509, he ensured Frescobaldi agent Ludovico della Fava was exempt from import rules and fees, ensuring the continuation of the ring. However, Cromwell could have had no way of knowing that the smuggling ring would have repercussions for the family once he returned to England.

While Cromwell worked in the Florentine office of the Frescobaldi, Ludovico della Fava worked in the London office for the king. Della Fava's influence on Cromwell was a mighty lesson in success, as della Fava ran a spiderweb of networks through Europe as a means of communication and information gathering.[23] These methods used by della Fava in London would be a similar method Cromwell would use to gain friendships with agents of powerful men, later making Cromwell a powerful ally at the royal court. These connections, built up while working for Frescobaldi, would later give Cromwell access to information and allies unattainable by others. While ambassadors worked for their rulers, it was information that ran through trading houses, wool warehouses, merchants' offices, bankers' meetings, and shipyards that could carry useful tips if you had access to the right people. Cromwell's largest talent, charming people and maintaining his friendships, worked perfectly with the business education gained from the mighty Frescobaldi, all entirely with their blessing. With these skills combined, Cromwell would climb the lofty heights to the king's affections, always being the finest Italian-Englishman possible. Thomas Cromwell was born in Putney, but his mind was entirely Florentine.

Chapter 3

1513–1520: Eminence

*'no sound taste nor judgement of religion, but was wild and
youthful, without sense or regard of God and his word'*

While the Frescobaldi flourished through the first decade of the sixteenth century, storm clouds brewed over the Republic of Florence. While Machiavelli captured Pisa for the Republic, there remained powerful rivals for the mighty province. The Medici had been out of power since 1494 and they wanted their city, and now had the backing of Pope Julius and his papal army.[1] The ongoing War of the League of Cambrai raged outside the Florentine borders for the entirety of Cromwell's time in Italy and encroaching Italian wars were a constant threat to the Frescobaldi. The reign of Piero Soderini and Niccolò Machiavelli ended abruptly in September 1512, when Cardinal Giovanni de' Medici took the city with a papal army, and became the Pope just one year later, ruling Florence from Rome.[2] This would bring remarkable change to Florence, leaving Florentines feeling as if they were part of the Papal States and not a republic. Safety and security were no longer assured in Florence.

That did not matter for Thomas Cromwell, who left the safety of his Florentine family when the Medici marched back into the city. While the Frescobaldi family was safe and able to do business as usual under Medici rule, perhaps there was no longer a place for the Italian-Englishman in Florence. The family had been doing well; Leonardo Frescobaldi gained a licence to trade wool and wine out of Southampton in 1512,[3] and the young Frescobaldi brothers had won the license to be lessees of tolls in Zeeland in the Low Countries.[4] Francesco Frescobaldi was now in charge in Florence, but the powerful new link with the Hapsburgs and their Antwerp trade is where the third Frescobaldi man, Tommaso Cremonello, found himself in the same year as the overthrow of Florence.

Cromwell's lifelong commitment to being an Italian-Englishman shows no negative reason for his departure from Florence. Whether it was the Florentine instability, the promotion to a role based in the Low Countries, or simply a desire to be his own man now he was nearly thirty years old, Cromwell moved on, with Bandello describing him as passing through Venice towards Antwerp. Cromwell had attended a spring merchant fair in Middleburg, Zeeland the previous year, as his enduring friend George Elyot wrote in 1535, recalling their meeting, 'the love and true heart that have held unto you since the Syngsson Mart (Whitsun fair) at Middelburg in anno 1512'.[5] The fairs held in Zeeland, Antwerp and elsewhere attracted many around Europe, and agents such as Cromwell had the chance to travel to the Low Countries, visiting the successive six-week fairs held between January and September.[6] With cloth being the primary international trading product, Cromwell would have felt quite at home, and his ever-strengthening language skills would have made him an ideal agent to send and negotiate trade deals.

Whether working for the Frescobaldi brothers or himself, Cromwell met a man who would be an integral part of his life for decades, John Hackett. Hackett acted as the Frescobaldi Chief Officer in Antwerp, and as a news source for England's royal court. Cromwell chose a fresh path for his life as a merchant and was well-placed in Antwerp to do so. Hackett was an Englishman from Calais and had lived in Flanders since 1505, giving Cromwell a well-connected friend to lean upon as he established himself. The pair continued to joke and write to one another usually in a mixture of English and French for the rest of Cromwell's life.[7]

Alongside Hackett and Elyot, Cromwell had another friend, made alongside the Frescobaldi as early as 1509. Harry Hotoft was an Englishman as near Italian as Cromwell, holding the role of Collector of Customs at Southampton port, and was in business with the Italians, Leonardo Frescobaldi chief among them.[8] Between his friends in Florence, Southampton and now Antwerp, Cromwell had the triangle of support he needed to make his own money.

Cromwell's name appears on documents in Antwerp, signing his name on papers relating to the merchant deals, as the legal middleman for English merchants in the prosperous city. Cromwell's role was akin to a clerk or secretary, a freelance man with the legal and trading knowledge to aid other merchants in foreign trade. This role would have required little capital to start, and after calling upon friends to find clients, Cromwell began handling the affairs of others for a modest fee per client. Cromwell had the skills for these basic legal tasks but no capital behind him to set up personal trading. When he left the Frescobaldi household on good terms, he had sixteen gold ducats in his pocket (about £60,000 today) and a horse.[9] These relatively straightforward administration roles would not have been high earning, but were a good start, and useful with his new legal, and even better, language skills.

Like much of Cromwell's early life, there is no certain date on which he returned to England, though it is often speculated anywhere from 1510 to 1515, but 1513 stands out for several reasons. Letters from Harry Hotoft place Cromwell still in the employ of Frescobaldi in 1509–1510,[10] and Cromwell only met George Elyot in 1512.[11] Cromwell likely had not travelled home to England since his departure at fifteen. Returning home would be a momentous occasion and an opportunity to make a little money in the Low Countries, before starting life in England, would have been advantageous.

By 1513, Cromwell was home and intent on starting a life in London. While only six miles downstream from Putney, London would still feel as far away as Florence 1,000 miles away. The Frescobaldi had their manor on Botolph Lane, not to mention the wide Italian community in the surrounding streets who would open their doors to a fellow Frescobaldi agent. The Italian community, which had flourished in London, were not always welcome. It was said that Londoners 'not only despised the way the Italians live, but curse them with uncontrollable hatred,' and that the English had a great antipathy of foreigners, and 'imagine that they never come into their island, but to make themselves masters of it, and usurp their goods'.[12] Cromwell grew up without a grudge for his humble upbringing in England, but he had also learned an appreciation for people that most of his fellow countrymen never experienced. This left Cromwell with a wide circle of people in which he felt most comfortable.

As soon as he arrived home, Cromwell put his newfound skills to work. He is registered as the plaintiff in the Court of Chancery as Cromewell v The Sheriffs of London in 1514. Cromwell stood as the lawyer for Antony Welys, who wanted repayment of a debt from William Thomas, 'contracted at Antwerp in the year 5 Henry VIII'.[13] He signed the paperwork as 'Thomas Crumwell, gentleman', meaning lawyer, and likely knew of the case from his time in Antwerp the year prior.

An accomplished honour for Thomas Cromwell came on his return to London when he was admitted to the Worshipful Company of Merchant Taylors,[14] with their grand Merchant Taylors Hall on Threadneedle Street in east London. By the sixteenth century, the Company thrived, with international business ever-growing in the city. Merchants were soon admitted, and like-minded men could fraternise on matters of business and religion. Here Cromwell would find himself among respectable gentlemen, those with connections to wealthy buyers, and once Martin Luther began his Reformation, men like himself who believed in the changes needed in the church. It had been suggested the sole surviving portrait of Thomas Cromwell was painted in the main hall of the Merchant Taylors' London building and he possibly even wore the master's robes.[15] Given that it was painted as late as 1532, when Cromwell was high in royal favour, shows that Cromwell never underestimated the honour afforded him by the Merchant Taylors.

As Cromwell toiled between working as a merchant and lawyer, he was hired to travel to Rome and argue a tithe dispute.[16] Having seen the 'factions and manners'[17] of the Italians for years, and able to speak fluent Italian and Latin, Cromwell was perfect for the job. In Rome, Cromwell stayed at the English Hospice, San Tommaso di Canterbury. The English Hospice at via Monserrato 45 (now The Venerable English College), sat a block from the Tiber river, and a two-mile walk to the Apostolic Palace. The hostel had been catering to English pilgrims to Rome for almost 200 years, and after renovation and reorganisation by King Henry VII, became an important hub for English diplomats visiting the city.[18]

On his stay, Cromwell met Lancelot Collins,[19] nephew to the hospice's master Cardinal Christopher Bainbridge, Archbishop of York, and resident English cardinal in Rome. This meeting between Cromwell and Collins would spark another genuine lifelong friendship, with Collins considered one of the kindest and most generous men in England by even cynical men.[20] Collins valued his friendship with Cromwell for over twenty years, even when, in later life, it would threaten his safety.[21] The meeting between the men at the hospice helps to date Cromwell's movements. Cromwell had already left Rome by 14 July when Cardinal Bainbridge was poisoned by Rinaldo de Modena, one of Bainbridge's chaplains, and rumoured lover.[22] When interrogated, Modena confessed to planning the murder with Silvester de Gigli, Bishop of Worcester and English ambassador in Rome, however, Modena was soon murdered in prison.[23] This whole tragic event meant Collins returned home and took up the treasurership of York Minster soon after, giving Cromwell a valuable new friend in the north.[24]

The trip to Rome was the start of Cromwell's success with his freelance legal business. For the next decade, his principal business was legal work, particularly in the Court of Chancery and the Star Chamber, both located around Westminster. Given that Cromwell had no formal legal training, it is no surprise that he stuck to easier tasks such as conveyancing, debt settlements, credit arrangements, equity law and setting up trusts. While full-time lawyers would be seen in the King's Bench or Common Pleas, Cromwell's name is never mentioned, and this allowed Cromwell to keep up with trading in the Italian quarter. Cromwell did not realise it, but he was enjoying the last of a golden period of Italian prosperity in London, as the Reformation would soon wipe away the Italian presence.[25]

Business successes aside, 1514 also marked an important turning point in Cromwell's family life. It is the final year in which his father Walter is mentioned in records. On 6 October, Walter was found to be leasing a virgate of land outside his grounds and was fined for the incident.[26] Then on 10 October, Walter was found to have been falsifying papers over the land he had fraudulently leased in Wandsworth. The Latin Court Rolls of Wimbledon does not specify the name of the lord in question but says that the lands were to be seized until the said lord settled the matter. While some have translated this ruling as Walter forfeiting all his lands and buildings, the Roll is ambiguous and may have only been a hold on land during the trial. Either way, Walter had gotten himself into a spot of legal bother. With Walter never appearing in records again, it can be assumed he lived little longer than 1514. Sadly, Cromwell's mother plays no role in the records, and her death cannot be pinpointed at all, though, given her son's boasting of her ability to bear children in older age, it is safe to assume Katherine Cromwell had already passed by this time. It is a shame that in Cromwell's life, a tale of loyalty and family, that the women in his life gained such little recognition.

As one part of Cromwell's family ended, another blossomed. About 1515, Cromwell met Elizabeth Williams, a Wandsworth local who had lost her husband Thomas Williams, a Welsh yeoman of the Guard.[27] They likely met through Cromwell's sister Katherine and her husband Morgan Williams, who lived in Wandsworth with their sons, Richard, Walter, and Gregory.[28] Thomas Williams was a cousin (possibly brother) of Morgan Williams, making them all close indeed. Another connection to the Williams family would be welcome, as Katherine disappears from records after 1517, leaving her young sons motherless.

Like Cromwell's mother, Elizabeth Williams' family history is difficult to trace. She was possibly born Elizabeth Wyckes, daughter of Henry Wyckes, a gentleman-usher to Henry VII, and his wife Mercy. Only a few things suggest Elizabeth was Wyckes' daughter – that Cromwell received a letter in 1523 from Harry Wyckes saying, 'my sister, your bedfellow',[29] and that there was a Henry Wyckes registered in Henry VII's papers as a gentleman-usher.[30] However, there is no record that Elizabeth ever had a brother, while her sister Joan is well-documented, and the girls inherited from their father, which they could not do with a living brother. Harry Wyckes also called himself 'your cousin, your servant, your beadsman',[31] in letters, so his actual connection to the Cromwell family is in doubt.

Another theory is that Elizabeth's maiden name was Prior, daughter of Sir John Prior and his wife Mercy, and co-heir to Prior's estate.[32] It is often assumed that Mercy Prior was married twice, given that a 'Mr Prior' was listed in Cromwell's inventory in 1527,[33] but this is a damaged and barely readable document. Sir John Prior was certainly either Elizabeth's father or stepfather. Sir John Prior's family were the Greys, his grandfather being Sir Edward Grey, 3rd Baron Rutheryn in Wales,[34] giving Cromwell an excellent connection to the Grey family which would soon become near kin to him. However, records only list Sir John Prior's first wife as Isabel/Elizabeth.[35] If Mercy was the incorrectly-named wife of John Prior, it would make her granddaughter of Robert, Lord Talbot, but doubt remains with several conflicting sources.[36] The other likelihood is that Mercy Prior was sister of gentleman-usher Henry Wyckes, and married Sir John Prior as her only husband.

Given these large inconsistencies, it is accepted that Cromwell married Elizabeth Williams née Wyckes-Prior, who, newly widowed, was heir to her husband's estate and co-heir of Henry Wyckes' estate after he died in 1512.[37] This would have made Elizabeth both wealthy and in need of a new husband, and the Williams family connection through Cromwell's sister made Elizabeth a perfect candidate. Between Cromwell's ambition and Elizabeth's inheritance, they could do well together. While it may have not been a love match, as successful marriages so infrequently were, it appears to have developed well over time.

Incorrect assumptions have made about Cromwell's life when he married Elizabeth, such as Cromwell working for Elizabeth's father, or that their fathers planned the match. As for Cromwell taking over Wyckes property and continuing its wool business after marriage, this is possible,[38] however, Mercy and Elizabeth could have also taken care of the business, along with Elizabeth's sister Joan and her husband John Williamson. Cromwell undoubtedly tapped into the wealth of the Wyckes-Prior lands once he married Elizabeth, but to suggest he went back to work as a sheep farmer and cloth fuller is foolish. Cromwell's days of working with his hands were long over – his mind now took precedence. Thomas and Elizabeth chose a city lifestyle now that he was a gentleman with the capital to back his further plans. The date for the marriage is as contentious as Elizabeth's identity, as there is nothing to suggest Cromwell and Elizabeth married before their son's birth in approximately 1520, and with no written proof before January 1522.[39] The marriage could have occurred any time between 1515 and 1520.

Cromwell and Elizabeth may not have had their own children in the early period of their marriage (just as Cromwell's sisters did not), but they did take on a ward, young Ralph Sadler. Cromwell met Henry Sadler from Hackney, who worked with Morgan Williams for Thomas Grey, 2nd Marquess of Dorset. In 1517, Sadler's wife Margaret died, leaving him with three young boys, Ralph, John, and infant Nicholas. Ralph, aged between seven to ten years old, went into Cromwell's household and simply never left, becoming a son to Cromwell in all but name. Cromwell and Henry Sadler remained friends throughout their lives, the pair dying just months apart, with Cromwell happy to aid the entire Sadler family.

In 1516, 'Thomas Crumwell, a gentleman', gained himself a new legal client, Sir Thomas Empson. Sir Thomas' father, Sir Richard Empson, was beheaded alongside Henry VII's other revenue collector and alum smuggler, Sir Edmund Dudley in 1510. Sir Thomas spent years in various courts on issues of titles, estates, and taxes. Cromwell represented Empson in court, and one file shows Cromwell's signature on papers filed as part of the 1512 case when Sir Thomas Empson gained his father's title.[40]

Cromwell's name does not appear in the paperwork and was not living in England in 1512, and he likely borrowed these papers while building the case surrounding Empson's unpaid debts in 1516.[41] The so-called 1512 paper bearing Cromwell's signature is undated and now exists to confuse historians about Cromwell's whereabouts (much like a file belonging to Cardinal Wolsey in 1514, which bears handwriting similar to Thomas Cromwell's, but again, bears Cromwell's signature as he had borrowed the documents for another case[42]). Cromwell's knowledge of the alum smuggling with the Frescobaldi family likely helped him win a client such as Empson.

As for Cromwell's former Italian patrons, the Frescobaldi family were not sharing in the success Cromwell found in England. The young King Henry VIII had been largely ignoring his offices and the alum smuggling ring fell into disarray. With finances now under the control of Thomas Wolsey, the new Archbishop of York after the murder of Cardinal Bainbridge in Rome, he ensured England imported papal alum from Tolfa, paying papal taxes.[43] This was a sign of England's commitment to Rome, as Wolsey had designs on the papal throne for himself. This left the Frescobaldi out in the cold after a decade of risking themselves for the English. Frescobaldi alum smuggling was Henry VIII's chief source of revenue after taxes, and yet his ambivalence saw the scheme collapse in 1518. This left Cromwell's friends Leonardo Frescobaldi and Giovanni Cavalcanti indebted to King Henry, Cardinal Wolsey, and John Heron for an eye-watering 24,000l (£12,500,000 today).[44] Some, including Cavalcanti, attempted to manipulate Henry VIII over alum, saying the Frescobaldi scheme had hurt him financially and expected the English king to pay compensation,[45] and this debt would be a noose around the Frescobaldi estate's neck for decades, as Henry VIII and Wolsey continued to make poor trading choices with alum.[46] The Frescobaldi family adapted and continued their banking, wool trading, and winemaking, while England floundered over mercantile decisions. King Henry went as far as rejecting an offer to buy the Tolfa alum mines, further damaging his finances and the wool trade in England.[47]

'Master Crumwell, gentleman', gained a further promotion in 1517, his self-taught education coming in most useful when the Boston Guild found itself in need of an English lawyer fluent in Italian. Our Lady's Guild in Boston, Lincolnshire, started as a merchant guild 250 years earlier and had expanded into the sale of indulgences, pardons given out to lessen the period one would spend in purgatory. This meant the Guild became wealthy in only fifteen years, travelling around England and into Ireland selling indulgences.[48] By 1517, the Boston Guild had a staunch competitor in the market, the English province of Austin Friars, who were only months away from having fellow German friar Martin Luther and his Reformation attack the church. While the Boston Guild and Austin Friars both had privileges to sell indulgences, the Boston Guild appealed to Thomas Wolsey to stop the Austin Friars from encroaching on the Guild's territory. Wolsey, now a cardinal, sent the appeal to Pope Leo X.

With so few Englishmen learning foreign languages, Thomas Cromwell in London was a splendid find for the Guild. The Boston Guild's Whitsun accounts show Cromwell travelled the 110 miles north to Boston and was paid for his time and expenses to the tune of 4l 6s 8d (around £2,800 today).[49]

The wheels of papal bureaucracy ambled along, and in the winter of 1518, Cromwell set off to Rome for a twenty-six-week round trip. Guild secretary Richard Chamber had unsuccessfully been to Rome on the same matter in 1517, and this trip which would take Chamber some forty-two weeks, punctuated by the assistance of smooth-talking assistant Cromwell to save the Guild's indulgence business, worth 1,550l a year (£800,000 today).[50] While Richard Chamber's account of the trip in the winter and spring of 1518–1519 is rather plain, discussing months of dreary meetings, Cromwell's experience was more fascinating.

Chamber, having been in Antwerp,[51] teamed up with Cromwell and they travelled well-furnished to Rome via Calais. Cromwell was 'given to adventure,' and 'loathe to spend much time, and more loathe to spend his money; and again, perceiving that the Pope's greedy humour must need be served with some present or other'. Cromwell was looking for the fastest, cheapest way to appease the Pope, and have a good time in the process. Cromwell and Chamber reportedly met Pope Leo in his hunting pavilion, regaling him with singers performing a three-man's-song, and presenting the sweet-toothed pope (a detail Cromwell already knew) with English jellies 'such as kings and princes only in the realm of England used to feed upon', or so Cromwell told Leo.[52] Before being styled as Pope Leo X, he was Cardinal Giovanni de' Medici, son of Florentine ruler

Lorenzo de' Medici the Magnificent, and brother to Piero de' Medici, the same who drowned at the Battle of Garigliano the morning teenage Thomas Cromwell fled the massacre. Whether Cromwell mentioned that he served at Garigliano alongside the Pope's brother is unknown, but it would have been foolish not to mention such a personal connection.

Taken with these Englishmen, Pope Leo granted the Boston Guild the right to sell indulgences and limited the powers of the Austin Friars. It was no simple grant Cromwell and Chamber proposed; in two pardons, they requested a wide range of religious grants, pardons, and religious relaxations, giving the Boston members wide-ranging freedoms, exemptions, absolutions and remissions.[53] Cromwell later told friend Thomas Cranmer that at the time of the visit, he 'had yet no sound taste nor judgement of religion, but was wild and youthful, without sense or regard of God and his word'.[54] Strong words for the man who would one day create the English Bible.

Having charmed the Pope, Cromwell skipped home, leaving Chamber to sort out the paperwork, but even this short meeting took six months. What else did 'wild and youthful' Cromwell do with his time? It would be nice to think he visited his Frescobaldi family. The Renaissance was alive and well in Italy; it was an extraordinary time for a man with language skills, an eye for books, education and a fantastic memory. Hot off the printing press was Desiderius Erasmus' second edition of *Novum Testamentum omne*, the Latin and Greek New Testament. After mixed reviews with the typo-riddled first edition, the new edition created deep repercussions throughout religious belief. Martin Luther used this second edition to create his German translation of the New Testament, which would then form the English translation. Martin Luther's *Ninety-five Theses*, or *Disputation on the Power and Efficacy of Indulgences*, was also available, discussing the very type of Catholic indulgences Cromwell fought to protect for the Boston Guild.[55] While Martin Luther had nailed his theses to a church in Germany, it was written in Latin and had been available to read since its initial display in October 1517. Cromwell already had wealthy merchant friends in London, such as William Lok and Richard Gresham, who embraced Luther's teachings.[56] Now, given Cromwell's recent tour to Rome to bribe a pope into granting petitions, the theses became more relevant to his own life. Luther wrote of the ills of indulgences and purgatory, while Erasmus was fighting to put three aspects into his new, easily accessible bible: fidelity, lucidity, and purity of language.[57]

Thomas Cromwell, by admission, had never embraced religion or God in his life. The emergence of new offerings from reformist Luther and humanist Erasmus sparked a new start for him. With his elegant Latin and Greek skills, John Foxe wrote that Cromwell, 'so continued, till, at length, by learning without book (formal education), the text of the New Testament of Erasmus' translation, in his going and coming from Rome, he began to be touched, and called to better understanding'.[58]

Cromwell returned to London having been paid 60l 19s 3d (almost £31,000 today) in fees and expenses for the trip.[59] He continued his relationships with those from the Boston Guild, especially John Robinson, the pair becoming personal friends.[60] Robinson wrote of travelling from Boston to London to visit Cromwell and Elizabeth at their Fenchurch Street home, deep in the heart of the Italian quarter. Cromwell never became a member of the Boston Guild despite his employment; this would have been a public display of religious views. However, he did continue working with them as late as 1524, helping them print religious pamphlets in London.[61]

In approximately 1520, Gregory Cromwell was born, possibly named after Pope Gregory, Apostle of the English, a Roman man who spread Christianity into England, a religious go-between for Italy and England. Cromwell's late sister Katherine also had a son named Gregory; perhaps the boys were both born in spring, around the time of Saint Gregory's feast day of 12 March.

At thirty-five, Thomas Cromwell had found the new religion, started a new family and would begin a whole new era in his life.

Chapter 4

1521–1523: Advancement

'he began to be touched, and called to better understanding'

Thomas likely felt comfortable with his life in 1521. He and Elizabeth had a home on Fenchurch Street in London,[1] surrounded by Italian friends. A steady stream of private legal clients continued to fund his lifestyle, along with work with merchants. Men like Cromwell, with legal and language skills, were essential to continue the trading practices of England's elite. The Cromwell family was ever-growing; son Gregory had been born, and Cromwell's mother-in-law Mercy Prior lived with the family. Katherine and Morgan Williams' sons Richard, Walter and Gregory were almost old enough to start apprenticeships, and Elizabeth and William Wellyfed now had three children, Christopher, William, and Alice. All six of these nieces and nephews would receive their uncle's attention, assistance, and money throughout their lives. Also, the household included Elizabeth Cromwell's sister Joan, and her husband John Williamson and their daughter Joan. The couple would live with Cromwell for the rest of his life, and John Williamson would go on to be one of Cromwell's closest stewards and friends.

By 1520, as King Henry and King Francis met at the Field of Cloth of Gold, and a year before King Henry would be titled Defender of the Faith by Pope Leo, the Reformation spread throughout Europe. Martin Luther's teachings circulated, generally resting on the arguments against purgatory, prayers for the dead, indulgences, and the sacrificial character of mass. Erasmus had taken it further with his humanist teachings, suggesting confession, fasting, vows and clerical celibacy harmed rather than affirmed spirituality.[2] Early Lutheranism suggested faith rather than good works would redeem a soul, and Catholics bitterly opposed this.[3] The Reformation caught on amongst merchants who travelled and associated with Europe,[4] and the fire of this new religion grew on English soil.[5] As groups of like-minded men began to gather, Cromwell found his good friends among them. What Cromwell learned now would come in helpful when creating the English church a decade later.

At this stage, Cromwell still lived on the edges of gentility, living in the Italian quarter near his friends Giovanni Cavalcanti, Antonio Bonvisi and Pier-Francesco de' Bardi, all just a street away from the Frescobaldi manor, and attended Austin Friars church within the precinct of St Peter-le-Poer. This church was the place that the Italians and other foreigners would worship, a welcoming home away from home.

Cromwell's Italian family helped him to sustain a household with a decent income. Diplomacy was key, and interactions between Rome and London were in constant need of men like Cromwell to work as interpreters, legal guides, or ambassadors. His friend Bonvisi, a man with broad connections in England and Italy, could introduce Cromwell to men like Silvestro Gigli, the Bishop of Worcester (who escaped his part in the murder of Cardinal Bainbridge in Rome), and Gigli's successor, Girolamo Ghinucci.[6] The bishop had a nephew named Augustine de Augustinus, who endlessly popped up in Cromwell's correspondence being a mixture of help and hindrance.[7]

While overseeing legal matters and increasing his religious knowledge and contacts, Cromwell never lost his links with the merchants. His friends Cavalcanti and Bardi were the leading importers of luxury black velvet, silks, and gold thread, and regularly spent time with King Henry and Pope Leo.[8] Cromwell also kept in contact with merchants in Southampton and Bristol, with the Frescobaldi family continuing to trade to pay off their enormous debt to the king. Cromwell made friends with William Popley, a regular client who worked for William Knight, King Henry's secretary and ambassador, another man who went to Italy in search of an education. All these little connections were stored up for later effectiveness.

Thomas Cromwell, unlike many others, did not attempt to try to ingratiate himself with anyone at the royal court, though they came to his part of town. On 13 May 1521, Edward Stafford, 3rd Duke of Buckingham was found guilty of speaking treasonous words against the king.[9] Four days later he was beheaded, and his body buried at Austin Friars. The friars were a sympathetic group willing to bury noble traitors. The Duke of Buckingham was tucked away from public view, so the faithful could not go to grieve and possibly plan revenge. The Austin Friars sat in the heart of a community of foreigners and had a reputation for helping kings in such matters (Perkin Warbeck was another of Friars' eternal guests).

Among the duke's wide retinue of staff was Sir Charles Knyvett, a ducal estate official. Naturally, once Buckingham was a head shorter, Knyvett was out of a job and sought to regain his position in overseeing the duke's estate. Knyvett had some fifty-five folios of paperwork on the work he did tending to the Buckingham estates, and he needed lawyers to prepare these folios, among them, Thomas Cromwell.[10] Knyvett and Buckingham had seemingly fallen out over issues, and Knyvett was dismissed from his roles, and had petitioned King Henry to be restored. But Knyvett had also taken a role with Lord Berners, Deputy of Calais in April 1521, just as Buckingham was arrested,[11] suggesting Knyvett shared information that helped secure Buckingham's conviction and won the king's favour. Knyvett claimed Buckingham had a secret plan to stab King Henry to death in a private audience, just as his father had planned to do to King Richard almost forty years earlier.[12] Among those on the jury to condemn Buckingham was his cousin Thomas Grey, Marquess of Dorset, employer of Morgan and young Richard Williams, and kin to Cromwell's mother-in-law Mercy Prior.

Cromwell's exact involvement with Buckingham and Knvyett is unknown, but it left a stark impression. Much of the work Cromwell did for Knyvett would have gone unnoticed, had he not received a letter bringing up the whole affair. John Gough, a Welsh cousin of Morgan Williams, wrote to Cromwell from Calais, reminding Cromwell he had still not paid the forty-seven angels (£10,000 today) he owed for items he bought from the seized Buckingham estate.[13] It is possible Cromwell travelled to Calais with Knyvett on his trip when Buckingham was sentenced to death, or gained items from Buckingham's estate through Buckingham's Welsh assets for Knyvett. What items Cromwell gained from Buckingham for such a large amount is untraceable, but for such a hefty cost, it shows how successful Cromwell had become with his private business.

Buckingham's wife, Eleanor Percy, soon remarried, but the duke left four adult children. Cromwell formed a close friendship with Buckingham's eldest daughter Elizabeth after her father's death. Poor

Elizabeth Stafford had been in love with the Earl of Westmoreland, only to watch him marry her sister, with Elizabeth married off to Thomas Howard, who became the Duke of Norfolk in 1524. Norfolk was thirty-five, Elizabeth only fifteen at their marriage. Norfolk lost his first wife, Princess Anne of York and all their children, and now Elizabeth was expected to provide an heir. By the time Cromwell came into Knvyett's employ, Elizabeth had given Norfolk four children and was fated to spend decades at the hands of her abusive husband. Cromwell and Norfolk went on to become bitter enemies, and Cromwell's constant listening, assisting and intercessions with Elizabeth cannot have helped matters.[14]

By this time, Cromwell lived a content and respectable life, and clearly had many close friends. He received a letter from John Creke, to his 'dearest friend in this world'. The letter, written in Italian, laments much, saying:

> the great friendship that has been between us cannot leave my memory, for the affection was so perfect, and if ever I come north, you shall know it. My love towards you rests in no less vigour than it did at our last being together. My heart mourns for your company and Mr Woodall's as ever it did for men. As I am a true Christian man, and I never had so faithful affection to men of so short acquaintance in my life, the which affection increases as daily, like a fire. God knows what pain I received in departing, when I remember our goodly walking in your garden, it makes me desperate to contemplate. I would write more, but my heart will not let me.[15]

Poor Creke was suffering either homesickness or loneliness on his trip to assist Emperor Charles in Spain, and fully embraced the flowery language of the age.

Another tricky situation popped up in a letter from Cromwell's 'well-beloved friend' Richard Chaufer, who requested help suing William Blount, Lord Mountjoy.[16] This may have been slightly difficult, as Mountjoy's wife was Dorothy Grey, sister of Cromwell's new master. Morgan Williams and his teenage son Richard had long been in the household of Thomas Grey, 2nd Marquess of Dorset, and by 1522, Cromwell joined his brother-in-law and nephew. Cromwell acted as a go-between for family members, as he spent much time ingratiating himself with Grey and his wife Margaret, Grey's many siblings, and Grey's mother Cecily Bonville, the Dowager Marchioness.[17] The role in the Dorset household was not a full-time position, given that he continued to have private clients and had a life outside the household.

Then came a privileged promotion, a place in parliament courtesy of Thomas Grey. With Wolsey as Lord Chancellor of England, parliament sat irregularly, with no sessions held between 1515 and 1523. Before the parliament session beginning in April 1523, Cromwell had been working on a petition for Thomas Grey, who wished to pass a bill stating that Holm Cultram in Cumberland should gain tax exemption due to military importance.[18] He was also working on paperwork for Grey's vast estates in the area,[19] before Grey's trip to the Scottish border. To see through this petition in parliament, it would be useful to have a man there in the seat of either Carlisle or Appleby to oversee proceedings. Sadly, neither of these locations recorded who represented them in 1523.

Entering the House of Commons gave Cromwell great opportunities; it was to become the great love in his life, and the opportunities to make friends countrywide exploded over the seventeen-week session. He soon picked up a new legal client in Sir Richard Cornwall, who wrote of Cromwell's kindness shown during the business in parliament.[20] The Speaker in Parliament was Sir Thomas More, who was not on good terms with Cardinal Wolsey at the time, which gave eagle-eyed Cromwell an insight into the men. Cromwell had no great desire to make himself popular in this parliament, and while the petition for Thomas Grey was eventually abandoned, Cromwell wrote himself a twenty-nine-page speech, arguing against King Henry, right before him in parliament no less, while being well prepared, cautious, and eloquent. Henry had it in his head to claim France, so Cardinal Wolsey attempted to extract a benevolence, a forced loan, from the people of England.[21] This was not ratified by parliament, leaving King Henry's 'Great Enterprise' 800,000l (£420,000,000 today) short for the war. Cromwell took it upon himself to inform King Henry he was wrong. After a thick layer of compliments to Henry, Cromwell laid out the basic facts: sending men into France was useless if they could not feed, clothe, and provision them. Cromwell broke it down to basic details, enough to show the plan had enough flaws in it to delay any invasion. War would have hurt trade through the Low Countries and into the Hanseatic regions in northern Germany. Between the loss of merchant ships being able to safely travel and the loss of men, Cromwell's, and his friends', thriving businesses would be harmed, not that those details entered his otherwise noble and patriotic speech.

Not long after the parliament finished, Cromwell wrote to his homesick friend John Creke in Bilbao saying, 'it is said that news refreshes the spirit of life'. Cromwell went on to tell Creke how he had spent seventeen weeks in parliament discussing:

> war, peace, strife, contention, debate, murmured grudges, riches, poverty, penury, truth, falsehood, justice, equity, distaste, oppression, magnanimity, accurate force, intemperance, treason, murder, felony, consuls … and how a commonwealth might be edified and continued within our realm. However, in conclusion, we have done as our predecessors have done that we left where we began …[22]

This casual and somewhat facetious letter also bears the first mention of old friends, especially of Stephen Vaughan, an English merchant who specialised in trade out of Antwerp and Brussels, and one of Cromwell's longest-serving agents and dearest friends. While the two men appear to have been very close, Cromwell had a level of ambition Vaughan never shared and often struggled in positions Cromwell sought for his friend.[23] Nevertheless, Vaughan benefitted from the friendship like all of Cromwell's friends and tried to promote him wherever he could. It was Vaughan's friendship and loyalty that never wavered.

Among all his work, Cromwell gained himself a space on the wardmote, a citizen committee gathered to discuss issues in the Broad Street ward of London where he lived, covering eight presentments. Most complaints to the committee were for damaged pavements, safety hazards, and people being called up for simple misdemeanours. Many of the complaints spoke of fires and chimneys not letting out enough smoke. Drains and gutters were defective, and a child had recently drowned. Several wives were singled out as scolds, though in Cromwell's area, St Peter le Poer, it was a Spaniard named John St John who was singled out for 'misbehaviour and evil conversation'. The book of the wardmote paperwork is written in Cromwell's hand, with his signatures some of only a handful, placed alongside the men who sought to make east London a safer and cleaner place to live.[24]

The pavement outside Austin Friars church was damaged and in need of urgent repair. It was likely soon replaced, for Cromwell had taken up the lease of the property against the friary to make into his own manor home. Cromwell and Elizabeth soon moved from Fenchurch Street into their small new home, followed by their whole extended families.

Of all the grand lands and estates Thomas Cromwell would eventually gain, it was Austin Friars in northeast London that forever remained the principal seat of the Cromwell family. The Order of Augustinian Friars had first opened in London in the 1260s, two decades after a group of Tuscan hermits worshipping under the Rule of St Augustine arrived in Norfolk.[25] The order grew over the next century, receiving grants of money and nearby buildings to expand their holdings, though they had diminished in number by the early sixteenth century. Much of the friary's lands bordered Broad and Throgmorton Streets, and Swan Alley led to the front door to Cromwell's new home. He would have felt in fine company in St. Peter's parish; the friary was dedicated to education, with a congregation of 'alien' parishioners, mostly Italian, German, and Flemish families.[26] Cromwell had friends all in the immediate vicinity; Giovanni Cavalcanti and Pier-Francesco de Bardi both lived in Austin Friars' buildings. Antonio Bonvisi lived just streets away.[27] With friends all around, along came fine guests; Bonvisi had taken over the lease from his friend, Sir Thomas More, at nearby Crosby Hall. Bonvisi also worked with Cromwell's acquaintance Girolamo Ghinucci, who worked for the Vatican. Gregory di Casali often rented a home from Austin Friars when in London and shared it with the secretary of Cardinal Giulio de' Medici, who would soon become Pope Clement VII.[28] While Cromwell was only a merchant, these people close to power already knew his name. But one most personal friendship began when Cromwell met Sir Henry Wyatt, his son Thomas and daughter Margaret. Sir Henry worked as Master of the King's Jewel House.[29] Young Thomas Wyatt had a love of all things Italian and while Margaret Wyatt was only eighteen when she first met Thomas and Elizabeth Cromwell, she would spend much time in their company, holidaying with Cromwell, marrying one of his servants and even naming one of her sons Cromwell.

While Cromwell's Austin Friars home would undergo sweeping alterations for the entirety of his time there, his first house remained a similar size until 1532. While the lease for this first decade has not survived, his mail was addressed to the 'dwelling at the Friar Augustine's gate',[30] putting the home between the friary churchyard and a home owned by Cavalcanti on Broad Street.[31] The Cromwell house boasted just fourteen rooms, plus a cellar and great space in the roof as servants' quarters. The 1527 inventory of Austin Friars, likely taken to establish a will, gives a detailed insight into Cromwell and his family before life in royal service.[32] The twenty-two-page list shows Cromwell's success and tastes. The walls had hangings in his favourite colours of red and green, with large green Persian carpets on the floor. The centre of the wide main hall bore a long detailed wooden table, surrounded by gilded chairs, stools and footstools of various sizes. Parlours could seat many around tables with comfortable seats covered with green cushions embroidered with red roses. Two leather chairs are singled out as fine Flanders creations, and one table is listed as bearing the image of the Lord in carved detailing. The walls bore both a canvas bearing Cardinal Wolsey's arms, and a portrait of Emperor Charles V. The house also had a private parlour, with wide windows so Cromwell and his Elizabeth could look out over their garden. Playing tables, made of wood and bone, were used for cards and dice, and sat with triangular stools, and long padded wooden seats lined the walls for guests to use, plumped with green cushions. On the parlour wall was a large canvas of a pair of lovers, while other rooms had various religious iconography. While Austin Friars was small, the family did not lack for anything, with rooms filled with plate for entertaining, a kitchen well stocked for parties, and bedrooms filled with fine clothing and fabrics.

Cromwell filled his bedroom with his favourite red and green, with golden bells adorning the curtains around his bed. He had featherbeds and goose feather quilts, like all the beds in the house, but his wardrobe was unmatched. The inventory details dozens of fine overgowns, made of fine wool, velvet, and damask, and almost all black. They were all lined with fine black and white sable, mink, and rabbit fur. Every coat had matching doublets, jerkins, and dozens of sets of hose. Black represented wealth and respectability, particularly in Italy and England, and suited men of an older age. Cromwell was now almost forty years old and probably felt well-entitled to wear this marker of success. But he clearly enjoyed bright coloured riding coats, made in vivid blues, greens and orange velvet. French caps, button caps, silk hoods, and Burgundian velvet hats sat alongside twelve pairs of gloves. Cromwell's experience in fabrics had paid off, as his clothing collection must have been quite an array of the availability of the period and showed a wealthy style for living even before his rise to power.

Elizabeth's rooms and wardrobes were no less impressive. She decorated in blues and yellows surrounding various statues of the Virgin Mary. Elizabeth owned many gowns in blacks, greys, and blues, mostly made of wool, velvet, satin and finished with wide black sleeves. Fine fabrics were stored all over the house, and rooms dedicated to Cromwell's mother-in-law Mercy displayed equal luxury and comfort. Throughout the 1520s, the Cromwell house was only one quarter the size it would eventually inhabit, though certainly big enough, and luxurious enough, for any well-established lawyer and merchant with a happy and respectable extended family.

Chapter 5

1524–1527: Enlightenment

'dangerous allusions to topical ecclesiastical and political affairs'

If a gentleman wished to call himself a lawyer in England, he needed to belong to one of the four Inns of Court dotted around the country. The Honourable Society of Gray's Inn sat one mile west of Austin Friars in central London, near Chancery Lane. Gray's Inn had been operating from its location since the 1370s, and in 1524, Thomas Cromwell was admitted and recognised as a lawyer. Thomas Cromwell, gentlemen of London, with no legal training, was legitimate in his role. Had his career peaked at this point, it would already have been a remarkable rise from his start in Putney.

Cromwell probably felt as if he needed this elevation. In early 1524, he left the service of Thomas Grey, Marquess of Dorset, and transferred to a position with Cardinal Thomas Wolsey. Wolsey held a stranglehold on England's power since the time Cromwell first returned to England. Wolsey swiftly rose in power after King Henry VIII's coronation in 1509, adapting his position on issues to whatever the young king wanted, leaving him constantly in Henry's good graces. Wolsey was the rarest of men; a common-born man surrounded by noble courtiers, meaning he had no choice but to work his way into power. Wolsey knew his allies and enemies; he slowly dripped poison into Henry's ear about whoever disliked him, while aiding and supporting those who could benefit him. Charles Brandon, the new Duke of Suffolk had little choice but to support Wolsey after he pleaded for the king not to punish Suffolk and his new bride, Henry's sister Mary Tudor, Queen of France, when they married without permission in 1515.[1] Acts such as this came not from kindness, but from necessity for Wolsey. Wolsey supported Henry's call for war in France in 1511 when others would not and gained the role of Canon of Windsor. By 1514, he was Bishop of Lincoln and Archbishop of York, and became a cardinal and then Lord Chancellor of England by

1515. Year on year, Wolsey's influence increased, ousted courtiers such as Archbishop of Canterbury William Warham, executed the Duke of Buckingham, limited parliament's power, and ensured his fortune.

Thomas Cromwell would be a perfect fit for Thomas Wolsey's household. The commoner, around twelve years older than Cromwell, son of Robert and Joan Wolsey, grew up as a butcher's son from Ipswich who attended Magdalen College at Oxford before becoming secretary to Richard Foxe, one of Henry VII's closest advisors. Henry VII took kindly to Wolsey's diligence and loyalty, making him an ambassador to Scotland in 1508,[2] paving the way for Wolsey to have access to Henry VIII just a year later. Wolsey, happy to take on a deluge of tasks others found too dull, suited the young new king perfectly, who never looked down on Wolsey for his humble background. A man without a noble background had no supporters, and thus, could never be a threat to the king.

Now, Wolsey needed a new lawyer fluent in Italian, and finding a common-born man with such tenacity created a personal and professional relationship. Thomas Grey likely mentioned Cromwell to Wolsey, as did Dr John Aleyn, Wolsey's Commissary-General since 1518, a staunch Italian-Englishman, and brother to Thomas Aleyn, who had been Cromwell's friend since they first worked together in 1519.[3] The Aleyn brothers had a colleague, a former London mayor also named John Allen, another friend to Cromwell,[4] and between them and Thomas Grey, Cromwell came highly recommended.

Cromwell, and perhaps even Wolsey himself, could not see it, but Wolsey's power over England was diminishing. The 1523 parliament had yielded no results for raising taxes to fund war with France. Wolsey had spent a decade brokering peace with Europe, all for little. The 1522 tax increases had drained the laity of funds and the clergy would not pay what was demanded, which was one-third of the profit of their goods.[5] By 1525, Wolsey had to enact viciously unpopular Amicable Grant taxes, forcing more money from the people, leading to uprisings quelled by the Dukes of Suffolk and Norfolk.[6] Wolsey always gave King Henry what he wanted but failed to fund the war. But, while being humiliated, Wolsey pressed on with his work as if he had lost none of the king's favour.

In Wolsey's offices, Thomas Cromwell could shine. Wolsey's magnificent tomb was still under construction at Windsor Castle, overseen by Italian artists. The head sculptor, Benedetto Rovezzano, was a Florentine, and an intermediary was needed between Wolsey's office and the men creating the structure of Florentine marble and brass; Cromwell's extensive knowledge of languages and Italian culture was perfect for the task. Rovezzano was financed by two of Cromwell's friends, artist Antonio Cavallari and merchant Antonio Bonvisi.[7] On the face of it, a role overseeing Italian artists did not seem like a taxing job, but it was the funds to pay for the work that needed the right Italian-Englishman for the job. Wolsey had multiple vanity projects; he was setting up Ipswich College and Cardinal College Oxford, the sites of his birth and his education, respectively. Fortunately, there was a precedent for raising funds for such works. During the fourteenth and fifteenth centuries, small monasteries with French connections were closed, punished for their connection during wartime. Henry VI had created Eton and King's Colleges off the back of the money and fittings of such monasteries, and Wolsey was ready to do the same.

Cromwell's time in Wolsey's employ started easily. In his papers appear two more men who would become lifelong allies. Sir Brian Tuke was secretary to Wolsey and worked extensively with Cromwell from the beginning of his time in the Lord Chancellor's offices. Among Cromwell's paperwork for private clients and personal friends, a letter for Wolsey's colleges, about closing the monastery at Lesnes outside London, Cromwell wrote a draft of a letter with a curious message: 'You wrote to me in your last letter that your errand was in good point. For God's sake forsake not that and make much of them that offers it till you know more. There can no man make me believe but as I have written. The 6th day at midnight, Master Pace has written to me, and he opened the letter, but there was no harm in it'. Tuke added a note underneath Cromwell's hand, likely a remembrance for Cromwell, 'look whether the letter that came from Rome be opened or not'.[8] Right from the beginning, Cromwell and Tuke appear in the thick of Wolsey's vast array of murky tasks.

Another introduction was Thomas Wriothesley, a young lawyer working for Archdeacon Stephen Gardiner, who occupied the ecclesiastical equivalent to Cromwell's laity position. Wriothesley's handwriting appears on several documents created by Cromwell, such as one for the Earl of Oxford, who had written to Wolsey on a matter of inheritance.[9] Much has been speculated about Wriothesley's early work for Cromwell, but Wriothesley sat firmly on Gardiner's side for the first decade since their first meeting. Thomas Wriothesley and Stephen Vaughan had identical handwriting, the typical legal clerk style of the time, which means the men have been often confused in archives. Cromwell and Vaughan had worked together closely since at least 1523 but Vaughan's handwriting is still often mistaken for Wriothesley's in archives. Wriothesley had precious little to do with Cromwell at this time, and was more than a decade away from Cromwell's employ. But Stephen Vaughan and Brian Tuke were part of Cromwell's daily life for the entirety of his time with Wolsey, and then through all of Cromwell's foray into public life for the court. Vaughan, worked for Cromwell in a personal capacity out of the Austin Friars house, and as his man in Antwerp and Brussels, as Cromwell never got the chance to travel to the Low Countries again. Among the variety of papers which exist for Cromwell's private clients in 1524, includes working for the Grey family, and acting as the lawyer overseeing Sir Henry Wyatt's resignation from the king's Jewel House.

Cromwell needed Vaughan at Austin Friars when he set off around the country at Wolsey's behest, to close underperforming monasteries. Yorkshire was first on the list for inspections, a trip that would cost more in expenses than Cromwell would make in a year as a monastery inspector, around 50l (£22,000 today). Cromwell wrote up the letters patent to begin the construction of Oxford College, and continued around Leicestershire, Essex, Suffolk, Herefordshire and London to visit monasteries, alongside a team of men. The project appears to have been as much a friendship-making exercise as a task that would draw extensive criticism through 1525 and 1526. Letters would talk of business, and then also ask if Cromwell's mother-in-law Mercy could send plasters for sore knees.[10] Legal papers would arrive alongside six dozen Calais quails for Elizabeth Cromwell,[11] or gifts of plovers and wine while asking after Elizabeth.[12] The sole surviving letter to Elizabeth Cromwell from her husband dates from 1525; much has been made of it over the years, suggesting Cromwell was a good husband. Cromwell was in Bayham in Kent in November 1525 and sent her a doe and asked her for news from others, signing the letter 'per your husband Thomas Crumwell'.[13] Hardly the most insightful or personal of messages. By this time, in addition to their son Gregory, the Cromwells were parents to a daughter, Anne.

By early 1526, Cromwell was still working privately for the Grey family, with Sir John Grey writing to his 'brother Cromwell'. Sir John knew how involved Cromwell had become in the monastery project and looked to scoop up freshly available land for lease in Buckinghamshire.[14] Cromwell also needed to oversee all the paperwork ensuring the creation of Ipswich College, and the project was no easy task, as Cromwell soon discovered, particularly in Kent. Tonbridge Priory resisted their closing, arguing their case without success. Alongside Cromwell was his friend John Aleyn, who soon became known as a man 'using rough fashion' when closing monasteries.[15] Aleyn picked up a reputation for being cruel to clergymen as they went about their business, whereas Cromwell seemed to pick up friends. But when Cromwell sent Stephen Vaughan to help close Lesnes monastery, so big the land was divided among twelve separate leases, Cromwell and Aleyn needed to seek licenses to have Vaughan and the other men protected from those who fought to stop the closure.[16] On Cromwell's visit to Bayham Abbey, a riot broke out, with rumours Archbishop Warham encouraged them.[17] These arguments only spurred on the project. But the uprisings that persisted on their travels between Kent and Sussex did not yield entirely poor results; for Cromwell had become known around the countryside as the man who closed monasteries, but people started assuming he was the man who could save monasteries. On a trip to Westminster Hall, Cromwell was cornered by several men who begged him to help with their monastery in Shulbrede, as their prior Robert Sherborne was to be ousted so the Bishop of Chichester could lease the monastery for profit. Cromwell called on Henry, Lord Percy, who could influence local affairs, and the monastery survived another decade, and Cromwell received a small annual pension from Shulbrede in thanks.[18] Bilsington Priory in Kent was earmarked for closure, and Sir Henry Guildford, friend to Cromwell as Guildford married Thomas Grey's sister, invited him to Leeds Castle to discuss the matter. Again, Cromwell was able to keep the local monastery open for another ten years.[19] Being able to call on the Guildfords in Kent allowed Cromwell to curate friendships in the gentry that would come in helpful later.

While working on monasteries in Suffolk, Cromwell met Thomas Rush, a member of the local gentry and member of parliament, and his stepson Thomas Alvard.[20] Rush and Alvard were traditional Catholics, while Cromwell continued with his readings of the evangelical religion. This bothered neither side of the argument, and the group began a friendship that lasted for years, with Cromwell turning to them when in dire need. Rush joined Cromwell closing Suffolk priories, and helping him obtain paperwork needed to help protect monastery inspectors from harm.[21]

St Frideswide's in Oxford was to become Oxford College, and it would have been plausible to assume that Prior John Burton would be upset to lose his priory, but after meeting Cromwell, they began a long-term friendship. Abbot Whalley at St. Mary's of York started sending a pension to Cromwell as a reward for his help. Thomas Frisby at Launde Priory sent Cromwell his favourite cheeses and asked him to visit again.[22] Abbot Stonewell at Pershore Abbey in Worcestershire remained Cromwell's friend for fifteen years after their meeting, while Abbot Richard Kidderminster at Winchcombe, a universally beloved man, clearly admired Cromwell, and became annoyed when Cromwell could not visit him at Christmas.[23] Kidderminster was a classic example of the fervently Catholic men Cromwell spent time with, even after his clear adoration for the new religion became obvious. While Cromwell was developing a reputation for doing Wolsey's dirty work, he always left a good impression of his character along the way, quite an achievement given the hostility over the endeavour.

By 1526, most of Cromwell's close personal friends that he could trust in later years were already in his life. At this stage, there was no advantage to being a friend of Cromwell and finding men truly loyal once he entered the king's employ would prove a challenge, with hundreds of letters arriving at a time, praising him and his work. But while he worked with Wolsey, Cromwell saw the true character of those about him. Working for Cromwell was William Brabazon, a long-time friend who would wade through the endless paperwork of monasteries on Cromwell's behalf. Another friend, John Gostwick, considered Cromwell his patron and fell over himself to be of good use to the man he considered so important.

An especially interesting friendship developed between Cromwell and Dr Miles Coverdale, a friar from Austin Friars Cambridge. Coverdale would become one of the main players in the creation of Cromwell's English Bible ten years later, but in 1526, was simply a friend, questioning his place as a friar. Coverdale believed Cromwell was a humanist patron and wrote of enjoying their time together at Easter, appreciating Cromwell's encouragement for the new faith.[24] Alongside Coverdale at Cambridge was Dr Robert Barnes, who had been imprisoned at Christmas 1525 for delivering a 'heretical' sermon, praising the new religion, and attacking the church's wealth. Barnes was accused of bringing together Lollards and Lutherans; the Lollards were a largely defunct group of people believing in illegal English bibles and questioning the church's wealth and power. The Lutherans were following Martin Luther's new faith which spread like wildfire through England, championing the end of indulgences and attacking church abuses. Barnes spent six months in Fleet Prison, but then gained an open house arrest at Austin Friars London, living next door to Cromwell. Given that Wolsey was light on heretics, it is not a stretch to suggest Cromwell sought to have Robert Barnes released. It was not in the church's interest to do so; Barnes started distributing William Tyndale's new English Bible from Austin Friars. Bishop Cuthbert Tunstall, an enemy to Wolsey, sent Barnes to Austin Friars Northampton, to keep him quiet, with little success.

Until this point, Cromwell had kept his opinions on religion quiet. He had only had his serious 'come to Jesus' moment late in life by standards of the time. Cromwell received no favours, roles or money from Wolsey. But Cromwell had gained an unusually high understanding of monastic life thanks to his tours of monasteries, something a layman never got to see. He worked with mostly ecclesiastical servants serving Wolsey but kept no outward religious views. Cromwell also met the nobility, doing a lot of work for men like Thomas Stanley, Lord Monteagle and Lord Darcy of Templehurst, yet he never attempted to gain favour with any nobles he encountered. Cromwell made himself something of a mystery without even trying.

It was only later that people attempted to put a title on Cromwell's religious leanings, labelling him a Lutheran or a Lollard for the sake of insults. But those seeking to pin down his beliefs would have struggled at every stage of his life. He had worked extensively for the Boston Guild, a group which would never betray its Catholic beliefs, and yet Cromwell made friends with the cascade of evangelicals that defected from the Guild, among them Thomas Garrett.[25] Cromwell had a close friend Donato Rullo of Venice, who was also friends with Reginald Pole, and the pair could not decide on Cromwell's true loyalties.[26] It was posited that Cromwell followed the style of Niccolò Machiavelli, his near neighbour back in Florence. He had come of age in Florence under the control of Piero Soderini, a firm Catholic, but the city had just endured almost a decade under the control of Girolamo Savonarola, a man who believed in cleaning up the abuses of the church and its corruption. Even at this early stage, Cromwell was establishing himself as a Nicodemite, one who did not show any outward appearance of their faith, a person of 'dangerous thoughts, dangerous allusions to topical ecclesiastical and political affairs'.

Cromwell did occasionally show hints of his leanings or at least gave others an impression. His friendships with Miles Coverdale and Robert Barnes made it clear he supported their views, and they were members of a group who, according to John Foxe, regularly met at the White Horse Tavern in Cambridge, nicknamed 'Little Germany', because of their reformist discussions. Besides Barnes and Coverdale, other members were Hugh Latimer, Thomas Cranmer, Nicholas Shaxton, John Bale, Thomas Bilney, John Clerk, and George Joye.[27] Being friends with such university men made no secret of what Cromwell discussed in his own time.

But Cromwell had another issue placed upon his shoulders. The project for closing the monasteries largely ended by late 1527, with the first half of 1527 bringing in 9,828l (or £4,300,000 today) to go towards the new Oxford University, but word of the endeavour spread. William Knight, secretary to King Henry, wrote to Wolsey, warning him that Henry was unhappy with the monastery project. Knight was off to Rome for the King's Great Matter and warned Wolsey never to send either John Aleyn or Thomas Cromwell to the king as a messenger, as, 'I have heard the king, and noblemen, speak things incredible of acts of Misters Aleyn and Crumwell', regarding their conduct at monasteries.[28] John Aleyn's rough behaviour at monasteries had travelled, tainting Cromwell in the process. With the Dukes of Norfolk and Suffolk, Thomas Boleyn, and William Fitzwilliam also mentioned in the same letter on other matters of secrecy, it is easy to believe all these men heard the words Knight was desperate to relay to Wolsey before his departure to Rome.

Cromwell had a tough month, with a letter to Wolsey dated 6 August 1527 sharing a frightening personal experience.[29] Wolsey was in France to gain support for Henry's annulment, with his men in charge of his York Place palace in London. As the plague season eased, men hiding in sanctuary at Westminster planned to escape and flee the country to avoid punishment. However, several prisoners were being held in the Gatehouse and the sanctuary men planned to break into the prison, free their friends and escape. While the Gatehouse had guards, the staff at York Place feared a riot at the palace, leaving a group of men, Cromwell included, to keep watch. On the night of 6 August, the sanctuary men, including three men named Penn, Sergier, and Servington lay in wait to kill Cromwell. While Cromwell fought off the would-be murderers, the prisoners were freed from the Gatehouse, and all made their escape. Once abroad, the men could not be tracked, leaving Cromwell's attackers permanently on the loose. Probably not a story he shared with Elizabeth when he returned home to Austin Friars.

By the close of 1527, Cromwell was listed as Receiver-General and Surveyor of Oxford College and he was settling Wolsey's accounts while his friend John Croke enjoyed a lavish time in France with the cardinal.[30] Cromwell also still worked with private clients, and the papers show friends and family serving as staff. While overseeing the case of the murder of Isabella Watson and her unborn child, listed is a young Ralph Sadler, Thomas Avery from Putney, and Cromwell's brother-in-law John Williamson.[31] Another client was Lady Alice Clere, sister of Thomas Boleyn, who needed her husband saved from prison due to debts.[32]

Cromwell, no doubt aware of his unpopularity over the closing of monasteries, continued with his plans with Cardinal College Oxford, as the university was ready to bring in new fellows. Wolsey had two well-respected Catholic men at the college, John London, and John Longland, who would soon send letters to one another in horror at what was occurring at the university. It was now Cromwell, not Wolsey, doing the hiring for the university, with he and Thomas Arundell receiving applications and granting positions.[33] When Cromwell appointed evangelical ally John Clerk as canon at the university, the staunch Catholics were aghast. Soon, Cromwell lured William Tyndale away from the Boston Guild, likewise John Frith, though friend Thomas Cranmer refused Cromwell's enticement to leave Jesus College in Cambridge. Cromwell's humanist friend George Elyot, who lived in Oxfordshire, was pleased to have Cromwell visiting him while he set up the new college,[34] but a scandal brewed, throwing open Cromwell's quiet beliefs.

Cromwell had dissolved Poughley Priory, twenty-seven miles outside Oxford, in 1525. Cromwell dealt with Edward Fetyplace, and all had gone relatively smoothly, with many of the fittings of the priory removed and transferred to the university.[35] But a letter from Fetyplace in 1527 complained that Poughley and its fittings were 'misused'.[36] A group of men, under the excuse of wanting to escape the plague in Oxford, had set up a heretical evangelical summer camp at Poughley in 1526. Wolsey dismissed the tale, not concerned by the trip or who attended, but Catholic stalwarts Longland and London at Oxford discovered a second summer gathering in 1527. This time, the information gathered showed John Clerk and Thomas Cranmer again running reformist sermons and readings at Poughley. Now Wolsey was angered, and Cromwell's fingerprints were all over the issue. All attendees mentioned were his friends, and letters still exist of Clerk writing to Cromwell about their 1527 visit,[37] and letters from whistleblower Fetyplace mentioned John Hidden.[38] Hidden came from a powerful family of Lollards, and his sister was Alice Doyley, a woman Cromwell had strongly represented in the Court of Chancery months earlier. The nest of heretics had risen in Wolsey's new college and Cromwell had not only taken part, but quietly created the nest right under Wolsey's nose while the cardinal worked on King Henry's annulment.

The 'Little Germany' meetings in Cambridge and the first summer readings had gone unpunished, but Wolsey could no longer turn a blind eye. Ten men were rounded up and imprisoned in a cellar filled with salted fish at Oxford, among them John Clerk and John Frith. Thomas Bilney, another of the original group, was already in the Tower for heretical sermons. But with the sweating sickness beginning its march through England, three prisoners died in the cellar.[39] The others were released and escaped to Germany, where William Tyndale, George Joye, Richard Bayfield, Miles Coverdale, and Thomas Hitton had already fled. The danger of being a reformer in England came into the light. For years they had slipped under Thomas Wolsey's radar, knowing his forgiving nature; Wolsey never burned heretics and rarely gave out harsh punishments. But upon Wolsey's fall, none of these men would be safe. Cromwell, the layman among them, remained unscathed; while he was a friend to these men, he did not make English translations or arguments against scripture. Thomas Cranmer, Hugh Latimer, John Bale and Nicholas Shaxton all stayed in England, allowed to continue their relatively quiet positions, but the days of going unnoticed had disappeared.

Despite being the man who funnelled these reformers into Oxford, Cromwell kept Wolsey's friendship and trust and would soon expand his role under the cardinal, while also looking to give his young son Gregory an evangelical Cambridge education. Around the end of 1527, Austin Friars had a new baby, Grace, a more unusual baby name for the period, but just as the Cromwells celebrated their third child, their household would soon undergo a tragically momentous shift.

Chapter 6

1528–1529: Lamentation

'cannot endure such taunts after the trouble I have taken'

What sadly lacks in archives is how Thomas Cromwell and Thomas Wolsey came to be close friends outside of their professional relationship. Certainly, spending so much time together would have allowed them to know one another as individuals, but why Cromwell over other loyal servants such as Stephen Gardiner, Rowland Lee, or Brian Tuke? Most people came to Wolsey through the usual channels – through their family's service to a noble house or their privileged religious learning. Cromwell likely felt like a novelty; a man with as low beginnings as Wolsey himself, coupled with a European adventure and an unorthodox education. Cromwell never failed to give a good first impression and had all the charm and mannerisms that endeared him to friends and colleagues. Was he an ambitious man? Surely to a certain extent, given his rise from sheep farmer's son to lawyer and gentleman. He worked hard and enjoyed the fruits of that work. He provided well for his immediate and extended family and friends. But did he serve men like Wolsey in the hope of advancement? In Cromwell's first four years of working for the cardinal, he made little advancement, and made nothing in the way of profit or offices. Cromwell did not use Wolsey as a stepping-stone to something more; he was living his own life, with his deals, clients, and beliefs, while working for Wolsey. Perhaps that sense of contentment and little demand for more sat well with the cardinal.

Another question is, how well did Wolsey know Thomas Cromwell? Cromwell had an air of mystery about him, from his origins and early life through to his education and career, all things other people boasted of, hoping to gain advancement through social connections. Cromwell's 1532 Holbein portrait shows just how carefully Cromwell managed this image. Wolsey was a devout Catholic, who had grown magnificently rich, while Cromwell was a humanist who, while enjoying all the comforts of a gentleman's income, made no serious attempt to show his success. From the outside, the pair could not be more different, yet it was the only friendship Wolsey became desperate to maintain.

While 1528 started in much the same vein as previous years, Wolsey, and likely Cromwell, noticed the slowly shifting sands. King Henry's attempts to gain a quiet annulment from Pope Clement had been unsuccessful, and now the situation was dire. Anne Boleyn rose in favour, and she could see as well as anyone that Wolsey, a man skilled in procrastination at the best of times, had no intention of ending Henry's marriage to Queen Katherine. Wolsey went to France to gain favour with no result, and since the Amicable Grant fiasco of 1525, Henry saw Wolsey as fallible.

The annulment issue hit a standstill after Pope Clement was taken hostage by Emperor Charles during the sack of Rome, and Charles had no intention of doing anything to risk harming his aunt Queen Katherine of England. As far as the world was concerned, Henry and Katherine had a solid and legitimate marriage. Henry's wandering faith in its legitimacy seemed to be borne mostly from a desire to impregnate a younger version of his wife. Anne Boleyn herself had risen in court life despite Henry's annulment failures of 1527 and had accepted her fate as the king's object of affection by 1528, wisely intent on being a queen.

While Wolsey had no interest in serving the Boleyn cause, he strived to satisfy Henry and sought to have Cardinal Lorenzo Campeggio come to England in his capacity as both Cardinal-Protector of England and the Holy Roman Empire, to rule alongside fellow legate Wolsey on an annulment. Wolsey sent several papal bulls in early 1528, written in Cromwell's fine handwriting. Campeggio had already ruled in favour of Katherine of Aragon to the Pope,[1] making the whole exercise pointless, but Wolsey was desperate and had Cromwell draft the paperwork for the case to be heard in England.

Among the varied jobs Cromwell took on over his forty-plus years of life, he probably never envisioned needing to appease and essentially babysit Wolsey's errant illegitimate children. The youngest of the three, Thomas Minterne, appreciated his lot in life and saw out his days in a respectable clerical role,[2] while Wolsey's slightly older daughter Dorothy rarely asked Cromwell for help, other than when she needed assistance while living as a nun at Shaftesbury Abbey.[3] The eldest son, Thomas Winter, was in constant need and regularly threw himself at Cromwell's feet. By 1528, Winter was living in Paris, and his father often withheld money owing to him, gained through preferments lavished on Winter by Wolsey, who then kept the money for himself.[4] From 1528 onwards, Cromwell received a steady stream of letters from Winter, and at times got annoyed with Winter's endless requests for money, and over-inflated praise of Cromwell's kindness. Cromwell had several weak spots, and one was helping those who knew Wolsey, and he certainly understood the feeling of being an outsider. Winter soon joined the league of young men under Cromwell's protective wing.

Wolsey was overloaded with the issue of the royal marriage, delegating more to his favourite lawyer in 1528. One enormous task which followed Cromwell was the estate management of Sir William Compton, one of the highest-ranked courtiers in the king's court.[5] Compton, enemy to Wolsey and close friend of the king, had long been seen (in the Wolsey household) as a hindrance. Compton died of the sweating sickness in June 1528, leaving behind one of the largest landholdings and richest accounts in England, with Wolsey in control over the estate and Compton's six-year-old son and heir.[6] Cromwell became the escheator of the entire case, overseeing the will in favour of Compton's pregnant wife, a case that took more than a decade.[7]

As Cromwell's workload increased, he continued his private affairs, gaining a license to sell corn in Nottinghamshire with close friends Thomas Cranmer and Richard Southwell.[8] Other friends called on him for his services, sending gifts such as barrels of salmon, and George Throckmorton sent him the gift of a greyhound in return for sturgeon and quails.[9] Cromwell continued to travel for the colleges, which Wolsey later wrote to him about saying they were, 'work of your own hands',[10] leaving Stephen Vaughan in charge of Austin Friars. But while in Oxford, Vaughan wrote to say he had locked up Austin Friars as Rodrigo, the local goldsmith and nearest neighbour of the Cromwells, had been stabbed to death in his own home by robbers. They also strangled Rodrigo's friend, an old lady who lived up the street, who had come to Rodrigo in search of a warm fire. Only two of the three murderers were captured, making Vaughan fear for the safety of his best friend's family.[11]

While the scandal of Cromwell's friends being outed as 'heretics' over their summer reading sessions continued, Cromwell was making personal decisions for his family. His son Gregory was now nine years old and in the care of Prioress Margaret Vernon of Little Marlow, whom Cromwell likely met while closing monasteries around Oxford.[12] Gregory had been receiving tutoring from Cromwell's old friend (and former tutor to Henry Fitzroy) John Palsgrave,[13] with little success, and Cromwell instead moved his son away to Pembroke Hall in Cambridge, alongside his cousin Christopher Wellyfed, and Nicholas Sadler, younger brother of Ralph Sadler. The three young boys, the 'Cambridge scholars', letters would call them, went into John Chekyng's care, with Chekyng informing Cromwell he had paid a full 51 (£2,000 today) for a book by Erasmus to use with the boys.[14] It has been speculated Cromwell was slow to pay for his son's education, resulting in letters complaining of non-payment, which seems a misinterpretation; rather, setting up the new home and schooling for the trio simply cost far more than expected, especially once sweating sickness began its rampant killing-spree through the summer of 1528, and Chekyng and the boys needed to flee to the country. The notion Gregory was not bright is another fallacy created from Chekyng's letters. Gregory was only nine, not fifteen or more as some scholars have misidentified, and rather than thinking Gregory slow, Chekyng denounced his former tutor Palsgrave for Gregory's poor introduction to education. Within two months of Chekyng's tutelage, Gregory wrote a letter to his father, with handwriting neater than many adults of the period, with excellent spelling and grammar skills, more than enough to silence any doubters.[15]

While the early half of 1528 had been much like previous years, with successes gained and issues surmounted, the sweating sickness epidemic could not be ignored. By early May, the sweat had broken out in London and quickly spread through most of the country and into Ireland. London suffered the worst, the illness being a summer disease that occurred at the same time as plague season. While many fled the city, King Henry included, this only spread the illness. The sweating sickness, possibly like hantavirus pulmonary syndrome, was a rapid illness that could kill in less than twenty-four hours, and half the sick would lose their lives. Rank made no difference; those as high-ranking as Cardinal Wolsey and Anne Boleyn themselves were afflicted soon after the death of Anne's brother-in-law, William Carey. But Cromwell stayed in London with Wolsey, writing letters to Sir Francis Bryan, who had gone to King Francis on Wolsey's behalf. Cromwell wrote an obvious lie, suggesting that King Francis send an ambassador, 'into England to see, know and understand of the prosperous estate and health of them both (Henry and Wolsey); which, lauds be given unto God, have escaped the great and furious anger of the pestilent plague of sweat lately visiting the realm of England; which plague at this day is well assuaged, and little or nothing heard thereof in any place'.[16]

Neither the sweating sickness, nor the plague, had abated. It was the fifth such outbreak in England in the forty-three years of the Tudor reign. The outbreak quickly spread outside England, infecting one thousand people in a matter of weeks in Hamburg, alongside the Low Countries and Germany. It spread through Germany and into Switzerland by December, before moving through Denmark and Norway and then east through Lithuania and Poland into Russia. While people knew of the sweat, their quarantine and distancing measures could not contain the virus, coupled with intermittent hygiene practices. They had no choice but to continue their lives as normal as possible, hoping God might save them if they were afflicted with the illness.

Cromwell's men at Oxford College suffered. Thomas Bird wrote to Cromwell on 1 September, telling them that four of their men died and another three looked to suffer the same fate.[17] Cromwell's family at Austin Friars were safe in London, and Gregory Cromwell and his classmates isolated in the Cambridge countryside, so Cromwell travelled seventy-five miles northeast to the opening of Ipswich College. All seemed fine; Wolsey received a letter, praising Cromwell's work in Ipswich, saying he had shown much kindness to all in the town.[18] Cromwell, alongside Stephen Gardiner, Geoffrey Pole and Rowland Lee continued closing monasteries and transferring items to the college throughout the month.[19]

But the fortunate position of avoiding the sweating sickness was not to last. Suddenly, Thomas Cromwell disappeared. Wolsey had serious issues to contend with, including the long-awaited arrival of Cardinal Campeggio, yet Cromwell was not working in the offices, nor from Austin Friars. The group working on monasteries at Ipswich disbanded and returned to London, but Cromwell had not returned to work. Cromwell's man Thomas Bird at Oxford wrote on 13 October, asking why payments for the men had not arrived,[20] but Bird got no reply. John Chekyng wrote from Pembroke Hall, to say that Gregory, Christopher, and Nicholas were safe and well, and ready to take up their studies at Cambridge again, and received money for the children's care, yet no news.[21] Nothing, either in Cromwell's correspondence or in Wolsey's offices bore any trace of Cromwell's presence at all. With work piling up, letters went unread, requests ignored, and confusion appeared among the delays and queries. Richard Thomlyn wrote to Cromwell in mid-November, assuming Cromwell was on leave from Wolsey's offices.[22] John Chekyng wrote again on 8 November, after hearing rumours that Cromwell suffered the sweat, but the rumours had turned out to be false.[23] Cromwell suffered the gravest of illnesses; grief. Elizabeth, his dearest wife of nearly fifteen years, was gone. Sweating sickness spared few, and regardless of age, wealth, or status, it picked off people without the slightest hesitation. Sweating sickness often hit middle-aged adults the worst, unlike plague which picked off the elderly or children. Elizabeth Cromwell is unlikely to have been the only casualty within the Cromwell extended family or the Austin Friars household. The illness likely also took the life of Morgan Williams, Cromwell's beloved brother-in-law, leaving three of Cromwell's nephews without parents. Elizabeth Cromwell's mother Mercy came through unscathed by the outbreak, and Stephen Vaughan wrote from Antwerp, calling her his most singular friend after Cromwell, the charming mother-figure to many among those grieving the loss of her eldest daughter.[24]

Cromwell, a man who oozed self-control and order, was missing in action. The death of his wife was likely sudden. They had built a life together, enjoying the fruits of their labour; three children, a home for themselves and their extended families. Cromwell had spared no expense on things like fine jewellery and fabrics for his wife and had ensured the best for their son's education. All had been on a steady rise for the couple until such a tragic event. Losing the only known woman in Cromwell's life, he would have felt nothing less than total devastation.

Cromwell remained almost a complete non-entity through the rest of 1528, only surfacing again in mid-January 1529, in a letter to Stephen Gardiner.[25] Cromwell tried to get back to work after the Christmas period and found a suitable distraction. Lesnes Abbey, twelve miles east of London near Greenwich Palace, had been swamped when the Thames burst its banks just after the Epiphany. Lesnes' land and fittings were extremely valuable and needed for the continuation of Ipswich College. Cromwell was instructed to report to Richmond Palace twenty miles east of Lesnes, so Gardiner wrote to Cromwell at Austin Friars. Cromwell sent back a complex list of ten important tasks that needed to be completed, all legal tasks involving paperwork to ensure the suppression of monasteries and creation of the college at Ipswich. Cromwell confessed all ten books were still not completed and he could not leave home. But Lesnes was just the thing to break Cromwell out of his spell at home, for the 350-year-old abbey and its surrounding woods and marshlands were in trouble. The river threatened to undo all the work done in the dilapidated abbey. Cromwell estimated more than 300l (over £130,000 today) worth of damage from the flood, with another 220l needed for fixtures and items needing removal from the site. Cromwell surveyed the damage and whipped up locals to help secure the abbey, rather than finishing his work for Wolsey. While the world continued to turn, and Wolsey began his spiral into disaster, Cromwell was not ready to return to work.

In late February, Cromwell's attendant Vaughan drew up a list of debtors who owed Cromwell money through statutes, bills, and obligations. These debts covered a huge period, from 8 December 1519 to 16 February 1529.[26] Why Cromwell had allowed debts to go unpaid for so long is not clear. Vaughan's list showed forty-one people owing Cromwell, among them his brother-in-law William Wellyfed, and close friends Thomas Rush, Sir John Gage, Thomas Somer, John Palsgrave, Thomas Aleyn, and Sir John Russell. Also on the list was Sir George Grey, Henry Percy, Duke of Northumberland, and Charles Knyvett. Many others had their professions listed; Cromwell had lent money to mercers, priests, parsons, clerks, brewers, and fishmongers.

With the list of these debts already past due, Cromwell took over the list and added another fifty names, among these men was Cardinal Wolsey, Thomas Grey, the Marquess of Dorset, Italian artist Antonio Cavallari, and both of Wolsey's new colleges, bringing up 4,500l, or £2,000,000 today. Cromwell was owed this enormous sum and wanted to call in his debts, something that must have frightened the myriad of people who sought him for loans. But after the shock of losing Elizabeth, Cromwell's forlorn attitude saw him preparing his personal affairs as if he expected the worst, or at least had been shocked into considering his mortality.

But even working for such a procrastinator as Cardinal Wolsey could only allow Cromwell to neglect his duties for so long. By March, he travelled back to Ipswich College to oversee its progress. He left Austin Friars in Stephen Vaughan's hands, with his brother-in-law John Williamson. One can only hope grandmother Mercy and Aunt Joan were enough for toddlers Anne and Grace Cromwell. Vaughan wrote to Cromwell, assuring him the family was well and awaiting his return.[27] By now, Mercy Prior was mistress of the household in London, with Vaughan leaving money for Cromwell in her safe hands.[28]

With the legatine court with Wolsey and Campeggio drawing near, Cromwell went back to London in early April, and among his workload was a letter of thanks from Thomas Winter for his help and money,[29] helping Stephen Vaughan buy books so he could learn French, and placating Thomas Howard, Duke of Norfolk, who had turned up at Felixstowe monastery, which he owned, to find it had been dismantled on Wolsey's orders.[30] The six-month mark was seemingly also the time in which a man of his standing should have been hunting for a new wife. Eleanor Scrope, daughter to Cromwell's friend Henry Baron Scrope, wrote to Austin Friars, sending him well wishes on finding a new bride.[31] The following week, old friend Edward Lewkenor wrote with similar wishes.[32] Yet Cromwell never once made any kind of overture to any other woman in his lifetime.

Cromwell's mood remained low as the months wore on, culminating in anger at John Chekyng about Gregory's progress at Cambridge. Chekyng replied to Cromwell's accusations, claiming he, 'cannot endure such taunts after the trouble I have taken', and that Cromwell's 'sons' 'have done as well as if they had many other teachers; others not so well as I could have wished, but if they have got little, they have lost nothing'. Chekyng raged he made no profit from educating the boys, that he could have educated seven boys in the same effort it took to educate just one of Cromwell's 'folks'. Chekyng swore the boys were happy with him, and felt angry that Cromwell only paid him 6l 13s 4d (almost £3,000), as Christopher had a habit of setting featherbeds alight.[33] Cromwell swiftly made an apology, mentioning that he had recently done a favour for Chekyng's chaplain and Chekyng's wife could have Cromwell's niece Alice Wellyfed to live in her household.[34] One hopes Cromwell consulted his sister Elizabeth before he made this offer, but it would have been a splendid opportunity for young Alice. Chekyng did not write so angrily again.

A week later, on 12 July, Cromwell had Vaughan write up his new will. The twenty-page document,[35] shows how precious a son was in the period; Gregory, still only around nine years old at the time, looked to have almost everything his father had ever amassed.

The first item on the will for Gregory was a sum of 666l 13s 4d (roughly 1,000 marks or £300,000 today), about sixty years' worth of a skilled tradesmen's wage, held in a trust and invested in land to go towards 'the education and finding honestly of my said son Gregory in virtue, good learning, and manner until he shall come to the full age of 22 years. During which time I heartily desire and require I said executors to be good to my son Gregory and to see he loses no time but see him virtuously ordered and brought up according to my trust'.

On top of this enormous inheritance, Gregory was to be gifted 200l (around £90,000 today) on his twenty-second birthday, and another 200l on his twenty-fourth birthday, as well as Cromwell's three best featherbeds, plush bolsters, blankets, tapestries, quilts, the best bed sheets, pillows, pillowcases, tablecloths. They had walked through Austin Friars and decided the best items from each room, including Cromwell's best Flanders bed and canopy, best Flanders carved wardrobes and cupboards, furs, and cushions.

It did not end there for Gregory. From age twenty-two, he would also receive the leases of Sutton-at-Hone, and Temple Hill in Dartford, close to one another in Kent, and their yearly profits from rents. Also, Cromwell's manor home in Canonbury, directly across the Thames from Hampton Court Palace gardens, and enough money to pay 40s a year to the poor of the area from the profits of the rents.

After the vast list of Gregory's inheritance, next came Cromwell's eldest daughter Anne, whose paragraph was entirely crossed out after her death. Anne was given just 100 marks (around 66l or £30,000 today), 'when she shall come to her lawful age, or happen to be married'. Cromwell's friend John Croke would also receive 40l to pay for Anne's upbringing and education until her marriage, suggesting he was her godfather. Cromwell's sister Elizabeth Wellyfed was high on his list of priorities, giving her 40l and numerous items, while her eldest son Christopher also received 40l and Cromwell's 'fifth best gown, doublet and jacket', while younger siblings William and Alice Wellyfed each received 20l. Elizabeth's husband William Wellyfed the elder sat slightly higher in Cromwell's esteem, gaining 40l and the 'third-best gown, doublet and jacket.'

In the initial draft, Cromwell gave his nephew Richard Williams (who changed his surname to Cromwell soon after the will was created) 66l 13s 4d and 'best gown, doublet, and jacket'. Much further down the list of priorities was Richard's brother Walter, who gained 20l, and the youngest Williams brother, Gregory, was not mentioned, possible due to his young age.

As expected, Cromwell wanted to be generous to Elizabeth Cromwell's mother, Mercy Prior. Mercy was granted 40l and much from the household at Austin Friars. Mercy's daughter Joan gained 10l, but her husband John Williamson gained 66l and many luxury items and fabrics. Their daughter, also named Joan, got 20l for her marriage.

Ralph Sadler was equally gifted well, with 200 marks, (almost £60,000 today), much better than many in the family, along with the second-best gown doublet and jacket, and the biggest gift of all, Cromwell's entire library. Stephen Vaughan was bequeathed 66l along with gowns, and a list of servants, Hugh Whalley, John Page, Thomas Avery, John Croke, Roger More, and John Horwood each receiving 6l 13s 4d.

What is interesting about the list is that there are no important names of note; merely friends who worked in Cromwell's household. By this time, Cromwell had amassed a large friendship base and larger client base and yet stuck to the everyday people in his life. Roger More, an Austin Friars neighbour and servant to the king's bakehouse, was chosen as overseer of the will when Cromwell could have chosen someone like Cardinal Wolsey.

Then appears a most curious name; Elizabeth Gregory listed as 'sometime my servant'. Elizabeth's role is undefined, is not connected to any family member or other servant. She bore the first name of Cromwell's wife, and her surname is the name of Cromwell's son, which, if a coincidence, is remarkable. Elizabeth gained an inheritance higher than other servants, with 20l and a household worth of items. Given that Cromwell's illegitimate daughter Jane was born around 1530, Elizabeth Gregory is perhaps Jane's mother, who remains unknown to this day.

Sadly, Elizabeth Gregory's entire paragraph is crossed out, meaning she died before the new draft was created in 1532.

The next paragraph is also crossed out and left to last; the inheritance of 'little Grace' Cromwell. Grace was given 100 marks, for her marriage, along with 40l for her education and upbringing, just like her elder sister Anne. This late edition suggests Grace was still very young, added to the will, likely born after the 1527 inventory was made, which probably had a will attached. Grace's care was left to Joan and John Williamson, her likely godparents.

Cromwell then turned to matters of his soul. He left 46l 13s 4d, to be spread evenly over seven years for the employ of a priest to sing for his soul. Then came 20l to pay for new roads and highways in the area, and 20s to be spread among London's friaries. Cromwell also allotted 40l to be shared among sixty poor women in the area to aid them in making marriages (13s 4d each, about three weeks' wages), and 20l to be shared among the Austin Friars household, and donations to poor parishioners in the area.

Many other of Cromwell friends were also added to the will. The standard 10 marks, or 6l 13s 4d went to friends Thomas Rush, Thomas Alvard, George Wilkinson, Richard Swift, Peter Mewtas, William Body, Thurston 'my cook', John Avery the yeoman of the bottle to the king, while William Brabazon received 20l, clothing and Cromwell's second-best horse. Just like with the bequeathing in his will, Cromwell also did not include anyone of note as an executor, instead choosing his friends John Croke, Stephen Vaughan, Ralph Sadler, John Smith, and John Williamson.

Cromwell would soon need these friends more than ever. While Wolsey toiled with the annulment case and the ensuing drama of the royal progress, Cromwell and the rest of Wolsey's household tried to carry on as normal. Cromwell travelled to Oxford College, his friend Thomas Alvard acting as a messenger for letters to the cardinal. In late September, Cromwell received a letter on Wolsey's behalf, from none other than his long-time Italian patron Francesco Frescobaldi. Francesco's brother Leonardo, who had been tending to the Frescobaldi merchant trading business in England, could not see Wolsey and discuss matters because of illness and died soon after Francesco sent the letter. The Frescobaldi family owed King Henry some 60,000l (around £26,500,000 today), part of their decades-long alum trading between the countries. Frescobaldi was desperate to discuss their repayment arrangement, which had come under serious pressure because of the vast changes in exchange rates of gold. Fortunately for the Frescobaldi family, Wolsey's coming collapse would help them stave off the payments for a while longer.

But in October, Cromwell's business went dark again, suggesting this was the period in which he lost his daughters Anne and Grace. Given their young ages, they would have been susceptible to a myriad of illnesses of the period, including plague, pneumonia, influenza, and scarlet fever. While sweating sickness rarely struck the very young, whatever crept the hallways of Austin Friars meant Anne and Grace were not so lucky this time. This would have been a dreadful experience for Cromwell; first his wife and now both his daughters. He may not have been at home when the sickness reached the household, keeping him safe, and Gregory was still safely away at Cambridge. Losing two precious daughters in the household would have been a shocking turn of events for a man who already felt his life slipping between his fingers. His best friend Stephen Vaughan had gone to the Low Countries, and wrote to Cromwell on 30 October, saying he was desperate to come home and help him, and could not, knowing the perilous situation in which Cromwell found himself personally and professionally.[36] Most of his immediate family was wiped out, and at age forty-four, Cromwell probably felt as if there was little left for him.

Chapter 7

1529–1530: Defiance

'and so to the Court, where I will either make or mar, here I come again'

Without a doubt, the flashpoint of Cromwell's career was the annulment trial of King Henry and Queen Katherine. Yet, despite being one of Wolsey's top lawyers and agents, Cromwell did not work on the case, though much Wolsey's work on the trial was destroyed.

Cardinal Lorenzo Campeggio had been in England over six months before the legatine trial began at Blackfriars in London.[1] A conglomeration of excuses and illness plagued the set-up of the legatine court, and in that time, Wolsey continued to woo the French to support the annulment, a task keeping Cromwell occupied. Before the start of the trial on 31 May, Cromwell's professional life centred mostly around Wolsey's colleges, likely familiar and helpful for him while he struggled with the turmoil of his home life. But his close friend John Aleyn was sent to Ireland and would become Archbishop of Dublin, leaving Cromwell with a handy contact for future endeavours. Most monastic houses marked for closure had been completed by 1529, but Wolsey had grander plans, which would have involved Cromwell had the project been allowed to continue.

By now, Thomas Cromwell had gained a unique insight into monastic life. His four years travelling the countryside to inspect and close these buildings gave him experience no other layman could boast. Cromwell had inadvertently become something of an intense anomaly; he had the knowledge of a clergyman when it came to monastic life, but without the religious attachment held by the people who lived and worked in such institutions. All the practical erudition, none of the sentiment. While Wolsey's closure of monastic houses is largely forgotten because of the greater upheaval of the 1530s, Wolsey had much more substantial plans, which would have been laid in the hands of his favourite layman, Thomas Cromwell. Plans were already afoot; monasteries with fewer than six men would be closed, and those with between six and twelve would be moved to other small monasteries nearby to bolster their numbers. As King Henry had spent his time on the throne largely ignoring monasteries, leaving them without royal funding, many houses were in a dire state, and Wolsey sought to tidy this issue.

Thomas Cromwell remained in his fragile state after Elizabeth's death by the time the legatine court began its proceedings. The legal charade lasted two months, with Wolsey and Campeggio bringing in King Henry and Queen Katherine among those to speak either for or against the royal marriage, including Katherine's impassioned speech to her husband.[2] Cromwell naturally would have wished for Wolsey's success, but his long-time friend Thomas Grey, Marquess of Dorset, was the man to testify Katherine and Prince Arthur had consummated their marriage. King Henry placed all his hopes in this trial and Wolsey; he was a papal legate and King Henry's choice of papal representative in England. Wolsey stood between Henry and the Pope and could argue any issue of papal jurisdiction. But this careful placement could be no match for Cardinal Campeggio, who had nailed his colours to the Pope long before he arrived in England. Campeggio adjourned the court in late July 1529, as Rome had broken up all courts and meetings for their summer harvest, and no decision would be made until Rome returned to court in October.[3] Queen Katherine now had months to send an appeal directly to the Pope, bypassing the legatine court's authority, leaving Henry back in no-man's-land.

While this decision was a masterstroke by Campeggio and Queen Katherine, Cromwell saw the disaster unfold the moment court adjourned. The same day, he wrote a hurried letter to colleague Sir William Claybrook, asking him to search Wolsey's archives for paperwork. Cromwell wanted the papers to show Wolsey could overrule Campeggio in England.[4] This was an act of defiance on Cromwell's part; until now, he had stayed in his lane, did what was asked, ever dutiful to his master. But this was not as a lawyer, but as a friend who strayed into the legatine fray to find a legal way to save Wolsey's skin. Claybrook returned the letter with a note on the back, thus preserving this vital private Cromwell document in archives.

King Henry did not immediately turn on his cardinal, and instead went on progress with Anne Boleyn, and invited both Wolsey and Campeggio.

Cromwell stayed behind, sending his friend Thomas Alvard in Wolsey's retinue to relay news. But by late September, Wolsey was relying on Cromwell's progress in ensuring his safety, as Alvard wrote to Cromwell, saying, 'I have delivered your letter to my lord's Grace (Wolsey), who immediately read them, and took them into his own possession. I say this because I never saw him do the like before. He heartily thanks you for your advertisement from time to time of such things as you have written to him'.[5]

By late September, King Henry was in one of his ever-whimsical moods. Henry allowed Campeggio to return to Rome but sent an angry letter to Pope Clement in Campeggio's luggage.[6] Queen Katherine too sent away her appeal on the annulment at the same time. Cromwell's mind was on the fate of his master, as shown in a conversation recorded by Reginald Pole. Pole recalled that Cromwell asked him, 'how a councillor of a Prince should conduct himself with that Prince, if at any time the Prince's inclination turned away from what generally seemed honourable, when he was not actually furnished with any authority in the matter that he sought'.[7]

Parliament had not sat since 1523 when Cromwell made his speech against a French war. Now, King Henry wanted his hand-picked MPs in London to decide on matters, rather than leaving them in Wolsey's hands. Finally listening to the whisperings of Anne Boleyn and other Wolsey enemies, King Henry ensured the cardinal's arrest on the charge of praemunire, abetting a foreign jurisdiction. The charge argued that, as the papal legate, Wolsey supported Rome over London. Henry took Wolsey's home of York Place and renamed it Whitehall Palace. A week after the charge, on 17 October, Wolsey was fired as Lord Chancellor, and days later stripped of all his seals of office and never saw the king again. But Henry did not send his friend to the Tower. Instead, Wolsey travelled up the Thames to Esher Place, a recently refurbished manor near Hampton Court Palace. In the brief time between Cromwell's meeting with Pole and Wolsey's banishment, Pole had gone to Paris, believing that Cromwell would be arrested alongside Wolsey. While Wolsey's crimes varied, Cromwell would be arrested for destroying monasteries. But while Henry's hate for the monastery project was well known, no charges were laid against anyone but Wolsey.

By this time, Cromwell was at breaking point. Just months after losing his wife, now Wolsey had toppled, and Anne and Grace Cromwell perished at Austin Friars. Given Cromwell's despondent mood over the last year, it would have been easy to give up. His friend Stephen Vaughan wrote from his trip in Antwerp, 'like as a true heart is never overthrown with no tempest, like so cannot the same in your trouble but be now much more thirsty to know your state, and more greedy to show you, if it were possible by works, how much it covets to serve you …' and tried to comfort his friend over the loss of his position in the cardinal's household, saying, 'you are more hated for your master's sake than for anything which I think you have wrongfully done against any man'.[8]

Pushed to his limit, it was hardly surprising that on 1 November, George Cavendish found Cromwell at Esher Place, crying against a window while reciting Our Lady Matins from a Latin primer. It would not be the only time that evangelical Cromwell reverted to his Catholic roots in times of great strife. But breaking down and reciting Catholic prayers, while totally out of character, came on the same day as something of an epiphany for Cromwell. He was a man who lived below stairs, never keen to put his head above the parapet. Cromwell never hustled Wolsey or anyone else for a higher station, promotion, or position. But Cromwell's turmoil, rather than breaking him, spurred him to make a change. While Cromwell cried to Cavendish that, 'I am like to lose all that I have travailed and that for all the days of my life, for doing of my master true and diligent service', he also swore to turn things around, saying, 'I intend, God willing, this afternoon, when my Lord hath dined, to ride to London, and so to the Court, where I will either make or mar, here I come again'.[9] No more despair; for Cromwell could not save his family, but he could still save Wolsey. Pulling together the Wolsey household, Cromwell suggested the chaplains personally pay Wolsey's servants, to keep them working and caring for their master. Cromwell was the first to offer his own money to keep Wolsey's household going, and the chaplains were forced to follow, as Cromwell argued that laypeople did more work in a day than clergymen in a year.[10] A secret plan was hatched at once, and Cromwell left Wolsey at Esher, riding to London that same night. Cromwell's will to survive had beaten his despair.

While the world fell apart around him, what Cromwell never lacked were friends. The ever-loyal Ralph Sadler was already on the ground in

London, laying the framework for Cromwell's audacious plan; to get a seat in parliament and argue Wolsey's innocence. Ralph went to fellow Cromwellian friend, Vice-Chamberlain Sir John Gage, who went to Thomas Howard, Duke of Norfolk, who went to the king and asked for Cromwell's permission to join parliament, only forty-eight hours away. Norfolk obliged Cromwell's request and even returned Cromwell's gift of a turquoise ring Ralph gave as a sweetener for the deal. Young Ralph went to Cromwell allies Thomas Alvard and Sir Thomas Rush, to see about taking Alvard's place in parliament. When that plan failed and Alvard missed out on a position, Ralph went to Cromwell's friend Sir William Paulet, who gave him the seat of Taunton in Winchester, one of Wolsey's dioceses.[11] After working in Wolsey's offices alongside Paulet for three years, Cromwell's connections paid off. All enacted in a single day.

But for all Cromwell's schemes, he could not control the king's whims. The same day Cromwell was seeing out this new plan, Henry sent Sir John Russell to Esher and gave Wolsey a secret pardon from all charges.[12] While Cromwell's plan was no longer needed, he learned much in a short time from Ralph, who gathered gossip on who had defected from the Wolsey camp, such as Stephen Gardiner. Cromwell appeared as a beaming light of loyalty in contrast, which pulled King Henry's focus. Cromwell had nothing to lose, and the opportunity in parliament was too good to turn away. Parliament opened on 3 November, and Cromwell had many friends as support. Sir John Gage was there, along with Sir Thomas Rush, and fellow Wolsey's servants William Fitzwilliam and John Morris. Close friends George Lawson and Richard Page had been selected, along with colleagues Reynold Littleprow, Thomas Chaffyn, Paul Withipoll, Sir Humphrey Wingfield, and Francis Hall.[13] The Commons had filled with Cromwell's allies. Cromwell had gained a splendid chance and would not waste it.

While Wolsey was safe, Henry still wanted the English clergy to oversee his annulment, but Wolsey's fall promoted an anti-clerical backlash in the Commons. Who better to argue against the clergy than Thomas Cromwell, who had just sought to financially punish the clergy in Wolsey's household? Sir Thomas Audley, Speaker of the House, and Cromwell colleague was appointed to create a panel of lawyers to combat clerical excess.[14] The surviving petition, while written in a clerk's hand, has Cromwell's corrections and changes on it, carefully checking the legal terms used to ensure those higher ranking in the church would come under penalties, while lay people working for the church would go unharmed. But not all shared these sentiments; there were those who, while critical of the church's behaviour, still believed Wolsey should be punished. Thomas, Lord Darcy of Templehurst, was unafraid to stick his neck out and speak ill of Wolsey in parliament, a grudge Cromwell squirrelled away for later use.[15] Arguments over religion flooded the Commons, which spilled into the House of Lords, raising the ire of Bishop John Fisher, who drafted in secular lords to quell anti-clerical criticism. While Fisher attempted to resist the anti-clerical sentiment, he was also anti-Wolsey, particularly over the dissolution of monasteries. A petition was drawn up against Wolsey again to be up on charges that could see him executed, which was signed by new Lord Chancellor Sir Thomas More on 1 December.[16] The whole situation had become less about Cardinal Wolsey, and more about church reform, leaving More in a vulnerable position in his new role. Dissolving further monasteries would be an ideal way to raise funds to pay the king's expensive annulment, but no one wanted that idea pitched to Henry.

While seeing his friend up on charges a month after his pardon upset Cromwell at a time he was in personal crisis, it gave Cromwell two things he needed – a task to distract himself, and a chance to speak in Wolsey's defence. Cromwell spoke of Wolsey's good works, his deeds, his faith in the king, words heard by Henry himself in the House of Commons. While people slunk away from any Wolsey association, Cromwell remained utterly loyal, despite overwhelming opposition. Cromwell had nothing to gain and probably felt as if there was nothing to lose either. Cromwell stood tall as the sole voice of loyalty and honour among a parliament session of fighting and rancour, and loyalty was the exact trait King Henry needed and respected. Cromwell's speech drew a new resentment – he spoke against everyone, and it irritated ministers because he had done so well.[17] Reports of his remarks left a good first impression on others, along with his loyalty, honest and intelligent words, and his spiritual and temporal understanding.[18] It would be a speech that would make people love or hate him, and Cromwell also generated overwhelming concern, as this quiet outsider appeared so calm, rational, forthright and original. After years of quietly flying under the radar, Cromwell stuck up for his friend in his hour of need and lost his personal anonymity.

Cromwell's new direction came slowly; King Henry gained everything in Wolsey's possession and kept most of those working on the various projects, including Cromwell as the mastermind of Oxford and Ipswich colleges and the Wolsey tomb at Windsor (whose Italian artists were fleeing and wanting payment).[19] Cromwell relied on his friends to help him continue with the projects.[20] But life was no longer simple; people such as the Duke of Norfolk had no desire for forward-thinking minds to be speaking before the king, and Anne Boleyn wished to erase all trace of Cardinal Wolsey. Wolsey was desperate to take up every waking minute of Cromwell's life as if he had nothing to cope with himself. From Esher Place, Wolsey wrote, 'if you love my life, break away this evening and come hither, to the intent I may open my mind unto you, and instruct you of the same which I cannot commit to writing … Forsake me not in this, my extreme need; and where, as I cannot, God shall reward you. Now is the time to show whether you love me or not'.[21]

Even after his grand gestures for his friend, Cromwell still had one chance to go back to his quiet life as a regular lawyer. However, his immediate family now only comprised of his son Gregory, along with his extended family; his comfortable mercantile life was finished. Cromwell likely could have stayed at Austin Friars and comfortably seen out his days, but Cromwell had caught King Henry's interest. Noblemen and women did not want a man like Cromwell in their sphere, but some could not help but sing his praises to Henry. First came the kind words of Sir Christopher Hales, King Henry's new attorney-general, and old friend of Cromwell. When asked about Cromwell, Hales spoke of Cromwell's lack of support for the Pope and his Italian connections as if they could benefit the king. Yes, Cromwell had been unpopular closing monasteries, but he also understood Henry's Italian adversaries, had shown unwavering loyalty, and raised enough money to create both Oxford and Ipswich Colleges. But King Henry wanted no mention of Cromwell, until Sir John Russell came to Cromwell's defence. Russell told of the undocumented secret trip he took to Italy many years earlier and found himself in 'great peril'. Cromwell had swooped in and saved Russell despite no obligation to do so. Russell believed Cromwell to be the best person to defeat Pope Clement. The story of Russell's secret conversation with Henry was documented by the newly arrived Eustace Chapuys, who wrote that Norfolk would not speak to Russell for a month over the crime of promoting Cromwell.[22] Cromwell needed men to support him, especially after the sudden death of his friend Thomas Grey, Marquess of Dorset, as the rest of his beloved Grey family spent little time at court.

News of King Henry's interest in Cromwell spread. Stephen Vaughan wrote from Antwerp, and asked about a rumour Cromwell would accompany George Boleyn to see the Emperor in Italy.[23] Thomas Cranmer reluctantly undertook the trip, but to be mixed up in a story over such a mission showed who was talking about Cromwell. Friends were not far wrong, for Cromwell was high in Henry's favour. On 10 February 1530, Cromwell had a private audience with the king, and two days later, Cardinal Wolsey was granted a full pardon on all charges.[24] Over previous months, Cromwell had been completing paperwork, transferring money, lands, and buildings from Wolsey to men at court whom Wolsey needed to bribe, with Wolsey heavily relying on Cromwell, writing, 'my only refuge and aide... I beg you to omit nothing that may be to my advantage'.[25] Each letter from Esher became more desperate, with Wolsey writing to his friend, 'my only comfort, at the reverence of God, leave me not now, for if you do, I shall not long live in this wretched world. You will not believe how I am altered, for that, I have heard nothing from you of your proceedings and expeditions in my matters...[26] my own good, trusty, and most assured refuge in this, my calamity'.[27]

Sadly, Cardinal Wolsey did not have Cromwell's subtlety or discretion; within days of his pardon, Wolsey complained about the money King Henry provided for his debts, protesting he was better off dead. Cromwell had to get on with his life, as Wolsey was as safe as he could be at Esher. Cromwell mixed his time working on the colleges for the king and working for his private legal clients, leaving his brother-in-law John in charge at Austin Friars.[28]

When Cromwell still had not made it to Esher by early March, Wolsey wrote to Cromwell, 'few things since my troubles have more grieved me than you not coming at this time when you could do me best in the advancement of my pursuits'.[29] King Henry gave Wolsey 1,000 marks (around £260,000 today) to travel 400 miles north to York, where Wolsey remained the archbishop. Cromwell could not travel with his friend, but among the vast train of servants was Sir John Gage, who reported Wolsey's entitled and over-privileged behaviour. Once Wolsey settled in the north, Cromwell wrote from St James' Palace and told Wolsey he had been to the king on his behalf again, telling Wolsey all would be well if he did not upset Henry any further.[30] But only two weeks later, on 17 May, Cromwell wrote to Wolsey, telling him the king would not reply to his request for money. Cromwell also told Wolsey that the letters he sent to Anne Boleyn had been given to her, but she had not promised to speak to Henry on Wolsey's behalf.

Cromwell's relationship with King Henry was sporadic, but with scholars from both Oxford and Ipswich in the king's company, it would be safe to assume Cromwell was somewhere close by as they discussed Martin Luther, with Cromwell remarking, 'I would (Luther) had never been born'.[31] Further letters went between the men in June, Cromwell aware that Wolsey's harassment of Sir Thomas More gained indignation.[32] But by 12 July 1530, Cromwell's mood had altered. Wolsey tried to regain control of his beloved colleges and attempted to halt the distribution of his other assets. Cromwell again went to the king on Wolsey's behalf but warned it was all too much. Cromwell could no longer go to the king and bother him with Wolsey's constant demands, stating he had personally paid 1,000l (almost £430,000 today) on supporting Wolsey's endeavours. He signed off, 'I entreat your Grace to be content, and let your Prince execute his pleasure'.[33] Wolsey took his request well, as Cromwell's next letter asked if Wolsey would take in one of Cromwell's distant cousins Henry Carbott as a chaplain in the cardinal's household.[34]

'My own loving Mr Crumwell ... you will show yourself my friend and comfort ... if you knew the heaviness of mind, your gentle heart would have compassion ... there is nothing here but lamentation and mourning, not knowing certainly what will follow...'[35] Wolsey wrote on 10 August, begging Cromwell to intercede with King Henry and the Duke of Norfolk about Wolsey's estates, titles, and the endless begging for money. Wolsey would not relent, although his pardon was not yet complete, and wrote to King Henry, the Duke of Norfolk, attorney-general Sir Christopher Hales, Master Secretary Stephen Gardiner, and various deans of universities around the country, begging for money and preferment. Cromwell had other matters to deal with; he had just ruled in judgement in a case against Wolsey and was summoned by King Henry to Hampton Court Palace to be on a panel concerning the annulment case.[36] King Henry went on progress to Ampthill, and Cromwell wrote a long letter to Wolsey and warned his friend:

Sir, some there say that your Grace keeps too great a house and family and that you are continually building. For the love of God therefore I (again), as I often have done most heartily, beseech your Grace to have respect to everything and consider the time to refrain yourself for a season from all manner of building, no more than mere necessity requires. I assure your Grace shall be good to yourself, shall sense and silence persons that much speak of the same.[37]

The letter went with an unnamed bearer, whom Cromwell begged to return at once, and was likely Ralph Sadler again given the task of delivering the important words.

Cromwell, as he regularly did, went away in September to visit his son Gregory at Cambridge, having his annual summer break. This holiday period bothered no one and business continued as normal, with letters to and from Cromwell resuming in mid-October. But this time away had been enough to enrage Cardinal Wolsey, who accused Cromwell of promoting himself, rather than Wolsey, to the king, and Cromwell likewise heard of Wolsey speaking ill of him to others. While Cromwell had been away at Cambridge, Wolsey wrote to Queen Katherine, the Holy Roman Emperor, and the Pope, hoping to be restored to his glory in England. King Henry had formally pardoned Wolsey by this stage but now was further incensed by Wolsey writing to England's 'enemies'. Cromwell too was angry, telling Wolsey:

I am informed your Grace has in me some diffidence, as if I did dissemble you, or procure anything contrary to your profit and honour. I much muse that your Grace should so think or report it secretly, considering the pains I have taken. Wherefore, I beseech you to speak without feigning if you have such conceit, that I may clear myself. I reckoned that your Grace would have written plainly to me of such things, rather than secretly have misreported me … Truly, your Grace, in some things you overshoot yourself; there is respect to be given in what things you utter and to whom.[38]

Cromwell wrote again weeks later, a much calmer letter discussing news from London and Gregory at Cambridge, but it was too late. While Cardinal Wolsey had been Archbishop of York for fifteen years, he had never been officially installed in York. Cardinal Wolsey's extravagant parade and ceremony was to take place in early November, with Wolsey acting as if he were king of the north. King Henry could no longer tolerate Wolsey's belligerent behaviour, and had Wolsey arrested at Cawood Castle. There was no more Cromwell could do for his friend; a year's worth of hard work came to nothing. Cardinal Wolsey died on 29 November 1530 at Leicestershire Abbey, on route to London for his imprisonment and execution, and Cromwell was summoned before King Henry in December, no doubt to clear himself of being involved in Wolsey's plans to reinstate himself.[39] The letters between Cromwell and Wolsey would have been ample proof of no plan, however, the interrogation is likely why so many of their letters are damaged or lost.

This meeting between Cromwell and King Henry was chronicled by Eustace Chapuys to Nicolas de Granvelle, Chancellor to the Holy Roman Emperor, who had asked for information on Cromwell. Sir John Wallop, ambassador to France and constant whiner, had laid a complaint about Cromwell to the king over a petty matter, but when Henry brought it up with Cromwell, it was quickly dismissed; Cromwell had the king's favour. Cromwell stood before Henry, 'whom he addressed in such flattering terms and eloquent language, promised to make him the richest king in the world, that the king at once took him into his service, and made him councillor'.[40]

Cromwell's rise in favour with King Henry had been a slow burn, much of it spent on maintaining the royal colleges, a dearly loved project, and trying to maintain a living as best he could. Cromwell worked diligently, no doubt using it to cope with the recent years of grief, and one bright spot in his private life likely happened in 1530. Cromwell had made (at least) one slip-up in his otherwise reserved, virtuous, and quiet private life, and his daughter Jane was born. Some scholars have suggested Jane was born before Gregory, a way of suggesting Cromwell never cheated on his wife, but this is unlikely. Cromwell did not cheat on his wife, at least, no suggestion ever came of this, and Jane was likely conceived after Elizabeth Cromwell's death. Mistress Jane took her father's surname, suggesting her mother never featured in her life, and Jane lived in the Cromwell household, old enough to live with Gregory once he married in 1537,[41] and old enough to gain an education in 1539.[42] Jane married in approximately 1550 and was recorded as having a nine-year-old daughter, Alice, in 1559.[43] Jane Cromwell married William Hough, son of Richard Hough, a gentleman from Oxfordshire and lacklustre servant to Cromwell,[44] who was most upset his son had married the bastard child of Cromwell. But in 1530, Mistress Jane was born into a household of a man about to be propelled into a position of power no commoner, or layman, could ever expect to achieve in England. An illegitimate child was usually paid for and squirrelled away, but Cromwell took in his daughter, suggesting she was a soothing presence after years of distress. Another other theory for Jane's parentage is that she was the illegitimate daughter of twenty-year-old Richard Cromwell, and she was taken into the Cromwell household, as Richard had no household of his own. But Jane believed herself Thomas Cromwell's daughter, and her judgemental Catholic father-in-law believed the same. Had Jane been a daughter of a Cromwell relative, she would have been recorded as such, but perhaps the lack of detail on her birth was beneficial for all involved.

Chapter 8

1531: Anonymity

'more valuable than all earthly goods'

After the intense strife of the previous few years, Cromwell no doubt relished the opportunity to have a quieter private life. For the new year, he celebrated by adding to his landholdings, leasing a rectory in Melbourne, Derbyshire, and leased 400 acres in Buckinghamshire including the parsonages of Brill, Worminghall, Oakley and Boarstall.[1] A few weeks later he leased the rectory of 'Gingemargaret', Essex, for thirty years.[2] His old friend, Henry Parker, Lord Morley, father of Jane Boleyn, Lady Rochford, wrote to Cromwell asking for help for a friend,[3] while newly-widowed Stephen Vaughan wrote regularly from Antwerp with news of the Emperor and the merchant trade.[4] Italian artist Rovezzano wrote to Cromwell, still working on the Wolsey tomb at Windsor,[5] and Sir John Gage wrote, saying he had left Cromwell purple and crimson velvet at Austin Friars to have a vestment made.[6]

Cromwell would need new clothes as a newly appointed councillor to the king; after the close of parliament in March 1531, he was permitted to wear the royal livery of a councillor. The king had made no official announcement of this new member of his Council, whose title and tasks were as vague as the Council meetings themselves. Cromwell's title as a Councillor of the King was not mentioned until parliament closed and he donned his new clothes, but the word of his rise in favour moved so fast the official announcement eventually meant little. If anyone thought Cromwell would wait for an announcement to start using his new role, they had no idea of the propaganda about to be unleashed.

Without question, having Wolsey die so far from London, so broken and dishonoured, would have brought grief to Cromwell, something he probably felt quite used to by the age of forty-five. But regardless of the endless outpouring of trouble, Cromwell continued to work in London through the latter part of 1530, attending the second Reformation parliament. His friend, Sir Christopher Hales, had previously tried and failed to put through a petition in parliament to see certain clergy members charged with praemunire over the Wolsey fiasco. The charge of praemunire could be settled with a fine of 100,000l (some £44,000,000 today).[7] Cromwell needed to make his new master rich and succeeded where the attorney-general failed. The anti-clerical sentiment was back in the Commons after the prior year's parliament and could not be abated; it is easy to imagine Cromwell at ease in parliament speaking against the clergy by late 1530. The Convocation of Canterbury could do little but agree to pay the immense sum to the king on 24 January 1531.[8] While the king basked in the win, and the church tried to spin the event as positive, it was all simply a step in a larger plan Cromwell devised to solve the King's Great Matter.

Only weeks later, King Henry wanted more from the Convocation; the grand command he was Protector and Supreme Head of the Church. In came 'Dominus Crumwell,' to speak privately with Archbishop Warham, who panicked at what he heard and tried to go to the king, flanked by a group of bishops. Henry wanted both the Convocation and parliament to ratify him as head of the church in England. Cromwell's handwriting did not appear on the official paperwork, as using a clerk's official handwriting was wiser, but the feeling that the king's new secret weapon had masterminded this plan spread so quickly, it instantly appeared in gossip over 100 miles away in Derbyshire near the home of Sir Anthony Babington, Cromwell's cousin.[9]

Cromwell's diligence was never in doubt; among papers of failed petitions to the Commons are Tudor copies of parliamentary papers from 1410. Someone had sought out these papers while studying, rewriting and inflaming claims against the clergy.[10] No one in the king's secret inner circle was pulling out old Latin texts and putting them into English for new parliamentary sessions in the Commons, except one man. Cromwell's plan to get Henry everything he wanted was underway, and it was only February. Soon after the praemunire pardon was granted, a second pardon soon passed for temporal subjects, meaning laypeople in the church, and all those working in the Commons, were spared from praemunire charges.[11]

Whether Cromwell felt any success from this high-stress parliament is unknown, as he had been working hard on a petition to reform treason laws, making sure the words of traitors spoken overseas would make them liable to face charges in England, but the law was not supported enough to pass in the Commons before the session closed.[12] Cromwell had six months before a new session would open, and he was ready to do the king's bidding.

While Cromwell had been shining in his favourite theatre of parliament, it was far from the only thing occupying his mind. Friends and allies needed his time and attention. Stephen Vaughan was still Cromwell's man in Antwerp and spent time sourcing books on religious reform. Cromwell was not powerful enough to spend personal time with the king, nor to go hunting or be invited to the privy chamber, but he had one ace up his sleeve – he collected and read as widely as the king. Vaughan sourced Reformation texts for Cromwell and tried to convince William Tyndale to return to England and convince King Henry about the new religion. Tyndale remained abroad along with many other Cromwellian friends, such as John Frith, Robert Barnes, George Joye, and Miles Coverdale. In January 1531, Vaughan succeeded in sending Cromwell and King Henry a copy of *A Disputation Between a Cleric and a Knight*, a thirteenth-century Lollard book, talking of defying the Pope.[13] Cromwell and Vaughan spent months trying to source books and provide safe passage home for at least Tyndale and Frith, knowing Sir Thomas More was already burning 'heretics.' More wrote against the Reformation and the annulment, while Tyndale wrote in opposition to More. Vaughan managed to secure a copy of Tyndale's writings to send to King Henry in March 1531, wary the books might not impress the king. Cromwell gently spoon-fed evangelical changes to the king, but Vaughan's delivery of Tyndale's *The Answer* pushed too far, and Henry outright hated Tyndale's words, too extreme in its reformist leanings. A long and rare letter of the period survives, written by Cromwell back to Vaughan, desperate to save his friend from the wrath of the king. Cromwell always wrote to his friend on the best of terms, but this letter spoke of anger, a draft with many crossed out ideas, increasingly harsh candour, and stern words to command Vaughan to stop sending evangelical writings and to stop promoting Tyndale and Frith to the king.[14] The king surely stood beside Cromwell when he penned the sharp words to his dear friend. Their personal project suffered a great setback.

Cromwell's other friends suffered lesser strife. John Creke wrote in panic, as he was bankrupt after his Spanish business fell apart and could not gain a position in Katherine of Aragon's household. Instead of fleeing into sanctuary at Westminster Abbey, Creke threw himself on Cromwell's mercy to get a job in the Treasurer's office, run by Sir William Fitzwilliam.[15] Italian friends were also coming in useful; Dr Augustine de Augustinus, once an agent and gossip master for Wolsey now worked for Cromwell and the Duke of Norfolk, reporting back on various movements, and Cromwell often got his neighbour at Austin Friars, Pier-Francesco de Bardi to translate Augustinus' whining letters into Latin from Italian to be more palatable for the duke.[16] Among all of Cromwell's friends aiding him in his climb beside the king was a late addition to the group, German Christopher Montaborino, who had been living in England for four years, and Cromwell gained his citizenship in England in 1531.[17] Mont became close to Cromwell, their evangelical leanings closely aligned, and Mont would serve as Cromwell's German translator.

But it was Cromwell's friend, Thomas Cranmer, who had the most to offer by Easter 1531. Back from Rome after only a few months, Cranmer, along with Edward Foxe, completed his *Sufficiently Abundant Collections*, which judged it unlawful for a man to marry his brother's wife, and that the Pope had no power to grant dispensations over the matter. This work had been completed for some time, but Cromwell published it in the latter part of 1531, and they went beyond the annulment matter, to say that the Pope had no jurisdiction over England in any matter, sowing the seeds for Cromwell's enormous and church-shattering acts in parliament soon after.

By this time, Cromwell and Cranmer had known one another for around five years and had developed their evangelical leanings at a similar rate. Cranmer lacked Cromwell's colourful and adventure-laden background, the son of minor gentry who, after losing his wife in childbirth, was ordained into the church at Cambridge. King Henry's international entreaties to gain support for an annulment fell on deaf ears, but the Cromwell-Cranmer pairing could advance the king's motives from home. They met new evangelicals from abroad; the men who fled overseas after the discovery of Cranmer's summer readings of 1526 and 1527 now yielded connections and friendships with other reformers. Petitioning the Pope or Catholic rulers no longer mattered, as after a meeting in February 1531, a league of evangelical rulers, formed mostly from Germany and Switzerland, boasted power, influence, and most importantly, a theological argument that the Pope did not rule over a king.

Having a man like King Henry support the Schmalkaldic League brought potential new alliances, with the Germans sending five embassies of men to England in 1531 alone. First Cromwell and Cranmer met Simon Grynaeus,[18] and soon after, Robert Barnes was able to safely return to England, now an ally of Martin Luther and Phillipp of Hessen, one of the strongest leaders in the Schmalkaldic League.[19] While everything moved at a glacial pace as King Henry mulled over his options with the new religion, deep fault-lines emerged; while Cromwell and Cranmer were sliding ever-deeper into the Reformation, former allies Sir Thomas More, Bishop Stephen Gardiner and Reginald Pole were more extreme in their Catholic beliefs. Cromwell and Cranmer, men of similar age, brought together by very different circumstances, privately decided to work together, one at home, one soon abroad, to ensure the king veered towards reform.

While Cromwell quietly toiled, the secret of being a royal councillor could not stay hidden, and in September 1531, the Venetian ambassador returned home from England. Lodovico Falier soon wrote of all he knew and named the most powerful men in the English court.[20] Falier named Cromwell alongside the all-powerful Duke of Norfolk, Duke of Suffolk, and Earl of Wiltshire, as well as Sir William Fitzwilliam and Stephen Gardiner. Now Cromwell was in the papers of the ambassadors of Europe, and the chance to sit quietly and work on private matters became harder.

Most of England already knew of Cromwell's appointment by April 1531. Letters came to him addressed to one of the king's most honourable councillors from Sir William Courtenay, Elizabeth Somerset, Countess of Worcester, and the Earl of Northumberland. Letters put him at the king's side at Hampton Court through the summer, but also at Austin Friars, particularly when writing to Stephen Vaughan, who persisted in finding reformist texts. By June 1531, Vaughan had copies of Philip Melanchthon's *Confessio Fidei*,[21] and Robert Barnes' *Supplication*, leaving Cromwell to constantly placate his friend's over-enthusiasm. At least Cromwell's friend John Hackett in Brussels worked with more diplomacy, sending letters back and forth to his friend, and aiding the Lord Privy Seal, Thomas Boleyn, with matters.[22] Whilst summer passed with multitudes of varied tasks given to Cromwell, his friend Henry Sadler wrote to thank him for his time,[23] as did Wolsey's son Thomas Winter, desperate for money and help, alone and confused in Italy and in need of a father figure, and addressing him as 'Clarissimo viro Domino Crumwello'.[24]

Cromwell's son fared better, still living at Pembroke Hall in Cambridge with Christopher Wellyfed and Nicholas Sadler. Cromwell did not get his usual time away in September with Gregory, and the Cromwell scholars moved into the Essex countryside for a summer break through September and October, staying twenty-five miles southeast of Cambridge at Yeldham and Toppesfield. In late October, Gregory wrote to his father, saying, 'I desire your blessing, which is more valuable than all earthly goods'.[25]

Cromwell could not visit his son in Cambridge because the king no longer had any desire to hide his alliance with his new councillor. In late August came a letter entitled 'Instructions by the King to his trusty councillor, Thomas Crumwell, to be declared to the Council, and undelayedly put in execution this Michaelmas term',[26] giving Cromwell explicit instructions to see to the king's debts and prepare everything required to open a new session of parliament. Not only did Henry trust Cromwell with the royal finances, but he also made him a de facto manager of parliament. Now all information would go through Cromwell. Need an exemption from attending? Ask Cromwell, not the king, for permission. Any bills that needed to be petitioned needed to go through Cromwell, a staggering amount of trust put in one man in such a short time. Cromwell also sought to change the way votes were cast; the usual loud shouting or yea or nay needed to be set aside. A system used once before in 1523, when tempers flared over proposed tax changes, saw each person casting a vote. Cromwell knew there would be enough yelling to go around in the Commons, and so created the official voting system.

King Henry initially requested parliament be opened in October, but delayed into December, not giving any clues why. This allowed Cromwell more time to work on the acts concerning the Catholic church's power over England. Cromwell had Stephen Vaughan monitor the movements and activities of Emperor Charles in the Low Countries with the German Lutherans.[27] Vaughan finally stopped promoting Tyndale and now focused on supporting Robert Barnes, who brought his reformist teachings to England in November. Their merchant business was never left out, with Vaughan constantly dealing with Cromwell's haberdasher friends around Austin Friars.

While trying to undertake the paperwork needed for parliament, Cromwell received a message from Sir Nicholas Carew, informing Cromwell he needed to start attending meetings of the Commissioners of the Sewers, who oversaw waterways and flooding maintenance, as he was now required to appoint the said commissioners.[28] Cromwell's varied workload expanded at a great rate. Until now Cromwell and Carew had little to do with one another, and Carew was a big supporter of Queen Katherine and Princess Mary, a position Cromwell quietly took himself, despite trying to become the mastermind behind the Reformation. Carew was not the only Katherine supporter keen for Cromwell's friendship; Charles Brandon, the ineffectual Duke of Suffolk, wrote to Cromwell, addressing him 'my loving friend', despite needing no alliance or goodwill from the Privy Council's junior member.[29]

By Christmas, Cromwell was still not ready to begin parliament, and the king gave no one any indication of the starting date. Even Cromwell's friend, the attorney-general Sir Christopher Hales had to write and ask for dates; everything hinged on Cromwell. Hales sent him many messages, along with a gift of a doe and wildfowl and they gossiped about mutual adversary Stephen Gardiner.[30] Gifts aplenty arrived at Austin Friars where Cromwell spent time with family rather than the king, with a parcel arriving from Sir John Seymour at Wulf Hall, sending Cromwell sheep as he heard Cromwell's kitchen already overflowed with gifts of venison.[31] A gift of Suffolk cheese and rabbits came from Cromwell's friend Richard Ingworth, Prior of Langley, one of the many religious houses Cromwell knew from his time of working on Wolsey's colleges.[32] The prior desperately wanted Cromwell to visit him at Christmas, but the visit was not to be, much to Ingworth's almost indignant disappointment.

Cromwell had little time for friends at present, and his days of crisscrossing the countryside for the Oxford and Ipswich colleges were over; King Henry dissolved both grand schemes. Ipswich was to be dismantled, though Cromwell ensured jobs and payment for those working there, while Cardinal College in Oxford would soon be reestablished as King Henry VIII's College, much to Cromwell's relief. It was not just parliament pinning Cromwell in London, he had also received letters from Ireland.[33] With his long-time friend John Aleyn now the Archbishop of Dublin, Cromwell began receiving letters from Piers Butler, Earl of Ossory, one of the key enemies of the FitzGeralds of Kildare, some of the most powerful, and most troublesome, Irishmen in the area. Not many Catholics of Ireland sought out Cromwell's friendship.

The long year finally ended, and Cromwell had gone from quiet agent to a 'right worshipful councillor to the king'. The final embassy to Emperor Charles on the annulment matter had proven fruitless, as had all the Schmalkaldic entreaties, but Cromwell paid this no mind, for he had his plan to help the king, planned entirely from the law parlour of Austin Friars. But Cromwell and Cranmer needed to be careful; Cranmer quietly going about his evangelical learning while Cromwell quietly dismantled Catholic powers through parliament. Sir Thomas More had already begun terrorising 'heretics', men who had been reading and sharing reformist books. Several of those who had escaped England in the late 1520s were back, and distributing these banned books, particularly through merchants in London, book-collector Cromwell right among them. Already, three men had been burned alive for possessing or preaching such beliefs (all eerily named Thomas), and in late November 1531, More tortured and burned Richard Bayfield, an English monk who had spent time abroad with Martin Luther and William Tyndale. The Cambridge scholar was no stranger to being persecuted, but now Bayfield suffered burning when he refused to stop distributing banned books.[34] Just a week later, John Tewkesbury, a leather merchant on Paternoster Row, the street filled with booksellers less than a mile from Austin Friars, was arrested and reportedly tortured at Sir Thomas More's Chelsea home. These heretical books were likely in Austin Friars' library, and yet Cromwell was expected to stand in parliament, knowing Lord Chancellor More would be listening and watching everyone's movements. More had John Tewkesbury burned at Smithfield just days before Christmas.[35] As Tewkesbury died defiantly, More also had London lawyer James Bainham tortured and interrogated at Chelsea.[36] Yet Cromwell pressed on with his work to free the king of his Catholic opponents, aware of the dangerous game he played.

Chapter 9

1532: Subjugation

'my whole trust next to God is in you'

When parliament opened in mid-January 1532, Thomas Cromwell had every intention of helping his king while maintaining his private persona. It was clear that there would be no conventional annulment for King Henry; Pope Clement again ruled in Queen Katherine's favour, though she had been ousted from court six months earlier and would never see her husband or daughter again. All European embassies sent to rally support for the annulment came to nothing, though Master Secretary Stephen Gardiner was in France over the matter. Having Gardiner out of the way made certain Cromwell had the access to the king he needed. Cromwell wrote to Gardiner in France, Thomas Wriothesley being the intermediary between the two former Wolsey attendants. Cromwell wrote that he had no news to give Gardiner, saying that Gardiner's friends gave him all news of court already, making it clear he was not among Gardiner's friends.[1] Cromwell mentioned an act in parliament, the Restraint of Annates, unsure if it would pass.

Cromwell wanted and needed the act to pass. His private place at the king's side was secure and yet relied on constant success. Cromwell gave the king a gold and ruby ring for New Year, engraved with the image of the French king's children, and the king gave Cromwell the gift of renewed power over the colleges at Oxford and Ipswich.[2] The odds of passing large acts of parliament swung in Cromwell's favour; in the House of Lords, Gardiner was away, Reginald Pole was overseas, Bishop Cuthbert Tunstall could not travel south, and Bishop John Fisher, despite his best efforts, was too ill to attend. But all did not start easily; two acts written by Cromwell and Thomas Audley failed to pass in the Commons and were tossed out, to Henry's fury.

Cromwell's first major bill of feudal tax reforms stumbled at the first hurdle,[3] but his Supplication of the Commons Against the Ordinaries passed.[4] It was not easy, but Cromwell was ready; the paperwork for the law was upwards of two years old by the time Cromwell could finally present it in the Commons. The Supplication Against the Ordinaries, or to Cromwell, *A Boke ayenst the Clergy for taking Excessive Fees*, was a Cromwellian masterstroke. With a long preamble and nine clauses, Cromwell sought to control the processes of the church. Naturally, the Commons were for the legislation, the Lords against. Cromwell wrote that in England all punishments should be overseen by the state rather than the punishments handed out by the clergy. He wanted better-worded laws and charges, to avoid laypeople tripping up when on trial, and to end the poorly planned and scheduled court hearings. Cromwell wanted to prevent clergymen from holding secular roles and offices, to stop charging people so much for their services, lower the costs of installing clergy in benefices, and stop church nepotism when clergymen installed their 'nephews' in church roles over more qualified people. The Supplication took power from the church, gave them guidelines to follow, and would see simpler punishments imposed on so-called crimes. The church also had an enormous number of holy days, which were not properly respected, and Cromwell sought to bring this issue under control. The Commons voted through this landmark Supplication in January, and on 8 March took it to King Henry, who needed time with the papers, knowing it would heap trouble upon him from the clergy and the Lords.

Cromwell undoubtedly knew of the coming outrage against his Supplication. Before it was presented to King Henry, Archbishop Warham in the House of Lords launched a spectacular attack on Cromwell and his Supplication. The other person sorely caught up in the battle was Lord Chancellor Sir Thomas More who lacked any ability to separate matters of church and state. Since his appointment to the role less than three years earlier, More transformed himself (in his eyes) into the man desperate to save the souls of Europe against reform. The Supplication Against the Ordinaries bound together the legal men of the Commons, the evangelical reformers, and the loyal royalists, and More was now their direct enemy, when he should have been the man closest to the king, performing his duty as the king's conscience.

An Easter break gave everyone time to consider their options in the debate. The king was the biggest concern; Henry was in no mood to be pushed around, but Cromwell's Supplications offered no downsides. The

Crown would gain powers over the church without giving 'heretics' any leeway, as Henry still had not come around to the reformist teachings. Henry was already angered, and while trying to relax on the Easter break, the king was twice accosted by Observant Friars at Greenwich, begging for Katherine's reinstatement at Henry's side. Too many people had pushed Henry too far.

Among all this, Cromwell's friends were still constantly calling on him for simple matters. Cromwell's Italian agent Augustine de Augustinus complained he was suffering overseas, supported by neither England nor the Frescobaldi family.[5] Thomas Frisby at Launde Abbey, who did not get his friend Cromwell to visit for Christmas, sent Cromwell some cheeses and wrote about a time they were walking in the snow and Frisby fell on his back, obviously a fun recollection for the men.[6] Hugh Latimer was languishing in Lambeth Palace jail,[7] though he was luckier than his friend James Bainham, who was burned by More in April. Stephen Vaughan returned Cromwell's Putney-born apprentice Thomas Avery,[8] who became one of Cromwell's closest private attendants. Lord Leonard Grey, son of Cromwell's favourite widow Margaret Grey, Marchioness of Dorset, wanted Cromwell's help in gaining favour with a rich widow, writing 'my whole trust next to God is in you'.[9] The lady in question, smartly, did not respond well to Grey's overtures.

On 12 April, Cromwell received his first official title from the king – Master of the Jewel House.[10] The role had stayed in one courtier's hands for so long it was barely ever mentioned. In 1524, Sir Henry Wyatt resigned the post after a whopping twenty-eight years, and Wyatt was promoted to Treasurer of the Household. His dear long-time friend Cromwell had been the lawyer to oversee the paperwork. Cromwell saw the benefit of this role; it was largely ignored at court, not a role anyone lobbied for or envied. In 1524, Cromwell oversaw the legal transfer of the role to another friend, Robert Amadas, a London goldsmith who died in April 1532. Cromwell simply had Stephen Vaughan pull out the old paperwork from 1524, crossed out Amadas' name and entered Cromwell as the receiver. But Wyatt was not to be Cromwell's boss in the role, as the Treasurer role now belonged to Cromwell's friend Sir Brian Tuke, Wyatt having retired in old age in 1528, a rare feat for any courtier under Henry VIII.

By this time, Cromwell was deep in the affairs of the king, and yet had nothing but his informal role on the Privy Council and now the Master of the Jewel House. It could have been seen as a slight; but Cromwell, as he had done with Wolsey, did not petition the king for roles, favours, or gifts. He simply did his job, and this meant he quietly edged towards gaining the king full powers over the church and the chance to annul his marriage without anyone noticing. Despite being in Henry's good graces, Cromwell knew to keep his head down, to avoid Anne Boleyn's wrath, and simply do his job. He was happy, he was comfortable, and now Cromwell and the king were ready to start a new phase in their quiet plan for annulment.

Any time King Henry needed money from the royal coffers, everything needed to be ratified and go through the Treasurer. While Cromwell was close to Sir Brian Tuke, sometimes a little flexibility was required, especially when seeing out projects King Henry wished to keep quiet or complete with efficiency. Cromwell also got to work reforming the Jewel House, with work beginning on its new building against the southside of the White Tower at the Tower of London in June 1532. With another of Cromwell's old friends, John Whalley, running the mint right beside the new Jewel House, the king's funds were in safe hands, and all within easy walking distance of Austin Friars. Access to the Jewel House gave Cromwell a financial foothold beside the king. The Jewel House likewise benefitted from Cromwell's involvement, not just with the move to the White Tower and convenient location beside the Exchequer, but Cromwell's careful and fastidious paperwork meant Henry's valuables were properly catalogued, monitored and maintained. Even as late as 1545, the king was still using Cromwell's paperwork for the Jewel House records.[11]

Placing Cromwell in a role such as Master of the Jewel House gained little attention, especially with parliament raging over his Supplication. But the gossipers in the taverns frequented by lawyers knew who to blame – Thomas Cromwell was the architect of coming upheaval. Sir George Throckmorton, a lawyer and MP went to King Henry with his concerns, and Henry put Cromwell at his side to give Throckmorton something of a telling-off, a warning to take back to the taverns and inns. But Throckmorton, either brave or probably stupid, uttered the infamous words, 'if ye did marry Anne, your conscience would be more troubled at length, for that it is thought ye have meddled with the mother and the sister'.[12] When Henry, a surprisingly prudish man, defended himself against sleeping with Anne Boleyn's mother Elizabeth, Cromwell had to jump in and lie, telling Throckmorton that Henry also never slept with Mary Boleyn. Not only did the meeting put out the wrong type of propaganda, it also showed Cromwell's closeness to the king, hardly something a man claiming to be a background character needed as the tale spread far and wide.

But Cromwell's Supplication dominated, and on 11 May, King Henry gave his notable speech that 'the clergy be but half our subjects, yea and scarce our subjects; for all the prelates at their consecration make an oath to the Pope, clean contrary to the oath that they make to us'.[13] Just three days later, the king prorogued parliament and its violent arguing, and sent the Duke of Norfolk to Archbishop Warham with the demand that the clergy submit all their power to the king, and revise canon law. Warham finally gave in, and on 16 May, the king was presented with the total Submission of the Clergy.[14] Cromwell's Supplication had done what had been considered impossible. Just five men witnessed the official document with the king, Cromwell with friend Sir William Fitzwilliam, and three random MPs, George Lord Abergavenny, John Lord Hussey, and John Lord Mordaunt.[15] Not only had Cromwell managed to break the back of the church, but there were surprising bonuses. First, the official signatures over clerical power was kept quiet, the five witnesses considered unimportant, keeping Cromwell's profile as low as possible. Second, Sir Thomas More was so outraged he resigned his role as Lord Chancellor.[16] Piece by piece, all the obstacles to Henry's annulment fell away.

Cromwell finally had some time to celebrate; the same day he signed the Submission of the Clergy, he also signed a ninety-nine-year lease to expand Austin Friars, taking over neighbouring buildings from his Florentine friend Giovanni Cavalcanti.[17] The buildings and lands extended Cromwell's home to the wall against the churchyard and on both sides of Swan Alley, the lane which had led to Cromwell's front door. This purchase began the extraordinary transformation of Austin Friars, transforming the fourteen-room home into a fifty-eight-room manor with a full acre of garden, home to his vast bird collection, beavers, and a leopard. One can only imagine the Cromwellians celebrated in their typical luxurious style, at least in private.

But what now for a man who had been sitting in an unofficial cloister for the last few years? He was no stranger any longer; now anyone who so much as saw Cromwell walking his spaniels wanted to call on him for favours. He snatched power from the Catholic church and accidentally orchestrated Sir Thomas More's fall. His minor role in the Jewel House came hot on the heels of more work; first, control over the enormous rebuild of York Place into Whitehall Palace, and the upgrade of Westminster,[18] and then in July, another title as Clerk of the Hanaper after its holder, Cromwell's friend from Ipswich, Thomas Hall, passed away.[19] Again, a small role, with a decent yearly fee and moderate power; he controlled the Hanaper that held all petitions needing the royal seal of approval. It was similar to the Jewel House; first, he gained power over the royal bank balance, now he had control over the writs and other documents the king would or would not see. These two small preferments gave Cromwell a decent amount of official power without attracting too much attention. That was how it would stay, for as long as Anne Boleyn sat at King Henry's side, Cromwell could never be titled like his peers.

But Cromwell could do several things to celebrate his successes. Apart from expansion plans at Austin Friars, Cromwell took over the lease on land in Rhymney in Wales.[20] Close to the Williams' family home in Glamorgan, the land came with the responsibility of overseeing civil law matters in the region. Cromwell also had his coat of arms made up, likely around September 1532, which were one of the few things that showed off Cromwell's position. Given the design, it was unlikely to be new; it bore the three lions rampant like the Williams' family arms, but also had the Wolsey golden chef through the centre as Cromwell's fess of a golden band featuring the Tudor rose (symbolising loyalty to the king) and two Cornish choughs (the symbol of Thomas Becket and all English Thomases). Given that Cromwell chose to keep this coat of arms now he was at court, emblazoned with two Thomases, is a glorious insight into his fidelity.

But the longest-lasting change Cromwell made was commissioning Hans Holbein to paint his portrait, the single picture which now defines how the world sees Cromwell. Cromwell must have been specific in his requests to Holbein; the portrait is as telling as it is mysterious. Hans Holbein had been working in royal circles since approximately 1526. Holbein's talent was without comparison; his work entirely shapes the view of the period. From his silverpoint sketches through to his full-size portraits, Holbein's ability to capture character, attention to detail, life-like reproductions and use of techniques continue to appeal. Yet Cromwell asked Holbein to put many of his talents aside for his painting.

Holbein's portrait of Thomas Cromwell is undoubtedly one of his least detailed, most simplistic portraits, without any desire to flatter or idolise. The portrait has been claimed to be a mockery of its subject. However, the portrait is loaded with specific humility, just as Cromwell must have requested. The most striking detail is that the portrait is done almost in profile, rather than in the more expressive three-quarter pose Holbein used with most subjects. This shows several key things about Cromwell. The profile portrait had been popular in Florentine art, constantly used in portraiture to an excellent degree of beauty. The profile style had been popular as it represented the ancient style of portraits that had been used on coins before portraits lost favour for almost a millennium. By Cromwell choosing profile over a more revealing pose, he appears more a symbol than a man. The private man with an adventurous and obscure past reveals almost nothing about himself.

The portrait does not have one central focus; Cromwell's face is not centred, nor his body, and he is set deep in the frame, almost untouchable or unreachable, a man keeping the world at arms-length. He sits in a rigid pose, a suggestion of substance and steadfastness, and Cromwell's eyes, up close a golden brown, are concentrated on an unknown focal point. His mouth offers absolutely nothing; his lips offer no emotion, though his face gives the impression of gritted teeth, his eyebrows likewise give no hint to Cromwell's feeling at the time of painting, though one sits a tiny fraction higher than the other as if his mind is on something specific.

Cromwell's choice of clothing offers no indication of his personality. Cromwell had a fine collection of clothes in various fabrics, yet he wore a featureless black velvet gown with brown fox fur. A glimpse under his gown offers nothing but black, likewise a plain black soft cap over dark hair, long enough to cover his ears and down into the back collar of his gown. Black was a symbol of wealth, certainly among Florentine merchants, plus wearing black showed no hint of allegiance. The only hint Cromwell's gown gives are the hints of light reflecting on his soft sleeve, suggesting there is a light source nearby, possibly a window in the distance.

Holbein did capture detailing in the blue wallpaper pattern in the background, alongside a red cloth over a table in the corner, which gives colour and texture, making Cromwell's ambiguous, steady look more severe. It is assumed the location is Austin Friars, though it has been suggested it may be the Merchant Taylors' Hall. Given that Draper's Hall moved into Austin Friars later may clear up confusion over which parlour is shown in the backdrop.

A simple portrait for a busy man, showing self-discipline with no outward idolatry. Cromwell has a paper in his left hand showing he is a lawyer, and his forefinger wears the heart-shaped turquoise ring listed in the Austin Friars 1527 inventory and even offered to Norfolk as a favour in 1529. The open letter on the table in front of Cromwell reads, 'To our trusty and right well-beloved Councillor, Thomas Crumwell Master of our Jewel-House', nicely dating the painting. On the table before Cromwell are also other papers with ribbons and wax seals, a devotional book, a quill, and a large pair of scissors to show his place as a cloth merchant. The table itself is covered in bright green cloth; the Board of the Green Cloth was a group of royal attendants headed by the Lord Steward of the Royal Household, who oversaw financial matters at court and dealt with legal offences committed within the court itself. Given Cromwell's ambiguous position at court, it is almost certain he was involved with the Board of the Green Cloth.[21]

The portrait shows a capable, skillful, observant man, and his merchant, legal and religious personality, almost exactly in the style of Sir Henry Wyatt's portrait, right down to the paper between his fingers. While the portrait lacks the detailing of Holbein's works, Cromwell must not have felt the need to have it softened in any way, unlike many other sitters. Cromwell perhaps had confidence in his outward appearance as he quietly continued to slip through the royal court. The portrait has been used by historians to describe Cromwell as a simple or cruel man, and reports of him walking with an 'awkward gait' or 'plodding walk' do not have any contemporary sources. Cromwell was in his late-forties by this time, and easily could have walked with an injury or limp after an exciting life, but the description seems more rooted in biased opinion than fact.

But what would have Thomas Cromwell made of the next big announcement at court? The role of Lord Chancellor was wide open; surely Cromwell would have flourished in this all-encompassing role above his peers. But without giving the role to anyone, King Henry gave the Great Seal, usually in the Lord Chancellor's hands, to Sir Thomas Audley. Audley could put King Henry's royal seal on official papers as Keeper of the Great Seal, while Cromwell got on with business in the background. As Lord Chancellor, Wolsey was endlessly overwhelmed with his workload, while Sir Thomas More floundered from the outset. Why would Cromwell want that on his shoulders? Sir Thomas Audley was a good lawyer from a decent family, not ennobled and without alliances, making him an excellent puppet for the king. Cromwell perhaps even suggested his friend Audley for the role, so that the Lord Chancellor role would be silenced while he and the king went about more important business.

The other major issue was the king's mistress; Anne Boleyn never liked Cromwell, being a Wolsey man, and perhaps the king could not give such a plum role to someone Anne disliked. The Duke of Norfolk would have been a similar dissenter if Cromwell became Lord Chancellor, though while Norfolk hated Cromwell for being a commoner, Norfolk also had little time for his niece Anne Boleyn's reformist religious views. Norfolk was powerful, more powerful than the Duke of Suffolk and his wife Mary Tudor, who were happy to defer to Cromwell in all matters. The fact Suffolk and Norfolk hated one another so much their servants came to blows was yet another relationship for Cromwell to balance (Cromwell's friend Richard Southwell, a Suffolk servant, murdered Sir William Pennington, a Norfolk servant, but purchased a pardon in 1532).[22] The other major issue was that Cromwell was still close friends with Norfolk's wife, Elizabeth. Norfolk hated and abused his wife and Cromwell always took Elizabeth's side. This selection of Audley as Keeper of the Great Seal kept everyone at arm's length from each other.

It is possible Cromwell got his annual September visit to see Gregory, as Audley wrote to Cromwell on 8 September, after hearing Cromwell had fallen ill,[23] and stopped by Austin Friars to find Cromwell not home (though Cromwell was known to make his servants lie to gain his solitude). This is the first of what would become a regular problem for Cromwell, falling sick among his tortuous workloads. Fortunately, this appears to have been a short-lived illness, as John Rokesbie wrote only ten days later, relieved to hear Cromwell was well again.[24] But by late September, Cromwell was back in London, as his sister Elizabeth

Wellyfed was gravely sick at Austin Friars, so much so the news travelled as far as the Duke of Norfolk at Windsor, who was wary of Cromwell returning to court with servants who might have aided Elizabeth.[25] While Elizabeth suffered, her son Christopher studying at Cambridge was put in isolation by his tutor, after one of his fellow students died of the plague. Fortunately, this time, everyone in the family survived.[26]

Things at court moved at a vast pace. Anne Boleyn was titled the Marquess of Pembroke in early September,[27] and the court prepared to head to France so King Henry could show off Anne and look for support from King Francis, both events planned and prepared by Cromwell. Work came at Cromwell from all directions, whether it was securing places at court for his former Wolsey men like Sir Richard Page, Sir Thomas Heneage, and Sir Anthony Browne, investigating the suspicious death of the Abbot of Holme,[28] or proofreading errors printed in King Henry's latest creation, *The Glass of Truth, or A Conversation between a Lawyer and a Divine*. It isn't hard to guess who Henry imagined as the lawyer in the tale.[29]

While Bishop Stephen Gardiner should have been dealing with the bulk of these issues as secretary, he was still out of King Henry's favour after rallying against the Supplication Against the Ordinaries earlier in the year. Richard Cromwell had been working in Gardiner's offices,[30] but Cromwell no longer required his prized nephew there, and by September, Richard was safely back home with his uncle full-time.

But the biggest bombshell was still to come. With Henry back in London, news came that Archbishop William Warham had died in Kent, aged an impressive eighty-two years. Now was the time to strike if King Henry was going to marry Anne Boleyn, and Cromwell was not about to waste it. Stephen Gardiner surely had his eyes on the role of Archbishop of Canterbury, but with his attitude being distasteful to Henry, Cromwell knew a far more forgiving man suitable for the post. Cromwell's good friend, Thomas Cranmer, still just Archdeacon of Taunton, was still abroad, writing just weeks earlier from Germany, where he was seeking reformist opinion (and taking a wife, which would be an issue for years to come). Cranmer was the perfect choice for archbishop; quiet, loyal, deeply evangelical, keen to reform the church, and able to rule on King Henry's annulment if all the legal aspects came together under Cromwell's preparations. The archbishop would need to be approved by Pope Clement VII in Rome, and the consecrated paperwork would need to arrive in London while Cranmer was recalled from the Emperor's court. Cranmer's less than prominent position could make it simple to slide the paperwork under the Pope's nose without any issues.

By the time the Calais trip was upon the court, Cromwell had all hands on deck; he had his friend Thomas Alvard working on his behalf in the Jewel House, who needed to prepare and deliver golden rings, tabernacles, bracelets, collars, necklaces and loose jewels, all totalling almost 300 diamonds, forty emeralds, 140 rubies and 600 pearls.[31] Cromwell's role in the Jewel House was already coming in handy; before departing for Calais, he had exchanged 20,000l (£8,800,000 today) in jewels and plate for ready money to be sent to his friend and in-law, George Lawson, on the Scottish border to help fortify the area, the whole endeavour signed off by Tuke and sealed by Audley without the delay of messy approval meetings.

Cromwell left Austin Friars in the hands of John Williamson as always, who first drew up Cromwell's personal Michaelmas accounts. Cromwell's loan clients owed him over 1,000l,[32] while Cromwell owed far less in return for trivial matters, like the cost of putting his nephew Christopher Wellyfed into a parsonage in Lincolnshire. Cromwell had also renewed his lease on his country home at Canonbury[33] and looked to his lands in Wales, which by all accounts were doing well and set to make a fine profit from corn.[34]

None of Cromwell's paperwork while away in Calais survives, and it is no wonder, considering how much celebrating Cromwell must have undertaken alongside his workload. While a cast of thousands went to Calais, some also had to carry on with the king to Boulogne, making for a hectic journey. The ever-elusive Cromwell is not mentioned at Boulogne, though he easily could have been in the background. Cromwell rented a manor separate from the homes of the royal visit, staying on 'the most wholesome street in Calais', with a large bed, plus another seven servants with their own hall and kitchens, stables for twenty-five horses and five tuns of wine (5300 litres/1400 gallons). Cromwell hosted some of his legendary-sized soirées on the visit, even taking his own musicians to attend him. He also, despite being told the house was fully furnished, took various pieces of furniture to liven up his party manor.[35] Cromwell servants on the trip were likely his nephew Richard, Ralph Sadler, Thomas Rush, and Sir Anthony Lee, not long married to Cromwellian friend Sir Henry Wyatt's daughter, Margaret.

Letters continued to arrive in Calais, which show Cromwell continued all his work as the unofficial Lord Chancellor while abroad with the royal court, including letters from Austin Friars as John Williamson gossiped about their mutual friend Sir John Allen lusting after a young woman he wanted to marry.[36] Cromwell also received a letter from John Legh, mentioning that he heard that Cromwell had been appointed Master of the King's Wards, and needed urgent help.[37] Sir Thomas Audley had stayed behind in London with the Seal, with he and Cromwell writing back and forward almost daily ensuring officialities were correctly sealed, and Audley reporting that while they were in Calais, the plague broke out in London, though everyone working in Austin Friars was safe. Williamson sent Cromwell 100 French copies of *The Glass of Truth* from Austin Friars to share among the French attendees.[38] Meanwhile, Wolsey's son Thomas Winter was in Padua and desperately poor, begging for 100l for provisions.[39]

Cromwell attempting to work as Lord Chancellor without being Lord Chancellor in Calais, combined with Audley back in London with the Great Seal, was not without its challenges. Due to the delay in delivery, daily letters crisscrossed one another, with instructions sometimes missing the messengers by mere hours. One letter sent in haste took six full days to reach Austin Friars. Cromwell had asked Williamson to send servant Thomas Fermour to Calais with Cromwell's vials.[40] A postscript showed that Williamson sent one of Cromwell's longest-serving gossip-masters, Richard Swift, with the box from the apothecary. The delay saw Cromwell waiting for ten days for what he desperately needed in Calais. Cromwell had told a friend, John Whalley, on 19 October that he was well in Calais, but their friend Sir Thomas Rush had hurt his arm.[41]

By late October, surely the effort of the trip was starting to wear on everyone. Christopher Hales wrote from Gray's Inn where he was working with Thomas Audley's man, Richard Rich and complained of plague in London, but Thomas Alvard wrote from Austin Friars to say the illness seemed to have lessened, except for Cromwell's French gardener, who suddenly dropped dead.[42] By 29 October, it was time for everyone to finally return to England. Tales of the success of the trip were underway, and Cromwell had John Gough write, and Wynkyn de Worde express print, the pamphlet 'The Manner of the Triumph at Calais and Boulogne'[43] detailing the glamour and success, real or perceived, of the trip. The mammoth task of getting back to England began, though it helped give the builders at Austin Friars more time to finish the huge renovations. The rumour circulated that the pressure and coercion on Anne Boleyn had finally forced her to sleep with King Henry, which was all the 'success' the trip would give the king. Anyone at court who hoped Henry would tire of Anne once she abandoned her moral fortitude would be sorely mistaken. While the king was likely riding high on his success of the Calais trip, Cromwell was bogged down with bills, paperwork, and endless requests from people, though, as Christmas approached, requests also came with seasonal gifts, mostly birds.

Cromwell's nephew, Christopher Wellyfed, had an unlucky time, almost dying in Cambridge when his featherbed again caught fire in the night.[44] That incident aside, the Cromwell household had a successful year, all coming through the plague outbreak and various illnesses unscathed, and their London home was better than ever. Gregory Cromwell had been spending time with Rowland Lee, one of Cromwell's closest friends, and was rapidly becoming a young man in the north of England.

By now, Cromwell's influence stretched far enough to get all his bills passed in parliament, and with the Convocation of Canterbury about to be in the hands of Thomas Cranmer, the friends were about to finally hold power together.

Chapter 10

1533: Triumph

By the time England rang in the New Year, the country had been without a Lord Chancellor for six months. But Sir Thomas Audley holding the Great Seal, and Thomas Cromwell holding everything else, simply could not be sustained. Cromwell continued to bear the burden of the workload through the festive season, with Audley stuck at home with kidney stones. On 26 January, King Henry summoned a group of his closest men, including Cromwell, Thomas Cranmer, the Duke of Norfolk, Thomas Boleyn, William Fitzwilliam, Stephen Gardiner, and William Paulet, and announced newly-recovered Thomas Audley was the new Lord Chancellor of England.[1] It was official; Cromwell again had missed out on the top job. Or had he? This role would keep Audley busy for the rest of his life, forever distracted by the role and complaining endlessly about the 'small' income. The role of Lord Chancellor was high profile, and not suited to the common man lurking in the background of the court. Cromwell was within striking distance of getting the king his annulment, and yet still held no title. This probably satisfied the king's need to keep Cromwell busy in his vague position at court, which allowed Cromwell freedom to pursue the needs of his king and kept Anne Boleyn at a distance.

Cromwell's workload must have seemed immense, so much so his nephew, Christopher Wellyfed, wrote to his parents at Austin Friars rather than his uncle when looking for help in obtaining a benefice in Cambridge.[2] Christopher later sent a note to his uncle, asking for books and a new gown, and mentioned Gregory was well, but 'has been vexed this Lent with the abscesses'.[3] During Lent, the boys probably would have liked the wheels of parmesan cheese fresh from Parma that Edmund Bonner sent Cromwell.[4] Cromwell probably had little time to enjoy his favourites. The skirmishes with Scotland meant frequent letters to and from his in-law George Lawson. Augustine de Augustinus kept writing as he travelled through Europe, collecting gossip and complaining neither Cromwell nor Frescobaldi would pay him for his work.[5] Cromwell was making good use of his Italian friends though, needing his Italian merchant colleague Arrigo Salvago to transfer 1,000l (£430,000 today) to pay for the paperwork needed to get Thomas Cranmer signed off as archbishop, and the costs associated with getting Cranmer swiftly back to England.[6] Cromwell had wanted Cranmer home before Audley's promotion, so had sent Stephen Vaughan on a dangerous winter voyage to Boulogne, who then walked twelve miles in the snow, then was thrown from his horse at Amiens on the way to Paris and then arrived in Lyon to find Cranmer. A staggering 430 miles plus sea voyage over eight days, all while fearing a broken leg.[7] The Cromwellians needed Cranmer home.

Cromwell's 1533 parliament would go down in history, as with his Statute in Restraint of Appeals, life in England would be blown wide open. This act, created in Cromwell's private office, cut off all avenues of appealing to Rome on any matter, essentially creating the Church of England. Its effect cannot be overstated. Cromwell worked on this bill for several years and finally could see its way through parliament. Ten copies survive in archives, with the wording carefully spaced as alterations could be made, including by King Henry, between its 4 February submission into parliament and its April approval in the Commons and Lords. The Restraints of Appeals meant, simply, as Head of the Church, Henry and England would decide on the royal annulment. Combined with the Submission of the Clergy, all ecclesiastic decisions within England would be made by a king rather than a pope.

While much is made of Cromwell's personal religious beliefs, whether he believed in the Catholic faith, or the Reformation, mattered none in this momentous piece of legislation. While it was obvious Cromwell was invested in the Reformation, the suggestion he made these changes to overthrow the Catholic church is without merit, for the paperwork shows a legal basis for the king's power; what Henry chose to do with that power was another matter. Rather than getting caught up in religious sentiment, Cromwell was the man able to set that aside and look at the issue of the royal annulment from a legal standpoint, setting him apart from all others attempting to help the king marry his mistress. Cromwell did not let his personal opinions follow him to work.

There would be no delay; on 5 April, Cromwell wrote an order to get Cranmer to sit in judgement and drafted bills to say the Convocation had ruled the royal marriage invalid and Henry could remarry, and on 11 April Crammer set off with the King's approval to decide on the Great Matter.[8] Ambassador Chapuys was beside himself with worry that Cromwell had finally found a way to end Queen Katherine's marriage for good, writing to Emperor Charles, 'for when this cursed Anne has her foot in the stirrup, you may be sure she will do the Queen all the injury she can, and the Princess likewise, of which the Queen is most afraid'.[9]

There could be no recourse from Cromwell's changes. The Convocation ruled 197–19 that the marriage between Henry and Katherine was illegal, Bishop John Fisher among those who voted no. Fisher soon went to the Tower on suspicions of colluding with Rome, to keep him out of the way for several months, before Cromwell got him released without charge.[10]

Cromwell had no time to celebrate; he had an inventory of his office done, listing all the papers he had in possession at the time, running into the thousands, including his personal opinion on the Great Matter, paperwork amassed while reviewing Calais the previous autumn, articles about a pope's powers versus a king's power, and a whole file dedicated to holding Cromwell's remembrances. This inventory also showed how Cromwell worked, how he pulled out old papers to research while he worked on his drafts. In his office, he had lists of how much it cost for King Edward III to have a retinue in France and Normandy, and a book about an argument between the Archangel Raphael and 'a certain gentleman of England'. Cromwell had made up notes on provisions for those starving, and ideas on how to repeal attainders. He pulled out the paperwork showing the official coronation speech for a king, presumably to alter it for Anne Boleyn's coronation. Cromwell was pulling papers from all over as his mind went between issues he sought to handle, all without an official court position. He also had a pile of important tasks to ask the king about, and each time he had finished a list, he had the king sign off on his notes, to prove he had the king's permission. Cromwell ensured anything he actioned did not come back to bite him later.

Cromwell likely never got his break at Easter; he got a letter from Gregory staying with his friend Rowland Lee, who was too sick to travel to vote on the king's marriage. But Cromwell did get one large return for his hard work. On 12 April, Cromwell was elevated to Chancellor of the Exchequer. This role as Chancellor would give Cromwell control of the king's and the realm's spending, taxation, and all monetary policy. He was well placed to get to work immediately to overhaul the office and be far more hands-on (which may not have been popular, as the workload would have increased for all those employed). Chancellor of the Exchequer was a highly prodigious role at the king's side, likely as high as Henry could elevate Cromwell without irritating his mistress.

But if anyone thought Cromwell planned to stick to monetary policy, they were wrong. At once he got back to work on a range of issues, including setting the Council over the Marshes of Wales to quell problems there, attempting to appoint his friend Rowland Lee to the position of overseeing justice throughout the country. While Cromwell and Lee were friends, Lee was not well-liked. Stephen Vaughan wrote an angry letter calling out Cromwell for the appointment, as Vaughan's new brother-in-law, John Gwynneth, wanted the position. Vaughan was one of the precious few who could speak to Cromwell in such a rude manner, warning his friend, 'remember God in all your facts, let no affections of persons lead you to condescend or work so evil a deed. You cannot undo that you have done ... Be you sorry for it, and help him with your good counsel, for I am more sorry for this deed done by you than for all the things that ever I knew you do'.[11] The letter from such a close friend must have been hard for Cromwell to swallow; Gregory was in Lee's care in the north, and here was his closest ally sending him a stinging rebuke. Cromwell recalled Vaughan home from the Low Countries late in the year, no doubt sick of Vaughan's endlessly complaining letters. Vaughan was constantly elevated by his friendship with Cromwell, but Vaughan somehow always managed to let him down.

Thomas Cromwell was now a man above all others, and with the division between England and Rome, he was bound to attract many enemies. At least now he had ascended to such a position, he had one friend alongside him who would never let him down – Thomas Cranmer. King Henry could not have asked for a better pairing to take on the church; two men, eminently faithful and loyal, clear-headed, and full of initiative. Cranmer was a calm man, restrained, orderly and obliging; Cromwell was adaptable, cunning, thick-skinned, and merciless in his use of the law. Cranmer had a glorious knowledge base; educated in classical literature, humanism, and philosophy, always the reserved scholar. Cromwell had next to no education whatsoever, had travelled Europe, pick-pocketing knowledge wherever he could, and was still doing so in his late forties when he took the role of chancellor, discovering an understanding of running the highest financial office in the land. They both collected books and read widely; they believed in easing England into reform with the complete blessing and support of their king. They collected all the banned books and read them without fear of being punished, and in Cromwell's case, patronised reformist authors and publishers. Cranmer was deeply invested in reforming the English church but lacked all political skill; Cromwell did not have ecclesiastical respect like Cranmer and needed him by his side as he pushed their agenda through civil law. The pair would be close until Cromwell's dying day.

Thomas Cranmer kept three books; one listed a summary of outgoing letters, another a summary of incoming, and a third listed letters from Cromwell. The third book did not last; it seems Cranmer had an interest in keeping his Cromwell letters private, with Cranmer's secretary, Ralph Morice, letting Cromwell's letters drift out of the records, likely to the benefit of both men.[12] Cranmer, the polite, unassuming clergyman, and Cromwell, the mysterious yet lovable rogue of the court may not have seemed like the likeliest friendship, yet Cromwell's sociable, charming and ruthless behaviour paired with Cranmer's calming influence had the power to change England. King Henry needed a new Cardinal Wolsey, and Cromwell was not that man; Cranmer was that man. Henry gave Cranmer Wolsey's archbishop's ring as a gift on his ascension. If Cranmer wanted to be more successful than Wolsey (and stay alive) beside the king, he needed protection. Thomas Cromwell did not stand beside the king as a man of God; he had no such sentimentality; Cromwell could stand tall and take the blame for the changes hated by the people of England, giving Cranmer the protection he needed. Cranmer may have been Henry's new Wolsey, but Cromwell was Cranmer's new Wolsey. All relied on one another for the explosive new era they were ready to begin.

For visibly pregnant Anne Boleyn to become queen, Cromwell had an entire coronation to prepare. On 28 April, Cromwell wrote up a list of items he still needed to organise, number one being the date and time for Anne's ceremony.[13] Cromwell also had to undergo what was probably an uncomfortable conversation with King Henry, as, on the back of a letter written by Henry arguing for new taxes on wool from Calais, he noted he had to prepare the formal judgement on Henry and Katherine's marriage, start the Act of Succession, and establish a new household for Queen Katherine. With all this going on, it is no wonder Chapuys wrote to Emperor Charles calling Cromwell, 'the man who has the most influence with the king'.[14]

Cromwell being Cromwell, he still made time for entertainment. He hosted Anne Howard, Dowager Countess of Oxford, and sister to the Duke of Norfolk, at Austin Friars, as a favour to Rowland Lee. When Lady Oxford travelled to London for the coronation, Lee asked Cromwell to hold a short-notice dinner party for her, as a friend welcoming a friend.[15] A widow in need and Thomas Cromwell? Of course he would make time for such an event. After all, Lady Oxford needed all the friends she could get; she had been married off as a child to then twelve-year-old John de Vere, Earl of Oxford, the 'incompetent wastrel'.[16] The hard-drinking, generally useless earl died aged twenty-six, leaving young Anne a widow to do as she pleased. Lady Oxford lived at Castle Camps, one of the original Norman castles in Cambridgeshire, and the earl's cousins constantly vexed her, stole from her, and once tried to poison her. Cromwell was just the man young Anne could write to in search of assistance. Lady Oxford continued to write to Cromwell in thanks for his great cheer and kindness,[17] just as the Duke of Norfolk's wife did every time Cromwell aided her (usually against her errant husband).

It was not until 23 May that Cranmer delivered the official verdict on the royal marriage at Dunstable, and he arrived back in London on 28 May. In a high gallery at Lambeth, Cranmer announced the marriage between Henry and Katherine void and legalised the secret marriage between Henry and Anne in late January. To all the world, Thomas Cranmer had created a new queen, Cromwell's name largely absent from the papers. Right on cue, the creation of a new queen could begin.

After two days of pageantry, on 31 May, Anne Boleyn's procession wound its way through London to much fanfare, even if the locals were not thrilled with the new queen. The procession weaved just a few streets away from Austin Friars where Cromwell had his friend Friar George Browne give an Easter sermon weeks earlier to promote Anne, though much of the congregation walked out. The following day, Anne was crowned at Westminster and sat beside Cranmer at the huge banquet held in her honour (with new Cromwell friend the Dowager Countess of Oxford at her service). Yet Cromwell had no position within any part of the procession, the ceremonies, or the coronation. After organising everything, he had no role to play and had not worked himself into the event. Cromwell had achieved the impossible and created a new queen and got nothing from it, ever the administrator in the background. Cromwell again got his writer John Gough and publisher Wynkyn de Worde to put out a pamphlet on the success of the coronation entitled, *'The noble triumphant Coronation of Queen Anne, Wife unto the noblest King Henry VIII',*[18] in English, French, and Latin.

Post-coronation, Cromwell had letters from relatives and friends piling up; his cousin John Babington was looking for a farm for his son and a place at Trinity Hall for another cousin;[19] cousin Nicholas Glossop needed Cromwell to strongarm the Merchant Taylors into giving him his annuity;[20] old friend Lancelot Collins asked for money due to a friend in York;[21] Anthony St Leger, once a friend to Cromwell's father, sent him the best buck he could find while out hunting, writing, 'half the living I have is by you'.[22] Even Princess Mary wrote to Cromwell, an informal letter asking for a favour for a friend. The letter suggests she had written to Cromwell in the past, no need for formalities. Others in Mary's household, such as Margaret Pole, Countess of Salisbury and John, Lord Hussey also regularly wrote to Cromwell asking for favours, so if the Katherine faction of the Great Matter saw Cromwell as the enemy, they had a very good way of hiding it. Old friend Sir Anthony Browne wrote from Paris, and added on the subject of the coronation, 'I think no man has deserved more thanks than you have, which is not a little comfort to your friends'. Meanwhile, a simple letter at home showed Cromwell's position, as he co-signed a letter with Thomas Audley over a matter of prisoners being delivered. Audley signed the letter 'Thomas Audley, Knight Chancellor,' while Cromwell was simply 'Thomas Crumwell'. A man with the weight of the realm on his shoulders had no title on which to affix said weight.

Cromwell's workload never ceased, even while staying with the king at Greenwich in the summer while Anne Boleyn waited to give birth. He had momentous tasks to begin – he had made a queen, now he had to keep her there. Cromwell needed to draft a Writ of Marriage Validity,[23] getting Queen Katherine to accept the end of her marriage,[24] start the Act of Supremacy over the church, the Act of Succession for the coming

royal baby and start work on an argument against any potential ex-
communication bull arriving from Pope Clement.[25] It was one thing to
create a queen and a new church, but now the laws to maintain these
changes were another thing entirely.

At this time, Cromwell placed spies Payne and Cornelius in the
Observant Friars at Greenwich, to listen to sedition and heresy being
spoken, as the friars fiercely supported Queen Katherine.[26] At the same
time, Chapuys started considering Cromwell an ally to Katherine and
Mary, writing to Charles V he would speak to Cromwell and, 'make him
feel how much he would gain in personal safety, and increase his power
and reputation if he would help in the Queen's restoration. Cromwell is
a man of wit, well versed in Government affairs, and reasonable enough
to judge correctly of them'.[27] If people at court were trying to figure out
Cromwell's loyalties, they certainly were not doing a great job.

One thing Cromwell had been doing quietly since his ascendancy to
court was dissolving monasteries, his own tried and trusty system of
gently cannibalising monasteries and other monastic buildings all over
England. Under his own volition, Cromwell set out to slowly enact
Wolsey's unfinished project. When it came time for a monastery and
its lands to change hands, the lands and income simply reverted to the
crown. A monastery would be dissolved, with the land leased out to those
on the lookout for a quiet little earner. In the immediate aftermath of the
expensive coronation, dissolved lands gathered in the last quarter came
in at a value of 12,000l, enough to pay a quarter of the enormous bill
to crown Anne Boleyn. Whether it was large abbeys such as Waltham
Holy Cross, Westminster Abbey, or the Sheen Charterhouse, or down
to small monasteries consisting of just a few people, Cromwell quietly
closed 150 monasteries between 1532 and 1534. Cromwell believed in a
reticent system of simply ending a monastery's life when the ownership
became vacant, rather than a systemic takedown.

In the summer of 1533, Cromwell began a new passion project, sending
historian and scholar John Leland across England and Wales in search
of manuscripts hidden in monasteries, abbeys, friaries, and priories.[28]
Leland had written much of the coronation speeches, and with a royal
commission, Leland went in search of papers for Cromwell to study
and keep in his libraries, along with items for the library at Lambeth
and the king's libraries. Fortunately, much of Leland's ten-year travels

around England have survived, along with records of what he discovered. Leland's appointment in this role turned out to be a masterstroke on Cromwell's part, as Leland's desire to preserve manuscripts and books throughout England and Wales, combined with maintaining libraries for collected works, meant much of history was saved through this difficult period. On top of Leland's enthusiastic commitment to his work, he also sought to protect historical sites in England and Wales and printed many books on the subjects he learned along the way. Leland was not the only one working on such tasks, as Cromwell set John ap Rhys of Brecon out on similar scholarly travels around Wales. Rhys married Cromwell's niece Joan Williams (daughter of Sir John Williams, brother to the late Morgan Williams), and set off on his trip to complement Leland's studies and enrich Cromwell's library.

September 1533 should have seen Cromwell at his happiest; the plague season had been slower than previous years, the royal marriage was confirmed, news from his agents in Europe brought no bad news, and Anne Boleyn was due to give birth to a son. No problems appeared; just Lord Lisle, the new Deputy in Calais, irritating Cromwell with pointless matters not worth his time,[29] while Lancelot Collins sent a note from York saying he had sent a token to Margaret More, Cromwell's neighbour; Collins suspected she would lose it gambling with Cromwell. Collins also arranged the delivery of his 'monstrous beast' to Austin Friars.[30]

But Cromwell's September holiday season was on hold when Anne Boleyn delivered earlier than expected. Rather than the son Henry, Cromwell, and Cranmer's plan needed, Anne delivered Princess Elizabeth. While Eustace Chapuys wrote of King Henry's disappointment, and his emotional fears over the fact baby Elizabeth would be a princess while Princess Mary lost her title, the whole affair was well received. Cromwell devised an elaborate coronation at Greenwich, forcing those Katherine-supporting Observant Friars to take heed, and King Henry put Cromwell's favourite Margaret Grey as godmother to baby Elizabeth, alongside Gertrude Courtenay, Marchioness of Exeter, another staunch Catholic Katherine supporter. The Duke of Norfolk and Thomas Cranmer stood in as godfathers, and Cromwell, as usual, placed himself outside the whole event.

But Cromwell looked after himself in other ways, and in mid-September set off for his new estate in Stepney, three miles east of London, to spend some free time. Cromwell signed a fifty-year lease for the Stepney manor and lands named Great Place from his friend Sir John Allen, who had taken it over from early humanist and reformer John Colet and the Mercer's Company.[31] Cromwell set to work right away, the manor being an 'ancient wooden mansion', though the rebuilding work was done in brick along the edge of Stepney Way, beside St Dunston's Church. It was a beginning and an end for the Cromwell family; as the Stepney manor began its rebuild, Walter Cromwell's old home on Wandsworth Lane was pulled down, to make way for new buildings.[32]

Stepney, three miles from London and surrounded by orchards, was to be a private retreat, but Chapuys followed Cromwell to Stepney in September and spoke with him while Cromwell enjoyed some time hawking. Chapuys relayed all to Emperor Charles, giving an insight into the nature of the personal relationship between Cromwell and Chapuys.[33] Chapuys wrote that Cromwell allowed him to speak ardently about Katherine and Mary, and allowed him to speak frankly on the matter of the king taking back his true wife, though Cromwell believed his laws on King Henry's new marriage would hold steady. The honesty between these men in an informal setting shows how Cromwell chose to do business; without any malice or anger, rather a casual conversation showing his confidence on such a weighty matter, and yet he allowed Chapuys to speak so honestly against him. Whether Cromwell simply placated the ambassador with his word, Chapuys could not tell, but Cromwell promised to do his best for Katherine and Mary saying, 'he watched all occasions to set matters right, but there were some things which he must lead with a long hand and discreetly' (give gentle guidance). While Cromwell created a world where Anne Boleyn could be Henry's wife, he never showed any kind of malice to Katherine or Mary, believing the pair unfairly 'injured' by the whole situation. Cromwell took the time to listen to Chapuys on many occasions, agreeing to read books Chapuys suggested and asking for Chapuys' advice. Cromwell, the creator of the new royal marriage and the Church of England, certainly never appeared to have harsh words for the Emperor's ambassador who stood against all Cromwell looked to build in England.

But while all appeared to be going well professionally, Cromwell endured yet another heartbreak at Austin Friars, with the death of his remaining sister Elizabeth and her husband William Wellyfed. Their eldest son Christopher wrote to both his uncle Cromwell and John Williamson at Austin Friars in late September, asking for help now he had no parents. Christopher wrote to Williamson, fearing he had angered his uncle Cromwell by not spending enough time with his mother as she was dying, but said he was not 'more delighted to search corners' in London rather than be with Elizabeth when she was ill, only that he was with his cousin Walter.[34] Christopher dared to write to his angered uncle, signing the letter X. W., begging for financial help.[35] By this stage, Christopher was no child; he would have been around the age of twenty. Cromwell had seen Christopher lavished with a fine education, which he had used to full advantage, and now seemed to think his uncle would support him through adulthood.

Elizabeth Wellyfed would have been in her early-to-mid fifties when she died, but regardless of her longevity compared to the rest of the Cromwell family, it cannot have been any easier for Cromwell to bear. His other sister Katherine had been dead sixteen years, his parents even longer, and with only Gregory and infant Jane, a person of any age would no doubt have felt this loss. Still, Austin Friars had Cromwell's mother-in-law Mercy, his sister-in-law Joan and her husband John, and their daughter Joan. He also had nephews Richard, Walter, and Gregory Cromwell-Williams at home, and the care of Christopher, William, and Alice Wellyfed. With William Wellyfed the younger studying at Cambridge near his elder brother, Cromwell turned his attention to his only niece Alice, writing up a pre-contract for her to marry one of his wards, Thomas Rotherham.[36] It is unclear when Rotherham married Alice, who was only seventeen in 1533, but in June 1535, Cromwell gained a manor in Dunton, Bedfordshire, taken over to be given to the future Rotherham couple.[37] The Cromwell family did not tend to get married young, and Rotherham continued to work as one of Cromwell's men, though was seemingly not especially liked. Alice was not listed as Mrs Rotherham until 1538 and gave birth to George Rotherham in 1543, just as her husband died. She was quickly remarried to Ralph Astrey by New Year 1544, giving Alice a comfortable life until she died at a similar age to her mother in 1561.[38]

If Cromwell needed time to mourn his sister, he was not about to get it. Princess Mary was stunned to see herself addressed as Lady Mary in letters from the king, Queen Katherine would not relinquish her title,

Cromwell needed to sit in the Star Chamber with Thomas Audley and have the seditious Observant Friars at Greenwich interrogated. People were still calling Anne Boleyn a whore, friend Hugh Latimer was again under suspicion for reformist preaching, and the Scots had finally signed the truce on the northern border. Cromwell even got a letter from his dearest friend Francesco Frescobaldi, who was in Marseilles awaiting the Pope's arrival. Frescobaldi was in dire financial strife at this stage of his life and begged Cromwell's help.[39]

Another calling on Cromwell was Thomas Wriothesley, who had gone with Stephen Gardiner to Marseilles to see the Pope and King Francis, complaining the trip was unpleasant and expensive. Cromwell gained Wriothesley the court role of Clerk of the Signet while gaining his friend Thomas Alvard a new place in parliament. Stephen Vaughan was in Antwerp having travelled through Julich-Cleves-Burg and Saxony, and most unhappy with his journey, going as far as saying if Cromwell did not write to Vaughan, he would die.[40] It was also at this time Cromwell received his new pet leopard, the 'monstrous beast', from old friend Lancelot Collins.[41] Cromwell's friend, Anthony Bonvisi, could have gone to see this beast, as he stopped by with gifts of birds and Italian gossip, helping Cromwell pass the time, no doubt aided by gifts of Spanish wine.[42]

Not that Cromwell had time to spare, as Chapuys told Emperor Charles, 'Cromwell has shown himself well disposed to your subjects, which is very important, as he rules everything', and spoke of how Cromwell privately continued to protect Katherine and Mary.[43] Publicly, Cromwell needed to deal with Elizabeth Barton, the Holy Maid of Kent, who had gone too far with her lies of prophesies against the king. Cromwell had Barton in prison, and sent her to be interrogated by Cranmer. But by late 1533, Cromwell had Barton's noble client list, who summoned her and paid for prophesies against the king and Anne Boleyn.[44] Barton's name was largely blackened by gossip of sexual misconduct with her counsel, and rumours of mental illness abounded.

Under interrogation, Barton confessed to lying about her claims, either out of repentance or in the hope of mercy. Cromwell and Cranmer used the classic good chaplain-bad chaplain method of interrogation. First Cranmer spoke with Barton, listening to her words, allowing her freedoms to pray and rest, treating her well and giving her confidence to speak freely.[45] Then Cromwell sent in Hugh Latimer (only just out of prison himself), claiming Barton's words were from the devil, twisting her words against her and eventually gaining the confession of her falsehoods. Barton was soon strung up at the open-air pulpit outside St Paul's Cathedral, alongside her chief conspirator, Edward Bocking from Christ Church Priory, and Richard Risby from Observant Friars, and slandered in a powerful sermon by John Salcot.[46] Cromwell had all 700 copies of Barton's latest book rounded up and burned, and had a pamphlet printed covering Barton's lies.

Cromwell's momentous year had come to an end, and yet 1534 promised to be one of equal dramatic change, and with a much darker tone. While Gardiner still clung to the title of Principal Secretary, it was undoubtedly Thomas Cromwell who was Chief Minister of the realm.

Chapter 11

1534: Precipice

*'if they once look you in the face, they shall not be
able to conceal anything from you'*

The days of being King Henry's quiet man in the background were over. The new year began with Cromwell hosting banquets for the Scottish ambassadors and was overheard saying 'the spirituality shall depart with their temporalities',[1] as Henry sort to strip the church of both its power and its wealth. But as 1534 opened, Cromwell knew the days of King Henry's slow changes to England were accelerating, and 1534 would herald drama, panic, and even murder in Cromwell's personal life. There was no turning back, and Cromwell would shoulder the criticism of failures as well as the spoils of success. Cromwell bought himself a New Year's gift, two houses on Broad Street, allowing him to further expand Austin Friars, which by this time, had upwards of 200 servants, and could serve 200 people from the poor community around the manor from its kitchens twice a day.

While Cromwell and Cranmer undoubtedly enjoyed the festive cheer of the season, they also had their own plans, sending Nicholas Heath to Germany and the Low Countries, alongside Cromwell's German agent Christopher Mont, Stephen Vaughan, and two of Cromwell's lawyers, Thomas Lee and William Paget. With King Henry still opposed to the Reformation, these men would canvas the leaders of the areas most associated with the new church, to find support for the new English church.[2] The group spent time visiting Lübeck and the Hanseatic League, the Duke of Bavaria, Frederick Elector of Saxony and his wife Sybille of Cleves, the Landgrave of Hesse, the King of Poland, and many archbishops along the way. They even attended the Diet of the Schmalkaldic League but could not officially represent England as a good ally against Pope Clement and Emperor Charles.

Not only did Cromwell write up an enormous remembrance list of tasks to be completed for early 1534, including controlling Wales and Ireland, he also had to open parliament again. Absences worked in Cromwell's favour; in the House of Lords, Archbishop Edward Lee, plus Bishops Tunstall, Fisher and Nix were all absent. But Cromwell's dear friend Sir John Gage said a tearful goodbye to court, to retire and become a Carthusian monk (to the surprise of his family). Cromwell ensured Gage's release from his role as Vice-Chamberlain for the king. Cromwell also ensured William Lord Mountjoy, friend and old Wolsey companion, could retire and see out his illness-ridden days working for Queen Katherine, who was suffering at Buckden Palace.[3] Henry Bouchier too begged Cromwell for help, as he was ill, and when trying to ride, fell from his horse, causing serious wounds. It would not be the first serious fall from a horse that would bring the Earl of Essex to Cromwell's attention.

While Cromwell excelled most in the cut-and-thrust atmosphere of parliament, they started with gentle laws being introduced, but large issues remained, with the Holy Maid attainders, and the Act of Succession also presented at once. Cromwell presented his monumental act, stating Anne Boleyn as queen, Princess Elizabeth as successor, and treason laws were expanded for speaking against the new royal family and Henry's control over the church. As soon as Cromwell present his act, he had to leave London with King Henry, travelling twenty miles to Hatfield to see Princesses Mary and Elizabeth.

While King Henry visited infant Elizabeth, Cromwell quietly sought out Princess Mary, begging her to accept her position as illegitimate, and that her mother was no longer queen of England. Princess Mary was no fool and would not accept, and not allowed to see her father, ambushed the king on his departure, forcing him to acknowledge her.[4] While Cromwell had to write laws to disinherit Katherine and Mary and needed to pass an act through parliament downgrading Katherine's lifestyle, it is unlikely Cromwell said anything negative to Mary, as he had developed a personal fondness for the girl wronged by her father. With one parent spurning her, the other forbidden to see her, Mary appeared grateful Cromwell could fill that void. Cromwell soon charged back to London, as he and Cranmer rarely missed days in session, one of the pair always present at Westminster if the other could not attend.

Parliament could not wait for Cromwell's attention, and disasters threatened. Gerald FitzGerald, Earl of Kildare was in London to explain why things were so dangerous and out of control in Ireland. He arrived nearly six months late, after receiving a gunshot wound during one of his various fights and generally lawless behaviour. Cromwell, in theory, should have sided with the Geraldines in the battles in Ireland, for Kildare had married Elizabeth Grey, sister to Thomas Grey. Elizabeth Grey's nephew, the new Marquess of Dorset, Henry Grey had just come to the royal court to marry Frances Brandon, the Duke for Suffolk's daughter. Dowager Margaret Grey had begged Cromwell to look after her wayward son.[5] The Geraldines had this undisputed connection to the Greys, and yet Cromwell did not take their side, instead being friendly toward Piers Butler, Earl of Ossory, the Geraldines' sworn enemy. It was the most confusing situation; Butler was kin to Thomas Boleyn, yet the Boleyns supported Kildare, getting him appointed the Lord Deputy of Ireland in 1532, a role he ruined with bloody battles and widespread thievery. Now Kildare and his wife Elizabeth Grey were in London, with Kildare expected to explain himself to the king and Cromwell, leaving his son, 'Silken' Thomas FitzGerald in charge.

The trouble was Cromwell was currently too distracted by domestic matters to notice Ireland and Wales languishing among his papers. The Exchequer demanded his time, parliament carried on to the continued distraction of those present, international diplomats needed Cromwell's instructions, clerical appointments needed attention, Ambassador Hawkins in Spain dropped dead in Los Balasses, and the Holy Maid executions needed to be scheduled. Something had to give.

Among the administrative bills going through parliament, which was finally free of Henry's Great Matter, was 'An Acte for the punishment of the vice of Buggerie'.[6] Who wrote and submitted the law was left blank, but it was Cromwell who needed to see it through the Commons and Lords. Whether Cromwell wrote the law is less important than what he did with it; by seeing it through parliament, he created a legal precedent. The Buggery Act was not the creation of a new law. Ecclesiastical courts had been overseeing cases of sodomy until this time, but the Buggery Act moved this process from canon to civil law. The law did not seek to punish gay relationships; it had very different specifications and was only intended to stay in force until parliament's next session. Buggery was not clearly defined in the law, making it easy to arrest anyone, and near impossible to defend oneself in court. Before 1534, sodomy related to sexual acts between men and women, and sex with animals was now included in the vaguely worded law. William Tyndale had been writing for years on the topic of clerical celibacy, blaming this as the reason there were sodomy 'crimes' to prosecute.[7] The law existed to punish the church's power, not same-sex relationships. No one voted against passing the Buggery Act, making it the perfect test case for Cromwell when removing church power. Once this was done, it showed the church's power to oversee laws and sentence the guilty could be removed, now in the hands of King Henry. Cromwell wanted to create the separation of church and state. The Buggery Act paved the way for laws to be handled by civil courts, and rather than existing to punish men, the act only saw around a dozen convictions between 1534 and 1660 when it was revised. Sadly, this law was used to punish relationships in the eighteenth and nineteenth centuries before being fully repealed and replaced in 1967, something not considered in the 1534 parliament. If only Cromwell had time to see through the removal of the act.

Another great issue looming over Cromwell was the matter of Bishop John Fisher and Sir Thomas More continuing to speak, write, and in More's case, publish against the king, his marriage, and his supremacy. The job of convincing Fisher and More to stop fighting the king fell to Cromwell, with a trail of letters going back and forth. Cromwell and Fisher spent the beginning of 1534 writing to one another, Fisher sick and away from parliament. It was not as if Fisher and More had not been given the luxury of time, for it had been almost two years since the Submission of the Clergy and a year since the creation of the Act of Supremacy. Fisher wrote to Cromwell in late January:

I must needs declare my conscience, the which, as then I wrote, I would be loath to do any more largely than I have done; not that I condemn any other man's conscience: their conscience may save them, and mine must save me. Wherefore, good Master Crumwell, I beseech you for the love of God to be contented with this, mine answer.[8]

Cromwell knew Fisher had spoken of things against his conscience before, and reminded the bishop of this, along with rebuttals for the issues Fisher raised, adding:

> beseech the king's grace, by your letters, to be your gracious lord, and to remit unto you your negligence, oversight and offence committed against his highness in this behalf. And I dare undertake that his highness shall benignly accept you into his gracious favour, all matters of displeasure past before this time forgotten and forgiven.[9]

Sir Thomas More was different. More felt he could choose to swear King Henry's marriage was legal, but not that Henry was Head of the Church, but Henry naturally wanted no one to pick and choose which laws they followed. More was an issue Cromwell could deal with through parliament. Cromwell and Audley managed to squeeze through altered heresy laws just before parliament ended its session. These, plus the Act of Succession, were law by parliament's end on 30 March, and Cranmer opened the Convocation of Canterbury on 31 March, forcing a vote that the Pope was simply a foreign bishop. To vote against this meant violating the new Succession laws. Cromwell and Cranmer now had total control.

With Elizabeth Barton and her enablers executed in April, the Thomas Philips case began to besmirch Sir Thomas More. More had arrested Philips months earlier on flimsy heresy charges, and the House of Commons oversaw his trial, exposing More's increasingly radical beliefs. Ultimately, Thomas Philips was found not guilty of heresy, and stayed at the Tower as a priest, a watchful eye for Cromwell and he introduced the English Bible to prisoners.[10] But all this had taken a dramatic toll on Cromwell; he was to meet Ambassador Chapuys at the Duke of Norfolk's London manor on 26 February, but Cromwell never arrived. He had fallen into one of his bouts of undefined illness, which usually lasted one to two months. Given Cromwell was sending off letters from dawn until after midnight, it hardly surprising he would go through periods where an illness would knock him back.

Regardless of his ill health, Cromwell had no choice but to work, for he was needed at court. Chapuys spotted Cromwell once at court in late March, so he must have been recovering,[11] and John Husee met with Cromwell on Lord Lisle's matters,[12] so he must have come through this bout without catching the measles outbreak in the city.

The situation in Wales had deteriorated after Princess Mary was left in limbo thanks to the annulment of her parents' marriage, and with Bishop Lee now in charge of the Welsh Marshes. Lee set off for Ludlow Castle, with Gregory Cromwell as his companion, where Gregory would spend the rest for the year in a miniature court. Gregory, as a son of the mighty Cromwell beside the king, was promptly welcomed into noble houses in the area.[13]

On 6 April, Bishop Gardiner left the court for Farnham, so far from the king's favour he needed to stay forty miles from London. Gardiner had been difficult through the parliamentary session, did not support Henry's new marriage or his supremacy, made a fool of England in front of the Pope and Emperor only six months earlier, and had been on the wrong side of Henry's religious disputes all year. He could no longer hold the title of Principal Secretary. There could be only one replacement – Thomas Cromwell was finally given a high-ranking role at court. Principal Secretary of State was the role that always had the king's ear. How had Henry got Anne to relent on her hatred of Cromwell? Possibly Gardiner's poor behaviour, rather than Cromwell's redemption softened Anne. By 15 April, Cromwell was signing letters as Secretary Crumwell,[14] including a letter to Gardiner himself a week later, almost rubbing Gardiner's nose in it as he asked for a favour.[15] Cromwell had been doing the job of secretary for several years with Gardiner constantly away, and Henry had a new project in mind for his secretary; retaliation.

On 13 April, Cromwell went to Cranmer's home at Lambeth Palace, where Sir Thomas More and Bishop John Fisher were summoned to sign the Act of Succession. This was it; Anne Boleyn was pushing Henry to accept no compromises, and so Cromwell had to push More to finally submit to his king's will. Neither man would sign and went to the Tower. Meanwhile, Chapuys was in a foul mood, concerned Lord Lisle had gone through letters between Emperor Charles and the Queen Regent of Flanders. Cromwell denied Chapuys' mail had been opened and read, but Chapuys told Charles, 'Cromwell's words are good, but his deeds are bad, and his will and inclination incomparably worse.'[16] Chapuys was right; in Cromwell's remembrances list written up by Stephen Vaughan, the very first item listed was 'Letters of the Emperor's intercepted'. [17]

By May 1534, Cromwell felt he deserved time away from court and London. He retreated to his home in Stepney, not that work left him in peace. William Marshall, a writer and printer under Cromwell's patronage, needed 20l to continue printing books, and sent Cromwell copies of *Gift of Constantine*, a work against the Pope. Marshall wanted to print copies of Erasmus' work *Maner and Forme of Confession*, sending Cromwell advance copies to enjoy. He wished to print *The Defender of Peace* by Marsilio da Padov from Latin into English, as well as the *De veteri et novo Deo* New Testament, giving Cromwell advance pages to see, in the hope Cromwell would (and later did) finance the endeavour.[18] Given Marshall's excellent work with publishing reformist propaganda, Cromwell soon got him to work on a radical new law he wanted to see through parliament, but the project had to wait. To add to Cromwell's Stepney reading pile was *Determination of the University of Cambridge* against the Papal Supremacy, hardly a relaxing holiday read.[19]

Marshall was not the only friend digging into Cromwell's time away from London. Augustine de Augustinus was in the Tower for offending the Duke of Norfolk and feared death from torture if Cromwell did not help him.[20] Merchants, domestic and international, wanted Cromwell's help, Thomas Audley needed Cromwell's signature on a treaty with Scotland,[21] and scholars at Oxford University had been dispensing canon law despite the Submission of the Clergy.[22] Though Cromwell made time for more widows in need; Elizabeth Ellis, widow to William Ellis, a judge on the Court of Pleas needed her son home but could not pay his debts.[23] Cromwell took care of Elizabeth's troubles just as Anne, Lady Berkeley's husband Thomas died, and Anne needed Cromwell to untangle her husband's legal mess. Old friend Sir Thomas Palmer also wrote, fearing he was about to die due to lack of money,[24] so Cromwell got him a job working for him in Calais.

Much closer to home, Cromwell's private life had two marvellous events, with Ralph Sadler and Richard Cromwell both marrying. The honorary sons, now in their mid-twenties, were not pushed into marriages, rather given the freedom to choose. Ralph chose from within the Austin Friars household; Ellen Michell had been working for Cromwell since 1530 and had two young daughters. Ellen was a relative of Cromwell's aunt Margaret Michell, and had married in 1526, before being abandoned with her children. Her husband being assuredly dead, Ellen went to live in the priory in Clerkenwell, but was then taken in at Austin Friars to work for Mercy Prior. Despite an age gap, Ralph and Ellen married for love by 1534.

Richard also married; initially he considered a marriage to Catherine St Leger, daughter-in-law of Sir William Courtenay, long-time good friend to Cromwell. Cromwell suggested Courtenay marry off his widowed daughter-in-law, who was also a relative of another friend, Anthony St Leger, to offset his debts. Richard wished to marry Catherine in 1533, but Anne Boleyn, related to Catherine's father through the Butler family, heard of the match and dripped poison on the idea, not wanting one of her ladies marrying a Cromwell. The couple and their families were left disappointed, and Anne had Catherine married off to John Baron Zouche. Luckily for Richard, he soon met Frances Murfyn, fourteenth child of former London mayor, Sir Thomas Murfyn. Frances Murfyn's stepfather, Sir Thomas Denys was another former mayor and Cromwell friend. Frances inherited property in Stepney and in London when she married Richard Cromwell, but both Richard and Ralph had made choices for their happiness rather than advancement.

Work forced Cromwell to leave Stepney for Richmond Palace, where he met with Ambassador Chapuys to discuss Queen Katherine and Princess Mary. Cromwell promised he would do his best for the pair and ensure Spaniards did not have to sign the Act of Succession. But Chapuys told Emperor Charles that Cromwell 'would do all he could to make things better, but I think he will not dare say a word for fear of the concubine'.[25]

Cromwell again tried to get away from court a little, spending time at his manor in Canonbury, three miles upstream from Richmond Palace. He left his clerks, led by Stephen Vaughan, to draw up an enormous inventory of Cromwell papers, running into the thousands in his possession, and stayed at home, doing favours for friends like Anthony St Leger, who wrote, 'I give you my heart, the greatest jewel I have',[26] and Thomas Cranmer's secretary James Barnard, whose father had been robbed. Cranmer wrote back in thanks, saying, 'if they once look you in the face, they shall not be able to conceal anything from you'.[27] Cromwell tried to stretch out some summertime for himself, bouncing between his homes at Stepney, a rented manor in Chelsea, and at Austin Friars, where he purchased eight buildings and four gardens belonging to Anthony Vivaldi on Broad Street, for 200l,[28] and the estate of buildings and land from William Wilford, also on Broad Street,[29] meaning the Austin Friars manor could be radically altered and expanded, again on its way to becoming one of the finest private homes in London.

Unfortunately, Cromwell barely had a moment to enjoy these new additions. Cromwell had been trying to work up a plan to quell the issues in Ireland, but the situation had deteriorated. Sir William Skeffington was appointed as Deputy of Ireland, to be accompanied by Piers Butler, Earl for Ossory, who was in England at the time. Skeffington wrote to Cromwell several times, doubting the entire plan, delaying with illness, and not especially interested in the position. Cromwell had copies of his new 'Ordinances of Ireland' printed up so the Earl of Kildare could not pretend to ignore the king's demands upon his return home to Dublin. The theory was to install an English style of governance in Ireland; the main problem being it would reduce power held by powerful families, like the FitzGeralds.

But the planning came all too late, as did correspondence from Ireland, taking three to four weeks, while letters could routinely get to Rome in a week to ten days. By early July, Ireland had descended into madness. In Kildare's absence, his son, 'Silken' Thomas FitzGerald had been in charge, which amounted to murder, violence, burnings, and robberies around Dublin.[30] The FitzGeralds committed treason and sedition, claiming to follow the Pope rather than the king, and took land and possessions and harmed anyone who stood in their way. The combination of appointing the English Skeffington to the Deputy role, the execution of Catholic Elizabeth Barton, combined with Cromwell's agents ransacking Bishop Tunstall's offices and the arrest of traitor Lord Dacre in the north (men loyal to the Geraldines), created a ticking timebomb. With the 'Ordinances of Ireland' set to strip the FitzGeralds of power, Silken Thomas took the bloody route to retaliation.

The biggest blow was yet to come. Cromwell's long-time friend John Aleyn had been Archbishop in Dublin for several years but had to leave the country at once. Silken Thomas and his men captured Aleyn as he tried to flee Ireland, Cromwell receiving the news in a letter dated 27 July. Cromwell had been friends with John Aleyn and his brother Thomas for nearly fifteen years, all living in the same area and working in the merchant business of London. Aleyn, fleeing Dublin Castle after hearing of a possible siege, fled to Artane Castle but was flushed out by Silken Thomas. Aleyn, wearing nothing but a shirt, begged for mercy.[31] Silken Thomas accused Aleyn of ordering the Earl of Kildare's death, and had two men slaughter Aleyn, only to claim a language misunderstanding

The edge of the Thames at Putney had not changed much between the fifteenth century and nineteenth centuries, despite the addition of Putney bridge, with boats being able to stop off in Putney for supplies, as seen here c.1865. (*Bequest of John Bonebrake, Cleveland Museum of Art, CC0, via Wikimedia Commons*)

Bayard sur le pont du Garigliano, the Battle of Garigliano Bridge, by Henri Félix Emmanuel Philippoteaux, painted 1840, where Piero de' Medici died and teenager Thomas Cromwell escaped. (*Henri Félix Emmanuel Philippoteaux, Public domain, via Wikimedia Commons*)

The Frescobaldi coat of arms
outside Frescobaldi Palace today,
as seen in Cromwell's time.
(*I, Cyberuly, CC BY-SA 3.0, via
Wikimedia Commons*)

PAGOLODINI
CHOLOFRESCH
ⱰBALDIꝂM·D·IIII~

Florence in the sixteenth century. Frescobaldi Palace is on the right hand side of the Arno River, with
its Ponte Santa Trinita the second bridge from the top. (*Unknown author, Public domain, via Wikimedia
Commons*)

The Frescobaldi Palace, with the Ponte Santa Trinita, and the Tower of the Palazzo Vecchio in Winter 1905. (*"Florence & Some Tuscan Cities", Painted by Colonel R.C. Goff. Described by Clarissa Goff; Published by A & C Black, London, 1905*)

The only surviving contemporary portrait of Thomas Cromwell, created by Hans Holbein in c.1532, a beautiful example of Cromwell's carefully curated image. (*Hans Holbein the Younger, Public domain, via Wikimedia Commons*)

Portrait possibly of Richard Cromwell, created by Hans Holbein in 1539. (*Follower of Hans Holbein the Younger, Public domain, via Wikimedia Commons*)

Portrait of Ralph Sadler, Cromwell's son in all but name, created by Hans Holbein in 1535. (*Workshop of Hans Holbein the Younger, Public domain, via Wikimedia Commons*)

Miniature created by Hans Holbein in 1537, commemorating Gregory Cromwell's wedding to Elizabeth Seymour. (*Follower of Hans Holbein the Younger, Public domain, via Wikimedia Commons*)

Cardinal Thomas Wolsey, Lord Chancellor of England, recreated from the original in c.1610. (*Sampson Strong, Public domain, via Wikimedia Commons*)

Cromwell's long-time friend Sir Brian Tuke had six portraits created by Hans Holbein, being the man to pay the royal painter for his work. This one dates from c.1540. (*Anonymous, after Hans Holbein the Younger, Public domain, via Wikimedia Commons*)

Archbishop Thomas Cranmer, Cromwell's endless ally, portrayed in 1545. After Henry VIII's death, he grew a beard in commemoration of his lost king. (*Gerlach Flicke, Public domain, via Wikimedia Commons*)

Sir Thomas Wyatt, sketched by Hans Holbein in c.1536, accomplished poet but unsuccessful diplomat for Thomas Cromwell, accompanied his master to the scaffold in 1540. (*CC BY-SA 4.0 via Wikimedia Commons*)

Lady Elizabeth Cromwell, by Hans Holbein, c.1542. Previously believed to be a portrait of Queen Kathryn Howard, now considered to be Gregory's wife Elizabeth. (*Hans Holbein the Younger, Public domain, via Wikimedia Commons*)

Sketch by an unknown author of Austin Friars, c.1540–1660, recreated in 1836, showing Cromwell's changes to his London home, with his unique turrets and oriel windows. (*Agga's Map, Public domain, via Wikimedia Commons*)

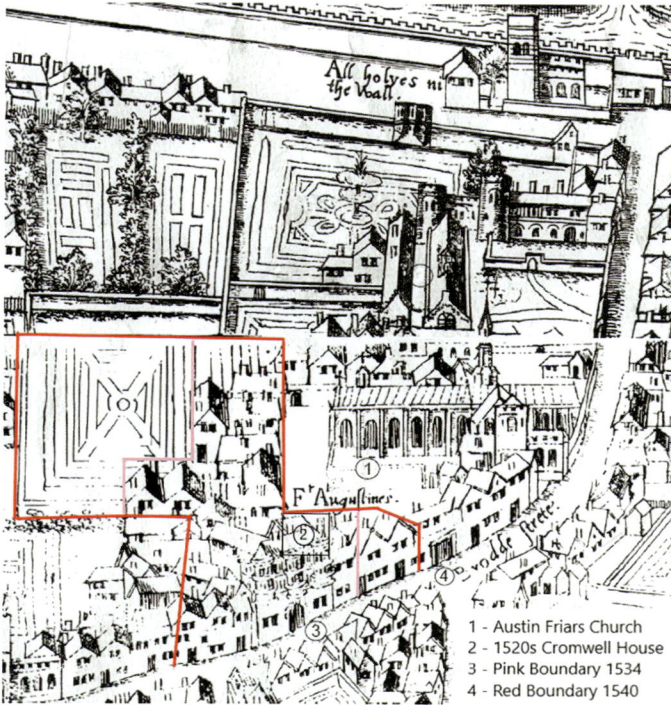

Sketch of London showing Cromwell's Austin Friars expansion between 1523 and 1540. (*Unknown author, Public domain, via Wikimedia Commons*)

1 - Austin Friars Church
2 - 1520s Cromwell House
3 - Pink Boundary 1534
4 - Red Boundary 1540

The Draper's Company removed Cromwell's knot gardens after their acquisition in 1543. After the 1774 fire, much of the house was rebuilt, and much of the garden was changed into a new great hall. Some of the Austin Friars garden still remains in London today, with detailed walking paths and fruit trees, now too small for the pond pictured here in the nineteenth century. (*Walter Thornbury, 'Throgmorton Street: The Drapers' Company', in Old and New London: Volume 1 (London, 1878), British History Online, no known copyright restrictions*)

The Cromwell banners of arms as seen after Cromwell's 1537 appointment as a Knight of the Garter, featuring the 'Two Thomases'. (*Rs-nourse, CC BY-SA 3.0, via Wikimedia Commons*)

The 1538 commemorative medal, with Cromwell's updated coat of arms to reflect Henry Cromwell's birth. The earl coronet must have been added just before Cromwell's death. (*British Museum, Public domain, via Wikimedia Commons*)

Canonbury Tower in Islington (spelled Canbury by Cromwell) in its original state. The house still stands today in a restored condition. An ivy vine needed to be removed in the later nineteenth century, being nine inches thick and destroying the main tower brickwork. (*British Museum, Public domain, via Wikimedia Commons*)

A print (1800–1830) of Dean Colet's house in Stepney, England, built c.1503, and leased by Thomas Cromwell in 1533. After his death the house went to Richard Cromwell, and then Queen Kathryn Parr. The wooden house still stood in the nineteenth century. (*Unknown author, Public Domain, via Wikimedia Common*)

422

430

One of Thomas Cromwell's remembrance lists, written in his own hand. A clerk often dictated the list, though Cromwell often took over himself. This one dates from a bunch collected in early 1534 covering miscellaneous small tasks. (*British Library, Shelfmark: Cotton MS Titus B I, with permission*)

All that remains of Cromwell's beloved offices at The Rolls of Chancery is the chapel, now part of the Maughan Library, c.1800. (*Samuel Ireland, Public domain, via Wikimedia Commons*)

Cromwell's lavish Hackney home was kept in its quality condition with photographs showing little change even in the twentieth century but was bombed during WWII. Seen here in 1750 from the south-east with its elaborate courtyard hidden. (*Ernest A Mann, Early views of Brooke House, in Survey of London Monograph 5, Brooke House, Hackney (London, 1904), created by Chatelain. 1750. British History Online, no known copyright restrictions*)

Cromwell's much redesigned and renovated home in Hackney, remained in his possession only one year, but survived until its demolition in 1954. Seen here from the north entrance in 1642. (*Ernest A Mann, Early views of Brooke House, in Survey of London Monograph 5, Brooke House, Hackney (London, 1904), created by W. Hollar, 1642, British History Online, no known copyright restrictions*)

Side entrance to Mortlake manor, c.1700. The house had been much changed by Cromwell, from an old timber and brick house to a fully brick manor home which dominated the shoreline at Mortlake for 300 years. (*Unknown author, Public Domain, via Wikimedia Commons*)

A View of Mortlake up the Thames, sketched in 1753, with Cromwell's Mortlake manor house against the river edge. (*A View of Mortlake up the Thames, 1753, Thomas Boydell, Maps K.Top.41.10.c, British Library's Collections for Flickr Commons, no known copyright restrictions*)

St James' Palace which Cromwell acquired as work and living places from 1536, seen in the 18th century. (*Thomas Bowles, Public domain, via Wikimedia Commons*)

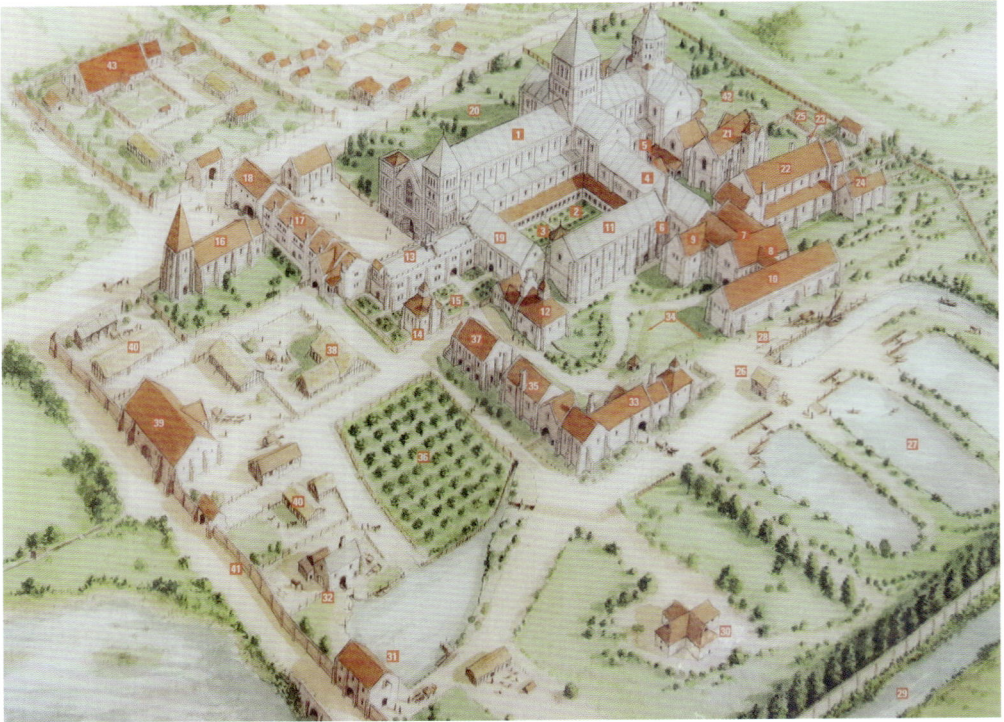

Lewes Priory before Cromwell's destruction overseen by Giovanni Portinari. 1 – Great Church, 2–15 prior and monks' living spaces, 16–19 great houses, 20 and 42 – cemeteries, 21–25 infirmaries, 26–30 livestock and fish spaces, 31–41 water-mill, brewery, brewhouse, bakeries, orchard, granary, barns, stables inside the boundary, 43 St James' Hospital. It was left as rubble in late 1538. (*Robert Eyers, CC BY-SA 4.0, via Wikimedia Commons*)

Leeds Castle as it is seen today, relatively unchanged since the years of Gregory and Elizabeth Cromwell. (*Robert Eyers, CC BY-SA 4.0, via Wikimedia Commons*)

when the Pope issued ex-communications for this behaviour. The still-living Earl of Kildare, in the Tower in London, grew rapidly ill, and was nursed by his wife Elizabeth Grey, but died of 'grief' on hearing of his son's behaviour and ex-communication. Murdering Archbishop Aleyn meant Silken Thomas lost the support of the clergy he needed to take control of Ireland. From this moment, Cromwell planned a campaign over three years to capture Silken Thomas, exploit the FitzGeralds' connection to the Grey family and have the entirety of their male line executed. No one was going to keep their heads after what happened to John Aleyn. For better or worse, Ireland now rested in Thomas Cromwell's hands.

Not only did this cause a great deal of tension, but it also caused dramatic issues within the royal court. Cromwell squarely placed the blame on the Duke for Norfolk and did not attempt to hide his anger. Cromwell openly stated Ireland could have been saved had King Henry's son Henry Fitzroy, the Lord Lieutenant of Ireland, been allowed to travel to Ireland.[32] But after Fitzroy married Norfolk's daughter Mary, in late 1533, Norfolk was reluctant to send Fitzroy abroad. Cromwell had wanted to send Fitzroy to Ireland as early as February before the violence erupted, but Norfolk refused. Cromwell managed to get Fitzroy away from Norfolk, travelling and working in Dorset to great acclaim. Norfolk was enraged by Cromwell's claim before the court and quickly retreated to his manor at Kenninghall, unable to stomach his continuing loss of power. The fact Norfolk and the Boleyns interceded to get the Earl of Kildare into power only two years earlier did them no favours, leaving Cromwell well-placed to fire his anger at his rivals without the slightest pushback from the king. Unlikely to be pleased about Norfolk's retreat was his wife, Duchess Elizabeth, who wrote to her friend Cromwell begging for food, as her husband would not give her anything. The fact Cromwell was having to feed Norfolk's wife on top of everything else surely only made for a hostile atmosphere.[33]

Sir William Skeffington set off for Ireland and Cromwell had to make a concession; he sent his dear friend William Brabazon as an agent for Skeffington. Cromwell and Brabazon had been friends since at least 1523, and now Cromwell needed someone he could trust in Dublin, despite the danger. Brabazon took the job and fellow loyal Cromwell friend, John Allen. Like murdered John Aleyn, Cromwell would never see Brabazon again. To get the initial outbreaks of violence in Dublin under control,

Cromwell also had to send his friend Sir William Fitzwilliam abroad, though Fitzwilliam was able to return once England soon after.[34]

Cromwell again tried to retreat from the court and stayed at his manor in Canonbury for several weeks. He received a letter from Queen Katherine, calling Cromwell her 'especial amigo', and begged to see Princess Mary, but Cromwell could not sway Henry, who was determined to maintain his cruelty to Katherine and their daughter. Cromwell sent Dr William Butts to Princess Mary, who reported on her stomach illnesses and headaches.[35]

But Cromwell received happier news from Rowland Lee that Gregory Cromwell was well, enjoying his time in the north, and was far away from the troubles which plagued his father.[36] Friend Richard Page wrote filled with thanks to Cromwell for overseeing justice for Page's niece who had been attacked,[37] and another friend, Thomas Godsalve, sent Cromwell a gift of six swans and thirty-seven kilograms of pears he grew himself.[38] Word must have gotten around Cromwell was in a sour mood.

People were right to think so. Cromwell was forced back to London to prepare the royal Michaelmas accounts and prepare the mammoth list of tasks to be carried out in Ireland. Even letters from Gregory de Casali talking of the Pope's imminent death did not rouse Cromwell's spirits. Chapuys reported on Cromwell's pain with glee to Emperor Charles, of how Cromwell refused to discuss Ireland at court, and in the state of confusion, a gag order was placed at court. Chapuys told Charles, 'indeed, so strict is the injunction that for some days past, Cromwell will not allow anyone at his table, or elsewhere, to mention the subject, which makes me think that affairs in that country do not exactly turn out as the king might wish.'[39]

If King Henry was mad over the situation in Ireland, he did not place the blame on Cromwell's shoulders. Archdeacon John Taylor, eldest of a group of triplets King Henry VII had cared for throughout their lives, died of illness on 8 October. Taylor had been the Master of the Rolls. It was a prodigious role, and one Cromwell could not miss, being granted it the same day as Taylor's death. Since the role began in 1286, the position had been held by a clergyman, until now. While Cromwell already had the powerful role of Principal Secretary and senior member of the Privy Council, this was a new type of honour. As keeper of the records at the Court of Chancery, Cromwell oversaw matters from all the courts in England, not bad for a man with no formal legal training who had only been admitted to Gray's Inn ten years earlier. The uneducated Putney boy was now the highest legal figure in the land after the Lord Chief Justice. The powerful role came with an annual salary of 300l (£130,000 today) and the manor on Chancery Lane, which Cromwell moved into almost immediately, allowing Austin Friars to finally function as a private home. Cromwell's private chapel in the manor is today in the Maughan Library, part of King's College, London. Cromwell loved the title and manor so much even when he had to relinquish the role to a friend, he remained living in The Rolls, much to the annoyance of his replacement.

October yielded more good news; Pope Clement VII was dead in Rome after almost eleven years on the papal throne.[40] The Pope who blocked King Henry's marriage was suddenly gone, and Alessandro Farnese, Dean of the College of Cardinals, soon took Clement's place as Pope Paul III. Clement had started life as Giulio di Giuliano de'Medici, rose to Archbishop of Florence, then was made a cardinal by his uncle Pope Leo. Clement was also the rumoured father of Alessandro de' Medici, now Duke of Florence, having brought Cromwell's Florence into the fold of the Papal States. No doubt Cromwell and the rest for the court knew life would be no easier under Pope Paul, who was naturally against the Reformation, and totally disinterested in King Henry's claim to be annulled from Queen Katherine.

By late 1534, what the Pope wanted from England no longer mattered. Cromwell's quiet alterations to law had brought about King Henry's every desire, and now they were living in the reality of Cromwell's efforts. Plenty of people signed the Act of Succession to accept Henry and his new wife, though many more believed in Katherine and Mary. Henry's new marriage had yielded Princess Elizabeth, the new rightful heir, but Anne Boleyn could not hold up her part of the deal; being a bride providing sons for the realm. With just Elizabeth and rumours of miscarriages, Anne must have felt permanently under siege, just like Queen Katherine before her. Cromwell had settled the Succession laws and the punishment was severe if these laws were not obeyed; Fisher and More still in the Tower were a testament to that, and while Cranmer had been installed as Archbishop of Canterbury, he was having a hard time himself, having spent all year trying to get the bishops of England on his side, with considerable pain for little advancement.

What Cromwell could control, if not Ireland or his temper, was parliament, submitting the First Fruits and Tenths Subsidy.[41] When Cromwell set up the Act of Restraint of Annates, England stopped paying taxes to Rome; now, the money entirely went to King Henry. These new payments were to start at New Year 1535, giving no monastic house any time to argue. Proceeds of the First Fruits went under the direct control of the Lord Chancellor and Master of the Rolls – Audley and Cromwell. The treason laws were also changed, removing the option of safety in sanctuary for traitors, but Cromwell added the word 'malicious' to the treason laws, so anyone offending the king could be arrested for treason as they had already proved evil intent with their words or deeds. Sir Thomas More was directly in the firing line.

As the year ended, Cromwell had a clerk run up a basic remembrance of his land holdings around England and Wales and their yearly value in rent.[42] His lands made a yearly income from rent alone was 416l (which, at the time, would take an average tradesman fifty years to earn). Sadly, the remembrance did not include the current value of Austin Friars, nor the manors at Stepney and Canonbury.

By 1534, it was well established Cromwell favoured slowly gathering monasteries and returning them to the crown when given the chance. But King Henry's desire for control over religion and wealth, coupled with Thomas Cranmer's continued trouble trying to establish the new Church of England, meant Cromwell's gentle plan for monastic lands would be twisted, exploited, and amplified for the world to see. Cranmer's inspection of friaries was underway with moderate success, but by November, King Henry commanded the project expanded to include an inspection of every single monastic house in England, Wales, and eventually Ireland. By this time, Cromwell was already deeply invested in Wolsey's, now Henry VIII's, College at Oxford and held the post of Visitorship of New College, Oxford, combined with being High Steward of Cambridge University, meaning they were already closely under his watch. King Henry wanted more; he appointed three men to be Commissioners of Royal Visitations, Cromwell, John Tregonwell and Thomas Bedyll, one of Cromwell's closest and so far, quietest agents and lawyers. By New Year, Cromwell would be given a title no man or woman ever held again in England, fall perilously close to death, and be assigned a project which would blacken his name for 500 years.

Chapter 12

1535: Affliction

'I have noted corruption took a great effort from you all'

Living at The Rolls rather than Austin Friars cut Cromwell's daily commute from 3.5 miles to 2.3 miles to Westminster and Whitehall. No more trotting down Throgmorton Street onto Cheapside, past St Paul's Cathedral and through Ludgate Hill. Now his trip was simply along Chancery Lane onto The Strand and straight to court or parliament. One person could no longer walk or ride with him; Thomas Alvard, his long-time friend, died of illness in February, Cromwell the executor of his friend's will. Alvard had been at Cromwell's side for so many important occasions, and his death would have come with sadness and a deep sense of loss.

How things had changed in five years for Cromwell; at the end of 1529, Wolsey was stripped of his role as Lord Chancellor and banished to Esher Place. More had become Lord Chancellor, and Stephen Gardiner was the new secretary to the king. Queen Katherine still held firm in her role, Anne Boleyn ready to pounce. But by the end of 1534, Katherine was out, and More sat in the Tower. Now Gardiner was banished to Esher Place, stripped of his title of secretary, given to Cromwell. Cromwell had been a contented but unremarkable lawyer who closed the odd monastery to build colleges. As 1535 dawned, Cromwell ran The Rolls of the Chancery, the heart of London's legal community, held parliament in his hand, created a queen and a new church. Probably the only thing unchanged was Anne Boleyn's hatred for Cromwell. Not everything could change.

By January 1535, everyone wanted a piece of Thomas Cromwell, but everyone needed to take second priority, as on 21 January, Cromwell, now Vicar-General of the Monasteries, was also granted the title of Vice-Gerent. As Vice-Gerent, Cromwell became Henry VIII's deputy. Given this role was undefined and never bestowed again, it meant Cromwell could extend his influence as far as required in England. Thanks to

Cromwell's Act of Supremacy, King Henry needed someone to do the work involved in establishing the English church, and Cromwell was the only person for the job.

As Vicar-General, Cromwell took the role as leader of the monastery inspections and sought to create the Valor Ecclesiasticus, literally a church valuation, of religious houses in England. What had been examinations in 1534 to seek out heretics was now an all-out inspection of all religious houses, checking to ensure clergy were practising the new faith, to root out any sedition or heresy, remove anyone under the age of twenty, and to give a 'broadly accurate' valuation of the buildings, lands, jewels, plate, and livestock.[1] Only friaries and nunneries were left largely untouched. Cromwell did not want women in monastic houses used by men, though was forced to change this rule when one of his favourites, Margaret Grey, informed Cromwell she would not be leaving her retirement home of Tilty Priory, and Cromwell ensured it stayed available for her use, along with eight monks for the rest of her life, along with her steward Henry Sadler. At this stage, the Valor Ecclesiasticus was not designed for dissolving monasteries, unless extreme failures were discovered; it was merely a way of cataloguing everyone and their land, eclipsing even the Doomsday Book of 1086.

Cromwell had little time to work as an inspector of religious houses, unable to leave London when parliament was in session. Ireland was still at war with the Geraldines, with Lord Deputy Skeffington endlessly sick and Cromwell's friend William Brabazon ever in need of money and reinforcements. Cromwell needed bishops throughout England to return their papal bulls swearing allegiance to the Pope and sign new bulls swearing allegiance to Henry and the English church. Some, like Bishop Lee, were happy to oblige;[2] Cromwell, in a mean streak, personally pulled Bishop Gardiner before the Privy Council and forced him, humiliated him, into admitting that the king now made and unmade bishops rather than the Pope.[3]

Religion dominated the most urgent business. While there were extreme papists such as More and Fisher in the Tower, the new reformist religion also had its own extreme factions – the anabaptists. These so-called radical reformers, who claimed the Reformation was not going far enough, started in Switzerland but popped up all over Europe. While Henry had wanted the Church of England, he was no reformer; he wanted the Catholic church to keep its nose out of England, but he had no plans to let in Lutherans. This meant while he punished priests, he also punished reformers, which kept rebellion to a minimum. On 11 February, friend William Lok wrote to Cromwell from the Low Countries, talking about anabaptists being burned.[4] As anabaptists were in danger, they looked to England as a potential haven; these perceived troublemakers were already finding their way to England by the time Cromwell received the news.

But despite Cromwell's already hefty workload, he had the distasteful task of satisfying the king's sudden need to renew an alliance with the French. Endless embassies and overtures into Europe had yielded no support for Henry's marriage to Anne, nor his religious changes, so now Cromwell entertained Ambassador Castelnau and various other delegations sent to discuss marriage for Princess Elizabeth to Prince Charles Duke of Angoulême (so arrogant he later killed himself during a dare). Cromwell also needed to discuss a possible French marriage for Princess Mary, who was ill, and Cromwell privately admitted concern over the ladies in her attendance, and poisoning rumours continued.[5] Cromwell seemingly only followed the king's orders for show, for when Chapuys sent a private message to Cromwell though a messenger, calling to dispel rumours the Emperor would arm the Irish against England, and fight for Mary's position, Cromwell 'showed himself very gracious and held his bonnet in his hand almost as long as my man did',[6] a show of his genuine words for Chapuys and the Emperor. But King Henry too seemed to switch up alliances; he had shrugged off his recent mistress for a new one, Anne's cousin, Margaret Shelton. If Cromwell had any interest in this gossip is impossible to tell; anything that kept the king occupied was useful in making sure he did not investigate Cromwell's business, which usually only slowed proceedings.

Between all the jostling for alliances, favours, rumours of war at home and abroad made the court a toxic environment in the early stages of 1535, and the Duke of Norfolk and the Duke of Suffolk left soon after, angered about their constantly side-lined positions. There were whispers many in court still preferred Katherine and Mary over Anne and baby Elizabeth, with Henry, Lord Montagu, muttering to the Duke of Norfolk he wished to shed blood for Katherine and Mary's position. Cromwell felt the same; behind closed doors, Cromwell wished to exact revenge on the French for their deplorable attitudes. Cromwell especially hated French Admiral

Philippe de Chabot, whom Chapuys reported Cromwell, 'covertly jeered at (Chabot) to me in a very emphatic way'.[7] The attempt to woo the French did nothing to ease Cromwell's stress.

Working at The Rolls offices and trying to appease Henry and Anne's desires to legitimise their marriage, Cromwell still made time for his friends and family. His nephew Christopher was accepted into King's Hall, Cambridge, obviously back in his uncle's esteem.[8] William Brabazon wrote from Ireland, the situation hitting a setback as they fought Silken Thomas' men outside Dublin. Cromwell's old friend Elizabeth Howard wrote from Kenninghall, sending a late New Year's gift of knives, 'for the kindness I have found in you, you shall have my heart during my life', and was unwell and neglected; her husband leaving the court for Kenninghall cannot have lifted spirits.[9] Stephen Vaughan too was in trouble; he caught a terrible ague and was seriously ill for two full weeks. Vaughan heard a rumour Cromwell was not well either and sent his brother-in-law John Gwynneth to attend him. Vaughan claimed Gwynneth, a Welsh priest and musician, could help with illness. This was a huge mistake, as Vaughan soon wrote again apologising for sending Gwynneth, and days later, begging for forgiveness as Cromwell had unleashed his indignation on his dear friend.[10] Between his strong papist leanings and lack of medical knowledge, Gwynneth fiercely annoyed Cromwell.

Everything annoyed Cromwell by March 1535. He suffered from a swollen face and retired to Austin Friars. Chapuys went to visit, and Cromwell had finally relaxed, still ill and swollen. Chapuys wrote:

> Cromwell went to dine in (Austin Friars' garden) intending to see his hawks fly. After dinner, I went there to see him and remained a long time … After several other conversations, Cromwell said that I and other agents of your Majesty acted like falcons, which flew very high to come down very low upon their prey, and that he knew very well that all our hunting was merely to get the Princess declared heir to the kingdom; but this was impossible, owing to the statutes made thereupon. I don't know if he did this to make himself feel better.[11]

But Cromwell was not well, and he could only deny it for so long. His old friend from Putney Thomas Megges spent an afternoon with Cromwell at The Rolls but then wrote a letter the following day, informing Cromwell he had become 'struck with ague', just as Vaughan suffered.[12] Cromwell isolated at The Rolls, only attending court if King Henry called for him. The Valor Ecclesiasticus inspection details were pouring in, Henry continued to jostle for a French alliance, and people continued to call on Cromwell's help, but he remained hidden in his Rolls rooms. Chapuys decided he would go to see Cromwell on 20 March, but Cromwell excused himself from court and returned to Austin Friars for Palm Sunday. By Monday, he tried to get out of bed to see Chapuys but could not even make it down the stairs.[13] Chapuys suspected lies and visited Austin Friars that same afternoon, but Cromwell was back in bed. When Chapuys' servant went the next morning to confirm a new appointment, Cromwell had deteriorated even further.[14] The king's most important servant was on the brink of death.

While Cromwell's illness was not defined, given Stephen Vaughan and Thomas Megges suffered ague suggests the same hit Secretary Cromwell. Ague, sometimes called tertian fever, mostly resembles malaria, prevalent in the sixteenth century. The illness could incubate for up to twenty-five days, and Cromwell had been visibly ill for some time. Once an ague set in, Cromwell suffered extreme fever, sweating, chills, seizures, bleeding gums, jaundiced eyes, plus all over pain, particularly in his back, with extreme headaches, nausea and vomiting. There was no alleviation for ague, and a person had to either fight off the fevers, which would come and go in three-day cycles, or die. Treatment was severely limited to trying to cool the patient or take liquids if they could swallow. On 3 April, an Italian physician was called to Austin Friars to help the suffering minister, already two weeks into his ague.[15] By this time, Cromwell should have recovered but was worsening. Most doctors of the time still worked on the theory of the four humours of the body and practices such as bloodletting and cupping, with no relief to the patient. Cromwell's Italian doctor was likely a local man from the Italian community, leaving Cromwell with plenty of help, but little remedy.

By 15 April, Cromwell had a guest at his bedside; King Henry himself.[16] The monarch, always terrified of illness, travelled to Austin Friars to see his chief minister personally. By this stage, it had already been six weeks since Cromwell was first noticed as unwell, but the king felt Cromwell was improving. Cromwell's signature on letters written by clerks shows he was at least able to sit up by this time and write a list of tasks he completed from his bed.[17] While it was touching for the king to go to Cromwell's bedside to see him, it was more likely Henry wanted something rather than feeling actual concern. But Henry had some patience; he waited another ten days before he sent a letter to Austin Friars, asking Cromwell to handle the interrogation of John Mores, surveyor of Syon Abbey.[18] Sir Thomas Arundell and Henry Bourchier, Earl of Essex, wrote to Cromwell, pleased to hear rumours of recovery, and Chapuys finally got a meeting with Cromwell. Despite the long illness, Cromwell tried to keep up with matters; seemingly no one paused their demands.

Now almost two months had passed, Cromwell was finally well enough to leave Austin Friars for brief trips. Cromwell met John Mores for interrogation, and while King Henry had approved torture, the interrogation was easy, with Mores happy to talk.[19] If the king thought John Mores would share information about Stephen Gardiner defying the Act of Supremacy, he was disappointed, with Cromwell satisfied they did not have enough information to arrest Gardiner.[20]

Cromwell could not escape other tasks. On 27 April he sat on the panel of judges on the case of the Carthusians monks who refused to sign the Act of Supremacy, and on 4 May, Prior John Houghton of London, Robert Lawrence of Beauvale, Augustine Webster of Axholme, Bridgettine monk Richard Reynolds of Syon Abbey, and priest John Haile of Isleworth, were all hanged, drawn and quartered at Tyburn.[21] A few weeks later, three more Carthusians from the London Charterhouse, Humphrey Middlemore, William Exmew, and Sebastian Newdigate, were arrested and bound upright in chains for weeks, before being tried and convicted on 11 June, and all hanged, drawn, and quartered eight days later.[22] Many others arrested on suspicion died in the cells in illness-infested conditions. This had been cruelty of the highest order, entirely for Henry's supremacy.

After the trial, Cromwell retreated to Stepney for a week to continue his recovery. His Act of Supremacy, born out of Henry's desire to marry Anne, was resulting in men being chopped up, their parts being displayed around London. King Henry never liked to do things by halves; in June, more than a dozen anabaptists were rounded up in England were burned as heretics.[23] Sir Thomas More burned men for reading the new religion; now England attempted to be a middle-way in religion, and Cromwell watched papists quartered and evangelicals burned, all so Henry could have the wife of his choosing. Now, with the church valuations, the quiet days of making laws in parliament and quietly closing monasteries probably felt like decades ago. Cromwell had almost worked himself to death and now worked to condemn others.

Back at work full-time, not all was well between the king and his favourite attendant. Henry decided he would not set up a treaty with France, and Cromwell needed to tell Chapuys so he could inform Emperor Charles. Unfortunately, in a rare fit of forgetfulness, Cromwell did not show Chapuys before sending the letters to France.[24] When Cromwell and Chapuys met up to discuss matters, Cromwell admitted King Henry told Cromwell he was a fool to his face. Cromwell again showed his opinion on the matter of the king's marriage, telling Chapuys, 'it was not in (Cromwell's) power, nor in that of any man, to alter the King's mind; nevertheless, he would try, at all hazards, what he could do'.

Cromwell tried to leave the whole France fiasco alone, leaving it to the Boleyns and the Duke of Norfolk. The valuation of monastic houses trickled along at a good speed; after five months, a large majority of buildings had already been inspected, and as Master of the Jewel House, Cromwell was interested in what jewels were being kept in monasteries, along with both seditious and downright offensive tales which came from inspectors.[25] At Cluniac Priory of St. Pancras in Lewes, homosexuality was 'out of control' among the monks, and the abbot preached he was 'the authority on God the Almighty, the authority on the King, and the authority on Master Thomas Crumwell'.[26] The Abbot of the Augustinian St. Mary and St. Lazarus house at Maiden Bradley in Wiltshire had six children and a license to keep whores because of his 'natures'.[27] Prior Edmund Streatham of the Crossed Friars in London had multiple whores for himself and others in the priory. He was found naked with a woman at the time of inspection and bribed inspectors to stay quiet (they accepted Streatham's bribe and reported him anyway).[28] Apart from the myriad of lewd reports, inspectors found monasteries dilapidated, enormous debts and running costs, but also monastic houses having inventories of gold and silver, yet no room for the poor. The entire system needed an overhaul. King Henry had never set aside alms for monasteries, and now they became a burden, as the houses sat on untended land.

The Valor Ecclesiasticus, despite its size, sped through England, without clear-cut rules and regulations. There were hundreds of inspectors, all keen to work for Cromwell and hoping for a slice of the profits off the church; after all, the monasteries Cromwell privately closed before 1535 were leased out at the king's blessing. As Vicar-General of the Monasteries, Cromwell ultimately had control over the project, but with so many other tasks, combined with his illness, even his deputies John Tregonwell and Thomas Bedyll could barely keep up with proceedings. The entire inspection process was ill-handled, especially by Cromwell's standards, but after seven months, 85% of houses were inspected.

The Visitation of the Monasteries needed Cromwell's attention, but with many other things going on, he could not give the project the firm hand it required, reminiscent of his issues over Ireland a year earlier. As a result, the Irish situation was ongoing; Silken Thomas' garrison had all been slaughtered at Maynooth Castle while their leader was absent, but the situation was far from resolved. Cromwell being overloaded at court resulted in the Irish situation escalating, and if Cromwell felt he had control over what Henry wanted out of the Valor Ecclesiasticus project, he was making a mistake. But that was reality; Cromwell held multiple offices, and people came to him on many issues, regardless of his official titles. He was the king's chief minister, and everyone looked to him. Alice More wrote to Cromwell, complaining she was struggling to pay costs with having her husband Sir Thomas in the Tower. Cromwell had already arranged for one of his Italian friends, Antonio Bonvisi, to ensure a continuous supply of the best wine and food to the Tower for More and Fisher. But unless Henry reconsidered, the men would not be set free, and Cromwell could do nothing.

Ultimately, the Pope decided for King Henry. Cromwell received a letter from his agent Gregory de Casali in Rome, stating Pope Paul had made Fisher a cardinal. Casali had been with the Pope, discussing the matter for alliances between France and the Emperor, but news came that the Emperor was moving troops in Spain. Instead of panicking, Cromwell took an evening trip to Chapuys' private home; if he wished to prevent war, he needed an ally of his own.[29] Cromwell and Chapuys met in private, Cromwell admittedly 'anxious and troubled'. Cromwell confessed to Chapuys he felt none of their embassies abroad had helped; no alliance formed from France, the German States, nor the Swiss. Chapuys told

Charles, 'as God has given (Cromwell) so much sense and intelligence it would be the more shame to him if he did not know how to successfully use such an opportunity'. Whether Cromwell truly trusted Chapuys or wished to be his ally can never be fully ascertained. Cromwell told Chapuys the valuations gathered from monastery visitations amounted to 500,000 ducats (around 2,000,000l, or 28,000 years' wages worth of skilled labour at the time), and Cromwell admitted Henry had become very greedy and would happily collect all the treasure of the country for his enterprises. Given how much Henry wasted on war in the past, Cromwell preferred to use these incomparable profits at home.

Among all the intrigues of the court, Cromwell made one remark that gave a glimpse into his relationship with Anne Boleyn, far different from simple letters and stiff formalities. Cromwell went as far as saying he and Anne argued on 2 June, and Anne told Cromwell, 'she would like to see his head cut off'. Chapuys wondered if this was true, given everyone thought Cromwell to be Anne's 'right hand'. There seems nothing to suggest Cromwell and Anne were ever on friendly terms, and she had blocked his advancement at every opportunity. Given Anne was already looking to disgrace her uncle, the Duke of Norfolk, it is more than likely she also wanted to be rid of the common-born minister. Chapuys felt Cromwell personally wanted to disgrace the aristocracy and planned to start with Norfolk, but Chapuys could not get a grip on the mysterious Master Secretary.

In between clandestine meetings with Chapuys, there was no shortage of sycophantic letters to Cromwell begging for help or favours. He received a desperately sad letter from his old friend Harry Hotoft, the Customs Surveyor in Southampton, who had been swindled by his Italian son-in-law and was now left in debt to the king for 1,340l (£580,000 today).[30] Poor Hotoft faced giving up everything he had, a small home and a ship for his merchant business and needed Cromwell's intercession with the king. As Hotoft wrote, 'you have known me about 25 years, and never to have done contrary to my word or promise … whatever becomes of me, be good to my son.' Cromwell could never let such an old friend remain in such calamity.

Soon after, Cromwell sent his son Gregory to Quarrendon to stay with Sir Robert Lee, the sheep farmer turned MP,[31] and then to his uncle Sir John Williams at Rycote Manor.[32] Unfortunately for Cromwell, he needed to put himself right in harm's way, as King Henry could no longer tolerate Bishop Fisher and Thomas More's behaviour. Cromwell sent interrogators to the Tower, among them Thomas Bedyll, Richard Layton, Henry Polstead, and John ap Rhys, to interview More and Fisher.[33] On 16 June, Cromwell sat on the panel of judges at Westminster, alongside him esteemed lawyers and peers of the realm, and in a single day, Bishop John Fisher was found guilty of high treason, based on evidence he said the king was not Supreme Head of the Church of England.[34] Fisher was unrepentant in his belief in the Catholic church and was sentenced to death at Tyburn. The Pope's decision to give Fisher a cardinal's hat to get him out of the country had pushed Henry too far.

The result of the Fisher trial was a foregone conclusion from the moment it began, and Cromwell did little work on the case. He had been to see Fisher numerous times, offered him ways to be released, and had seen he had minor luxuries in his cell far longer than many others. If Cromwell had a troublesome time in passing judgement on Fisher, he hid it well. Cromwell wrote an enormous list of remembrances the same day as the trial, not mentioning Fisher at all, save for a note to send Ralph Sadler to tell the king about the trial. Cromwell was personally more interested in what the king wanted to be done with Sir Thomas More.

The situation in Ireland dominated Cromwell's mind, with a new Deputy of Ireland appointed, Lord Leonard Grey. Grey was brother to Elizabeth Grey, wife to the late Earl of Kildare, who had died in the Tower after hearing his son had murdered Archbishop Aleyn a year prior. Lord Leonard was also brother to Cromwell's dear friend Thomas Grey. Leonard Grey was not sent into Ireland to negotiate; he took the post with great anger, even threatening the outgoing Deputy William Skeffington with a dagger, treating his men harshly and had no conscience when killing everyone in his path. Had Cromwell's friend William Brabazon not also been in Ireland, things could have been even more catastrophic. Brabazon was the calming influence the English needed. At once, the Irish parliament sat and drew up new laws to defeat the rebels, many of their requests on Cromwell's remembrance list.[35] Cromwell wanted Ireland and revenge against the FitzGeralds.

Among everything going on, talks between England and France had broken down, with Cromwell delighted. Cromwell, before the king and Chapuys said, 'he would die the cruellest death to see a friendship between (Emperor Charles) and the king firmly established.'[36] Cromwell also received a gift from friend Henry, Lord Morley, father of Jane Boleyn, with a letter, 'as you will spend this summer in sporting, I send you a greyhound, fit for a gentleman to disport withal'.[37] But relaxing on summer progress probably felt like a lifetime away.

On 1 July, the panel of judges at Westminster had swollen with more peers of the realm there to preside over Sir Thomas More's trial. More was charged that on, '7 May 27 Hen. VIII., at the Tower of London, before Thomas Crumwell … saying "I will not meddle with any such matters, for I am fully determined to serve God, and to think upon His Passion and my passage out of this world"', and writing, after hearing of Fisher's trial, 'the Act of Parliament is like a sword with two-edges, for if a man answer one way it will confound his soul, and if he answer the other way it will confound his body'.[38] The trial also included the now infamous testimony of Thomas Audley's protégé Richard Rich, sent to More's cell to play a game of hypothetical questions in which More admitted resisting the Act of Supremacy.

More was unceremoniously beheaded at Tower Hill on 6 July, the same level of shock and outrage generated as Fisher's just weeks before. Fisher's head was thrown in the Thames so More's could replace it on London Bridge. Cromwell recorded nothing on the trial, and when writing of the situation (or when others wrote to him), would only comment on the death as, 'Fisher and the other'.[39] Both Fisher and More may have been guilty, but did the punishment fit the crime? It was a question so many of Henry VIII's victims would lament. Either way, while Fisher did not weigh on Cromwell's conscience, More clearly did. If Sir Thomas More could be killed, then what would stop the king from killing anyone?

Correspondence to Cromwell continued as if the beheadings never occurred. Among them was friend Robert Barnes, sent to see Philip Melanchthon, in hopes he would come to England and promote the Reformation to the king. Cromwell also sent off his own Stepney priest Simon Haynes with Christopher Mont to Germany to find support for England. Propaganda was in full swing, with John Stokesley, the stuttering Bishop of London, giving off-the-cuff sermons about the invalidity of the marriage of Henry and Katherine. Cromwell was best pleased with Stokesley's work, privately telling Chapuys he 'would have paid 1,000l. sterling that (Emperor Charles) had heard a sermon made by the bishop of London a few days ago on the validity of the first marriage and the usurpation of the Pope'.[40] Cromwell was also uninterested in the French, reportedly hiding in his backyard at Austin Friars playing bowls, getting attendants to tell the French ambassador he was not home.

Cromwell had many things to tie up before leaving to join King Henry and Anne on their glorious summer progress, a propaganda trip to promote their marriage and get signatures on the Act of Supremacy. Among many things needed was help for his old friend Thomas Megges, who had been robbed and wanted to avenge the murder attempt of one of his servants.[41] Cromwell also needed to keep his own homes safe while he was away, The Rolls left in loyal Thomas Thacker's hands, and Austin Friars as always under John Williamson's care, aided by new Italian attendant Richard Tomyou. The plague was especially bad in London, meaning Cromwell needed to have his homes sealed from the threat. People continued to die around Austin Friars all summer, though no one in the manor itself was ill; life continued, with deliveries of mail, money and new falcons arriving regularly.[42] Cromwell was enjoying himself on progress, ordering a new black damask gown in London, having his attendants ship it to him at Thornbury,[43] along with another of velvet and one green riding cloak from Austin Friars. A rare receipt of the period survives, showing Cromwell's July costs for his labourers, Hackney costing 36l, Austin Friars 22l, while other vast amounts poured in for all manners of business.[44]

Cromwell's magnificent new manor in Hackney came along nicely; a grand staircase from his rooms into the gallery added, four new chimneys, a new roof added through August, the all-new kitchen, buttery, and scullery were done, with labour costing 44l (enough to pay seventy-five men full-time).[45] Austin Friars continued to become more lavish than ever, with a vast kitchen, scullery and offices all looking out onto the street being rebuilt, and the roof of the entire manor raised. Cromwell's new private rooms, with a chamber and gallery above them, went in, with large oriel windows being added on the street front, giving the manor a very distinctive look in the neighbourhood. Despite the plague, Cromwell regularly kept twenty workmen in Austin Friars at a cost of 20l a month. Another sixty-seven carpenters, costing Cromwell 25l a month worked at Cromwell's new manor at Ewhurst by the river, needing 600 loads of timber delivered just in time to raise the roof over the wide hall. Given Cromwell's monthly costs, Sir John Dudley, writing to say he would start repaying the 2,000l (£880,000 today) he owed Cromwell, would come in handy.[46]

With Cromwell on progress, work never ceased, mostly matters on church inspections and rumours coming from overseas agents. Sir Thomas Audley attempted to deal with Ireland, hopefully providing Cromwell with some relief,[47] as he could not return home to London due to plague.[48] While the royal propaganda progress trailed on, with Henry and Anne happier than ever, Cromwell followed the progress through Gloucester, staying at Tewkesbury, Berkeley, and Thornbury, but then had to make a detour, as his monastery inspections project was out of hand. His chief inspectors Richard Layton and Thomas Legh had been at loggerheads for months, Legh constantly writing to Cromwell, complaining about Layton, despite Layton's successful visits. Layton too began criticising Legh's behaviour. Cromwell knew both men personally; Layton was one of Cromwell's men from Stepney, and Legh was a relative of Cromwell's ally Rowland Lee. Layton met with Cromwell at Tewkesbury monastery, and a week later reported many significant matters of corruption in monastic houses.[49] But Legh was ruining Cromwell's monastic inspections with his behaviour.

A monk named John Musard wrote privately to Cromwell on 8 August about Thomas Legh, who had imprisoned Musard on false charges.[50] More letters came in about Legh's behaviour at monastery visitations, which Cromwell took seriously, and tried to force the heavy-handed inspector to stop with his behaviour.[51] It was all in vain as Cromwell carried on with the court to Bromham House and then Wulf Hall.

Unfortunately, while Cromwell had been away from court, King Henry had gone through Cromwell's vast mail backlog and his large remembrances lists. The last thing Cromwell needed was the king poking his nose in his business. The relationship between Cromwell and Henry had been good all summer; they had published a copy of the Vulgate Old Testament and the New Testament in July, albeit in Latin, agreed on most business, and got along well. Whenever someone criticised the king, they blamed the 'evil' men at Henry's side. Seeing Cromwell and Henry travelling, entertaining, hunting and working together across many regions of England would silence any doubters; if they tried to criticise Cromwell, they would criticise their king too.

But the issues around Thomas Legh would not desist. John ap Rhys, husband of Cromwell's niece Joan Williams, wrote to Cromwell as progress neared its end, admitting he knew about Legh's abuses on the visitation trail, but ap Rhys thought Cromwell did not care for such news, or worse, condoned it. Ap Rhys wrote that Legh's 'abuses, excesses and insolences' at Bruton, Bradstock, Stanley, and Edington, were so bad surely Cromwell knew. He wrote, 'wherever he comes he handles the fathers very roughly, many times for small causes, as for not meeting him at the door... More modesty, gravity, and affability would purchase him more reverence than his satrapike (henchman-like) countenance. He is young and of intolerable elation.'[52] Rhys revealed Legh had been violent to clergymen if the bribes were not to his liking and had twelve men in his livery, dispensing 'justice' as Legh saw fit, and forbidding nuns their 'rights' as their houses were seized and valued. Legh had taken Cromwell's loose guidelines and given the whole Valor Ecclesiasticus a name for violence and corruption. Legh wrote to Cromwell in his defence, obviously receiving an incensed letter from the Master Secretary, and Legh admitted, 'it would be folly in me to excuse myself if my actions did not correspond; and though a man is given to sensual appetites, I am not addicted to such notable sensualities and abuses as you are informed'.[53] While no record of Legh's sexual crimes remains, they had cast a long shadow over the church valuations, something the dissolution project would never shake. Cromwell soon had to change what should be considered an offence during visitations, especially considering the sex scandals of the clergy, and now his inspectors.

No wonder Cromwell was not in a great mood when he finally arrived back in London, rightly or wrongly sending rude, angry letters to Audley and Cranmer. The former begged forgiveness, while the latter showed his closeness to Cromwell by firing back and defending himself from petty arguments.[54] At least Gregory Cromwell was well, asking his father to thank so many for their generosity over the long summer.[55] Cromwell also became a godfather yet again, this time to the Duke of Suffolk's new son, Henry.[56] Given the plague in London, Cromwell retired to his home in Stepney, noticing in his personal accounts at Austin Friars that he had earned 468l (£200,000 today) from various pensions, but spent 749l (£330,000 today), on rebuilding works on his various properties.[57]

Cromwell prorogued parliament until after New Year and set about putting together the Valor Ecclesiasticus in its ultimate form to present to the king. Of the 9,000 monks and nuns in England, only around 1,700 had been removed from their houses, mostly because of the cutoff age of twenty (rounded down from twenty-four after Dorothy Wolsey called in a favour). Cromwell looked at the project as an opportunity for re-education. Even the University of Cambridge was not immune from Cromwell's anger about their behaviour, noting in a scathing letter, 'I have noted the corruption took a great effort from you all.'[58]

Under Cromwell's new idea, the Carthusian monasteries, all closed earlier in the year, would be reopened, reformed, and provide evangelical teachings, a new monastic house for a new age. Right through the year, Cromwell privately investigated redesigning the monastic houses, so they took on the new teachings of the church, spreading King Henry's supremacy. But with the profits of closed houses going to Henry, Cromwell's desire for reform had to beat the king's desire for wealth. To finish the Valor Ecclesiasticus, Cromwell needed to inspect the remaining houses himself around London and produce the work to the king by 13 November.[59] Anne Boleyn was freshly pregnant after the progress, so it could not have been a better time to present the work and his ideas. Combined with Cromwell's knowledge of the monastic houses around the country, monasteries could provide education, healthcare and help for the homeless. Another quiet plan Cromwell began started with a freshly translated work by his publisher William Marshall, an English copy of *The Forme and maner of subuention of helpyng of pore people, deuysed and practyced in the cytie of Hypres in Flaunders, whiche forme is autorised by the Emperour, and approued by the facultie of diuinite in Paris.*[60] With this, Cromwell started his enormous 1536 Act for Punishment of Sturdy Vagabonds and Beggars, to present to the next parliament.[61] Having the records of these houses from the Valor Ecclesiasticus would be useful in his new welfare programme. Cromwell began work on the huge act, detailing how the poor and homeless would be given housing, medical care, food, and work, allowing needed infrastructure works to begin all around the country, along with education and care of children.

Cromwell was working, but still not back to his old self. While he worked at The Rolls, Stepney, or near the king at Richmond, he refused Ambassador Castelnau's audience five or six times, leaving the French ambassador standing outside without hope of conversation. Castelnau reported to Ambassador Chapuys this behaviour had 'caused him to feel it so deeply he fell into a fever,' accused Cromwell of 'carelessness and indiscretion' and had written to Cromwell, saying he, 'would never visit or address Cromwell again, unless under the express command of the king.' Cromwell was probably relieved. Chapuys bumped into Cromwell at the Lord Mayor's banquet, only for him to disappear into his offices again to avoid everyone.

While Chapuys could not gain an audience with Cromwell, both Emperor Charles and his Chancellor Antoine Perrenot de Granvelle both wanted to know more about the enigmatic secretary. Chapuys shared Cromwell's life story, or at least what Cromwell had carefully curated and shared, saying, '(Cromwell) speaks well in his language, and tolerably in Latin, French, and Italian; is hospitable, liberal both with his property and with gracious words, magnificent in his household and building'.[62] Emperor Charles wrote a personal letter to Cromwell to thank him for his care of Katherine and Mary; while the king cared none for them, it was obvious they had a personal ally in Cromwell.[63] It had been Cromwell who soothed Chapuys a year earlier, saying King Henry loved Princess Mary one hundred times more than Princess Elizabeth; Cromwell's alliances were firmly on the Spanish side. But while Anne Boleyn remained with the king, Cromwell could never create an Imperial alliance.

While pregnant Anne was safer than ever on her throne, Queen Katherine was dangerously ill, and after a year of wholesale killings to appease Henry's whims, Cromwell had been stretched to his limits. Soon, King Henry would need his chief minister to go far beyond the realms of tolerable behaviour and commit his gravest sin of all.

Chapter 13

1536: Vengeance

'it was in his power to undo part of what he had already done'

… although Crumwell was at one time the adviser and promoter
of the demolition of the English convents and monasteries, yet
perceiving the great inconveniences likely to arise from that measure,
he has since made attempts to thwart it, but the king has resolutely
declined to make any modification of it whatsoever and has even
been somewhat indignant against his secretary for proposing such
a thing.[1]

T homas Cromwell's inconspicuous system of closing monasteries
was completely out of hand. With most religious houses already
valued by the dawn of 1536, Drs Legh and Layton were in
Yorkshire, finishing the final northern houses. Cromwell's quiet proposals
for reforming certain houses had not gone to plan, and others, such as the
Duke of Norfolk, began actively closing monasteries privately for financial
gain. The cash-grab that would become the Dissolution of the Monasteries
look set to begin, destroying Cromwell's personal work and plans.

Even the opening week of the year brought challenges to distract
Cromwell. On 7 January, the great Queen Katherine died at Kimbolton
Castle, aged only fifty, likely of cancer, though poison was suspected.[2]
The news came to court at once. Cromwell was tasked with preparing
Katherine's funeral procession. He tried to plan the most elaborate funeral
possible at St Peterborough's Cathedral, down to the finest detail, only
to have King Henry command the procession drastically scaled back.[3]
Cromwell also needed to take care of Katherine's will, and sent ten men
to Kimbolton, among them Ralph Sadler, to carefully oversee the dead
queen's household.[4] Cromwell admitted to Chapuys having Katherine
gone simplified things,[5] as an audacious plan to eliminate another English
queen began.

Stephen Gardiner was in France as ambassador, and wrote to Thomas Wriothesley, who had finished in Gardiner's household and newly transferred to Thomas Cromwell. Gardiner and Cromwell wrote to one another on an almost daily basis, despite their fractured personal relationship. Wriothesley received a letter from Gardiner talking of rumours in Paris about Anne Boleyn's adultery.[6] Wriothesley informed his new master at once, who made the bold choice to tell the king. King Henry took the news as expected – a foreign court saying your wife was a cheat would hurt even the most rational monarch. He ordered Cromwell and Wriothesley to make inquiries, a quiet investigation into where these rumours came from, and left it in their hands. If Cromwell was going to use this information to his advantage, he had to bide his time.

Cromwell started gathering all the pieces in the chess game that would bring down Anne Boleyn. Her hatred for Cromwell was already obvious for the entire court to see; she hated his position as Vice-Gerent and the destruction of the monasteries. Anne's religious outlook was as fervent for the Reformation as Cromwell's; they simply could not work together due to their personal opinions. Cromwell was too lowly in Anne's eyes; Anne was a usurper in his. While Anne may have played an absolute masterstroke in getting herself from lady-in-waiting to queen, over the years she had increasingly made her hate for Cromwell ever more obvious, which showed her weakness. The Boleyns had pushed their way into power, but never capitalised on it, creating a power vacuum. It had been their lack of foresight that had allowed covert Cromwell to slip in and gain the king's ultimate trust in the first place. Now Anne openly wanted to toy with Cromwell, the man who had overcome far more than Anne could ever imagine and had risen in power despite her presence, hindering Henry from giving Cromwell what he deserved. Cromwell cleared the way for Anne to be queen, and to turn on him so aggressively was such a reckless blunder. As Chapuys wrote of Cromwell, 'it was in his power to undo part of what he had already done'.[7]

Finding people to rally against Anne in a clandestine plot was no arduous task; she had no allies. Anne certainly had champions, predominately religious men who fluttered about her, like moths to whatever flame could further reform. The reality was Anne had no power, but she had a royal baby in her belly. Cromwell needed to be exceedingly careful. With Queen Katherine dead, and Henry and Anne openly thrilled, Anne's marriage was now legitimate, especially if she had a son, and would remain a constant thorn in Cromwell's side. Cromwell first recruited Sir Nicholas Carew, who openly hated Anne Boleyn. Cromwell and Carew had little in common, one evangelical, another papist, but both had Henry's friendship and protection. Cromwell, overseeing Queen Katherine's will and items to go to Mary, sent Carew to Hunsdon to see the princess. Carew took Italian Richard Tomyou with him, Cromwell's Clerk Controller, who had once worked in Queen Katherine's and then Mary's households. Cromwell privately wanted to get Mary back in her father's favour, but she had to accept Henry's position as Head of the Church. Carew and Tomyou swore to Mary she had the Master Secretary's allegiance.[8]

Business of the realm continued in all corners in the hands of friends. Cromwell's old friend Lancelot Collins had a dying Dean of York on his hands,[9] while Richard Southwell, Thomas Legh and Richard Layton all had serious abuses to contain in northern monasteries.[10] Thomas Bedyll inspected Ramsey Abbey, and found a charter from King Edgar, solidifying England's claim to be an empire.[11] Fortifications at Dover and Calais needed endless money, and Thomas Cranmer was living at Knole in Kent (with his wife Margarete and daughter Margaret), outside the drama of the court.[12] But while Cromwell prepared to open parliament, King Henry fell from his jousting horse in the tiltyard. While the myth tells of King Henry unconscious for two hours (a story made up in Europe at the time), Chapuys wrote Henry sustained no injury, and everyone marvelled how Henry was unharmed by the fall. Chapuys mused Henry cheated death and perhaps God had further misfortune planned.[13] He accidentally predicted the future; days after he wrote those words, the day of Queen Katherine's funeral, Anne Boleyn miscarried her baby. It is yet another situation bathed in myth; tales of a deformed fetus were born decades later, and whether the baby was a boy is not confirmed with any evidence. Also, the tale the Duke of Norfolk caused Anne's miscarriage by upsetting her with news of Henry's joust fall is the stuff of myth; pregnant women and their babies could handle much more than uncles with blunt manners or husbands flirting with ladies-in-waiting. Poor Anne was struck with the same problem as Queen Katherine; a husband who rarely produced healthy offspring.

Cromwell opened parliament on 4 February, to pass a list of sixty-two acts. Cromwell's own important, complex, and eventually troublesome acts were the Statutes of Uses and Statutes of Enrolments, designed for King Henry to gain taxes from the process of land changing hands after someone's death. Given Cromwell and Audley tried to push through such measures in 1529 and again in 1532 without success, this would have finally felt like a success. Another enormous act was The Law in Wales Act, officially annexing Wales into an English style of governance.[14] While it would seem like success to Cromwell in Westminster, it ignored the needs and cultures of the Welsh people, and it would take until 1993 to have the act fully repealed. Cromwell also passed the Jurisdiction in Liberties Act, bringing uniformity to the legal processes around England.[15]

Unfortunately, Cromwell's time in the nine-week parliament would not see total success. He set out to pass his Act for the Punishment of Sturdy Vagabonds and Beggars, which stated 'sturdy vagabonds', had to be put to work.[16] The poor could no longer simply be punished for being poor, and the men in power would be punished if they did not aid beggars. Taxes were not levied to cover these costs; collection would be organised through a common box, to pay for people to be put to work, for the sick to be healed so they could recover and find work, and those who could not work would not be left to beg. There were still harsh punishments in place for those who refused to abide by these rules, but this was the birth of real aid for the poor. Cromwell's draft went into fine detail – those who could, would report for work starting Easter 1537, though to Michaelmas 1540. Jobs would be created, mostly in creating infrastructure, roads, waterways, and repairing ports, with results that benefitted the population. The workers would be paid a fair wage, along with meat, drink, and a clothing allowance. Doctors would be arranged for the sick and injured; medicine, beds, food, and warm fires would be provided for those who needed them. Children between five and fourteen could be educated and apprenticed in jobs, but only those over twelve would be whipped for failure to work. Cromwell had finely tuned what he could see would be a legacy; changing the way the poor lived and bettered themselves, help he personally needed in his youth.

Cromwell had King Henry sit in the Commons to hear him pitch this act to the Commons, which did not go well. Those in the Commons and the Lords would be the ones paying and would have to abide by the rules, some being the men overseeing such audacious schemes. The act was put to the Commons in February and eventually was only voted through as a simplistic, watered-down version of Cromwell's sweeping plan. No taxes were levied, but parish leaders could not leave people to beg and starve, though no other help was given. The revolutionary plan would have changed England forever, and yet it fell at the first hurdle, which after Cromwell's extensive planning, must have been both angering and severely disappointing.

The worst was yet to come. The Valor Ecclesiasticus, complete and showing the value of the church, was something just too good for a greedy king to leave in the hands of the clergy. Cromwell's notion of reforming monasteries for creating colleges of learning, or helping the poor in need, never stood a chance compared to Henry's desire for money. Lord Chancellor Audley was happy to step in and propose the Act for the Dissolution of the Lesser Monasteries, leaving Cromwell, as Vicar-General, no choice but to oversee closing small religious houses.[17] The law quickly passed in parliament, and lawyer Sir Richard Rich, long in Audley's patronage, was appointed as the Chancellor of the Court of Augmentations, to oversee the dissolutions. While everyone had to report to Cromwell as the Vice-Gerent and Vicar-General of England, Richard Rich, described as immoral, dishonest, and treasonous, began sending arrogant letters to Cromwell and his inspectors. The quiet collection of monasteries was over, and Cromwell's name would forever be tied to the dissolution of English religious life.

By March 1536, Cromwell needed some good news. Peter Berkwithius sent Cromwell a new book entitled *A Book of Certain Verses in the Praise of My Lord Master ... Heroic and other verses in honour of Thomas Crumwell, and in dispraise of the bishop of Rome*' which called Cromwell 'a man of great virtue and erudition'.[18] Cromwell so desperately wished to see through the changes to England, but while he used to work without too much interest from the people of England, he was now the most hated person, the man who sent out monastery inspectors and tax collectors. Scholars such as Erasmus still believed in Cromwell's moves, writing to express his approval and asking for Cromwell's help,[19] likewise Martin Luther,[20] while friends continued with their endless pleads for favours, such as Antonio Bonvisi sending news from Spain, and others sent fresh merchant goods from India.[21] Cromwell had his Rolls office flooded with monastery visitation papers and he snapped at Stephen Vaughan several times, his nerves not coping with attendants who could not comply with their master. Cromwell's Italian-Englishman in Venice, Richard Morison, begged bitterly to return home. Meanwhile, in London, Cromwell and Francesco Frescobaldi dramatically reunited, a reversal of their 1503 meeting, with Cromwell now the wealthy powerbroker, Frescobaldi seeking to save his family's fortunes. Bandello wrote that Cromwell was happy to return the favour.[22]

Whispers around the court continued after the rumours of Anne Boleyn's adultery surfaced in France. Cromwell had sworn to protect Princess Mary and heard comments made by Anne about how she wished Mary would die like her mother. After Anne's January miscarriage, rumours and whispers continued unabated; Henry and Anne were not speaking or living at the same palace. Sadly for Anne, by March, rumours also started that Henry was fixed on Jane Seymour after seemingly not noticing her for the five years she had lived at court.

Cromwell, ever the one to see out the king's wishes, and always with express permission on every issue, overreached himself and started making plans of his own. Cromwell met with Chapuys at night outside the Austin Friars church, which sat against their respective city homes, to discuss an English alliance with the Emperor.[23] Cromwell knew it was risky; the Boleyns, the Dukes of Norfolk and Suffolk, and even his friend Treasurer William Fitzwilliam, all wanted an alliance with France, who paid them handsome pensions. Cromwell and Chapuys went as far as talking terms of an alliance. Henry needed to return to the Pope, Princess Mary needed to be heir, and England had to help Emperor Charles against the Turks. Cromwell had neither the position nor power to talk terms of any alliance; that was best left for kings and their appointed ambassadors. All this was discussed in the shadow of Austin Friars, and Cromwell knew the danger; he sent Gregory north to Woodrising Manor in Suffolk to live with friend Richard Southwell, away from the drama of court.[24]

Anne Boleyn picked a terrible time to inflame the already overwhelmed chief minister. Now aware of rumours she was no longer in the king's favour, Anne turned her attention to the Dissolution of the Lesser Monasteries. Anne went to the Vice-Gerent and in no uncertain terms expressed how she felt the monasteries project was a cash-grab for personal gain. She was not wrong; while the first 200 houses to be closed would go to Henry's exchequer, people were already climbing over one another to lease the land and buildings. To complain to Cromwell was futile, as while he oversaw the new dissolutions, profits were directed to Richard Rich's office, and it was the king himself who approved the project. But Anne could not cry to her husband, for he enjoyed Jane Seymour's company. Cromwell had even emptied one of his rooms at Greenwich for the Seymour family to use, with free access to the king's rooms, and Edward Seymour was now a member of the privy chamber. While Henry's greed for money squashed Cromwell's monastery reformation project, Henry's greed for women and attention swept Anne aside, making Cromwell's alliance with the Emperor easier to prepare.

Anne's anger towards Cromwell was grand entertainment for Cromwell's friends, with Henry Grey, Marquess of Dorset, his aunt Elizabeth Grey, and Henry, Lord Montagu all gossiping with Chapuys, making delightful dinner conversation. Chapuys disagreed with them; he feared for Cromwell's safety, saying he hoped for a new queen if only to keep Cromwell safe.[25] Cromwell privately admitted he regretted paving the way for Henry's marriage to Anne, only promoting it as the king desired the change. Cromwell mockingly commented to Chapuys he believed Henry would remain in a 'chaste and marital life' with Anne. When Chapuys called Cromwell on his sarcasm, Cromwell had to lean back against a window and cover his mouth to hide his smile and told Chapuys not to worry about the rumour of King Henry taking a French bride, as Henry had chosen wife number three.

Cromwell's risky position was no longer a secret. On 2 April, Anne had her almoner John Skip give a sermon that decried Cromwell as evil and King Henry as an adulterer. As secret alliance negotiations continued with the Emperor, Chapuys reported to his master that Cromwell:

was aware of the precarious nature of human affairs, to say nothing of those appertaining to royal courts ... He has, however, admitted that the day might come when fate would strike him as it had struck his predecessors in office: then he would arm himself with patience and place himself for the rest in the hands of God ... (Cromwell) would have to implore God's help if he wishes to escape from dangers and inconveniences of that sort ... and he would, besides, do his utmost to avoid danger.[26]

Cromwell had John Skip arrested, interrogated, and suitably frightened, but Anne was the real threat. Parliament closed on 14 April after a busy session, in time for Easter. Cromwell gave the precarious job of Archbishop of Dublin to George Browne from Austin Friars and hoped Ireland would settle down;[27] Silken Thomas FitzGerald was now in the Tower with his five uncles. FitzGerald's younger brother was safe in England with his mother Elizabeth Grey, while Elizabeth's brother Leonard Grey murdered his way through the Irish rebels. With one country hopefully under control, Cromwell needed to unveil his alliance with the Emperor, something no one else offered the king. Cromwell hosted a private dinner party at his lavishly rebuilt home in Hackney, where he and Chapuys completed their plans. The Emperor was ready to accept Anne as queen and the Pope was prepared to suspend Henry's looming ex-communication.

It would be a disaster, on top of all the other setbacks Cromwell endured through the year. At Greenwich on 18 April, word of Cromwell and Chapuys planning an alliance reached the king's ears. King Henry pulled Chapuys to one side at the Easter banquet and asked him of the matter, and Chapuys shared the news Henry could have an alliance with the Emperor over the French. Chapuys left to chat with Edward Seymour, leaving Henry and Cromwell talking in a far corner in a window bay, and a fight between the king and his Vice-Gerent broke out before everyone in the presence chamber. Cromwell charged off, his anger and exhaustion on full display as he sat down out of sight of everyone and called for a stiff drink. The king later told Chapuys he could not consider an alliance with the Emperor that was not in writing, but more likely, Henry's ego was harmed, as Cromwell and Chapuys had tried to solidify a deal without his opinion. The Emperor would accept Anne as queen and be an ally against France in return for Henry rolling back religious harm and restoring Princess Mary, while each country would be an ally in any potential wars. It was a good alliance, but without Henry's express command, Cromwell had so deeply overreached that the king refused the offer.

Cromwell took this loss and humiliation as best he could, telling Chapuys he would not give up on the deal but warned, 'that before asking an injured person for favour... it was necessary to acknowledge old favours'.[28] Cromwell and Chapuys met privately the morning after the disastrous banquet, with Chapuys shocked at how devastated Cromwell looked, barely able to speak, though mentioned he, 'had never been as stunned by a person's reaction as he had been with the king'. Chapuys suggested they drop the entire plan and concentrate on aiding Princess Mary, and Cromwell, 'suddenly recovered his wits, and said that the game was not entirely lost and that he had still hopes of success'.[29] Cromwell had a plan, and none of it would be good for Anne Boleyn. Chapuys believed Cromwell took to his bed with an attack of anxiety and disappointment.[30] Instead, Cromwell was busy in private.

The Privy Council met days later, pleading Henry to accept the alliance. This excited Chapuys that not all was lost, but Cromwell woefully remarked, 'whoever trusts in the words of princes… or relies on them or expects the fulfilment of their promises, is not a wise man, as I experienced.'[31] Cromwell then turned away from Chapuys, the Imperial ambassador unable to get any time with the secretary, who was deep in a plot that saw his other tasks go quiet, his correspondence non-existent.

Cromwell only needed twelve days to create a master plan to eliminate Anne Boleyn. Anne had stood in Cromwell's way for years, unable to advance as high as he deserved at court because of her hatred. Now she looked to put her opinions into Cromwell's monasteries project, which was already out of control. Anne also tried to take over the plan to reform England, years after Cromwell and his faction started their work. Anne had been promoting reform to Henry, but she had never made any meaningful change, while others toiled in parliament and the convocations. Several of Cromwell's crucial parliamentary reforms had failed in 1536, the monasteries were going to be closed, and Cromwell's long-held dream of an Imperial alliance had been shot down by a king distracted by his wife and mistress. King Henry was due to leave for Dover to inspect fortifications, and George Boleyn busied himself with the trip, while Margery Horsman planned Anne's preparations; Cromwell even mentioned he might go to Calais himself to oversee works there; these fake trips acted as a delightful distraction for everyone. On Sunday 23 April, a new Knight of the Garter was to be chosen, and with the king away, Henry Percy was chosen to oversee the selection process, which saw Sir Nicholas Carew chosen over George Boleyn.[32] Carew had been Cromwell's partner in crime in the Boleyn adultery investigation, and now Carew's allegiance was sealed with this grand honour.

By Monday morning, Cromwell was back at work, overseeing the suppression of the monasteries and getting oyer and terminer papers drawn up in Middlesex and Kent, the papers needed to set up a grand jury for matters of treason.[33] Days later, Cromwell sent out a summons to bring parliament back for an extra session; if a major issue needed to be passed, they all needed to be present.[34] Bishop John Stokesley met Cromwell privately to discuss the matter of annulling royal marriages.[35] Richard Sampson, Dean of the Royal Chapel, spent four days at Cromwell's home at Stepney, discussing the religious aspects of annulment.[36] Convincing Henry there needed to be a full-scale investigation into the rumours of adultery against Anne was simple; the king was infatuated with Jane Seymour.

If Cromwell wanted Anne Boleyn to be an adulterer, she needed to have co-conspirators. Who Cromwell chose was less important than who he did not choose to be condemned. There was a revolving door of men who worked in the king's privy chamber. Many were friends of Cromwell, old Wolsey allies, and MPs sympathetic to passing Cromwell's parliamentary bills. This meant regulars such as Sir Thomas Heneage and Sir William Fitzwilliam were safe. Sir Francis Bryan joined his brother-in-law Sir Nicholas Carew, who was staying with Jane Seymour at Chelsea, ready to become a queen. Edward Seymour was safe, being prepared as a new brother-in-law to the king, and William Fitzwilliam's brother Sir Anthony Browne was married to Alice Gage, daughter to Cromwell's long-time friend, Sir John Gage. Sir Thomas Wyatt was harder to deal with; Sir Henry Wyatt was one of Cromwell's dearest friends, but his son needed to be arrested as a co-conspirator, as did Cromwell's friend Sir Richard Page, to give the project an air of authenticity. One of Anne's priests, William Latimer, was also arrested, but this was over banned books. All three would be released after Cromwell completed his destruction of the court.

This left four regulars in trouble. Sir Henry Norris had no connection with Cromwell and was also supportive of Anne. Sir Francis Weston was an inexperienced courtier who spent time in Anne's room with Norris. Sir William Brereton was a thorn in Cromwell's side; he had John ap Gryffith Eyton killed on unproven charges in Wales even after Cromwell tried to save his friend. Only one man would be enough, but the more Cromwell had to choose from, the better.

Another man then proved himself the most helpful – Mark Smeaton, the court lute player. Anne rebuked Smeaton for being too familiar with her in her rooms. These words were overheard, and Smeaton being a commoner, Cromwell could interrogate him easier than others. Smeaton was arrested and taken via boat from Greenwich to Stepney for interrogation (a source claiming torture is tenuous).[37] Henry knew what was happening; Henry and Anne were seen arguing the same day, Elizabeth in her mother's arms. Smeaton knew far less but was transferred from Stepney to the Tower. The fake royal trip to Dover was cancelled, and yet the coming storm was not immediately obvious.

Overnight, Cromwell prepared the paperwork, and on 1 May, Henry and Cromwell left the Greenwich May Day celebrations for Whitehall; the following morning Anne Boleyn was arrested at Greenwich and sent to the Tower just after 6.00 am, and Norris was arrested later that day. Weston, Brereton, Wyatt, and Page were all soon rounded up and put in the Tower as well. Cromwell did not need to say much; as soon as gossip got around and people panicked, the accusations flew, innocent comments twisted, and simple tales misrepresented. The women in the Tower to accompany Anne into the Queen's rooms reported her every word. Anne's regular ladies too were interrogated; Margery Horsman had been investigated several times throughout the year and was helpful. Elizabeth Somerset was sister to Cromwell's friend Fitzwilliam and would say anything needed. Everyone was scared, then comments about Anne's relationship with her brother George came up, and this incredible arrest was also made at Whitehall, where George had gone to defend his sister. Jane Boleyn, George's wife, refused to speak lies against him, and being the daughter of Henry Lord Morley, one of Cromwell's close friends, no harm came to Jane, just as it would not come to Wyatt and Page.

Whether anyone was innocent or guilty became meaningless. Henry commanded Cromwell to find all those accused guilty, and Cromwell was more than happy to oblige. Henry's cruelty, combined with his foolish decision to rush into marriage, and angry finger-pointing in panic created evidence for the court cases. Cromwell simply sat back and let everyone undo one another. The dates given as evidence of salacious encounters, or guilty comments and flirtatious behaviour made little sense, but it did not matter. In case the evidence did not convince the judges, Cromwell gifted his incredible new house at Hackney back to the king, so it could be gifted back to Henry Percy, who had lost it to pay debts a year earlier. Henry Percy needed to say he was pre-contracted to Anne, but he would not budge. Cromwell had now lost his manor at Hackney for nothing.

Only Archbishop Thomas Cranmer came to Anne's defence, twenty-five miles away at his favourite manor, Knole, and innocent in Cromwell's plan. Cranmer wrote to Henry in defence of the queen, only to pull back his support when hearing the charges from Cromwell and Audley. There would be no point in saving Anne, as Chapuys told Charles on 2 May, 'that (Cromwell) hath done, and would do, marvels'.[38]

By 8 May, Cromwell had everything he needed, complete with Mark Smeaton's confession after interrogation in the Tower, Anne's comments about Henry's sexual dysfunction, and sufficient conjecture about Anne's incest with George Boleyn. Four days later, a panel of anti-Boleyn judges gathered, with Smeaton, Norris, Weston, and Brereton, all guilty the same day. Anne and George faced their charges and fate on 15 May. Two days later, the men were all beheaded at Tower Hill, Anne brave as she was famously beheaded by an expert swordsman two days later. Just like that, it was over. Cromwell worked for four years to end Queen Katherine's marriage, and only four weeks to end Anne Boleyn. Those twelve days between Easter and the end of April saw a plan prepared to kill an English queen, entirely aided by King Henry's fragile manhood. Thomas Cranmer annulled the marriage between Henry and Anne before her death, but Henry's hatred was so deep it made no difference. A group of innocent people all died, and Cromwell could sit back and marvel at how simple it was, and how quickly people turned on one another.

Cromwell and Chapuys soon met up again, and Cromwell, 'extolled beyond measure the sense, the wit, and the courage of the deceased royal mistress, as well as of her brother,' and Cromwell confirmed the whole scheme was solely to end Anne and continue his plans, with Cromwell telling Chapuys, '...he had taken a great deal of trouble, and that, owing to the displeasure and anger he had incurred upon the reply given to me by the King on the third day of Easter, (Cromwell) had set himself to arrange the plot, to fantasise and conspire the affair...'[39] While Cromwell had come up with the idea off the back of Gardiner's rumour of adultery at Christmas, it was Henry who ultimately sealed Anne's fate. Jane Seymour became queen on 30 May, and Cromwell looked to ensure Princess Mary's safety throughout this troublesome time. Finally, Cromwell had no one holding him back.

Anne Boleyn quickly vanished, just as the annulment papers disappeared from records. Cromwell friends were soon elevated; Edward Seymour was made Viscount Beauchamp, while Richard Sampson was made Bishop of Chichester. Thomas Heneage took Norris' place as Groom of the Stool, Ralph Sadler was made an official member of the Privy Chamber, and Henry Parker, Lord Morley, was given the Stewardship of Hatfield Park.[40] Jane Boleyn had remained loyal to her husband George throughout the saga and wrote to Cromwell, worried about her future.[41] Cromwell ensured she received her monies owed from her father-in-law, and she soon became a lady for the new queen, as did Margery Horsman. Cromwell also made certain Sir Francis Weston's young wife was not left with his vast string of debts worth 1,000l (£430,000 today) and ensured Sir Thomas Wyatt's mistress, Lady Elizabeth Darrell, or Bess as Cromwell called her, was cared for while he was imprisoned.[42]

Within a week of the king's new marriage, parliament reopened on 8 June, no one complaining over changes to the succession and treason laws. While there were no recriminations for the Boleyn saga, Thomas Cranmer, the sole voice to defend Anne, was passively punished by being asked to give up swathes of land to the king, including the area of Wimbledon outside London, and the traditional archbishops' manor at Mortlake.

Cromwell had not given up on any of his personal religious beliefs, despite serving a king still weak on reform, and a queen with no evangelical connections. But first Princess Mary had to be protected, as Cromwell had promised. The Duke of Norfolk and Bishop Sampson were sent to threaten Mary to swear the oath of her father's role over the church in England, and to agree to her illegitimacy. Cromwell sent Mary an angry letter, no doubt read by the king, as it did not follow the usually informal and kind notes he sent. He sent her a book of articles to read, and a message for her to copy in her hand to send to her father, submitting to his will. Cromwell ended his letter, 'I take Christ, whose mercy I refuse if I write anything unto you, I have not professed in my heart and know to be true.'[43] Cromwell was helping her through the threats from her father. Norfolk had already professed to want to use violence against the princess. Mary told Cromwell the same day as his letter, 'you will see I have followed your advice, and will do so in all things concerning my duty to the King, God and my conscience not offended; for I take you as one of my chief friends next his Grace and the queen.[44]

Princess Mary finally submitted to her father's will and protected herself, and friends Cromwell and Chapuys were most relieved for her safety. Cromwell and Thomas Audley had investigated people sympathetic to Mary and her Catholic cause, forced to arrest friends William Fitzwilliam and Anthony Browne, who then spoke out about Nicholas Carew and Lady Mary Hussey. All were released, but it caused a dramatic fracture in Cromwell's friendship with Fitzwilliam.[45] King Henry used Cromwell's home at Hackney to meet Princess Mary, and Cromwell also got to see her, and told Chapuys he would 'die proudly knowing that he had the chance to reunite the king with his daughter'.[46] Mary felt the same for Cromwell, writing, 'Good Master Secretary, how much I am bound unto you, which has not only travailed, when I was almost drowned in folly, to recover me before I sunk and was utterly past recovery'.[47]

Cromwell did not personally benefit from seeing out Henry's desire to have Anne Boleyn executed. Neither did anyone else; positions became available and were offered, and all remained quiet about their part in the coup. But now Cromwell had Princess Mary's position settled, and thus any threat from Spain or the Empire, so there was room for reward. On 2 July, Cromwell publicly received the plum role of Lord Privy Seal. Given Cromwell was Vice-Gerent, Vicar-General, Principal Secretary, Master of the Rolls, and Chancellor of the Exchequer, he had previously done little work for the Privy Seal's office. He was now the holder of the king's private seal, the fifth of the nine high offices in England. Thomas Audley still held the Great Seal of Office in the highest office in the land. Given Audley also remarried to Elizabeth Grey, daughter to Cromwell favourite, the late Thomas Grey, Cromwell's alliance with Audley would never falter. The Duke of Suffolk was the Lord High Steward and Lord President of the Council, positions two and four respectively in the land, and Cromwell shared a good relationship with his fellow counsel. That only left Norfolk ranked higher than Cromwell as Lord Treasurer. Cromwell sent off his son Gregory to stay in the north with Norfolk, in an effort to smooth over their relationship.

Cromwell simply could not rise any higher in the land than Lord Privy Seal but could stretch his reach wider. He was also granted the title of the Receiver of Petitions to Parliament. Plus, while Cromwell had been acting at Vice-Gerent for a year in secular matters, he was given the title of Vice-Gerent of the Spirituals, meaning he sat over both archbishops in the Convocation, which he would put to good use.

Amassing titles and roles was something Cromwell had become adept at and needed to relinquish some work to continue being successful. Cromwell could not work as Lord Privy Seal and Master of the Rolls, so the job went to his good friend Sir Christopher Hales. However, Cromwell would not give up his private rooms in The Rolls Manor, so while Hales could work there, he had to live elsewhere.[48] Cromwell had Ralph Sadler work jointly with him, as Clerk of the Hanaper, Sir John Williams, Cromwell's brother-in-law, collaborated in the Jewel House, while William Paulet worked with Cromwell as Master of the King's Woods. Cromwell no doubt held a lavish celebration for this grand promotion and bought himself Newington Belhouse Manor in Kent.[49]

But it was not over; while Cromwell had amassed roles under Anne Boleyn, he could not become a peer of the realm. On 8 July, Henry corrected this error and made him Baron Cromwell of Wimbledon, giving him the lands taken from Cranmer a month earlier. Cromwell was now in possession of the lands around his home in Putney, and the enormous manor at Mortlake, where his relatives once worked as servants. Cromwell could not be Lord Cromwell until the close of parliament on 18 July, so he could continue to control the House of Commons. Otherwise, that role would fall to Sir Richard Rich, whom no one liked or trusted, and who had already fallen foul of several high-ranking courtiers by being rude in his role in the Court of Augmentations.

Cromwell's glorious new manor at Mortlake stretched along Lower Richmond Road to the bank of the Thames, a two-winged brick building with high walls. The manor was created for the sumptuous requirements of archbishops, and royal progresses stopped there. The house became known as Cromwell House for several hundred years. Cranmer had left the manor unused, and Cromwell immediately started work to make it grander than ever, suitable for royalty once again. Mortlake had been a manor for the Archbishop of Canterbury since 1099, and a popular Plantagenet summer house, and to be granted Mortlake and all its lands was a grand honour for the man changing the church.

After an enormous celebration party at Mortlake,[50] Cromwell tried to get back to work, close to the king all the time, including travelling on progress with Henry and Jane. Nasty rumours sprang up; Cromwell's attempts to be kind to Princess Mary, such as sending her a horse and saddle so she could go outdoors and recover her health,[51] or making her a beautiful medallion coin engraved with a picture of the king and queen, plus a poem talking of Mary's humility, were being misconstrued as romance.[52] Mary was only twenty years old, not much more than Gregory. Of course, being kind to Mary helped Cromwell; it aided his plan for an Imperial alliance, but suggestions Cromwell wanted Mary in marriage was a laughable notion. Cromwell was kind to Mary, something she rarely got from her own father, the same way Ambassador Chapuys was kind to Mary, and yet Cromwell was slandered with inappropriate notions.

King Henry's family issues kept Cromwell busy. Henry's niece Lady Margaret Douglas had married Lord Thomas Howard (brother of the same name to the Duke of Norfolk), and the pair were arrested for engaging in a secret marriage.[53] But news came to Dover, where Cromwell and Henry were on delayed progress to oversee fortifications. Henry Fitzroy, the king's only son, had died at St James' Palace. Henry was naturally distraught to hear that his son, only just seventeen, was dead of a lung illness. In a fit of anguish, Henry ordered Norfolk to remove and bury Fitzroy in secret, but a few days after the burial, King Henry changed his mind and wrote to Norfolk, furious at his son's arrangements. Norfolk wrote to Cromwell at once. Fearing he would go to the Tower, he prepared his will and made Cromwell the executor, just in case the worst happened. Norfolk also wrote of young Gregory, saying:

> your son is in good health here, sparing no horseflesh to run after the deer and hounds. I trust you will not be discontent that I now cause him to forbear his book. Be sure you shall have in him a wise, quick piece. From Kenninghall Lodge, Saturday at 10 at night, 5 August, with the hand of him that is full, full, full of choler and agony.[54]

Cromwell continued on progress, staying in Oxford and Woking, while Cromwellian servants sent him the costs for his work on Austin Friars and Mortlake for the month, amounting to 651 (£30,000 today), a fifth for the cost for Mortlake's windows alone. Austin Friars had ninety-seven tradesmen on its own, and Thomas Thacker, who looked after accounts at The Rolls, needed an extra 40l of lead to line the windows. The walls and doors in Cromwell's chambers at Austin Friars also had wainscot, engraved and detailed wooden detailing, added for his comfort. Thacker was also instructed to send Cromwell a new quiver and a dozen arrows for his crossbow, so Cromwell was not spending all day working on progress.[55] Given he travelled with all his dogs, hawks, falcons, and leopard, Cromwell knew how to travel in style.

Friends wrote to Cromwell on many matters over the summer; among them all asking for favours, he received a letter from his nephew. William lived St John's College at Cambridge, and it was a disaster. William wrote to his uncle:

> I never think about the kindness of my uncle Cromwell without blaming myself for not taking more pains to preserve your honour and fulfil your duty... I accuse myself of having despised God's laws, abused your kindness, and wasted your time and money... and I beseech you to lay aside your anger. You cannot inflict a greater punishment than I deserve, nor greater than I will willingly undergo. There is another thing which alone grieves me, which if I could overcome, I would be considered not as a relation, but as one of your hired servants ... I remember the faults of my old life with tears. I enlarge on your kindness to me, and I offer to submit to any punishment.[56]

Fortunately for William Wellyfed, his uncle focused his anger elsewhere.

As Cromwell and the royal couple progressed to Grafton in September, murmurs of disruption appeared in the north. There had been many changes for the people of England, and pushback would be expected. Now Cromwell sat at the top of the Convocation, he and Cranmer pushed through the *Ten Articles devised by the King's Highness' Majesty to establish Christian quietness and unity among us*, five articles to define rules for doctrines, another five dealing with ceremonies. As Michaelmas loomed, tax collectors headed out across the country, and changes in festivities for local saints also came into force. Cromwell had worked hard for his religious changes, finally free to push forward, showing how dearly he held the Reformation. Cromwell wrote the *Injunctions of the Clergy* and decreed adults, and children should learn the Ten

Commandments, Lord's Prayer, and the Ten Articles in English so they could better understand their faith. Throughout Europe, reformers were trying to find consensus, with little luck. William Tyndale was in prison in Brussels (and Stephen Vaughan and Cromwell tried to help with no luck),[57] though Cromwell prepared to print Miles Coverdale's English Bible, based on much of Tyndale's work. Several reformed books were being printed in England regardless of the laws, Cromwell turning a blind eye in the hopes Henry accepted the books. Stephen Gardiner's *De vera obedientia* was distributed in England and Europe, and Reginald Pole reviewed it, saying, 'Gardiner's book is written with the highest art, but... the arguments are weak',[58] and then published his defiance of King Henry and his new church, *Pro ecclesiasticae unitatis defensione*. Cromwell in reviewing this treatise commented he, 'would make (Pole) eat his own heart'.[59]

But a fresh problem arose; while for years, England could begrudge Anne Boleyn, now their hatred needed a new target. At the monastery of St Albans, Prior Ashwell was hoping Cromwell would be in the Tower by Michaelmas and asked, 'what should we pass upon these statutes, which be made by a sort of light-brained merchants and heretics, Cromwell being one of the chiefs of them?'[60] Rumours were rife across the country as the new laws struggled to be understood and people increasingly panicked.

After months of discontent in the north, on 1 October, Thomas Kendall, vicar of Louth, gave a sermon denouncing religious changes and whipped up fear over the town's local houses. John Heneage had arrived to elect officials for the new season and was seized by the angry crowd, but escaped, being the brother of one of King Henry's privy chamber men and promised to speak to the king on their behalf.[61]

Four miles from Louth was Legbourne Priory, owned by Cromwell. Three Cromwellian servants, John Milsent, John Bellow and George Parker were gathered by an angry mob and imprisoned,[62] while households belonging to friends of Cromwell and Cranmer were burned. Within a day, over 3,000 men gathered, and at Bolingbroke, John Raynes, the chancellor of the Diocese of Lincoln, lay on his sickbed and was murdered, along with a cook. By the time news reached Cromwell, panic had spread, stories were out of control and crowds of upwards of 10,000 formed.

King Henry dispatched the Duke of Suffolk north with an army, and Cromwell prepared his nephew Richard to defend London north of the city, Richard ready to handle a retinue of men and artillery from the Tower. The rebels sent a list of demands; among them, the rebels wanted Cromwell, Cranmer, Rich, Hales, and Bishops Latimer, Lee, Longland, Goodricke, Barlow and Hilsey ripped from power. Poor Cranmer had to go into hiding in Kent while Cromwell took charge in London.[63]

King Henry and Queen Jane retreated to safety at Windsor Castle, and Richard Cromwell went north with 100 men, mostly labourers from Mortlake Manor.[64] It was a brave move, given the hatred for the name Cromwell and despite the nerves of Richard's young wife, Frances. Cromwell wanted to do more, sending 160 men from his various homes to fight, including his cook at Austin Friars.

The Duke of Suffolk took his army north, and Norfolk guarded East Anglia, where Gregory Cromwell remained out of harm's way. The Duke of Suffolk charged into Lincolnshire, bringing them under control, and by 23 October, Norfolk had negotiated with the rebel leaders of upwards of 20,000 men. A Yorkshire-born, London-based lawyer, Robert Aske was now the rebels' leader and belonged to Gray's Inn in London just like Cromwell. Many of Cromwell's friends and commissioners were stuck in the north, and some escaped south but lost everything. Cromwell's in-law Sir George Lawson was north of York, too afraid to leave the region, and was forced to host the rebels in his home as an act of humiliation.[65] Lancelot Collins at York felt the same and was forced to take down Cornwell's arms in his home or have the place burned to the ground. Tens of thousands of people revolted against Cromwell's work and wanted his head.

The rebels' demands went to Windsor to the king, and he then wrote a scathing proclamation in response.[66] Henry openly defended all on his Privy Council, except Lord Cromwell, Archbishop Cranmer, and Chancellor Audley. Was it to distance them from the Privy Council to appease the rebels? To suggest they were not as powerful as the rebels suspected? To keep them safe, or to show them they were on the brink of ruin?

Cromwell moved between Mortlake Manor and The Rolls during this time and was gone long enough it was suggested he had been diminished. Vaughan and Wriothesley stayed close to their master, Sadler with the king. On 5 November, Cromwell received two late-night messages, from Thomas Heneage and William Fitzwilliam at Windsor, warning him to stop Sir Ralph Ellerker and Robert Bowes, the rebels' ambassadors, from leaving London. The men were stopped, Henry's proclamation destroyed. Ellerker and Bowes left with an updated version of the king's proclamation a week later, which now read, 'we, by the advice of our whole Council before named, did elect and choose into our Privy Council, and also into their rooms, Sir Thomas Audley knight, our Chancellor, and Lord Crumwell, Keeper of our Privy Seal, thinking them men in, all our opinions, most mete for the same rooms'. Cranmer was squeezed into the list of men carefully chosen to Council. The fact the proclamation had to be intercepted and revised must have been of grave concern to Cromwell.

The crowds in the north disbanded and headed home, thinking they would be listened to and pardoned. Henry went to Richmond Palace, and Cromwell was just two miles away at Mortlake. Cromwell spending time in the king's company saved him; Cromwell's ability to talk anyone into anything prevailed yet again. As Henry's next proclamation read, '(Henry) will not forego my Lord of the Privy Seal for no man living'.[67]

What had started as being against taxes was now fully a religious matter. Robert Pakington, London merchant and MP who reported to Cromwell, was murdered one misty morning while crossing his street to St Pancras Church at Cheapside, only a few hundred metres from Cromwell's Rolls office. Pakington was a loyal evangelical and Cromwell supporter and shot dead while the killer was neither seen nor caught, despite a hefty reward. The Catholic church was quickly blamed, with multiple theories springing up in years to come. But negotiations with the rebels continued throughout November, and the commoners and nobles who followed the insurrection thought they were gaining ground; Henry promised pardons, but the armies were not disbanded.

King Henry set out a huge Christmas celebration at Greenwich Palace, his first Christmas with Queen Jane, who must have wondered what she married into over the past several months. Cromwell finally got Gregory home from Norfolk; the pair had not seen one another since Cromwell sent his son away before Anne Boleyn's death. Cromwell's nephew, Gregory Williams, was always grateful for his uncle; he received two benefices on Anglesey despite still being a teenager. The Cromwell family continued to grow, with Ralph Sadler and his wife Ellen welcoming their first child, a son appropriately named Thomas after his godfather. The household also had a departure; Edward Sutton, son of John, Baron Dudley and Cecily Grey, who had been in Cromwell's household while his parents suffered issues (mostly Baron Dudley's mental state), left to join his uncle Lord Leonard Grey in Ireland.

Cromwell spent several weeks at his manor in Stepney before going back to work at The Rolls, as King Henry and Queen Jane rode in procession through the city streets to great fanfare. Cromwell went back to biding his time, buried deep in his offices. Upwards of 40,000 men had marched to see Cromwell eliminated, and it had harmed him none. All those leaders involved in the uprising were recorded in Cromwell's papers, monitored and ready to be condemned. Soon a letter arrived, saying they had uncovered the original vicar Thomas Kendall of Louth, and Cromwell could begin interrogations. Now was the time to kill for the new religion.

Chapter 14

1537: Prestige

'there is no man so ill-beloved'

Sir, Your Majesty allows yourself to be governed by a tyrant named Crumwell ... It is you, Lord Crumwell, who is the original cause of this rebellion ... The blame lies on the King's councillors; all is run and started by Crumwell ...[1] Crumwell, it is thou that art the very original and chief causer of all this rebellion and mischief, and... though thou wouldes procure all the noblemen's heads within the realm to be stricken off, yet shall there one head remain that shall strike off thy head.[2]

Without a doubt, the words said by the rebels would have been both hurtful and infuriating. By January, while the rebels disbanded and were silenced, things were far from peaceful. Cromwell had been in the king's court since 1530 but had largely been left to his own devices. Even the Privy Council had little effect on Cromwell's plans and ambitions until now. The demanded changes in the Privy Council were largely the rebels' only gain, and so far, Cromwell's only loss. The group needed to be formalised, each position justified and reasoned, even a minute book of meetings created. The Privy Council had been a group of men close to the king who gave advice; now there were formal management meetings, and rather than serving Cromwell's aims, it would control his movements. Had Cromwell not destroyed Anne Boleyn and became both a peer and a member of the top-nine councillors in England, perhaps it would not have happened. Cromwell's elevation had also seen his freedom severely restricted.

Cromwell received a letter from the Earl of Cumberland on 12 January, and plainly stated, 'the commons in every quarter throughout this county are so wilfully minded against you ... and as yet they continue in the same fury against you, so that in case any man speaks of you, he is despised of all the county'.[3] The fact the hatred remained was no secret; while brawn had beaten back the rebels, Cromwell was ready to use brains to finish them. That was where his plans for psychological defeat came in, with the king's full support. Cromwell knew the rebellion needed to be picked apart from within, and he had three ways to do it; the gentry had to be separated from the commoners, power needed to be solidified in the hands of those loyal to the crown, and a propaganda sweep of published pamphlets needed to be unleashed. These pamphlets needed to talk of the physical and moral dangers of rebellion, along with support for national unity and peace.[4]

It is easy to imagine Cromwell sitting alone, worried and distracted through this difficult period, but if he was concerned, he certainly did not show it. In January 1537 alone, Cromwell's personal monthly income, aside from all his official roles, was a little over 1,000l (£430,000 today) made up of rents, fees and annuities owed, mostly from clergy or religious houses. His accounts show Cromwell receiving unmarked bags of 'various gold' in January, likely New Year's gifts. Cromwell regularly received unmarked payments and also gave out unmarked payments at New Year, as well as 'white money', his version of petty cash.[5]

Cromwell's accounts remain a treasure trove of who was important to him and how he spent his time. While Cromwell stared down a rebellion to destroy him, he did not sit quietly at court, lavishing a large gold cup on Queen Jane for New Year, and sending Princess Mary 40l (almost £17,000 today). Cromwell hosted a party at Austin Friars where they enjoyed pheasants and puddings and everyone dined with gilt silver cutlery and received gifts of brooches and gold chains, and enjoyed new falcons, hawks, and the bowling alley in the garden, which now had its own keeper. Cromwell also lost 24l (over £10,000 today) on playing dice on 5 January, no doubt celebrating the epiphany in grand style. He redecorated his offices, at a cost of 57l, and bought Gregory two new caps trimmed with gold and put 6l in his son's purse when he left London with Sir John Williams on 19 January. Accounts showed how Cromwell tipped servants when they came by, such as the man who bought meat sent to Cromwell from the king's cooks or to Ralph Sadler's servants for bringing gifts; tips ranged from 2s to about 10s (almost £200 today). On the lighter side, Cromwell only paid 1s 1d for a boat ride from Westminster to Stepney or Greenwich to visit the king, and six weeks rent for all his servants to stay at Greenwich only cost 25s (£500 today), while Gregory alone regularly cost his father 12l (£5,000 today) a month in expenses, travel, and clothing. In contrast, Cromwell paid his falconer Richard 45s, an illustration of Gregory's comfortable lifestyle at his father's behest.[6]

Despite everything going on, Cromwell could find time to enjoy life, paying the queen's actors to perform, the Earl of Rutland's minstrels to sing and ordering marchpane and oranges for his guests. Richard Cromwell also paid 12l to a man for the costs of 'my Lord's part of the masque', so memorable evenings by the Cromwell household were certainly being had despite the rebellion. Cromwell also sent Thomas Wriothesley to Princess Mary, with a gift of 15l as he was her 'Valentine', which was unlikely to stifle puerile rumours of Cromwell's interest in the woman. Cromwell called his surgeon, Mr Forrest, to attend him, at a cost of a mere 5s, while Cromwell's yearly fee to his London baker was only 40s, or 2l (around £800 today). Given the expenses, Cromwell was unwise to lose some 45l (almost £20,000 today) gambling at Sir Edward Seymour's house on 1 March.[7]

While things may have felt calm at court or in the Cromwellian manors, the north suffered lingering bitterness and danger. By the second week of January, the commoners who had returned home were already sceptical, as 'Crumwell and other evil counsellors should have been banished from Court, and they are now in higher favour than ever they were before'.[8] Rebel leader Robert Aske left London 8 January after warning Henry 'there is special grudge against lord Crumwell as the destroyer of the Commonwealth'.[9] The rebels wanted, 'to put down the lord Crumwell, that heretic, and all his sect'.

While Robert Aske believed King Henry would stick to his words, and Cromwell's propaganda pamphlets began to spread into the north, the loyal lords prepared for more disharmony, and the commoners prepared to rise again. Cromwell even had men like Layton and Legh start dissolutions again, and taxes still needed to be collected. The rebels tried to take Hull on 16 January, but the Duke of Norfolk and his men easily overthrew the rebellion.[10] Without the support of the nobles in the area, the commoners could not group as they had before, nor have safe places to retreat. Ralph Sadler was in York, reporting to Cromwell of the uprisings and general disquiet in the area, and it was clear that any peace promised at Christmas was lost. The commoners thought Cromwell controlled Henry, and that Cromwell wrote the king's letters of peace and pardon, rendering them invalid. Ralph Sadler went in search of a haven in Scotland; one of Cromwell's most beloved men was not safe.[11] Even Norfolk worried the plan to separate the nobles from the commons may not work and sent a box to Cromwell in London, 'which I require you to keep unopened while I live', alongside Norfolk's will.

Among the confusion and infighting of the north, Sir Francis Bigod's rebellion of 5,000 men was soon quashed by Norfolk, who was no longer sympathetic to the commoners. Bigod slandered Cromwell in another letter, stating 'it is reckoned surely that Lord Crumwell has caused this statute (punishment of Lady Margaret Douglas and Lord Thomas Howard) to be made because he would himself have had her to his wife'.[12] Why Bigod would suspect Cromwell of wanting to marry the king's niece is a mystery.

Sir John Bulmer and his wife Margaret Stafford tried to begin a new uprising in Ryesdale, but they too were soon beaten back, especially now that executions and punishments were being handed down. None of the agreed points during negotiations were adhered to; Cromwell stood firm in the king's heart, the monasteries closed, and taxes were collected. Many of the leaders – Robert Aske, Sir Francis Bigod, and a dozen others were all executed, along with six abbots, sixteen priests, thirty-eight monks and another 150 people involved in the rebellions. For Cromwell, there was some satisfaction to be had, for he believed Lord Darcy of Temple Hurst, who had famously defected to the rebels' side, had planned to blow up Cardinal Wolsey in 1529 with gunpowder.[13] Cromwell had held that grudge for almost eight years and finally got revenge when Darcy was beheaded at Tower Hill. Cromwell was the master of biding his time.

While the trauma of the northern rebellion continued, Cromwell remained busy with the issues of Ireland. Lord Leonard Grey continued his murderous control of the country, but the Council of Ireland, Cromwell's friends well-placed among them, regularly reported back their distaste for Grey and his cruel and reckless behaviour. It was not a good time to be a traitor to King Henry; among the anger and bitterness of the northern battles, King Henry also decided that the Irish rebels, Silken Thomas FitzGerald and his five uncles in the Tower, would be executed at Tyburn on 3 February. Silken Thomas was beheaded and buried, but his uncles were hanged, drawn and quartered, and their parts were scattered as a warning.

Despite all the drama of the north, other issues did not abate. King Henry's perpetually ungrateful cousin Reginald Pole had been made a cardinal. Pope Paul did this to both irritate the king and embolden the northern rebels. Any kind of cordial friendship Cromwell had shared with Pole was long over, but one of Pole's servants, Michael Throckmorton, planned to travel to the Low Countries and wrote to Cromwell wanting a meeting.[14] Pole wanted to meet Cromwell in Flanders to discuss possible peace and understanding on matters of religion. Cromwell of course could not just leave England, and he and the king saw this as a trap and possible assassination attempt.[15] Cromwell sent his friend John Hutton in Brussels to watch Pole, who found Throckmorton had Henry Phelips working for him, the same man who had exposed William Tyndale's hiding place to authorities.[16] Tyndale had been recently strangled and burned, but Cromwell had no intention of stopping his plan to create the English Bible using Tyndale's words.

But with all the drama of the past few months weighing on Cromwell, one personal bright spot emerged. Elizabeth Seymour Lady Ughtred, sister to Queen Jane, wrote to Cromwell asking for help.[17] Elizabeth was still only nineteen but a widow of three years and had two young children. She had suffered one of the most unjust cruelties of the period; married off at twelve, to a man forty years her senior. Elizabeth gave Sir Anthony Ughtred a son three years later, and fortunately, she was widowed while carrying her daughter. Elizabeth Seymour needed a new husband, so Cromwell began negotiations with Elizabeth and her brother Sir Edward Seymour so she could marry into the Cromwell family. While popular fiction has suggested Elizabeth thought she would marry Cromwell himself, from the outset it was clear Cromwell wished Elizabeth to marry Gregory, now seventeen. Gregory Cromwell had spent the last few years travelling the countryside with Cromwell's friends and needed to start living like an adult. This would make Gregory Cromwell brother-in-law to the king of England.

The glorious news of Queen Jane's pregnancy appeared in early April among the works to end the rebellion.[18] Arranging the marriage between Gregory and Elizabeth was the ultimate Cromwellian opportunity now Queen Jane had finally conceived. It was time to push even further and set up a Vice-Gerential synod. Cromwell sat the head of the assembly for the first few days, outlining religious issues around the country, before leaving it in the hands of Cranmer (while paying Alexander Alesius 5l a month to gather gossip from the bishops).[19] The synod needed to debate and finalise the Ten Articles on Cromwell's behalf, as well as the English Bible.

With rebels still to be condemned to death, Henry wanted religious control elsewhere. The Carthusian London Charterhouse, which Cromwell privately tried to convert to a centre for reformist teaching, still refused the King's supremacy. Cromwell sent his men to demand the thirty monks swear King Henry was the Head of the Church. Fortunately, twenty signed the act.[20] All ten dissenters were chained upright in Newgate prison, where five died in the illness-infested summer conditions within a month, another two near death before Cromwell heard of the situation. Nine of the ten monks died of horrid conditions, plague and typhus running rampant, and the final monk was executed in 1540. Meanwhile, two of their monks who had been exiled to Yorkshire were hanged in chains. Again Cromwell's personal endeavours had been ruined by Henry's greed.

As negotiations for Gregory and Elizabeth Seymour's marriage continued, Cromwell received a letter from this dear friend Elizabeth Howard who had been tied up and abused by the Duke of Norfolk's mistress Bess Holland.[21] Sir Thomas Wyatt needed guidance, freshly arrived at the Emperor's court as the new ambassador, and out of his depth.[22] Sir Henry Capell heard gossip between commoners in Stoke that Henry Courtenay, Marquess of Exeter, had tried to stab Cromwell to death, but Cromwell, wearing armour, was saved and threw Courtenay in the Tower.[23] How they came to make up this ridiculous story is a mystery. It sits alongside another false story earlier in the year that said Richard Cromwell had been murdered in the north, and the murderer wanted to burn off his own hand because it had not murdered Thomas Cromwell.[24] Richard Cromwell was alive and well with his uncle, beloved by the king for his hard work, and awaiting the arrival of his first child with wife Frances.

Cromwell had no time for gossip; he had an engagement party to hold at Mortlake Manor for Gregory and Elizabeth. The court stayed at Hampton Court Palace just six miles upstream from Mortlake, now the most luxurious manor imaginable. Elizabeth Seymour had been staying at her brother Edward's house in Twickenham, neatly between Mortlake and the court. The party was a glorious sight, with a porpoise centrepiece, and Cromwell spent 60l (£25,000 today) on new green coats for his servants for the occasion. The wine bill alone came to an astonishing 400l, almost £340,000 today, double the cost for all of Cromwell's servants and labourers for the month at all his manors. Gregory was dressed in a velvet cape trimmed with gold, given fine new shirts and doublets and even a sword and dagger for the occasion, the outfit costing 15l, while Cromwell got himself a new cape, at a cost of a mere 6s.[25] By this time, Cromwell had his own group of actors, the Lord Crumwell players, who could perform anywhere in the country, spreading the good word of the new religion, though hopefully the party shows were livelier.[26]

Gregory Cromwell and Lady Elizabeth Seymour married at Mortlake Manor on Friday 3 August. Gifts and supplies came from all over the place, artichokes from Edward Seymour, quince from Princess Mary, apples and pheasants from Mordaunt, stags from Henry Grey, and a special delivery of ginger nutmegs, while Cromwell's gift to his son on his wedding day was 50l (£21,000 today).[27]

Cromwell no doubt felt he had started the year at his lowest ebb, and now could not rise any higher. The north was under Norfolk's control, the West Marshes were being set up, and monastery dissolutions now carried on without any restrictions. But even a baron and uncle-in-law to the king could not escape the scourge of Tudor summer illness. The year had already claimed two of Cromwell's oldest friends, Thomas Rush and John Whalley, and summer claimed his faithful lawyer, Thomas Bedyll. The court was on progress, Henry in a good mood as Queen Jane's pregnancy advanced without complications.[28] Cromwell travelled with the court, but while away, one of his servants, Thomas Bolde, suddenly died of the plague. Someone dying so close to someone dear to the king and queen was impossible to miss, and Bolde had also visited Ralph Sadler after Henry Percy's funeral. Percy had been allowed to go home to Cromwell's Hackney place to die of illness, and Sadler was given leave to attend Percy's burial, close to Sutton House, the manor Cromwell had purchased for Sadler. Sir John Russell rushed to the king to tell him Cromwell and Sadler had been exposed, and while Henry was happy for Cromwell to re-join the court (sadly not Sadler), Queen Jane was nervous for her baby.[29] The court was already in self-isolation away from illness, and they devised a plan for Henry and Cromwell to spend time together while protecting Jane. Each day, Cromwell met King Henry outdoors, riding, hunting and other activities they enjoyed, practising social distancing. Rather than staying at court, Cromwell stayed at nearby manor homes, such as Kingston next to Hampton Court, and enjoyed homes belonging to Sir Richard Weston, Sir Anthony Browne, Henry Courtenay, and many more.[30] By all accounts, the plan worked well; Queen Jane kept herself quarantined away from illness, and Cromwell, who did not fall ill, was able to enjoy the progress without any interruption.

Ralph Sadler did not have such luck. He could not stay home with his wife, Ellen, who was pregnant, nor at Mortlake where Gregory was with Elizabeth.[31] Plague also infected The Rolls in London, though thankfully Austin Friars remained healthy.[32] Cromwell put Sadler in The Neat at Westminster, and fortunately, he did not contract plague. With The Rolls closed, Thomas Thacker worked from Austin Friars for his master, and the house was starting to fill with relics, statues and treasures from closed monasteries, the manor becoming an unlikely storage facility for items Cromwell did not believe were real, but had nowhere else to go.[33]

After a month of sheltering against illness, Cromwell was able to return to indoor meetings at court, and not a moment too soon. King Henry decided to call a one-time special meeting for Knights of the Garter to appoint a new member. Cromwell had seen his enemy Lord Darcy executed after the Pilgrimage of Grace, creating a space in the order that only allows twenty-four members at a time. After only one round of voting with the five present knights,[34] Henry looked over the twelve names suggested and announced Cromwell could join the Order, the highest of honours, without hesitation or discussion. All was a formality in the king's closet at Hampton Court, for Henry had decided to enlist Cromwell specifically, who at once fell to his knees before his king in thanks. Henry placed the chain of the Order around Cromwell's neck and raised him again.[35] Cromwell also gained the elaborate Garter gown, borrowed from Thomas Boleyn, and Cromwell's updated coat of arms, his own conjoined with the Seymour banner, plus bleeding pelicans to symbolise Christ's sacrifice for humanity, now hung in St George's Chapel at Windsor.[36]

Now was the perfect time to offer King Henry a copy of the new Cromwell Bible. The Vice-Gerential synod was complete, with Cranmer excitedly telling Cromwell all issues had been resolved. Cranmer wrote from Forde Place in Kent where he hid from plague, sending Cromwell a copy of the English Bible, the original copy made during the synod. Cromwell showed the bible to Henry at once, who promised to allow it to be published after he read and revised the teachings. It was to be 'engraven on the hearts of our said people' and decreed it should be read in every parish every Sunday.[37] Given that Henry never properly read through it, Cromwell and Cranmer were able to slip through the reformist teachings they wanted, without gaining any anger from their king. Creating the English Bible would be Cromwell's greatest achievement; however it was published under a false name, the author being the imaginary 'Thomas Matthew', hence its nickname the Matthew Bible. In reality, it was the Cromwell Bible, nicknamed the Cranmer Bible after Cromwell's death. The celebrations in Cromwell's rooms and manors must have been in overdrive throughout August, almost as busy as Cromwell's laundry women, who were in full-time preparation to keep their lord clean and healthy around the pregnant queen.[38]

September showed a return to normality, not that it would last. The previous eighteen months had been inconceivable, but progress and relaxation while avoiding the plague seemed the priority. Cromwell's manor homes were quieter than normal, with only Austin Friars undergoing construction, while Cromwell and his enormous entourage of servants, falcons, hawks, greyhounds, and spaniels spent private time at both Mortlake and Stepney after leaving Wulf Hall.[39] Sir Edward Seymour wrote how Cromwell had left the manor, and missed him and his dogs for their hunting and Cromwell's huge collection of hawks and falcons for entertainment. Seymour wrote of his sister Elizabeth and new husband Gregory, 'I pray God to send me by them shortly a nephew', showing Elizabeth's already advancing pregnancy was known to the family.[40] One month into marriage, Elizabeth Cromwell was three months pregnant.

Ireland continued to take up Cromwell's time, the Council was unable to make any firm decisions on even minor matters, often getting a sharp reply.[41] Cromwell also wrote to Reginald Pole's servant Michael Throckmorton, a cutting insight to someone facing Cromwell's wrath.

Cromwell considered Reginald Pole a lost cause, and while Nicholas Heath was going to the Low Countries to speak with Throckmorton, Cromwell saw the man as an ungrateful traitor. Cromwell wrote, in a long and angry letter that:

> I now remember myself too late … I might better have judged that so dishonest a master could have but even such a servant as you are. No, no, loyalty and treason dwell seldom together … You have blurred my eyes, and your credit shall nevermore serve you so far to deceive me the second time. I take you as you are … Pity, it is that the folly of one brainsick Pole, or to say better, of one witless fool, should be the ruin of so great a family … If you continue in your malice, and perverse blindness; doubt you not, but your ends shall be as of all traitors … I have done what I may, to save you. I must I think do what I can to see you condignly punished. God send you both to fare as you deserve, that is either shortly to come to your allegiance or else to a shameful death.[42]

While Cromwell tried to vanquish Henry's enemies, he accidentally renewed one of his own. Cromwell and the Duke of Norfolk had been getting along rather well over the past year, the pair communicating regularly over the Pilgrimage of Grace, and Norfolk seemed polite, thankful, and civil towards the commoner he never liked. But now Norfolk, who also had to stay away from court due to illness among his men, returned to see Cromwell a Knight of the Garter, uncle-in-law to the king, rewriting the Bible, and even the new Dean of Wells Cathedral, despite being a layman.[43] Cromwell had wanted to move Gregory and Elizabeth to his new manor at North Elmham near Norfolk's home base, but that would only anger the jealous duke even further. But Cromwell and Norfolk met in the garden at Mortlake Manor and did a deal; Norfolk would help Cromwell gain the extraordinary Lewes Priory in Sussex for Gregory if Cromwell helped Norfolk gain Castle Acre, twenty-eight miles north of Norfolk's home at Kenninghall.[44] This would help ease tensions between the king's closest men. But both Cromwell and Norfolk had far bigger issues than where Gregory and Elizabeth Cromwell would raise their children.

Illness was still rampant; Queen Jane isolated at Hampton Court Palace with King Henry three miles away at Esher Place. Norfolk could not get to court, and Ralph Sadler had to again self-isolate at Hackney after being exposed to the plague, his wife Ellen safe at Lesnes. Sadler was less worried about Ellen than he was of losing his place in the Privy Chamber, making sure Cromwell kept his position safe, even though Sadler's servants were dying around him.[45] Sadler managed to make it back in time to the joint royal courts before Queen Jane gave birth to Prince Edward on 12 October. The king finally had a legitimate son, and Cromwell's future grandchildren would be first cousins to the future king. There would be no higher contentment for either man, not that they knew it at the time. Cromwell was at St James' Palace in London, safe from plague, when the news came from Queen Jane herself,[46] and Cromwell celebrated by giving out money to the ninety commoners living around St James[47] as well as tipping the midwives to the queen well for their service, and even his spaniels got a treat.[48]

As with Princess Elizabeth's christening four years earlier, Prince Edward brought together all sides of the divides at court. Cranmer, Norfolk, and Suffolk stood as godfathers, Princess Mary as godmother alongside Gertrude Courtney, as Margaret Grey was unable to attend due to a plague outbreak. Yet in all the planning, Cromwell did as he always did; he did not include himself in the official proceedings, simply walking in with friend Thomas Audley in the procession.[49] Instead, as Principal Secretary, Cromwell created and pronounced the gifted titles of Earl of Southampton to old friend William Fitzwilliam, and Earl of Hertford to new friend Edward Seymour. Cromwell seemed content to treat himself to new capes for himself and Richard, accompanying the endless spending for Gregory.[50]

The Cromwell and Seymour families barely had time to celebrate their golden new world before it turned to dust in their hands. On 24 October at St. James', Cromwell received a panicked letter from the Duke of Norfolk, saying, 'my good lord, I pray you to be here tomorrow early to comfort our good master, as for our mistress there is no likelihood of her life, the more pity, and I fear she shall not be alive at the time ye shall read this'.[51] Norfolk was right; by the time Cromwell rushed to Hampton Court, Queen Jane was dead, likely from a blood infection or clot after struggling to recover from her horrendous birth.

For Cromwell personally, the devastation could only have been soothed with hope, combined with the ability to control the situation. He had given his precious son Gregory to the Seymour family. Technically the situation had not changed; infant Prince Edward was the heir to the throne, Gregory the uncle to the future king. But Edward was a newborn without a mother, his delicate claim to the throne fragile as crystal. The Seymours felt precarious, and if the king were to marry again, an expectation rather than a suggestion, any future children could also have a claim to the throne. All Cromwell could do was manage the situation as best as he could.

Three days after the death of Queen Jane, Cromwell penned an angry letter to Stephen Gardiner and Lord Edmund Howard in Paris.[52] The first half told of Jane's demise, and how the Privy Council had discussed a new bride with the king. France had two options; the teenage Princess Margaret of France and the preferred Mary de Guise, Madame de Longueville, who was in negotiations to marry King James of Scotland. Cromwell wanted Edmund Howard to find out more about possible marriages and then went on to vent his anger and disappointment at Gardiner. King Henry wanted Esher Place for himself, pressuring Gardiner to gift it to the monarch. Gardiner had been speaking ill of many, Cromwell in particular about the whole issue. Cromwell wrote, 'you do both me and others wrong to be angry with us without cause … I am sorry, my lord to see you so contentious and to have so little care of your friends'.[53] Their attempts to find at least a civil or polite friendship had already fallen away, over an earlier petty argument about Cromwell sending Gardiner a horse, Gardiner forgetting about it and then calling Cromwell a liar. The absurd fight had dragged on for months, the king even needing to step in, as the pair appeared unable to work together.

Cromwell also wrote to his friend John Hutton in Brussels, to enquire over potential royal brides with the Queen Regent Mary. After listing a few unsuitable women, Hutton suggested either sixteen-year-old widow Christina of Denmark, Duchess of Milan, or reclusive twenty-two-year-old Anna von der Marck, Duchess von Kleve, adding weight to Cromwell's list of potential brides when King Henry was ready to choose.[54]

Cromwell's correspondence of the period showed him as sharp and impatient with people on several issues. Queen Jane's funeral preparations lasted for weeks, and on 12 November, twenty-nine-year-old Queen Jane was laid to rest in an elaborate funeral at Windsor.[55] His sister-in-law's funeral became Gregory's first public duty, one of the chief mourners alongside Richard Cromwell. All sides of the religious and political divide attended, the chief mourner being Princess Mary. Cromwell got the king's niece Lady Margaret Douglas released from Syon Abbey to attend, and her traitorous husband Lord Thomas Howard conveniently died in the Tower, one less threat to the fledging new line to the throne. The same day as Queen Jane's funeral, Cromwell fired off an angry letter to his cousin John Babington, who had been running riot at Kingston Manor, causing massive damage, and overcharging his own relatives rent. Cromwell was not in the mood to indulge him.[56]

Work did not abate for the frazzled Lord Privy Seal. Ireland had ongoing complaints, friend Sir Thomas Wyatt was not doing well with the Holy Roman Emperor, and Rowland Lee, strangely, was not being harsh enough on criminals in Wales, despite his penchant for being cruel.[57] Cuthbert Tunstall, the new president of the Council of the North, asked Cromwell, 'of (the king's) mirth, all our mirth depends, and of his heaviness all our heaviness; wherefore my singular good Lord, show yourself a solicited and diligent servant, as I am sure ye do'.[58] All Cromwell could do to aid the grieving king was to keep the country going in Henry's absence.

Cromwell did have things to soothe himself; his personal income was upwards of 1,200l a month (£500,000 today). He now spent the bulk of his time at St. James' Palace, fit for a man of his stature, rather than at The Rolls. He had a fine Italian coat made for Jane's funeral, coupled with a 2,000l (almost £850,000) diamond and ruby ring, but also needed to call for a doctor and surgeon in early November.[59] Richard Cromwell took over domestic matters for his uncle, taking care of the Lewes Priory acquisition with the Duke of Norfolk and ensuring errant nephew, William Wellyfed, was finally under control. Preparations for Gregory's new home at Lewes cost his father 1,000l (£430,000 today) in a single month.[60]

By mid-December, Cromwell had been pushed too far; he left London and retired to Mortlake, everyone under strict instructions not to visit or request anything. Only King Henry could ask for Cromwell's time. Cromwell was considered 'somewhat acrazed',[61] and needed time with Gregory and Elizabeth. The new Cromwell couple were supposed to leave for Lewes, while Cromwell himself was to have a new manor near them at Fletchling, but Cromwell needed his son and daughter-in-law with him at Mortlake. Cromwell hosted a private family Christmas at Mortlake, with actors from the king. Thomas Audley and Henry Courtney lost money playing cards at the manor, and Gregory received a gift of Arctic falcons to take to Lewes.[62] Ralph Sadler's wife, Ellen, had given birth to their second son, named Edward after the new prince, and Richard Cromwell's wife, Frances had their first child, a son named Henry, more godsons, practically grandsons, for Cromwell. These were in addition to other godchildren throughout the year; Thomas Wriothesley's wife, Jane, gave birth to their second daughter Mary, and Henry Grey and his wife, Frances Brandon, had their first daughter, Lady Jane Grey. The Cromwell-Williams-Williamson-Wellyfed-Sadler family were all well and safe after a year of severe trial, but it would be 1538 that threatened the family in a deep, personal, and betraying way.

Chapter 15

1538: Atrocity

'you may rejoice in being the only man in his place who has never forgotten his old friends'

By 1538, Cromwell, now barrelling towards his mid-fifties, could be excused for feeling tired at the prospect of playing queenmaker yet again. First, he hobbled Queen Katherine, then killed Anne Boleyn. Just when Queen Jane looked solid, sixteenth-century medical care dashed her away. Now, the greatest challenge yet; a queen to meet impossible expectations. King Henry wanted a European noblewoman, young, beautiful, fertile, able to quell the religious fights at home and abroad with her mere presence. Did such a woman exist? Why would she want Henry?

Cromwell never concerned himself with gaining another wife. While men of all social classes replaced their deceased wives as if they were misplaced tools or livestock, Cromwell made no overtures to any woman. Why would he? His personal life was rich with family instead, and after soothing quarrels for so many other couples, no one could blame Cromwell for seeing the benefit of the single life. Cromwell spent New Year at Greenwich with the king, not leaving out anyone with gifts and preferments. Cromwell bought himself the New Year gift of land at Havering Park and spent 37l on gifts at court. He shared 70l between men in the king's rooms, while Cromwell, Sadler, Vaughan and Wriothesley were all given gifts from the king. With celebrations in full swing, Cromwell lost 56l (£23,000 today) gambling at New Year. Cromwell got himself a new girdle to wear at court and had a small velvet purse made for Will Somers, the king's fool; he had puddings and capons delivered, lost a game of bowls against old friend Sir John Russell, costing him 20s, and purchased a huge roll of fine crimson velvet at a cost of 22l (almost £10,000 today), more than enough for new outfits. Cromwell also purchased a wide range of items, from guns to handkerchiefs, and gave out 18l in alms to the poor.[1] He could well afford to be so liberal with money; throughout the year, Cromwell's average personal monthly income in 1538 was over 1,000l (£430,000 today) and he would have thought nothing of buying Fyndon Manor near Lewes from Sir Richard Rich,[2] or Wingrove Manor in Buckinghamshire from John Neville and his wife Kathryn Parr.[3]

The holiday period did not last long, with Cromwell back at work at The Rolls by 7 January. A peculiar and persistent problem trickled in; rumours of the king's death, along with vague accusations of witchcraft involving dolls filled with pins.[4] Cromwell sent Cranmer and Wriothesley to deal with various rumours[5] and kept to more pressing work, such as managing the Council of the North and chasing up clergymen not sticking to new teachings.[6] But Cromwell was not immune to the constant trickling of sedition around the country; in Oxford, Thomas Bright was visiting a friend's party when John Hampson, who was openly speaking against the king, said, 'nay, nay, that Crumwell, that traitor that has destroyed many a man, and I were as nigh him as I am you, I would thrust my dagger into the heart of him'. Poor Bright was beaten with a staff for trying to defend Cromwell.[7]

Monasteries were closing at an effective rate and widows continued to seek out Cromwell. His dearest friend Margaret Grey, Dowager Marchioness of Dorset, continued to write about her lazy son Henry Grey,[8] and young Mary Howard, Dowager Duchess of Richmond, had not been paid her dower from the king after Henry Fitzroy's death eighteen months earlier.[9] But the most important work issue facing Cromwell and Cranmer, the issue of finding a bride aside, was the English Bible, which needed constant revisions from Henry's whimsical religious leanings. Cranmer was at Lambeth, both interrogating prisoners and gaining Lutheran information from his secret wife's uncle in Switzerland,[10] while Cromwell continuously presented the English Bible to Henry in the hope he could finally use his licence to print the books.[11]

International diplomacy may have been filling Cromwell's in-tray, but his personal life was endlessly busy, with his son Gregory taking centre stage all year. Lewes Priory was well underway, Cromwell in demolition mode, eager to destroy the entire monastery, a building 420 feet by 150 feet, with a steeple of 90 feet.[12] Cromwell seemingly took out his anger at the church on poor Lewes Priory. Newly married Cromwellian

Richard Tomyou tried to suggest Cromwell ease up on the magnificent building, without luck. Cromwell hired Italian Giovanni Portinari, son of Cromwell's old Florentine friend, Francesco Portinari, and by late March, the transformation of Lewes Priory began, leaving parts available for Gregory to live and work in, given a job as a Justice of Peace in Sussex. The other big news was the arrival of Henry Cromwell.

The birth of baby Henry, Gregory's first son, Cromwell's first grandson, and the king's nephew, goes unrecorded, which is curious and unfortunate. Cromwell paid the midwife the customary 30s (around £600 today) usually paid by the godparent, on 1 March. However, Cromwell's records state it was for Mr Richard's nurse and midwife, paid by Mr Gregory. The payment suggests several possibilities; that Gregory's wife, Elizabeth, gave birth at Stepney, and Richard Cromwell arranged the local midwife.[13] But it could suggest Richard Cromwell's wife, Frances, gave birth in late February (their son Henry is listed as born in 1537, and on the Julian calendar it was still 1537 at the time).[14] Cromwell had many godchildren in 1538, and in every entry in his expenses, it lists the name of the father, and who passed on the 30s gift from Cromwell. This payment, calling for Mr Richard's midwife is exceptional from all other entries. This is not impossible, as this was a special occasion, and possibly Richard Cromwell stood as godfather, with the expense entry incorrect. Princess Mary's expenses show she was godmother to baby Henry Cromwell, giving the customary gift of a cup, the item listed in her April expenses.[15] As items were not necessarily paid for the month they were received, it is still possible Elizabeth Cromwell gave birth in late February. The other hint in Cromwell's expenses is the huge cost of 44l for 'Lady Ughtred, by Mr Richard, for things she needed at her lying down' (almost £19,000 today).[16] Given Richard paid the costs suggests Elizabeth gave birth at Stepney, not Mortlake, and certainly not at Hampton Court, where Cromwell attended the king in late February and early March. Expecting Elizabeth to give birth at the same location she watched her sister die only months earlier is improbable.

Another hint of Henry Cromwell's birth is Cromwell's expenses showing him hosting a masque at court with Henry in early March. Portinari was the choreographer, for which Cromwell needed to pay 25l (£10,000 today), in addition to the twenty-seven horses and extra men needed for just four days at court. Sadly, this alone does not show Cromwell celebrating the birth of his grandson; perhaps he simply kept King Henry entertained while preparing Philip Hoby and Hans Holbein's trip to France to paint various potential brides and prepping Sir Thomas Wyatt to push for an alliance with the Emperor.[17] Similarly, in late February, Cromwell had held a grand party, his players constantly on the move, and working with Thomas Audley and the Duke of Suffolk's players as well, with Cromwell buying them a new lute.[18] A large party is no indication of a special occasion; Cromwell loved to entertain. But Cromwell had a table engraved with the Cromwell banner made in early March, which could make an excellent item for a man who had a new grandson who was the first cousin to the future king. The Cromwell family had never been more successful.

Gregory Cromwell left for Lewes on 11 March, and it seems unlikely, and cruel, to make Elizabeth Cromwell travel with him after only days of recovery. But it is unlikely Gregory left before the birth of his son, and Elizabeth Cromwell's cart of items did not leave Stepney until mid-April.[19] Had Elizabeth already given birth in late February, the baby would likely have been conceived at the massive Mortlake Manor engagement party two months before the wedding. The Cromwell and Seymour families would have been thrilled by the new baby boy, and Gregory and Elizabeth had clearly made opportunities to make the pregnancy happen, though as Gregory would soon point out when it came to women, he did not take no for an answer.

Richard Cromwell, John Williamson, and Giovanni Portinari had been travelling to ensure Lewes Priory was to be a grand demolition and rebuild, and Gregory reported in mid-April he and Elizabeth were most happy with their new life.[20] Meanwhile, Richard Cromwell was rewarded with Hinchingbrooke nunnery, sixty miles north of London. Richard did not share his uncle's desire for demolition, rather rebuilding and redesigning the grand building to create a manor home worthy of the Cromwell name.[21]

Other Cromwell godchildren came in quick succession throughout the period, Sir Anthony and Anne Knvyett, Sir Edward and Anne Seymour of Hertford, and Sir Edward and Anne Kerne, all appointed Cromwell godfather. Edward and Isabel Baynton, and Sir George and Anne Brooke of Cobham appointed both Cromwell godfather and Princess Mary godmother, the same as Robert Radcliffe, Duke of Sussex, and his wife Mary, though sadly their daughter Anne died soon after.[22] Even the Duke of Norfolk wanted Cromwell involved in the birth of his grandson, born to Henry Howard and his wife, Frances. Lady Frances went into labour two weeks early, but Norfolk could not get her or the baby to London for christening before his godfathers Cromwell and King Henry, with plague rampant at Kenninghall.[23] Another baby was on the way; Cromwellian Sir Brian Tuke had finally married Grissell Boughton and had their first of six children in six years.

While Cromwell was busy destroying monasteries and hurrying along with the English Bible, none of his international issues eased. From Ireland came one of the most insightful letters about Cromwell's life. Anthony St Leger, someone Cromwell could endlessly trust, wrote of rumours about fellow Council of Ireland member George Paulet, who was speaking seditiously against Cromwell. He soon put another Cromwellian, John Allen, in charge of investigating rumours, and Paulet frankly shared his opinions on Cromwell. Paulet told Allen:

> and as for my Lord Privy Seal, I would not be in his case for all that ever he has, for the King beknaveth him twice a week, and sometime knocketh him well about the pate; and yet when he has been well pummelled about the head and shaken up, as if were a dog, he will come out into the great chamber shaking of the (hair) with as merry a countenance as though he might rule all the roost.[24]

Paulet was critical of Cromwell trying to make peace instead of being harsher on the Irish, because:

> the Lord Crumwell was so affectionate unto the same land because his ancestors were born there, and had been the cause of the King wasting his treasure in suppressing the Geraldines, and afterwards squandering the revenues thus acquired ... Cromwell was the greatest briber that ever was in England ... and that the King has six times as much revenue as his predecessors, and all is consumed by the Lord Privy Seal ... (Cromwell) was a great taker and briber, like his old master the cardinal, but he spent it honourably and freely like a gentleman (though he were none) and helped many honest men and preferred his servants well.

Paulet could hardly be trusted; he also believed in prophecies about magic pelicans, and he was soon sent to the Tower. Cromwell had suppressed the violent Geraldines after they murdered his friend Archbishop John Aleyn. Cromwell's hatred and anger at the Geraldines was no secret. One month after Paulet's outburst, Cromwell's servant, Jerome Flynn, was murdered in Drogheda, an unwitting symbol for the Irish's hatred of English control.[25] Cromwell did not have the level of control over Ireland he needed to secure the country.

When it came to a potential royal bride, friends Cromwell and Cranmer had a rare clash. Cranmer believed King Henry should marry an English woman, pick a wife for love and comfort; Cromwell disagreed and argued there were no suitable women in England. Henry had made a disastrous choice in Anne (as judged by its ending) and had jumped into marriage with Jane on a whim. Now, finally, Henry had the chance to make a calculated decision, and fortunately, Henry agreed with Cromwell. England needed an alliance, as the Emperor and the French king were close to finally finding an alliance of their own, and England could be left with powerful Catholic enemies. As much as Cromwell could fulfil personal desires by gaining an Imperial alliance, he could also ensure the Seymours' standing would not be diminished by the new bride. He needed to control the narrative at every opportunity.

Cromwell sent out friends to find brides, but by May, negotiations undertaken by Thomas Wyatt, John Hutton and Peter Mewtas had done little but go in circles. In earshot of several Privy Councillors, French Ambassador Castillon told King Henry he thought Cromwell was 'so proud and ungracious', to which Henry replied Cromwell, 'was a good manager, but not fit to intermeddle in the affairs of kings', and others mused Cromwell's 'Spanish passion' got in the way of honest negotiations.[26] The cruelty was intense; King Henry's ulcers were in a grave state, but that was no excuse to treat his most faithful servant in such a manner. At least Cromwell could be certain Henry would not marry Mary de Guise, for she rebuffed Henry and his need for a big wife, saying she 'was a big woman, but only had a small neck',[27] and married King James of Scotland by proxy.

Cromwell was losing on all fronts. Henry spent more time with Castillon and French-loving Norfolk than Cromwell and Imperial Ambassador Chapuys, who toyed with the idea of getting Princess Mary out of England.[28] Emperor Charles and King Francis were to meet and sign the Treaty of Aigues-Mortes, and Bishop Edward Foxe, one of Cromwell's staunched reformist allies, died of illness at Hereford.[29] On top of this, one of Cromwell's oldest friends, Lancelot Collins, died in York.[30]

Henry, with his leg ulcers so bad he could barely walk, set off to Havering Manor, seventeen miles outside London. Cromwell had planned the progress but received a message to say he was banned from attending court and Privy Council meetings. Henry hovered on the brink of death with his ulcers for twelve days, and Castillon remarked Cromwell, 'would not be safe if he did not quickly cross the sea'.[31] Richard Cromwell went to court and the Privy Council meetings and reported Henry would not open Cromwell's letters, instead choosing to entertain the French ambassador. No one situation points to any falling out between Cromwell and Henry, and yet Henry froze his relations with Cromwell simply to appease the French.

Cromwell knew how to handle the volatile and changeable king. He planned an extravagant banquet at Havering, spending 50l (£22,000 today) on a dinner with a porpoise centrepiece, accompanied by quail, heron, salmon, capons, and cherries. With the sumptuous meal, Cromwell sent six Cornish wrestlers he borrowed from his friend William Godolphin.[32] It worked; John Williamson and Richard Tomyou went to Havering and bestowed all on the king, and Henry soon read Cromwell's letters and sent word to St James' Palace. But time apart was not kind to Cromwell; Castillon had almost convinced Henry to marry Princess Mary to the Duke of Orleans and reported he had, 'gained the battle against the Lord Privy Seal... the Lord Privy Seal holds the King's hands at the expense of the crucifix'.[33] The French ambassador was correct; but Henry instructed Cromwell to go to Castillon and be 'gracious and more amiable to France than ever' and reported Cromwell walked with a limp, possibly after coming off his horse in late May. While Cromwell had been employing doctors and surgeons for servants, none attended Cromwell personally, so his pain could not have been too serious.[34]

Rumours continued to swirl; Ambassador Chapuys feared Princess Mary would marry the Duke of Cleves, and Henry would marry Duchess Anna.[35] Cromwellian Richard Morison entertained the German ambassadors, who were reminded of:

Crumwell's favour by the warrants sent them ... they shall return to Germany witnesses of Crumwell's love for religion ... and say idolatry would continue still were it not for his lordship ... My own prayer is to bind my friends to Crumwell. I dislike fickleness in friendship, which should be like marrying, for better, for worse. You may rejoice in being the only man in his place who has never forgotten his old friends. His lordship should try true from false friends.[36]

Cromwell's placating behaviour soothed King Henry, and Cromwell travelled on progress soon enough, to Havering, Eltham and Gravesend in June, and Lambeth, Fulham and Oaking in July, his huge entourage of servants, horses, greyhounds, spaniels, falcons, hawks, and cages with birds travelling with him.[37] Cromwell even bought himself a new 'cast of lannerets', African falcons, and purchased Sir George Somerset's house at Kew, right beside Richmond Palace.[38] When not travelling with the king, Cromwell stayed at a manor in Chelsea, next door to Thomas More's manor where Ambassador Castillon lived, but travelled by barge to Putney several times over several months, giving out money to the poor. More godchildren continued; Thomas Thacker, Cromwell's personal clerk, had a son named Thomas for his father and godfather. Also added to the Cromwell family of godchildren was a son for Sir Arthur Darcy and his wife Mary, plus the child of another of Cromwell's servants, sadly unrecorded.[39] The same month, Richard Woodall, one of Cromwell's old merchant friends, wrote in a panic to his master, telling him that he would die of ague if he did not have his master's comfort, which he gained, and fortunately survived.[40]

The mammoth transformation of Lewes progressed at a speedy and expensive rate, with Gregory preparing for the royal progress to pass through.[41] Cromwell and his men were well-prepared; Thacker had purchased yellow velvet for clothing costing 53l (£22,500 today), along with lengths of cloths to make hose for Cromwell, and lace to create ribands for Cromwell's glasses. For the second time in as many months, Peter the apothecary was called for Cromwell, costing 33s (close to £700 today). Cromwell needed silver cutlery for Lewes and the costs of finishing Gregory's house ran into the thousands ahead of King Henry's visit.

Cromwell travelled through Petworth, Portsmouth, Arundell Castle, Mayfield, Sheffield Park, and Firle where friend Sir John Gage lived (no longer a monk and back at court), just five miles from Gregory's home at Lewes Priory.[42] Cromwell found time to enjoy himself, losing 1ll at dice at Mayfield, another 10l (£4,300 today) at Arundell, and bought beavers for his menagerie.[43] The court travelled through Kent and Cromwell stopped in Canterbury, where Thomas Becket's bones were removed from Canterbury Cathedral and destroyed.[44]

Over the summer, Cromwell wrote his draft entitled *Touching the Reading of the Bible*. The English Bible would be freely available in all churches and homes, to be read and spoken in a language everyone could understand. Cromwell wrote to the clergy, 'Where it has pleased the king's Majesty... to permit and command the Bible being translated into our mother tongue, to be sincerely taught and declared by us the curate, and to be openly laid forth in every parish church, to the intent that all his good subjects... and so, by your good and virtuous example, to encourage your wives, children, and servants to live well and Christianly...'[45] This soon became the Injunctions to the Clergy, making it law to provide bibles and religious instruction in English and the reformed faith.[46] Cromwell also expected all clergymen to record local births, deaths and marriages, something forever beloved by historians and genealogists.

Cromwell had friend Miles Coverdale print the first 2,500 copies of the Bible in Paris, and they tried to organise an English printer in London for the remainder,[47] and by mid-September, Cromwell's greatest achievement was now real, complete with a cover that featured King Henry, Archbishop Cranmer, and Cromwell himself, handing books to the people. Given the dissolutions and the new Bible, Cromwell and Cranmer could feel as if their reformation finally made progress.

As queenmaker, Cromwell felt less successful. King Henry had not met with the German and Schmalkaldic embassies all summer, and the Cromwellians sent to hold Imperial alliance meetings were similarly disappointing. Vaughan and Wriothesley were in Brussels, but Wriothesley caught an ague on arrival and immediately was unable to move,[48] and Cromwell sent his personal apothecary Philip to Brussels.[49] Cromwell's friend Dr Edward Kerne volunteered to head to Brussels, Wriothesley relieved of the back-up, writing to Cromwell he, 'hoped to raise almost from death to live and serve my master'.[50] Vaughan was no better, unable to meet with Queen Regent Mary, confiding in Cromwell that he thought himself unworthy, calling the meeting, 'a charge far weightier than is mete for a man of so slender learning and judgement'.[51]

By Christmas, Wriothesley was still too sick to undertake any work, and negotiations to marry Duchess Christina of Milan lost another three months of progress.[52] As Duchess Christina had already remarked when Philip Hoby and Hans Holbein went to create her portrait, 'if I had two heads, one should be at the King of England's disposal'.

Cromwell also needed to deal with treason on his doorstep. Sir Geoffrey Pole had been in the Tower for months on suspicions of communicating with traitor Cardinal Pole, and interrogations began in September. After several attempts to gain information, Pole suffered a mental breakdown and tried to kill himself. Still, information was gathered; Cardinal Reginald Pole still wanted England to revert to the old religion, and as a result, all correspondence with him into England was banned. Seemingly, his brother Geoffrey, plus Henry Pole Lord Montagu, Sir Edward Neville, along with Henry Courtenay, Marquess of Exeter, had no interest in obeying this law. The king's cousins corresponding with a direct traitor posed a serious threat to Henry and his crown. Cromwell's man in Padua, Thomas Theobald, told Cromwell that Cardinal Pole claimed, 'but for my crafty and subtle conveyance, Crumwell would have beheaded me, not considering that I am a person whose life can neither hinder nor further the King or Crumwell'.[53] Theobald did fine work for Cromwell, though when getting Italian verses translated and sent to England, he accidentally included 'villainous verses' in the packet and was terrified Cromwell would be mad. They surely were not the first 'villainous' Italian verses Cromwell had read in his time.

The worrying reality was the Pole and Courtenay families were happy to topple Henry. Margaret Pole, Countess of Salisbury, had just seen her Bisham Abbey destroyed before her eyes, only a year after its founding, the final straw for the Catholic royal cousins. They saw themselves as the last 'White Roses', believed in Princess Mary as heir and had seen many of their allies already killed, like More, Fisher, the Holy Maid of Kent, and Pilgrimage traitors Darcy and Hussey. Rumours of Reginald Pole's desire to revert England, and rumours he could marry his cousin Princess Mary (despite being a cardinal), circled all summer. If Reginald Pole could not be captured, the rest of the Pole family could substitute. Cromwell's interrogations of Geoffrey Pole began on 26 October, fifty-nine questions put to the weakest Pole brother, mostly about his illegal correspondence with Reginald. Henry Pole Lord Montagu also had correspondence to and from his brother and ferried correspondence to others in England.

Montagu had Sir Thomas More's works in his possession, letters against the king's religious changes, and letters of how Cardinal Pole tried to get foreign aid to the Pilgrimage rebels. Sir Geoffrey's mental state meant he spilled the details, naming his family and allies as enemies of the king. By early November, Montagu and Exeter were in the Tower as royal cousins who thought themselves suitable to be king.

Exeter's wife, Gertrude Courtenay, who had rallied against King Henry on multiple occasions, confessed she knew of the conspiracy and Sir Edward Neville's involvement (as uncle to Montagu's wife Jane). Neville, 'trusted this world would amend and that honest men should rule one day', and Gertrude confessed she knew her family would be safe during the Pilgrimage of Grace as 'good northern lords would rule one day after the knaves, such as King Henry and his men, were put down'. The Exeter conspiracy papers survive in part, with Cromwell's handwriting as he took a personal interest in arrests, proceedings, and interrogations. While most of the information needed was completed by 7 November, interrogation against relatives and servants continued through the month. Exeter and Montagu's trial began on 3 December, Cromwell ranked third on the list of judges (below only Norfolk and Suffolk).[54] Geoffrey Pole and Edward Neville had a separate trial on the same day, as while they were involved, they did not see themselves as suitable replacements for the king.[55] All was well-planned, and the men were certainly guilty, and the result saw Exeter, Montagu and Neville swiftly executed. All guilty co-conspirators were dead by January, but Sir Geoffrey Pole was pardoned and released after his second suicide attempt at Christmas. These were King Henry's cousins; Exeter had been brought up in the same household as the king and had once been married to a member of the Grey family. The threat was close to King Henry's heart.

By 17 December, King Henry was finally, officially, excommunicated from the Catholic church. The whole incident did little more than anger the king further, giving Cromwell the chance to further the Reformation in England. Sir Edward Neville had been the Constable of Leeds Castle, and Cromwell received the title. Just before the trial, Cromwell had purchased the Guildford estates at Halden in Kent from Sir John Dudley, who needed the money (and was the son of Cecily Grey, who begged for Cromwell's help). Cromwell had also received Mottenden Priory, which accompanied vast lands through Mottenden, Plushenden, Plomford, and Delmynden.[56] Halden sat just fourteen miles from Leeds Castle, and it was quickly assumed Cromwell condemned Neville to gain Leeds Castle, which seems more like a coincidence given the dates of purchase. Halden cost Cromwell 3,500l, in addition to other purchases that month Golston and Lees Manors at 800l, Folkeston and Walton for 1,574l all in Kent, plus 1,000l for Brampton Manor, as a gift to Richard Cromwell.[57] Taking over Leeds Castle from Neville was not planned, but certainly looked like a conspiracy from the outside. Reginald Pole was happy to continue the theory of Cromwell as England's Machiavelli. Cromwell must have felt a little nervous; in late 1538, he called his armourer over from Antwerp, bringing with him new high-quality German rivets to build added protection.[58] Ralph and Ellen Sadler gave Cromwell more need to be careful, with yet another son, baby Henry, added to the family.

Cromwell was deeply in need of land in Kent by late 1538, and Leeds Castle now available was a lucky acquisition. He needed luck; for his personal life, so carefully curated and managed, had completely collapsed during the Exeter Conspiracy. Cromwell had been at odds with former ally Bishop Sampson of Chichester for some time, and when a storm broke, Sampson could not turn to the Lord Privy Seal and went to Richard Cromwell for help. In a letter misidentified as 17 June (but is likely late November or early December), Sampson wrote of an unfolding disaster in Sussex. The letter, now mutilated, concerned Gregory Cromwell at Lewes. Sampson wrote, 'the young man' needed to attend church at Chichester, forty miles west of Lewes Priory on a Sunday, 'and with a low voice, to the priest that shall sing mass, say, I knowledge myself to have offended Almighty God and the world, and I desire mercy of God', and then distribute bread to the poor. Sampson added, 'the young man has been with me this morning and scornfully refused this penance. Wherefore, I advertise you of it, praying you to weigh it as a matter that touches much the honesty of your friend. For surely if there be any business for it, I will advertise the King's Majesty of the whole. And I doubt not but when my Lord Privy Seal shall hear the truth, he will assist me in it'.[59]

Sampson was amid having his Chichester cathedral dissolved and its relics stripped, including the shrine of St Richard. Given Sampson needed to give out punishment to Gregory Cromwell, and Richard knew of the situation by the time this letter was written, suggests only two crimes; heresy or sexual assault.[60] Eighteen-year-old Gregory had been left to enjoy the high life since childhood, given everything without having to earn it, so it is not reasonable to think he may have made an off-hand comment that could have been insulting or even sound heretical to the Catholic bishop. But Gregory was no scholar, no politician like his father, and never showed any interest in religion. Also, that a heretical comment could receive a small punishment but provoke his father in such a wild manner is at odds with reality, leaving only sexual crimes. The church tended to turn a blind eye to (men's) adultery, equally seduction or coercion without consent. Whatever Gregory did, Sampson said it would affect Gregory's 'honesty', which in turn would harm the 'reputation' of Elizabeth, sister to late Queen Jane. Whatever sexual assault Gregory committed (and it cannot have been against Elizabeth), it was enough to potentially make a scandal of the Cromwell family. Given that sexual crimes are rarely punished even today, particularly by the Catholic church, Gregory must have done something especially heinous.

Cromwell had nurtured his only son, given him the world, gained him a noble bride, and had just finished spending countless thousands on Lewes Priory. Suddenly, the young Cromwell household needed to be broken up, Gregory whisked out of Sussex entirely. Sir John Gage nearby offered to lease the Lewes lands so Cromwell could get out at once,[61] and now Cromwell was the largest landowner in Kent, he had somewhere to hide his useless son. Gregory was shipped up to Mortlake Manor, and a letter from Elizabeth Cromwell arrived, stating she would stay half a mile from Mortlake Manor. Elizabeth wrote, 'this letter from you is more pleasure to me than any earthly good, for my trust is now only in you ... your humble daughter-in-law'.[62] Cromwell needed to pay for Gregory at Mortlake for Christmas and pay servants to attend Elizabeth, who was six months pregnant while she cared for ten-month-old Henry.

Loyal Henry Polstead and John Williamson from Austin Friars, who had worked tirelessly to prepare Lewes Priory throughout the year, began works to remove all trace of the Cromwells in December 1538, a four-month process.[63] At the same time, Cromwell received Oakham in Rutland and put the manor and lands in Gregory and Henry Cromwell's names,[64] but possibly did not have the heart to banish his family 100 miles north from London, when the now-empty Leeds Castle was only forty miles east. Within six months, all trace of the Cromwells' life and manors in Sussex were gone. This crime undermined everything Cromwell created for Gregory, and yet has largely been erased from records, and the year came to an end in a way that would have put Cromwell near the end of his rope.

Chapter 16

1539: Malady

'you were born at a happy hour, for do or say what you,
the King will always take it well at your hand'

With all Cromwell's land purchases over the last several months, he likely updated his will. Given how hard life was about to become, the Cromwellian servants probably felt as if they needed that will on hand. But as New Year was upon the court, at least outwardly, all seemed well in the Cromwell household. Cromwell's official New Year gift was the role of Constable of Leeds Castle.[1] In return, Cromwell gave King Henry a customary gold cup, gifts to the men of the court to the value of 150l (£63,000 today) and gave out forty-two ounces of silver-gilt spoons. Gifts arrived from all over England from the Duke of Norfolk, Ellen Sadler, the Earl of Oxford, Edward Baynton, Anthony Bonvisi, Lady Elizabeth (Grey) Audley. Cromwell spent six weeks at Greenwich with the king, ordering two stools to rest his legs on, suggesting he was not feeling his best. Cromwell had a private barge that went up and down the Thames regularly to make sure the Lord Privy Seal could keep up with work over the festive season. The Cromwell household enjoyed pheasants, partridges and apples, new clothes, and cash rewards for the servants. Cromwell spent 10l on his part in a masque, employed Prince Edward's minstrels for their music and had his own players perform a show for the household. Gregory, despite his appalling behaviour, continued to siphon money from his father's accounts, for shoes, a new saddle and various other 'bits'. Cromwell gave cash gifts to his precious nephew Richard, his niece Alice, and her brother William Wellyfed, and 6s 8d (about £150 today) to 'a poor woman for bringing a nightingale', and 90l (£38,000 today) on luxurious black sable fabric.[2] Yet none of Cromwell's accounts show the usual parties, celebrations, and gambling usually prevalent at this time of year. Gregory's despicable behaviour and evacuation from Sussex put a damper on spirits.

Cromwell's bank account was equally healthy, starting the year earning almost 2,000l in gifts, rents, pensions, income for his ward John Lord Conyers, loan repayments, and gifts given in semi-anonymous ways; 80l in handkerchiefs, 12l in a pair of gloves, 6l in a white purse, 20l in a black velvet purse, all coming one after another during the festive season, the givers unrecorded.[3] All of these would go well towards the gift Cromwell bought himself; lands and manors around Dunsford, Wandsworth and Wimbledon, now owning more land around where he was humbly born many years earlier.[4]

Despite being the master of the Exeter Conspiracy, Cromwell had no cause to see any of the men dead, while King Henry pushed for executions. It was not over; Henry was suspicious of Sir Nicholas Carew, despite not having the dynastic connections of the others. Carew was a well-known papist; he sided with Cromwell to bring down Anne Boleyn and was friends with Exeter and Montagu. When Carew was on the jury for the Exeter trials, he doubted the evidence and legal process, but a rumour stated Carew and the king played bowls and joked together early in the new year, and Carew hit a sore spot of Henry's fragile ego. Cromwell was godfather to Carew's grandson; Elizabeth Cromwell was close friends with Carew's son-in-law. Either way, Cromwell had no choice but to arrest Carew on Henry's orders.

Carew suffered the same way many did; Henry's current angry mood saw the conservative Princess Mary supporter out of the king's favour. Letters belonging to Carew were represented as vague treason, and he was convicted on 14 February.[5] Nothing of the situation survives in Cromwell's collection on the matter, though his attendant Richard Pollard wrote up Carew's interrogation (as he had for the Exeter arrests), and Cromwell sat in judgement over his former ally.[6] Cromwell's man in the Tower, Thomas Philips, is said to have converted Carew with English Bible readings in the Tower, but Carew was executed on 3 March at Tower Hill. All Cromwell could do was respond to Lady Elizabeth Carew's letters to ensure she had access to money and lands for herself and her children.[7] Both Cromwell and his nephew Richard sent her money until all was finalised six months after the execution when Henry calmed down.

Cromwell was not happy with the Exeter Conspiracy killings; he had hoped the Duke of Norfolk would be condemned, as he posed a far more dangerous threat to court. Yet again, Norfolk remained elusive. Cromwell interrogated Lady Gertrude Courtenay in the Tower multiple times about Norfolk, and people were surprised Cromwell would question a woman so 'harshly'.[8] He was in a foul mood; Lady Lisle had a brief trip from Calais and stopped Cromwell at court on a trivial matter, and he snapped at her too, leaving her feeling shaken by his uncharacteristic outburst.[9]

Cromwell still had reasons to be cheerful; Henry named him Chief Nobleman of the Privy Chamber and removed conservatives Sir Francis Bryan and Sir Anthony Browne from his retinue, and replaced them with Philip Hoby, Richard Morison and John Lascelles, all Cromwellian friends.[10] A new council to control the West Country was set up, headed by Cromwell's dear friend Sir John Russell, newly made a baron. Lord Chancellor Audley was also made a baron, though Cromwell pushed the king for a higher honour for Audley.[11] Things may have been positive domestically, but internationally they fell apart.

The Exeter Conspiracy had emboldened the Irish papists and the FitzGeralds considered themselves the Irish equivalent of the White Roses. Lord Leonard Grey sympathised too much with the papists.[12] But Cromwell's faith in the Grey family meant Lord Leonard kept his head. Cromwell's childhood friend Anthony St Leger was considered a replacement for Grey, but then letters arrived from others in the Irish Council, Cromwell's other men William Brabazon, John Allen, and Archbishop Browne, who hated Grey's seditious behaviour, but also feared St Leger embezzled the king's funds while paying the army.[13] Parliamentary sessions and masses still took place, but it was not enough. On 3 February, King Henry appointed Cromwell Vice-Gerent of Ireland, to run their government and close religious houses there, just as in England and Wales. Cromwell's men would be the new deputies to the project and report to Cromwell directly, not Deputy Grey. At once Cromwell's men got to work, and almost immediately, Christ Church Cathedral's priory in Dublin was suppressed and reopened with a dean and chapter, to begin life as a reformed college, just as Cromwell had opened in Norwich the previous year.[14] For a rare moment, peace came to the Irish Council.

Negotiations in Europe fared no better. As early as 1 January, bedridden Wriothesley wrote from Brussels, warning he, Kerne and Vaughan no longer felt safe. France and Scotland had been making idle threats towards England, and with the French-Imperial alliance advancing, King Henry had a right to feel threatened.[15] Without any official words said, it was clear international tensions were mounting against England. King Henry went to Dover, to oversee fortification plans, leaving Cromwell in charge in London, with Ralph Sadler at the king's side on Cromwell's behalf. Henry announced he wanted all nunneries closed, to finance any potential defences needed against the Emperor. Nunneries were full of noble daughters and Cromwell had left them alone throughout the dissolution process, but King Henry's fears meant they were no longer safe.[16] Emperor Charles slowly headed to Germany to handle the states breaking away from the Empire, and Cromwell dispatched Christopher Mont and Thomas Paynell to Cleves, to negotiate a marriage between King Henry and Duchess Anna. If the Catholic nations were gathering, the Reformation states needed to do the same.

The first open sign of trouble came in early February when French ambassador Castillon met with Cromwell at Austin Friars. Castillon was desperate to meet with the king and Cromwell discovered Castillon wanted to return to France, only one year into his job. Cromwell first took Castillon on a private tour of his vast Austin Friars manor and spent time in the armoury. Cromwell was clearly showing off, having much of the leftover armour and artillery used by Richard Cromwell during the Pilgrimage of Grace, enough to arm hundreds of men. Cromwell boasted there were more than twenty lords in England who could raise an army in defence of their king should an enemy surface, not being even a little subtle with the French ambassador.[17]

Though it rarely happened, Cromwell personally needed help from France. His blessed English Bibles, the first 2,500 copies, which had cost 2,000 crowns (£430,000 today), were confiscated by the Inquisitor-General in the Paris Faculty of Theology at the Sorbonne.[18] The wary Catholics were suspicious of the English Bibles, and Cromwell needed to make a deal. Luckily, he had a card to play; the Rochepot Affair. Over the years, several situations arose where international ships came to grief with one another, the issues passing over Cromwell's desk at regular intervals. Cromwell and Chapuys resolved these issues without too much trouble. But a French ship, owned by François de Montmorency, Sieur de la Rochepot, was one of three which attacked Easterling (northern German) merchant ships. When Rochepot's ship docked in England, it was confiscated as a pirate ship, the attack first appearing in Cromwell's remembrances in November 1537. The ship sat stuck in port through 1538 and into 1539, and now, Cromwell could release Rochepot's ship if France released the bibles. The French thought Cromwell wanted Rochepot's ship for its precious cargo of wine and wool, but there has never been any evidence to support the claim. It worked; the Constable of France allowed the release of the bibles just before the escalating European tensions. King Henry did not allow Cromwell to release the ship in return, but in his defence, there were more pressing issues.

Wriothesley reported to Cromwell from Brussels; he had finally made some recovery from his ague after four months, and had a guest; Henry Phelips, the man who betrayed England's William Tyndale, leading to this execution in late 1536. Despite anger from Cromwell and King Henry, Wriothesley wrote, 'the fellow has a great wit, he is excellent in language, he is no man of estimation nor can do any manner of hurt at any time hereafter, he has freely yielded himself, thinking it better to be hanged than to live a traitor, his experience is great and may serve if the fellow may be well won'.[19] Cromwell wanted to get his hands on Phelips, but international tensions prevented this (and it probably did not help that Frances Cromwell's uncle was one of Phelips' servants); Wriothesley and Edward Kerne were suddenly invited to court with Queen Regent Mary and the Duchess of Milan, despite more than a year of stalled marriage negotiations.[20] The pair were treated to a sumptuous event, only for Mary to then impose blockades against all English ships in ports throughout the Low Countries. All trade halted, and Wriothesley, Kerne and Stephen Vaughan were prevented from leaving. Queen Mary would lift the embargo only if King Henry sent her Ambassador Chapuys.[21] A permanent ambassador in England was a sign of peace and amity, and losing Chapuys sparked great worry, especially with no promise of a replacement. King Henry controlled Dover for the defence of the coast, and Richard Cromwell was the man to oversee Calais and head up fortifications and preparations.[22] Cromwell wrote up long remembrance lists for preparations for Dover, Calais, and Berwick in the north, ordered work on all coastal beacons, and started work on mustering men for battle. Emperor Charles was ready to declare war on behalf of Christendom.[23] All ships in England were ordered to be held in port, sparking anger from the merchants, with Norfolk sending all the complaints to Cromwell's desk.[24]

King Henry did not wish to release Eustace Chapuys, but Cromwell wrote to Henry at Dover, quietly trying to get the ambassador released, and got him a new passport. The man had become something of a close friend, one of the few Cromwell made at court.[25] Eventually, Henry agreed to swap Chapuys for Wriothesley and Kerne, and Chapuys fled to Calais. He sent Cromwell a letter a week later, written in Spanish to 'Milort Crumuel', apologising for his flight without saying goodbye, and swore to stay there until he knew Wriothesley and Kerne were safe.[26] Now was the time to ally with Saxony and Hesse, get Wriothesley and Kerne evacuated from Brussels, and see if the errant Imperial ambassador Wyatt could finally report useful news.[27]

While everything happening abroad seemed little more than posturing, England could not afford to hope for the best. Thomas Wyatt got the news he longed to hear; Cromwell wrote to tell him to leave the Emperor's court and return home.[28] His mistress Bess Darrell had been worried for some time, writing to Cromwell for Wyatt's safe return.[29] Cromwell began mustering men himself, having to travel to his lands to find tenants and servants ready to fight. But it was the most nervous ambassador of all, endless ally Stephen Vaughan, left behind in Brussels, who stepped up for Cromwell. Not only did Vaughan enquire about getting 1,000 men in the Low Countries to fight on Henry's behalf, but he also went on a mission to see which ships were leaving Antwerp in defiance of the Emperor and got more information from Queen Mary's court than Wriothesley and Kerne managed in six months of work. Vaughan heard the Turks were looking to attack Imperial areas, distracting the Emperor from invading England.[30]

Cromwell could have been forgiven for neglecting domestic or personal affairs but on 6 April, he started putting together names for parliament, the first session in three years, to tidy up loose ends within the country. Despite all his current issues, Cromwell still found time to do what he did best; hiding away in his offices for long periods and creating bills and drafts to be put to parliament, using his legal and administrative skills to best effect. Cromwell had multiple ideas; plans to improve his failed Poor Laws of 1536, spread the English Bibles, make changes to religion, destroy shrines, ban indulgences, and change religious holidays.

Dissolution of the Monasteries had come a long way in three years, and Cromwell looked again to halt dissolution in favour of reforming and reopening them as colleges, places of education, charity, and assistance for the communities they served. With the arrival of the English Bibles in April, including Cromwell's personal beautiful painted copy, Cromwell reopened the London Greyfriars as his publishing house for the outstanding 6,500 copies.

Cromwell did not have the final say on which MPs entered the Commons; that belonged to the king, who chose many of Cromwell's friends; Edward Baynton, John Gage, John Gostwick, William Godolphin, John Heneage, Richard Pollard, Richard Southwell, and Thomas Pope. Cromwell also received a gift from Lord Morley after his son Henry Parker was selected, fresh copies of Machiavelli's *History of Florence* and the famous *The Prince*, with a note saying they would be useful in dealing with the Privy Council.[31] Cromwell's adopted sons Richard Cromwell and Ralph Sadler were listed, as was his own son, Gregory, as an MP for Kent. The fact Cromwell wanted to push forward Gregory after his recent behaviour seemed to give the nineteen-year-old the kick he needed to get himself together.

Just before being summoned for parliament, Gregory was still with his father while Cromwell prepared Leeds Castle. John Williamson from Austin Friars, along with Richard Pollard and many other attendants, readied Leeds Castle in record time, building work going ahead along with livestock being brought up from Sussex, including the huge falcon collection Gregory had amassed at Lewes Priory. Cromwell regularly spent a great deal on his falconers, 50l (a solid annual wage for three men) throughout the year. The costs of setting up home at Leeds Castle for the Cromwells ran into the thousands, but Gregory did not leave London permanently for Leeds until late May, by which time, his wife Elizabeth reconciled with him and their second son, named Edward after his cousin the prince, was born.[32] Also going to Leeds was Cromwell's nine-year-old daughter Jane, and Cromwell paid 12l 14s 6d (almost £5,500 today) for Mistress Jane's new apparel.

Cromwell received a letter from Prioress Vernon, who had helped care for Gregory when he was still very young, saying, 'I hear there is a little gentlewoman with Master Sadler which I would very fain have the governance and bringing up, as it were to my comfort now in mine age'.[33]

It is possible Vernon meant Jane Cromwell, who would have been the perfect age for beginning education and could have been in the Sadler household, having lived at Austin Friars with Ellen Sadler for some time in her earliest years. Ellen Sadler also had her two daughters from her first marriage, who would have been around ten and eleven and may have stayed with their mother after she married Ralph Sadler. Whether Jane Cromwell remained in Leeds with Gregory, went to be educated with Prioress Vernon, or stayed with Mercy Prior at Austin Friars, remains a mystery. Ralph and Ellen Sadler needed all the help they could get. By 1539, they had three sons, Thomas, Edward and Henry, and a newborn daughter, Anne, all barely surviving a measles outbreak in Hackney.

Cromwell's personal life was mooted in contrast to other years; while he spent 38l on a masque about King Arthur's knights at the beginning of the year, other activities were rather quiet, though Austin Friars got a huge refit of a new gallery. Cromwell spent his time giving out alms in multiple places, giving money to staff in royal kitchens, lending money to other nobles, and buying items from Thomas Cranmer, such as satin gowns and fur sables at a cost of 21l, which he did not need.[34] Some other purchases were indicative of the period; he needed new tents for his mustered men, 109lbs of gunpowder, hay brought in from his manor at Stepney for new horses and he ordered 100 extra bow staves in case the Emperor invaded.[35] His nephew, William Wellyfed, was again in need, while William's siblings, Christopher and Alice, were self-sufficient. Cromwell also gained another four godchildren; Sir Anthony Lee and his wife Lady Margaret Wyatt had their fourth son, named Cromwell Lee, and Cromwell gave a generous 45s as payment to the midwife. George Brooke Lord Cobham, and his wife, Anne, also had another child, though this baby seems to have soon died. Sir Thomas Poyninges and his wife also received a payment for their new child, as did Peter Mewtas and his wife Lady Jane Astley for their son Thomas.[36] Soon after, Cromwell dispatched Mewtas with Hans Holbein to Germany to negotiate King Henry's marriage to Duchess Anna of Cleves.[37]

Among Cromwell's endless correspondence was the usual array of unhappy wives and widows. Old friend Elizabeth Howard was complaining the Duke of Norfolk tried to poison her, her children were ungracious, and needed money,[38] while Elizabeth Whettyl in Calais thanked Cromwell profusely for all his help, including taking her son

Gilbert into his service.[39] Cromwell also needed to pay the debt of his nephew Walter Cromwell, who owed the king money, likely taxes.[40] All these accompanied a sad letter; news from agent Thomas Theobald that his godfather, Thomas Boleyn, had died at Hever Castle.

Cromwell needed to be ready for parliament, but John Husee reported on 4 April that Cromwell was at Austin Friars and had not been seen in two days. Parliament was due to open on 28 April; German ambassadors had again arrived for a two-month summit on matters of alliance and religion, and worryingly, King Henry was writing religious doctrine. The last thing Cromwell and Cranmer needed was Henry interfering. Cromwell had lost a few friends too, a rare occasion. Sir William Fitzwilliam and his brother Sir Anthony Browne, Wolsey men who rose alongside Cromwell, had cooled their allegiance, and Sir William Paulet, who had helped Cromwell into parliament in 1529, leaned conservative even before Cromwell had Paulet's brother George thrown in the Tower for treason.

Cromwell remained tucked away at Austin Friars but wrote to Henry at court about the changes abroad, and news about the Emperor and the German States.[41] Ten days after Cromwell was last seen, on 12 April, his regular surgeon Forest arrived and was paid 20s (about £400 today) for whatever treatment he administered. Cromwell's dreaded ague had returned. A repeat of his 1535 disaster, Cromwell had again contracted ague, or malaria, after working night and day to prepare for parliament. The same illness had hobbled Wriothesley for months in Brussels and now had struck the Lord Privy Seal. On 19 April, Cromwell wrote to Henry as he was supposed to attend court:

> tomorrow, I might have waited and given my due and promised attendance upon your highness, but that I find upon me some grudge of an ague, and think that withstanding the first brutes by the sparing of one or two days, I shall be the better able to continue my duty of service towards your grace many months and years ... I shall not be idle but intend to your Majesty's service as I have done hitherto and shall as long as God shall give me breath and power to stir.[42]

Cromwell simplified his situation, but he could not hide forever. With ague giving the patient headaches, sweating, bleeding gums, jaundiced eyes, vomiting and bouts of fever so bad they caused seizures for days, Cromwell tried to work between these episodes. He sent Henry a letter four days later, discussing his thoughts on the international alliances and various ambassadors.[43] Cromwell wrote in English and Latin a day later to recommend Ambassadors Francis Burgartus and Ludwig von Baumbach from Saxony and Hesse who had arrived from Germany. Cromwell thanked Henry for allowing him to stay home, but admitted, 'this night I have had evil rest, this is the day of the access of my fit. If I can escape it, I hope to be some recovered. If it shall continue, then yet will I do my best to overcome it the soonest I can, for I think the time very long till I be better able to serve your Majesty'.[44]

Woefully, Cromwell was far from well. Parliament opened on 28 April, and he was not there. Cromwell's administrative diligence meant his bills could still be proposed through the Commons and Lords, and everything passed as required, but he could not be there to hear the debates and votes, nor see Gregory in the Commons alongside Ralph and Richard. But among it all came two acts Cromwell did not create: one incredible, another calamitous.

The House of Lords Precedence Act 1539,[45] written by King Henry, recreated the order of precedence of members in the House. This had not been done since the initial creation of English governance and was the true revolution of the Tudor government.[46] A lord's precedence was defined by bloodlines and birthrights, and Henry sought to change that, and thus diminish anyone with a claim to the throne. Instead, King Henry decided precedence on titles held; those who had worked their way into titles on merit. The entire noble ladder in the House of Lords, from barons up to dukes and bishops, would be changed. Cromwell was the lowest-ranked baron and now, as Principal Secretary, would become the highest-ranked baron in the land. Apart from being the head baron, as Vice-Gerent, Cromwell now sat as the highest man in the House of Lords, ranked above Archbishop Cranmer, then Archbishop Lee, and the bishops of the Privy Council. Henry then ranked men in the lords based on the top ten titles (Cromwell being fourth as Lord Privy Seal and tenth as Secretary), followed by nobility based on rank. As Vice-Gerent, Cromwell was only outranked by the king, and it neatly put him on the (right) clerical side of the house, far away from Norfolk on the (left) noble side, as Norfolk was the only one to complain (though being ranked second behind Chancellor

Audley, Norfolk promptly closed his mouth). King Henry had created an incredible shift in politics and nobility, entirely for personal gain, but for Cromwell, it shot him into superiority. All dukes, marquesses, viscounts and barons not holding a working title could no longer claim power over anyone working for their position close to the king. While we can see the list as making perfect sense today, at the time, it was a complete revision of what was known as power in England.

Regrettably, King Henry was not done. He put forward the Act of Six Articles, to replace Cromwell and Cranmer's Ten Articles written in 1536. Henry put forward his six issues to a synod of eight bishops, four from each side of the debate, with the Duke of Norfolk overseeing the discussions while the Vice-Gerent was too sick to attend. As Vice-Gerent, Cromwell should have been there to make decisions and was the best politician to see through the debates. The synod went ahead on 6 May, and soon after, Cromwell was seen for the first time, able to travel one mile from his home at Austin Friars to his office at St James' Palace, unable to move any more, let alone work with his ague. It was a highlight of King Henry's cruelty; he gave Cromwell ultimate power with one act, and then denied him the right to use his power by hosting the Six Articles debate during Cromwell's illness.

Of the six issues debated, the Reformation lost on five of the six articles; the Eucharist was again the true body of Christ, clerical celibacy was compulsory, vows of chastity and widowhood had to be obeyed by law, and private masses were again the law. Reformers gained a little ground in the final law; confession was still necessary, though not divine law. To break any other of the articles meant a death penalty or substantial imprisonment, at odds with reformist doctrine.

Married clergymen such as Cranmer had less than a month to 'put away' their wives and families.[47] Margarete Cranmer had been in England for four or five years by this time, an open secret among Cranmer's homes with their daughter Margaret, who was around six in 1539. At once, Cranmer was forced to send them to Germany, and not see them for eight years. Cromwell away with his ague had caused a great deal of pain. Cromwell's long-time friend from Austin Friars turned Archbishop of Dublin, George Browne, had a wife and three children, he too was among Cromwell's closest friends who had been harmed.

At once, things started spiralling into panic. Cromwell's two long-time reformist bishops, Latimer and Shaxton, both quit their dioceses in protest and were put under house arrest. Alexander Alesius, who Cromwell had teaching at Cambridge, quickly fled the country to Germany to escape the coming onslaught. Cromwell and Cranmer likely gathered to discuss the Articles and it would have been easy to panic, but the Cromwell Bible still belonged to Henry and his Thomases. Cromwell and Cranmer could still feel confident they could push forward with the Reformation, though they were losing support around them.

While all the drama of parliament continued, the potential battles against international foes did not stop. On 8 May, as the muster of men around London paraded through the city before the king, Cromwell was able to stand on his balcony at St James' to see the occasion. Ralph Sadler led the 20,000 men from Stepney through the city to Whitehall and the king, with Richard and Gregory Cromwell both leading the Cromwell contingent of 1,500 armed men, at a cost of 400l (£170,000 today) for uniforms and weapons from the Austin Friars armoury.[48] Despite his illness, Cromwell was able to plan the muster and parade through his friends at the London Council but could do little on the day due to his ague, yet another occasion missed.

Two months after first becoming ill, Cromwell got back to work, but any chance of peace and unity in religion was lost, and as friend Bishop Shaxton wrote to Cromwell in early July when parliament closed, 'Our Lord save you from all the power of your adversaries'.[49] At least the Catholic states were appeased by the Six Articles, but the Germans now considered Henry weak.

The worst was yet to come. Cromwell stayed at Stepney, and then at Mortlake to recover from his ague, missing the entire parliamentary session. After years of leasing Canonbury Manor, he purchased it for himself for the odd figure of 296l and sent Henry his leopard, with a velvet collar made especially for the new royal pet.[50] On 2 July, Henry, already off on progress, commanded Archbishop Cranmer to host a banquet at Lambeth Palace, with both sides of the religious divide ordered to attend, as everyone remained in London. Henry did not attend, but Cromwell, starting to return to health after three full months, could attend his first public occasion. The banquet would go down in infamy.

As a man freshly recovered from a torturous illness, Cromwell was far from the calculating, charming man he portrayed at court. Cranmer's secretary Ralph Morice recorded the evening, which formed the basis of John Foxe's later book detailing the event. Cromwell and Cranmer were warmest friends and allies, two leaders of the Reformation in England. Morice recalled a rarely recorded argument between the pair. Cromwell muttered to Cranmer:

> you were born at a happy hour, for do or say what you, the King will always take it well at your hand. And I must needs confess that in some things I have complained of you unto His Majesty, but all in vain, for he will never give credit against you, whatsoever is laid to your charge, but let me or any other of the Council be complained of, his Grace will most seriously chide and fall out with us.[51]

Whether this uncommon, disrespectful, and candid complaint came before or after the main fireworks is unknown, as Cromwell again made a scene, publicly fighting with the ever-present, ever-meddling, Duke of Norfolk. Norfolk gave a speech about King Henry's love for Cranmer, and compared Cranmer to Wolsey, calling Wolsey 'a churlish prelate ... who could never abide a nobleman ... you know well enough Lord Crumwell, for he was your master ...'[52] Morice then put down his quill, unwilling to record the awful things Norfolk insinuated about Wolsey and Cromwell.

Cromwell, only just out of his sickbed, and already surrounded by enemies and a tense meeting of religious views, stood up to defend Wolsey. He told the room he did not regret his time with Wolsey, well-paid and well-provided for during their six-year friendship. Cromwell then roundly turned against Norfolk, giving him a caustic sixteenth-century dressing down, among other things, saying, 'I was never so far in love with (Wolsey) as to have waited upon him in Rome if he had been chosen Pope, as I understand (Norfolk) would have done'. The exchange does not sound hostile now, but it implied Norfolk was prepared to serve the Catholic faith and the Pope over his king, which would be treason. Norfolk bellowed a denial to the claim. Cromwell, through a lack of manners and a vast memory, told everyone Norfolk received 50,000 florins to transport Wolsey to Rome in 1523 when Wolsey was in place to become the Pope. The florins were proof of Norfolk's plan to go to Rome with Wolsey. While Cranmer and others at the banquet diffused the screaming match, which was unquestionably complemented by bountiful wine and strong egos, the match had been lit between the men. Neither needed to wear the mask of courtesy again, as the peers of the realm had seen and heard all. Cromwell did not know it, but this banquet was the beginning of his ultimate downfall.

A few days later, new French ambassador, Charles Marillac, wrote to the Constable of France, saying Cromwell, 'made so honest a reply that if he were as strong in keeping promises as he is bold in making them, (Marillac) might have good hope',[53] concerning the settling of the Rochepot Affair. Cromwell had his English Bibles, but Henry wanted to hold the trial against the pirating ship in England, so Cromwell could not release the ship. Cromwell instead worked on the business of the Earl of Desmond attempting to rebel in Ireland, before setting off on progress, meeting King Henry at Oatlands on 11 July. The Cromwellian household moved from St James' to Mortlake, requiring three barge trips just to carry Cromwell's apparel. On progress, all his falcons journeyed with him, plus his sixteen spaniels, spaniel wrangler Humphrey getting an extra tip for all the work. Cromwell even took his own bed to each stop on the progress.[54]

As the progress moved through Guildford, Farnham, and Oaking, Cromwell took time to catch up on proceedings in parliament,[55] and Edward Seymour was keen to hear rumours of how Anna of Cleves could still be an option of a royal bride.[56] The Duke of Suffolk had also heard the rumour and wanted to hear it directly from Cromwell.[57] The rumour was true; the king still needed a marriage, and despite the Six Articles now being law, the conservatives had not made the progress that they hoped. As soon as Cromwell was at Henry's side again, he was pulling the royal strings. Alexander Alesius, freshly free of England, wrote from Germany, trying to convince others that Cromwell still adhered to the new faith, and England could still ally with the German States.[58]

By 2 August, Elizabeth Cromwell, newly pregnant yet again, was living at Leeds Castle with Gregory; the hard-won marriage had been repaired, the family settling in with babies Henry and Edward. John Williamson had been with Gregory and Elizabeth in Leeds but had fallen ill. Many of the Cromwell family were there; Richard Cromwell's wife Frances and baby son Henry, and Richard's brothers Walter and Gregory, whose young son was also stricken ill. Fortunately, all soon recovered.[59] At Austin Friars, Henry Farlion, the king's apparel-maker, suddenly died while working on Henry and Cromwell's tents being made for troops. Thacker shut away the body and all the royal tents in case of illness.[60] Fortunately, everyone else at Austin Friars also survived.

The Norfolk incident had not gone unacknowledged; now-enemies William Fitzwilliam, William Kingston and Anthony Browne got together to plan a coup against Cromwell, to oust him from the Privy Council. They went to Bishop Cuthbert Tunstall, the one to approach the king on the matter. The men badly mistimed their coup; Cromwell was at the king's side most days and knew when to, and when not to approach a king angry with painful ulcers. The coup fell apart at once.[61] Cromwell was no fool; he could see he needed to regain power on the Privy Council after three months away, and convinced Henry to eject enemies Stephen Gardiner and Bishop Sampson from Council, which would have been a pure delight. Bishop Stokesley of London, whom Cromwell long hated, politely dropped dead, making life a little simpler.

Progress carried on through Surrey and Oxfordshire, Cromwell stopping at Newbury, Burford, Woodstock, the new build at Nonsuch Palace, then Grafton, Ampthill, and Langley. Cromwell received a gift from Lubeck, two elk, which he would keep at Stepney.[62] His servants were busy with the falcons, hawks, dogs, and horses travelling with Cromwell, with extra tips in his monthly bills for them, falconers Roger, Davy, and Richard in particular. Cromwell's laundry bill listed fifty-five dozen items washed in September, showing he had plenty to do through the summer.

All the relaxation of progress had calmed Henry and given him time to consider marriages and alliances. With Emperor Charles distracted, and France seemingly uninterested in England, Cromwell assigned Christopher Mont and Nicholas Wotton to go into Germany to discuss marriage to Anna of Cleves and create an alliance with the Schmalkaldic League.[63] At the same time, Duke Wilhelm of Cleves sent ambassadors to England; one group from Cleves stayed with Cranmer at Lambeth to discuss marriage, and a second group from the Schmalkaldic League would stay at St James' Palace with Cromwell to discuss alliances.[64]

In mid-September, Cromwell left the king at Ampthill, and went to visit his old friend George Cavendish, losing 51 at dice, before visiting

Richard Cromwell's new home Hinchingbrooke Manor, before a quick
trip back to London, purchasing a new satin gown on the way.[65] He
received a letter from court, announcing the king had fallen ill. Thomas
Heneage wrote he delayed Cromwell's servant at court because King
Henry wished to send Cromwell a unicorn (narwhal) horn, but his illness
meant Heneage was unwilling to press Henry for the horn. Given the
alleged healing properties of the unicorn horn, the gift was quite an
honour. But Henry was suffering 'a very fair siege' with the privy stool,
and no one dared press Henry about the gift.[66]

Cromwell had no time for the king's intestinal eruptions, after two
years of stalled marriage considerations, Henry suddenly wanted a new
bride. By September, Cromwell's remembrances were nothing more than
marriage preparations, planning the legal aspects of a union.[67] Everyone
was excited to see Hans Holbein's new portrait of Anna of Cleves, but
Cromwell was squirrelled away in his offices at St James' Palace, preparing
the mountain of paperwork required at both ends to ensure the marriage
could go ahead at Henry's sudden insistence.

On 6 October, the fourteen-page Latin marriage treaty was signed by
the king and his closest men – Cromwell, Cranmer, Audley, Suffolk,
Fitzwilliam, and Tunstall. Henry was so taken with Anna he agreed to
waive the dower, and German delegates Henry Olisleger, Lord John a
Doltzike, William ab Harff and Francis Burgartus were equally thrilled.[68]
Cromwell would prepare everything, Anna was coming by land to 'protect
her beauty', and he prepared her passports when the Cleves delegation fell
short. Cromwell's endless ally, Stephen Vaughan, was ready to receive
Lady Anna in Flanders but also warned of large troop movements in the
area.[69]

All was not well; Henry could marry Anna, but the Schmalkaldic
League were not impressed with the English Reformation. Martin
Luther wrote plainly:

Henry VIII acting against his conscience is clear... He has many
pious preachers like the deprived Bishop Latimer and Crumwell ...
Yet he used this very teaching which he now persecutes for a time
for his advantage ... He urges great kings to set up religions for
their convenience ... Henry cares nothing for the honour of God
... He cared little for this learning but meant to make a religion for

himself ... The King is a sophist (deceitful) and covers everything with glosses.[70]

The alliance between England and the German States was falling apart before the unwitting bride had even left home. French ambassador Marillac wrote on 25 October, 'his desire of issue (as he has only one male child), which he could not better have than with the said lady, who is of convenient age, healthy temperament, elegant stature, and endowed with other graces'. But the French too could see the cracks emerging, and the Emperor was unhappy with the match, warning Henry 'should never enjoy this sister of the Duke of Cleves', a direct threat.[71]

The Germans were not concerned, convinced the Six Articles would be abolished, saying Cromwell and Cranmer were, 'both excellent men, and most friendly to the purer doctrine of the Gospel. But God in his mercy seems to have turned the wicked counsel upon the heads of its authors, for these excellent men are now in greater favour than ever, and the papistical faction has no ways obtained its hoped-for tyranny'.[72] Cromwell needed to make sure the Germans felt safe; he ordered three abbots executed for defying monastery inspectors. The three men were hanged, drawn, and quartered and other large monasteries soon started surrendering, realising the end was near. Cromwell would have his reformation.

Ambassador Chapuys arrived back in England and went to King Henry with Ambassador Marillac, a rare occasion to voice concerns over the anti-Catholic marriage. Henry and Cromwell were outraged at their behaviour, and Henry suggested the pair were going to draw Scotland into a joint invasion of England. Emperor Charles' idle threats shook the court. Marillac wrote:

this very strange language, especially from Crumwell, who has the principal rule, as showing the extreme jealousy and fear they have fallen into, which in truth, is so great that nothing is said now except about defending themselves, everybody believing, despite all denials on my part, that the conclusion of treaties between Francis and the Emperor is only with a view of attacking them.[73]

Lady Anna's progress was slow; by 13 November, Anna, and her train of 350 servants had not completed the ninety-mile trek from Swan

Castle to Antwerp, where Stephen Vaughan awaited her.[74] Cromwell busied himself with getting more English Bibles printed but was angry at Vaughan for not sending updates on the future queen. Vaughan defended himself and had news to share; they anticipated the Emperor in Antwerp would meet his sister Queen Regent Mary, and the Emperor would marry a French princess, securing a vast Catholic alliance.[75] The Duke of Cleves was concerned by the presence of Emperor Charles and his army, King Henry waited for a bride to arrive, but no one knew where she tarried, and mail was not arriving; the whole situation sent nerves through the English court. Emperor Charles was moving north due to his anger with Henry and Anna's marriage treaty and was ready to stop the Protestant German States from falling away from his control, particularly Guelders, newly in Wilhelm of Cleves' hands. Emperor Charles and Duke Wilhelm both believed they had equal rights to the small German duchy of Guelders and were prepared to go to war over it. King Henry was about to marry the sister of a man ready to go to war with Emperor Charles, which would force England to side with Cleves in a battle they might not win.

Cromwell kept busy preparing for Lady Anna's arrival, purchasing blue velvet decorations, ivory flutes, golden cups, and Cromwell even bought himself two diamonds to add to his St George's medal.[76] He prepared the lists of who would go to meet Anna in Calais, William Fitzwilliam in charge, and his attendant would be Gregory Cromwell. Cromwell tried to include as many people as possible, even asking Mary Boleyn to join, along with Mary's daughter, Lady Catherine Carey. His friend Edward Baynton was named vice-chamberlain for Lady Anna's household. Elizabeth Cromwell would meet Lady Anna at Dover with the other ladies, unable to travel abroad, as she was already advanced in her third pregnancy less than three years into her marriage. Cromwell himself planned to meet Anna at a magnificent ceremony with the king, Richard Cromwell and Ralph Sadler beside him, along with all the closest friends he could gather at once.[77]

Vaughan and the merchants of Antwerp gave Lady Anna a beautiful welcome in early December, and the 350-strong train was a sight to behold on its multi-stop trip to Calais. Gregory reported from Dover of the upgrades to the city, the lavish jousts and the 500-gun salute planned.[78] But by 16 December, storms kept Lady Anna and her train stuck in Calais,[79] but Gregory sat with the future queen as she chose to dine with the men of King Henry's court, eager to learn more about her husband and her new home.[80]

Cromwell also needed to get himself and the Cromwellian household ready, regularly buying new clothes for his servants, and ordering 176 yards of black velvet, always his personal favourite. He had sent Gregory off in finely embroidered apparel and had ordered 152oz of gold thread for the work, and 3lbs of silver. He picked a much simpler gift for Lady Anna when she arrived of fifty gold sovereigns, worth £30,000 today, which Archbishop Cranmer would personally deliver. It was also that time of year again, where gifts and payments arrived in unmarked bags. Cushions under the gallery windows at Austin Friars made an interesting hiding place for discreet payments; a glove containing 20l appeared, a white leather purse containing 100l was found under a cushion, as did another bag containing 10l a few days later. A week later, a small red leather purse containing 50l appeared under this popular cushion under the middle gallery window. Cromwell discovered 120l in a white leather purse personally, not recording its origin, and his nephew Walter Cromwell found another white purse containing 10l. Unfortunately, there is no record of who visited in the lead-up to the festive season.[81]

Meanwhile, among Cromwell's usual costs were three new godsons; monastery commissioners Francis Cave and wife Margaret had baby Thomas, and Roger Ames and his wife had a son, plus one of Cromwell's servants at Leeds, Jasper Smyth, and his wife, had a son. This is where the 366-page booklet of Cromwell's 1537–1539 payments ends, giving us no further insight into Cromwell's personal spending habits or godchildren.

The weather finally allowed the entire royal group to cross from Calais to Dover on 27 December, and Cromwell had prepared the most elaborate and beautiful arrival for Anna just outside London, no expense spared. Meanwhile, Lady Anna's brother was quietly preparing for war with Emperor Charles, and the French were terrified of war on their border. Cromwell's new queen had been placed in a position of men's making, binding countries together, and far apart.

Chapter 17

1540: Immortality

'it shall not be in the King's power to resist me'

Lady Anna of Cleves planned to meet her new husband between Shooter's Hill and Blackheath on Saturday 3 January 1540. Once in the company of her new English ladies at Dover, Anna travelled on to meet Archbishop Cranmer at Canterbury and then travelled to Rochester to meet the Duke of Norfolk. Among the ladies were those loyal to Cromwell; his daughter-in-law Elizabeth, and Jane Wriothesley, though both women were trapped in a semi-permanent state of pregnancy and would not stay long. Jane Boleyn, Lady Rochford was there too, always reliable with information.

King Henry could not wait any longer meet his bride. Henry left Greenwich Palace to meet Anna on 1 January at Rochester 'to nourish love'.[1] It was a fifty-mile round trip, and Cromwell did not go with the king, but eight privy chamber men did; presumably, Ralph Sadler among them. Anna grew up in a court where men and women did not mix informally, and now, a group of strangers burst into her private rooms while she watched a bear-baiting competition below her windows. Probably flustered, Anna received a gift of a crystal cup inlaid with gold and jewels, paying little attention to the guests. Henry, who was in disguise, retreated and returned in his kingly purple velvet apparel, brazenly kissed Anna, and spent the day with her. He stayed overnight nearby, and had breakfast with Anna and her German contingent, before travelling back to Greenwich.[2]

Cromwell arranged a joyous meeting three miles from Greenwich with a guard of honour of 5,000 horses. After arriving back at Greenwich on 2 January, Henry told Cromwell that Anna was 'nothing so well as she was spoken of … and if I had known as much before as I know now, she should not have come within this realm'. Still, Lady Anna had arrived, and Cromwell had no choice but to push on with proceedings.

Under gold cloths of estate, Lady Anna was presented to King Henry and his most important men. Cromwell was there beside Audley, both given permissions to wear rich purple velvet for the day. Marillac mentioned Cromwell as looking more like a 'post-runner than anything else, running up and down with his staff in his hand',[3] ensuring the day went perfectly. Marillac, from his distant position from Lady Anna, described her as:

> about 30 years of age, tall and thin, of medium beauty, and very assured and resolute countenance, showing that in her the turn and vivacity of wit supplies the place of beauty. She brings from her brother's country 12 or 15 damsels inferior in beauty even to their mistress and dressed so heavily and unbecomingly that they would almost be thought ugly even if they were beautiful[4]

The wedding was delayed by a day, showing something was not quite right. Cromwell did not yet have the German paperwork showing Anna's void pre-contract with the Duke of Lorraine. But Cromwell had created a marriage contract with no out-clauses; if Henry wanted out, he had asked the wrong man to create the paperwork. When the contract was created, there had been no suggestion Wilhelm of Cleves and Emperor Charles would go to war over Guelders. The Germans were still unhappy with the lack of alliance with England over matters of religion, and now King Henry could be forced to fight against Emperor Charles on his new wife's behalf. It would give even a level-headed groom nerves. King Henry's initial feelings about Anna, probably from her quiet and reserved demeanour, had hurt his pride, and he confided in Cromwell, 'my lord, she is nothing so far as she has been reported, howbeit, she is well and seemly'.[5] Cromwell called together a meeting of the marriage council; Norfolk, Suffolk, Cranmer, Fitzwilliam, and Tunstall, to find a way out. While the paperwork was not ready, there was no reason to put off the marriage without gravely offending the Germans and the Schmalkaldic League. King Henry reported to Cromwell that famous line, 'I am not well handled', adding, 'if it were not that she is come so far into my realm, and the great preparations that my states and people have made for her, and for fear of making of a ruffle in the world, (meaning) to drive her brother into the hands of the Emperor and French king, I would never have nor marry her'.[6] It was easy to place the blame on the possibility Henry found Anna unattractive (and vice versa), but in reality the marriage placed England into an international furore it sorely did not need. When Henry realised his councillors could not find a solution, he admitted, 'I must need against my will, put my neck in the yoke', of pushing his country towards potential war.

The wedding went ahead early on 6 January, bride and groom both adorned in gold. The Earl of Essex did not arrive to walk the bride down the aisle, and Henry appointed Cromwell to the job, but he managed to get himself replaced. He returned to the king's rooms, where Henry told him, 'my lord if it were not to satisfy the world and my realm, I would not do that I must do this day for no earthly thing'. The bride probably felt the same, given how late she was for the ceremony. Cranmer married the pair, the ceremony witnessed by only a few in the king's closet, Cromwell likely among them. They attended mass and had spiced wine before going about their day. Cromwell was the one to ask Henry how the wedding night went, and Henry, who believed Queen Anna was not a virgin based on a quick grope, told Cromwell, 'surely my lord as you know I liked her before not well but now I like her much worse … I have left her as good a maid as I found her'. Cromwell had the misfortune of having to ask this question twice more in February, and the king could not manage his duty.[7]

After a week of marriage, various jousts and celebrations were held, Queen Anna in English fashions with French hoods to show off her beauty. Everyone appeared to like the new queen except Henry. Stephen Vaughan wrote with gossip from Antwerp, remarking he was glad Cromwell, 'found his judgement true of the Queen'.[8] The French were eager for gossip on the new royal marriage too; Marillac reported on 17 January that Cromwell hosted the closest men of the Privy Council (likely, Norfolk, Suffolk, Fitzwilliam, Tunstall, and Audley) with German ambassadors Baumbach, Burkhardt, Olisleger and Hoghestein to discuss the royal marriage. Olisleger had not yet proved the paperwork of Queen Anna's pre-contract to the Duke of Lorraine, so in return, Cromwell would not share the paperwork showing Anna had been granted the lands promised in the marriage treaty.[9] Whether Cromwell discussed war or already looked for a way out of the Cleves marriage is up to interpretation.

Cromwell had to say goodbye to Ralph Sadler, off as ambassador to Scotland again. King James looked to ally with France, and the new Scottish queen, Mary de Guise, was pregnant. There had been fighting on the Scottish border and Sadler was sent north to negotiate peace and sow seeds of discord among the Catholic clergy.[10] At least while having to send away a man he loved as a son, Cromwell also got to send the Duke of Norfolk to France as an ambassador, as Edmund Bonner had been doing a terrible job.[11] Norfolk was able to sweet-talk the French, leaving Bonner, now a firm enemy of Cromwell despite being given preference and honours, at home to plot against the Vice-Gerent with the other snake of the court, Stephen Gardiner.

By the end of January, rumours of the king's dislike of Queen Anna spread, as did the suggestion all was Cromwell's fault for choosing her. Cromwell retaliated, screaming he only followed the king's orders, and as for those who expected Cromwell to take the blame, 'if the lords would handle me so, that I would give them such a breakfast (defeat them with ease) as never was made in England, and that the proudest of them should know'.[12] The proudest, most arrogant of them all was the Duke of Norfolk. Not an ounce of civility had passed between the pair since the screaming match at Lambeth Palace.

By late February, things calmed again. Queen Anna wrote to her family, saying she was happy and grateful to be in England. King Henry would go to Anna's bed every few nights but not touch her, which probably helped her disposition. The vague paperwork concerning Anna's pre-contract to the Duke of Lorraine arrived at long last, the legal wording poor, making it perfect for a lawyer of Cromwell's quality. If Henry wanted out of his marriage, this paperwork would secure an annulment.[13] But Queen Anna was key to the alliance with the reformist countries Cromwell longed for and giving up so easily just because of Henry's bedroom deficiencies was not in the plan. Cromwell had recently finished an incredible reconstruction of the gallery ceiling in St James' Palace, Italian style, to commemorate Henry and Anna's wedding; he still believed in Queen Anna.

After the work put into Henry's four marriages, Cromwell was probably relieved to work on other matters. Parliament was to be opened in April, and Cromwell knew it was time to work harder than ever. He was in the Lords now, and while the Commons would remain unchanged, the Lords had made a sharp change due to resignations, arrests, and executions. For Cromwell, it was now or never to make his mark in parliament again. Many of the acts were standard administration that needed trusty eyes and concentrated minds to work on, as it required care but offered no glory. These were building roads, refining tax laws, regulating lawyers and wills, horse breeding and naval maintenance. Cromwell set about tying up loose ends. On top of the workload, he also sat as Commissioner of the Peace in ten counties, meaning a varied array of paperwork crossed his desk.

King Henry and Queen Anna moved from London to Hampton Court Palace where Prince Edward lived. Cromwell was lucky to be able to stay behind and get on with his work. But the Elector of Saxony wrote, eager to push England into changing the Six Articles and conform to more Lutheran ideas of reform, which helped no one.[14] Cromwell also had the added concern of Lord Leonard Grey in Ireland, who was on his way to England to explain his terrible management. Cromwell's old friends Chancellor John Allen and Vice-Treasurer William Brabazon sadly could not travel with the endless warring nation needing some leaders still in charge.

Not all was bad; the Dissolution of the Monasteries was finally complete, with the final one, Waltham Abbey, closed on 23 March 1540. Second to last was Thetford Priory, which belonged to Norfolk's family, and Cromwell waited to close it while Norfolk was meeting the French king. Naturally, Norfolk was furious, but it was too late, and Cromwell would not turn Thetford into a new college of learning. Westminster Abbey had also freshly closed, and was now a reformed college, as was Christ Church in Canterbury. Norfolk wanted Thetford to be reformed just like Burton and Thorton colleges which were closed at the same time, and Cromwell denied him, yet another issue to drive hatred between them. The new gospel was being preached, the English Bibles had been distributed and Cromwell's dream of founding colleges of learning finally came to fruition. Now the monasteries were gone, the men and women pensioned off or moved to new colleges, the project could again be Cromwell's plan, to put new life into the Church of England.

If Cromwell felt like his religious goals were complete, reality soon came knocking. Bishop Stephen Gardiner had been preaching the old doctrine at St Paul's. Days later, old friend Robert Barnes did the same, preaching the reformed doctrine. King Henry heard of these outbursts and ordered Gardiner and Barnes to appear before him to explain themselves. It was not simply two men forced to explain themselves, as the king was 'scandalised' by their words. It was Gardiner's words against Cromwell's words, Barnes simply the mouthpiece. Henry, unhappy with his German marriage, could turn his anger against the Reformation instead of its real target, bringing Cromwell and Gardiner's long-running feud to its bitter end.[15] Barnes was one of three Cromwell men, the others Thomas Garrett, chaplain to Bishop Latimer, and William Jerome, Cromwell's personal vicar at Stepney, who angered the king. Cromwell sent Gregory to Stepney at once to see what Jerome had been preaching, as suggestions of Cromwellian heresy were uttered to the king.[16] Everyone needed to be silent to appease the king's current mood, so Barnes recanted his words in late March,[17] and Cromwell made a concession; he invited Stephen Gardiner to dinner at Austin Friars.

If the Lambeth Palace banquet was a flashpoint in Cromwell's fortune, the Austin Friars dinner party would go one step further. What should have been two men finding a truce, instead turned into a bitter dispute, free of the civility of court. Rumours were already flying; people believed Cromwell would lose the Vice-Gerent and Lord Privy Seal positions.[18] With Henry turning from the Reformation due to his marital bed problems with Queen Anna, Cromwell needed to defend all he had done, just as Gardiner felt he needed to defend the papacy. A withering and acrimonious shouting match ensued with Cromwell screaming at Gardiner, 'if the King would turn (from the Reformation), yet I would not turn! And if the King did turn, and all his people, I would fight in the field in my person, with my sword in my hand, against him and all others'.[19] Cromwell, holding a knife (claimed Gardiner), added, 'if this dagger was not thrust into my heart in battle, and if I would not die in that quarrel against them all, and I live one year or two, it shall not be in the King's power to resist me'.

Cromwell had made a huge mistake, not unlike several inappropriate outbursts over recent months. A man who could have his enemies cornered before they realised the hunt had begun, suddenly began making missteps for no apparent reason. Gardiner kept this treasonous argument quiet, and Cromwell needed to get ahead of him. Cromwell surrendered the position of Secretary of State to the king, a job he held in an official capacity for six years. Secretary Cromwell was no more. The position that gave so much power beside the throne slipped away, but only just. The position would be divided between two people, a plan used regularly in the future, separating the immense power of the position. Ralph Sadler and Thomas Wriothesley were both given the job. Cromwell would not be the secretary at the king's side each day, but he would have two of his closest allies there, one a son in all but name. Cromwell was already passing tax laws through parliament and needed to deflect the blame from Henry onto himself, to appease a king who never liked to accept blame for his own decisions.[20] Ralph Sadler and Thomas Wriothesley received knighthoods as well as the title of Principal Secretary, and Cromwell addressed letters to Ralph as secretary immediately, as Ralph needed Cromwell's help on most matters while the changes took hold.[21]

For a moment, things seemed to calm again; Princess Mary wrote to Cromwell, calling him, 'her sheet anchor against the wind',[22] and Cromwell took time to council his dear friend Sir John Gage when his daughter Lady Alice Browne died, Gage thanking Cromwell for his 'charitable and prudent counsel'.[23] Parliament opened on 12 April, Cromwell listed first among those in attendance as Vice-Gerent. He was busy; he needed all new jerkins, jackets and robes all lined with furs, and wondered whether to pick new furs or reuse sables he already owned.

But Ambassador Marillac thought Cromwell was in trouble; Gardiner had not said anything, but Marillac, either listening to bad sources or simply sharing lies, wrote to King Francis, 'Cromwell is tottering'.[24] Marillac could not have been more wrong. On 17 April, King Henry astounded Cromwell and his friends and foes, telling him that he would become the 16th Earl of Essex (1st Earl, sixth creation),[25] accompanied with a list of lands and manors five pages long. Henry Bouchier, whose family had held the Essex titles for eighty years, broke his neck after coming off his horse a month earlier, a sudden opportunity for Cromwell to be elevated. One day after this shock announcement, Cromwell was again bestowed with glory: the title of Lord Great Chamberlain, head of the royal household. The Earls of Oxford had held the role for the past 400 years, but John De Vere had died at home just a week after Henry Bouchier, leaving a vacancy at court.[26]

Cromwell received these new titles on 18 April, along with the official ceremony of knighthood for Ralph Sadler and Thomas Wriothesley, the

Cromwellian circle higher than ever in favour. In an elaborate ceremony, Cromwell received a patent for his new role as Chamberlain, made by Sadler and Wriothesley, and was presented with the staff of the office and the robe to mark his new earldom. King Henry and Queen Anna left to dine alone (or apart), and the present dukes and earls dined as a group, before formally hearing Cromwell's new title; Thomas, Lord Crumwell, Earl of Essex, Vice-Gerent and High Chamberlain of England, Keeper of the Privy Seal, Chancellor of the Exchequer, and Justice of the Forests beyond the Trent.[27] But to stay high in power, Cromwell needed to make another grand sacrifice; he gifted Henry lands in Surrey, the barony of Wimbledon, his extraordinary house at Mortlake and all the lands around his old home of Putney. This meant King Henry's lands extended from London to the new Nonsuch Palace and hunting grounds of Woodstock, so Henry could go on progress without travelling far on his toxic, ulcerated legs.[28] The grant was kind and appeasing to Henry but must have been a serious weight to bear for Cromwell.

French ambassador Marillac was forced to eat his words, writing, 'Cromwell has been made earl of (Essex) and Grand Chamberlain of England, and is in as much credit with his master as ever he was, from which he was near being shaken by the Bishop of Winchester and others'.[29] The Cromwellians kept rising; on 23 April, Cromwell was among the earls to choose the newest member of the Order of the Garter, selecting Lord Chancellor Thomas Audley, for the role.[30]

On the heels of these grand occasions came the May Day jousts. Among the many fights hosted, with Gregory Cromwell competing among them, the king's main event had six champions. Henry chose three men and Cromwell chose three. Cromwell chose his nephew Richard, plus Sir John Dudley and Sir Thomas Seymour, doing friends a favour. King Henry chose Sir George Carew (brother-in-law to Cromwell's attendant Richard Pollard), Thomas Poyninges (personal friend of Cromwell) but also Sir Anthony Kingston, son of Sir William Kingston, one of Cromwell's enemies. Richard Cromwell was the winner of the event, and King Henry dropped a diamond from his finger to Richard and gave him a knighthood, Henry calling Richard 'my diamond'.[31] Richard Cromwell was as close to his uncle as Gregory was to his father, and for Richard to be knighted in such a grand fashion (so grand a wall-sized portrait of the occasion still exists at Hinchingbrooke House) must have felt like the grandest of occasions. If only Gregory had been as talented, intelligent, and loyal as his cousin Richard, who had all the love and trust of his uncle. Richard was now a member of the king's privy chamber, a knight and member of parliament, the king's diamond. Cromwell could not have asked for more.

Another personal moment for Cromwell was the completion of Austin Friars. After taking out the ninety-nine-year lease in 1532, Cromwell had successfully purchased the properties and gardens around his manor over three years (including moving one house on rollers and confiscating a strip of another property). Austin Friars had become the largest pre-Dissolution property in London, spread over 2.3 acres, the large garden taking 1.5 acres. The building accounts have not survived, but cost Cromwell more than 1,000l with enough labourers that he was able to draft a small army. The four-year building programme was overseen by Giovanni Portinari, who used Austin Friars as a practice model for grander schemes later in his career. Portinari built Cromwell's love for all things Italian into the bones of his family home. The buildings lasted without any need for maintenance or changes for the next 100 years.[32] Austin Friars' frontage onto Throgmorton Street was approximately fifty metres long, with two main entrance gates, one leading to the larger courtyard leading to the main hall and the enormous kitchens, and a smaller gate leading to the stables and private chapel.[33] The frontage was built with brick, along with the east side wall of the main courtyards (an outside wall of the original house), approximately two feet thick, while all other walls were timber. The windows were built in pale green Reigate sandstone from Surrey, contrasted with the red roof tiles.[34]

Thirty-two rooms, galleries, stairways, and courtyards sat on the bottom floor of the property, with three kitchens, one dedicated to pastry, plus larders, stores, pantries, butteries, sculleries, a large wine cellar and the armoury. The main kitchens had their own third courtyard, leading to a back entrance to the property. Galleries ran over all the courtyards, one of the final parts to be completed in the main courtyard in late 1539.[35] Another nineteen rooms sat on the second level, with ornate oriel windows looking out on Throgmorton street, hosting private bedrooms, heated private parlours, and luxury rooms to host guests. The third level had seven simple bedrooms, all looking out over the main street, with attic rooms in the roof, likely for servants. The house had four main chimneys in the front, generally situated directly above the kitchens, spread throughout the manor.[36] Plans show how the house stood out dramatically from those around it; the three wooden turrets with large oriel windows gave the house an outstanding change in design, and the interior galleries likely had these oriel windows looking out into the courtyards as well. Cromwell's rooms were away from the street front on the north-west side of the manor, overlooking the garden at the back, and had an adjoining bathroom and built-in wardrobes, while street-front bedrooms would have been for Cromwell-Sadler-Williams guests, and the most trusted of attendants.[37] Mercy Prior, Cromwell's ever-faithful mother-in-law, had her rooms, with notes about her private area of the manor needing new doors in 1540, the same time Wriothesley's private room in the manor was being emptied so he could work at court.[38]

Cromwell's garden was as glamorous as his rooms. Set almost fifty metres back from the road, the 1.5-acre garden was interlaced by mazes, hedged knot gardens and gravel walkways that required six gardeners to maintain in 1540.[39] One corner had a stable, another had a small house. The southwest corner had a gaming or gambling room, surely well used, and a bowling alley sat along the western edge, and plans were made for a tennis court.[40] While the outlines of the house can be seen in papers, sadly, the interior of the house was not given a firm inventory. The walls would have been lined with tapestries, possibly some of those that hung in the original house, and a Flemish arras of the Virgin Mary and baby Jesus was taken by King Henry in 1540.[41] Each of the bedrooms had large beds with canopies made in velvet, damask, and cloth of gold.[42] Cromwell still seemed to particularly like red and dark green colour schemes.

Despite the vast array of homes Cromwell amassed, Austin Friars was undoubtedly personal. It was a family home created to reflect him, his family and to show his endless elevation in status. Even after acquiring St James' Palace for work in 1536, Austin Friars' construction and improvement continued. It was a symbol of all Cromwell had learned; his building and construction projects undertaken for Cardinal Wolsey showed his management skills; his Italian friends and interests showed his flair for style, and the fact it was run by the families of his wife and sisters showed how important his home was to him. Cromwell's other manors were symbols of success, places to stop while travelling with the king, but Austin Friars was deeply personal, and when he lost his family, he simply could not bear to let it go and start over. Nowhere was as important as the Cromwell family home.

In around May 1540, Gregory and Elizabeth Cromwell had a third son, named Thomas.[43] The resurrection of their marriage would have felt like a personal victory to Cromwell, and a third healthy grandson in less than three years of marriage would have left him feeling like a king himself. His near-son Ralph Sadler's family was also ever-growing, with three sons and daughter Anne, and Sir Ralph and Lady Ellen now had baby Mary. With Ralph Sadler and Richard Cromwell knighted and in parliament, Cromwell could turn his attention to gaining more for Gregory.

Chapter 18

Perpetuity

'I have been a great traveller in this world,
and being but of a base degree, was called to high estate'

While Cromwell had a succession of personal successes, King Henry's fateful marriage to Queen Anna could not be ignored. Sir Thomas Wyatt was finally home from the Emperor's court, telling Cromwell the Cleves delegation in Ghent, 'are not drawn by courtesy, friendship, or equity, but by interest'.[1] Cleves and the Emperor had been trying to negotiate peace, without success, for months. England may have married into the Cleves family, but had offered no support, religious or military, for any of Cleves' German battles. To make matters worse, King Henry was now fooling around with young Lady Katheryn Howard, one of his wife's ladies, a favourite hunting ground for the obese, ageing king. Among Cromwell's papers was a land transfer to Lady Katheryn, confiscated from murderers in Sussex, an odd gift from the king to his teenage victim. There was little time to worry about Henry's attempts to successfully bed anyone, as Cromwell's friend Christopher Mont was still away in Cologne, trying to entreat with German leaders on King Henry's behalf, but at this stage, whether Henry cared is impossible to tell.[2]

On 9 May, King Henry invited Cromwell to a private meeting at Westminster, 'concerning weighty business concerning the honour and surety of the King's person and the tranquility of his subjects'.[3] Henry now wanted to appease the French, forcing Cromwell to go to Ambassador Marillac to show his singular affections to the country, lying to Marillac that he was no longer an Imperialist.[4] But among Henry's instructions was a curious occasion; on 11 May, as Bishop Sampson (the man who punished Gregory for sex crimes in 1538) was invested as Bishop of Westminster. Henry allowed the investiture to go ahead, no doubt knowing Cromwell would have Sampson arrested and thrown in the Tower that same afternoon. The new Bishop of Westminster was arrested for heresy, and the king did not even flinch, as Ralph Sadler reported a few days later.[5] Henry was allowing Cromwell to personally go after his enemies.

There were plenty of enemies to go around, as the only men higher in rank than Cromwell, the Dukes of Norfolk and Suffolk, were both in London, and while Suffolk was a simple man who did as he was told, Cromwell and Norfolk could not spend time together. Lord Lisle was in London and Henry had no qualms about throwing his uncle into the Tower for his shameful lack of control of heretics in Calais. Lord Leonard Grey was in London as well, as Ireland suffered from rebels who burned towns, overran castles, and caused a hung Irish parliament.[6] Being a member of the Grey family would protect Lord Leonard no more.

Ambassador Marillac remarked how calm Henry and Cromwell had been when Bishop Sampson was arrested on the day of his Westminster investiture, the same day as all his goods were confiscated and he was attainted, calling it, 'as horrible to tell as frightful to see'.[7] Marillac knew Cromwell had a list of six bishops to topple, Sampson simply being the first scalp. With Sampson in the Tower, Thomas Cranmer stepped up and gave a powerful reformist sermon at St Paul's, usually never one to stick his neck into political fights if he could avoid them. Cranmer needed Cromwell's protection but felt he had it. Marillac wrote, 'those who lately shook the credit of Master Cramvel, so he was very near coming to grief', were next to be toppled. If Cromwell did have such a list, Stephen Gardiner would be firmly at the top, with Bishop Cuthbert Tunstall close behind him. Conservatives Nicholas Heath at Rochester, John Salcot at Salisbury, and John Bell at Worcester must have also been feeling nervous.

King Henry ended the imprisonment of reformist bishops Latimer and Shaxton at the same time, and one of Cromwell's long-time enemies, Sir John Wallop, came back from France, and Cromwell was sent to investigate whether Wallop should be arrested. Bishop Sampson wrote to Cromwell from the Tower, trying to clear Gardiner and Tunstall of any suspicion of heresy, a clear sign the conservatives were gathering while Cromwell destroyed his adversaries.[8]

In an inopportune turn of events, just as Cromwell's chance to turn on the bishops came, the king called Cromwell to court on 6 June, where

Henry confessed his impotency.[9] Henry confessed this only to Cromwell and friend-turned-foe William Fitzwilliam. Cromwell had listened to Henry complain of his marriage to Anna multiple times over Easter, and again through Whitsun week in mid-May, but confirmation of the lack of consummation and Henry's suggestion of annulment could not wait any longer, no matter Cromwell's opinion.[10] The alliance between England and Germany was non-existent, and the Emperor and France were not looking to go against England. Henry had no reason to hold on to a woman he did not like, no matter how much Anna was liked by others, or how suitable and well-chosen she was for England. King Henry had also been sneaking out of court to spend time with Lady Kathryn Howard at Stephen Gardiner's Winchester Palace.

Cromwell travelled home to Austin Friars, where Thomas Wriothesley met him; Cromwell appeared exhausted and worn out by events. In Wriothesley's deposition, he asked Cromwell, 'what one thing rested in his head which troubled him'. Cromwell, believing his home would afford him privacy, told Wriothesley the king's marriage remained unconsummated. Wriothesley pushed the belief they could solve Henry's issue, or 'they should all smart for it', but Cromwell replied it was a 'great matter'. Wriothesley kept pushing his master, and Cromwell replied again it was a great matter, but stopped himself from revealing impotence. Still, the damage was done.[11]

While Cromwell was at home feeling despondent and disillusioned, Stephen Gardiner prepared his attack. Since returning to England, he had reconnected with Thomas Wriothesley. Wriothesley claimed to be utterly loyal to Cromwell since late 1535 but was no such thing. Given how many people openly detested Wriothesley, it came as no surprise he would easily swap to old allegiances. Another Cromwell man, Edmund Bonner, who had bonded with Gardiner over their shared disastrous times as French ambassadors, turned against Cromwell, though, like Wriothesley, there appears to be no incident which caused a shift. Bonner's position was likely his religious beliefs; Wriothesley was likely greedy. Wriothesley knew who else was close to the king and was happy to turn against Cromwell; William Fitzwilliam and his brother Anthony Browne, Master of the Horse. Both men were on the Privy Council and the king would readily listen to their opinions. With Wriothesley fresh appointed co-secretary to the king, and Fitzwilliam the only other person aware of the impotence besides Cromwell, Gardiner could easily collude with these men to destroy the new Earl of Essex.

Thomas Wriothesley, who had been just another man in Wolsey's household, plucked to work alongside Stephen Gardiner, and then taken into the Cromwell household as one of his own, was only too eager to betray his noble master. Thomas Cromwell had overseen the grandest changes of Henry VIII's reign. He destroyed the Catholic hold over England and ended the monasteries in favour of reformist colleges. He found the way to bring down Queen Katherine of Aragon. He beheaded Anne Boleyn so Henry could bat his eyelashes at Jane Seymour. Cromwell created the Church of England and made King Henry the supreme leader, ended paying taxes to Rome, and saw off threats from the Pope and Emperor Charles. Cromwell had engineered the execution of countless men, clergy and laity, when they did not agree with the king's current mood, regardless of their innocence or guilt. He ensured the beheadings of noblemen who died for the king's ever-grasping power and enriched Henry in a way not thought possible. Cromwell spent years in the background, learning, studying, and working with his legal skills while other courtiers fluttered around the king and whatever woman had Henry's fancy. The English Bible was a reality because of all the endless work by Cromwell and Cranmer, two great men of learning trying to help the people of England, Wales, and Ireland. Cromwell endured years of taunts as a man walking around like Wolsey's ghost behind the king, suspected of being a heretic for his learning, and was openly called a traitor for trying to advance the king's desires. King Henry heard all these taunts, and defended Cromwell, even when 40,000 rebels called for Cromwell's head. For over half of Cromwell's time at court, he gained almost no personal advantage to himself, despite the enormous upheavals he created. Gregory Cromwell was finally established as an adult, while Richard Cromwell and Ralph Sadler were now knighted Privy Councillors and honorary sons of whom Cromwell could be immensely proud. From the scandals of the summer reading sessions of 1526 and 1527, Thomas Cranmer had become the Archbishop of Canterbury, with Cromwell at his side. Robert Barnes was in the Tower and needed Cromwell's help, likewise Thomas Garrett and William Jerome. Miles Coverdale had successfully created a translation of the Bible, and Hugh Latimer, Nicholas Shaxton and John Clerk were now bishops, while John Bale had been writing evangelical plays for Cromwell for years and enjoyed safety in Cromwell's protection. All of Cromwell's old friends – Stephen Vaughan, John Williamson, John Gostwick, John Russell, Roger More, Richard Pollard, Peter Mewtas, Philip Hoby, Thomas Thacker, William Body, Richard Morison, Richard Tomyou, Thomas Avery, Brian Tuke, Henry Grey, John Gage, John Allen, William Brabazon, Giovanni Portinari, Thomas Legh, Richard Layton, every single one rose at court alongside Cromwell; no one was forgotten, no one disloyal. Yet one whisper of impotence to Wriothesley at Austin Friars was enough for King Henry to forget every single one of Cromwell's good deeds in His Highness' name and sign an arrest warrant.

Only Ambassador Marillac's letters remain on the detail of the arrest of Thomas Lord Crumwell.[12] On 10 June, it was recorded Cromwell arrived late to a Privy Council meeting after a morning in parliament. There was no reason for Cromwell to be late, it is more likely the Council was summoned slightly early without his knowledge. Among those in the Council were those close to Cromwell's heart; Ralph Sadler, Thomas Cranmer, Thomas Audley, John Gage and John Russell. There were men there who had made Cromwell godfather to their children, the Duke of Suffolk, Edward Seymour, and Robert Radcliffe. Many enemies were present; Stephen Gardiner, the Duke of Norfolk, William Fitzwilliam, and traitor Wriothesley. Men who were like brothers or sons to Cromwell could only sit and watch as the nightmare unfolded. Sir William Kingston from the Tower was there with four guards to arrest Cromwell on arrival. Still dressed formally for parliament, wearing his Garter ribbons, collar of St George and his sable fur robes, Cromwell never got to say a word, nor realised anything was untoward before Kingston announced the arrest. Shocked, Cromwell ripped his black cap from his head and threw it on the table and cried,

'I am no traitor! Is this the reward for good service done unto His Majesty the King? I put it to your consciences; am I a traitor as your accusations imply? Well, no matter, for I renounce all pardons or grace needed, for I never offended the King, and it matters only if the King himself thinks me a traitor, and he would never have me linger long!'

The words were not dissimilar to Wolsey's eleven years earlier.

Fitzwilliam untied Cromwell's garter from his leg while Norfolk took Cromwell's golden collar. The intention was clear; an attainted man could not be a member of the Garter. This was not a spur-of-the-moment plan; Norfolk had spoken to King Francis in Paris of the plan to destroy Cromwell back in February.[13] Cromwell was taken from a water gate at Whitehall to the Tower with relative anonymity and housed in the Queen's apartments, just as Anne Boleyn had been four years earlier. Wriothesley began the Council's letters for around England and Europe, sharing the news before anyone at court or parliament even knew the arrest occurred.[14] Poor Ralph Sadler later had to go through King Henry's letters and read happy reactions from France.[15]

In London, news of the arrest spread when Sir Thomas Cheyney (uncle of Jane Wriothesley) arrived at Austin Friars to confiscate the entire property. Cheyney had two dozen archers at his back for the occasion, despite the fact there would be no resistance at the surprise invasion. At the time, Mercy Prior still lived at the property, as did John and Joan Williamson and their children. The Williams and Wellyfed siblings likely had rooms at the house, as did loyal personal servants like Thomas Thacker. All would now be homeless, unable to access any of their belongings. All the servants, falconers, gardeners, dog handlers, stable hands for Cromwell's 100 horses, would be left in limbo. The private items belonging to Gregory, his lost mother and sisters, and Cardinal Wolsey would be taken for their value. Cromwell's daughter, Jane Cromwell, was hopefully away at Leeds Castle at the time of the arrest, though poor Gregory would have been in London for parliament and was likely staying at Austin Friars. Cheyney's men knew what they wanted, and what they needed to find. Cromwell had 7,000l (almost £3,000,000 today) in coin on the property, plus silver plate and jewels all through the house. Rooms were decimated, from the linens, to bejewelled church relics in storage, to the vast armoury, whose inventory boasted 400 pikes, 272 handguns, 459 hooked halberds, 759 bows and armour for at least 600 men.[16] Cromwell had shown Ambassador Castillon the armoury and boasted of his power; now it could look like a plan to destroy Henry. Coupled with Cromwell's argument with Gardiner in March, that he would 'fight the king, sword in hand' over religion now looked and sounded like treason.

Cheyney's men wanted to see Cromwell's offices, and the papers in his possession. A vast number of state papers were at Austin Friars, as Cromwell regularly took files to study while creating new laws or overseeing changes. They found letters Cromwell received from German Lutheran lords and more extreme Calvinists in Switzerland as he debated religion. These were now seen as plans to overthrow religion in England with extremism. The letters and files in Cromwell's rooms also discussed a great many other issues, but as they did not cast any negative assertions, they were conveniently ignored by evidence collectors. King Henry said he wanted to abolish all memory of Cromwell, a comment he would regret within weeks.

Items of immediate value were taken; plate, jewels, and Cromwell's vast collection of clothes were soon missing. King Henry personally wanted Cromwell's large bed, plus three other bed frames, and nine sets of fine linens, which included the elaborate canopies and curtains, quilts, and sheets, made in luxurious damask, velvet, and cloth of gold. Certain personal items appealed to Henry; he wanted Cromwell's gilt silver engraved with the Cromwell banner of arms, as if to remove Cromwell from the world.[17] It did not work; at once, Ralph Sadler got hold of the 1532 Holbein portrait of Cromwell and hid it away. Loyal account-keeper Thomas Avery snatched a table with Cromwell's golden portrait engraved into the wood. Servants were left to take whatever they wanted, but surprisingly, many items were left behind, as seen in a partial inventory that still survives, as if leaving space for Cromwell to return to one day. In a mark of cruelty, Austin Friars was placed in Thomas Wriothesley's hands, but perhaps the ghosts of his crime were too much to bear, and Wriothesley spent no time in the manor, which sat untouched for the next three years, except for the books King Henry ordered stolen from the library.

One day after Cromwell's arrest, Thomas Cranmer wrote in despair to the king:

who cannot be sorrowful and amazed (Cromwell) should be a traitor against your Majesty, he that was so advanced by your Majesty; he whose surety was only by your Majesty; he who loved your Majesty, as I ever thought, no less than God; he who studied always to set forwards whatsoever was your Majesty's will and pleasure; he that cared for no man's displeasure to serve your Majesty; he that was such a servant in my judgement, in wisdom, diligence, faithfulness, and experience, as no prince in this realm ever had ...'[18]

Only Cranmer had the king's protection and could write such words. No one could speak in Cromwell's defence, or they would be soon tarnished with accusations too. All Cromwell's friends could do was keep up his work. If Cromwell could not work for any reason, such as his illnesses, his men could carry on without him, and his planning and style of governance meant nothing fell apart. Gregory was able to retreat with his family, and Cromwell's friend Anthony St Leger was appointed to oversee Leeds Castle, keeping Cromwell's family safe. Ralph Sadler and Richard Cromwell suffered no ill-effects after the arrest, staying quiet and gathering news. Rowland Lee controlled Wales, John Russell controlled the west and Bishop Holgate controlled the north. Henry Polstead was put in charge of Austin Friars and its inventory, his loyalty meaning Cromwell's correspondence could be destroyed, clearing his name of any further blackening. Cromwell had so many friends in so many places his work could continue, and even his acts would finish going through parliament.

Several drafts of Cromwell's attainder went through parliament, the final passing on 28 June, only eighteen days after his arrest. Cromwell had written a letter to Henry on 12 June, outlining his defence against accusations of heresy and treason, writing a coherent, measured, and calm response to the charges. Cromwell's threat to fight the king, made over dinner with Stephen Gardiner, was one piece of evidence, Cromwell crying he would give the arrogant lords a 'breakfast' was another. Cromwell was accused of taking bribes and pushing his religious agendas on the country, over the will of the king. The attainder completed:

> the said Thomas Crumwell, Earl of Essex, for his abominable and detestable heresies and treasons, by him most abominably, heretically, and traitorously practised, committed, and done, against Almighty God and Your Majesty, and your realm, shall be convicted and attainted of heresies and high treason, and is adjudged an abominable and detestable heretic and traitor... Crumwell shall suffer such pains of death, losses, and forfeitures of goods, debts, and chattels at the pleasure of your most royal Majesty ...[19]

Despite being legally dead, Cromwell still had to work. King Henry still wanted his annulment from Queen Anna and Cromwell readied the paperwork in the Tower. Sir Anthony Browne made up a story about the disastrous first meeting of Henry and Anna, claiming Henry thought her ugly and foul-smelling, the meeting rude, confusing, and unpleasant. Cromwell wrote up his versions of events, Henry's nerves, concerns, and lack of communication. The letter famously ended with the final lines:

> I am a most woeful prisoner, ready to take the death when it shall please God and your Majesty. Yet the frail flesh incites me continually to call to your Grace for mercy and pardon for my offences and in this, Christ save, preserve, and keep you. Written the Tower, this Wednesday the last of June, with the heavy heart and trembling hand of your highness' most heavy and most miserable prisoner and poor slave. Most gracious prince, I cry for mercye, mercye, mercye.[20]

Even this would not change Henry's mind, for Cromwell had been attainted, and to grant mercy to a prisoner after the attainder would create a legal precedent no one wanted to touch. Still, the king had Ralph Sadler read the letter aloud thrice. But by 9 July, people were going to the king for advice instead of Cromwell, making Henry realise just how hard Cromwell had been working for a full decade. The realm needed Cromwell at the helm, as Henry had no interest in working as hard as his faithful servant. From now on, King Henry's kingdom would never run as smoothly, and regret sank in.

By this stage, Henry's annulment from Anna was complete, Cromwell's paperwork enough to aid the process, with Cranmer annulling the marriage. Gossip poured in from Europe, particularly from France, and Marillac told King Francis that Cromwell's death, scheduled after parliament's closing on 15 July, 'will be the most ignominious in this country'.[21] As the French and the Emperor rejoiced, despite Cromwell's years of work to gain an Imperial alliance, Richard Pate at the Emperor's court wrote:

> while Thomas Crumwell ruled, slander and obloquies of England were common, men saying the sacrament of the altar was abolished, and all piety and religion banished... the rumours will perish with their author, a plain gentile, a traitor, and a heretic ... what service that wretch did our sovereign lord, that neither regarded his master's honour nor his honesty.[22]

Cromwell's final letter from the Tower went to the Privy Council on 24 July, about the Rochepot Affair, with France still angry about the seizure of the ship. The issue could now be resolved by forcing Cromwell to take all the blame, seizing the ships for its goods (which remained untouched). Cromwell explained the situation of the delayed trial against the ship, and signed the letter, 'this, my good lords, I pray the eternal Redeemer to preserve you all in long life good health with long prosperity. At the Tower, the 24th day of July with the trembling hand of your beadsman'.[23] Only time would show Cromwell's innocence in the Rochepot Affair, long after his death.

Several days later, on 27 July, a package arrived at Hampton Court Palace, addressed to Cromwell. It was a large collection of clothes newly made for summer progress. Henry ordered them handed out to eight courtiers, Cromwell's friends Thomas Heneage and Edward Baynton among them. But Henry ordered Cromwell's exquisite 'garter robes of crimson and purple velvet' be kept untouched at Hampton Court.[24] One can only hope Henry felt guilt when looking at the unworn robes when he realised his mistake too late.

For such a momentous day, Wednesday 28 July barely survives in reliable records. Cromwell learned of his execution at dawn on 28 July from William Laxton and Martin Bowes, the sheriffs in the Tower.[25] It was a sunny summer's day and after breakfast and prayer, Cromwell, dressed in black, only had a brief walk from his rooms in the Queen's rooms, past the Jewel House he had created, and out across the moat to Tower Hill. One thousand halberdiers had been summoned for the day, to line Cromwell's walk from the moat bridge to the scaffold, armed thanks to an unfounded fear Cromwellians would mount an escape bid among the immense crowd.[26] Cromwell did not have to face the scaffold alone, as Sir Thomas Wyatt was selected to be with Cromwell on the final day. Cromwell was not the only one being executed, as Walter Hungerford would also die for his crimes of buggery, incest, and wife-beating. The theory was Cromwell would be shamed by being killed before such an atrocious man, but Hungerford has remained a footnote, an unremarkable man of little consequence among thousands who reported to Cromwell over the years. Hungerford had lost his mind, and Cromwell tried to calm him, saying 'there is no cause for you to fear. If you repent and be heartily sorry for what you have done, there is, for you, mercy enough from the

Lord, who for Christ's sake, will forgive you. Therefore, be not dismayed and though the breakfast which we are going to be sharp, trusting in the mercy of the Lord, we shall have a joyful dinner'.[27]

Cromwell was afforded the death of an earl by being beheaded, not the 'shearman' he was labelled in his attainder, who would be hanged, drawn, and quartered. The king had shown some mercy. Cromwell left behind a wide extended family, natural and adopted, and his words would be held against them if he spoke out of turn on the scaffold. Cromwell stood before the large crowd, Wyatt close behind him, giving a long speech, acknowledging his sins and ready to die. In this long speech, Cromwell said:

> For since the time that I have had years of discretion, I have lived a sinner, and offended my Lord God, for the which I ask him heartily forgiveness. And it is not unknown to many of you, that I have been a great Traveller in this World, and being but of a base degree, was called to high estate, and since the time I came thereunto, I have offended my Prince, for the which I ask him heartily forgiveness, and beseech you all to pray to God with me, that he will forgive me.[28]

Cromwell said he would die believing in the sacrament of the true faith, wisely not pointing out what he believed was the true faith. He then went on to pray, giving a long and thoughtful prayer, finishing, 'when death hath taken away the use of my Tongue, yet my heart may cry and say unto thee, Lord, into thy hands I commend my Soul, Lord Jesus receive my spirit, Amen'. Cromwell removed his back gown, said goodbye to Wyatt, and on seeing his tearful friend's pain, he added, 'gentle Wyatt, pray for me'. He prayed the executioner would take his head with a single blow,[29] but what came next is conflicted in many reports. With each letter written across England and Europe, the story changed to the stage where Cromwell was burned, quartered, all number of cruel imagined punishments, showing how twisted the tale became. The most likely tale is Cromwell's head was simply chopped by a single blow, as early reports mentioned.[30] But other tales told of more explicit details; that the axeman was a 'ragged and butcherly wretch' and the first blow instead hit Cromwell's skull, or that it took half an hour to cut through Cromwell's neck.[31] Such a tale relies on dramatics and exaggeration, no doubt wishful thinking on behalf of Cromwell's enemies. Even in poor executions, the victim would die or be unconscious within seconds. The king's great polymath was gone, buried unmarked at St Peter ad Vincula within the Tower walls, unable to be buried in his Italian part of London after the closure of Austin Friars. 'The judgement of men belongs to Christ, who knows the hidden things of the heart', so Reginald Pole in Italy wrote after hearing of Cromwell's death.[32]

Epilogue

'they made him put to death the most faithful servant'

If anyone thought King Henry would become Catholic again, the reissue of the English Bible in 1541 would have concerned them; Cromwell's banner of arms was removed, a large white hole in the otherwise decorated cover. An artist drew a beard on Cromwell next to the king. This man was no one; just as Cromwell had once been at court. Cromwell left a hole in every respect; Cromwell's enemies jostled for the Vice-Gerency, but Henry awarded it to no one, and the role would never be given out again by any monarch.

Elizabeth Cromwell was the smart one, writing to King Henry to thank him for the mercy shown to the Cromwell family throughout this difficult time, possibly to spur Henry into showing said mercy.[1] Elizabeth timed her letter to perfection; King Henry burned preachers Robert Barnes, William Jerome and Thomas Garrett, getting his fill of punishment on Cromwellians. By the end of the year, Gregory was made a baron, and the new generation of Cromwells moved north to Launde Abbey. Gregory and Elizabeth stayed quiet at Launde, having two more children, Katherine in 1541, and Frances in 1542. Gregory diligently attended parliament each year but achieved nothing. If anything, Gregory was one of those peers Cromwell never liked; those who were rewarded for their status rather than their effort. But the disease that claimed his mother and sisters, sweating sickness, remerged in 1551, killing Gregory at age thirty, and his son Edward, not yet a teenager.[2] Elizabeth quickly remarried, and young Henry Cromwell married his stepsister Mary Paulet, granddaughter of one of the Grey sisters Cromwell once served, and produced a line of Irish Cromwells who lived with mixed success. Thomas Cromwell the younger went into English politics with Ralph Sadler and a friend, Seymour servant William Cecil, and served Queen Elizabeth with the level of skill, respect and intelligence shown by his grandfather.[3] Thomas became a parliamentary historian, creating papers still useful in studying the Elizabethan era today.

King Henry's mercy fell on stronger Cromwellian shoulders; Sir Richard Cromwell was allowed to openly mourn his uncle at court. In 1541, Richard was in parliament and High Sheriff of Cambridgeshire and Huntingdonshire, around the enormous manor of Hinchingbrooke, which Henry allowed Richard to buy just before Cromwell's execution. A year later, Henry lavished more monasteries, lordships, and manors on Richard, in particular, his uncle's Great Place Manor in Stepney. When war broke out in France, Richard responded by joining 6,000 men siding with Emperor Charles in battle.[4] Sadly, Sir Richard Cromwell died of illness in October 1544 in his mid-thirties, just a year after his wife Frances. Their children, Henry and Francis, were left obscenely wealthy and cared for by the Cromwell-Williams families, both going into politics, with Henry's grandson Oliver beheading King Charles I.

It was surrogate son Sir Ralph Sadler who defied the odds. Arrested in early 1541 with Thomas Wyatt on very undefined terms, he managed to smooth-talk his way out of prison and remained in the privy chamber and Privy Council and was ambassador to Scotland.[5] But Wriothesley bullied Ralph from his shared role as secretary, although he did his best to avenge Cromwell. Ralph, after learning how to end Queen Katheryn Howard, did his best to destroy Stephen Gardiner and the Duke of Norfolk, both men in the Tower for all of King Edward's reign. Sadler came to grief in 1545, when his wife Lady Ellen's first husband reappeared, not dead after all, but the king had parliament ratify Sadler's marriage and legitimise his children Thomas, Edward, Henry, Anne, Mary, Jane, and Dorothy. The Sadler family lived comfortably and in favour for the rest of their days, Ralph living until 1587.

Jane Cromwell's life after her father's death remained quiet, not showing up in records until her 1550 marriage, and her daughter Alice's birth in 1559. Mercy Prior never appears in records again after her mention in 1540 just before Cromwell's execution. Christopher and William Wellyfed lived out their days in the church, while Alice Wellyfed lived happily with her second husband until 1561.[6] John and Joan Williamson, and their daughter Joan, remained very quiet after Cromwell's demise, likely living peacefully in Gregory Cromwell's home at Launde Abbey.

Stephen Vaughan ended his time in the Low Countries in 1544, and returned to England to work in parliament, before dying in 1549, thirty years after meeting Cromwell in merchant trade.[7] Vaughan had more luck than fellow ambassador Thomas Wyatt, who died in 1542, after falling foul of the king and then fell ill, leaving his mistress Bess with three children.

The one who suffered Cromwell's loss more than any other was Thomas Cranmer. Not only had he lost his ally, but he also lost a friend and his protection. Cranmer never developed Cromwell's political skill, and in 1543 was accused of various crimes, though fortunately the king took his side and did not sign an arrest warrant. Cranmer stubbornly fought back against Catholics like Stephen Gardiner, still in Henry's favour at his death, and wrote the Book of Common Prayer in 1549 under King Edward.[8] Under Edward's rule, Cranmer was finally able to reunite with his wife and daughter, and a son Thomas was born, but Queen Mary's accession chased Margarete, Margaret, and baby Thomas back to Europe. Mary arrested Cranmer in 1553 and Cranmer delayed his death with false recantations but was burned to death as an example in 1556, crying out in favour of the Reformation as he burned.[9] Of Queen Mary's various crimes, Thomas Cranmer's death was among the worst.

The Grey family suffered a mixture of fortunes. Henry Grey, 3rd Marquess of Dorset, later a duke, tried to put his daughter Jane on the throne, resulting in their deaths. Elizabeth Grey's son Gerald FitzGerald in Ireland spent much of his life captive or on the run.[10] Elizabeth's niece of the same name, married to Thomas Audley, was widowed in 1544 when Audley, still Lord Chancellor, died suddenly of illness, leaving the king without his conscience. While Cromwell's beloved Grey family struggled, the Frescobaldi family in Florence, marred by bankruptcy in 1581, adapted and adjusted, and still work in the wine trade today.

On 3 March 1541, Ambassador Marillac wrote to Paris, saying he and Ambassador Chapuys worried for King Henry, whose leg caused him anguish, that he ate and drank continually, leading to immense weight gain, and his mood had become 'contrary even to itself'. Men fell foul for seeing through the king's instructions, as instructions could change within the same day. The king blamed his ministers for all his troubles, and on occasions even, 'reproaches with Crumwell's death, saying that, upon light pretexts, by false accusations, they made him put to death the most faithful servant he ever had'.[11]

Thomas Cromwell never intended to climb the greasy pole of politics to the glamour of the royal court. His quiet legal and merchant life suited him just fine for the first forty-five years of his life, and his choices, such as holding his family and old friends close, and refusing to remarry, shows Cromwell as a man who had found what he wanted in life before King Henry looked to exploit his talents. The final ten years of Cromwell's life, where he created true government in England, showed commoners were capable of leadership, and revolutionised how a country should be run, was the cherry on top of a life already lived. Cromwell's tireless administrative toiling changed England, and subsequently laid the governing foundations for every country borne out of her colonising invasions. True governance, public service and freedom from Catholicism is a remarkable legacy.

Notes

Chapter 1: 1485–1503

1. The Antiquary: vol 2, p.166
2. *The Complete Peerage of England*, vol 1, p.420
3. *The Complete Peerage of England*, vol 3, p.555
4. SP. 2/551i-ii, 9 Mar 1538
5. *The Complete Peerage of England*, vol 3, p.555
6. Ibid
7. Ibid
8. Ibid
9. LP ix no. 862, 21 Nov 1535
10. Court rolls of the manor of Wimbledon, p.75
11. The Antiquary: vol 2, p.166
12. Manorial Records, p4
13. Court rolls of the manor of Wimbledon, p.75
14. Wandsworth Historical Society Papers, p.31
15. Walford, p.489
16. Bennett, *Ale, Beer, and Brewsters in England*, p.67
17. HC 1509–1558 2, 597
18. HC 1509–1558 1, 356
19. HC 1509–1558 1, 356
20. SP 1/74 f. 25, 13 Jan 1533
21. SP 1/77 f. 77, 24 Jan 1533
22. LP viii no. 802, 29 May 1535
23. SP 1/42 ff. 101–116, 16 Jun 1527
24. Ibid
25. Ibid
26. Ibid
27. Foxe, 1570
28. LP ix no.862, 21 Nov 1535
29. LP viii no.802, 29 May 1535
30. Wandsworth Historical Society Papers, p.31
31. TNA C1/199/35
32. *The Complete Peerage of England*, vol 3, p.557
33. *Holinshead Chronicles of England*, vol 6
34. MacCulloch, *A Life*, p.37
35. Ibid
36. Bandello, vol 4, p.117
37. Foxe, 1570
38. Bandello, vol 4, p.117
39. Mallett and Shaw, p.27
40. Guérard, p.132
41. Mallett and Shaw, p.44
42. Tavuzzi, p.134

43. Mallett and Shaw, p.61
44. Bandello, vol 4, p.117
45. Fowler, p.137
46. Ibid
47. Ibid
48. Hibbert, *The House of Medici: Its Rise and Fall*
49. Paoletti, p.11
50. Gelčić, Piero Soderini profugo a Ragusa: memorie e documenti
51. Viroli, pp.81–86
52. Bandello, vol 4. p.117
53. Carteggio inedito d'artisti del sec. XIV, XV, XVI, p.454–463
54. Najemy, *Between Friends, Letters of 1513–1515*
55. Strauss, *Thoughts on Machiavelli*

Chapter 2: 1504–1513
1. LP iii no. 2394, 17 Jul 1522
2. Ross, Florentine Palaces, pp.105–107
3. Pizan, *The Book of the City of Ladies*
4. Pierotti-Cei, *Life in Italy During the Renaissance*
5. Ibid
6. Alberti, p.200
7. Herald, *Renaissance Dress in Italy*
8. Johnson, p.152
9. de Roover, p.10
10. Ibid, p.15
11. Goldthwaite, p.25
12. MS. Harl. 295, f. 103, 17 May 1503
13. CSPV no.509, Materials vol 1, p.299
14. Setton, vol 3, p.239
15. Ibid
16. Finot, p.424
17. BL Add. MS 59899 f 64
18. MSS. Adv. 204: Royal 13 B. ii. No. .58, 12 Feb 1508
19. Adv. MS. 203, 12 Feb 1508
20. Penn, p.253
21. MS Bodley 488
22. Ibid
23. Penn, p.199

Chapter 3: 1514–1520
1. Giovio, De vita Leonis decimi Pont. Max. libri quatuor. Accesserunt Hadriani sexti Pont. Max. et Pompeii Columnae Cardinalis vitae, May 1548.
2. Ibid
3. Platt, p.204
4. SP 1/87 f. 81, 7 Dec 1534
5. SP 1/104 f. 211, 28 Jun 1535
6. Van Houtte, pp.191–193
7. Rogers, *The Letters of Sir John Hackett 1526–1534*
8. Platt, p.244
9. Bandello, vol 4, p.107
10. SP I/93, f. 77, 16 Jun 1535
11. SP I/104 f. 211, 28 Jun 1535
12. Williams, vol 5, p.196

13. TNA c/1/483/33, 1518
14. TNA, CP 40/1038
15. Ibid
16. Parks, vol 2
17. SP I/43 f. 74, 13 Feb 1538
18. SP 1/118 f. 268r, 24 Apr 1537
19. Chambers, p.77
20. SP 1/131 f. 91, 14 Apr 1538
21. SP 1/118 f. 268r
22. MacCulloch, *A Life*, p.9
23. Vitell. B. II., 9, 28 Aug 1514
24. Le Neve, p.15
25. Harte and Ponting, p22–49
26. Lawrence, p.73
27. Merriman, vol 1, p.12
28. Gerhold, p.31
29. SP I/29 f. 26, 2 Nov 1523
30. LP ix no. 862, 21 Nov 1535
31. SP 1/29 f. 26, 2 Nov 1523 and SP 1/128 f. 136, 29 Jan 1539
32. Blomefield and Parkin, vol 9, p.488
33. SP I/42 ff. 101–116
34. Blomefield and Parkin, p.488
35. Ibid
36. WARD 2/59A/228/24, 31 May 1512
37. LP ix no. 862, 21 Nov 1535
38. SP 1/27 f. 286, 10 May 1523
39. LP iii no.1963, 15 Jan 1522
40. SP 3 f. 73, 4 Nov 1512
41. TNA c244/163/92
42. Nero. B. VI., 25, 26 Aug 1514
43. SP 9, f. 101, 28 Aug 1514
44. Indenture, 22 Feb. 8 Hen. VII (1517)
45. LP iii no. 182, 12 Apr 1519
46. LP iv no. 1865, 3 Jan 1526
47. Vit. B. VIII. 138, 11 Oct 1526
48. Swanson, pp.172–4
49. MS Egerton 2886 f. 112r, May 1518
50. Swanson, p.375
51. Foxe, 1570, 1385
52. Ibid
53. Ibid
54. Ibid
55. Disputatio pro declaratione virtutis indulgentiarum, 1517
56. MacCulloch, *A Life*, p.45
57. Barral-Baron, L'humaniste chrétien face à l'histoire
58. Foxe 1570, 1385
59. BL MS Egerton 2886 f. 112r, May 1518
60. LP iii no. 3015, 10 May 1523
61. LP iii no. 3015, 10 May 1523

Chapter 4: 1520–1523
1. LP iii 1963, 15 Jan 1522
2. MacCulloch, *The Reformation*, p.119

3. Marshall, p.146
4. MacCulloch, *The Reformation*, p.202
5. Marshall, p.124
6. Wyatt, p.58
7. BL MS Harley 6989 f. 17, 27 December 1532
8. Hayward and Kramer, pp.93–104
9. Guy, p.97
10. MacCulloch, *A Life*, p.45
11. SP 1/69 f. 189
12. LP iii 1284 ii
13. SP 1/69 f. 189
14. One example is MSS Vesp. F XIII. 79., 23 Aug 1534
15. LP ii no. 2394, 7 Jul 1522
16. LP iii no. 2557, 22 Sep 1522
17. Vesp. F. XIII. 91 14 Aug 1522
18. SP I/41 f.157r
19. SP I/233 ff. 315–316, 22 Dec 1523
20. SP I/55 f. 129, 28 Sep 1523
21. Fletcher and MacCulloch, p.22
22. SP I/28 f. 154
23. SP viii 509, 17 Oct 1538
24. LP iii no. 3657, 21 Dec 1523
25. Roth, 1249–1538
26. Holder, p.142
27. Blackburn, p.51
28. Sicca, p.172
29. LP iv no. 643, 10 Sep 1524
30. From Stephen Vaughan LP v no. 291 (201), 18 Apr 1531
31. TNA SP2/L, ff. 205–10, nos 183–8
32. SP I/42 ff. 101–116

Chapter 5: 1524–1527
1. Harris, pp.59–88.
2. Mackie and Spillman, *Letters of James IV*
3. SP 1/31 f. 72
4. SP 1/53 f. 37v
5. Fletcher and MacCulloch, p.22
6. Guy, p.103
7. Bodl. MS Jesus College 74 ff. 189r–191r
8. LP iv no, 99, 9 Feb 1524
9. LP iv no. 167, Feb 1524
10. LP iv no. 1385, 5 Jun 1525
11. LP iv no. 1620, 5 Sep 1525
12. LP no. 1768, 31 Oct 1525
13. Ellis vol 2, no. 125
14. LP iv no. 1881, 12 Jan 1526
15. SP 1/44 f. 3
16. SP 1/52 f. 38
17. SP 1/34 ff. 240–48
18. TNA, SP 2/O f. 133
19. SP 1/108 f. 114
20. MacCulloch, *Suffolk and the Tudors*, pp.227–30
21. LP 4 i no. 2024vi, 4 Mar 1526

22. BL MS Cotton Titus B/I f. 358
23. SP 1/235 f. 346
24. SP 1/65 f. 238
25. BL MS Egerton 2886 f. 202r, ff. 295r–296v
26. SP 1/233 ff. 334–8
27. Haigh, p.58
28. SP 1/131, 19 Aug 1527
29. Ellis, vol2 no. 62
30. SP 1/235 f. 216,
31. LP iv no. 3212, Jun 1527
32. LP iv no. 3741, Dec 1527
33. SP 1/106 f. 4r
34. SP I/235 f. 280
35. SP 1/52 f. 219
36. SP 1/59 ff. 104–5
37. SP 1/49 f. 196
38. SP 1/44 ff. 144–5
39. Foxe 1583, 1086

Chapter 6: 1528
1. Cardinal Lorenzo Campeggio, legate to the courts of Henry VIII and Charles V
2. SP 1/104 ff. 118–19 (1538) and SP 1/72 f. 117 (1539)
3. SP 1/98 f. 48, 23 Oct 1535
4. LP iv no. 5446, 9 Apr 1529
5. SP 1/49 f. 3, Jun 1528
6. SP 1/59 f. 127, 14 Mar 1529
7. SP 1/49 f. 3, dated 8 Mar 1522
8. LP iv no. 3819, 20 Jan 1528
9. LP iv no. 4628, 12 Aug 1528
10. Bodl. MS Jesus College 74 f. 193v, Feb 1530
11. LP iv no. 4107, 28 Mar 1528
12. Erler, p.88
13. SP 1/49 f. 152, 27 Jul 1528
14. LP iv no. 4314, 1 Jun 1528
15. LP iv no. 4561, 27 Jul 1528
16. LP iv no. 4656, 21 Aug 1528
17. LP iv no. 4690, 1 Sep 1528
18. Titus, B. I. 275, 26 Sep 1528
19. LP iv no. 4755, 18 Sep 1528
20. LP iv 4843, 13 Oct 1528
21. LP iv no. 4837, 2 Oct 1528
22. LP iv 4934, 15 Nov 1528
23. LP iv 4916, 8 Nov 1528
24. LP iv 5034, 15 Dec 1528
25. Ellis, vol 2, no 113, 18 Jan 1529
26. SP I/53 f. 37v, 23 Feb 1529
27. LP iv no. 5398, 23 Mar 1529
28. LP iv no. 5459, 12 Apr 1529
29. LP iv no. 5446, 9 Apr 1529
30. SP I/52 f. 174r, 12 Apr 1529
31. SP I/736 f. 76, 6 Apr 1529
32. SP I/736 f. 77, 13 Apr 1529
33. LP iv no. 5757i, 5 Jul 1529

34. LP iv no. 5757ii, 5 Jul 1529
35. SP I/54 ff. 234, 12 Jul 1529
36. Ellis 3 Ser, II p171, 30 Oct 1529

Chapter 7: 1529–1530
1. Hall vol 2, p.144
2. Singer, p.72
3. LP iv no.5791, 23 Jul 1529
4. SP 1/53 f. 19v
5. Vit. B. XII. 173, 23 Sep 1529
6. Vit B. XI 21, 30 Sep 1529
7. Mayer, vol 1, p.212
8. Ellis, vol 2, p.171
9. Singer, p.270
10. Ibid, p.260
11. BL MS Cotton Otho C/X f. 218v
12. Singer, pp.270–71
13. SP 1/55 f. 198
14. SP 1/236 ff. 168–9
15. SP 1/54 f. 208v
16. Herbert, pp.266–74
17. SP 1/68 f. 58
18. Herbert, p.274
19. Bodl. MS Jesus College 74 ff. 189r–190r
20. LP iv no.6099, 19 Dec 1529
21. Cott. App. XLVIII 10
22. Spanish Calendar, iv no.267, 6 Feb 1530
23. SP 1/46 f. 227
24. Rym. XIV, 366
25. Cott. App. XLVIII. 23
26. Cott. App. XLVIII, 19
27. Cott. App. XLVIII. 18
28. LP iv no.6223, 18 Feb 1530
29. Cott. App. XLVII. 11
30. MSS. Jesus Coll. in Bibl. Bodl. Oxon. c.74, p.262 ff
31. Ibid
32. Ibid
33. Ibid
34. Ibid
35. Cott. App. XLVIII. 13
36. Wien, Rep Fasc c.226
37. MSS. Jesus Coll. in Bibl. Bodl. Oxon. c.74, p.262 ff
38. MSS. Jesus Coll. in Bibl. Bodl. Oxon. c.74, p.262 ff
39. Spanish Calendar v no.228
40. Wien, Rep Fasc 229 ½ ii, 30
41. LP xiv.ii no.782, f. 31, f. 117, Jul 1538
42. LP xiv.i no.130, 24 Jan 1539
43. MacCulloch, *A Life*, p.102
44. C. Johnson, p.22

Chapter 8: 1531
1. LP iv no.47vi, 15 Jan 1531
2. Add. MS. 28,583 f.59, 13, 6 Feb 1531

3. LP v no.23, 1 Jan 1531
4. LP v no.26, 3 Jan 1531
5. LP v no.32, 7 Jan 1531
6. LP v no.36, 9 Jan 1531
7. Lambeth MS 751, 55–75
8. TNA, E 135/8/36
9. SP 1/68 f.109
10. Cleop. F. II. 223. B. M., 16 Jan 1531
11. Parl. Roll. 22 Hen. 8.c.16
12. LP v no.52, 16 Jan 1531
13. BL MS Cotton Galba B/X f.46r
14. MSS Galba B. x 338, May 1531
15. SP 1/81 f.95, Apr 1531
16. BL MS Cotton Galba B/X f.10, 3 Jun 1531
17. LP v no.506i, 3 Oct 1531
18. MacCulloch, *Thomas Cranmer*, pp.60–66
19. Maas, pp.25–6
20. Venetian Calendar 4 no.694, at 297, Nov 1531
21. LP v no.303, 19 Jun 1531
22. LP v no.315, 30 Jun 1531
23. LP v no.333, 11 Jul 1531
24. Nero, B. VI. 163. B.M, 14 Jul 1531
25. Ellis, 3 Ser. I. 340, LP v no.496, 25 Oct 1531
26. B. M. St. P. I. 380, Aug 1531
27. Titus B.I. 368, 14 Nov 1531
28. LP v no.429, 23 Sep 1531
29. LP v no.431, 4 Oct 1531
30. LP v no.620, 31 Dec 1531
31. LP v no.646, 1531
32. LP v no.596, 22 Dec 1531
33. Lambeth MS 616 f.46, 2 Jan 1532
34. Moynahan, p.260
35. Foxe 1570, p.1204
36. Foxe 1570, p.1211

Chapter 9: 1532
1. SP I/69 f. 40, Jan 1532
2. LP v no.701, 9 Jan 1532
3. Lehmberg, pp.138–46
4. Wilkins, III, p.750
5. Vit. B. XIII. 144. B.M. 5 Jan 1532
6. Titus, B.I. 353. B.M., 14 Jan 1532
7. Harl. MS. 425, f.13 b. B.M., 11 Mar 1532
8. LP v no.789, 8 Feb 1532
9. SP 1/70 f.56, 24 May 1532
10. LP v no.978 xiii, 12 Apr 1532
11. Howard, p.131
12. MacCulloch, *Thomas Cromwell*, p.167
13. Hall 2, pp.209–11
14. Lambeth MS 751, pp.91–3
15. Pocock, II., p.257
16. St. P. VII. 370, 16 May 1532
17. SP II/L ff.183–188, 16 May 1532
18. LP v no.1086, 11 June 1532

19. LP v no.1207 xxxvi, 16 Jul 1532
20. LP v no.1065 xxxiii, 17 May 1532
21. MacCulloch, *A Life*, p.174
22. McSheffrey, pp.1–3
23. LP v no. 1300, 8 Sep 1532
24. LP v no.1318, 16 Sep 5132
25. LP v no.1369, Sep 1532
26. LP v no.1318, 16 Sep 1532
27. Lansd. MS. 261, f.140. B.M., 1 Oct 1532
28. LP v no.1317, 16 Sep 1532
29. Ellis, vol II, 196, 18 Sep 1532
30. LP v no.s791, 807
31. Royal MS. 7 C. XVI. f. 40. B.M, 1 Oct 1532
32. LP v no.1285, 2 Sep 1532
33. LP v no.1339, 23 Sep 1532
34. LP v no.1342, 24 Sep 1532
35. LP v no.1386, 5 Oct 5132
36. LP v no.1442, 16 Oct 1532
37. LP v no.1447, 18 Oct 1532
38. LP v no.1454, 20 Oct 1532
39. LP v no.1452, 20 Oct 1532
40. LP v no,1464, 23 Oct 1532
41. LP v no.1743, 26 Oct 1532
42. LP v no.1472, 25 oct 1532
43. LP v no.1284, 1285, Camusat, 106, 29 Oct 1532
44. LP v no.1578, 26 Nov 1532

Chapter 10: 1533
 1. Rym. XIV. 446, 26 Jan 1533
 2. LP vi no.70, 23 Jan 1533
 3. LP vi no.221, 10 Mar 1533
 4. LP vi no.103, Jan 1533
 5. Vit. B.XIII. 144, 5 Jan 1533
 6. MSS Titus, B.I., 419, 11 Mar 1533
 7. LP v no.1620, 9 Dec 1532
 8. Harl. MS. 283, f.97, 12 Apr 1533
 9. LP vi no.324, 10 Apr 1533
10. Rym. XIV. 454, 5 Apr 1533
11. SP 1/80 f.75, 1 Nov 1533
12. MacCulloch, *Thomas Cranmer*, p.135
13. Egerton MS. 985, f. 57b, 28 Apr 1533
14. LP vi no.351 15 Apr 1533
15. SP 1/75 f.167, 24 Apr 1533
16. Ross, *The Foremost Man of the Kingdom*
17. SP 1/76 f.33, 11 May 1533
18. RSTC 656, May 1533
19. LP vi no.603, 8 Jun 1533
20. SP 177 f.77, 24 Jun 1533
21. LP vi no.612, 9 Jun 1533
22. LP vi no. 604, 8 Jun 1533
23. Pocock, II. 487, Jun 1533
24. Otho, C. X. 199. B. M. 3 Jul 1533
25. Rym.XIV.476, 29 Jun 1533

26. SP 1/78 f.25, 23 Jul 1533
27. Wien. Rep. P. Fasc.,c. 228, no.46, 30 Jul 1533
28. Carley, De uiris illustribus
29. Lisle Letters, I, 46, 1 Sep 1533
30. LP vi no.1159, 27 Sep 1533
31. Mercers' Co. Archives, MS. Acts of Ct. 1453–1527, f. 6d
32. The Antiquary, p.167
33. LP vi no.1164, 27 Sep 1533
34. LP vi no.1182, 30 Sep 1533
35. LP vi no.1181, 30 Sep 1533
36. SP 2/O ff. 119–131, 1533
37. LP viii no.962 xxii, 25 June 1533
38. Waters, *Genealogical memoirs of the families of Chester and Astry*
39. LP vi no.1215, 4 Oct 1533
40. St. P. VII. 516, 21 Oct 1533
41. LP vi no.1354, 1355, 26/27 Oct 1533
42. Vesp. C. XIII. 257, 15 Nov 1533
43. LP vi no.1445, 20 Nov 1533
44. LP vi no.1468, Nov 1533
45. MacCulloch, *A Life*, p.235
46. LP vi no. 1460, 24 Nov 1533

Chapter 11: 1534
1. Wien, Rep. P.C., Fasc. 229, no.8, 28 Jan 1534
2. Harl. MSS. 6148, f.81, 5 Jan 1534
3. SP 1/79 f.158, 10 Oct 1533
4. LP vii no.83, 17 Jan 1534
5. LP vii no.153, 4 Feb 1534
6. 25 Hen. 8 c. 6
7. Cocks, p27
8. MSS Cleo. E. vi. f.101, 31 Jan 1534
9. MSS Cleo. E. iv, f.101, 27 Feb 1534
10. MacCulloch, *A Life*, p.245
11. LP vii no.373, 25 Mar 1534
12. LP vii no.386, 28 Mar 1534
13. Otho. C. x. 171, 5 May 1534
14. LP vii no.483, 15 Apr 1534
15. Add. MSS. 25,114 f. 348, 24 Apr 1534
16. LP vii no.530, 22 Apr 1534
17. LP vii no.586, Apr 1534
18. LP vii no.423, 1 Apr 1534
19. Wilkins, III. 771, 2 May 1534
20. LP vii no.599, 2 May 1534
21. Rym. XIV. 529, 11 May 1534
22. LP vii no.619, 6 May 1534
23. LP vii no.658, 13 May 1534
24. LP vi no.675, 16 May 1534
25. LP vii no.690, 19 May 1534
26. LP vii no.862, 20 June 1534
27. LP vii no.776, 3 June 1534
28. LP vii no.944, 3 July 1534
29. LP vii no 977, 15 Jul 1534
30. SP 60/2 f.48, Jul 1534

31. Webb, *Archbishop John Allen*
32. LP vii no. 1141, 19 Sep 1534
33. MSS Vesp. F XIII. 79., 23 Aug 1534
34. LP vii no.1161, 18 Sep 1534
35. LP vii no.1129, 2 Sep 1534
36. LP vii. no1194, 27 Sep 1534
37. LP vii no.1173, 21 Sep 1534
38. LP vii no.1189, 24 Sep 1534
39. Wien, Rep. P.C., Fasc. 228, no.57, 23 Sep 1534
40. LP vii no.1185, 24 Sep 1534
41. 26 Henry VIII 8 c.3, MSS Cleo. E. IV. 174, Nov 1534
42. MMS Titus BI 413, 7 Dec 1534

Chapter 12: 1535
1. Knowles, pp.241–54
2. LP viii no.195, 11 Feb 1535
3. LP viii no.189, 9 Feb 1535
4. LP viii no.198, 11 Feb 1535
5. LP viii no.263, 26 Feb 1535
6. LP viii no.263, 26 Feb 1535
7. Ibid
8. LP viii no.107, 26 Jan 1535
9. LP viii no. 319, 3 Mar 1535
10. LP viii no.301, 302, Feb 1535
11. Wien., Rep. P.C., Fasc. 229½, f.46, 7 Mar 1535
12. LP viii no.299, Feb 1535
13. Wien., Rep. P.C., Fasc. 229½, f.46, 7 Mar 1535
14. Ibid
15. LP viii no.501, 3 Apr 1535
16. Wien, Rep. P.C., Fasc. 230, no.23,17 Apr 1535
17. MSS Titus BI 425, 10 Apr 1535
18. MSS Vesp. F. xiii. 71 b, 26 Apr 1535
19. Ibid
20. Ibid
21. LP viii no.661, 4 May 1535
22. Harl. MS. 530, f.54, 19 Jun 1535
23. Brigden, p.270
24. Wien. Rep. P. C., Fasc. 229½, ii. f.29, 23 May 1535
25. Wien. Rep. P. C., Fasc. 229½, ii. f.29, 23 May 1535
26. Cook, pp.55–56
27. BL Cotton MS Cleo. E iv f.249, Aug 1535
28. BL Cotton MS Cleo. E iv f134b
29. Wien, Rep. P.C., Fasc. 229½, 5 Jun 1535
30. LP viii no.878, 16 Jun 1535
31. LP ix no.422, 24 Sep 1535
32. SP 1/96 f. 209, 25 Nov 1535
33. SP. 1/431–436, 14 Jun 1535
34. Cleop. E. vi. 178 b, 17 Jun 1535
35. MSS Titus, B.I. 474, 17 Jun 1535
36. LP viii 948, 30 Jun 1540
37. LP viii no.957, Jun 1535
38. LP viii no.974, 1 Jul 1535
39. Titus, B. xi.425, 14 Aug 1535

40. LP viii no.1105, 25 Jul 1535
41. LP viii no.1088, 22 Jul 1535
42. LP ix no.132, 139, 20 Aug 1535
43. LP ix no.131, 20 Aug 1535
44. LP ix no.1142, 30 Sep 1535
45. LP ix no.66, 11 Aug 1535
46. LP ix no.193, 27 Aug 1535
47. Titus, B. xi. 425
48. SP 1/438, 7 Aug 1535
49. LP ix no.42, 7 Aug 1535
50. LP ix no.51, 8 Aug 1535
51. LP ix no.191, Sep 1535
52. LP ix no.622, 16 Oct 1535
53. LP ix no.651, 21 Oct 1535
54. Titus B.I., 360, 3 Oct 1535
55. LP ix no.422, 24 Sep 1535
56. LP ix no.386, 18 Sep 1535
57. MSS Titus B. I. 412, 2 Oct 1535
58. MSS Cleo. E. VI. 253b, 15 oct 1535
59. Close Roll 27 Hen. viii. m. 11d, 13 Nov 1535
60. STC 26119
61. BL MS Royal 18 CVI
62. LP ix no. 862, 21 Nov 1535
63. Wien, Rep. P.C ,Fasc. 229½, ii. 72, 13 Dec 1535

Chapter 13: 1536
 1. Wien, Rep. P. C., Fasc. 230, 1–4, 1 Apr 1536
 2. LP x no.200, 29 Jan 1536
 3. LP x no.76, 11 Jan 1536
 4. MSS Otho. C. x. 216, 7 Jan 1536
 5. Wien, Rep. P.C., Fasc. 236, no.3, 21 Jan 1536
 6. TNA, SP 70/7 ff. 6r-7r
 7. SC v no.29, 23 Feb 1536
 8. SP 1/142 f.202rv
 9. LP x no.84, 11 Jan 1536
10. Cleop. E. iv. 115, 13 Jan 1536
11. Cleop. E. iv. 203, 13 Jan 1536
12. Vesp. F. xiii. 79 b, 18 Jan 1536
13. Wien, Rep. P.C., Fasc. 236, no.3, 21 Jan 1536
14. A.D. 1535 Anno vicesimo septimo Henrici VIII c. 26
15. Elton, *The Tudor Constitution*
16. BL MS Royal 18 CVI
17. Hardy, p.257
18. LP x no.356, 26 Feb 1536
19. MSS Vit B. xiv. 278, 15 Mar 1536
20. Harl. MS. 6,989, f.56, 9 Apr 1536
21. LP x no.368, 28 Feb 1536
22. Nero, B. vi. 130, 28 Feb 1536
23. Wien, Rep. P. C., Fasc, 25 Feb 1536
24. MSS Cleo. E. iv. 230, 20 Mar 1536
25. Wien, Rep. P. C., Fasc. 230, 1–4, 1 Apr 1536
26. Ibid
27. LP x no. 597. 47 i -ii, 10 Mar 1536

28. Wien. Rep. P. C.,Fasc. 229½, 1–4, 21 Apr 1536
29. Ibid
30. LP x no.700, 21 Apr 1536
31. Ibid
32. Anstis' Order of the Garter. ii.398, 23 Apr 1536
33. LP v no.848i, vi, 24 Apr 1536
34. Close Roll, 28 Hen. VIII. m.43 d, 27 April 1536
35. LP x no.753, 29 Apr 1536
36. Ibid
37. Hume, p.91
38. LP x no.783, 2 May 1536
39. Wien, Rep. P.C., Fasc. 230, No. 32, 6 June 1536
40. LP x no.1256 ii, Jun 1536
41. BL MS Cotton Vespasian F/XIII f. 199, May 1536
42. MSS Titus, B. I. 444, 13 May 1536
43. MSS Otho. C. x. 273, 10 Jun 1536
44. MSS Otho, C. x. 262 b, 125, 10 Jun 1536
45. Wien, Rep. P.C. Fasc. 229½, 1 Jul 1536
46. Wien, Rep. P.C., Fasc, 8 Jul 1536
47. Hearne's Sylloge, 144, 23 June 1536
48. BL MS 163 f.95
49. LP xi no.135, 21 Jul 1536
50. LP xi no.321, 18 Aug 1536
51. MSS Otho, C. x. 267, 1 Jul 1536
52. LP xi no.148 i-ii, 23 Jul 1536 i
53. SP. v. 58, 12 Aug 1536
54. LP xi no. 233, 5 Aug 1536
55. LP xi no.335, 20 Aug 1536
56. LP xi no.548 – 551, 5 Oct 1536
57. LP x no.663, 13 Apr 1536
58. LP x no.276, Jul 1536
59. BL MS Cotton Cleo. E/IV f. 323r
60. LP xci no.354, 24 Aug 1536
61. SP 1/110 f. 133rv,
62. SP 1/109 f. 1r, 21 Oct 1536
63. MacCulloch, *Thomas Cranmer*, pp.170–71
64. Spanish Calendar v no. 104, 7 Oct 1536
65. SP 1/115 f. 41
66. SP 1/506, 2 Nov 1536
67. SP 1/111 f.56, 11 Nov 1536

Chapter 14: 1537
1. Thomas, *The Pilgrim*
2. LP xii.ii no.976, 19 Apr 1537
3. SP 1/114 f.77, 12 Jan 1537
4. Bush and Bownes, p.151
5. LP xiv.ii no.782, f. 82
6. Ibid
7. Ibid
8. LP xi no.506, Mar 1537
9. LP xii.i no.6, 1 Jan 1537
10. LP xii.i no.201, 23 Jan 1537
11. MSS Calig. B. II. 344, 28 Jan 1537

12. LP xii.i no.533, Feb 1537
13. SP 1/118 f.43
14. LP xii.i no.429, 15 Feb 1537
15. LP xii.i no.430, 15 Feb 1537
16. SP 1/120 ff.205–7, May 1537
17. 2 LP xii.i no.678, 18 Mar 1537
18. Titus B. I. 489, 3 Apr 1537
19. LP xiv.ii no.782, f.82
20. MS Cotton Cleopatra E/IV f.256, 14 Jun 1537
21. Titus B.I. 383a, 16 Jun 1537
22. Harl. MSS.282, f.203, 6 Jun 1537
23. LP xii.ii no.51, 7 Jun 1537
24. LP xii.i no.891, 10 Apr 1537
25. LP xiv.ii no.782, f.82
26. SP 1/116 f.157, Feb 1537
27. LP xiv.ii no.782, f. 82
28. LP xii.ii no.242, 11 Jul 1537
29. LP xii no. 242, 11 Jul 1537
30. Ibid
31. LP xii.ii no.300, 21 Jul 1537
32. LP xii.ii App 44, Oct 1537
33. LP xii.ii no.299, 21 Jul 1537
34. Anstis' Order of the Garter,ii. 407, 5 Aug 1537
35. Ibid
36. Anstis' Order of the Garter,ii. 408, 26 Aug 1537
37. Cranmer's Works, 469, 13 Aug 1537
38. LP xiv.ii no.782, f. 82
39. LP xii.ii no.629, 2 Sep 1537
40. LP xii.ii no.629, 2 Sep 1537
41. SP v. 2ii, 28 Sep 1537
42. SP 1/125 f. 71, Sep 1537
43. Hearne's Trokelowe, p271, 1 Oct 1537
44. SP 1/126 f.58, 4 Nov 1537
45. LP xii.ii no. 827, 4 Oct 1537
46. Nero C. x. 1, 12 Oct 1537
47. LP xiv.ii no. 782, f. 82
48. Ibid
49. Add. MS. 6,113, f.81, 15 Oct 1537
50. LP xiv.ii no.782, f.82
51. LP xii.ii no.971, 24 Oct 1537
52. SP viii, 368, 27 Oct 1537
53. Ibid
54. SP. viii. 5, 4 Dec 1537
55. Heralds' College MS. I. 11,f. 37, 12 Nov 1537
56. Belvoir Castle MSS, 12 Nov 1537
57. MSS Titus B. I, f.416, 5 Dec 1537
58. SP 1/126 f. 118v, 13 Nov 1537
59. LP xiv.ii no.782, f. 82
60. Ibid
61. SP 1/127 f.49, 14 Dec 1537
62. LP xiv.ii no.782, f. 82

Chapter 15: 1538
1. LP xiv.ii no.782, f.31, f.117 Jan 1538
2. LP xiii.i no.190xi, 14 Jan 1538
3. LP xiii.i no.312, 18 Feb 1538
4. LP xiii.i no.41, 4 Jan 1538
5. LP xiii.i no.76, 14 Jan 1538
6. MSS Cleo. E. iv, f.7, 7 Jan 1538
7. LP xiii.i no.306, 17 Feb 1538
8. LP xiii.i no.236, Feb 1538
9. LP xiii.i no.13, 2 Jan 1536
10. Harl. MS.6,989, f.80, 24 Jan 1538
11. Royal M.S.7. C. xvi. 19, 25 Jan 1538
12. LP xiii.i no.590, 24 Mar 1538
13. LP xiv.ii no.782, f.31, f.117 Mar 1538
14. Add. MSS. 5,498, ff. 1–2, Feb 1538
15. Madden, pp.66–69
16. LP xiv.ii no.782, f.31, f.117 Apr 1538
17. Harl MSS. 282, f. I78, 1 March 1538
18. LP xiv.ii no.782, f.31, f. 117 Jan 1538
19. LP xiv.ii no.782, f.31, f. 117 Apr 1538
20. Ellis, 3d Ser.iii. 192, 11 Apr 1538
21. Noble, vol 2
22. LP xiv.ii no.782, f.31, f.117 Mar 1538
23. LP xiii.i no.504, 14 Mar 1538
24. SP. ii. 551.i-ii, 9 Mar 1538
25. LP xiii.i no.771, 15 Apr 1538
26. Kaulek, 49, 14 May 1538
27. LP xii.ii no.1286, May 1538
28. Spanish Calendar 6 i no. 7, 31 Aug 1538
29. Haigh, *English reformations*
30. Parks, vol 2
31. Kaulek, 49, 14 May 1538
32. SP 3/4 f.35, May 1538
33. Kaulek, 54, 31 May 1538
34. LP xiv.ii no.782, f.31, f. 117 Jun 1538
35. Spanish Calendar 5.ii., No. 225, 17 June 1538
36. LP xiii.i no.1297, Jun 1538
37. LP xiv.ii no782, f.31, f.117 Sep 1538
38. LP xiv.ii no. 782, f.31, f.117 Jul 1538
39. LP xiv.ii no782, f.31, f.117 Sep 1538
40. LP xiii.ii no. 1250, 18 Aug 1538
41. LP xiii.i no.1282, 29 Jun 1538
42. LP xiv.ii no. 782, f.31, f.117 Sep 1538
43. Ibid
44. Barlow, *Thomas Becket*
45. MSS Cleo. E. v, f.344, Jun 1538
46. Burnet iv. 341, 5 Sep 1538
47. LP xiii.ii no.336, 12 Sep 1538
48. LP xiii.ii no.551, 6 Oct 1538
49. LP xiv.ii no.782, f.31, f.117, Oct 1538
50. SP viii 509, 17 Oct 1538
51. SP viii 509, 17 Oct 1538
52. LP xiii.ii no.1124, 22 Dec 1538

53. Nero B. vi.132, 1 Oct 1538
54. Baga de Secretis, Pouch XI. Bundle II
55. Baga de Secretis, Pouch XI., Bundle I
56. LP xiii.ii no.967, Nov 1538
57. LP xiv.ii no.782, f.31, f.117 Nov-Dec 1538
58. Ibid
59. LP xiii.i no.1200, (misdated 17 Jun 1538)
60. MacCulloch, *Thomas Cromwell*, pp.482–83
61. LP xiii.ii no109, 18 Dec 1538
62. LP xii.ii no.881, filed as 10 Oct 1537 but undated
63. SP 1 f.46, 14 Mar 1538
64. *Topographical History of the Country of Norfolk*, vol 9, p.489

Chapter 16: 1539

1. LP xiv.i no. 18.ii, 4 Jan 1539
2. LP xiv.ii no. 782, f.59, f. 117 Jan 1539
3. Ibid
4. MS Harl. 47 A. 50, 16 Jan 1539
5. LP xiv.i no. 204, 2 Feb 1539
6. LP xiv.i no. 189, Jan 1539
7. LP xiv.i no. 498, 11 Mar 1539
8. BL MS Cotton Titus BI f. 101r, Dec 1546
9. SP 3/1 f. 52a, 3 Dec 1539
10. SP 1/142 f. 1, Jan 1539
11. LP xiii.ii no. 962. 52, 29 Nov 1538
12. SP iii. 118, 16 Feb 1539
13. SP iii 116, 18 Jan 1539
14. Murray, pp.122–3
15. SP. viii. 524, 21 Jan 1539
16. Ribier vol 1, 364, 26 Jan 1539
17. MSS Titus B. I, f. 263, 5 Feb 1539
18. Lanz, II. 297, 9 Jan 1539
19. LP xiv.i no. 247, 7 feb 1539
20. LP xiv.i no. 321, 19 Feb 1539
21. SP viii. 176, 7 Mar 1539
22. LP xiv.i no. 478, 9 Mar 1539
23. Spanish Calendar, 6 i. no. 43, 8 Mar 1539
24. LP xiv.i no. 541, 17 Mar 1539
25. P xiv.i no. 651, 11 Mar 1539
26. LP xiv.i no. 579, 21 Mar 1539
27. SP viii, no. 531, Mar 1539
28. Harl. MSS. 282, f. 195, 12 Apr 1539
29. LP xiv.i no. 212, 2 Feb 1539
30. MSS Vit B. XXI. 177, 14 Apr 1539
31. LP xiv. No. 285, 13 Feb 1539
32. LP xiv.ii no.782, f.59, f. 117 Aug 1539
33. LP xiv.i no. 130, 24 Jan 1539
34. LP xiv.ii no. 782, f.59, f. 117 Apr 1539
35. Ibid
36. Ibid
37. MSS Vit C. XVI. 264, Jun 1539
38. Titus B.I. 391 B. M, 29 Jan 1539
39. LP xiv.i no. 169, 30 Jan 1539

40. LP xiv.i no. 992, 20 May 1539
41. MSS Titus B.I. 261, 16 Apr 1539
42. Titus B. I. 265, 19 Apr 1539
43. MSS Nero B. vi, f. 5, 23 Apr 1539
44. MSS Cleo. E. v.172, 24 Apr 1539
45. Parl Rolls, 31 Hen. 8 c. 10
46. MacCulloch, *A Life*, p500
47. Haigh, p.153
48. LP xiv.ii no. 782, f.59, f. 117, 1539
49. SP 1/152 f. 118, Jul 1539
50. LP xiv.ii no. 782, f.59, f. 117 Jun 1539
51. Foxe, Book of Martyrs, 1570, p.1337 and p.2075
52. MacCulloch, *A Life*, p.505
53. Kaulek 108, 5 Jul 1539
54. LP xiv.ii no. 782, f.59, f. 117, Jul 1539
55. LP xiv.i no. 11 Jul 1539
56. MSS Vesp. F. XIII. 104, 17 Jul 1539
57. LP xiv.i no. 1348, Jul 1539
58. MS Nero, B. VI. 56, Jul 1539
59. LP xiv.ii no. 12, 2 Aug 1537
60. Ellis, 3 S. III. 87, 15 Aug 1539
61. SP 1/155 ff. 154v, 157rv, 16 Dec 1539
62. LP xiv.ii no. 85, Aug 1539
63. Harl. MS. 6,89, f. 4, 19 Aug 1539
64. MSS Vit C. XVI. 275, 4 Sep 1539
65. LP xiv.ii no. 782, f.59, f. 117, Sep 1539
66. LP xiv.ii no. 149, 11 Sep 1539
67. Harl. MS. 296 f 185, 25 Sep 1539
68. MSS Vit C. XI., f. 213, 4 Oct 1539
69. LP xiv.ii no. 356, 19 Oct 1539
70. Corpus Reform, III. 796, 23 Oct 1539
71. Kaulek, 138, 25 Oct 1539
72. Rymer XIV. 649, 14 Nov 1539
73. Kaulek 143, 13 Nov 1539
74. LP xiv.ii no. 315, 13 Nov 1539
75. LP xiv.ii no. 541, 17 Nov 1539
76. LP xiv.ii no. 782, f.59, f. 117, Nov 1539
77. Harl. MS. 295, f. 153 b, 22 Nov 1539
78. LP xiv.ii no. 638, 5 Dec 1539
79. LP xiv.ii no. 693, 16 Dec 1539
80. SP 1/155 f. 111v, 13 Dec 1539
81. LP xiv.ii no. 782, f.59, f. 117, Dec 1539

Chapter 17: 1540

1. Cecil Papers, 124–7, 30 Jun 1540
2. *Hall's Chronicle*, p.852
3. Kaulek, 15, 5 Jan 1540
4. Ibid
5. Cecil Papers, 124–7, 30 Jun 1540
6. Ibid
7. Ibid
8. SP viii, 554, 15 Jan 1540

9. LP xv no.91, 21 Jan 1540
10. MS. Adv. Lib., Edinb., Sadler State Papers, i. 46, 22 Feb 1540
11. SP viii, 560, Jan 1540
12. Burnet, pp.187–192
13. Harl. MS. 1061, 8 Jul 1540
14. MSS Cleo. E. v, 2357 Mar 1540
15. Add. MS. 33,514, f.36, 7 Mar 1540
16. MSS Cleo. ff.405–406, 29 Mar 1540
17. Foxe App. no. vii. 436, 27 Mar 1540
18. Ribier I, 513, 10 Apr 1540
19. Burnet, vol 1, pp.187–99
20. Herbert, p456, 12 Apr 1540
21. Roy. 7 C. xvi, f.149, 7 Apr 1540
22. MSS Vesp. F. xiii., 202, 15 Apr 1540
23. LP xv 477, 8 Apr 1540
24. Ribier, I, 513, 10 Apr 1540
25. LP xv no.611, 37, 17 Apr 1540
26. Mortimer, p.115
27. Harl MS. 6,074, f. 57b. 18 Apr 1540
28. LP xv no. 498, 36, Apr 1540
29. Kaulek 179, 24 Apr 1540
30. Anstis' Order of the Garter, ii. 413, 23 Apr 1540
31. Noble, pp.5–20
32. Johnson, vol 3, p.107
33. Draper's Company pp.759–62
34. The Medieval Friaries of London, p.167
35. LP xiv.ii no.782, f.117, Feb 1539
36. Draper's Company, A XII 121
37. The Medieval Friaries of London, p.167
38. LP xv no.1029 vii
39. BL, Royal MS Appendix 89, f. 70
40. TNA, E36/153, f. 21
41. Starkey and Ward p.181, no. 9015
42. Ibid
43. Given the events of the second half of the year, it is unlikely Elizabeth gave birth any later than May and still named the baby after her father-in-law. As Edward Cromwell was born in May 1539, it is unlikely the child was born any earlier than May 1540

Chapter 18: Decimation

1. Harl. MS. 282, f.243, 5 Apr 1540
2. SP viii 590, 11 May 1540
3. Titus B. I. 406. B.M, 9 May 1540
4. Kaulek 181, 8 May 1540
5. SP i 627, 19 May 1540
6. SP iii, 206, 17 May 1540
7. Kaulek 187, 1 June 1540
8. MSS Cleo. E. v., 300, 7 Jun 1540
9. Burnet, *The History of the Reformation*
10. Bodl. MS Jesus College, 74, f.299r
11. Strype, 459, 7 July 1540
12. Kaulek 193, 23 Jun 1540

13. Kaulek 191, Jun 1540
14. SP 1/160 ff.140, 10 Jun 1540
15. MS Harley 288 ff.47, 16 Jun 1540
16. Kaulek 193, 23 Jun 1540
17. Starkey and Ward p181 no.9015
18. Cranmer's Works, 1846, p401, 11 Jun 1540
19. Parl. Rolls, 32 Hen. 8,c.62
20. MSS Otho C. x, f. 247, 30 Jun 1540
21. Kaulek 197, Jul 1540
22. SP viii, 613, 12 Jul 1540
23. SP 1/642, 24 Jul 1540
24. LP xv no.917, 27 Jul 1540
25. Herbert, Bodleian Library Oxford, Folio 624, 462
26. Hume, p.104
27. Foxe, 1563
28. Hall vol 2, pp.306–7
29. Cox, Parker Society MS 168 f. 209rv
30. Ibid
31. Galton, *The Character of Times of Thomas Cromwell*
32. Epistolarum Reinaldi Poli Collectio iii. 62, 11 Sep 1540

Epilogue
1. MSS Vesp. F. xiii. 157, 30 Jul 1540
2. Venn, Alumni Cantabrigienses, vol. 1, 1922
3. Carthew, Hundred of Launditch, ii. 522, 1878
4. Noble, Memoirs of the Protectorate-house of Cromwell, p.15
5. Kaulek 261, 18 Jan 1541
6. Waters, Genealogical memoirs of the families of Chester and Astry
7. Fry, pp.78–95
8. MacCulloch, The Reformation, p.411
9. Ayris and Selwyn, *Thomas Cranmer*
10. Lennon, p.151
11. Kaulek 274, 3 Mar 1541

Bibliography

PRIMARY SOURCES

Alesius, A., *A treatise concernynge Generall Councilles, the Byshoppes of Rome and the Clergy …* (London, 1538, *RSTC* 24237)

Anstis, J., *The register of the most noble Order of the Garter… usually called the Black Book* 2 vols (Barber, London, 1724)

Bandello, M., *The Novels of Matteo Bandello Bishop of Agen now first done into English prose and verse, ed. and trans. J. Payne* 6 vols (Villion Society, London, 1890)

Barlow, W. *A dyaloge describing the originall ground of these Lutheran faccyons …* (London, 1531, *RSTC* 1461)

Brewer, J. S. et al, *Letters and Papers, Foreign and Domestic of the reign of Henry VIII 1509 – 47* 21 vols (London, 1862 – 1932)

(BL) British Library, London
Additional MSS Charters
Arundel MSS
Cotton MSS
Cotton MSS Appendix
Cotton MSS Caligula
Cotton MSS Claudius
Cotton MSS Cleopatra
Cotton MSS Galba
Cotton MSS Nero
Cotton MSS Othello
Cotton MSS Titus
Cotton MSS Vespasian
Cotton MSS Vitellius
Egerton MS
Harley MSS and Harley Charters
Landsdowne MSS
Royal MSS
Western Illuminated MS

Bullen M. W. and A. H., *A Dialogue Against the Feuer Pestilence, by William Bullein, from the Edition of 1578, Collated with the Earlier Editions of 1564 and 1573* (EETS extra series 52, 1888)

Carthew, G. A., *The Hundred of Launditch and Deanery of Brisley* (Miller and Leavins, Brisley, 1877)

Cavendish, G., *The Life of Cardinal Wolsey* (Harding and Lepard, London, 1827)

Chirbury, E. Lord Herbert of., *The Life and Raigne of King Henry the Eighth* (London, 1649, Wing H1504)

Cokayne, G. E., Gibbs, V., et al, *The Complete Peerage of England, Scotland, Ireland, Great Britain and the United Kingdom, Extant, Extinct or Dormant*, 14 vols (St Catherine Press, London, 1910)

Dilly, C., *The British Plutarch: Containing the Lives of the Most Eminent Statesmen, Patriots, Divines, Warriors, Philosophers, Poets, and Artists, of Great Britain and Ireland, from the Accession of Henry VIII. to the Present Time. Including a Complete History of England from that Area* (London, 1791)

Dymond, D., *The Register of Thetford Priory II: 1518–1540* (Norfolk Record Society, 60, 1996)

Ellis, H., *Original Letters illustrative of English History... from autographs in the British Museum and... other collections* 11 vols (Bentley, London, 1824, 1827, 1846)

Erasmus, D. *Liber ... de praeparatione ad mortem ... accedunt aliquot epistolae seriis de rebus, in quibus item nihil est non novum ac recens* (Basel, 1534)

Finot, J., *Le Commerce d'alun dans les pays-as in* (Imprint Nationale, Paris, 1903)

Foxe, J. *The Unabridged Acts and Monuments Online or TAMO* (HRI Online Publications, Sheffield, 2011). Available from: http//www.johnfoxe.org

Foxe, J., *The first volume of the ecclesiasticall history contaynyng the actes and monuments of thynges passed in every kynges tume in this realme... The second volume of the ecclesiastical history, contenynyng the actes and monumentes of martyrs* (Daye, London, 1570)

Foxe, J., *Actes and monuments of matters most speciall and memorable, happenyng in the Church* (London, 1583, *RSTC* 11225)

Foxe, J., *Actes and Monuments of these latter and perillous dayes ...* (London, 1563, *RSTC* 11222)

Foxe, J., *The first volume of the ecclesiasticall history contaynyng the actes and monumentes of thynges passed in euery kynges tyme in this realme ... The second volume of the ecclesiastical history, conteynyng the actes and monumentes of martyrs* (London, 1570, *RSTC* 11223)

Franciscus, A., *Itinerarium Britanniae, A Journey to London in 1497* (Barcelona, 1953)

Fry, G. S., *Abstracts of Inquisitiones Post Mortem For the City of London, Part 1* (London, 1896)

Gaye, G., *Carteggio inedito d'artisti del sec. XIV, XV, XVI* (Florence, 1839–40)

Giovio, P., *De vita Leonis decimi Pont. Max. libri quatuor. Accesserunt Hadriani sexti Pont. Max. et Pompeii Columnae Cardinalis vitae.* (Laurentius Torrentinus, Florence, 1548)

Gough, W., *The noble tryumphaunt coronacyon of quene Anne, wyfe vnto the moost noble kynge Henry the .viij* (London, 1533, *RSTC* 656)

Gough, W., and Crumwell, T., *The maner of the tryumphe at Caleys (and) Bulleyn* (London, 1532, *RSTC* 4350, 4351)

Hall, E., *The Triumphant Reigne of Kyng Henry the VIII* 2 vols (London, 1904)

Hatfield House, *Calendar of the manuscripts preserved at Hatfield House, Hertfordshire* 24 vols (Historical Manuscripts Commission, London, 1883–1976)

Haus-Hof-und.-Staats Archiv, Wien, Austrian State Archives, Department of House

Hayward M., and E. Kramer, E., *Textiles and Text: re-establishing the links between archival and object-based research* (Archetype Publication, London, 2007)

Hearne, T., *Titi Livii Foro-Juliensis, Vita Henrici Quinti, Regis Angliae : accedit, Sylloge Epistolarum, a variis Angliae Principibus scriptarum* (Oxford, 1716)

Hitchcock E. V., *The Lyfe of Sir Thomas Moore, knighte, written by William Roper ...* (Early English Text Society original series 197, 1935)

Holder, N., *The Friaries of Medieval London: from foundation to dissolution* (Woodbridge, London, 2017)

Holinshead, R., *Holinshead's Chronicles of England, Scotland and Ireland* 2 vols (London, 1577)

Hume, M. A. S., *Chronicle of King Henry VIII of England* (Bell and Sons, London, 1889)

Johnson, A. H., *The History of the Worshipful Company of the Drapers of London* 5 vols (Clarendon, Oxford, 1914–22)

Johnson, C., *The travels and trials of a sixteenth-century Wirral recusant* (Cheshire History 47 2007–8)

Kaulek, J., *Corrrespondance Politique de Mm. De Castillon et de Marillac* (Alcan, Paris, 1885)

Lawrence, P. H., *Extracts from the court rolls of the manor of Wimbledon, extending from 1 Edward IV. to A.D. 1864* (Wyman, London, 1866)

Leland, J. *De Uiris Illustribus: On Famous Men*, ed. J. P. Carley (Toronto, 2010)

Leland, J., *The itinerary of John Leland in or about the years 1535–1543*, ed. L. Toulmin Smith (5 vols., repr. London, 1964)

Lott, T., *Account of the Muster of the Citizens of London in the 31st Year of the Reign of Henry VIII* Archaeologia 32 (Cambridge, 1847)

Luther, M., *Disputatio pro declaratione virtutis indulgentiarum* (Germany, 1517)

Machiavelli, N., *The Prince*. Penguin Books, New York, 1981)

Mayer T. F., *The Correspondence of Reginald Pole: a calendar* 3 vols (Aldershot, 2000–2004)

Merriman, R. B., *Life and Letters of Thomas Cromwell* 2 vols (Clarendon Press, Oxford, 1902)

MS Jesus College 74: *Thomas Master collection for Lord Herbert's Life of Henry VIII* (Western manuscripts at the Bodleian Libraries)

Parks, G., *The English Traveller in Italy* 2 vols (Edizioni di storia e letteratura, Rome, 1954)

Phillips, J., *The Cromwell family, Antiquary 2* (1880), *The Cromwells of Putney', Antiquarian Magazine and Bibliographer 2* (1882), *Wandsworth Notes and Queries* (1898)

Pocock, N., *Records of the Reformation: the Divorce, 1527–33* 2 vols (Oxford, 1870)

Pollard, A. F., *Thomas Cromwell's Parliamentary lists, Bulletin of the Institute of Historical Research* 9 (1931)

Ribier, G., *Lettres et mémoires d'estat... sous le règnes fe François premier, Henry II et François II* 2 vols (Paris 1666)

State Papers published under the authority of His Majesty's Commission, King Henry VIII 11vols (London 1830 – 52)

Strype, J., *Ecclesiastical Memorials, relating chiefly to Religion ...* 3 vols (London, 1721)

The National Archives, Kew
SP 1; SP 2; SP 6; SP 10; SP 11; SP 12; SP 15; SP 46: State Papers, Domestic, Henry VIII–Elizabeth
SP 3: Lisle correspondence
SP 5: Exchequer: King's Remembrancer papers
SP 7: Wriothesley correspondence
SP 60: State Papers, Ireland

Thomas, W., and Froude, J. A., *The pilgrim: a dialogue on the life and actions of King Henry the Eighth.* (London, 1861)

Thoroton, R., *Norwell, Woodhouse and Midlethorpe* 3 vols (Throsby, Nottingham, 1796)

Tyndale, W., *A Treatyse of the Justificacyon by faith only, otherwise called the parable of the wyked mammon* (Southwark, 1536, *RSTC* 24455)

Tyndale, W., *The Institution of a Christen man, conteynynge the Exposytion ... of the commune Crede, of the seuen sacramentes, of the .x. Commandementes ...* (London, 1537, *RSTC* 5164)

Van Houtte, J. A., *Les foires dans la Belgique ancienne* (Ed. de la Librairie Encyclopédique, Brussels, 1953)

Walford, E., *Old and New London* (Cassell, Petter & Galpin, London, 1878)

Walford, E., *The Antiquary* 2 vols (Stock, London, 1880)

Waters, R. E. C., *Genealogical memoirs of the families of Chester of Bristol, Barton Regis, London, and Almondsbury, descended from Henry Chester, sheriff of Bristol 1470 [microform] : and also of the families of Astry of London, Kent, Beds, Hunts, Oxon, and Gloucestershire, descended from Sir Ralph Astry, Kt., lord mayor of London, 1493* (Reeves and Turner, London, 1881)

Webb, A., *A compendium of Irish biography comprising sketches of distinguished Irishmen, and of eminent persons connected with Ireland by office or by their writings* (M.H. Gill & Co., Dublin, 1878)

Wilkins D., *Concilia Magnae Britanniae et Hiberniae* 4 vols (London, 1737)

SECONDARY SOURCES

Andrews, F., *The Other Friars: The Carmelite, Augustinian, Sack and Pied Friars in the Middle Ages, Monastic Orders* (Woodbridge: London, 2006)

Ayris, P., and Selwyn, D., *Thomas Cranmer: Churchman and Scholar* (Boydell Press, Suffolk, 1999)

Barlow, F., *Thomas Becket* (University of California Print, Berkeley, 1986)

Barral-Baron, M., *L'enfer d'Érasme. L'humaniste chrétien face à l'histoire* (Droz, Geneva, 2014)

Battista Alberti, L., Watkins, R., *The Family in Renaissance Florence 1443* (Columbia, South Carolina, 1969)

Bennett, J. M. Ale, *Beer, and Brewsters in England: Women's Work in a Changing World* (Oxford University Press, 1999)

Bindoff, S. T., *The History of Parliament: the House of Commons 1509–1558* 3 vols (London, 1982)

Blackburn, E. L., *An Architectural and Historical Account of Crosby Place, London* (John Williams, London, 1834)

Blomefield F., and Parkin, C., *An Essay towards a Topographical History of the County of Norfolk* 11 vols (Forgotten Books, London, 2018)

Brigden, S., *London and the Reformation* (Oxford, 1989)

Bruce J., and Perowne, T. T., *Correspondence of Matthew Parker, D.D., Archbishop of Canterbury : comprising letters written by and to him, from A.D. 1535 to his death, A.D. 1575* (Forgotten Books, London, 2015)

Burnett, C., Mann, N., *Britannia Latina : Latin in the culture of Great Britain from the Middle Ages to the twentieth century* (Warberg Institute, Londo 2005).

Bush M., and Bownes, D., *The defeat of the pilgrimage of grace : a study of the postpardon revolts of December 1536 to March 1537 and their effect* (University of Hull Press, 1999)

Cardinal, E. V., *Cardinal Lorenzo Campeggio, legate to the courts of Henry VIII and Charles V* (Chapman & Grimes, Boston, 1935)

Carey, V., *Surviving the Tudors – The 'Wizard' Earl of Kildare and English Rule in Ireland, 1537–1586* (Four Courts Press, Dublin, 2002)

Chambers, D. S., *Cardinal Bainbridge in the Court of Rome 1509 to 1514* (Oxford University Press, 1965)

Chisholm, H., *Wyat, Sir Thomas* (Cambridge University Press, 1911)

Cox J. E., *Cranmer's Works* 2 vols (London 1884, 1846)

Davies., M and Saunders, A., *The History of the Merchant Taylors' Company* (Maney Publishing, Leeds, 2004)

de Pizan, C., Richards, J., *The Book of the City of Ladies 1405* (Picador, London, 1982)

de Roover, R. A., (1948), *The Medici Bank: its organization, management, and decline* (Oxford University Press, 1948)

Elton, G. R., *The Tudor Constitution: Documents and Commentary* (Cambridge University Press, 1962)

Erler, M. C., *Reading and Writing during the Dissolution* (Cambridge University Press, 2016)

Fletcher, A and MacCulloch, D., *Tudor Rebellions* (Harlow, London, 2004)

Fowler, K., *The Age of Plantagenet and Valois* (Ferndale Editions, London, 1967)

Galton, A., *The Character and Times of Thomas Cromwell: a sixteenth century criticism* (British Library, London, 2010)

Gelčić, J., *Piero Soderini profugo a Ragusa: memorie e documenti* (Regusa, Dubrovnik, 1894)

Gerhold, D., *Thomas Cromwell and his Family in Putney and Wandsworth* (Wandsworth Historical Society Papers 31, 2017)

Goldthwaite, R. A., (February 1987), *The Medici Bank and the World of Florentine Capitalism, Past & Present* (Oxford University Press, 1987)

Guérard, A., *France: A Modern History* (University of Michigan Press, Ann Arbour, 1959)

Gunn S., and Lindley P. G., *Cardinal Wolsey: Church, State and Art* (Cambridge University Press, 1991)

Guy, J., *Tudor England* (Oxford University Press, 1988)

Haigh, C., *English Reformations: Religion, Politics, and Society Under the Tudors* (Clarendon, Oxford University Press, 1993)

Hamilton W. D., *A Chronicle of England ... by Charles Wriothesley* 2 vols (Camden Society, London, 1965)

Hardy, W. J., and Gee, H., *Documents Illustrative of English Church History* (Macmillan, London, 1910)

Harris, B., *Power, Profit, and Passion: Mary Tudor, Charles Brandon, and the Arranged Marriage in Early Tudor England* (University of Michigan Library, 1989)

Harte, N. B., and Ponting, K. G., *Textile History and Economic History: essays in honour of Miss Julia de Lacy Mann* (Manchester University Press, 1973)

Hayward, M., Ward, P., and Starkey, D., *The Inventory of King Henry VIII* (Harvey Miller Publishers for the Society of Antiquaries, London, 2011)

Heale, M., *Dependent priories and the closure of monasteries in late medieval England, 1400–1535', EHR* 119 (2004)

Heer F., *The Medieval World* (Welcome Rain, New York, 1998)

Herald, J., *Renaissance Dress in Italy 1400–1500* (Bell & Hyman, London, 1981)

Hibbert, C., *The House of Medici: Its Rise and Fall* (Allen Lane, London, 1974)

Higgins, A., 'On the work of Florentine sculptors in England in the early part of the sixteenth century: with special reference to the tombs of Cardinal Wolsey and King Henry VIII', *Archaeological Journal* 51 (1894)

Howard, M., *The Building of Elizabethan and Jacobean England* (Yale University Press, 2007)

Hoyle, R. W., *The origins of the dissolution of the monasteries, HJ* 38 (1995)

Johnson, H., *Vintage: The Story of Wine* (Simon and Schuster, New York, 1989)

K. Lanz, *Correspondenz des Kaisers Karl V ...* 3 vols. (Leipzig, 1844–6)

Knowles D., *Religious Orders in England III* (Cambridge University Press, 1959)

Le Neve, J., *Fasti Ecclesiae Anglicanae 1300–1541* (Athlone Press University of London, 1963)

Lehmberg, S. E., *Reformation Parliament* (Cambridge University Press, 2009)

Lehmberg, S. E., *The Later Parliaments of Henry VIII 1536–1547* (Cambridge, 1977)

Leland, J., Carley, J. P., Brett, C., *De uiris illustribus: On Famous Men* (Pontifical Institute of Mediaeval Studies, Toronto 2010)

Lennon, C., *Sixteenth-century Ireland- the Incomplete Conquest* (Gill and Macmillan, Dublin, 1994)

Maas, K. D., *Reformation and Robert Barnes: history, theology and polemic in early modern England* (Boydell Press, Woodbridge, 2010)

MacCulloch, D., *Suffolk and the Tudors: politics and religion in an English county 1500–1600* (Clarendon, Oxford, 2011)

MacCulloch, D., *The Reformation: A History* (Penguin, London, 2005)

MacCulloch, D., *Thomas Cromwell: A Life* (Viking, London, 2018)

Mackie, R.L. Spillman, Anne, *Letters of James IV* (Scottish History Society, Edinburgh, 1953)

Madden F., *Privy purse expenses of the Princess Mary* (Pickering, London, 1831)

Marshall, P., *Heretics and Believers: A History of the English Reformation* (Yale University Press, New Haven, 2017)

Marshall, P., *The shooting of Robert Packington, in Marshall, Religious Identities in Henry VIII's England* (Aldershot, 2006)

Matusiak, J., *Wolsey: The Life of King Henry VIII's Cardinal* (History Press, 2014)

Mayer, T., *Correspondence of Pole* (Routledge, London, 2017)

McEntegart, R., *Henry VIII, the League of Schmalkalden and the English Reformation* (Boydell & Brewer, Woodbridge, 2011)

McSheffrey, S., *Seeking Sanctuary: Crime, Mercy, and Politics in English Courts, 1400–1550* (Oxford University Press, 2017)

Moynahan, B., *God's bestseller: William Tyndale, Thomas More, and the writing of the English Bible – A story of martyrdom and betrayal* (St Martin Press, New York, 2003)

Murray, J. A., *Enforcing the English Reformation in Ireland: clerical resistance and political conflict in the diocese of Dublin, 1534–1590* (Cambridge University Press, 2011)

Najemy, J. M., *Between Friends: Discourses of Power and Desire in the Machiavelli-Vettori Letters of 1513–1515* (Princeton University Press, 2019)

Paoletti, C., *A Military History of Italy* (Greenwood Publishing Group, Westport, 2008)

Penn, T., *Winter King: Henry VII and the Dawn of Tudor England* (Penguin, London, 2011)

Pierotti-Cei, L., Tallon, P., *Life in Italy During the Renaissance* (Liber, Geneva, 1977)

Platt, C., *Medieval Southampton: the port and trading community, A.D. 1000–1600* (Routledge, London, 1973)

Roberts, J., *Holbein and the Court of Henry VIII: drawings and miniatures from the Royal Library Windsor Castle* (National Galleries of Scotland, Edinburgh, 1994)

Rogers, E. F., *The Letters of Sir John Hackett 1526–1534* (West Virginia University Library, Morgantown, 1971)

Ross, J., *Florentine Palaces & Their Stories* (JM Dent and Company, London, 1905)

Ross, J., *John de Vere, Thirteenth Earl of Oxford 442–1513, The Foremost Man of the Kingdom* (Boydell Press, Woodbridge, 2010)

Roth, F., *The English Austin Friars, 1249–1538* (Augustinian Historical Institute, New York, 1966)

Setton, *The Papacy and The Levant 1204–1571* 3 vols (Simon & Schuster, New York, 1989)

Shaw, C., Mallett, M., The Italian Wars: 1494–1559 (Routledge, Oxford, 2018)

Sicca, C. M., *Consumption and trade of art between Italy and England in the first half of the sixteenth century: the London house of the Bardi and Cavalcanti company* (Renaissance studies, V. 16, n. 2, June 2002)

St. C. Byrne, M., *The Lisle Letters* 6 vols (University of Chicago Press, London and Chicago, 1981)

State Archives

State Papers Online, 1509–1714: https://www.gale.com/uk/primary-sources/state-papers-online

Stoney, *A Memoir of the Life and Times of the Right Honourable Sir Ralph Sadleir* (Longmans, Green & Co, London, 1877)

Strauss, L., *Thoughts on Machiavelli* (University of Chicago Press, Chicago, 1958)

Stuart, D., *Manorial Records* (Phillimore & Co, Chichester, 1992)

Swanson, R. N., *Indulgences in Late Medieval England: passports to paradise?* (Cambridge University Press, 2007)

Tavuzzi, M., *Renaissance Inquisitors: Dominican Inquisitors and Inquisitorial Districts in Northern Italy, 1474–1527* (Brill, Leiden, 2007)

Vasari, G., *Lives of the Painters, Sculptors and Architects* 2 vol (Harry N Abrams Inc, New York, 1979)

Williams, C. H., *English historical documents 1485–1558* 5 vols (Eyre & Spottiswoode, London, 1967)

Wyatt, M., *Italian Encounter with England* (Cambridge University Press, 2012)

Index

BANDON
County Cork

A Social History
of
North Main Street
and Kilbrogan Hill

CATHERINE FITZMAURICE

who purchased the leases of many of the houses on North Main Street in the early 1800s and who also held the Kingston Buildings. George Kingston's grandson, Charles Cameron Kingston was Premier of South Australia from 1893 to 1899. Thomas Holland became a freeman of the Corporation of Bandon Bridge.

J. Bernard lived in a large property which had been an inn and which reverted to an inn (The King's Inn) sometime before 1787. He was likely to have been one of the Bernards of Castle Bernard.

Thomas Baker, an attorney and woollen manufacturer, John Garvan, a woollen manufacturer, J. Fielding, a linen draper, Richard Abbott, a tanner, Dr Joseph Ledbetter, a medical doctor, Arthur Bernard, the brother of Judge Francis Bernard of Castle Bernard[13] and Rev Dr St John Brown, the rector of Christ Church all had sizeable residences on the street. By the 1800s many of those with a similar social background had moved into large residences outside the town.

The leases were concentrated in very few hands. The principal lease-holders in 1775 included Stephen Winthrop who held all the sites from the Provincial Bank to the front entrance of Christ Church, John Lapp, Roger, George and William Connor, Arthur Bernard Esq, Anthony Harris and John Jones.

By the early 1800s the street changed substantially as builders such as Benjamin Forde bought up multiple leases and erected new houses. The occupiers were mostly middle class protestants until the early 1900s.

---

[13] Arthur Bernard also occupied Palace Anne near Murragh

6

harness makers, leather sellers, spirit dealers and woollen drapers were amongst the mix of retail trades.

A significant change in industry had occurred by 1775. Business had flourished throughout the early 1700s and those who benefitted from the buoyant economy sought superior residences. The area became dominated by medium sized houses. Large houses were an exception and several were described as new.[9]

Tanning had declined dramatically. In 1775 just one tannery was recorded which was sited between Church Lane and the bottom of Kilbrogan Hill[10]. Historians have suggested that the tanneries moved to other areas such as Watergate Street where access to water, an essential ingredient in the industry, was far more efficient with direct access to the Bandon river. A significant amount of water was required for cleaning the hides prior to treatment. The larger tanyards would have had slaughter pens, glue yards, drying houses and a place where the leather was softened and finished by applying greases. The finished product was then sold to the footwear and saddler trades.[11] As a result of this industry, Bandon became a major producer of leather and finished goods. Shoemakers, saddlers and harness makers occupied houses in the street throughout the 1800s and well after the tanning industry had relocated to other areas in the town.

One large malt house was recorded in 1775 which belonged to John Williams and was sited north of what became the Bridewell prison. Three had existed in 1750.

A few of the larger residences in 1775 were occupied by wealthy and influential townspeople at the time. Thomas Holland, a linen draper, grocer, spirit merchant and stamp distributor, lived in a house which was on the site of the Provincial Bank (No 1).[12] He leased the property from George Cornwall, the brewer. The house was recorded as a new slate house with an office, yard and garden. Thomas Holland's daughter Hester married George Kingston Esq

---

[9] Bandon Historical Journal. No 5. Bandon in the Eighteenth Century. Patrick O'Flanagan.

[10] Scale's Map of 1775

[11] Bandon Historical Journal. No 23. "Smelly Old Bandon". The Tanyards of Yore. Paddy O'Sullivan

[12] See Appendix. Biographical Details & Lucas Directory. 1787

- **Henry Rice, Junior.** East Side 1 ½ storey dwelling & tanyard
- **William Lapp.** East Side. Good 2 storey dwelling & large tanyard.
- **Widow Haddock.** East Side. 2 storey dwelling & small tanyard.
- **John Whelply.** East Side. 1 ½ storey dwelling & small tanyard.
- **Thomas Biggs.** East Side. 2 storey dwelling & tanyard.
- **William Bull.** East Side. 2 storey dwelling & tanyard.
- **Timothy Sullivan.** East Side. Large low house & tanyard. (Near the Modern Day Post Office Sorting Office)

One malt house was referred to:-
- **William Lapp and Solomon Burchill.** East Side. 1 ½ storey dwelling with 2 tenements, back houses and a large malt house. The likely location was north of the Bridewell Prison where the malt house was outlined on the Scale map of 1775.

In 1748 the north side of the town was still described as being chiefly inhabited by tanners with up to fourteen tanyards (as opposed to just one recorded on the south side of the river). It was evidently a profitable business. Biggs became very wealthy and diversified into other industries. John Sullivan had a tanyard on Watergate Street[6]. He acquired considerable wealth which was inherited by his sons. Two of his sons, Thomas Kingston Sullivan and William Connor Sullivan, became prominent business men and were also very much involved in the political life of the town in the mid 1800s. William Connor Sullivan operated a tannery and dyeing house on Watergate Street well into the mid 1800s.[7]

Three malt houses were located on North Main Street by the 1750s.[8] Few reference are made in early records as to what kind of shops existed in the 1700s though it is likely that shoemakers,

---

[6] The holding may well have been the premises occupied previously by Timothy Sullivan near the Post Office Sorting Office.

[7] See Appendix. Biographical Details.

[8] Bandon Historical Journal. 5. Bandon in the Eighteenth Century. Patrick O'Flanagan.

Scale's map of 1775 is the earliest surviving detailed record of the street. The original maps of 1717 and 1775 were accompanied by terriers which gave information about the immediate lease holders and the head tenants. Some of the indexes survived. The absence of maps to accompany the survey of 1717 makes it difficult to plot exactly where the holdings were located. However, the information was divided into east and west North Street and the prison, mill, church lane and one or two tenements were identified which makes it possible to make a rough guess at probable sites of some of the holdings.

Bandon was a thriving industrial town in the 1700s with milling, malting, brewing, tanning woollen and linen trades. A mill was sited on the north side of the river to the west of the modern foot bridge at the bottom of Mill Lane on the present site of the public car park and Cluid premises. North Street was the most populated area of town where the largest houses were located. The houses weren't particularly grand and they fronted straight on to the road as in the present day streetscape. Even as early as 1717 there were a number of 1 ½ and two storey slate roofed houses particularly those houses which had tanyards.

In 1717 most of the tanyards listed below were recorded as being on the east side of the street. These businesses would have had access to the stream which runs through the glen at the back of the properties.

- **Thomas Legg**. West Side. Tanyard & dwelling
- **Widow Skinner**. West Side. Next door to Legg & seven properties distance from the Market House. The former holding of John Ines. Tanyard & dwelling
- **Daniel Connor**. East Side. Near Potters Messuage (Modern Day Kilbrogan Place) – Slated House & tanyard.
- **Widow Barker**. East Side. Slated House & tanyard
- **Richard Ward**. East Side. 2 storey dwelling & tanyard
- **Richard Ward**. East Side. 2 storey dwelling. (Woodleys). Tanyard.
- **Richard Harris**. East Side. 1 storey & small tanyard.

Jury rooms on the upper floor. Access was via an outside staircase. The markets for grain, wool and other produce as well as weighing and measuring equipment were on the ground floor. The building stood for 185 years until 1802 when it was demolished.

The estimates for the large Shambles meat market at the bottom of Kilbrogan Hill were submitted to the Duke's Agent on 11th July, 1816.[2] Paul Williams and Patrick Sullivan won the tender and the Shambles was completed in 1817. The total estimate was £1258. The circular walls still stand but a large part of the plot within the perimeter was developed into housing during the economic boom in about 2007. There are several references in early deeds to an old Shambles which stood next to the main bridge on the site of No 4 Bridge Place.

Town walls and ramparts were erected for the protestant population as a defence against incursions by Irish chieftains. In the early days, the jurisdiction of the provost and burgesses did not extend beyond the walls. On 20th June, 1620, the first foundation stone of the Bandon wall was laid. Sir Richard Boyle paid Richard Crofts and Captain Newce for the work.[3] The circuit of the wall was about a mile long which incorporated an area of about 27 statute acres. There were four gates; North Gate, South Gate, West Gate and Water Gate. On the North side of the river the wall stretched from Water Gate at Bank Place in front of the Post Office to behind Christ Church as far as where North Gate was located.[4]

The North Market House adjoined the north gate. The wall continued until it arrived 30' to the west of the barracks[5]. It ran due south until it reached the bastion in the river which was known as the round tower. According to George Bennett, the walls were mainly composed of a thick, black slate brought in from Twoomey's glen and the adjoining quarries in the park. They were about nine feet thick and varied in height. The walls were completed in 1628. Fifty nine years later during the rebellion of 1687 sections of the wall were destroyed and were never rebuilt.

---

[2] Lismore Papers
[3] The Diaries of Sir Richard Boyle
[4] Between House Numbers 41 & 43 (valuation record number).
[5] The present site of Trunwits

CHAPTER 1

THE EARLY HISTORY OF NORTH MAIN STREET

Bandon was built on lands which were granted by Queen Elizabeth I following the failure of the rebellion by the Earl of Desmond in 1583. Phane Beecher acquired 14,000 acres on the south side of the river and Hugh Worth was granted the lands of Kinalmeaky on the north side of the town which included North Main Street (or North Street as it was known in earlier years). The lands were quickly colonised with loyal English settlers who were mostly protestants and many of whom came from the south west of England.

Worth's holdings on the north side of the river were acquired by Captain Newce who, at one stage, considered building a rival town at Newcestown. On 20th June 1613, Richard Boyle, who later became the first Earl of Cork, purchased Newce's interests. Phane Beecher's son, Henry, sold his holdings to Boyle on 2nd May 1619. By that time, Boyle had amassed a vast estate in the south west of Ireland. In 1602 he had already purchased holdings from Sir Walter Raleigh who had been granted 42,000 acres in 1586 as part of the Munster Plantation.

When the north and south of the town were still under different ownership in 1613, the town of Bandon was separated into two parishes with the Bandon River as the dividing line. They were connected by a bridge (the first bridge having been in existence as early as the 1300s). There were two protestant churches and two market houses. The North Market House was built in 1617 and bore the name Wednesday's Market House. It was situated on North Street.[1]

The Market House was a two storey structure which accommodated a courthouse, municipal apartments and Market

---

[1] The Ancient and Present State of the County and City of Cork. Charles Smith. North Street incorporated North Main Street, Kilbrogan Hill and Kilbrogan Place (the lower part of Convent Hill)

In more recent years residents have moved to modern houses on the perimeter of Bandon leaving some of the historic buildings vacant and in a few cases derelict. The economic boom has somewhat diminished hope of their revival as the mass of new housing elsewhere deters investors from costly renovations.

Kilbrogan Hill is little changed since the early 1800s and it remains a fine Georgian streetscape with well built houses which have survived the passage of time.

PREFACE

Bandon has a rich history which is core to its identity yet has often been overlooked. The purpose of this book was to compile a social study of a street which was originally one of the principal areas in the town and which was occupied for over 250 years by a predominantly protestant population. In the 1700s it was filled with malt houses, tanneries, shops and dwelling houses. A major transformation took place in the late 1700s as industry moved to other areas of the town and the street became residential. The part now known as Kilbrogan Hill evolved into a very fashionable place to live with mostly protestant families and their relatives taking up residence side by side.

All the houses were leased from the Devonshire Estate, many on long leases to immediate lessees who sub-contracted to tenants on either long term, monthly or weekly terms. It wasn't unusual for some tenants to frequently move house within the street possibly by choice or perhaps because the Devonshire Estate agents or the immediate lessees required occupiers to move in order to avoid being challenged by sitting tenants.

The valuation records which commenced in 1856 indicate that very few of the properties were ever vacant for any length of time despite challenging economic times. Ejectments for non payment of rent did occur but were relatively few in number. This suggests that rents were fair and as a consequence the tenants were loyal. There was, however, a turnover of tenants in some of the properties who did not move to other Devonshire properties in the immediate area. The high levels of emigration at the time was one reason for such regular movements of residents away from the town.

By the early 1900s the protestant families had almost all departed and the street had changed dramatically. The turnover of tenants was less frequent and many of the shops and businesses gradually ceased trading as South Main Street became the dominant retail area of the town.

DEDICATION

In memory of Patsy O'Shea, a descendant of the Loane family of the Devonshire Arms Hotel, who spent many years researching her family and the history of Bandon. She helped to contribute to material posted on www.bandon-genealogy.com and she compiled Chapter 6.

CONTENTS

About the Author

Catherine FitzMaurice has undertaken detailed research into Bandon family history over the past ten years and maintains the website *www.bandon-genealogy.com*

CHAPTER 2

THE DEVONSHIRE ESTATE AND THE ADMINISTRATION OF NORTH MAIN STREET

The history of the Devonshire's Estate, in so much as it relates to Bandon, is important to consider when reviewing the social history of the street.

The Boyle Estate passed to the Devonshires in 1753. The fourth Earl of Cork (1694-1753), also Richard Boyle, did not have a son. His eldest daughter, Lady Charlotte Boyle, married William Cavendish in 1748. Richard died in 1753 and his vast estate was inherited by Lady Charlotte and her husband William who became the fourth Duke of Devonshire in 1755 on the death of his father, also called William. For 144 years from 1753 until 1897, the land on which all the premises of North Main Street were built was owned by the Devonshire Estate.

The Fifth Duke of Devonshire succeeded to his position in 1764 when he was just sixteen. He went on to lead an extravagant lifestyle, running up sizeable debts which were inherited by his son who became the 6th Duke. He paid little attention to his property interests. He relied instead on his auditor in London to oversee his Irish Estate which consisted of 61,000 acres. Included were 18,800 acres situated in and around the town of Bandon. A large portion of the holdings was within the area of the walls.

Bandon, like other plantation towns, was administered by agents for the landlords. The agents kept rent rolls and account books which are an invaluable resource when recording the social history of the street.

Three generations of the Connor family were involved in the management of the Boyle/Devonshire Estate in Bandon. An insight into the Connor family history provides an interesting picture not only of the power that they had within the borough of

7

Bandon Bridge but also of how leases were distributed amongst family members and relatives along North Main Street.[14]

Cornelius O'Connor married Joane Splane in 1670.[15] Cornelius was murdered by soldiers of Cromwell's army and their son Daniel was brought up by his mother, Joane, at Gallow's Hill in Bandon. She changed her surname to 'Connor'.

Daniel became a wealthy merchant. He purchased the confiscated estates of Justin McCarthy in 1698 and those of Donogh McCarthy, the Earl of Clancarty in 1702. Margaret Sloane became his wife in 1698.

Daniel served as the receiver of rents for Boyle's Bandon Estate which included North Main Street. He was also provost in 1706, 1722, 1735, 1743, 1748 and 1750. Daniel and his wife Margaret had at least seven children and there is plenty of evidence in the family tree to suggest that they may well have extended favours within their own family. This generosity appears to have commenced before the Devonshires inherited the estate from the Boyles.

Daniel's son William married Anne Bernard in 1721. Anne Bernard was the daughter of Arthur Bernard of Palace Anne near Bandon and the grand daughter of Judge Francis Bernard, a powerful landlord, who lived at Castle Bernard. Whilst we don't know if this was a marriage of convenience, the Connor family was undoubtedly politically motivated and was deeply involved in the Corporation of Bandon. Such a marriage would have helped to enhance their power within the borough.

At the time of his marriage in 1721, William Connor was working for the Earl of Cork. He became the agent for the Bandon estate in 1739 and was appointed as the overall Irish agent in 1748. He acted as the Earl of Cork's attorney from 21st March 1753.

When the Estate passed to the Devonshires in 1753, William Connor and his family were politically compromised. On the one hand, William junior held the role as the Duke's agent in Ireland

---

[14] http://alison-stewart.blogspot.ie/2013/02/the-connoroconnor-family-of.html

[15] The Biggs family were related to the Connors through the Splane family

but at the same time he was closely related to the Bernard family who vied with the Devonshire Estate for power within the Corporation.

The Corporation of Bandon was controlled by just thirteen people and nearly always included a member of the Bernard family. Such a small corporation meant that the seats and role of provost were extremely important particularly to the Devonshire and Bernard Estates. The Connor family's control in the Borough during the 1700s was very significant particularly given the small size of the corporation and the fact that only its members had the power to elect two members to the Irish Parliament.

William senior was provost in 1741. William's brother George was provost in 1761 and 1767 and his grandson William was provost in 1779 and 1785.

The Connors and their extended family acquired a number of leases from as early as 1717. By 1775 they had extended their holdings significantly. Devonshire correspondence infers that the leases were at very favourable terms to those individuals and at the expense of the Devonshire Estate.

In 1775 Arthur Bernard of Palace Anne was recorded as the lease holder of a large slate house beside the mill (Floraville). He had leased the site from at least 1738. William Connor's sons William and Roger also held leases on North Main Street in 1775.

Daniel and Margaret's daughter Jane married John Lapp, a merchant of both Bandon and Cork. Lapp held the leases on a large portion of North Main Street in 1775.

Their daughter Elizabeth Connor married Richard Gumbleton. He was assigned Devonshire Estate leases in East Cork which were the subject of much dispute because of how Gumbleton obtained them.

The Connors were cousins of the Biggs (both families married into the Splaine family). The Biggs also held leases on the street.

Elizabeth Connor of Ballybricken married Francis Fielding of Bandon. In 1775 the Fielding family who were linen merchants also held a lease on the street.

William Connor, the younger, was forced to resign his position as the Duke's Agent in July 1792 following a period of gross mismanagement which included granting favours to his own family and relatives such as the Biggs, Splaines and Gumbletons and most likely also to the Lapps and Fieldings. He was also accused of pursuing his own political career at the expense of the Duke's, taking back-handers before issuing leases and keeping very poor records and accounts which he failed to prepare in a timely manner. He had frequently avoided meetings with the agents. When he was elected provost of Bandon, he excused himself from meetings with other agents and auditors on the basis that his role as provost was consuming all his time. The more likely reasons were because his records were in considerable disarray and also because he was running the Estate to benefit his own family so had no wish for the management details to be revealed.

Following the forced resignation of William Connor, the Estate employed English agents who reported directly to the auditor in London. Connor's immediate successor was Henry Bowman who took up the position in 1792.

Thomas Knowlton recounted in 1806 that the Duke's interests in Bandon and his other Irish estates had been nearly annihilated by 1792 when Henry Bowman was appointed agent following the forced resignation of William Connor. Henry Bowman acted as agent for just five years from 1792 until 1797. Thomas Knowlton was his successor.

The Devonshire Estate agents appear to have made a clean sweep of most of the former lease holders. The leases were not renewed for the very large holders on the street such as Stephen Winthrop, John Lapp, the various Connor Family holdings or the Bernards. There may have been many reasons for this. Perhaps they were offered renewals at unattractive terms or perhaps they sought more lucrative investments elsewhere though it's more likely that the estate sought a break from the corruption which had occurred in the 1700s so hand-picked those who were to replace them when the leases matured. Furthermore, the leases were assigned to a far greater number of middlemen avoiding the concentration of power in the hands of very few intermediate lessees as had occurred in the 1700s. There was also a marked difference in the type of lease holders in the 1800s. They were nearly all resident in Bandon and only a handful were landed gentry.

Bowman most likely faced very challenging conditions in his employment as the Irish agent. He was preceded by a dynasty of Connors who had manipulated the Estate to their advantage and had kept the accounts in considerable disarray, all of which he was left to unravel. In addition, Bowman would have had to encounter some potentially challenging middlemen as Connor had chosen his friends and relatives as the leaseholders. These lessors would have remained loyal to Connor. Bowman's wife refused to move to Lismore so Bowman would have had to make frequent trips to England and may have been considered an absentee landlord. The law agent, Thomas Garde, was in pursuit of Bowman's position so made life very difficult for him. He was appointed in 1770 so had been in the position from well before Bowman's appointment. A local Irish law agent, often a solicitor, was retained by the Estate to undertake all legal transactions which included any necessary court cases such as those relating to evictions as well as the preparation and recording of all the leases and notices to quit.

Thomas Garde was replaced as legal agent by Benjamin Popham in 1807. Popham, born in 1780, was the son of Robert Popham and Mary Dowe. His father was a local Bandon farmer and malster with a property at Mossgrove in 1787 and at Kilmore near Brinny in 1820. Popham was responsible for the legal affairs of both Cork and Bandon until 1817 when Thomas Seward was appointed to take care of the Waterford Estate. From that time onwards Popham's empire was significantly reduced. The Estate had begun to defend its property rights far more diligently during this period which required much more input from the law agents, hence the need to split the role.

In 1801 Benjamin Popham married his cousin Elizabeth Popham, the daughter of Thomas Popham. He was sympathetic to the plight of tenants and townspeople during the immensely challenging times but he was often accused of acting unethically in land dealings. The Estate papers contain many references to complaints about Popham's behaviour. He fell out of favour with the Duke in the 1840s and when he died in 1847, his affairs were found to be in some disarray. Two years following his death on 27th April, 1849 Regina Popham was ejected from her house on North Main Street for non payment of rent, Robert Popham was ejected from his house at Mawbeg and Anna Maria and Elizabeth Regina were ejected from their father's dwelling at Mawbeg (he was their natural guardian).

The Bandon agents were active in local administration. They served as magistrates and sheriffs, they were appointed to the board of the poor law and they sat on the grand jury. The agents employed stewards and bailiffs. David Craig was appointed Steward of the Bandon Estate in the early 1800s and he was succeeded by his son James Craig. Jonathan Tanner acted for a period as a bailiff.

The Estate's sub agent in Bandon reported to the agent in Lismore and submitted the accounts to him. He was responsible for the administration of the estate which included valuing properties, collecting rents, organising the lease arrangements and tenancies, enforcing the terms of the lease convenants and the overseeing the properties and any renovations which required to be carried out in cases where the Estate was responsible for the maintenance. In addition to these tasks, the agent was responsible for securing a profit and achieving political influence.

The Lismore agent's duty was to carefully inspect the Bandon accounts and to oversee the sub agent's activities. John Swanston held the Bandon sub agency until 1837 and it then passed to his son, Alexander Swanston, who continued in the position until 1859. He resigned following a serious dispute with the Duke. He had presented himself as a parliamentary candidate in Bandon thus potentially pitting himself against his own employer. Furthermore, the Duke refused to allow him to act as a trustee for his brother's affairs in England whilst at the same time carrying out his role as the Duke's Bandon agent. Alexander continued to be active in politics following his resignation and sat as a Liberal MP for Bandon between 1874 and 1880.

Swanston's successor was John Rawdon Berwick who handed over to Richard Hodson in 1889. Richard Hodson held the position until 1897 when the estate was sold to Sir John Arnott.

The Bandon agents reported to the head agent at Lismore. When Bowman resigned, Thomas Knowlton took up the position and held it for more than twenty years. Both Bowman and Knowlton were English and most likely spent considerable time in England so were viewed as absentee landlords. Colonel William Currey took up the position in 1817. He was the first of three generations of the Currey family act as the head agent. His son, Francis, succeeded him and he was followed by Chetwynd. The local agents in Bandon reported to Currey.

In the early 1800s a number of the Estate's lease holders and tenants sat on the corporation. Even Lord Bandon's park was under lease from the Duke. The Duke's agent was able to use the expiry of the lease in 1799 to force Lord Bandon to re-instate the 1767 agreement allowing the Duke the alternate nomination for the borough. (In 1790 Lord Bandon had reneged on the previous agreement to share power). However, the corporation was to remain in Lord Bandon's hands and from 1826 onwards there is little evidence that the Duke actively sought political influence in the borough.

By providing employment, improving the local economy and offering favourable leases, landlords such as the Devonshires may have believed that they would be assured of votes. The 6th Duke succeeded his father in 1811 at the age of 21. He was known as the Bachelor Duke as he never married. His first visit to Bandon took place in 1812 just a year after he became Duke. Following that visit he engaged in a huge investment in the town. Buildings on North Main Street such as the Court House, the Shambles and the Devonshire Arms were all erected during his lifetime. He seemed motivated to display his wealth and power and that applied to his English Estates as well as to those in Ireland.

Many of the long leases on the street were assigned in 1816.[16] Given the large number of term leases which were assigned in that year, it seems likely that maturing term leases from the 1700s were extended on a short term basis until 1816. Surviving records relating to the expiration of the lease for the Methodist Church on North Main Street imply that the Duke and his agents worked out their future plans very carefully without necessarily consulting those who held term leases which had already expired or were about to expire. It hasn't been possible to ascertain how many of the new leaseholders in 1816 previously held leases on the street though it is more than likely that from the time when Bowman

---

[16] See Appendix. Leases

assumed his role in 1792, some of the leases which began to expire from that date were agreed to only on a short term basis, possibly annually, until 1816.

The Duke was regarded as a sympathetic landlord and a good employer. He increased expenditure substantially in spite of the fact that he had been left with sizeable debts by the 5th Earl. A severe financial crisis was to affect the Duke in 1844-5 and from that period on, the Estate ceased to expand.

The 6th Duke was succeeded in 1858 by his cousin William who became the 7th Duke. William died in 1891 and was succeeded by Spencer Compton Cavendish. In 1894 the 8th Duke sold his Bandon Estate. Most, but not all, of the properties on North Main Street and Kilbrogan Hill were purchased by Sir John Arnott.

CHAPTER 3

THE MIDDLE MEN
AND THEIR UNDER TENANTS

Relatively little information survives about the assignment of
leases before the street passed into the possession of the
Devonshires. However, there is no doubt that the Boyle and
Devonshire Estates, as head landlord of North Main Street, were
part of an elite group of fewer than 1,000 head landlords in County
Cork[17]. The agents of the Estates assigned the leases for varying
terms, some for 99 years but more often for two or three lives of
young people named in the lease, at times with a concurrent term
of thirty one, sixty one or ninety nine years. Some of the leases
which the Devonshire Estate inherited from Boyle did not mature
until as late as 1820.[18]

Under the penal laws of 1704, catholics and protestant dissenters
(mostly presbyterians) were forbidden from taking up leases for
any term exceeding thirty one years or for lives. They were also
prevented from inheriting lands from protestants. Furthermore,
the estates of catholic landowners had to be distributed equally
amongst the male heirs. Other penalties included catholics being
barred from practising law or from being a member of a grand
jury, the municipal corporation or even Parliament or from service
in the army or navy. This system survived until the Catholic Relief
Act was introduced in 1778.

As a result of the penal laws, the street was almost exclusively
protestant throughout the 1700s and for most of the 1800s even
following their repeal. The surviving records of 1717 suggest that
the tenants were mostly the holders of the leases and did not sub-
let. Short biographies of a number of these early tenants and
leaseholders are included in the appendix. There were just a
handful of middlemen namely, Charles Abbott, Herbert Love,
William Lapp, Kurtis, William Bull, Ralph and Richard Clear,
Widow Langton and Cornelius Connor. However, none of these
appeared to have had substantial holdings at that stage.

---

[17] The Land and People of Nineteenth-Century Cork. James S. Donnelly, jr
[18] The Duke of Devonshire's Irish Estates 1794-1797. Barry, J.

As the town prospered in the 1700s, a thriving system of intermediate lessors and under tenants developed and was particularly evident in the Scale records of 1775. As can be concluded from some of the biographies, the leaseholders were primarily protestant middle class families who had built up successful businesses in the town and who sought the leases as investments. As mentioned previously, in the case of most of the 1700s when the Connors were agents, many of these middlemen were relatives or family of the Connors. The practice of middlemen was to continue right through the 1800s. There are only a handful of examples in the 1800s where the lease holder and the tenant was the same person on the street. In some instances individual lessors became tenants of other lessors.

Following the mismanagement of the Devonshire Estate in the 1700s, Connor's successor, Bowman, carefully analysed how other estates were maintained. He advocated reducing the number of leaseholders between the landowner and the tenant. He also recommended letting directly to the occupying tenants and increasing the use of annual rather than leasehold tenancies. There is evidence in North Main Street that the annual, weekly or monthly tenancies became more widespread in the mid 1800s.

When Bowman assumed his position in 1792, holdings were generally let out to intermediate lessees for leases of various terms, many on North Main Street for three lives and/or 99 years. The middlemen subsequently divided the land into smaller parcels and erected houses. They derived their income from the profit they made in leasing a larger plot, dividing it up and erecting more houses and letting on a shorter term basis to the tenants.

The Duke as the head landlord, had no control over how the leases were sub let into shorter periods though it was stipulated in some of the leases as to how many houses were to be built on any given plot. This is particularly obvious when examining the leases of North Main Street during the 1800s. Benjamin Forde, one of the most prolific builders on North Main Street, leased a few larger plots on the street from the Estate, built multiple houses on the land and let out each of the houses on short term leases, far shorter than the lease he had executed with the Duke's Estate in the hopes of reaping much greater rewards.

The Duke also reserved the right to nominate the people whose lives the leases involved. Presumably this was in order to keep track of whether or not the lives nominated were actually still living or were deceased.

The 1700s was a buoyant period in the Bandon economy. Most of the Bandon leases had been set in the early 1700s at fixed terms for up to three lives. Some had been granted by William Newce long before the Devonshire's assumed control and they were for long terms with expiry dates as far out as 1820. This prevented the Duke from benefitting from the increase in property values during the very profitable times of the mid 1700s as he was unable to make any adjustments to the terms of the leases. Meanwhile, the intermediate lease holders enjoyed bumper profits particularly around the time of the Napoleonic wars as they were able to increase the rents to their tenants who would all have been on very short rental terms.

When Bowman became agent, leases expired on four or five houses on the Estate which were to be let again from Lady Day 1794. (Lady Day was a traditional name for the Feast of the Annunciation of the Blessed Virgin on 25th March and most of the lease repayments were set to be paid on that day and at the end of September).

The new leases which were conveyed in 1794 were to be building and repair leases[19]. This meant that the tenant was responsible for the building and its maintenance. The objective was to set terms which would not only encourage the lessees to take up the leases but would also result in the houses being well kept. They were for three lives despite Bowman's recommendation to the Duke that the Estate should seek shorter leases between the Estate and the tenant in an effort to cut out the middleman. The Estate would, therefore, benefit in future years from economic booms such as those which had occurred in the 1700s. The conveyance of leases for lives was presumably because the houses were in such bad

---

[19] When Arthur Young toured Ireland in the late 1770s he observed that the middlemen were not resident and were also not promoting any kind of improvements. In correspondence with the head agent at Lismore, Bowman commented that the houses in Bandon were generally in bad repair.

repair that the lessees were only willing to contract for a longer period as they would have to either re-build or undertake substantial renovations to the existing houses. Leases of too short a duration would not have been profitable for the investors as it would not have given them enough time to recoup their investments and turn a profit.

The Act of Union in 1801 was a very significant event in Irish politics as was the Catholic Relief Act of 1793. Following 1801 the number of Irish seats in parliament was reduced from 300 to 100 and there were an additional 32 seats for peers and bishops. From that time, elevation to the peerage had become much more important to those who had political ambitions. The first Earl of Bandon, by means of a strategic marriage, received his peerage in the late 1700s so was assured of a seat in parliament.

Bandon had had two representatives in the Dublin Parliament but that number was reduced to a single member following the Act of Union in 1801. The 1793 Catholic Relief Act had an impact on how the seats were taken up. The protestant ascendency needed to find sympathetic voters in a protestant borough in order to achieve their political ambitions. Bandon was one of just thirteen towns in Ireland where the right to vote was limited to a small section of the population namely the corporation and which was still a protestant borough. The corporation was made up of a provost, free burgesses and common council men. Therefore, the key to any political success in Bandon lay in influencing a very small minority of people as they were the only people who were permitted to vote.

The Devonshire Estate had substantial holdings in Bandon so, in theory, should have had a major say in the government of the Borough. However, the Bernards managed to hold a tight grip on local politics.

The composition of the Borough and its voting system meant that the town remained in protestant hands for years following the Catholic Relief Act of 1793. The street remained largely protestant until after the Devonshires had sold their holdings in 1897.

Deeds and leases contain very valuable early information about the street. The Registry of Deeds was established in 1708 to provide a system of voluntary registration. The books held in the archive contain a synopsis of the deeds. Information for the street is somewhat limited prior to 1800 and in the early 1800s the deeds executed between the Duke and his immediate lessees do not appear in the Registry. However, numerous deeds exist between the lease holders and parties to whom these lessees passed on title. There were often many links in the chain of a deed which had been originally executed with the Estate and over which the Estate had no control. The leases were traded like share investments today. The Duke of Devonshire Estate would enter into a lease at a fixed term which might change hands several times before the lease expired. The prolific builders such as Benjamin Forde frequently entered into short leases which were all recorded in the Registry of Deeds.

The Duke of Devonshire permitted some of the lease holders who built properties on their plots to apply to the Clerk of the Peace for the registration of the freehold of the building. A number of such freeholds in North Main Street were registered with the Courts in May, 1829[20]:-

- William Kingston of Bandon – A dwelling house and premises
- Benjamin Forde, Builder – Several messuages, tenements or dwelling houses with their appurtenances and premises situated in North Main Street
- George Harris, Pawn Broker – Several messuages, tenements or dwelling houses with their appurtenances and premises situated in North Main Street
- William Lovell. A dwelling house, messuages, appurtenances and premises located in North Main Street

Leases and other types of deeds of the 1700s and 1800s generally did not record house numbers. The plot was defined in measurements such as breadth and depth and occupiers or lease holders of adjoining properties were sometimes mentioned in the deed. Oftentimes the occupiers or lease holders mentioned referred to the original lease rather than to when the lease was re-negotiated or conveyed to another purchaser. This makes it difficult to establish the exact location of the property without having access to the individual house deeds.

---

[20] Southern Reporter. 14th May, 1829

The Devonshire Estate Collection contains some details relating to leases. Most of the houses on North Main Street were not built by the Estate. The land was leased and lessees erected either a house or several houses on the plot which had been leased to them. The lessees either rented the houses to annual, monthly or weekly paying tenants or assigned the leases for varying intervals or in some, though not many, instances, the lessees lived in the properties themselves.

Many of the leases in the 1800s which were assigned for lengthy terms by the Duke of Devonshire were transacted in 1816 with most of the rest being assigned in the years from 1816 up to 1825[21]. A large percentage of the houses were rebuilt when these new leases were taken up. The leases were lengthy and stipulated whether repairs or a new house construction was to take place. The deed also specified the minimum amount to be expended by the lessee, the time frame in which the work had to be carried out as well as how many houses were permitted to be erected on the site and whether they were to be for commercial or residential use. Oftentimes there was a map attached to the deed specifying the exact size of the plot and the ownership of the holdings which bounded the site.

The occupations of the immediate lessees during this period included shop keepers, a brewer, medical doctors, a watch maker, builders, a worsted manufacturer, tanners, a boot and shoemaker and a pawn broker. Very few were described as landed gentry and almost all the leases were assigned to people who lived and worked locally.

The names of leaseholders in the 1700s such as Connors, Lapp, Bernard, Ledbetter, Love, Winthrop and Watkins had disappeared in the 1800s. However it's likely that the Roche, Harris, Clear, Sullivan, Holland, Bennett, Bull and Williams families of the 1800s were all descendants of the leaseholders of the 1700s. There is also no reason to suggest that these families who continued to hold leases in the 1800s were in any way involved in the corruption which was attributed by the Devonshire Estate to the Connor family and their relatives.

---

[21] See Appendix. Leases

In the 1800s the handful of lessees who held their original leases until expiry or surrender included Eliza and Martha Jenkins, David Bushe, William Hunter and William Kingston, the pawn broker. A small number of the lessees were ejected for non payment of rent, eg Joseph Bullen, a shop keeper who was ejected in 1848, Robert Fuller, a shopkeeper (no 87), Samuel Sullivan, a shopkeeper who was ejected before 1830 - His lease was re assigned to Richard Cole who built a new house on the site (No 25). The Representatives of Benjamin Popham (the Duke's Legal Agent) were ejected in 1849 shortly following his death.

The Griffiths Valuation Record was the first large scale valuation of property in Ireland. It was overseen by Richard Griffith and was published between 1848 and 1864. Its objective was to determine liability to pay the poor rate to support the poor and destitute within areas which were divided into Poor Law Unions. The records for North Main Street were compiled in 1851.

The Valuation Office Records for North Main Street commenced in 1856 and from that time onwards, a schedule was kept of the rateable valuation of each house, the property number, the occupier and the lease holder. A number of pre-valuation records existed throughout the country including records for 1849 for the street.

The records in the valuation office which relate to the lease holder are, at times, inconsistent with the records which appear in the Registry of Deeds. This implies that the records of the immediate lessees were not as up to date as the register of occupiers of the properties.

The valuation records are an extremely important resource for genealogical data in the absence of census returns before 1901. A very detailed protestant census for the parish Ballymodan still exists for 1834 and 1845 but there are no surviving similar records for North Main Street which was in the parish of Kilbrogan, Barony of Kinalmeaky, on the north side of the river. In 1837 a list of occupiers of the houses along with estimated annual valuations was put together by Edward Doherty, the town clerk, in the absence of valuation records which were required to be compiled. These records, although not detailed, provide valuable information about the street in 1837.

The valuation office records which commenced in 1856 were hand written and colour coded. Some of the entries are difficult to read making some names and dates indecipherable. Whilst the census of Ballymodan contained details of every person in the property, the valuation office record only reported the immediate lessor and the head tenant. For the most part it is not possible to determine who was residing in the house with the head tenant. Many tenant names are recorded in church and other records as living on North Main Street yet the names do not appear in the valuation records presumably as they were not the head tenants in whichever property they resided in. Furthermore, there are a few names of head tenants who are also recorded as living elsewhere, eg Thomas Kingston Sullivan, William Christopher Dowden and Henry Cornwall Nash. This suggests that they may have taken on the lease for other family members or in some cases employees.

A few immediate lessors on North Main Street hired agents to manage their properties and to collect the rents. Agents such as Richard Wheeler Doherty often appeared as acting on behalf of the immediate lessor. There are instances where the valuation office recorded the legal agent as the immediate lessor rather than the actual lessor. (On 30th September, 1863 Richard Wheeler Doherty purchased all Benjamin Forde's leases in North Main Street[22] and he re-assigned some of the leases for varying durations)

It is not possible to establish who built all the houses. The most prolific builder in the street was Benjamin Forde and to a lesser extent Paul Williams and Edward Preston. In the earlier deeds Benjamin was recorded as a slater and subsequent deeds refer to him as a builder. His eldest son, also called Benjamin, became an architect. In 1838 Benjamin Forde built several new dwellings between the front entrance to Christ Church and the Provincial Bank. The properties were bounded on the north by Edward O'Brien's field. In 1824 William Hosford was recorded as having built two houses on the east side of the street.[23]

Prior to 1803 all the shop windows in the town were unglazed. They consisted of timber framework in which two or three shelves

---

[22] Registry of Deeds 1863 37 132
[23] Lismore Papers

were placed. The shelves were equidistant from one another and were parallel to the pavement. Samples of the shops wares were piled up on the shelves in order to attract customers. For the first time in 1803 a shop owner installed a glass window.[24]

North Main Street was, for many years, the prime residential location in the town. Whilst the lessees were mostly business people from the town, in the mid 1800s the street was populated with nearly four times as many resident gentry and clergymen than any other street[25].

---

[24] The History of Bandon. George Bennett
[25] Irish Historic Towns Atlas

Catherine FitzMaurice

CHAPTER 4

EARLY SURVEYS AND MAPS

In Scale's survey of 1775 a number of holdings, messuages and tenements were referred to.

- **Love's Holding** – (Held by Major Herbert Love[26] in 1717). The present Post Office Sorting Office stands on part of the holding. A tanyard once occupied part of the site, possibly that of Timothy Sullivan. Love's holdings in 1717 ran as far as the church yard.
- **Hill's and Magee's** – 2 Tenements on the South Side of North Main Street. William Recroft held Magees in 1743. It was held by Stewart Tresilian in 1803. (not recorded in Scale but recorded in the Lismore Papers)
- **Hussey's Tenement** – Near valuation no 39. Abraham Watkins had the lease from at least 1743 & was still registered as the lease holder in 1775. Richard Lloyd had the lease in 1800 and in 1801 except for the part held by Corless Welch.
- **Lane's Messuage** – Partly held by Corless Welch, a saddler in 1800
- **Margett's Tenement** – Near valuation no 44. The original lease was granted in 1610 by Captain Newce and was to run for 200 years. It became part of the holdings of the First Earl of Cork in 1613 following his purchase of Captain Newce's interests. Solomon Burchill held the lease from at least 1743 at a rent of 6s 8p and the terms of the lease imply that his predecessors held it before him[27] He appears to have held it until its expiry. Jonathan Clerke was recorded as the tenant in 1817.
- **Daniel's Plot** – Near valuation no 75
- **Clarke's and Roche's** – Near valuation no 78. See also index of 1717, Numbers 55 and 59 belonging to Richard Clarke and Andrew Roche. The leases for numbers 55 to 59 were held by Dennis Kelly in 1748 (he held No 58 in 1717) and the tenement was recorded as Clarke's and

---

[26] See Appendix. Short Biographies
[27] Lismore Papers

Roche's.[28] Dennis was granted the lease on 25th March, 1720 for three lives & 21 years namely, William Giles, only son of Mary Giles, daughter of William Giles of Bandon, shoemaker and Mark Legoe, son of Mark Legoe of Bandon, clothier. The lease described the holding of Dennis Kelly as a 'part lot'.[29]

- **Webb's and Bramble's tenement** – Near the Shambles. Andrew Roche held the lease from at least 1722 to 1775. Corless Welch, a saddler had the lease in 1803. Elizabeth Barry shared part of the area by a lease of 1730 and she still held it in 1817.
- **Shinner's Holding** – Near valuation no 83
- **Snooks Messuage** – Near valuation no 92. Snooks appears on the list of English settlers who arrived some time before 1620. They seem to have fled either following the invasion of 1641 or after the rebellion of 1685. The messuage was held by Widow Taylor until 1720. The original lease was dated 1613. Anthony Harris had the lease from 1722 & was still registered as the lease holder in 1775

---

[28] Registry of Deeds. 136 70 90546 of 18th January 1748
[29] Lismore Papers

1717 NORTH STREET – THE EAST SIDE
Bounded on east and north by a small brook & the lands of Kilbrogan

81	**Francis Jenkins**	Low thatch. Part of Potters Messuage (Now Kilbrogan Place)
82	**Daniel Conner**	Slate house & thatched house to street, **tanyard** & all houses belonging to it
83	**Robert Giles**	1 ½ storey slated house & thatched house adjoining **tanyard** & another thatched house
84	**Widow Barker**	1 ½ storey slated house, thatched house, back house, **tanyard**
85	**Widow Barker**	Good arable ground at back of Peters Field (Potters)
86	**Richard Ward**	2 storey, out house, gable end to street, **tanyard**
87	**Richard Ward**	2 storey, low back house, **tanyard** (Wadleys/Woodleys?)
88	**John Sullivan & Edward Spelane**	Front house in 2 tenements. 1 storey. garden
89	**Stephen Moxley**	2 storey corne house, 2 low back houses, large back yard
90	**Henry Rice Snr**	2 storey. 2 small low houses & ground at back
91	**Richard Harris**	1 storey. Back yard. Small **tanyard**
92	**Henry Rice Snr**	Low thatched stable & garden & another low thatched house jutting into street.
93	**Henry Rice Jnr**	1 ½ storey. Low house adjoining. Large back house. **Tanyard**
94	**Francis Kaple**	Low house, back side, garden
95	**William Heazle**	Low thatched house, back side, garden
96	**Henry Rice Jnr**	Good meadow from former garden to Knockbrogan bounds
		The parcels are bounded on North East by Knockbrogan lands & West by North Street & South by street & William Lapps holdings
97	**William Lapp**	Good dwelling. 2 storey, large outhouse 1 storey high. Large **tanyard** with houses for the trade. Garden plot extending to Knockbrogan.[30] (no 47-53 of map of 1775)
98	**Widow Haddock**	2 storey. 2 low outhouses, back house, small **tanyard**
99	**John Loane**	2 storey. 4 out houses, backside & garden
100	**William Murry & Jeremiah Regan**	1 ½ storey, large back house, garden
101	**Gilburn Stephens**	2 storey. Back house, garden

[30] Assigned to John Lapp as part of his marriage settlement to Ann Falkiner. Registry of Deeds. 126 430 88201 of 4th March 1747

102	John Whelply	1 ½ storey. Small **tanyard**.plot entering Knockbrogan
103	John Hammet, Daniel Stanfield	1 ½ storey. Back house, garden extending to Knockbrogan
104	George Collins	2 storey. Back house, garden
105	Richard Brabbin	1 ½ storey. Back house, garden
		These 6 entries under Francis Bernard under William Lapp as chief tenant
106	Thomas Biggs	2 storey. Low house adjoining. 3 out houses, backyard, **tanyard**
107	William Orchard	1 ½ storey. Garden extending backwards
108	Edward Draper	Low house to front converted to **forge**, dwelling house lying backwards of James Dammel's house, garden & plot extending to Knockbrogan.
109	James Dammel	2 storey. Back house, large plot extending to brook
110	William Lapp, Solomon Burchill	Front house 1 ½ storey, 2 tenements, backhouse, **malt house**, garden
111	William Bull	Part 1 ½ storey. Part 2 storey. 2 outhouses, **tanyard**, garden plot extending to brook.
112	William Morris under William Bull	2 storey, backhouse, back yard, garden
113	Ralph Wright under William Lapp	2 storey, linny, outhouse, backside, garden
114	Sarah Blewett under William Lapp	2 storey, back house, garden extending to brook
115	Rev Solomon Foley	Several good outhouses. Fine garden. Well planted with summer house
116	Rev Solomon Foley	Large 2 storey, return & stair case, small front yard, offices[31]
117	Richard Clear	2 storey linny, back house, garden
118	William Madden	2 storey, small linny, back yard, back house adjoining fronting the **Church Lane**
119	Andrew Roche	2 storey. Back house in Church Lane
120	Piercy Smith	4 low houses fronting Church Lane from William Madden's back house, 199ft length with garden lying between Richard Clear's & **Town Wall**
212	Andrew Roche	Plot part within & part without Town Wall
213	John Curtis	Garden plot on south side of **Church Lane**
214	William Madden	2 storey, low backhouse, backyard, **Franklyns**
215	John Briers	2 storey, linney, backyard. **Dunkins**
216	Widow Tresilian	2 storey, back house,
217	John Curtis & Barnaby Brown	2 storey. 2 returns, 2 tenements, linny, outhouses, garden plot
218	John Curtis	Plot of Ground lying within **Town Wall**
128	Isaac Bare	2 storey. Backhouse. Yard & garden
129	George Woods	2 storey, large back yard
130	Henry Jones	2 storey, back yard & garden
131	Abraham Davis. Under Kurtiss	2 storey. Back house, linny, garden

[31] See No 37 in 1775 map. Situated by the North Market House

132	**William Moxly**	Garden & back yard
133	**William Harden**	1 ½ storey, small linny, back yard, garden
134	**Timothy Sullivan**	2 storey, linny, back house, garden
135	**Daniel Beamish**	2 storey, back house, yard on west side of entry to **Church**
136	**John Harris**	1 ½ storey, garden east side of **Church** entry
137	**The Church Yard**	Handsome church in form of cross & large church yard
138	**Daniel Sullivan** under Herbert Love[32]	Low dwelling house, large garden **adjoining church yard**
139	**James Rice** under Herbert Love	Large house part of it double with 2 returns. Part next the street 2 storey. Rest 1 ½ storey. Large stable house & garden
140	**James Rice** under Herbert Love	Long strip of land on outside of town wall
141	**Timothy Sullivan** under Herbert Love	Walls of ruined house to front & back yard in common, **tanyard**, large low house thereunto belonging
142	**Stephen Winthrop** under Charles Abbott	Large thatched house & garden outside of Watergate on north side of street
143	**Robert Spilane**	Garden & waste plot without Watergate on **south side of street**
144	**Robert Spilane**	**Corn house** 1 ½ storey, back house out of repair
145	**Widow Brown**	1 ½ store, back house & back side
146	**Waste**	Waste plot without house
147	**PRISON**	Front house 1 ½ storey & backyard adjoining **bridge**

[32] Herbert Love's holdings were assigned to his son John Love. In 1727 they passed to Thomas Bryan, Clothier who passed them to Jn Stammers in 1737.

1717 NORTH STREET – THE WEST SIDE

No	Name	Dwelling
40	William Millet	2 storey with **Presbyterian Meeting House** adjoining, backyard, large garden
43	William Stephens, Widow Hicks, Alexander Bull, Richard Edwards under widow Langton	On plot lying on corner of Sugar Lane are 2 houses 1 ½ storeys hight fronting North St. & 2 low houses fronting Sugar Lane. Garden plot belonging to poor of parish
44	Ralph Clear Jun	2 storey, a low house & garden
45	Benjamin Wheeler	2 storey, 2 low outhouses, garden
46	Waste Plot	Open to street. No house
47	William Langton	2 storey, linny, backhouse, garden
48	William Conner	1 storey, 2 low backhouses, garen
53	Abraham Davies[33]	Good **Mill House** newly built, garden bounded on west by town wall and by river, 2 grist & mills, fish house. Salmon weir runs from mills. Barracks in front
54	John Whelply	Low house. Good garden.
55	Richard Clarke[34]	2 storey. Garden. (Pitmans)
56	Widow Bennett	Large 2 storey. Gable end to Sugar Lane. Good garden
57	John Jones & William Bennett	Good new 2 storey with stair case, outhouses. Very good garden
58	Dennis Kelly	1 storey & garrett, nr **Market House.** Garden
59	Andrew Roch[35]	1 storey, low garrett, garden
60	Abraham Bare[36]	Low thatched house, garden
61	William Snow	Garden plot. Adjoining road to Mill
62	William Snow[37]	Large House, 2 returns to front. 2 storey. A yard, offices, terrace walk behind house, small pleasure garden. fishpond
63	James Martin	Low house. 1 storey, garrett & garden
64	William Stephens	Low house. 1 storey. Back house & garden
65	Thomas Legg[38]	1 ½ storeys, linney, **tanyard** & outhouses

[33] Abraham Davies also had 10 acres for the Mill Bog and 2 small islands. Arthur Bernard had this holding in 1775.

[34] See Clarke's and Roche's tenement on map of 1775

[35] See Clarke's and Roche's tenement on map of 1775

[36] See Webb's and Bramble's tenement on map of 1775. Boyle lease dated 1720 to Andrew Roche, Cooper.

[37] Agent for the Earl of Cork and Burlington's Estate in Bandon between 1711 and 1720.

[38] Surrendered in 1740 (See Legg Biography) Also ROD 100 478 71307 of 1740

66	**Widow Skinner**	1 ½ storey. Back house adjoining another low house & **tanyard** (late John Ines)
67	**Sion? Hill**	2 storey. Back house, linny, low back house, ½ of another house and garden
68	**Joseph Wheeler**	2 ½ storey, back house and garden
69	**Daniel Conner**	2 storey, linny, 2 large outhouses & garden
70	**Jasper Kievell**	Low dwelling, 2 cabins
71	**Waste**	No house
72	**Edward Jenkins**	2 storey, out house, garden
73	**John Crousell**	2 storey, back house, garden
74	**Thomas Loane**	2 storey, back house, garden
75	**Samuel Brown**	2 storey, back house, garden
76	**John Whelply**	2 storey, gable end to street, linny, garden
77	**Thomas Brien**	2 storey, linny, back house, garden
78	**George Alby**	2 storey, linny, back house, garden
79	**Daniel Sullivan**	2 storey, back house, garden
80	**Waste**	Waste next to bridge

1775 NORTH STREET – THE EAST SIDE

No	Tenant & Immediate Lessor	Dwelling
1	**Thomas Holland**. I.L Stephen Winthrop	[39]New slate house, office, yard, garden. 45' arp 1.6
2	**Robert Williams**. I.L. Stephen Winthrop	House, yard, stable. 33.6' arp .6
		[40]LOVE'S HOLDING
3	**Henry Hudson**. I.L. Stephen Winthrop	House, garden. 57.6' arp .24
4	**Patrick Vance**. I.L. Stephen Winthrop	Small house, yard. 19.3' arp .4
5	**Jas Bernard**. I.L. Stephen Winthrop	Large slate house, office, yard, garden, formerly an inn. 48'
6	**Widow Huson**. I.L. Stephen Winthrop	Small house.
7	**Widow Dant**. I.L. Stephen Winthrop	Small house.
8	**Richard Hammett**. I.L. Stephen Winthrop	Small house, office.
9	**Richard Hammett**. I.L. Stephen Winthrop	House, office and garden
10	**Jonathan Roe**. I.L. Stephen Winthrop	House, office, yard
11	**Thomas Baker**. I.L. Stephen Winthrop	House, office, yard
12	**William Lisson**. I.L. Stephen Winthrop	House, office, yard
13	**Benjamin Hales**. I.L. Stephen Winthrop	House, office, yard
14	**John Williams**. I.L. J. Kingston	House, office, yard
15	**John Garvan**. I.L. Widow Leg	House, office, yard
16	**Thomas Child**. I.L. Thomas Child	House, office, yard
17	**Thomas Child**. I.L. Thomas Child	House, office, yard
18	**J. Fielding**. I.L. William Moxley	Small house, office
19	**J. Williams**. I.L. Alex Martin	House, office

[39] Site of Provincial Bank & present day Post Office
[40] Once the site of a tanyard. A large holding which extended to the churchyard.

20	**Alex Martin.** I.L. Alex Martin	House, office, yard
21	**J. Hodges**	House, yard
22	**Robert Band.** I.L. Fran Pool	House, yard
23	**Robert Band.** I.L. Fran Pool	House, yard
24	**Richard Abbott.** I.L. Samuel Jarvis	House & **tanyard**
25	**J. Sullivan.** I.L. Sam Jarvis	House, office, yard
26	**Edward Davis.** I.L. Isaac Jones	House, office
27	**Edward Davis.** I.L. Isaac Jones	Small ?
	CHURCH LANE[41]	
28	**Thomas Denning.** I.L. Barry Walsh	Small house. North corner of Church Lane & North Main Street
29	**John Griffith.** I.L. William Baldwin	Small house
30	**J. Moxley.** I.L. William Baldwin	Small house
31	**Thomas Kingston.** I.L. William Baldwin	Small house
32	**John Manzer.** I.L. David Barry	Small house
33	**Widow Holland.** I.L. Widow Holland	Small house & garden
34	**John Manzer.** I.L. David Barry	Small house & garden
	NORTH MAIN STREET (cont)	
35	**Jane Moxley.** I.L. J. Moxley	House, yard
	LANE'S TENEMENT[42]	
36	**Widow Clear.** I.L. Richard Clear	House, yard, office
	HUSSEY'S TENEMENT[43]	
37	[44]**Jn Travers. I.L.** Abraham Watkins	Large slate house, yard, small garden

---

[41] MS 43 215/3 Lismore Papers. John Hosford, Chandler, rented a garden in Church Lane on 25th March 1800 for 5s. It had formerly been in the possession of John Jones.

[42] MS 43 215/3. Lismore Papers. Corliss Welch, sadler, rented part of Lane's & Hussey's messuages, lately in his possession from 25th March 1800 for £2

[43] MS 43 215/3 Lismore Papers. On 25th March, 1801, Richard Lloyd of Bandon, Clerk rented the part of Husseys not in occupation by Corless Welch.

38	**Thomas Stephens** John Lapp	Small house
	MARGETT'S TENEMENT	
39	**Dr Ledbetter. I.L.** John Lapp	Large house, office, yard
40	**Matthew Russel. I.L.** John Lapp	House, yard, garden
41	**George Giles. I.L.** John Lapp	House, stable, yard
42	**Widow Biggs. I.L.** Widow Bull	House, garden
43	**Jn Lamb. I.L.** Widow Bull	House, stable, yard
44	**Widow Bull. I.L.** Widow Bull	House, stable, yard
45	**Adam Hoel. I.L.** Widow Bull	Small house
	[45]**METHODIST MEETING HOUSE**	
47	**William Peaton. I.L.** John Lapp	House, yard[46]
48	**Richard Gillman. I.L.** John Lapp	Small House
49	**William Gifford. I.L.** John Lapp	House & Yard
50	**John Williams. I.L.** John Lapp	[47]**A Large Malt House**
51	**William Banfield. I.L.** John Lapp	Large house, office, yard, garden
52	**Ralph Clear. I.L.** [48]John Lapp	House, office, yard & ?
53	**John Shorten. I.L.** John Lapp	House & yard
54	**Samuel Kingston. I.L.** Richard Clear	House, office, yard & garden
55	**Samuel Kingston. I.L.** Jas Bernard	**New** house, office, garden
56	**Major Alexander. I.L.** Jas Bernard	**New** house, office, garden
57	**Robert Blare. I.L.** Jas Bernard	House & garden
58	**Widow Hanes. I.L.** Jas Bernard	House, garden

[44] Provost in 1775. Directly behind the Market House. See also 115 & 116 on preceding 1717 map (Registry of Deeds. 49 80 30974 date 4th June 1724
[45] Situated behind the site of the Bridewell
[46] William Lapp had tanyard and land between No 47-53. All were assigned to John Lapp in 1747 on his marriage to Ann Falkiner. ROD 126 430 88201
[47] Also on site of the Bridewell
[48] Possible site of No 111 on 1717 index assigned by William Bull to Richard Ward in 1725 & by Richard Ward to Ralph Clear in 1747

59	**William Rogers**. I.L. Jas Bernard	House, stable, garden
60	**Thomas Harris**. I.L. Jas Bernard	House, garden
61	**John Shine**. I.L. Jer Regan	Small house
62	**John Riely**. I.L. Jer Regan	House, office, garden
63	**Waste**. I.L. John Lapp	House, stable
64	**Rev Dr. Brown**. I.L. John Lapp	[49]Large house, office, yard.
65	**Rev Dr. Brown**. I.L. John Lapp	An Orchard
65	**Rev Dr. Brown**. I.L. John Lapp	Field, meadow
65	**Rev Dr Brown**. I.L. John Lapp	Field, meadow
65	**Rev Dr Brown**. I.L. John Lapp	A field arable
66	**Richard Gillman**. I.L. John Lapp	Slate House &?
67	**William Chambers**. I.L. John Ward	Small House
68	**William Niedham**. I.L. John Ward	Small House
69	**Thomas Horneybrook**. I.L. John Ward	Small House
70	**Waste**. I.L. John Ward	Small House
71	**Robert Wanderton**. I.L. John Ward	House & Stable
72	**Edward Duke**. I.L. John Ward	House & yard
73	**Daniel Dawson**. I.L. John Ward	House, yard, stable 32' arp .6
	[50]**POTTERS MESSUAGE**	
74	**Richard Mellefont**.I.L. John Lapp	Large Slate House, office, yard 43.9 arp 2.22
75	**Richard Mellefont**. I.L. John Lapp	Meadow arp 1.0.24
76	**Richard Mellefont**.I.L. John Lapp	Meadow arp 2.12
77	**Richard Mellefont**. I.L. John Lapp	Meadow arp 1.0.4
78	**Horatio Carty**. I.L. John Ward	House, Yard 32'

[49] Present site of Kilbrogan House
[50] Present Site stretching from Kilbrogan Place to Kilbrogan Street.

1775 NORTH STREET – THE WEST SIDE

No	Tenant & Immediate Lessor	Dwelling
1	**Richard Sullivan. I.L.** Richard Clear	House, stable, yard, garden 60'6" arp 1.0
2	**Richard Williams. I.L.** Isaac Servat	House, stable, yard 48'4" .14
3	Waste. I.L. Roger Conner	House, garden 29'6" arp .12
4	**Joseph Lisen.** I.L. Roger Conner	House 20'
5	**Edward Scuce**. I.L. Roger Conner	House, garden 26' arp .9
6	**John Hammet.** I.L Roger Conner	House, garden 38'8" .11
7	**George Hammet.** I.L. Roger Conner	House, garden (shared with 8) 22'6"
8	**Alexander Hammet.** I.L. Roger Conner	House, garden (shared with 7) 20'
9	**Goodman Atkins**. I.L. William Conner	House, yard 28'8" arp .6
10	**Widow Conner**. I.L. George Conner	House, office, yard, garden 67' arp 1.33
11	**Widow Milliner.** I.L. George Conner	House, office, yard 28' arp .23
12	**Jn Bennet**. I.L. Jos Williams	House, yard, garden 18'8" arp .22
13	**Widow Popham.** I.L. Kirks	House, shared yard & garden with No 14 21'6"
14	**Thomas Holland**. I.L. Kirks	House with shared yard & garden with No 13 23' arp1.0
15	**Widow Beamish**. I.L. George Conner	House, yard, garden 31' 8" arp .12
16	**Robert Shearman**. I.L. George Conner	House, yard, garden 28'6" arp .8
17	**Widow Alcock.** I.L. Thomas Holland	House, yard, office & craft 33'6" arp 1.0
18	**Joseph Davis**. I.L. Richard Ward	House, stable, yard 31' arp .9
19	**Capt Liter.** I.L. Thomas Holland	House, yard, garden 32' arp .36
19	**Capt Liter.** I.L. Thomas Holland	Field, meadow arp 1.0.
20	**Samuel Shorten.** I.L. George Conner	House, garden 19.6' arp .8
21	**William Cook.** I.L. George Conner	House, garden shared with No 22 19.8'
22	**Jn Oliffe**. I.L. George Conner	House, stable. Garden shared with No 21 22' arp .11

1775 NORTH STREET – THE WEST SIDE

		DANIELS PLOT	
23	**John Wheeler.** I.L. Robert Dunkins & Thomas Wheeler	House, yard, garden 44.6' arp 1.26	
24	**John Wheeler.** I.L. Ralph Clear	House, yard, garden 36'6" arp .12	
25	**William Shine.** I.L. John Williams	House, garden 29' arp .10	
26	**Widow Callaghan.** I.L. George Conner	House, office, yard 46'9" arp .19	
27	I.L. Roger Conner	**ALMS HOUSE & YARD** 21' arp .10	
28	**Jn Bull.** I.L. Dr Joseph Ledbetter	House, garden 18' arp .8	
29	**Waste.** I.L. Dr Joseph Ledbetter	House, garden 18' arp .8	
30	**DISSENTING.** I.L. Dr Joseph Ledbetter	**PRESBYTERIAN MEETING HOUSE, YARD & GARDEN** arp 1.4	
31	**Jn Hosford.** I.L. William Connor	House, yard 29' 8" arp .6	
32	**David Abbot.** I.L. William Baldwin	House, yard 23' arp .9	
33	**William Strike.** I.L. William Baldwin	House 14'	
		CLARKE'S AND ROCHE'S	
34	**Jn Moxley.** I.L. Dennis Kelly	Small house, stable, yard 35' arp .9	
35	**Thomas Belcher.** I.L. Dennis Kelly	House, yard 25'6" arp .8	
		WEBB'S AND BRAMBLE'S TENEMENT[51][52]	
36	**Jas Roache.** I.L. Andrew Roache	House, stable, yard 33' arp .8	
37	**Widow Burke.** I.L. Andrew Roache	House, yard 33' .19	
38	**Widow Burke.** I.L. Andrew Roache	Shop 22' 3"	

[51] See No 60 of 1717 West Side. Lease from Boyle to Andrew Roche dated 1720 in possession of Abraham Beare for lives of Richard Clarke, Daniel Deason and Hannah Luskin

[52] MS 43 215/4 Lismore Papers. Corliss Welch, salder, was renting this house and tenement on 29th September 1803 at £8

39	**William Gash**. I.L. John Jones	Large Slate House, office, garden 57' 9" arp 2.3
40	**Arthur Bernard Esq.** Tenant and I.L.	Large Slate House, garden. Site of **Bandon Mill and town hall** 62.3' arp 2.3
40	**Arthur Bernard Esq.** Tenant and I.L.	Garden arp .33
40	**Arthur Bernard Esq**	Cooks Meadow – situated east of Main Bridge arp 8.2.38
40	**Arthur Bernard Esq**	Cooks Meadow – situated east of Main Bridge
41	**Francis Bursted**. I.L. John Jones	House, yard, garden 37' 9" arp 1.4
42	**Henry Grant Esq**. I.L. John Jones	House, yard, garden 30' arp .33
43	**David Barry**. I.L. Anthony Harris	House, stable, garden 35' 7" arp .26
	SHINNER'S HOLDING	
44	**Jn Decourcey**. I.L. John Jones	House, stable, garden 16' arp .2
45	**Dr Rowland**. I.L. Anthony Harris	House, yard, stable, garden 32'6" arp .33
46	**Jas Wheeler**. I.L. Anthony Harris	House, yard, stable, garden 34'
47	**Widow McCarty**. I.L. Anthony Harris	House, stable, yard, garden 28' arp .19
48	**Widow Conner**. I.L. Anthony Harris	House, stable, yard, garden 25' 8" arp .9
49	**Thomas Gaunt**. I.L. Anthony Harris	House, stable, yard, garden 27' arp .16
50	I.L. Anthony Harris	Waste Plot 78' 7" arp 1.6
51	**Richard Clear**. I.L. Anthony Harris	House, stable, yard, garden 28'4" arp .22
52	**William Parrot**. I.L. Anthony Harris	House, office, yard, garden 42' arp .30
53	**Jas Grant**. I.L. Anthony Harris	House. Garden shared with No 54 15' 8" .16
54	**Edward Brown**. I.L. Anthony Harris	House, yard. Garden shared with No 53
55	**Robert Brooks**. I.L. Anthony Harris	House, stable, garden 14' 4" arp .11
56	**Joshua Sullivan**. I.L. Anthony Harris	House, stable, yard 24' arp .10
57	**Rev Ja Cluxton**. I.L. Anthony Harris	House, office , yard 43' arp .16
58	**John Sullivan**. I.L. Anthony Harris	House 31'
59	**Arthur Maynard**. I.L. Anthony Harris	House, yard 36'
60	**John Humphry**. I.L. Anthony Harris	House, yard 27' arp .6
61	**Widow Faros**. I.L. Anthony Harris	House, yard 23' arp .7
	PRISON	
62	I.L. John Jones	The gaol in ruins 23'
63	I.L. John Jones	Waste House and garden 25' arp .11
64	**Giles Varian**. I.L.	House, garden 24' arp .8

	John Jones	
65	**William Moxley**. I.L. John Jones	House 16'8"
66	**John Scott**. I.L. John Jones	House 28'6"
67	**William Harris.** I.L. John Jones	House & Yard 24' arp .7~

1775 MAP OF NORTH STREET

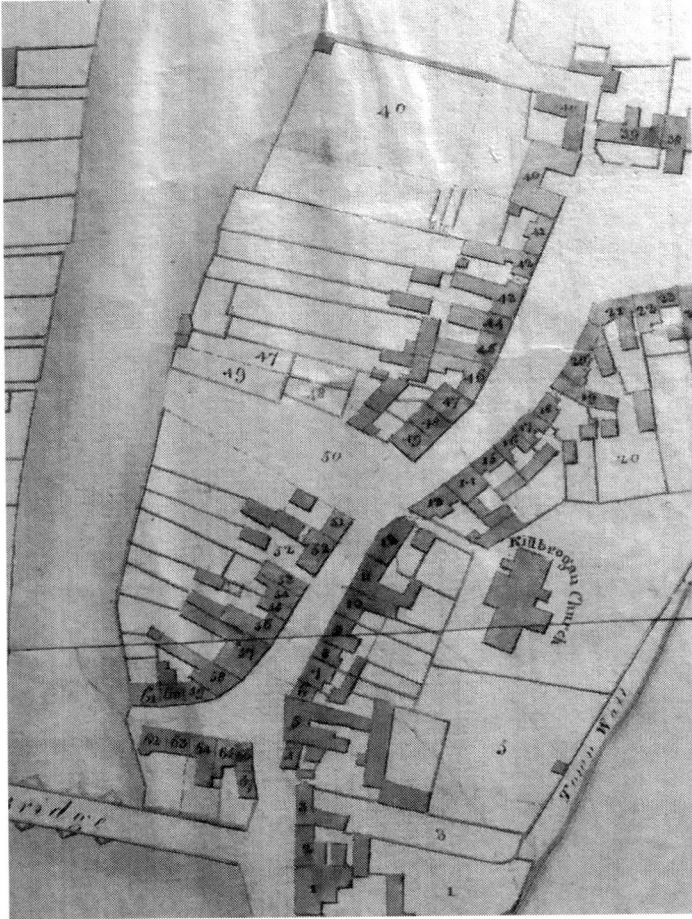

1775 MIDDLE SECTION OF NORTH STREET

1775 UPPER SECTION OF NORTH STREET

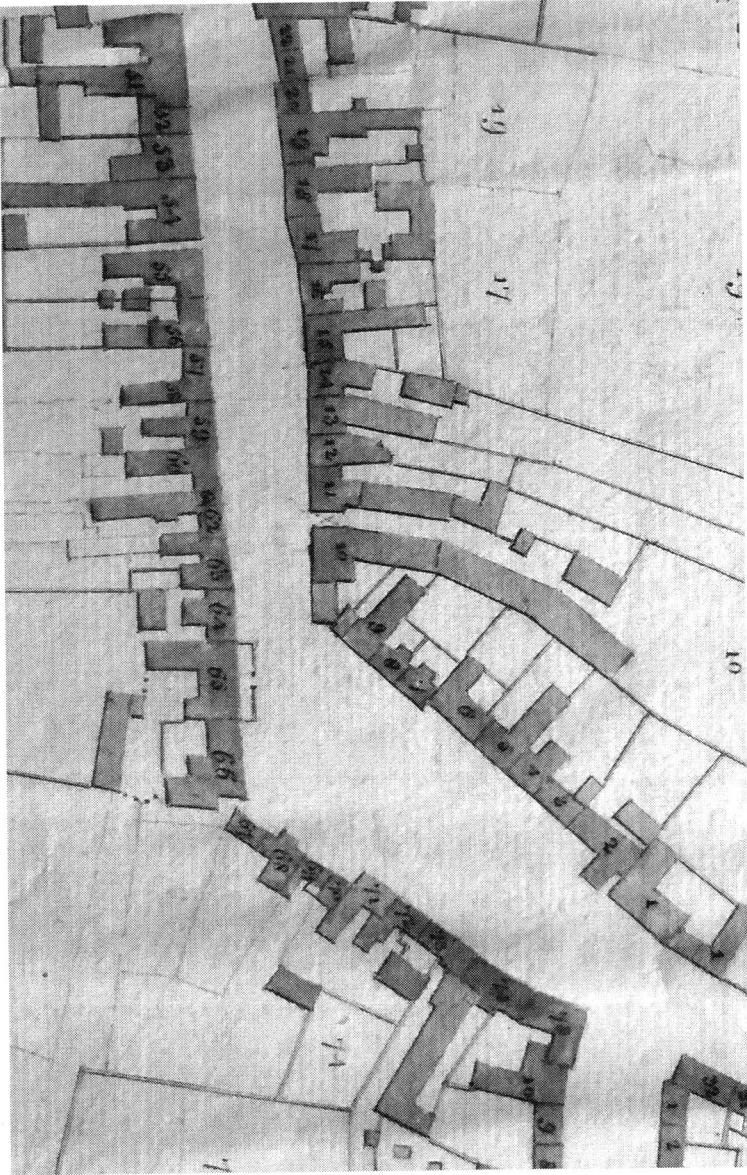

ORIGINAL GRIFFITHS MAP OF
KILBROGAN HILL

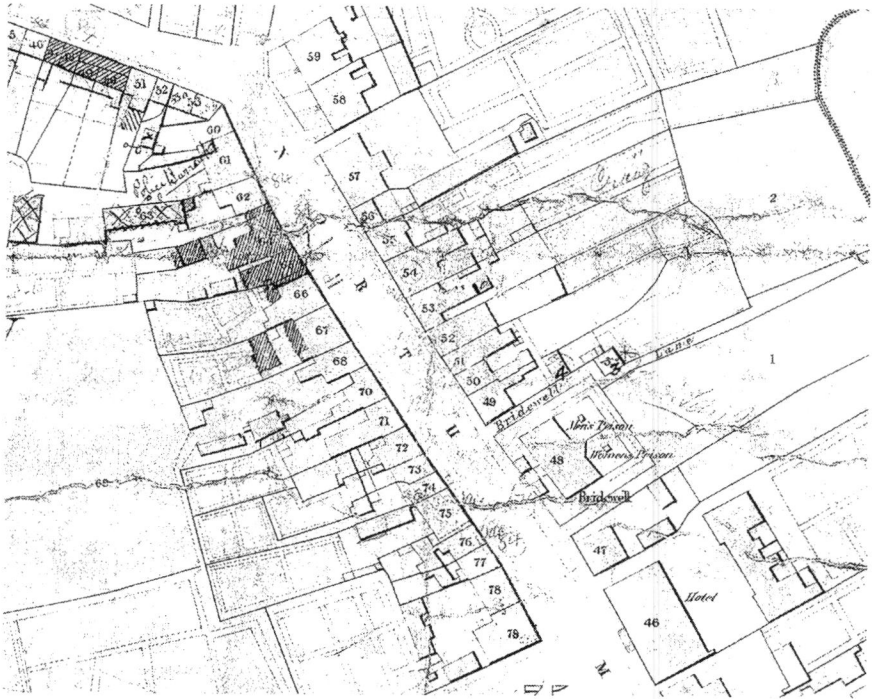

ORIGINAL GRIFFITHS MAP OF THE SHAMBLES

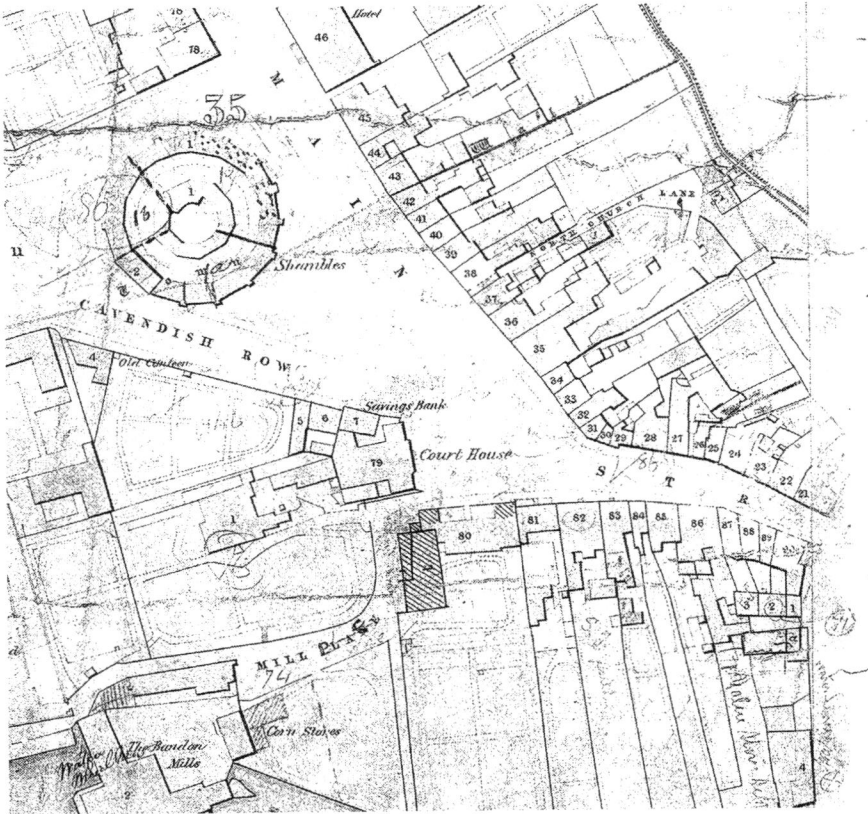

CHAPTER 5

A HISTORY OF THE HOUSES AND PUBLIC BUILDINGS

Without access to individual property deeds, the compilation of data for each house was challenging. Any inaccuracies are unintentional. The data is divided into immediate lessors and occupiers as represented in the valuation records. The numbers of the houses are those which appear in the valuation office and they rarely reflect the same numbers as today's postal addresses. Numbers also varied in each of the two censuses. Where known, the different numbers used for each house are reflected.

It has not been possible to determine how many of the houses pre-dated 1816. A comparison of the 1775 map and index in the previous chapter with the data for the houses in the 1800s provide some interesting revelations. Where new houses were built in the early 1800s, old out buildings were often left untouched making comparisons between the maps somewhat easier.

Very little is known about the occupiers of the houses during the early 1800s as the first record was dated 1837. There is a gap in data between 1837 and 1849 when the pre-valuation records were compiled and again between 1849 and 1856. From 1856 onwards the information is, more or less, complete except in some cases where the records were difficult to read. The absence of any data in the valuation records relating to the immediate lessors and tenants themselves sometimes makes it impossible to determine who some of the occupiers were.

No 1 – BANK HOUSE – built in the early 1870s on the site of former houses

1837 Number 1 – Valuation £42

1851 Number 1 – Valuation £30 10s 0d

1874 – Converted to a new premises

1901 Census Number: 1 – The Provincial Bank

1911 Census Number: 101 – The Provincial Bank

Immediate Lessors

1775 Stephen Winthrop (He held all the sites up to the front of Christ Church which were previously held by Herbert Love)

1816 George Kingston Esq[53]

1817 William Holland Kingston Esq (eldest son and heir)

1832 Hester Waring (to secure a loan of £200 to William H. Kingston – The 61 year lease which was to be held by Richard Tresilian)

1864 Richard Wheeler Doherty (possibly on Richard Wheeler's behalf)[54]

1868 James Moriarty

On 25th March 1816 the lease on this property was granted by the Duke of Devonshire to George Kingston Esq. The term was for 73 years. William, the eldest son of George, inherited the lease following the death of his father on 23rd August, 1817

In 1868 the lease was held by James Moriarty, a shop keeper in Bandon[55].

---

[53] See Appendix. Biographies
[54] Registry of Deeds. 1837 21 57
[55] Registry of Deeds. 1868 14 67. See also Appendix. Biographies

Occupiers

In 1775 there was a large 'new' slate house on the site with an office, yard and garden. It was occupied by Thomas Holland, a linen draper and spirit merchant.[56]

The Bank was opened in Bandon in 1834. The occupier in 1837 was John Johnson Thomson Esq, manager of the Provincial Bank. Robert Tresilian Belcher was Director of the Bank in 1844 and Hezekiah O'Callaghan was the teller.[57]

John Thomson died on 13th August, 1853, aged 52. He had been the manager of the bank for over nineteen years. An auction of all the contents of the house took place on 6th October, 1853 and was conducted by Mr Pennington, an auctioneer. The venue was the ball room at the Devonshire Arm's hotel and the contents included carpets, beds, a piano, furniture, a shower and hip bath and kitchen ware.

Hezekiah O'Callaghan assumed the role of manager following the death of John Thomson. He was recorded as being in residence at the time of the first valuation record in 1856[58]. In 1851 he was living at No 61 North Main Street.

Hezekiah married Catherine Tresilian in Bandon in 1848. Catherine's mother, Dorothea Tresilian, was living with them at Bank House when she died on 24th April 1862. She was the widow of Josias Tresilian of Mohonagh, Co Cork.

Hezekiah retained his role as manager until 1867 when Henry James Simms took over the position. In 1865 Henry Simms married Emily Teresa Curling, the daughter of Edward Curling, MP, of The Castle, Newcastle. The marriage took place at Newcastle West. Henry was recorded in the register of vestrymen in Christ Church, Kilbrogan in 1870.

In the early 1870s a new bank was built incorporating No 1, 2 and 3 North Main Street.

---

[56] See Appendix. Biographies
[57] W.A. Spiller. A Short Topographical and Statistical Account of the Bandon Union
[58] Slater's Directory of Bandon, 1856

On 20th August 1874 the Bank moved its business for a time to Mr. R. Hunter's premises. The occupier of Bank House is listed in some subsequent valuation records as the Provincial Bank.

While Henry and Emily Teresa were living at the property, they had a daughter, Catherine Curling born in 1872 and a son John Curling on 19th January, 1874. Henry was manager of the Bank until 1876. He was recorded as Manager of the branch in Ennis in 1893.[59]

In 1881 Robert H. Chapman succeeded Henry Simms. He continued in the position as manager until at least 1893. His residence was at No 4 North Main Street for some of this period.

Samuel P. Gordon (52), Church of Ireland, was described as the Bank Manager in the 1901 census. He resided at the property with his wife Marion (51), Mary Mahony (20) who was a domestic servant and Michael Devine (53), a porter at the bank.

At the time of the 1911 census, Harry Stuart Pearson, Bank Manager, aged 43 was in residence. He lived with his wife, Eva Isabella aged 43, daughter Helen Adelaide aged 14, son Harry Stuart aged 11, daughter Dorothy aged 3, domestic servant and nurse Mary Josephine O'Neill aged 19 and porter Charles Morris aged 39. In 1912 Harry Stuart Pearson was promoted to manager of the Youghal branch of the bank.[60]

T.W. Martin was the manager in 1915[61]. A.T. Johnston was the accountant and the two cashiers were J.F. Flood and J.F. McGrath

In 1921 V.D. Garde was the manager.[62]

A.H. Holloway was the manager of the bank in 1944.[63]

---

[59] Teresa was executor and a beneficiary of the will dated 1928 of Miss Frances Napier Curling who lived at No 2 Devonshire Square.
[60] Christ Church Vestry Minutes of 31st July 1912.
[61] Cork and Munster Trade Directory. 1915
[62] Guy's Directory of 1921
[63] Thom's Directory of 1944

The Provincial Bank was taken over by Allied Irish Banks Ltd in 1974 and after a period in private ownership, An Post, became the tenant in 1988.

No 2 – Became Bank House
1837 Number 2 – Valuation £13
1849 Number 6
1851 Number 2 – Valuation £9
1874 Converted to a new premise

Immediate Lessors
1775 Stephen Winthrop (He held all the sites up to the front of Christ Church)
George Kingston Esq
Thomas Hornibrook
William Holland Kingston
1836 The Provincial Bank[64]
Thomas Fuller Esq[65]
1845 George Fuller Esq (son and heir)
1850 Rev Thomas Glasson Bennett (brother in law to George Fuller Esq)

William Holland Kingston entered into a lease with the Provincial Bank on 27th March 1836. The property was described as 44' in breadth, 188' in depth and bounded on the south by North Main Street, on the north by the stream separating the premises from the lands of Knockbrogan and on the west by the premises in occupation by the under tenants of Thomas Fuller and the garden of Dr Clerke and on the east by the stream and the other premises demised by William Holland Kingston to the Provincial Bank to hold for 42 years to commence on 29th September 1834 paying a yearly rent to William Holland Kingston of £28 9s.[66]

This holding was included in a marriage settlement in 1850.[67] George Fuller Esq, a barrister at law, transferred the lease to Rev Thomas Glasson Bennett of Innishannon and Charles Johnston of Mt Jerome, Dublin. George Fuller married Charlotte Matilda

---

[64] Registry of Deeds. 1836 7 209
[65] Died 25th March, 1845 aged 70
[66] Registry of Deeds. 1836 7 209
[67] Registry of Deeds. 1850 4 275

Elkins of Oswerby, Salop, UK in Pancras, London in early 1850. The witness to the deed was Mr Edward Elkins. No 3 was also included in the settlement.

Rev Thomas Glasson Bennett married Mary Fuller who was the daughter of Thomas Fuller and sister of George Fuller.

Occupiers
In 1837 the occupier was Robert Baker who was a dyer.

The occupier in 1849 was Jeremiah Mahoney, a spirit dealer, who was still resident up to the 1870s. William Foley was the last tenant before the building was converted into the new bank in 1874. He held a month to month tenancy agreement.

No 3 – Became Bank House
1837 Number 3 – Valuation £18
1851 Number 3 – Valuation £12
1874 The building was converted into the new Bank.

Immediate Lessors
1775 Stephen Winthrop (He held all the sites up to the front of Christ Church)
The original lease was to George Kingston
Thomas Fuller Esq[68]
1845 George Fuller Esq (son and heir)
1850 Rev Thomas Glasson Bennett (brother in law of George Fuller)

This holding was also part of George Fuller's marriage settlement of 1850. (See No 2). (The immediate lessor is recorded as Thomas Fuller Esq in the Griffiths Valuation of 1851).

Occupiers
In 1837 the occupier was Edward Murphy.

By 1851 the occupier was Timothy Murphy who was a tailor as well as a publican. He vacated the premises in 1864 and was succeeded by William Tanner who was in residence until 1867. John Burke

---

[68] Died 25th March, 1845

became the occupier in 1869 but was moved out in 1874 when the building was converted into the new bank. He was a butcher. He married on 5th February, 1874.

No 4 – Bank Place – For Many Years a Medical Hall. Present site of ODM.

1837 Number 4 – Valuation £45 (Divided into 2 in 1847)
1851 Number 4 – Valuation £19 10s
1901 census Number 2 – Medical Hall
1911 census Number 100 – No entry

Immediate Lessors

1775 Stephen Winthrop (He held all the sites up to the front of Christ Church)
1816 Jonathan Clerke – 99 yr lease
1837 Thomas Shadwell Clerke
1838 John Lovell, Tanner
1847 William Lovell (brother of John Lovell)
1847 Elizabeth Lovell, spinster
1870 David Hunter, Merchant
1875 Charles Cooper, Surgeon
1901 Dr John Reid

By indenture of release dated 1st April, 1816, the Duke of Devonshire demised the holding to Jonathan Clerke, a Medical Doctor. A new house was built on the site in 1816 and was occupied by Dr Jonathan Clerke. The holding measured in front 42' 9", at the rear 30' and from front to rear on the west 211' and on the east 190' 9". The term was for the life of His Highness R Leopold of Saxe Coburgh and for 99 years to run concurrently at an annual rent of £12 payable half yearly.[69] Jonathan Clerke,

---

[69] Registry of Deeds. 1838 10 178

Medical Doctor was admitted to the Corporation of Bandon as a Freeman in 1797.

The premises were bounded on the north by the bleach field known at the time as Wheelers Bleach. A lane ran from the Old Cork Road to the Kilbrogan River and on towards the rear of Christ Church. It was known as Bleach Lane.[70] The plot was described as being bounded on the east by the holdings of George Kingston and on the west partly by Thomas Lovell's holding and partly by the holding of Paul Williams.[71]

Jonathan Clerke's will was published on 17th February 1837. Sir Thomas Shadwell Clerke, a Major in the army at the time, was the eldest son and heir to his father's estate. He assigned the lease to John Lovell of Bandon, a tanner. John Lovell paid Sir Thomas £300 for the remainder of the lease and he was also subject to the yearly rents documented in the original lease.

John Lovell Esq, a tanner, died intestate on 2nd April 1847 at this residence. His death notice recorded that he died of a fever which he caught in the discharge of his public duty as Poor Law Guardian. He had pursued a long commercial career with honour and integrity.[72]

The premises passed to his brother, William Lovell by deed of 8th May 1847.

Following John Lovell's death, the house was divided into two. William resided in one of the houses up to his death and the second house was occupied by Anne Robinson as a tenant of William's.

Occupiers

In 1837 the occupier was Jonathan Clerke, a Medical Doctor.[73] He died on 7th April 1838 aged 74 and his wife, Mrs Eliza Clerke died on 13th March, 1842, aged 74.

---

[70] Bandon Historical Journal. No 9. The Laneways of Bandon. Sean Connolly
[71] Ms 6189 Lismore Papers
[72] Southern Reporter. 3rd April, 1847
[73] See Appendix. Biographies

John Lovell became the tenant in 1838 and following his death William was in residence for a short period.

William Lovell died in 1847. By the terms of his will of 23rd July 1847, Elizabeth Lovell, a spinster, inherited the property for the residue of the term of the lease. William Lovell charged the entire head rent on the adjoining house and appointed Thomas Clear and David Hunter as executors to his will. Thomas Clear's mother was Jane Lovell.

In the valuation records of 1856 the occupier was recorded as the Representatives of William Lovell, namely Thomas Clear and David Hunter. By an agreement dated 14th October 1858 they assigned the property to Elizabeth Lovell for the residue of the term of the lease. Elizabeth Lovell's name appeared in the valuation records of 1861. She died in 1863. In her will dated 22nd November 1863, she assigned the lease on the property to David Hunter.

Robert H. Chapman, the Manager of the Provincial Bank, was the occupier for a period in the 1870s. In 1879 Charles Thomas Cooper, a medical doctor, took up residence. He paid David Hunter £60 for the remainder of the lease.

When Charles Cooper became the occupier in 1884, the building was much improved and a new roof was added. His name appeared on the electoral register of 1884. The property was described as a house with offices yard and garden with a rateable valuation of £25.

He resided at the premises until sometime in 1898 when Dr John Reid succeeded him.

Dr. John Reid.

Dr. John Reid was not married when he took up residence. He was the son of Henry Reid of Grange House, Ovens and his wife, Sarah Anne (Rice). He was born in June 1871 and was educated at Fawcett Collegiate School, Cork and at Queen's College, Cork. He took graduate courses in medicine and surgery in Dublin, London and Paris. He married Isabella Josephine MacNamara in 1906. She was the daughter of Rev MacNamara, the rector of Ballymoney. Dr John and his wife had two sons, Arthur Maurice and John Lewis.

In the 1901 census he was described as Church of Ireland, aged 29. He was living at the premises with his sister Ellen (26), a visitor Jane Biggs (44), a servant, Annie Kidney (25) and a boarder, Charles Cox (22).

Dr John Reid was also recorded as a resident of Devonshire Square a short time afterwards. He then moved to Glensalney on the Dunmanway Road.

In 1915 J. Reid was recorded as operating a chemist.[74]   He left Bandon in 1919 and was succeeded by Patrick O'Driscoll[75].   In 1934 Mrs Maud O'Driscoll was recorded as the occupier.   In 1939 the property became vacant.   Michael O'Reilly took over the tenancy in 1941 and in 1955 he was succeeded by Jeremiah O'Shea.

The building was substantially altered in recent years.   In 1978 it was converted into offices.

No 5 –Robinsons Wine and Spirit Merchant and Grocer. Present Site of Ho Kee
1837   Number   4   (See   previous house. Divided into two in 1847)
1849 Number 9
1851 Number 5 – Valuation £16
1901 Census Number 3 – Public House
1911 Census Number 99 – Public House

BANDON[76]
IMPORTATION OF WINES

A. ROBINSON has lately Imported, direct from
Oporto and Cadiz, several Hogsheads of Superior
PORT and SHERRY, shipped by First-class Houses in the
Trade. These wines can be depended upon as Genuine,
and will be Sold at the Lowest Prices.
Cognac Brandy, Hollands' Gin, &c,, direct from the Cus-
tom-house; Choice OLD WHISKEY, off Sherry Casks,
Bass's Pale and Burton Ales, Drogheda Ale, Jameson's and
Pim's E.I. Beer, Guinness's Double Stout, in fine condition
in Bottle.
      WINE, TEA, AND GENERAL GROCERY STORES,
                  NORTH MAIN STREET.
Bandon, 16th April, 1862   (1696)

---

[74] Cork and Munster Trade Directory. 1915
[75] Christ Church, Kilbrogan. Vestry Minutes of 17th September 1919

[76] Cork Examiner. 30th May, 1862

Immediate Lessors
1775 Stephen Winthrop (He held all the sites up to the front of Christ Church)
1816 Thomas Lovell – 99 years
1847 Thomas Lovell Esq
1847 William Lovell Esq (brother to Thomas)
1879 Winspeare Hungerford Toye

Thomas Lovell entered into a lease with the Duke of Devonshire on 1st April, 1816 for the lives of William and John Lovell and William Hunters and 99 years running concurrently at a rent of £4 4s. The site was described as a plot whereon an old house was standing which was in the occupation of Thomas Lovell, 19' in breadth and 46' in depth. It was bounded on the south by the street, on the north and west by the inn and livery stables which were in the possession of Paul Williams and on the east by a new gateway leading to the livery stables.

Occupiers
In approximately this location in 1775 J. Bernard had a large slate house with an office, yard and garden

In March 1824 John Swanston, the Duke's Agent in Bandon, wrote to the Lismore Agent, William Currey, outlining a plan of the old inn and the adjacent premises which included this property. He requested that the outline be shown to Mr Swete explaining a division which he proposed to make with an entrance running between Dr Clerke (No 4) and Mr Lovell (No 5). The adjoining premises (No 7) at the time was to be offered to Mr Swete at £10 pa. Swanston considered that the division was the best way of giving Mr Lovell a back yard.[77]

According to a deed of 1838 relating to No 4[78], this property was once occupied jointly by Thomas Lovell (the husband of Mary Barrett) and Paul Williams. The latter was described as a builder, contractor and Inn Keeper who operated it as The King's Arms Hotel in the early 1800s before he moved to the Devonshire Arms in October 1822[79]. It was subsequently occupied by John Swete

---

[77] MS 43 382/22 Lismore Papers. See also page 64
[78] Registry of Deeds 1838 10 178
[79] See also Property No 6.

and William Lovell. William Lovell's occupancy is confirmed in the records of 1837. It is likely that William ran the inn with his brother in law James Robinson.

James Robinson (1777-1844) married Mary Lovell on 1st May 1806 at Christ Church. James was recorded as an inn keeper when his second son, Thomas, entered Trinity College Dublin in 1835 (Thomas qualified as a clergyman and married Susan Starkey on 1st August, 1838 at Christ Church, Innishannon with the permission of the rector of Ballymodan). James's eldest son William married Anne Hunter on 6th January 1838 (Anne was the daughter of William and Catherine Hunter, grocers and linen drapers of North Main Street). William and his wife Anne operated a Wine and Spirit Store at the premises

Anne and William had three children, Catherine, baptised on 23rd April 1839, James baptised on 18th October 1840 and Mary Anne baptised on 11th December 1844.

WINE AND SPIRIT STORES, 5, NORTH MAIN[80] STREET, BANDON.

WILLIAM ROBINSON, in returning thanks to his
Numerous highly respectable supporters, begs leave
To say that he has always on hand a large Stock of all the
Best, Bottled Wines in general use.
Wise's Best Old Housekeeper's WHISKEY, STRONG
ALES, Guinnes's EXTRA STRONG BROWN
STOUT, WARRANTED GENUINE.
W.R. Rests his claim for a continuance of public favor
on his determination to Sell the Best Articles ONLY on
the LOWEST TERMS.   NOV. 3, 1840

William Robinson died of a fever aged 35. His death notice appeared in the Cork Examiner of 21st April, 1847.

Anne Robinson, a widow, was recorded as the occupier in the pre-valuation records of 1849.

---

[80] Southern Reporter, 7th November, 1840.

In 1856 the names of Anne Robinson and David Hunter as Representatives of William Robinson were recorded as the occupiers. Anne and David's parents were William and Catherine Hunter who were buried at Christ Church.

Anne was in the property until the early 1860s when the names which appeared in the records were both David and Mary Hunter. David may have been Anne's brother.

Anne Robinson and David Hunter entered into a deed of annuity dated 1876 for the annual payment to be made to Anne of £52 for the house, shop and premises then in occupation of David Hunter.[81] David married Mary Hamilton. David was described as a grocer and wine merchant at the time of the baptism of their daughter Thomasina Elizabeth on 4th October, 1854[82]. They also had Catherine Anne, born 31st October, 1855, Frances Mary born 16th May 1857, Hamilton Bryan born 27th July 1858, Frederick born 27th September 1859, Eliza Jane born 25th March 1861. They moved to live at Mount Prospect, Ballymodan in 1862 and had Eva born 1st December 1862, Mary Hamilton born 28th June 1864, Florence born 8th March, 1866 and David born 21st November, 1870

Anne was living in South Main Street in 1882 and the Hunters held the tenancy until 1879.

The Hunters were succeeded by Alexander Stuart Gash, a wine merchant[83], who also had a mineral water factory.[84] He was born in 1838. He married Dora Christina Hayes, the daughter of Rev Richard Hayes of Mishells House (She died in 1919). Alexander may have used No 5 for his business as his residence was recorded as River View not far from Mishells House. Alexander and Dora had at least nine children, Charlotte Popham (b 1870 and married Mr Craven), Mary Stewart (b 1872 and married Thomas Gill), Thomas Warren (b 1873), Richard Horace (b 1876), Dora Marguerite (b 1878 and married George Samuel Levis), Kathleen

[81] 1876 29 213
[82] All their children were baptised at Christ Church, Kilbrogan even after they moved to Ballymodan in 1862-
[83] Slater's Directory of 1881
[84] Guy's Directory of 1886

Frances (b 1879), Alexander Stuart (b 1881, died Kenya), Vincent Gordon (b 1884), Massy (b 1885).

In the electoral register of 1884 Alexander Gash was recorded as the occupier. The rateable valuation was £20 and the premises was described as a house and offices.

The rent of the property was reduced in 1889 and a note added that the valuation was out of all proportion to similar properties. Alexander Gash was the tenant for sixteen years. He died on 16th February, 1898 at River View. Probate was granted at Cork to Dora C. Gash of River View, his widow. His effects amounted to £1,728 15s.[85]

He was succeeded by John Howard in 1895. He was also a vintner. He died on 21st October, 1896. The administration of his estate was granted at Cork to Mary Howard of North Main Street, his widow. His effects were £271 13s.[86]

In 1897 the Representatives of John Howard became the occupiers of the property. A notice appeared in the Freeman's Journal of 17th May, 1897 which recorded that Mrs Howard, a respectable shopkeeper, was found sitting on a chair inside her counter 'quite dead'. She had been widowed for a few months and earlier in the evening had appeared in good health. She left a large young family who were too young to understand the double loss of both their father and mother within a short space of time.

In 1899 Timothy Coffey had taken up residence.

Timothy Coffey was a licensed vintner who also had a drapery business. At the time of the 1901 census he was aged 28 and was living at the premises with his wife Margaret Mary (30), infant daughter Kathleen Mary aged 2 and a servant, Mary Cahill (17).

By 1911 Timothy had a son John Baptist Coffey and his servant was Minnie Lordan. He occupied the premises until 1914 when Jeremiah Keane took over. The Keanes were resident for many years. In 1927 Julia Keane's name was recorded as the tenant.

---

[85] Calendar of Wills. National Archives of Ireland
[86] Ibid

She was succeeded by Hanna Maria Keane in 1950. Donal O'Donovan became the next tenant in 1977. It is currently occupied by Ho Kee Restaurant.

From the Lawrence Collection
With permission of the National Library of Ireland

No 6 Formerly the site of the King's Arms Hotel with Livery also known as Burchills. – Demolished in 1957
1837 Number 6 - £30
1849 Number 10
1851 Number 6 – Valuation £15
1901 Census Number 4 – Private Dwelling
1911 Census Number 98 – Shop

Immediate Lessors
1775 Stephen Winthrop (He held all the sites up to the front of Christ Church)
Pre 1822 Paul Williams
1822? William Lovell Esq
1860 Thomas Clear
1890 Richard Clear (son of Thomas)
1901 Richard Clear
1828 Dr Shinkwin

J. Bernard's house may have stretched across this plot as well as No 5 and it is likely that the inn incorporated both No 5 and No 6 at one time.

A note on Scale's index of 1775 recorded that the house was previously an inn which suggests that it became an inn again sometime after J. Bernard vacated the property. In the Lucas Directory of 1787, Ann Landers was recorded as the occupier of the Kings Arms Inn (or the 'Kings Inn'). The will of James Landers of Bandon, Inn Keeper, was proved in 1785.[87] The Inn passed to John Burchill at some point after 1787 and he held it until 1813 when Paul Williams took over. In 1811 the freemasons met at 'Burchills'.[88]

Paul Williams agreed to take on the Devonshire Arms as a tenant on a yearly basis from 29th September, 1822 and in return, he surrendered this premises which had been in his possession.

Occupiers
In 1837 the occupier was William Lovell. He had split the neighbouring house into two.

Thomas Clear was recorded as the occupier in 1849. His wife was Mary Robinson whose mother was Mary Lovell. (See also No 5 and No 81).

Thomas was described as a grocer and flour factor of Old Cork Road in the Slater's Directory of 1846. It's not know where he moved to between 1851 and 1856 when Margaret Sullivan's name appeared on the register as the resident for five years until Thomas Clear returned to the property in 1856. He stayed for five years until 1861 and then moved to No 81 where he resided until 1868 two years before his death in 1870. (See No 81 for his biography).

In 1861 Charles Rice Wade, a haberdasher, moved into the property and was the occupier until his death in 1871. He was recorded in the register of vestrymen of Christ Church, Kilbrogan in 1870

---

[87] Kinsale Council Book
[88] 275 Years of Freemasonry in Bandon. David J. Butler & Alwyn C. Williams

Charles had had a haberdashery business on South Main Street in 1856 though was recorded as a shoemaker in the Ballymodan census of 1845 and at that time was living with his wife Jane and son Denis. His business had moved to his residence on North Main Street by the 1860s.[89] He married Jane Hunter in 1842. They had at least a son Charles, baptised on 16th February 1845 in Ballymodan and a son Denis.

Charles Rice Wade died on 26th August, 1871. Letters of Administration were granted at Cork to Denis Wade, his son and only next of kin. Charles left effects of under £800.

Denis Rice Wade was recorded as the occupier following the death of Charles in 1871. His name appeared on the electoral register of 1884. The property was described as a house with offices and yard at a rateable valuation of £15.

Denis Wade remained at the property until 1896. He married Sarah Isabella, a daughter of George Appelbe who had a business in No 7. They had at least Mary Gertrude born 10th September 1873, Charles born 7th October, 1874, George Applebe Rice Wade, born 28th December 1875 Denis died in Bandon on 29th November, 1918. At the time of his death his address was given as Lee's Hotel and his occupation was a retired Bank Manager. Probate was granted in 1919 to his granddaughter, Henrietta Gertrude Langhorne (Denis's daughter Mary Gertrude married William Henry Langhorne).

Joseph Allshire, a grocer took up residence in 1896. He died on 4th March 1898 and was succeeded by his son William Henry Allshire.

In 1897 John Reen rented an office and yard from Richard Clear. The arrangement changed in 1903 when Jeremiah Keane took over as the occupier.

By the time of the 1901 census Charles Payne[90], a Methodist, was described as aged 45, a carrier. He was living at the property with

[89] Coghlans Directory of 1867
[90] Charles Payne may have been related to the Allshires as he was executor to the estate of Thomas Allshire of Castle Road, Shoemaker who died 9 April 1916

his wife Sarah J. Payne (35), daughters Rachael (9) and Susan (8) and sons, William Joseph (7) and H. Roberts (1).

Shortly afterwards Susan became the occupier and by 1903 Hannah O'Mahony had moved in. Hannah occupied the property until 1905 when Charles Coffey took up residence and held it until 1910. In 1910 he was replaced by Nora Coffey.

In 1911 James Coffey, a boot and shoemaker was living at the property with his wife Nora. The premises was recorded as a house and shop. James was recorded as a boot maker in 1915.[91]

In 1903 the valuation records record that Nora Coffey was renting the shop part of the premises from Charles Payne.

Nora Coffey died on 2nd December 1926[92]. The Coffey family continued to occupy the premises until 1928. In 1930 Ellen Crowley became the tenant. It became vacant in 1936 and in 1938 Matthew Nooney took on the tenancy.

In 1914 the office and yard were rented from Richard Clear, the lessor. That part of the property was recorded as 6a and it was described as a shed and a yard. Jeremiah Shine had it for a while and he was succeeded in 1930 by Bartholomew. John Lyons took it over in 1933 and by 1938 Michael O'Reilly had become the occupier.

Michael O'Reilly was succeeded by Matthew Nooney, David Crowley in 1940, Timothy Coleman in 1943 and Timothy Daly in 1946. James Daly, a shoemaker, became a tenant in 1952. The building was demolished in 1957.

---

[91] Cork and Munster Trade Directory 1915
[92] St Patrick's Church

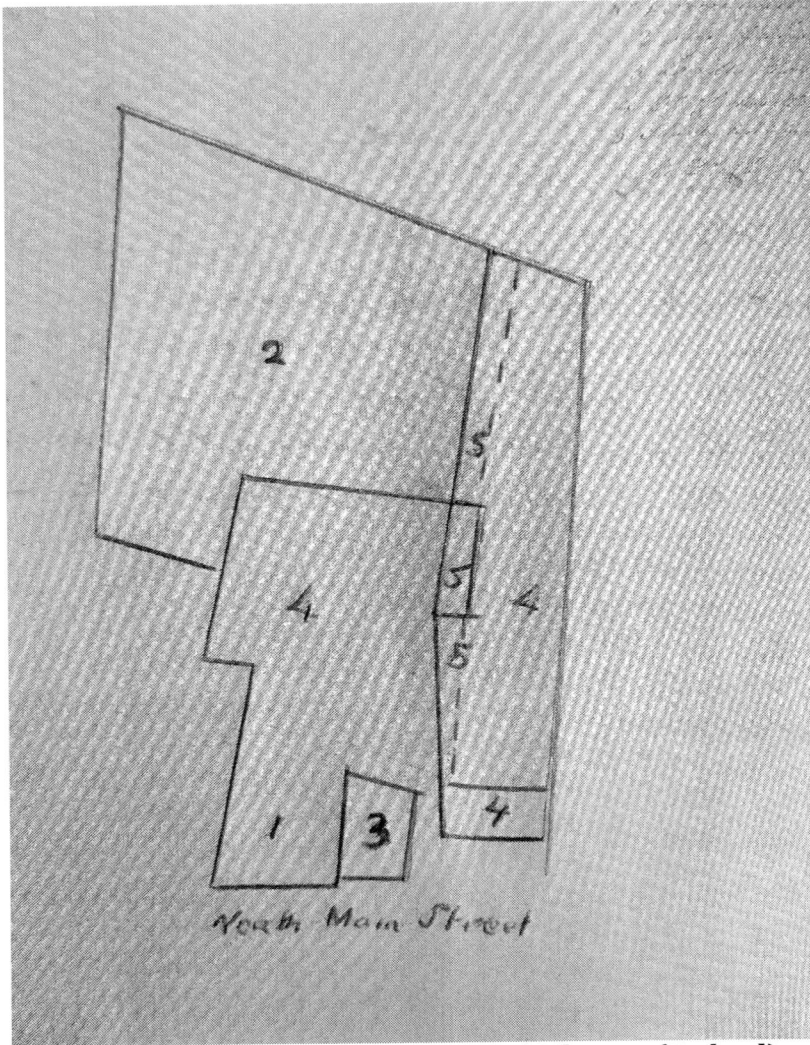

(with permission of the National Library of Ireland)

This plan of the houses numbered below was included in the Lismore Estate Papers[93]

1. Inn and Yard (No 6)	4. Dr Clerke's House (4)
2. Garden	5. Stable & Ground given to Dr Clerke
3. Lovell's House (No 5)	

---

[93] Lismore Papers. Ms 43,382/22 Plan of Old Inn

No 7 – Formerly George T. Appelbe's. Presently De Barra's Pub

1837 Number 6 – Valuation £24
1849 Number 11
1851 Number 7 – Valuation £16
1901 Census Number 5 – Public House
1911 Census Number 97 – Public House

Immediate Lessors

1775 Stephen Winthrop (He held all the sites up to the front of Christ Church)
1825 John Swete – 99 years to 25/3/1929
1851 Mrs Blood/Mrs Bowen
1863 George Thomas Appelbe
1901 Edward Appelbe

An entry in the valuation record reads as follows:- 'Mrs Blood is now Mrs Bowen and she is a lunatic daughter of late Mr Swete'.[94]

In a lease dated 31st December, 1825, the Duke of Devonshire demised the site to John Swete and his heirs for the lives of William Belcher, Henry Belcher and John Belcher, sons of William Belcher, apothecary or 99 years. The site was 48' in breadth at the front, 89' at the rear with a depth of 281'. In 1863 the surviving trustees, Alicia Lysaght Perry of Rock Lodge, Cork and Thomas Lucas of Richardstown, Cork assigned the remainder of the lease to George Thomas Appelbe and his heirs together with other houses built on the site by John Swete[95]. (See Property No 8)

Occupiers

William Hunter and his wife Catherine (1783-1836) and family were the occupiers in 1837 and were still in residence in 1849. In

---

[94] See Mill Place. Floraville
[95] Registry of Deeds. 1863 30 66

1829 William Hunter of the North Main Street was admitted as a freeman of the Corporation of Bandon.[96] William was a grocer, haberdasher and linen and woollen draper.[97] Their son John (b 1810) died aged 25 in 1836 and was buried with William and Catherine at Christ Church. Their daughter Anne (b 1811), married William Robinson. (See No 5), Frances (b 1813-1889) married Thomas Lovell in 1848, David (b 1817) married Mary Hamilton (see also No 5). Their son James, born 1819 died in 1875.

By the time of this first valuation in 1856 George Thomas Appelbe had taken up residence. George was the son of Edward Alexander Appelbe who married Sarah Thomas. He was a grocer, iron monger and seed merchant[98].

George Thomas and his wife Annie Mary had a daughter Anne on 21st January 1856 whilst living at this address. They also had a son George Thomas, born on 7th May 1857 (he died aged 2 in 1859), a daughter Isabella Mary born on 13th October 1859 (she married Denis Rice Wade of No 6) and a daughter, Ann Mary born on 12th July 1862. Their son Edward Alexander who was born in 1853 became a surgeon and died in Winchester. Their daughter, Anna, born in 1856, died in Bandon in 1895.

Annie Mary, died in August 1862 shortly after their last child was born.

George's name appeared in the register of vestrymen at Christ Church, Kilbrogan in 1870.

---

[96] Southern Reporter. 23rd April, 1829
[97] Slater's Directory of 1846
[98] Slater's Directory of 1856

In 1883 the following advertisements appeared in the Eagle relating to businesses conducted by George Appelbe.

BANDON

TO BE LET

SEVERAL GOOD HOUSES, Furnished
Or Unfurnished, on Very Reasonable
Terms. Apply to
GEORGE T. APPELBE,
(494-2683-6r)   BANDON

GOULDING'S MANURES
ARE THE CHEAPEST AND THE BEST

AGENT FOR BANDON:
GEO. T. APPELBE
(495-2683-6t)

The rental on the property in 1884 was £18 10s.

In 1887 George was recorded as the Deputy County Surveyor. George remained listed as the occupier until his death in 1896.

The will of George Thomas Appelbe who died on 5th September 1896 was proved at Cork by Edward Alexander Appelbe of South Gate Road, Winchester, Hampshire, a medical doctor and son of the deceased. George left effects of £9,312 4s 1d

Thomas Turpin took up residence in 1897 and he was the occupier by the time of the 1901 census. He was described as Church of Ireland, aged 38, a shopkeeper, living with his wife Sarah (34). The property was recorded as a public house. Thomas died on 2nd

June 1909. Probate of his will was granted to Dr John Reid. His estate was valued at £1112.

In 1911 Sarah Turpin was recorded as the occupier and the property was listed as a public house.

Thomas Tanner moved into the licensed premises in 1914 and continued in occupation until 1929 when he was succeeded by Michael O'Reilly.

No 8 – Presently De Barra's
1837 Number 7 – Valuation £52
1849 Number 12
1851 Number 8 – Valuation £40 15s 0d
1901 Census Number 6 – Public House
1911 Census Number 96 – Public House

Immediate Lessors
1775 Stephen Winthrop (He held all the sites up to the front of Christ Church)
1851 Representatives of John Swete and Mrs Bowen
1861 William Connor Sullivan
1867 George Thomas Appelbe
1897 Sir John Arnott
1901 Edward Appelbe
1954 Arnott Estate

Occupiers
In 1837 John Swete was the occupier.

Richard Dowden was recorded as the occupier in 1849. The property was described as a large premises with many stores. The annual rent was £33. On 4th February 1847 a newspaper advertisement announced that Richard Dowden had just received at his stores in North Main Street 100 tons of prime African Guano which he wished to sell at very reasonable terms. Wholesale buyers were encouraged.

Rev Dominick Murphy was resident in 1851. By 1864 he was living at Douglas Road, Cork and was a Parish Priest.

By the time of the first valuation in 1856 William Connor Sullivan, a tanner, had become the occupier.

Joseph Lane, a grocer, became the occupier in 1860. A note in the valuation record states that 'it was leased in 1860 and the tenant put in a new shop front. The lease is the same as before'.

In 1867 Eliza Emerson, a chandler, leased a section of the building from William Connor Sullivan. The premises were divided into 8a and 8b.

By the 1870s Joseph Lane, a baker, grocer and publican[99], leased the shop, office and garden.

Joseph Lane continued to occupy the property until 1893 when Richard Kevin Lane took over. His name appeared on the electoral register of 1884. The property was described as a house, offices and yard with a rateable valuation of £21. The garden with offices and a yard were recorded separately at a valuation of £7 10.

In the 1901 census Richard Kevin Lane aged 31 resided at the premises with his wife Mary (3) and daughters Mary (7) and Gertrude (5) and son John Joseph (4). Richard was described in the census as a journalist and his wife as a shopkeeper. The property was described as a public house.

Joseph Lane's wife died on 22nd April, 1903 at an advanced age following a long illness. She was buried at the Kilbrogan Cemetery. She pre-deceased her husband who was one of the chief mourners at her funeral.

The Lanes lived at the premises until 1908 when they were succeeded by Patrick Murphy. There is no entry for the property

---

[99] Slaters Directory of 1881

in the 1911 census. By 1913 William Hurley had taken up residence. The property was vacant in 1915 and in 1916 Michael O'Reilly became the tenant and held the premises for many years.

By at least 1910 the premises was divided into 8a (licensed premises, house and office) and 8b (office, yard and garden). 8b had been occupied by Sarah Turpin who had No 7. In 1914 the tenant of No 7 was Thomas Tanner and he also held 8b.

The name of the tenant in 1962 became Michael O'Reilly Ltd. The property became vacant for a short period in 1993.

No 9 – Formerly a Bakery
1837 Number 8 – Valuation £16
1849 Number 13
1851 Number 9 – Valuation £9 5s 0
1901 Census Number 7 – Bakery and dwelling house
1911 Census Number 95 – Bakery and dwelling house

Immediate Lessors
1775 Stephen Winthrop (He held all the sites up to the front of Christ Church)
1851 The Duke of Devonshire
1897 Sir John Arnott
1901 Sir John Arnott

Occupiers
In 1837 the occupier was Anne Clerk.

Ann Clerk and Eliza Emerson were still the occupiers in 1849[100] and paid an annual rent of £4. They were earthenware dealers

---

[100] Slater's Directory of 1846

and grocers. They were recorded as A. Clerk and E. Emerson in the Griffiths valuation record of 1851. The valuation was £9 5s.

By 1861 Eliza, a chandler, had become the sole tenant. In 1869 Eliza was replaced by William Tanner, a chandler, baker and grocer.[101] William Tanner was recorded in the register of vestrymen at Christ Church, Kilbrogan in 1870. In the electoral register of 1884 the property was described as a house with offices and a yard at a rateable valuation of £12.

William Tanner remained as the occupier of the premises until 1927 when he was replaced by Elizabeth Wood. She occupied the dwelling until 1937 when she was succeeded by Miss Mary B Daly.

In the 1901 census William Tanner was recorded as Presbyterian, aged 60, a baker, living with his wife Anne, aged 58 and a daughter Minnie aged 38, an assistant in her father's shop, a son William aged 30, a baker, a son Edward aged 26, a baker and a son Richard aged 23, a baker along with Robert Harman aged 8, a grandson and a servant Mary Coughlan.

Mary B. Daly was succeeded by Kathleen Daly in 1955. In 1962 Donal Connolly became the occupier. He was succeeded by Seamus Farrell. The building was recorded as being in poor condition.

---

[101] Coghlans 1867 Street Directory and Guys Directory of 1893

No 10
1837 Number 9 – Valuation £14
1849 Number 14
1851 Number 10 – Valuation £10
1901 Census Number 8 - Shop
1911 Census Number 94 – Shop

Immediate Lessors
1775 Stephen Winthrop (He held all the sites up to the front of Christ Church)
1851 Matthew Hunter
1856 Representatives of William Lovell Esq
1901 Sir John Arnott
1910 Reps of William Lovell Esq
1930 Mr Barry Deane

Occupiers
In 1837 the occupier was Anne Joyce.

George Forde, a wool comber, was the occupier in 1849. He paid an annual rent of £4. He lived at the premises with his wife Mary and family. His son Thomas who was born in 1846 became a publican. George was recorded in the register of vestrymen at Christ Church, Kilbrogan in 1870.

George Forde remained at the address until 1888 when Denis Ryan became the occupier. He was succeeded by his wife Anne Ryan.

In the 1901 census Annie Ryan (50), a shop keeper and widow was living at the premises with her daughter Mary Anne (29), a daughter Helena (26), a son Thomas (22) and a National School Teacher, a daughter Kitty (21), a daughter Annie (17), a daughter Birdie (16) and a relative, Mary Walsh.

In the 1911 census Anne Ryan (64), shop keeper and widow who had had seven children, was living at the property with a daughter, Mary Anne Ryan (45), a daughter Helena Ryan (40), a son Thomas (33) and Mary Lee (5), a granddaughter.

Anne Ryan remained as occupier until about 1940. Ellen Ryan succeeded Anne. In 1950 Kathleen O'Brien became the tenant.

No 11 – Merged with 12
1837 Number 10 – Valuation £11
1849 Number 15
1851 Number 11 – Valuation £6
1901 Census Number 9 - Shop
1911 Census Number 93 Merged with 92 – Shop

Immediate Lessors
1775 Stephen Winthrop (He held all the sites up to the front of Christ Church)
1851 Matthew Hunter
1861 William Hunter
1870 Alfred Hunter
1901 Sir John Arnott
1910 Alfred Hunter
1930 Michael O'Reilly

Occupiers
In 1837 the occupier was Thomas Hornibrook

In 1837 the occupier was Mary Rutledge (In an electoral list of 1832 John Rutledge was described as a pensioner).

Sheares Ollive was the occupier in 1849. He paid an annual rent of £2.

Diana Williams, a book seller, dress maker and milliner[102] was the occupier in 1851.

Isabella Peters became the tenant in 1864 and in 1866 her name was replaced by Richard Cole Brady, a woollen draper and haberdasher. Isabella and Richard Brady married on 30th August

---

[102] Slater's Directory of Bandon, 1856

1865 at St Nicholas Church, Cork. Isabella was the daughter of Thomas Peters.

Richard was recorded in the register of vestrymen of Christ Church, Kilbrogan in 1870.

Richard Wheeler Doherty administered the rentals for Alfred Hunter. Richard Brady's payment of rent is recorded in the cash books for the house and premises from 1876 until 1877 at a rate of £1 13 4 per month paid quarterly.

Richard Brady moved to No 13 in 1883 and the property was vacant before John Hosford assumed occupancy in during 1884.

In 1890 Daniel O'Driscoll, a saddler and harness maker,[103] took up residence and was at the property during the 1901 census. He was listed as a harness maker, aged 51, living with his wife Jane aged 50, son Michael aged 30 also a harness maker, son Cornelius aged 23, a harness maker, son James aged 16 a law clerk, daughter in law Julia O'Driscoll aged 27 a house keeper, granddaughter, Jane O'Driscoll aged 7, a journey man John O'Sullivan, Daniel Fenton, apprentice harness maker aged 20. The property was described as a shop.

Daniel O'Driscoll died sometime between the two census and the premises was occupied by his representatives.

The property was vacant for a while before Michael O'Reilly took up occupancy in 1921. He was succeeded by Kate Quinlan in 1931 and by Michael in 1932. In 1936 Cornelius Crowley became the tenant and Michael O'Reilly was the lease holder. Ellen Crowley succeeded Cornelius in 1955. She remained as the tenant until 1964. In 1979 No 11 and No 12 were amalgamated.

---

[103] Guys Directory of 1893

No 12 – The Social & Family Protection Office.
1837 Number 11 – Valuation £11
1849 Number 16
1851 Number 12 – Valuation £6 5s
1901 Census Number Appears to be merged with 11
1911 Census Number 92 – Shop
2015 Number 96 North Main Street

Immediate Lessors
1775 Stephen Winthrop (He held all the sites up to the front of Christ Church)
1851 Matthew Hunter
1861 William Hunter
1901 Sir John Arnott

Occupiers
In 1837 the occupier was Mary Rutledge (In an electoral list of 1832 John Rutledge was described as a pensioner).

George Turpin, a watch maker, was the occupier in 1849. He paid an annual rent of £9. On 5th June 1857 George and his wife Maria had a daughter Susanna Jane who was baptised on 14th June 1857 at Christ Church. They had a daughter Georgina Maria born on 14th April 1862.

In 1864 George Turpin moved from this premises to No 94. The next occupier was recorded as Alfred Hunter. He remained at the premises until 1877 when William Tanner[104], a tallow chandler, took up residence. By 1880 William O'Brien had moved in and by 1883 the occupier changed again to Miss Granger. In 1898 she was replaced by Daniel O'Driscoll who was the occupant at that stage of No 11 and 12.

---

[104] Slaters Directory of 1881

By the 1901 census Numbers 11 and 12 appear to have merged.

In 1911 the occupant, Jane O'Driscoll was recorded as aged 69, a widow living with son Michael O'Driscoll aged 45 a harness maker and married, his wife Julia aged 40, a son James aged 25, a solicitor's assistant, a grandson Michael Joseph aged 6, a grandson Cornelius aged 4, a granddaughter Julia aged 3, a grand daughter Mary Christina aged 1, a niece Catherine McDaniel aged 13, a harness maker Stephen O'Driscoll aged 60, Cornelius McCarthy, a harness maker aged 19 and Patrick Daly, a harness maker aged 18.

By 1917 Michael O'Driscoll was no longer recorded as the occupier and the house became vacant.

A photo of Michael O'Driscoll in the doorway

In 1919 when Mr Cullinane became resident for a year. In 1920 Michael O'Reilly took over. Michael took over as immediate lessor of this premises. In 1938 the property was occupied by Daniel O'Sullivan.

The property was listed as having a shop and store in 1938. In 1979 the property was amalgamated with No 11.

No 13
1837 Number 12 – Valuation £18
1849 Number 17
1851 Number 13 – Valuation £15
1901 Census Number 10 - Shop
1911 Census Number 91 – Shop

Immediate Lessors
1775 Stephen Winthrop (He held all the sites up to the front of Christ Church)
1851 Matthew Hunter
1860 The Duke of Devonshire
1882 William Hunter
1938 Eugene Duggan

Occupiers
In 1837 the occupier was James Morgan.

Johanna Murphy, a publican and baker[105] was the occupier in 1849. Sometime between 1856 and 1860 Joseph Lane took up residence. William Hunter, a baker, was the occupier from 1860. He remained in the property until 1877 when William Tanner succeeded him. He was registered at the address until 1880. He was succeeded by Denis Ryan and by Richard Cole Brady[106], a confectioner and grocer, who moved from No 11 in 1883. The rateable valuation in 1884 was £20. Richard's wife, Isabella, died on 29th July 1886 aged 65. Her burial took place at St Peter's, Ballymodan.

---

[105] Slater's Directory of 1856
[106] Slaters Directory of 1881. (He was also described as a tea merchant in the will of Robert Baker who died in 1888)

Richard Cole Brady remained at the property until his death on 14th May 1895 aged 58. His burial also took place at St Peters, Ballymodan. Laurence Johnson became the next occupier in 1895. According to the valuation record, he pulled down the rear of the premises.

In the 1901 census, Lawrence Johnson, Church of Ireland, aged 62 and a shop keeper and widower was living in the house with his sister Mary aged 54, daughter Eliza aged 20, daughter Sarah aged 15, daughter Gertrude aged 12, Thomas Small, a lodger aged 37, an engineer, a lodger William Harding aged 31 in the ordinance survey, Robert Hoxley aged 24, a bank agent.

In 1911 the Johnson family moved out and William Nagle became the occupier.

William Nagle, a Methodist, aged 60, a shop keeper was living with his wife Katie aged 50, son George aged 15, Annie D Somervill a boarder and dressmaker aged 26, William Thomas Brookes a boarder and iron monger aged 24, Benjamin Northridge a boarder and apprentice apothecary aged 18.

William and family moved out in 1922 and the property was vacant for a while. In 1923 Samuel Northridge took up residence.

In 1931 David Gallagher became the occupier and remained at the property until 1953. The property was still listed as a shop. Eugene Duggan became the lease holder in 1938. He was succeeded for a time by Nora Reale (nee Gallagher). She kept lodgers.

No 14 The address was also referred to as Church Place.
1837 Number 13 – Valuation £16
1849 Number 18
1851 Number 14 – Valuation £12 15s
1901 Census Number 11 – Singer Sewing Machine
1911 Census Number 90 - Shop

Immediate Lessors

1775 Stephen Winthrop (He held all the sites up to the front of Christ Church)
1817 William Sloane – The lease expired in 1851
1851 The Duke of Devonshire
1897 Sir John Arnott

Occupiers

William Sloane, a cordwainer, was both the immediate lessor and occupier of the property from 1817 until his death. He entered into the lease on 1st April 1817 for the lives of George and Thomas Sloane, sons of William and 41 years concurrently. William Sloane was contracted to spend £50 on repairs within the first year of the lease. The rent was £5 5. The property was described as being 23' in breadth with a depth of 101'. It was bounded on the south by North Main Street, on the north by the churchyard and on the east by the holdings of Ellis and on the west by the holdings of William Hunter and Benjamin Forde.

William Sloane died whilst living on North Main Street on 28th March, 1851 aged 92[107] He was buried in the family grave at Christ Church, Kilbrogan. His wife Ann died on 19th July, 1836, aged 69 and is buried in the same plot.

---

[107] Cork Examiner. 9th April, 1851

Robert Baker[108] was the occupier from at least 1849 until he died on 25th December 1888. He was a dyer and wool comber. In 1849 his rent was £8. Robert was recorded in the register of vestrymen at Christ Church, Kilbrogan in 1870. The rateable valuation in 1884 was £12 15s and Robert was recorded as the tenant.[109]

There were a number of occupants in very short succession following Robert Baker. Richard Cole Brady, a tea merchant, was in the property in 1892. He was the sole executor of the will of Robert Baker which was proved at Cork on 29th April 1889. (See also No 13). Robert Baker died on 25th December 1888. He left effects under £35.

He was succeeded by Julia Halloran and James Turpin. The Singer Sewing Machine Co occupied the premises from 1900 until 1905 when Maria West became resident.

In the census of 1911 Maria West aged 43, a widow, was living with her mother Johanna Marshall aged 70, niece Eva May McMorrough aged 22, a single teacher, niece Lucy McMorrough aged 20, single, in the hosiery business, Francis McMorrough, a nephew aged 17, Bertie McMorrough, a nephew aged 15, Dora West, a step daughter aged 29 and Thomas Kelleher, a lodger aged 26 and a chauffeur.

In 1915 Mrs West was recorded in the Cork and Munster Trade Directory as having apartments as a business.

Maria West continued to live at the premises until she was succeeded by John Marshall in 1949. William McCarthy was the occupier in 1953 and John Skinner became the tenant in 1957. He was succeeded by Cornelius Bolster in 1983.

---

[108] Slaters Directory of 1856
[109] Electoral Register of 1884.

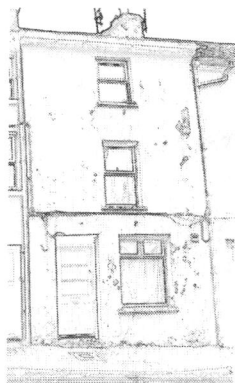

No 15 – Formerly a Public House
1837 Number 14 – Valuation £14
1849 Number 19
1851 Number 15 – Valuation £7
1901 Census Number 12 – Public House
1911 Census Number 89.1 – Public House

Immediate Lessors
1775 Stephen Winthrop (He held all the sites up to the front of Christ Church)
1817 William Hunter (from Duke of Devonshire) – 41 years
1851 William Hunter
1856 The Duke of Devonshire
1858 Edward Preston
1879 Joseph Calnan
1886 James Clugston Allman
1917 Beamish and Crawford
1932 Sir John Arnott

William Hunter took on the lease from the Duke of Devonshire on 1st April 1817. The lease was for the lives of William Hunter and Thomas Hunter, sons of the lessee and 41 years to run concurrently. £70 was to be expended on repairs to the property within one year of the lease. The annual rental was £4 15s. The site was described as being 12'5" in breadth with a depth of 43'. It was bounded on the south by the main street, on the north and west by the holdings of Benjamin Forde and on the east by William Sloane.[110]

He retained it for his tenure until he surrendered it some time prior to Edward Preston acquiring a new lease.[111] The note in the Lismore papers states that the property was let to Edward Preston along with the adjoining premises.

---

[110] MS 6189. Lismore Papers
[111] Lismore Papers

On 29th September 1858 Edward Preston of Bandon, Builder, entered into a lease with the Duke of Devonshire for No 15 and No 16 (referred to as two messuages) for 39 years. By a lease dated 8th December 1862, Edward Preston assigned the two premises to George French for the remainder of the term.[112]

In 1886 Joseph Calnan assigned the lease to James Clugston Allman of Watergate Brewery for 40 years at an annual rent of £40 to run from 29th September.[113] The property was recorded in the lease as being bounded on the east by Robert Baker and on the west by the Church.

Occupiers
In 1837 the occupier was James Craig.

William Hunter was the occupier in 1849 at a rent of £3 per annum.

At the time of the Griffiths Valuation in 1851, Timothy Desmond was resident in the property.

By the time of the first valuation record in 1856 William Peyton[114] was the occupier but he moved to No 65 shortly afterwards.

The house was vacant until 1858 when John Daly, a spirit dealer, took up residence. He remained at the premises until 1879 when Mrs Crowley[115], a publican, became the occupier.

In 1888 Patrick Desmond[116], a vintner, became the occupier and by 1890 the tenant was listed as Ellen Desmond.

The 1901 census recorded Ellen Desmond, aged 42, a widow and publican, who was living with her brother Patrick Desmond, aged 38, a cattle dealer, a boarder Benjamin Shorten aged 19 and a drapers assistant, a boarder Jeremiah Crowley aged 19 and a harness maker, a boarder John Collins aged 16 and also a harness maker, a boarder James Cotter aged 23 and a coach man, a

---

[112] Registry of Deeds. 1862 40 19
[113] Registry of Deeds. 1886 24 63
[114] See No 65 for biographical details
[115] Slaters Directory of 1881
[116] Guys Directory of 1893

boarder David Ahern aged 26 and a coach man and a boarder Mary Aherne aged 25.

The 1911 census recorded Ellen Desmond aged 60, a widow and vintner who was living with a relative Patrick Desmond aged 45, a cattle dealer, Michael O'Neill, a lodger, aged 50, Bat Donovan, a lodger and widower aged 50 and Katie Manning a relative aged 25 and single.

Patrick became the occupier in the records in 1922. He was succeeded by Miss Kate Manning in 1942. Margaret Sugrue followed her in 1947. Samuel Fitzell became the tenant in 1948, G. McCarthy in 1954 and Frank Lyons in 1958.

The property became vacant in 1960. Timothy Whooley was the next tenant in 1963. There have been several tenants since that period.

No 16
1837 Number 15
1849 Number 20
1851 – Number 16 – Valuation £9 10s
1901 Census Number 13 – Public House
1911 Census Number 88 – A Private Dwelling

Immediate Lessors
1775 Stephen Winthrop (He held all the sites up to the front of Christ Church)
1817 Benjamin Forde – 41 years
1858 Edward Preston, builder
1885 James Clugston Allman
1917 Beamish and Crawford

On 1st April 1817, Benjamin Forde, a builder, entered into a lease for the lives of Hon R.B. Bernard and Hon W.S. Bernard and 41 years running concurrently. He was contracted to spend £100 for repairs within one year by the terms of the lease. The annual rental was £6 6s. The property was described as being bounded on the north by the church yard, on the east partly by William

Hunger's holding and partly by the holding of William Sloane and on the west by the holding of George Harris.[117]

On 24th April, 1858 Benjamin Forde, Architect, of Summer Cove, Kinsale, the son of Benjamin Forde, surrendered the lease. The house had been occupied by his father but was unoccupied in 1858.[118]

On 29th September, 1858 the lease was assigned by the Duke of Devonshire to Edward Preston for 39 years. On 7th July 1860 Edward Preston assigned the remainder of the lease to George French. The lease also involved No 15.

Occupiers
In 1837 the occupier was Anne Forde. She was recorded as living at the property for another 14 years.

Anne Forde of the Old Bake House was the occupier in 1849 at an annual rental of £5.

In 1851 Hannah Duke was recorded as the resident.

By the time of the 1856 valuation Benjamin Forde appeared both as immediate lessor and occupier. For a short while Thomas Bradfield resided at the property. Thomas Bradfield married Mary Herrick in Templemartin on 16th October 1850. Thomas was born in 1821 and was the son of James Bradfield and Edith Shorten. They lived at Moneen, Templemartin parish. Thomas and Mary had been living in Castlenalact, Templemartin where they had two children, John, baptised on 17th August, 1851 and Thomas baptised on 10th December, 1854. They had a son, Edward baptised on 22nd July 1863.

According to the valuation records of this period, the property was in a dilapidated state, almost in ruins.

In 1858 James Ryan, a flour dealer, became the occupier. He continued to occupy the property until 1881 when Jeremiah

---

[117] MS 6189. Lismore Papers
[118] MS 43 215/5. Lismore Papers

Donovan took up residence. The property became vacant in 1884 and in 1885 James F. O'Regan moved into the premises.

In 1890 Mary Desmond took up residence. In the 1901 census Mary Desmond aged 72 was living with her husband Patrick aged 85, a retired farmer, with their daughter May aged 45, a vintner, a son Michael aged 30, a clerk, a boarder Cornelius Crowley aged 21, a singer sewing machine agent and a servant Margaret Canniffe aged 16.

Mary Murphy became the next occupier in 1909.

The 1911 census recorded William Murphy, a cattle dealer, aged 50 living with Mary B. Murphy aged 38, a sister and dress maker.

Mary Murphy continued to live in the premises until 1935 When William Murphy was recorded as the tenant. In 1938 Timothy Coleman became the tenant. He ceased to be the occupier in the 1960s.

No 17 – now a grave yard
1837 Number 17
1849 Number 24

The original lease was dated 1st April, 1817 and was between the Duke of Devonshire and George Harris senior for the lives of his sons William and Henry or 41 years. On 12th August 1858 George Harris transferred the lease to Rev Charles Brodrick Bernard, rector and church wardens John Keys and Stewart Tresilian, both of North Main Street.

Occupiers
In 1837 the occupier was John Desmond, a baker and publican.

In 1849 Robert Creech occupied a house on the site at an annual rent of £2.

The Griffiths Valuation of 1851 recorded the immediate lessor as John Harris and the occupier as Robert Creech who was a worsted manufacturer and wool comber in South Main Street. By 1856 the occupier had become John Crowley. Following the transfer of the lease from George Harris to the church, the property together with the two neighbouring properties, 18 and 19, had become church property with no tenants. These properties were taken down and the land became part of the grave yard of Christ Church.

No 18 - now a graveyard
1775 Number 12
1837 Number 18
1849 Number 22

Stephen Winthrop was the immediate lessor of the house on this site in 1775 and William Lisson was the occupier.

In 1837 the occupier was Benjamin Forde

George Harris was the resident in 1849.

The Griffiths Valuation recorded John Harris as the immediate lessor and the occupiers were 'lodgers'. By the time of the first valuation record in 1856 the occupier was Charles McCarthy and shortly afterwards James O'Leary took over as a tenant. The lease was transferred by George Harris to the Church in 1858.

CHRIST CHURCH, KILBROGAN
Now the West Cork Heritage Centre

The first vicar of the parish of Kilbrogan was recorded in 1481. Christ Church was built in 1610 and a stone which was inscribed 'Momento Mori' was placed over the original entrance. One of the first rectors in the new building was Robert Sutton who became the incumbent in 1615 in addition to acting as vicar of both Desertserges and Ballinadee. In 1625 additions were made near the entrance on the northern side and the church was considerably enlarged. The entrance was moved to the southern side shortly afterwards.

On 11th May, 1635 Rev John Snary who had been admitted as prebendary and vicar received a patent uniting the rectory of Kilbrogan to the prebendary and vicar of Kilbrogan and Desertserges, posts which he already held. The association with Desertserges appears to have continued throughout the 1600s.

Most of the settlers in the early 1600s were Puritans, a group founded shortly after Elizabeth 1 became Queen of England. Their wish was to purify the Church of England of what they considered to be Roman Catholic practices. Many Puritans emigrated to Ireland, the Netherlands and Wales in the late 1500s and early 1600s as they were prevented from making changes to the established Church of England. The Puritans in Bandon worshipped in Christ Church until the Act of Uniformity was passed in 1662. The act prescribed the Book of Common Prayer to be followed in all rites in the Church and Episcopal ordination of ministers was explicit. Many of the Puritans left. Some became Presbyterians. The name of the first Presbyterian minister in Bandon dates from about this time.

Family members of some of the clergy married into local families throughout the generations and many of their extended families lived on North Main Street. A few of the clergy requested in their wills to be buried in the chancel.

From 1692 until 1796 the parish of Murragh was held with Kilbrogan. It was located within a quarter of a mile of Desertserges. The rectory of Murragh which adjoined the church yard incorporated 60 acres upon which rectorial tithes were levied. The parish stretched as far as Bandon. In 1700 there were more Protestants in the parish of Murragh than Roman Catholics. Of the hundred protestant families at that time, twenty were dissenters who worshipped in Bandon. Arthur Bernard and Major Herbert Love held significant leases on North Main Street in the 1700s but resided in Murragh.

In 1796 Ambrose Hickey became the new rector of Murragh at which time it ceased to be connected with Kilbrogan. A new church was built in 1811 on the lands of Farranthomas which were granted by Thomas Ware of Woodfort.

Rev Richard Synge who became predendary of Christ Church in 1669 and Archdeacon of Cork in 1674 was also recorded as vicar of Aglish in 1674 when Rev George Synge succeeded him at Christ Church. The parish of Aglish then became connected to Kilbrogan and from that time on, except for a period from 1739 until 1746, the prebendary at Christ Church had possession of the Aglish rectory and received part of the rectorial tithes which amounted to £39 in 1700. That union appears to have continued into the early 1800s. Aglish church was situated just three miles from Moviddy Church. It was no longer standing in 1833 and by 1837 no curate was employed. Services were held in a house licensed by the dioceses for that purpose for some time.

The first rector of Christ Church whose descendants were known to have lived in the town was Rev Solomon Foley who took up his post in 1704 following the death of Rev Daniel Lord[119]. As well as acting as the prebendary, rector and vicar of Kilbrogan, he was also rector and vicar of Murragh. He was resident on North Street as it was then called and his house was described as a large two storey property with a small front yard, offices and a fine garden with several good outhouses. A marriage settlement deed of 1736 recorded that he had a house on lease from William Lapp deceased. William's son, John, inherited his father's estate and was recorded in 1775 as holding numerous leases on the street.

Rev Solomon Foley directed in his will of 1738 that he should be buried near his deceased wife Margaret in the chancel of the church. The burial took place on 26th February, 1738. His daughter, Susannah, married his curate, Rev Robert McClellan in 1736.[120]

Rev William Jackson succeeded Rev Foley as prebendary, rector and vicar. He was also rector of Aghlish near Crookstown and rector and vicar of Murragh like his predecessor. He was priested in Cork in 1737 and served in Brinny before moving to Bandon. He married Mary Nash of Brinny. He died on 1767 and bequeathed his property to his wife. His son James Jackson was provost of Bandon in 1716. James married a daughter of Rev Solomon Foley.

William Jackson resigned as rector of the parish in 1736 and was succeeded by Rev William Robinson[121]. The Robinsons were some of the earliest settlers in Bandon and their descendants lived in the town for generations. They inter-married with families such as the Clears, Lovells and Hunters and therefore had extensive connections to properties on North Main Street, eg No 5 – Robinsons Wine and Spirit Merchants. Many of the family were buried in the cemetery at Christ Church. Rev William was born in 1679 in St Michael's, Kirkham, Lancashire and was the son of Rev Thomas Robinson. Rev William had at least one brother, Ralph, who lived at Thornton Hall in the parish of Poulton, Lancashire. Ralph left his house in Lancashire to Rev William. A church bell

---

[119] See Appendix. Short Biographies
[120] Registry of Deeds. 86 170 59831 1736. Marriage settlement.
[121] See Appendix. Short Biographies

still hangs in St John's Church, Poulton le Fylde, Lancashire with the inscription 'Ralph Robinson 1741.' Rev William died in 1746.

Following Rev William's death, Rev St John Browne[122] became the prebendary, rector and vicar and he was also the rector and vicar of Murragh, the rector of Killowen, chancellor of Ross and the rector of Innishannon and Leighmoney. He lived at Kilbrogan House (No 57).

On 18th June 1790 a vestry meeting was held to discuss a large sum bequested by William Connor of Mishells and dated July 1761.

Walter Travers bequeathed a legacy of £200 to the incumbent and church wardens with a direction that they distribute the interest to ten old poor protestant inhabitants of the parish who were to be chosen by them. The executors of his will were Miss Mary Travers, Robert Travers and John Campbell Esq and the first vestry meeting to discuss the bequest took place on 24th February 1795.

The following poor of the parish were chosen to receive the payment:- Katherine Holland, widow, Jane Bond, widow, Parnel, wife of Philip Clerk, a black smith, James Webb, a shoe maker, Robert Wanderton, a linen weaver, William Lego, a camblet weaver, Robert Lisson, a camblet weaver, Thomas Landon, a camblet weaver, Susanna Belcher, widow, a hay maker.

The vestry agreed at that meeting to put twenty more names on the poor list of the parish as follows:- Francis Shine,, Tim Regane, Mary Skuse, widow, Widow Lewis, Widow Dawson, Widow Hosford, Widow Dudley, Widow Allice Wright, Widow Hornibrook, Widow Blair, Widow Bennett, Widow Shorten, Widow Northridge, Widow Garrett, Widow Bevil, Widow Richardson, Widow Lindsay, Widow Haines, Thomas Moxly, Jane Bond.

It was further agreed that the list would not exceed twenty and that William Cambridge would be the next person to fill a vacancy on the list.

---

[122] See Appendix. Short Biographies

Rev Dr St John Browne died in 1796 and was succeeded by Rev John Kenny who acted as prebendary, rector and vicar of Kilbrogan, vicar of Kinneigh and rector of Dunderrow.

On 31st July 1799 a vestry meeting was held for the purpose of imposing a 'due observance' of the Sabbath following the Act of Parliament which regulated the issuance of licenses for the sale of spirituous liquors by retail. The purpose of the meeting was to ensure that:-

a)   No person licensed to retail spirits was to entertain any persons in their houses on Sunday before 4pm nor after an unreasonable hour or in the morning of any day before sunrise. Thirty shillings was the penalty for the first offence, five pounds for the second and for the third offence the licence would be withdrawn

b)   Any magistrate who neglected to carry out the rules would forfeit £50.

A list of parishioners was drawn up to oversee the act and to enforce obedience. The list included the church wardens, Francis Travers and Thomas Cluxton. Also included were Philip Splaine, Robert Travers, Newth Jenkins, Lawrence Hornibrook, Mr Bull, Mr Young, B. Hodges, Richard Donovan, Horatio McCarthy, William Banfield, Thomas Welsh, Richard Williams, William Keyms, William Mellifont, Richard Dudley, William Moxley, Benjamin Hales, Jn Tresilian, Frances Fielding, Robert Ford, Jn Sullivan, Henry Jenkins, Thomas Williams, George Wheeler, George Harris, Jn Wheeler, Jn W. Sullivan, Richard Gash, John Sullivan of the Bridge, Jn Cotter, Paul Loane, Jn Lovell, Samuel Hosford, Joseph Hosford, William Stanley, Ralph Clear, William Banfield, Thomas Gash and Horatio Hosford.

It was further concluded that 200 copies of the notice be printed and that each publican throughout the parish would be supplied with it.

At a vestry meeting which took place on 25th September, 1802, it was agreed that £30 be raised from the inhabitants of the parish to repay the expenses incurred in paving two thousand three hundred yards of the street within the said parish between Watergate and Dr Clerke's house on North Main Street. The following were appointed to 'applot' or apportion the sum to be raised:- George Kingston, George Cornwall, John Wheeler, Philip

Splane, William Moxley, the church warden for that year, George Harris, Frances Fielding, Newth Jenkins, George Wheeler, James Sweeny, John Sullivan and Richard Hammett.

Rev Kenny died in 1814 and Rev Verney Lovett, DD, became the next incumbent until 1818 when he resigned and was followed by Rev Horatio Townsend Newman who remained as rector until 1842. The Board of First Fruits spent £200 on improvements to the church in 1829.

In the early 1800s a dispute arose in relation to a pew No 17 which had been the property of William Moxley[123] who died in March 1822 without issue[124]. He left no freehold property and his widow Jane was his residuary legatee. On 3rd June 1788 the pew had been registered in the name of William Moxley and Jane and Anne Oliffe who were sisters. Jane became the wife of William in 1793.[125] Anne married William Medley.[126] In 1813 and in 1820 the pew was registered in William Moxley's sole name as Anne Medley was not residing in the parish at the time. However, in 1822 when a new numbering system was introduced, only Jane's name appeared as the holder of the pew even though her sister Anne, a widow, had returned to reside in the parish. Jane died in 1823 and bequeathed all her property to her trustee to pay the interest to Anne and following her death to various relatives. A second claimant to the pew was Richard Perrott, a nephew and heir at law who was living in Cork when William Moxley died in 1822. He made over his rights to the pew to his cousin John Lovell who was residing in the parish.

As a result of the confusion, both John Lovell and Anne Medley claimed rights to the pew.

The Hon & Rev Charles Brodrick Bernard the second son of James, the 2nd Earl of Bandon, became the next vicar. During his tenure in 1856 the church was enlarged and was re-opened in March 1857. It was lengthened by twelve feet, re-floored, roofed with dark oak, re-pewed, a new organ was installed and a tower and spire were erected. Some headstones were allegedly used not

---

[123] William Moxley was the son of William.
[124] Christ Church, Kilbrogan Vestry Minutes.
[125] William Moxley and Jane Oliffe were married in Ballymodan in 1793.
[126] The Medleys were buried in Ballymodan.

only as foundations but also in the construction of the tower. The improvements cost £3030 and the work was carried out by a Mr Parrott. The rector of Ballymodan, Rev Henry McClintock[127] was the preacher at the service at the time of the re-opening. He commented in his address that the church had been founded by the Great Earl of Cork and was restored by the 'piety and zeal' of Rev Hon Charles Brodrick Bernard.

Rev Richard Hussey Loane[128] was curate in 1860 along with Rev James O'Sullivan. There were 1038 in the parish at the time and at Christmas there were about 200 communicants.

In 1866 Rev Hon Charles Bernard was appointed Bishop of Tuam and was succeeded at Christ Church by Rev Robert Eccles.

Rev Eccles was rector at the time of the disestablisment of the church in 1869. Up to that time, the established church had been supported by a tithe paid by the entire community. William Gladstone, the leader of the Liberal Party, believed it to be a particularly unfair arrangement given that out of a population of over 5,700,000 in the country only 690,000 belonged to the established church. He was instrumental in bringing about the reforms.

To partly compensate for the loss of income from the tithes, in 1871 the Duke of Devonshire gave an endowment to the parish of £2000 for the benefit of both Kilbrogan and Killowen. He also gave £500 to Murragh, £500 to Templemartin and £500 to Ballymodan. A long dispute evolved as to how the £2000 should be allocated between Kilbrogan and Killowen.

Rev Eccles died in 1880 and was succeeded by Rev Benjamin Christmas Fawcett[129]. In 1888 Killowen was joined with Christ Church following the death of the rector, Rev John Ashe. At that time there were 430 in the union of Kilbrogan and Killowen. The curate resided in the glebe at Killowen. In 1902 the curate was Rev E.A. Golding who married Eveline, a daughter of Rev Benjamin.

---

[127] Rev Henry was made a freeman of the Corporation of Bandon Bridge in 1831
[128] See also House No 67 and No 80
[129] See Appendix. Short Biographies.

During Rev Benjamin Fawcett's time as rector, white marble steps were built at the approach to the chancel and at the Communion rails. A red marble base and steps were added next to the lectern. The gifts were memorials from George Appelbe (See No 7). He had played a prominent part in the interest of the parish acting as church warden, parochial nominator and synods man.

The Inside of Christ Church. Lawrence Collection
with permission of the National Library of Ireland

The brass eagle in the church was presented by Mrs Milnes Gaskell of the Baldwin family of Brookfield.

In 1917 an approach was made by Rev Popham of Ballymodan requesting a conference to discuss the idea of merging the parishes of Kilbrogan and Ballymodan. A meeting took place but the parishioners of Kilbrogan voted to remain independent.

The Kilbrogan Glebe was built in 1813 at a cost of £2861 (the previous glebe had been on the site of Kilbrogan House). It had 32 acres of land attached to it.

One of the oldest memorials in the church is a brass tablet erected in memory of Richard Croft who was one of the original twelve burgesses of the Bandon Corporation and was provost in 1617 and captain of the town militia.

A flat stone recording the burial place of the well known 'Shane Dearg' also survives. The original inscription read: "Here lies the body of Captain John Nash, who departed this life 18th of February, in the 75th year of his age, and in the year of Our Lord 1725."

For many years Christ Church Kilbrogan parish had a school known as Kilbrogan School which was located on Kilbrogan Street. In 1906 following the resignation of the teacher, Miss Syms, the rector advised the vestry that the population of the protestant community in the parish had significantly decreased. He recommended that the school be closed so that it would strengthen the other protestant schools.

The parish eventually merged with St Peter's Ballymodan and was deconsecrated in 1973 after a period of 363 years. The West Cork Heritage Centre is now located in the building.

No 19. – The Sexton's House – No longer standing
1837 Number 19.
1849 Number 23 Kilbrogan Church

Immediate lessors
1851 The Hon and Rev Charles Brodrick Bernard
1860 Rev Eccles
1880 Rev Benjamin Christmas Fawcett
1938 The Church of Ireland

Occupiers
In 1837 William Turpin was resident in a house on this site.

Emily Lisson, aged 71, died at the sexton's house on 16th May 1854. The house was situated at the back entrance of the church yard. In 1861 the occupier of the house was recorded in the valuation records as William Lisson.

The Christ Church vestry minutes of 6th June 1898 recorded that the attendees resolved that Thomas Turpin, the sexton, give up his house and garden in his occupation and resign his position as sexton on 9ᵗʰ July 1898. Mr William Whelan was appointed as the new sexton on 29ᵗʰ August 1898 at a salary of £ 1.13.4 per calendar month. The treasurer at the meeting was authorized to pay Mr Sullivan for the costs of evicting Thomas Turpin.

William Whelan continued in occupation until shortly after 1932 when he was succeeded by Joseph Macklin.

According to the valuation record of 1959 the building was almost a total ruin.

George Bennett recorded that a portion of the space occupied by the main entrance to Christ Church was the site of an old two storied house, whose big bay windows, high pointed gables and conical roof, formed and appropriate residence for its well known inhabitant.[130] According to Bennett, the tenant's name was Katty Holt. She was described as a thin, skinny, wicked old woman who never stopped talking until she was asleep. She used to allow her neighbours to pass through her house to access the church and in time, the passage became a regular thoroughfare on Sundays as it saved them from having to go via North Church Lane.

---

[130] The History of Bandon. George Bennett

No 20 – Built by Benjamin Forde[131]
1849 Number 24
1901 Census Number 15.2 and 15.3 - Shop
1911 Census Number 86 – A Shoe Maker's Shop
2015 Number 12 North Main Street

Immediate Lessors
1817 George Giles from Duke of Devonshire
1824 Benjamin Forde (from Duke of Devonshire)
1836 Richard Williams, Pawn broker
1860 Richard Wheeler Doherty

George Giles entered into a lease on 1st April 1817 for the lives of George and William Giles, sons of the lessee at £12 12. The plot was described as being ground on which two old houses stood which were bounded on the north by the church yard, on the south by the Main Street and on the east by the gateway and entrance to the church yard and on the west by the holding of John Gosnell. The lease stipulated that £300 be spent on building a good substantial house within one year from the date of the lease. [132] This lease must have been surrendered.

The Duke of Devonshire demised the plot of land to Benjamin Forde in 1824 along with the land on which No 21 was built. In 1836 he assigned the lease to Richard Williams for £150. The house was in the possession of Benjamin Forde and was the eastern one of the two dwellings which he built bounded on the

---

[131] Registry of Deeds. 1836 16 109
[132] MS 1689. Lismore Papers

east and north by the church yard and on the west by other houses in possession of Thomas Bennett and his under tenants and on the south by North Main Street.

In 1860 he assigned the lease of No 20 to Richard Wheeler Doherty.[133] He had sold the lease of No 21 to Thomas Bennett shortly after he had built the two houses.

Occupiers
Richard Joyce was the occupier in 1849 at a rent of £6. He was a boot and shoe maker.[134]

By the time of the Griffiths Valuation in 1851 the property was unoccupied.

Shortly before 1861 Daniel Leary became the occupier and he remained in the house until 1886 when he was succeeded by Mary Riely. Daniel's name appeared on the electoral register of 1884. The property was described as a house and office with a rateable valuation of £9. A work shop, offices and the use of the yard were recorded separately with a valuation of £7.

James Donohue became the occupier in 1900 and by 1901 James Lordan had taken up residence.

The 1901 census recorded Mary Lordan as the occupier, aged 39, a house keeper, living with a daughter Elizabeth aged 7, a daughter Mary aged 5 and a daughter Eva Ellen aged 3. The census was split into 15.2 as above and 15.3 which had as occupier, Mary Ann Hughes aged 61, living on own means.

In 1910 Frank Dowling, a shoe maker, who was born in Co Cork, ran his business from the property. He was recorded in the 1911 census as Frank Charles Dowling aged 48, married for 30 years. He and his wife Anne, also born in Co Cork, aged 45 had had seven children, 6 still living at the time. A daughter Susan Jane aged 15, born Woolwich, England and a daughter Anne aged 13 born in Aldershot, England and a son aged 12 also born in Aldershot were

---

[133] Registry of Deeds. 1860 19 52
[134] Slater's Directory of 1846

98

also living at the property. Frank was recorded at the premises in 1915.[135]

In 1916 Frederick Dowling was succeeded by Daniel Regan and by a Mr Crowley in 1919. In 1922 the occupier was recorded as Catherine Crowley. Michael Crowley took over in 1932 and the property at that stage was listed as a shop. He remained in residence until 1940 when his representatives took over from him. Jessica Heath held the property in 1949; Timothy Coughlan held it in 1950. It became vacant in 1951 and by 1959 it was almost a total ruin. The next tenant took up occupancy in 1963.

No 21 – Built by Benjamin Forde[136]
1849 Number 25
1901 Census Number 16 - A Bakery
1911 Census Number 85 – A Bakery
2015 Number 13 North Main Street

Immediate Lessors
1817 George Giles from Duke of Devonshire (See entry for No 20)
1824 Benjamin Forde (from Duke of Devonshire)
Before 1836 Thomas Bennett

In 1824 the Duke of Devonshire conveyed the interest in the site for this house along with the site for No 21 to Benjamin Forde for the lives of the lessee, Henry Belcher and John Belcher and for the life of the longest liver from 1824 or 99 years at an annual rent of £4 7s.[137]

---

[135] Cork and Munster Trade Directory 1915.
[136] Registry of Deeds. 1836 16 109
[137] Registry of Deeds. 1856 1 296

No 21 and No 20 were erected by Benjamin Forde. He assigned this property to Thomas Bennett[138] some time before 1836.

1851 Rev Thomas Glasson Bennett

Occupiers
In 1849 William Baldwin was recorded as the occupier at an annual rent of £5. He was a shop keeper and dealer in sundries. By 1856 Elizabeth Keleher[139], a publican, had taken up residence.

Elizabeth Keleher was succeeded by James Mahony, a spirit dealer, in 1858. He remained at the property for 14 years until 1872. In 1870 Timothy O'Keeffe succeeded Patrick and by 1882 the occupier was Thomas McCarthy who was a baker[140]. His name appeared on the electoral register of 1884. The property was described as a house with offices and a yard. It had a rateable valuation of £8.

Thomas McCarthy aged 68 was recorded in the 1901 census as a baker and widower who was living with his daughter Hannah McCarthy aged 24, a house keeper, three sons John aged 32, a business man, James aged 30, a baker and Thomas, aged 26, a baker.

Thomas McCarthy had died by the time of the 1911 census and the representatives of Thomas McCarthy appeared as the occupiers in the valuation papers. The 1911 census records James McCarthy aged 44, a baker and Thomas McCarthy, his brother, aged 36 and also a baker.

Thomas McCarthy was recorded as a baker in 1915.[141] He died sometime between 1915 and 1919 as the tenant was recorded as the Representatives of Thomas McCarthy. In 1921 James McCarthy was listed as the occupier.

In 1934 the McCarthys were succeeded by John O'Neill. Ellen followed him and Julia became the tenant in 1950.

---

[138] Registry of Deeds. 1860 19 52
[139] Slater's Directory of Bandon, 1856
[140] Guys Directory of 1893
[141] Cork & Munster Trade Directory 1915

No 22 – Former Public House
1837 Number 20 – Valuation £14
1849 Number 26
1851 Number 22 – Valuation £11 5s
1901 Census Number 17 – Public House
1911 Census Number 84 – Public House
2015 Number 14 North Main Street

Immediate Lessors
1817 John Gosnell
1851 Henry Cornwall
1858 Duke of Devonshire on expiry of lease
1863 Timothy Taylor
1897 Sir John Arnott

John Gosnell entered into a lease with the Duke of Devonshire on 1st April 1817 for the lives of the lessee and of Hon William S. Bernard and 41 years to run concurrently at a rent of £9 11s. The house was described as being 29' in breadth at the front and being bounded on the north by the church yard and on the south by the Main Street, on the east by the holdings of George Giles and on the west by William Shine's holding. He was contracted by the terms of the lease to spend £200 on repairs to the property within one year of the commencement of the lease.[142]

The lease passed to Henry Cornwall and expired on 25th March 1858. Timothy Taylor took on a lease on 25th March, 1863.

Occupiers
The occupier was James Hurley in 1837.

---

[142] MS 6189. Lismore Papers

John Desmond was the tenant in 1849. He paid an annual rent of £7.

Jeremiah Donovan was the occupier in 1851. By 1856 Timothy Taylor[143], a publican and baker, had succeeded Jeremiah.

Timothy Taylor died on 25th September 1877. Probate was granted at Cork to his daughter, Annie Taylor who was living with him. He left effects under £100.

In 1878 Anne Taylor succeeded Timothy Taylor and by 1879 Matthew Taylor had succeeded Anne. Matthew's name appeared in the electoral register of 1884. The property was described as a house with offices and yard at a rateable valuation of £11 5s. He was succeeded by Margaret Taylor in 1887.

At the time of the 1901 census Margaret Taylor, aged 46, a widow as well as a publican and farmer, was living with her daughter Mary Taylor aged 17 and sister, Mary Connor aged 36. The property was recorded as a public house with seven windows at the front. Seven rooms were being occupied by the family

Margaret Taylor was succeeded by Anne Lynch in 1905. In the 1911 census Mary Lynch, a widow aged 68 was living with Anne Lynch, a daughter aged 27, a vintner, John Lynch, a son aged 26 and a carpenter, Julia Lynch, a daughter aged 23 and a national school teacher and Annie McCarthy, a visitor aged 23 and also a national school teacher.

In 1922 Anne Lynch was succeeded by Anne Gawles. Ann Lawless took over in 1929. She died on 22nd October, 1932.

In 1934 Jeremiah Lynch was recorded as the occupier. Miss Bridget Lynch succeeded him in 1941. In 1947 Lena Galvin became the occupier. The West Cork Bottling Co became the tenant from 1968 to 1970.

---

[143] Slater's Directory of 1856

No 23
1837 Number 21 – Valuation £16
1849 Number 27
1901 Census Number 18 - Shop
1911 Census Number 83 – Private Dwelling
2015 Number 15 North Main Street

Immediate Lessors
1816 William Shine, boot & shoe maker (from Duke of Devonshire)[144] 41 year lease
1851 The Representatives of William Shine
1856 The Duke of Devonshire
1867 Walter Bullen
1901 Rev Thomas Brown
1902 Sarah MacCarthy

William Shine entered into a lease with the Duke of Devonshire on 1st April 1816 for lives and for 41 years to run concurrently. By the terms of the lease, he was contracted to spend £150 within a year making repairs to the house. The rental was £9.13.10 pa. The property was described as being bounded on the south by North Main Street, on the north by the garden of Mrs Jenkins, on the west by Mrs Jenkins house and on the east by John Gosnell's holding. Following William's death, the house was left to Martha Shine, a daughter. She died in May 1850 and her sister Charlotte went to live in London. She wrote to her brother requesting that they surrender the lease as there were only a few years to run on it, emphasising that they did not own the property.[145]

William Shine was the immediate lessor as well as the tenant. The lease was not recorded as being passed on during its tenure and it expired following his death

---

[144] Lismore Papers
[145] MS 6189. Lismore Papers

Occupiers

William Shine was the occupier in 1837 and was still recorded at the property in the pre-valuation records of 1849. He was a shoe maker.[146]

In 1851 Denis O'Leary was in residence. In 1853 Eliza Johnston[147], gentry, had become the occupier. Eliza was the widow of John Daunt Shorten. (See also No 33 & 34). She took the property on a yearly tenancy.[148]

Eliza Johnston remained until 1864 when she was succeeded by Walter Bullen, a chandler and grocer. The property valuation was £16[149]. On 29th September 1867 Walter Bullen purchased a 41 year lease on the holding from the Duke of Devonshire.[150]

On 24th March 1868 he was paid an allowance by the Duke of Devonshire's Estate of £25 for permanent improvements during the period 1867-68 in addition to the outlay agreed to be made by him in exchange for obtaining his lease.[151] He recorded his address as Church Place, Bandon.[152]

On 23rd November, 1877, he sold, assigned and transferred the lease of the shop, dwelling house, tenement and premises to James Moriarty, a shop keeper, of South Main Street. Walter was recorded in the deed as the auctioneer. The property was described as being bounded on the west by the holdings of Joseph Good (No 24) and on the east by the representatives of Timothy Taylor deceased (No 22).

Sarah McCarthy took up residence in 1879. She was a bookseller, stationer, confectioner, tobacconist, linen and woollen draper.[153] In 1884 Patrick A. McCarthy, a postmaster, was also living at the address. The sitting room for his use was recorded as being at the

[146] Electoral List of 1832
[147] Slater's Directory of 1856
[148] MS 6185. Lismore Papers
[149] See No 86 for Biography of Walter Bullen
[150] Registry of Deeds. 1877 48 204
[151] Lismore Papers. MS 7058
[152] Chirst Church Kilbrogan Vestry Minutes reported in the Skibbereen Eagle of 3rd April 1869
[153] Slater's Directory of 1881

rear of the first floor and he also occupied a bedroom at the front on the second floor.[154]

John Nash, a Wesleyan Minister, was also a tenant at the house in 1884. He had a bedroom at the rear of the first floor and a sitting room at the front on the first floor. The rateable value at the time was £13.

Sarah was described in the 1901 census as aged 57, single, a Methodist and a shop keeper. She was living with Anne Appelbe, aged 26, a shop assistant, Margaret Coffey, a servant aged 19, William Eyre, a boarder aged 36 with a private subscription. They had a total of six windows at the front of the building and eight rooms were being occupied by the family. It was described as a 1st class house.

In 1902 Rebecca Bradfield became the occupier. Rebecca was born on 16th May, 1869. She was the daughter of Thomas Bradfield (1816-1890) and his wife Ann Harrold (1834-1908) who married at Moviddy on 21st February, 1854. Rebecca had a sister, Sarah Bradfield who was baptised on 19th February, 1863 and who married Joseph Nagle in 1889.

By 1910 Mary Murphy had succeeded Rebecca and had also taken over the shop.

The occupiers in the 1911 census were Cornelius Murphy, a labourer, aged 72, married with 12 children, 7 of whom were still living and as living with daughter Nellie Murphy aged 40, daughter Minnie Murphy aged 38, son Michael Murphy aged 36, son Maurice Murphy aged 32 and a barber, daughter Lizzie Murphy aged 26, son Patrick Murphy aged 23 and a postman, boarder John Ahern aged 18 and a post office clerk, boarder William Fitzgibbon aged 40 and a baker, boarder Daniel Crowley aged 65 a widower and farmer and boarder Norah Crowley aged 40 and married.

Mary Murphy continued to occupy the premises until 1940 when the property became vacant. In 1948 Fitzgibbon and Galvin

---

[154] Electoral Register of 1884. Borough of Bandon Bridge

became tenants and in 1954 Charles O'Brien succeeded them. John F.M. Carruthers was the next occupier in 1956.

No 24 - Present Day Concept Design
1837 Number 22 – Valuation £16
1851 Number 24 – Valuation £10
1901 Census Number 19 – lodging house
1911 Census Number 82 – Private Dwelling
2015 Number 16 North Main Street

Immediate Lessors
1816 Eliza and Martha Jenkins (from the Duke of Devonshire) – 41 yrs
1851 The Duke of Devonshire
1866 Eliza Johnson
1870 Mary Jane Hart
1900 Rev Thomas Brown

On 1st April, 1816 Eliza, Ann Jenkins and Martha Jenkins entered into a lease for lives with 41 years to run concurrently. The site was 22' in breadth and 75' in depth. It was described as being bounded on the south by North Main Street, on the north by the church yard, on the east by William Shine's holding and on the west by the holding of Samuel Sullivan.

Occupiers
The Misses Jenkins took up residency in this property in 1816 and they resided at the property for 36 years. They were the original lease holders as well as the tenants. Devonshire Estate papers record that the property was bounded by the Kilbrogan church yard wall and on the east by William Shine.

Miss Elizabeth and Martha Jenkins surrendered their lease of the house on 19th April, 1852. An entry in Swanstons's diary referred to a doorway leading from the garden of the house to the Kilbrogan church yard. The sexton had put a padlock on the gate when Elizabeth and Martha left. Once the padlock was removed, the Duke's Agent, Swanston, put a new lock on the gate from the inside.

Sometime between 1856 and 1861 Daniel Corcoran became the occupier. He was succeeded shortly afterwards by Eliza Johnson. In 1864 a section of the property was occupied by Mary Jane Hart, a grocer.

In 1866 Mary Jane Hart was the occupier. In 1868 Joseph Good was listed as an occupier in part of the house with Mary Jane Hart in the shop.

The Duke of Devonshire's Estate contributed £25 towards permanent improvements to the house in addition to the outlay agreed for the lease on 24th March, 1868.[155]

In the early 1870s Joseph Good, an earthenware dealer and grocer, became the tenant. He was recorded in the register of vestrymen at Christ Church, Kilbrogan in 1870. He remained at the property until the 1902 when Rebecca became the occupier. In 1884 the house was described as having offices, a yard and a small garden with a rateable valuation of £13. Rebecca Wilson took over the shop in 1892.

In the early 1900s Michael Desmond became the occupier.

Michael Desmond was recorded in the 1901 census as aged 45, a general labourer, living with his wife Hannah aged 43, a boarder Robert J. Brophy aged 30 and a reporter to the press, a boarder Michael Collins aged 17 and a shop assistant of a grocery. The house had five windows at the front and 7 rooms were occupied by the family.

From 1902 Thomas O'Keeffe became the tenant in the shop and he was succeeded by Maurice Murphy in 1907.

---

[155] Lismore Papers. Cash Book MS 7058

At the time of the 1911 census the house was occupied by Michael Desmond, aged 55 and a general labourer, his wife Hannah aged 66 and a boarder Timothy O'Driscoll, aged 26, a shop man in a drapery and Timothy Murray, a boarder aged 18 and a shop man in a grocery.

Part of the premises was occupied by John Murphy aged 70, a gold miner, born in Cork.

Another part was occupied by Thomas Armstrong aged 57, an RIC pensioner.

Maurice Murphy moved out of part of the house in 1915 and that part became vacant until Richard Collins moved in during 1919.

Richard Collins had assumed occupation of the whole building in 1919 and Mary Fahy did also when she succeeded him in 1920. The description in the valuation records changed from shop to house, office and yard.

Mary Fahy was succeeded by Mary O'Keeffe in 1922 and she held the tenancy for many years.

No 25
1837 Number 23 – Valuation £18. (Split into 25 and 26 by Griffiths Valuation of 1851)
1851 Number 25 – Valuation £8
1901 Census Number 20 – Public House
1911 Census Number 81 – Public House
2015 Number 17 North Main Street

Immediate Lessors
1817 Samuel Sullivan, shop keeper
1832 Richard Cole (from Duke of Devonshire)
1831 Richard Williams
1851 The Representatives of Richard Cole
1856 The Representatives of Richard Williams
1870 Thomas Sherlock
1909 Allman Dowden & Co (formed in 1885 when Dowden & Co was dissolved)
1930 Travers Jeffers

The original lease dated 1st April 1817 was for the two lives of Samuel Sullivan's sons, Samuel and John at a yearly rent of £8 payable half yearly. Samuel Sullivan was ejected for non payment of rent. The terms of the lease required him to spend £150 on repairs

The property was subsequently assigned to Richard Cole who built a new house on the site. On 1st November 1831 Richard Cole, a shop keeper, entered into a mortgage with Richard Williams, a pawn broker, for the sum of £100.[156]

Richard Cole's lease was assigned to him by the Duke of Devonshire on 25th March, 1832 to run for 99 years until 1931 at an annual rental of £7 7 8.[157]

---

[156] Registry of Deeds. 876 581905
[157] Lismore Papers. MS 6185

Occupiers

William House was the occupier in 1837 before the property was split into two.

Edward Grainger was recorded as the tenant in 1849.

By 1856 Jeremiah Hyde[158], a publican was resident in the premises and he remained for eight years until 1864.

In 1864 the new tenant was Margaret Deacy. She stayed for three years. In 1867 John Finnegan[159], a spirit dealer, took up residence.

John Finnegan also spent just three years at the property. The next occupier was John Buckley senior who moved in during 1870. John Buckley senior was succeeded shortly after 1870 by John Buckley junior.

Denis Donovan moved into the premises in 1779 and from that time on until 1884 there was a succession of tenants, namely Michael Desmond in 1779, Jeremiah Sullivan in 1882 followed by Daniel Murray in 1884. His name appeared on the electoral register of the same year. The property was described as a house with offices and yard and a rateable valuation of £9 5s. In 1895 John Howe replaced Daniel Murray as a vintner.

In the 1901 census John Howe was described as a publican, aged 38 who was living with his wife Maria aged 26, daughter Helena aged 8, Hannah Maria aged 6, Rebecca aged 5, son Thomas aged 3 and son Desmond aged 1 and Robert James. Sister in law Bridget Desmond aged 15, brother in law Humphrey Desmond aged 20 and boarder Bartholomew Mahony aged 18, a drapers clerk were also in residence. The house was described as 2nd class with five windows at the front and five rooms occupied by the family.

John Howe's name appeared on the parchment which lists the committee members responsible for erecting the Maid of Erin statue

---

[158] Slater's Directory of 1856
[159] Coghlan's Directory of 1867

In 1903 John Howe was replaced by McCarthy and in 1909 by Hannah Mahony.

In the 1911 census Hannah Mahony, vintner, aged 30 was recorded as living at the premises with her sister Mary Mahony aged 26

Hannah remained as a resident until 1927 when she was replaced by Mary Donovan. There have been a few occupiers since Mary Donovan.

No 26
1837 Number 23 – Valuation £18 (Subsequently divided into two)
1851 Number 26 – Valuation £9
1901 Census Number 21 – Shoe Maker's Shop
1911 Census Number 80 – Shoe Maker's Shop
2015 Number 18 North Main Street

Immediate Lessors
1817 Samuel Sullivan
Before 1831 Richard Cole
1851 The Representatives of Richard Cole
1856 The Representatives of Richard Williams
1870 Thomas Sherlock
1909 The Misses Sherlock

Occupiers
The house was part of No 25 in 1837 and was subsequently divided into two separate properties.

Richard Cole was recorded as the occupier in 1849 at a rent of £5

By 1851 Richard Topham had taken up residence. He was a boot and shoe maker.

Mary Jago became the occupier in 1856. She was followed shortly afterwards by Norman Allshire who in turn was followed by Joseph Allshire, a grocer, who took over before 1861. Joseph was married to Rachel Burchill and they had a son, William Henry who was born on 27th July 1857 and was baptised at Christ Church on 29th July 1857. His occupation was recorded as currier and shop keeper. Their daughter Sarah Jane was baptised on 15th February 1863.

Joseph Allshire remained in the property until 1870. He transferred premises to No 99 North Main Street.

John Buckley senior became the next occupier in 1870. In 1878 James Donohoe[160], a grocer, was recorded in the property. He resided there until 1887. The property was vacant for a year and in 1888 Denis Driscoll took up residence. In 1894 he was succeeded by Cornelius Regan, a shoe maker.

In the 1901 census Cornelius Regan aged 50, a shoe maker, was living at the property with his wife Mary aged 45, daughter Lizzie aged 21, son Jeremiah aged 19 and also a shoe maker and daughter Mary Ellen aged 16. The property was recorded as a second class premises with just three windows at the front and five rooms occupied by the family.

In the 1911 census Cornelius Regan, aged 69, a boot maker and widower was still living at the property with his daughter Elizabeth Regan aged 30, a son Jeremiah Regan aged 28 and also a boot maker and a daughter Mary Regan aged 24.

Cornelius Regan was in the property until 1918[161] when he was succeeded by E. O'Donoghue and by Richard Collins in 1919. William Duggan moved in very shortly after that. He was succeeded by Anne Hurley in 1926 and in 1928 by Mary Harold. Timothy Murphy became the next occupier in 1945, Ellen M. Regan in 1951, Mrs Bridget Hallihan in 1949 and David McNamara in 1963.

---

[160] Slater's Directory of 1881
[161] Cork and Munster Trade Directory. 1915

No 27 – Once a Salt Manufacturer's Premises

1837 Number 24 – Valuation £17
1851 Number 27 – Valuation £13 20s
1901 Census Number 22 – Private Dwelling
1911 Census Number 79 – Private Dwelling
2015 Number 19 North Main Street

Immediate lessors

1816 Richard Gash
1845 Thomas Buckley
1856 The Duke of Devonshire
1897 Sir John Arnott

Thomas Buckley, a merchant of Bandon, entered into a deed with Richard Gashe of Bandon, a shop keeper and Richard Pierce Gash of Co Cork Esq on 4th January 1845.[162] The duration of the lease was for 41 years from 1816. It included this property as well as No 28.

Occupiers

In 1837 the occupier was John Williams, a salt manufacturer.[163] Salt was an essential ingredient for the preservation of hides, fish and other produce. At that time marine salt was made by either using the sun to evaporate the salt from sea water or by boiling the sea water over a furnace until the water evaporated and a crust of salt was left. The Corporation of Saltmakers of Bandonbridge was founded in 1627 but was shortlived. Amongst other issues preventing the success of the salt corporation, the manufacture of salt was heavily dependent on being able to source cheap fuel.[164]

---

[162] Registry of Deeds. 1845 1 118 of 4th January 1845. See also No 28
[163] Slater's Directory of 1846
[164] Bandon Historical Journal. No 10. Salt Politics: The Corporation of Salt Makers of Bandonbridge. Dr Charles G. Ludlow

In 1841 100 tons of rock salt was being manufactured into coarse salt in the town.[165]

In the pre-valuation records of 1849, John B. Williams was still registered as the occupier in a house which contained various salt stores. The valuation was £8.

Elizabeth Williams was recorded as the tenant in 1851. By the time of the first valuation record in 1856, the occupier was Thomas Williams and he was followed very shortly afterwards by Anne Williams. Dennis Lynch[166], a salt dealer, moved in before 1861 and he remained at the premises until 1884 when Ellen Callaghan replaced him. Andrew Healy took up residence during 1885.

It was noted in the valuation records of 1892 that the shop was in poor condition and was to be taken down and rebuilt. The building was vacant for a time before being occupied by John Buckley in 1899.

In the 1901 census John Buckley was recorded as a building contractor, aged 54, who was living with his wife Ellen aged 58, son John aged 26, a mason, son Daniel aged 25, a mason and mother in law Ellen O'Mahony aged 90 and a general servant Lilly Waton aged 40. The property was described as a second class house with five windows at the front and seven rooms occupied by the family.

John Buckley was for a time a member of the Bandon Town Council. He was the father of Sean Buckley and his name appears on the list of the committee who originally erected the Maid of Erin statue.

In the 1911 census John Buckley aged 35, single, a builder was living at the property with Ellen Buckley, a widow aged 71 and Kate McSwiney, a servant aged 22. The property was described as a second class house with four windows at the front and a total of eight rooms occupied by the family.

---

[165] W.A. Spiller. A Short Topographical and Statistical Account of the Bandon Union
[166] Slater's Directory of 1870

John was described as a builder and contractor in 1915.[167]

In 1920 M. Walsh became the new occupier and he remained in the premises for nine years until Mrs Josephine Kerr took up residence in 1929. The property became vacant in 1940 until E. Gumbleton moved in during 1941. Leslie Gumbleton was recorded as the tenant in 1942. The property became vacant again in 1945 and in 1946 Annie Canty took over.

No 28
1837 Number 25 – Valuation £16
1851 Number 28 – Valuation £10 10s
1901 Census Number 23 – Public House
1911 Census Number 78 – Public House

Immediate Lessors
1816 – Richard Gash
1845 Thomas Buckley
1856 Anne Williams
1897 Sir John Arnott

A note in the lease of 1816 from the Duke of Devonshire to David Bush (No 31) stated 'east Joseph Lisson, Richard Gash'

On 4th January 1845 Richard Pierce Gash Esq entered into a deed relating to this property with Thomas Buckley, a merchant of Bandon. The lease may have also included No 26. The measurement was 46' at the front and it was bounded on the north

---

[167] Cork and Munster Trade Directory. 1915

by the church, on the east by holdings of Samuel Sullivan and on the west by a holding of William Lisson. The duration of the lease was for 41 years from 1816. Richard Gashe, a shop keeper, was also named in the deed.[168]

Occupiers
William Barry was the occupier in 1837. He was recorded as a grocer and baker on the electoral register of 1832.

In 1849 Williams was the occupier of the property at an annual rent of £4.

Ralph Fuller, a pawn broker, was the tenant in 1851.

By the time of the first valuation in 1856 the occupier was Cornelius Callaghan, a spirit dealer.[169] In 1866 his rent was increased from £7 10s 0d to £10[170]

The Devonshire Estate carried out repairs to his house in 1868.

Cornelius Callaghan remained in the property until 1877 when Ellen Callaghan took over. It passed from Ellen to John Callaghan in 1885. John B. Callaghan was an accountant. A clerk, William Lynch, was also living at the premises in 1884. The sitting room and bedroom were on the second floor at the front of the building.[171] It became vacant in 1886 with a comment in the valuation record that it was dilapidated. In 1892 it was occupied by Andrew Healy as a licensed premises.[172]

Andrew was resident at the time of the 1901 census. He was recorded as aged 52, a vintner, living with his wife Catherine, daughter Hannah aged 16, son Daniel aged 15, son Cornelius aged 13, son John aged 11, daughter Nellie aged 10 and boarder Patrick Callaghan aged 50, a carpenter. The property was described in the census as first class with six windows at the front and seven rooms occupied by the family.

---

[168] Registry of Deeds. 1845 1 118 of 4th January 1845
[169] Slater's Directory of 1856
[170] Lismore Papers. Cash Book 1867-68 MS 7058
[171] Electoral Register of 1884. Borough of Bandon Bridge
[172] Guys Directory of 1893

By the time of the 1911 census Andrew was aged 63, a vintner, and living with his wife Kate, aged 57, son Cornelius aged 24 and a carpenter, daughter Nellie aged 20, brother in law Patrick Callaghan aged 62, a carpenter, a nephew John Forde aged 11 and a boarder, Timothy Cahill, aged 34 and a creamery manager. The property was described as a first class house with six windows at the front and ten rooms occupied by the family.

Andrew died on 13th February, 1921 and was succeeded by his wife. In 1925 their daughter Nellie Healy's name appeared on the valuation record. She was succeeded by John Healy in 1958.

No 29
1837 Number 26 – Valuation £7
1849 Number 33
1851 Number 29 – Valuation £4 5s
1901 Census Number 24 – Private Dwelling
1911 Census Number 77 – Private Dwelling

Immediate Lessors
In 1816 – Joseph Lisson and Richard Gash
1851 The Duke of Devonshire
1897 Sir John Arnott

Occupiers
William Lisson was resident in 1837 and was still the occupier in 1849. A note in the Lismore Papers regarding David Bush's lease of 1816 (*No 31*) stated 'east by Joseph Lisson and Richard Gash' which suggests that Joseph Lisson may have resided in this property prior to William. Richard Gash was in No 28.

In 1851 the tenant was John Forde. John was listed in the register of vestrymen at Christ Church, Kilbrogan in 1870 and in the electoral register of 1884. The property had a rateable valuation of £7 and was described as a house with offices and a yard.

John Forde remained at the property until 1897 when he was succeeded by Henry Forde.

At the time of the 1901 census Henry Forde aged 48, Church of Ireland, a plasterer, was living at the property with his sister Jane aged 30. The property was described as second class in the census with four windows at the front and four rooms occupied by the family.

In the 1911 census Henry Forde, a builder aged 58, was living with his sister Jane aged 36 both single. The house was described as having four windows at the front and five rooms occupied by the family.

Henry was described in the Cork and Munster Trade Directory of 1915 as a builder and contractor.

Henry was listed as an occupier until 1939 when Jane took over. She remained in the property until 1957 when it became vacant for a time.

No 30 and 31

1837 Number 27 - Valuation not recorded

1851 Number 30 – Valuation £2 10s

1901 Census Number 25 – Private Dwelling

1911 Census Number 76 – Private Dwelling

Immediate Lessors

1816 David Bushe (from Duke of Devonshire) – 41 years
1851 Thomas Bushe. The lease expired on maturity in March 1857
1872 The Duke of Devonshire
1895 Mr Craig
1934 James Melville Craig

David Bushe entered into a lease on 1st April 1816 for lives and for 41 years to run concurrently at a rent of £8 8s. The premises measured 48' in breadth with a depth of 84'. It was described in the lease as being bounded on the west by North Main Street, on the south and east by the holdings of Joseph Lisson and Richard Gash and on the north by the holdings of John Shorten. David Bushe was contracted by the terms of the lease to spend £100 on repairs to the building.

Occupiers

Margaret Giles was the occupier in 1837

John Sheerman was recorded as the tenant in 1849 at an annual rent of £1

In 1851 the occupier was Owen Sullivan.

By the time of the first valuation record in 1856 Mary Lehane had become the resident.

In 1872 Catherine Nagle succeeded Mary Lehane. In 1883 the house became vacant until 1887 when it is occupied by the Representatives of D. Lynch. It became vacant again shortly afterwards.

By 1895 it was recorded along with number 31 with the residents Thomas Bushe and Constable Connell took up residence during 1895.

In the 1901 census Anna Bell O'Connell, born Kilkenny, aged 28, married was recorded as the occupier along with her daughter May aged 11, born Kilkenny, daughter Anna Bell, aged 10, born Limerick, James Frances aged 9, born Kilkenny and Maurice Dan aged 4 and born in Cork. The building was described as having five windows at the front of the house and five rooms occupied by the family. In the valuation record of 1901-1910 the property was listed with Number 31. Constable Connell was replaced by Corporal Hunt in 1908 and by 1910 P Downey was the occupier.

The 1911 census recorded Daniel Downing as a pawn broker's manager, aged 33 living with his wife Mary Jane aged 29 and a daughter Mary Brigid aged 2.

Richard Drew took over as the occupier in 1916 and was succeeded by Margaret in 1928, then by Timothy Donegan in 1930 and then by Frank McMorrogh in 1934.

From the Lawrence Collection
With permission of the National Library of Ireland

No 31

1837 Number 28 – Valuation £6
1851 Number Number 31 - £4
1901 Census Number
1911 Census Number –

Immediate Lessors

1816 David Bushe (from the Duke of Devonshire)
1851 The Duke of Devonshire
1895 Mr Craig

Occupiers

A lease dated 1816 was executed between the Duke of Devonshire and David Bush. The lease was not recorded in the Registry of Deeds as being transferred which suggests that the Bush family remained in the premises until its expiration in 1865.[173]

In 1837 the occupier was David Bushe. The tenancy had passed to Thomas Bushe by 1849 and he was still in residence in 1851. Thomas Bushe was a letter carrier. His daughter Jane was a straw bonnet maker. On 2nd February 1865 he was gored by a bull at Coolfadda and was killed.

The Devonshire lease to the Representatives of David Bush expired on 10th December 1865.

The Duke of Devonshire's Estate contributed £10 5s 1d towards repairs to Thomas Bushe's house and towards Tim Desmond's house on 25th March, 1868.[174]

In 1884 Thomas Bushe was recorded as the occupier of the house, offices and yard rated at £4. He also had another house and yard at Barrett's Hill.

By 1895 the property was grouped together with Number 30.

---

[173] A lease dated 1816 for David Bush is recorded in the Lismore Papers
[174] Lismore papers. MS 7058

No 32
1837 Number 29 – Valuation £6
1851 Number 32 – Valuation £5
1901 Census Number 26 –
Private Dwelling?
1911 Census Number 75 –
Tailor's Shop

Immediate Lessors
1816 David Bushe (from Duke of Devonshire)
1851 Thomas Bushe
1867 The Duke of Devonshire
1895 Mr Craig
1934 Marshall Moore Craig

Occupiers
In 1837 the occupier was Richard Topham and he was still registered at the property in 1849 and in 1851.

Dennis Connor was the occupier at the time of the first valuation in 1856. He remained in the property until 1867.

Timothy Desmond moved into the property during 1867. A notice appeared in the Cork Examiner of 19th October, 1866 as follows: 'Application for a spirit licence from Timothy Desmond of 44 North Main Street, Bandon. Granted at the Bandon Quarter Sessions.' The magistrates on the bench included Colonel Bernard MP and George Beamish Teulon who was living at that time in No 58 and Major Cornwall.

Timothy Desmond paid his rent on a monthly basis.

Johanna Desmond succeeded Timothy in 1876. Shortly afterwards Cornelius Desmond took over. He was recorded as the occupier on the electoral register of 1884. The rateable valuation of the property was £5 and the property was described as a house and offices. During 1884 John O' Callaghan, a tailor, became the occupier.[175] His name appeared in the electoral records of the Borough of Bandon Bridge in 1884. The property was described as a house and office with a rateable valuation of £5.

John O'Callaghan was recorded in the 1901 census as aged 40, a tailor, living with his wife Mary aged 32, son Daniel aged 3 and daughter Margaret aged 1. The house was described as a private dwelling, second class with 3 windows at the front and five rooms occupied

The 1911 census recorded John O'Callaghan aged 50, tailor and clothier with six children, his wife Mary aged 40, son Daniel aged 13 and an apprentice, his daughter Margaret aged 11, son John aged 9, son Humphrey aged 7, daughter Hanora aged 4, and daughter Mary aged 9 months. The house was described as a tailor's shop with 3 windows at the front and 5 rooms occupied by the family.

In 1916 John O'Callaghan was no longer the occupier and the building became vacant for a year. Daniel O'Regan took up occupancy in 1917. He was recorded as a saddler.[176] His representatives were recorded as holding the tenancy in 1948.

---

[175] Guys Directory of 1893
[176] Guy's Directory of 1919

No 33 – A Public House
1837 Number 30 – Valuation £16
1849 Number 37
1851 Number 33 – Valuation £10 10s
1901 Census Number 27 – Public House
1911 Census Number 74 – Public House

Immediate Lessors
1816 John Daunt Shorten from the Duke of Devonshire
1818 Henry Jenkins
1851 Elizabeth Johnston
1870 Frances Charles Hunter
1885 Allman Dowden & Co (formed in 1885 when Dowden & Co was dissolved)
1949 Beamish & Crawford

Eliza Johnston was the widow of John Daunt Shorten, a shop keeper of Bandon and she was the administrator of his will.

By lease dated 1st April 1816, the Duke of Devonshire demised to John Daunt Shorten the land called ' Shorten land'. There was an old house on the site and the holding measured 20' at the front, 33' 6" at the rear and 198' in depth. At the time of the lease, the holding on the north side of the site (No 34) was another property which belonged to John Shorten. The premises on the south (No 32) belonged to David Bushe. The plot was bounded on the east by the church wall.

John Shorten held the lease for the lives of John Shorten, Joseph Stanley and Jane Shorten and for a term of 99 years to run concurrently from 25th March 1816 at a yearly rent of £3 17s 6 ½p which was payable on 25th March and 29th September of each year.

John Shorten built a house on the site and on 1st December 1818 he leased his holding to Henry Jenkins for 56 years. Henry had died with 10 years still left to run on the lease. As a result, in 1864 the lease reverted to Eliza Johnston, as the widow and beneficiary of the estate of her husband. In 1864 she sold the lease to John Hurley Esq for £90. The witnesses to the deed were Thomas Kingston Sullivan, solicitor, Richard Brangan, writing clerk and Samuel Cottrell, law clerk.[177]

Occupiers
According to a deed of 1864, the leaseholder from 1818, Henry Jenkins, lived at the property for some time. He was a coal dealer in South Main Street.

In 1837 the occupier was John Palmer. He is likely to have resided at this address in 1832. He was recorded as a publican of North Main Street on the electoral list of that date.

Frances Palmer was the occupier from at least 1849 until 1856. She was a publican[178].

By 1856 the occupier was James English, a yearly tenant. At that time the garden was in the tenancy of James Elliott also as a yearly tenant.

James English was replaced in 1867 by Samuel Cottrell, a confectioner and spirit dealer.

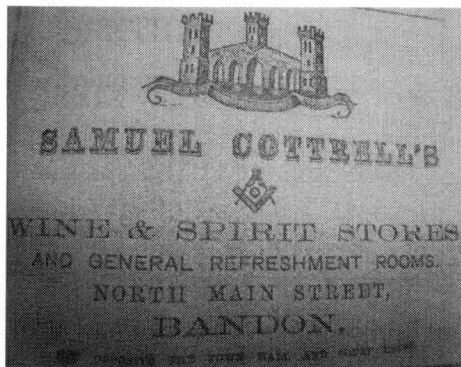

SAMUEL COTTRELL'S
WINE & SPIRIT STORES,
AND GENERAL REFRESHMENT ROOMS.
NORTH MAIN STREET,
BANDON.

---

[177] Registry of Deeds. 1864 39 240
[178] Slater's Directory of Bandon, 1856

In 1870 John Driscoll took over as occupier from Samuel Cottrell. John was recorded on the electoral register of 1884 as the occupier. The property had a rateable valuation of £11 10s. Jeremiah Driscoll succeeded John Driscoll in 1892.

Jeremiah O'Driscoll was recorded in the 1901 census as a vintner, aged 39, living with his wife Kate aged 29, daughter Mary aged 8, daughter Kathleen aged 6, son Dani aged 5 and daughters Nellie aged 4 and Elizabeth. The house was described as first class with six windows at the front and eight rooms occupied by the family.

In 1908 Kate Long moved into the property. She was recorded in the 1911 census as aged 38, single, licensed publican living with her uncle Edward Long, a retired farmer, boarder Cornelius Lynch aged 24, a harness maker, Jeremiah Mullins, a boarder aged 35 and an army canteen superintendent, Julia O'Callaghan a boarder aged 14 a scholar. It was described as a second class house in this census with six windows at the front and five rooms occupied by the family.

In 1931 Anna Hurley became the occupier and by 1937 Hanna Deasy was in residence.

No 34 – Private House – New house built in 1820

1837 Number 31 – Valuation £22
1849 Number 38
1851 Number 34 – Valuation £14
1901 Census Number 28 – Private Dwelling
1911 Census Number 73 – Samuel Johnson

Immediate Lessors

1816 Original lease from Duke of Devonshire for 99 years (see also No 35)
1817 William Kingston to Joseph Hosford of Tullyglass
1820 Benjamin Hosford (only son & heir to Joseph Hosford of Tullyglass) to William Kingston
1851 The Duke of Devonshire
1861 Henry Ormston
1867 The Duke of Devonshire
1868 Eliza Johnston
1872 The Duke of Devonshire
1897 Sir John Arnott

On 7th May 1817 a mortgage was extended by William Kingston, shop keeper (pawn broker), to Joseph Hosford. By 1820 Joseph Hosford of Tullyglass had died intestate and Benjamin of Teadies was the only son and heir. For £300 he made over the plot to William Kingston upon which he built a new house. The plot was 41' in front, bounded on the west by North Main Street, on the east by a lane leading to the church, on the south by John Shortens holding and on the north by the holdings of John Bennett and George Heazle as demised to William Kingston by the Duke of Devonshire for 99 years from 25th March 1816[179]

---

[179] 1820 758 514862

Occupiers

In 1837 the occupier was Mary Applebe

Eliza Johnston was the occupier in 1849 at an annual rent of £8 and was still recorded as the occupier in 1851. Henry Arnold had succeeded her by 1856.

Henry and his wife Sarah had a daughter, Sarah Elizabeth born on 24th January 1859 and baptised at Christ Church on 20th February. His occupation was recorded as Principal of a Training Institution. They also had a daughter Mary Augusta Fanny born on 28th March 1861 and baptised on 24th April.

By 1861 the occupier was James Elliott. He leased the garden of No 33.[180]

James Elliot moved out in 1866 and was replaced in 1868 by Rev James O'Keeffe. In 1870 George Gabriel became the occupier and in 1878 Arthur Thomas Greaves took up residence. Samuel Johnston moved in during 1884. His name appeared on the electoral register of that year. The property was described as a house with offices, a yard and a small garden at a rateable valuation of £15.

On 31st July, 1888 Samuel and his wife had a daughter at the house.[181] He was recorded in the register of vestrymen at Christ Church, Kilbrogan in 1870.

Samuel Johnston was an assistant to the land agent and in conjunction with David Craig and Daniel Crowley of the Shambles, he was responsible for collection the rents for Sir John Arnott's Estate in Bandon.

In the 1901 census he was recorded as Samuel H. Johnston aged 58, assistant to land agent who was living with his wife Martha Johnston aged 37, son Henry J. Johnston aged 16, daughter Olive J., aged 14, son Charles J aged 11, daughter Lillian M aged 10, son Gilbert S aged 5 and Kate Baldwin, a servant aged 17. The house

---

[180] Registry of Deeds. 1864 39 240

[181] Belfast Newsletter of 7th August, 1888

was recorded as a private dwelling with ten windows at the front and ten rooms occupied by the family.

By the time of the 1911 census Martha Johnston had died and Samuel, aged 68, a widower and land clerk was living with his daughter Olive J aged 24, Lillian M aged 20 and a governess, Gilbert S aged 15 and Catherine Baldwin, a servant aged 26. The house was described as a private dwelling with eleven windows at the front of the house and nine rooms occupied by the family.

Lily Johnston took over the property in 1935. It became vacant in 1938. Patrick Hawkes junior was the tenant in 1942, it became vacant again in 1946, Patrick Griffin was the occupier in 1947, William Slattery in 1949 and J. McElligott in 1951.

No 35 – Private House and Pawn Brokers Shop – Hilton House

1837 Number 32 – Valuation £45
1849 Number 39
1851 Number 35 – Valuation £35 5s
1901 Census Number 29 – Pawn Office
1911 Census Number 72 – Shop

Immediate Lessors

1816 William Kingston from the Duke of Devonshire – 99 years
1851 The Duke of Devonshire
1897 Sir John Arnott
? Allman Dowden & Co (formed in 1885 when Dowden & Co was dissolved)
1956 Mrs Lorna Roddie

Wiliam Kingston entered into a lease with the Duke of Devonshire on 1st April 1816 for the lives of the Prince Regent, the Duke of York and Princess Charlotte with 99 years to run concurrently at a rent of £20 10. The site was described as a plot whereon an old house was standing and which was in the occupation of William Kingston. It had a breadth of 41' and a depth of 140'. It was bounded on the west by the street, on the east by a lane or passage leading to Kilbrogan Church and on the south by Mr Shorten's holding and on the north by the holdings of J. Bennett and George Heazle.[182]

Occupiers

On 9th May, 1829, with the agreement of the Duke of Devonshire, William Kingston applied to the Clerk of the Peace in County Cork to register the freehold of the dwelling house and premises.

In 1837 the occupier was Dora Kingston, the widow of William Kingston who died on 15th April, 1831 and was buried in the family vault at Christ Church, Kilbrogan. William was a pawnbroker.

In 1849 William and Dora's son, William Kingston, was the occupier. The building was described in the record as a large property with shop, house, P. Barkers shop, chandlers and candle store and a snuff house

The occupier at the time of the Griffiths Valuation was still William Kingston, a pawnbroker[183]. William married Ellen Rebecca Vickery at Christ Church, Innishannon on 7th February 1854. They had a daughter also named Ellen Rebecca born on 6th November 1857 and baptised at Christ Church, Kilbrogan, a daughter Eliza Anne born on 7th March 1859 and baptised at Christ Church on 20th April, a son George Thomas born on 28th August 1862.

William was recorded in the register of vestrymen at Christ Church, Kilbrogan in 1870.

In 1884 John D. Swan, a cashier in the Provincial Bank of Ireland, also resided at the house. He occupied a front sitting room and front bedroom which were both located on the second floor. William Kingston lived at the house and also operated his business from the address. The rateable value was £35 5s.[184]

---

[182] MS 6189. Lismore Papers

[183] Slater's Directory of 1856, 1870 & 1881. Coghlans Directory of 1867

[184] 1884 Electoral Register. Borough of Bandon Bridge.

William continued to reside at the property until he died on 3rd October, 1895 aged 71 years. He left £2,769 in his will to his wife. He was buried in the family vault at Christ Church, Kilbrogan. His wife, Ellen Rebecca Kingston succeeded him.

In the 1901 census Ellen Rebecca Kingston aged 70, a widow and pawnbroker, was living at the premises with her sons James aged 35, a pawnbroker, George aged 39 a pawnbroker, daughter Elizan aged 42, Daniel Downing, an assistant aged 21 and Margaret Crowley a servant aged 18. The house was described as a pawn office with ten windows at the front of the house and thirteen rooms occupied by the family.

Ellen Rebecca died aged 69 on 27th June 1901. Probate was granted to her son, James S. Kingston who was described in her will as a photographer. She left effects of £1,724.

In 1903 James S Kingston became the occupier. In the census of 1911 he was described as single aged 45, a pawnbroker living with his brother George aged 48 an assistant pawnbroker, their sister Elizan Kingston, a house keeper aged 50 also single and a servant Margaret Crowley aged 28.

In 1915 James S. Kingston was recorded as a pawnbroker, clothier, outfitter, shipping agent and photographic artist.[185]

James S. Kingston lived in the property until the 1930s. He died on 8th August 1950 and was buried in the family vault at Christ Church, Kilbrogan. His brother George was also buried in the same plot. He died in March 1944 and their sister Elizan died in March 1946.

The house was divided into flats following the departure of the Kingstons in the 1930s.

---

[185] Cork and Munster Trade Directory. 1915.

No 36 – a Licensed Premises and for a period undertakers
1837 Number 33 – Valuation £28
1849 Number 40
1851 Number 36 – Valuation £17
1901 Census Number – Public House
1911 Census Number 71.1 and 71.2 – Public House

Immediate Lessors
1816 Timothy Murphy
1851 The Duke of Devonshire
1897 Sir John Arnott
1907 John Murphy

Occupiers
In 1775 one house occupied the site of No 36 and No 37. The immediate lessor was Isaac Jones and the occupier was Edward Davis.

Timothy Murphy appears to have been both the immediate lessor and occupier of the property from 1816. His occupation was recorded as shop-keeper. He was still the tenant in the register of 1837 and again in 1849 in the early valuation records at which time his occupation was described as a publican.[186]

Hanoria Murphy[187], a publican, had become the resident by 1856. She was also recorded as a grocer in 1867.

Hanora had died by 1873 and Catherine Murphy took over the business. Catherine died on 18th January, 1874. She was a spinster. John Murphy succeeded her. In 1879 Dominick Frances McKeon was recorded as the occupier and in 1880 Thomas McGrath became the tenant.

---

[186] Slater's Directory of 1846
[187] Slater's Directory of 1856

By 1882 Dominick Francis McKeon, a baker, wine and spirit merchant and grocer[188] was the occupier. In 1884 W. Catterson Smith, a cashier in the Bank of Ireland, was also recorded at the premises. He occupied a front sitting room on the second floor and a front bedroom on the third floor.[189] The landlord, Dominick McKeon, occupied the dwelling both as a place of business and as a residence and the rateable valuation at the time was £20. He sold wines, spirits and sundry goods. Dominick acted as a town commissioner during at least 1893.[190]

In the 1901 census Dominick Frances McKeon aged 49 was recorded as a shopkeeper and widower living with his daughter Mary J. McKeon aged 16, son Michael J. McKeon aged 15, a servant Joseph Robinson, a car man aged 20.

The occupiers were Catherine Shine (1904), John Hennessey (1907) and Michael Tobin (1910)

The 1911 census recorded Michael Tobin as aged 32, a licensed vintner living with his wife Margaret Tobin aged 30 having had five children, three of whom were still alive and also residing at the property daughter Johanna aged 3, daughter Julia Anne aged 2, niece Margaret Tobin aged 20, boarder Margaret O'Sullivan aged 26 and a dress maker and a boarder Bridget O'Sullivan aged 19 and also a dressmaker.

In another part of the house in 1911 John Nelson Goode aged 29, married and a farrier was living with his wife, Bessie aged 28 and son Alec aged 1 month.

In 1915 M. Tobin was recorded as operating a posting establishment.

The Tobins resided at the property for years.

---

[188] Guys Directory of 1893
[189] Electoral Register for Bandon Bridge. 1884
[190] Guy's Director of 1893

133

No 37 – A Private House

1837 Number 34 – Valuation £16

1851 Number 37 – Valuation £11 10s

1901 Census Number 31 – Private Dwelling

1911 Census Number 70 – Private Dwelling

Immediate Lessors

1851 The Duke of Devonshire

1885 John Murphy

Occupiers

The site of No 36 and No 37 was occupied by a house and office in 1775. The immediate lessor was Isaac Jones and the occupier was Edward David.

Anne Swanton was recorded as the tenant in 1837 and was still resident in the early valuation records of 1849 and in the Griffiths Valuation of 1851.

By 1856 the occupier was James B. Swanton. James and Phoebe had a son, Samuel, baptised on 20th October 1861. James's occupation was scripture reader.

Ellen Bull became the occupier before 1861 and resided at the property until 1876 when Miss Turner took up residence.

Rev James Stephenson moved into the property in 1885. Josephine Calnan was a resident in 1899 and Mary McNamara by 1901.

By the time of the 1901 census Isabel J. McNamara aged 25, an organist and teacher was living with Mary Anne Payne, a general servant, domestic aged 60.

The next occupant was Percy Jeffers in 1909 followed by James Good in 1911. The house was vacant at the time of the census

Timothy Sullivan moved in during 1915 and the house was once again vacant in 1917.

The family of William Parker Appelbe Heron (b 1852 in Bandon and the son of John Heron and Esther Edwards) became the next occupants. They were Methodists. William married Mary Jane Fuller, the daughter of Joseph Fuller and Mary Williams of Castletreasure, Ballineen. He ran a grocery and hardware business on South Main Street. William and his wife Mary had Hester Anne, John S., Thomas Henry, Mary Eileen, Georgina Claire, James A. and Ellen.

William died in 1920 and the property then became that of his wife Mary Jane Heron. She died in Bandon in 1936. William V. Harte became the next occupier in 1927. Hester Harte succeeded him in 1957.

THE CHURCH LANE DIVIDES THESE PROPERTIES

The lane was known for some time as Church Lane North and also as Tobin's Lane. "North" was used to differentiate it from the Church Lane at St Peters, Ballymodan.[191]

Church Lane was the original entrance to Christ Church. The Sexton's House was built at the end of the lane next to the entrance to the graveyard. In the 1700s there were many small houses along the lane.

On 29th September, 1801 John Hosford, George Heazle and Corless Welch jointly rented holdings in Church Lane (North Main Street) at a rent of £5 5s for the year.[192]

---

[191] Bandon Historical Journal. No 9. The Laneways of Bandon. Sean Connolly
[192] Lismore Papers

Church Lane North

No 1
Immediate Lessor
1856 Ellen Bull
1870 The Duke of Devonshire
1897 Sir John Arnott
1938 Michael Tobin

A house existed on the site in 1856 which was occupied by Henry ?[193] It became vacant before 1860.

By 1867 John Corcoran had taken up residence. John Murphy became the tenant in 1870. He was succeeded by John Corcoran in about 1886. James Corcoran succeeded John in 1908 and remained in the property until 1919. In 1921 Thomas Tobin became the tenant. In 1928 the property was improved and part of it was used as a carpenters store room. Michael Tobin succeeded Thomas Tobin and in 1938 he purchased the freehold from Sir John Arnott

No 2 - LAND
Intermediate Lessor
The Duke of Devonshire
1867 Richard Wheeler Doherty

There was an office with land attached on the site in 1856. Robert Wheeler was the occupier. He held the lease on the office and the Duke of Devonshire had the lease on the land.

In 1864 Eliza Wheeler had succeeded Robert Wheeler as the occupier of the land. She held the lease on the office but it had become vacant.

By 1867 Matthew Lee had become the tenant of the land. The entry for the office was crossed out in the valuation record which suggests that it may have been taken down.

---

[193] Surname illegible

In the early 1870s Matthew Lee was succeeded as the occupier of the land by George Lane, William Lovell Hunter and then R.H. Chapman.

R.H. Chapman was succeeded in 1879 by John Payne followed by Joseph Lane in 1881. The land passed to Rev Benjamin Christmas Fawcett in 1891 and he held it until 1907 when it passed to Rev Maurice W. Day. It then passed to Rev J.C. Lord in 1921.

In 1937 the representatives of Rev J.C. Lord assumed the tenancy and in 1938 the occupier of the land was recorded as Rev Alfred McConnell.

Rev Charles Allen became the next tenant of the land in 1941. By 1960 the entry had been changed to Bandon Select Vestry.

No 3
1901 Census Number 2

Intermediate Lessor
1856 Mary Hunter
1867 James Hunter
Ca 1880 Reps of James Hunter followed by Mrs Hunter.
1930 William Loane
1962 George Beare

James Hunter was an architect who died on 20th August, 1875 His wife, Catherine Hunter, was the sole executrix of his will which was proved at Cork on 29th September, 1875. He left effects under £300.

There was a house and yard on the site which was occupied by 'lodgers' from at least 1856 until 1879 when John Daly became the tenant. He was succeeded by Charles Cunningham in 1894. In the 1901 census he was described as aged 50, a rural postman, living with his wife Mary aged 44, daughter Hannah, aged 18, son John aged 16, daughter Julia aged 14, daughter Margaret aged 12, daughter Norah aged 9 and daughter Teresa aged 6.

The Cunningham family were succeeded by John Seymour in 1913 and by Charles Cullinane in 1920. William Loane became the immediate lessor in 1930.

Richard Walsh was registered as the tenant in 1939. The property became vacant in 1962.

No 4
Intermediate Lessor
1856 Mary Hunter
1867 James Hunter
Ca 1880 Reps of James Hunter followed by Mrs Hunter.
1930 William Loane
1962 George Beare

There was just a house on the site also occupied by 'lodgers' from at least 1856 until 1901 when Catherine Kehily became the tenant. In the 1901 census Catherine was described as aged 70, a widow living with her daughter Jane (36), also a widow and involved in laundry work. Her children Nellie (11), Daniel (6), Robert (4), Michael (1) were also recorded. Catherine was succeeded by Daniel Kehily in 1921. Thomas Barry became the tenant in 1930 and he was followed by Margaret Barry in 1938.

The North Market House was situated on the road between Church Lane and the North Gate. It was built by Richard Croft in 1617 to accommodate a court house, market jury apartments and a market area. It was demolished in 1800. It was a three storey fortified building with a lead sheeted roof, ports for cannons and portcullis gate and apartments for the Earl of Cork.[194] Ministers from the Methodist Church which was built in 1760 at the site of the Bridewell preached in front of the market house.

---

[194] A Historical Walk through Bandon. Paddy Connolly.

No 38

1775 Site of Number 28

1837 Number 35 – Valuation £30

1849 Number 42

1851 Number 38 – Valuation £21 15s

1901 Census Number 32

1911 Census Number 69 – Private House

2015 Number 1 Lower Kilbrogan Hill

Immediate Lessors

1816 William Jenkins – 99 year lease (see also No 39, 40)

1840 Eliza Barter

1851 Miss Barter

1856 Benjamin Forde

1869 Richard Wheeler Doherty

1884 Miss Doherty

The holding was demised by the Duke of Devonshire to William Jenkins on 1st April 1816.[195] In a lawsuit in 1840 between Roderick Connor Esq, Master of Chancery, Susanna Barter of Hinckly, Leicestershire, William Jenkins of the USA, James Splaine Biggs, James Edward, Jackson Rickard, Mary Roe and Rev Thomas Roe and Elizabeth Barter of Patrick Street, Cork, Susanna was the plaintiff and William Jenkins and several others were the defendants. William Jenkins surrendered the piece of ground formerly in his possession to Elizabeth Barter for her to hold for the remainder of the 99 years which commenced on 25th March 1816 on payment of the original annual rent as agreed in 1816. This agreement appears to have included the site of No 39.

Some time between 1840 and 1851 Eliza Barter sold the lease to Martha Matilda Garde. The lease was subsequently transferred to Benjamin Forde.[196]

---

[195] Registry of Deeds. 1840 9 67

[196] Registry of Deeds. 1864 19 50

Occupiers

A small house (no 28) facing towards Church Lane occupied the site in 1775. The immediate lessor was Barry Walsh and the occupier was Thomas Denning.

Edward O'Brien was the resident in 1837. His occupation was described as gentleman in the electoral list of 1832 and he was living in North Main Street at the time possibly at this address.

In 1849 Rev John Pratt was the occupier. He was living in Kilbrogan Street by 1856.

Henry Ormston, a medical doctor, was recorded as the occupier in 1851.

Henry Baldwin Ormston was a physician to the Bandon Dispensary and Fever Hospital. On 18th May 1849 he wrote a letter to the Southern Reporter confirming that an outbreak of cholera had occurred and that two fatal cases were diagnosed in Bandon. He was a member of the Masonic Lodge No 82.

On 15th September 1849 Henry married Maria Anne Tresilian, daughter of Richard Tresilian, at the Scots Presbyterian Church in Bandon. Henry was a brother of Catherine and Jane Hawkesby Ormston (she was born in 1812 and died on 16th June 1876. Her executor was her niece Dorothea Hayes). Born in 1812, he died on 19th April 1868 aged 56. Henry and Maria had a stillborn child in November 1851. They had a son Robert Henry, born 1856, who died in Portsea UK of malarial fever. Henry graduated as a Medical Doctor at the University of Glasgow in 1837.

Dr Henry Ormston died on 19th April 1868 in Bandon. Letters of Administration were granted to his wife, Maria Anne Ormston, on 12th April, 1869. He left effects under £800.

The subsequent occupiers were the representatives of Henry Ormston and in 1878 Rev George Smith took up residence.

Rev John Robert Porte became the occupier in 1879 and he was followed shortly afterwards in 1880 by Mrs Gillman.

Mrs Unkles, Mrs Craig (1891), Rev John O'Rourke (1895) and Rev John W. Ballard (1898)

By the time of the 1901 census the occupier was Rev Stewart Smith aged 57, a Methodist minister who was living at the property with his wife Susan and Mary E McClelland aged 43 and also Methodist. She was a visitor

Sarah McCarthy became the occupier in 1905 . It was vacant for a period in 1909. In 1910 Chambre Baldwin took up residence.

The 1911 census recorded Chambre Baldwin as aged 47, born in Australia and a fellow of the surveyors institute, a land agent and a land valuer. He was living with his wife Beatrice, aged 41 and born in England. They had six children. The following were living at the property, Beatrice aged 20, Laura aged 19, Godfrey aged 14, Walter aged 10, Violet aged 7 and a servant Kate Quinlan aged 22. The children were all born in Dublin. A son Chambre aged 17 and listed as a bank clerk was crossed out.

The Baldwins were succeeded by Thomas Seandun (?) in 1913, Hugh C Green in 1918, T Tweedy, a county inspector in 1919 and Joe Callanan in 1921 who resided at the property until the 1930s. Joseph Calnan in 1944 was succeeded by Eileen Mary Calnan in 1953.

No 39 – A school for a short time in the early 1800s.
1775 Site of Number 35
1837 Number 36. Valuation £20
1849 Number 43
1851 Number 39. Valuation £14
1901 Census Number
1911 Census Number 68 – Private House
2015 Number 2 Lower Kilbrogan Hill

Immediate Lessors
1816 William Jenkins (See also No 38) – 99 year lease
1851 Miss Barter
1856 Benjamin Forde
1870 Richard Wheeler Doherty
1884 Miss Doherty

Occupiers
In 1834 Richard Hayes, AB, TCD was recorded as having moved his school to a 'most healthful and eligible situation in the North Main Street and would take charge of a few young gentlemen as boarders who would derive, under his care, all the combined advantages of public instruction and the domestic comforts of a private family.' Parents or guardians who were desirous of reposing such trust to him were invited to apply to Mr Bolster's at Patrick Street, Cork or to Mr Hayes in Bandon either in person or by letter to learn the terms.[197]   Hayes was still registered as the occupier in 1837.

Mrs Powell was recorded as the occupier in 1849 and she was still at the property at the time of the Griffiths valuation of 1851. She also ran a school.

---

[197] Cork Constitution. 24th April, 1834

In the valuation records of 1856 the occupier was named as Sarah Powell, presumably Mrs Powell who had been in occupation in 1849. She left before 1858.

Henry Arnold took up residence in about 1859 and Valentine McCreight, aged 20, succeeded him in 1861. Valentine McCreight was one of ten children of William McCreight who married Mary Milner Badwin of Lisnagat. Valentine was born in about 1841 and died in 1914.[198] His mother, Mary, died at No 75 in 1862 and his father died in 1861 (See entry for No 75).

Henry Robinson Unkles succeeded him shortly before 1864 and he was succeeded by Thomas Hunter in 1866. John Shine Hunter moved in during 1868. He was a photographer[199] Both Thomas Hunter and John Shine Hunter occupied the house together. Their names appeared in the electoral register of 1884 as living on South Main Street in addition to a house, office and yard on Watergate Street.

Peter Brennan took up residence in 1882 for one year. In 1883 George Lamb and Devonshire Penrose Hawkes and families lived at the property having moved from No 77. They resided at No 39 until 1900 when they moved to Barryshall in Timoleague. They were recorded at Barryshall in the 1901 census. Meanwhile Devonshire's wife, Sara's mother, Anna Maria, a widow, lived at the address with a daughter Anna Maria.

The 1901 census lists Anna Maria Hosford aged 70 as living on money devised from land and living with daughter Anna Maria Hosford, aged 39, granddaughter, Josephine Mary Price aged 7, governess Florence H.M. O'Callaghan aged 21 all Church of Ireland and servant Kate Corcoran, Roman Catholic.

Anna Maria who was born in 1828 died aged 74 in 1902 and her daughter Anna Maria became listed as the occupier until 1908.

Mary McNamara moved in during 1908.

---

[198] The Baldwins of Lisnagat by Alexandra Bugahair.
[199] Coughlans Directory of 1867. Also William J. Hunter of Bandon married Ann, daughter of John Shine of Bandon on 22nd September 1829 at St Nicholas, Cork.

The 1911 census recorded Mary E. McNamara as a widow aged 73 who had had seven children with six still alive. She was living with a domestic servant aged 22, Margaret Lane.

In 1917 Patrick Joseph McCarthy, a solicitor, moved from Kilbrogan House to this property. He lived at the property until 1927 when Margaret M. Beechiner became the occupier. The property became vacant in 1955. Patrick O'Reilly was the occupier in 1957 and Patrick Staunton in 1958. The property became vacant in 1960.

No 40
1775 Site of Number 35
1837 Number 37 – Valuation £22
1849 Number 44
1851 Number 40 – Valuation £14
1901 Census Number 34
1911 Census Number 67 – Private House
2015 Number 3 Lower Kilbrogan Hill

Immediate Lessors
1816 William Jenkins (See also 38, 39) – 99 year lease
1851 Miss Barter

William Jenkins entered into a lease with the Duke of Devonshire on 1st April 1816 for the lives of the Prince Regent, Duke of York and Princess Charlotte and 99 years running concurrently at a rent of £12 10s. The site was described as a waste plot which was already in the possession of William Jenkins. It had a breath of 60' and a depth of 263'. It was bounded on the west by the main street, on the east by the stream, on the north by the holding of Cornelius Hagarty and on the south by the lane or passage leading to Kilbrogan Church.[200]

---

[200] MS 6189. Lismore Papers

Occupiers
In 1837 the occupier was Thomas Barter.

Miss Jane Clarke was recorded as the resident in 1849.

The property was unoccupied at the time of the Griffiths Valuation in 1851.

By 1856 the occupier was Catherine Hayes. Her father was George Hayes who married Catherine Jenkins. The father of Catherine Jenkins was William Jenkins who married Catherine Tresilian. Catherine was succeeded in 1873 by Dora Hayes, her sister. Dora and Catherine had seven other siblings, Anne, Elizabeth, Georgiana, Wilhelmina, Alicia, Maria and Jane. Dora, a spinster, died on 7th December 1906. Probate of her will was granted to Archibald O. Hayes, a retired County Inspector, RIC. She left effects of £385.

John Jones junior moved in during 1895. He was succeeded by Sarah McCarthy in 1897.

In the 1901 census Sarah McCarthy was living with Thomas Wingrave Ashton, a boarder and law agent, Church of Ireland, aged 25 and Mary Brien aged 29 female servant

Patrick Murphy took up residence in 1905 and remained in the house for three years.

Matilda Fawcett became the occupier in 1908 presumably having relocated from the Kilbrogan Glebe following the death of her husband. She was the widow of Rev Benjamin Christmas Fawcett who had been rector of Christ Church, Kilbrogan.

In the 1911 census Matilda Eleanor Fawcett was recorded as living in the property aged 73, a widow who had had 8 children with 5 still alive. Her daughter, Matilda S. Fawcett, was living with her as were Arnie Houghton, a visitor, aged 43 and Catherine MacCarthy, a domestic servant aged 17.

Frances and Sarah Fawcett succeeded Matilda in 1933. The house was vacant in 1936 before James Neville moved in during 1937. M. Brady was the next occupier in 1941. The property was vacant in 1955. In 1956 Humphrey Lynch became the tenant. The property was vacant again in 1959 and in 1960 Patrick Gallagher became the occupier.

No 41 – Fairview House. Built at the same time as No 42.
1775 Site of Number 36
1837 Number 38 – Valuation £22
1851 Number 41 – Valuation £13
1901 Census Number - 35
1911 Census Number 66 – Private House
2015 Number 4 Lower Kilbrogan Hill

The Town Wall ran through part of the garden of this property.

Immediate Lessors
1816 Cornelius Hagarty (from Duke of Devonshire) See also No 42
1851 James Hagarty
1856 Cornelius Hagarty
1860 Bartholomew Daly
1883 Sarah McCarthy
1926 Catherine McCarthy

The Duke of Devonshire demised the plot to Cornelius Hagarty, a ropemaker, on 1st April 1816 for 99 years and two lives at £8. On 25th March, 1800 Cornelius had leased 5 fields in Coolfadda at an annual rental of £14 16s and on 29th September 1801 he rented part of the lands of Coolfadda for a year together with William Cames and John Hagarty at an annual rental of £45 15s.[201]

Hagarty erected two houses on the site (No 41 and 42). On 14th August 1847 his son and executor of his will demised the lease to Bartholomew Daly at an annual rental of £20. On 27th April, 1852 it was assigned to Maurice Dominik Daly and Michael Sullivan and

---

[201] Lismore Papers

on 14th June 1853 they assigned it to Mathew Regan also at an annual rent of £20 paid twice yearly.[202]

Occupiers

In 1837 the occupier was Eleanor Austin.

Dr Magrath was recorded as living in the property in 1844[203] and he was still resident in the early valuation records of 1851.

In 1856 the occupier was Richard J. O'Mahony and was succeeded shortly afterwards by Rev Nyhan. By 1860 Rev Timothy Holland had taken up residence.

Rev Timothy Holland moved out in 1864 (he was living at Highfort, Innishannon in 1870) and he was succeeded by Charles McCarthy, a medical doctor. He was succeeded by Catherine Unkles in 1878.

In 1883 Rev Denis McCarthy became the occupier. His name appeared on the 1884 electoral register and the property was described as a house with offices, yard and garden at a rateable valuation of £15.

Rev Denis McCarthy remained until 1889 when Jeremiah Coghlan took up residence. He was followed by Abraham Haynes in 1895

The 1901 census the occupier was recorded as Abraham Haynes aged 48, single, Clerk of Union and District Council who was living with Helena Fuller, servant, aged 24.

There was a succession of tenants between the two censuses. Sarah McCarthy was recorded as the occupier in 1907, Annie Bartlett in 1908, Elizabeth Halburd in 1910 and David Gillman Scott in 1911.

The 1911 census recorded David Gillman Scott as an accountant, aged 40, married with one child and living with his wife Amelia Emily Frances, son James Erie aged 5 months and domestic

---

[202] Registry of Deeds. 1853 21 107

[203] W. A. Spiller. A Short Topographical and Statistical Account of the Bandon Union (1844)

servant Mary O'Sullivan aged 16. He was living in a part of the house (66.3).

Rev John Armstrong, a lodger, and curate assistant of Kilbrogan and Killowen aged 26 was recorded as the occupier in part of the house (66.2).

Dora Christina Gash, aged 66, a widow who had had nine children was living with her daughter Kathleen Frances Gash aged 29, grand child Dorothy Georgina Levis aged 5, visitor Dorothea Lucy Halahan aged 35 and servant Catherine Connor aged 22 was living in the part of the house recorded as 66.1.

In 1926 Eliza Tanner succeeded David Gillman Scott as the occupier. She was succeeded by Margaret, Marie and Sarah Tanner in 1927. Patrick McGrath became the next occupier in 1944. He was succeeded by Jeremiah in 1960 and by Christopher Callanan in 1961.

No 42 – Built at the same time as No 41

1775 Site of Number 36
1837 Number 39 – Valuation £22
1851 Number 42 – Valuation £12 10
1901 Census Number 36
1911 Census Number 65 – Private Dwelling
2015 Number 5 Lower Kilbrogan Hill

Immediate Lessors

1816 Cornelius Hagarty (from Duke of Devonshire) See also No 41
1851 The Duke of Devonshire
1864 Thomas Kingston Sullivan
1882 Miss McCarthy
1897 Sir John Arnott

The Duke of Devonshire demised the plot to Cornelius Hagarty on 1st April 1816 for 99 years and two lives at £8. Hagarty erected two houses on the site (No 41 and 42).[204]

Occupiers

In 1837 the occupier was Lydia Hagarty. There is a reference to Mr Wigglesworth as being the occupier in 1844.[205] James Hagarty's name appeared as the tenant in 1849. He was a rope maker and was still in residence in 1851[206]

A note in navy blue ink in the valuation record reads as follows: 'Cornelius Hagarty claims to be jointly rated with his brother, James, for this and some other concerns for the Borough but he was not able to show me that he had any legal right to be so rated? His father left this house to James and No 41 to Cornelius Hagarty.'

---

[204] See No 41 for further details.
[205] W.A. Spiller. A Short Topographical and Statistical Account of the Bandon Union.
[206] Slater's Directory of 1856

In 1864 James and Cornelius Hagarty were no longer recorded as resident at the property. Henry Hassett, JP, became the head tenant. At the time of his death on 28th November 1870, he was living at Woodlands, Bandon which suggests that he may have held the tenancy for other family members.

William Christopher Dowden and George Lyons were registered as the occupiers in 1872 though this is entry is also somewhat confusing as William was also recorded as living at Floraville[207]. They may have taken on a short term lease for staff or family. William was born in 1801 and died in 1887. He was one of the principals in Allman, Dowden & Co, brewers and was mentioned in Slater's Directory of 1870 as a corn and linen merchant of South Main Street. He was the younger son of Christopher. His older brother Christopher was recorded as a manufacturer.

Messrs Dowden and Lyons were succeeded by John W. Watson in 1873. The property became vacant for a year in 1879 and in 1880 James Hegarty took up residence. By 1882 John Halley had succeeded James Hegarty. John Halley's name appeared on the electoral register of 1884 and his property was described as a house with offices, yard and a small garden. It had a rateable valuation of £14 10s.

James Hegarty remained in the property for four years and was succeeded in 1886 by Widow McCarthy. Two years later in 1898 Margaret M and Amelia McCarthy were recorded as the occupiers.

In the 1901 census Amelia McCarthy was described as aged 60, living on her own, single and depending on income derived from house rent.

The 1911 census recorded Margaret M MacCarthy aged 60, single, living with her cousin Jane Clerke aged 78

Shortly afterwards in 1911 Eliza Tanner became the occupier and she was in the property for eight years.

The house was vacant during 1919 and in 1920 Miss S. Tanner was recorded as the occupier. Matthew Nooney succeeded her in 1921.

---

[207] Guy's Directory of 1875

The property became vacant in 1939. In 1940 Conor James Kennedy was the occupier. He was succeeded by William McElroy in 1950.

No 43 – Part of the site of the Provost's House in 1775
1775 Site of Number 37
1837 Number 40 – Valuation £16
1849 Number 47
1851 Number 43 – Valuation £16 10s
1901 Census Number 37
1911 Census Number 64 – Private Dwelling
2015 Number 6 Lower Kilbrogan Hill

Immediate Lessors
(See also entry for No 44)
1817 Thomas Hornibrook of Keamagara
1851 John Thomas Hornibrook
1897 Sir John Arnott

Occupiers
James Dawson, a coal dealer and courier[208] was recorded as the tenant in 1837.

Thomas Hornibrook Sullivan became the next occupier in the late 1850s[209].

John Keys Esq took up residence during 1861. He was an accountant at the Provincial Bank of Ireland. He died at this residence on 13th September 1864 following a short illness.[210] The auction of the contents of the house was carried out by William

[208] Slater's Directory of Bandon, 1856
[209] See Appendix. Short Biographies. Thomas Hornibrook Sullivan
[210] Cork Examiner, 19th September, 1864

Marsh & Son on Monday, 10th October, 1864. Furniture, rugs, curtains, a piano, beds and kitchen ware were amongst the items sold.

In 1866 Thomas Kingston Sullivan was recorded as the occupier. [211]Miss Scott moved in followed shortly afterwards by John Donovan, a saddle and harness maker[212] who moved out in 1871.

Mrs Wells was recorded as the occupier in 1879.

Henry Slorack, a Medical Doctor, took up residence in 1880.

By 1883 the property became vacant. Franklin Baldwin became the occupier during 1886. He was succeeded by Thomas Cooper in 1896.

In the 1901 census Thomas Cooper was described as 57, an accountant at distillery, who was living with wife, Henrietta aged 51, both Church of Ireland and servant, Mary Skelton aged 26.

The property was vacant at the time of the 1911 census but shortly afterwards in the same year Dora Gash took up residence. She remained in premises for eight years until 1919 when Mary Murphy became the occupier.

Margaret Murphy succeeded Mary Murphy in 1920 and she was in residence until 1935 when David Reen succeeded her. Rita Reen was recorded as the occupier in 1961.

---

[211] See Appendix. Biographies.
[212] Slater's Directory of 1867

No 44 – North Gate.
The North Gate Market House stood in front of the property.

The site of part of provost's house in 1775.

1775 Site of part of Number 37
1837 Number 41 – Valuation £30
1851 Number 44 – Valuation £20 15s
1901 Census Number 38
1911 Census Number 63 – Private Dwelling

Immediate Lessors
1715 Abraham Watkins held the lease on a site which included the house now standing on this plot. The occupier in 1715 was Rev Solomon Foley[213] (See No 115 & No 116 on map details of 1717). Abraham Watkins died before 1724 and his widow Mary Watkins, a resident of Cork City by that time, assigned the lease to John Travers who was still recorded as the occupier in 1775.[214] The house on the site in 1724 had a slate roof. Rev Solomon Foley had at least one daughter Susanna, who married Rev Robert McClellan.[215]

1851 John Thomas Hornibrook[216]
1885 Mrs Hornibrook

Occupiers
In 1837 the occupier was Mary Travers.

Robert Cross Denton was recorded as the occupier in 1849 and he was still in the residence in 1849 and in 1851.

Robert was the Bandon Collector of Excise and Quit Rent and he and his wife, Charlotte occupied the house.[217] Their son, Robert

---

[213] See Appendix. Short Biographical Details
[214] Registry of Deeds. 49 80 30974 4th June 1724
[215] Registry of Deeds. 86 170 59831 20th October 1736
[216] See Appendix. Short Biographical Details

Cross died on 22nd April, 1849 aged 4. On 20th March 1852 their daughter, Edith, died aged 18. Both of the children are buried at Christ Church, Kilbrogan.

Robert Cross Denton died in Bridlington in England on Sunday 13th February 1859 aged 63.[218] His widow, Charlotte, died on 7th April, 1875.[219]

By 1856 the occupier was James Black, an excise collector[220]

W.R. Hickey moved into the property in 1861. He was succeeded in 1869 by Thomas Derham. Part of the property was used as an Ireland Revenue Office and a section was used as an excise office which was exempt from valuation taxes.

Thomas and his wife Rose had a daughter Rose Lucy on 19th October 1865 and his address was given as Kilbrogan Hill. His occupation was recorded as 'in customs department'. He was listed in the register of vestrymen at Christ Church, Kilbrogan in 1870.

Thomas Derham was the occupier for ten years until Alexander Appelbe took up residency in 1879. Alexander's rental in 1884 was £17.[221] He was succeeded by Miss Baldwin in 1885

The notes which recorded that 'part of the premises are used as an excise office' were crossed out.

Walter[222] became the tenant in 1891.

Dora Hayes was recorded as the occupier in 1895 and she was succeeded in 1901 by Francis Ormston. (The entry in the subsequent valuation book is for Francis Ormston Hayes)

In the 1901 census Francis Hayes was described as aged 65 depending on income from land and house property and living

---

[217] Dublin Almanac of 1847

[218] Obituary of Saturday, 19th February, 1859

[219] New York Herald of Saturday, 10th April, 1875

[220] Slater's Directory of 1856

[221] Electoral Records of 1884

[222] Surname not known

with sister Rosa Hayes aged 70, dependent on lands and dividends, sister Catherine Hayes aged 67, brother Alexander Hayes aged 50, living from houses and property, all Church of Ireland and servant Julia Sullivan aged 20. None were married

Alex Hayes was recorded as the occupier in 1909.

By the time of the 1911 census the house was vacant.

In 1913 William Hallahan became the tenant and he remained at the property until 1919 when it became vacant for one year.

J.J. Acton took up residency in 1920 and he was succeeded by William Foley in 1921[223] and by Daniel Murphy in 1934. The representatives of Daniel Murphy took over in 1962.

No 45
1837 Number 42 – Valuation £30
1849 Number 49
1851 Number 45 – Valuation £20
1901 Census Number 39
1911 Census Number 62 – Private Dwelling

Immediate Lessors
1775 John Lapp
1851 John Thomas Hornibrooke[224]
1879 Mrs Hornibrook

Occupiers
A large house with an office and garden stood on approximately this site in 1775. It was occupied by Dr Joseph Ledbetter.

---

[223] A death of a William Foley is recorded in the St Patrick's burial register dated 30th June 1932.
[224] See Short Biographical Details in Appendix. He died in 1876 & his estate passed to his widow, Mrs Hornibrook.

In 1837 the occupier was John Popham. He may have been in residence in 1832 as he was recorded that year as a resident of North Main Street and his occupation was described as a gentleman.

Fanny Baldwin (Frances Elizabeth Marsden) was the occupier in 1849. She was born about 1810 and was the daughter of William Baldwin of Lissarda Castle and Nelson Place by his second wife, Mary Franklin Kirby whom he married in Castletownsend. Her brother was Franklin Kirby Baldwin of Castle Baldwin who married Barbara Morris Evanson. (See entry for No 81, the residence of Franklin and his family).

Fanny continued to reside in the property until her death on 23rd November 1891. She left a personal estate of £980. Probate was granted to Catherine Pilkington Baldwin, the personal legatee for life. She was the daughter of Godfrey Baldwin who married Anna Louisa Pilkington. Catherine was born on 17th July 1835 and she died on 6th November, 1904.

The 1901 census described Catherine P Baldwin as aged 50, single, living from interest with a servant Mary Casey aged 42.

Abraham Haynes became the next occupant following Catherine's death in 1904.

The 1911 census described Abraham Haynes as aged 63, Clerk of the Union, living with his wife Martha Emily, aged 45 and a visitor Dora Breck aged 48 and Hannah Aherne a general servant aged 27

The Haynes family continued to live at the property until 1920 when Col. E. Sullivan moved in. He spent just one year in residence and was succeeded by Mrs Mary Sullivan in 1921. By 1925 Mrs C. O'Driscoll had taken up residence. Mrs Mary O'Driscoll became the next tenant.

No 46 – DEVONSHIRE ARMS HOTEL (Also known for a time as the Williams Inn). Erected in 1822. See also Chapter 6.

1837 Number 43 – Valuation £65
1849 Number 50
1851 Number 46 – Valuation £71 10s
1901 Census Number 40.1
1911 Census Number 61 – Hotel

Immediate Lessor
The Duke of Devonshire's Estate was responsible for the construction and maintenance of the hotel and held the lease.
1897 Sir John Arnott

Occupiers
The hotel was opened in October 1822 by Paul Williams formerly of the King's Arms (No 5 & 6). He ran it for eighteen years until his death in 1840. His youngest daughter, Mary Dawson was recorded as the occupier in 1849. She married firstly in 1840 William Dawson and secondly, in 1848, Abraham Loane who was recorded as the occupier at the time of the Griffiths Valuation in 1851.

Abraham's sister, Anne Loane was recorded as the occupier in 1880 and she was succeeded by David Forsyth in 1882 (David married Rebecca Loane, the daughter of William Loane in 1881). David Forsyth married secondly, Margaret Murphy. David was recorded as the occupier on the electoral register of 1884 and the property had a rateable valuation of £65. It was described as a hotel, offices, yard and garden. David died in 1887 and in 1890 his wife Margaret Forsyth was recorded as the occupier.

In the 1901 Margaret Mary Forsyth was described as aged 40, a widow and hotel keeper, Roman Catholic, living with her son Michael aged 16, two servants Kate Duggan (20) and Bridget Walsh (18) and a boarder Arthur F. Corr aged 27, a bank clerk

In the 1901 census Herbert R. Baldwin (4) was recorded as living in part of the property. He was single and was living on his own means.

In the 1911 census Margaret Mary Forsyth was described as aged 50, a hotel proprietor and widow who was living with John Forsyth, aged 25, son and assistant, a daughter Marion aged 22, an assistant. John Gough, a visitor aged 30, a bank clerk, Mary O'Shea, a servant aged 30, Bridget Connor aged 20, a servant and Denis Long aged 32, boots.

Herbert Baldwin was still living in a part of the property in the 1911 census. He was described as aged 50 and a retired farmer. He was still in residence in 1915.[225]

The 1911 census recorded Maurice Francis MacEnerny as a lodger. He was aged 49 and was a supervisor of customs and excise.

Michael J. Forsyth became the occupier in 1921

The property was commandeered as an RIC barracks in 1922. A temporary hut and latrines were erected.

Michael J. Forsyth continued to occupy the premises after the RIC moved out. Marion Healy joined with him in 1927 and they retained it until 1943. Edward O'Farrell took over in 1944 and he was succeeded by Rennie Ashton in 1950 and by Edward O'Farrell in 1951.

The hotel was destroyed by fire in 1976.

---

[225] Cork and Munster Trade Directory of 1915

No 47

1837 Number 44 – Valuation £11
1851 Number 47 – Valuation £10
15s
1901 Census Number 41 – Public House
1911 Census Number 60 – Public House

Immediate Lessors

1851 Abraham Loane
1880 Anne Loane

Occupiers

In 1837 the occupier was James Connor.

The tenant in 1849 was Edward Hornibrooke, a publican[226]. He was still the occupier at the time of the Griffiths Valuation of 1851.

Jeremiah Desmond moved in shortly after 1856 and he remained in the property until 1867. The Representatives of Jeremiah Desmond held it until 1869.

Denis Canty moved in during the mid 1870s and remained in the property until 1933 when Margaret Mary Canty took over. In 1884 the rateable value was recorded as £9 and Denis Canty's name appeared as the resident.[227]

In 1893 Denis Canty was described as a vintner and also a car owner.[228]

In the 1901 census Denis Canty was described as aged 52, a publican and Farmer who was living with wife his Hannah aged 49, son Timothy Canty aged 22, a clerk, daughter Margaret Mary Canty, aged 18, daughter Kathleen Canty aged 15, son John Joseph

---

[226] Slater's Directory of 1856
[227] Electoral Register. 1884
[228] Guy's Directory of 1893

Canty aged 13, son Denis Canty aged 12, son Michael Francis
Canty, aged 10, son Daniel Patrick Canty aged 7.

In the 1911 census Denis Canty aged 69, a farmer was living with
his wife Johanna aged 62. They had had 8 children. Also
recorded as living in the house were Timothy Canty, a son aged 31
and an accountant, Margaret Mary, a daughter aged 27, Catherine,
a daughter aged 25, John Joseph, a son aged 23 and Michael
Francis a clerk aged 20 and Daniel a son aged 17, a farmer

Denis Canty was succeeded by Margaret Mary Canty in 1933.
Daniel Canty was recorded as the tenant in 1952.

There was a shop and store registered at No 47a in 1949 which was
occupied by Lily Seaman.

A Hatchery was also registered in 1949. Mary Collins was the
tenant and she was succeeded by Mary Sheehan in 1953 and
Timothy and Mary in 1955.

No 48 The Bridewell

The Wesleyans built a chapel on this site in 1760. It was described by Wesley as 'a very neat and lightsome building'. It became too small and a new chapel was constructed in 1789 on the site of Riverside House (No 91).

The Bridewell was built by the Duke of Devonshire who paid for its upkeep. The buildings for male and female prisoners were separated and a maximum of 24 prisoners were accommodated.

The Old Bridewell building had no roof in 1919 went it became vacant and was described in the valuation register as in ruins. The previous tenant was recorded as Michael Collins.

In 1934 a new technical school was built on the site by Messrs Jones & Co, Builders of Bandon. On 20th March 1934 Michael O'Reilly, Auctioneer and Valuer of Bandon, held an auction at the new school to sell off the surplus building materials which were left over following the construction project.

The school relocated in 1979 and more recently the building was converted into a block of apartments.

The Lane at the side of the Bridewell which was known as Bridewell Lane ran down to the stream at the back.

Governors
In 1846 Robert Hovendon was governor of the Bridewell.

Henry Burke was the keeper of the Bridewell in 1848. Henry and his wife, Catherine, had a daughter born on 23rd January 1848.

Thomas Allen, Bridewell keeper and his wife Catherine had a son born on 28th May 1857 and baptised on 11th July 1857. He was forced to resign his post following the execution of his son, William Philip Allen, who became known as one of the Manchester Martyrs.

BRIDEWELL LANE

No 1 & 2
A garden was recorded at the site in 1856 and the occupier's name was listed as the Duke of Devonshire. By 1860 William Gore Brett was the tenant of the garden and shortly afterwards Robert Topham held the tenancy. He still held the garden in 1897 when the immediate lessor passed from the Duke of Devonshire to Sir John Arnott.

Denis Canty took over as occupier of the garden from Robert Topham in the early 1900s. He was succeeded by Margaret Canty in 1933. By 1934 the County Cork Vocational Committee had become the occupier.

No 3
In 1856 Joseph Bennett was recorded as both the occupier and the lease holder of a coach house. There was no record of the holding in the 1860 valuation. However in 1867 Timothy Taylor was the occupier and George Bennett held the lease. The property on the site was described as an office. William Tanner succeeded Timothy Taylor in 1882. He was still recorded as the occupier of an office in 1894 when the immediate lessor passed from George Bennett to his wife, Kate Anne Bennett. The property became vacant before 1920.

Jane Anne Wright succeeded Kate Anne Bennett by 1938 and Cecil Mills became the tenant.

Cecil Mills was succeeded by Jane Anne Wright in 1841. Joseph Hyde took it over in 1962.

No 4

A stable must have been built on a site near the Lane by 1867 as an entry for No 4 appears in the valuation records. J. Rodwell, S.J. was the tenant and Rev Thomas Wakeham was the intermediate lessor. In the early 1870s Rev Thomas Wakeham became the tenant as well as being the lessor and shortly afterwards the holding became vacant. It was classified as a vacant store in 1882 and was still vacant in the 1890s.

Richard Clear was the tenant of the store in the early 1900s. The store was once again vacant by 1920.

Alice Ambrose became the immediate lessor in 1938 and Richard Walsh was recorded as the tenant of an office.

Elizabeth Walsh took over the property in 1954. It became vacant in 1960 and in 1961 Thomas J Tubridy became the occupier. It appears to have become vacant again in 1962.

No 49 – Built by Benjamin Forde[229]

1837 Number 45 – Valuation £30
1849 Number 55
1851 Number 49 – Valuation £18 10s
1901 Census Number 32
1911 Census Number 58
2015 Number 12 Kilbrogan Hill East

Immediate Lessors

? Duke of Devonshire to Benjamin Forde
1836 Joseph Bennett
1851 The Duke of Devonshire

---

[229] Registry of Deeds. 1836 16 120

1856 Joseph Bennett
1872 The Duke of Devonshire

On 15th August, 1836, Benjamin Forde sold his lease to Joseph Bennett, a Pawn Broker and father of George Bennett[230]. The sale included the leases on No 50, No 51 in the occupation of Mrs Catherine Donovan and No 52 which was in the occupation of James Dixon. Henry Baldwin Esq was living next door to Dr William Belcher at this time.[231] The four leases were sold for £754 10/.

Occupiers

In 1837 the occupier was William Belcher, a Medical Doctor. His widow, Anna, continued to live at the property and was recorded on the valuation record of 1849 and at the time of the Griffiths valuation of 1851.

By 1856 William Gore Brett had taken up residence.

William Gore Brett originated from Dunmanway. He married Catherine Anne Donovan, a native of Bandon, on 1st January, 1834 at Christ Church, Innishannon. He acted as a Sub Inspector of Police in Bandon. They had a number of children including Francis Hingston Brett born 1847, Henry St John Septimus Brett born 1850, Pilkington Jessop Brett born 1851 and Charlotte Catherine and Alexander Brett born 1854. Two other children, Hannah Tyndall Gore and Charles Tyndall Gore (Baptised on 7th February 1846) died young and are buried at Christ Church, Kilbrogan.

George Bennett replaced Joseph Bennett as the immediate lessor in about 1858 and William Sillefeul replaced William Gore Brett in 1861.

In 1864 Henry Lucas took up residence and remained until 1867 when Rev Thomas Wakeham became the occupier. Henry Lucas and his wife Emma Hardcastle Haldane had a son Henry John born on 13th June 1865. His occupation was recorded as Captain and adjutant of the South Cork Militia.

---

[230] See Appendix. Biographies
[231] Registry of Deeds. 1836 16 120

Rev Thomas Wakeham was a curate in Christ Church Kilbrogan from 1867 to 1872. He was born in Youghal on 17th February 1819, the second youngest son of Rev Thomas Wakeham. He was a curate in Ballymodan, Bandon from 1847-1851. He moved from Christ Church Kilbrogan to become rector of Clonfert in Cloyne where he remained from 1872 until 1887.

He married in December 1859 Catherine E., the fifth daughter of the Rev William Townsend, Rector of Aghada, Cloyne and by her he had two daughters. Charlotte died on 22nd April 1892. He retired in 1901.

The building was vacant until 1874 when George Bennett became the occupier. [232] He was succeeded by Mrs Hornibrook in 1877. She remained in the property until 1883 when Mrs George Bennett became the tenant. She moved out in 1895 and Joseph Wheeler took up residence.

By 1898 Richard Clear had become the occupier. He had lived in No 81 from 1873-1879 which was the residence of his father from 1861 to 1868.[233] He also lived briefly at No 57 (Kilbrogan House) and at Janeville on Watergate Street.

Richard Clear, an active Methodist, was born in Bandon on 31st May 1846. He married Elizabeth Belcher in the Methodist Church in Passage West on 17th August, 1870. They had four children, Emma Mary born 1871, Thomas Albert born 1873, Mabel Elise, born in 1881 and Richard William born in 1883.

Richard was aged 54 at the time of the 1901 census. He was a Justice of the Peace and an owner of land. His wife was Elizabeth, aged 48, was born in England in 1853. Mabel Eliza, aged 19, and Richard William, aged 17, were living with them along with two servants Johanna McCarthy, aged 55, and Mary Crowley, aged 44.

By the time of the 1911 census Richard Clear was still residing at the property with his wife Elizabeth and two servants, Anne Carley and Margaret Griffin. Richard was living from income derived from houses and lands. He died on 26th April, 1917.

---

[232] See Appendix. Short Biographies.
[233] See No 81 for the Biography of Thomas Clear, Father of Richard

The Clear Family was recorded as living at the premises until 1919 when it became vacant until 1921 when Richard Walsh took up residence. In 1953 the tenant was recorded as the representatives of Richard Walsh. Elizabeth Walsh became the occupier in 1954 and in 1960 Thomas Tubridy succeeded her. The property became vacant in 1962.

No 50 – Built by Benjamin Forde[234]

1837 Number 46 – Valuation £20
1849 Number 54
1851 Number 50 – Valuation £12 10s
1901 Census Number 44
1911 Census Number 57
2015 Number 13 Kilbrogan Hill East

Immediate Lessor

Duke of Devonshire to Benjamin Forde
1836 Joseph Bennett
1856 Joseph Bennett
1858 George Bennett

Occupiers

On 15th August, 1836 Benjamin Forde, an architect, entered into leases with Joseph Bennett, a pawn broker[235], in the amount of £754 10s which included No 49, 50, 51, 52.

In 1836 and 1837 the occupier was Henry Baldwin Esq.

Samuel Beamish was resident in 1849.

---

[234] Registry of Deeds 1836 16 120
[235] See Appendix. Biographies

In 1851 Joseph Bennett, a pawn broker and father of George Bennett, was recorded as the occupier.

By 1856 Miss Hornibrooke had become the tenant. Miss Hornibrooke remained as the occupier until 1861. At that stage the name Anne Hornibrook Bickford appeared in the records. She is likely to have been the same person.

In August 1864 an account appeared in the Derbyshire Times about a burglary experienced by Miss Bickford at 2am one morning. She was residing by herself in the 'fashionable' part of the North Main Street when she was woken by a strange noise. She became alarmed and went into the kitchen to discover a burglar. The intruder escaped.

Miss Anne Hornibrook Bickford lived at the address until she died aged 64 on 29th June, 1874. She was the daughter of Philip Peterson Bickford and Jane Hornibrook who married at Christ Church Kilbrogan on 25th October, 1799.[236] James Lane, a solicitor, was the sole executor of her will which was proved at Cork on 4th February, 1875. She left effects under £1000.

Miss Giveen succeeded Anne Bickford in 1874. She remained at the property until 1883 when Mrs Peard took up residence and the immediate lessor switched from George Bennett to Mrs George Bennett.

Mrs Peard was succeeded by Mrs George Bennett in 1882. Joseph Wheeler was recorded as the occupier in 1883 and in 1895 Mrs George Bennett moved back into the property

In 1901 census Kate Anne Scott Bennett was described as aged 70, living from land and houses. She was born in London. She was living on her own with a servant, Anne Crowley.[237]

Annie Healy was the next occupant following the death of Kate Bennett.

[236] See Appendix. Short Biographies. Thomas Hornibrook
[237] See Appendix. Short Biographies

At the time of the 1911 census Annie Healy was living in the house with a niece, Mary Gollock, and three lodgers, Eustace Nigel Crew, a brewer, John Doran, a bank cashier and Michael Crowley, a book keeper.

Annie was succeeded by Mary Gollock in 1914. She remained at the property until 1934 when Jane Anne Wright took up residence. Joseph Hyde became the next occupier in 1952 and the representatives of Joseph Hyde were registered as the tenant in 1961.

No 51 – Built by Benjamin Forde[238]
1837 Number 47 – Valuation £15
1849 Number 55
1851 Number 51 – Valuation £11
1901 Census Number 45
1911 Census Number 56
2015 Number 14 Kilbrogan Hill East

Immediate Lessors
? Duke of Devonshire to Benjamin Forde
1836 Joseph Bennett
1851 Joseph Bennett
1858 George Bennett
1892 David Craig

Occupiers
On 15th August, 1836, Benjamin Forde assigned this lease (and others including No 49, 50 and 52) to Joseph Bennet, a pawn broker (the father of George Bennett) for the sum of £754 10/.[239] At the time of the lease agreement in 1836, the occupier was Catherine Donovan, a widow.

---

[238] Registry of Deeds. 1836 16 120
[239] See Appendix. Biographies

In 1837 Catherine Donovan was recorded as the occupier in the valuation record.

William Spiller was resident in 1849.

By 1851 the occupier was William Barter.

Thomas Sullivan had become the occupier in 1856 and shortly afterwards he was succeeded by Thomas G. Walker

In the late 1850s Ellen Mathew had taken up residence.

In the early 1860s Thomas Hornibrook Sullivan became the occupier. He had moved to the property from No 43. He was born in 1806. He remained at the premises until his death on 2nd August 1874, aged 68. His wife Anne continued to reside at the property until 1892 when she was succeeded by Maurice Healy.

An advertisement for the Healy business in 1883

Maurice Healy was living at the premises by the time of the 1901 census along with his wife Margaret and six children, Mary G aged

16, Anne aged 15, Kathleen aged 14, Margaret M aged 11,
Bernadetta aged 10, Patrick John aged 7 plus a servant, Michael
Driscoll. He was a merchant who had been born in Bandon as had
all his children and his wife

Albert Vickery moved in during 1911. He was described in the
census as living with his wife Elizabeth Ann and six children. All
were born in England except for the youngest child, Horace, aged
6 months who was born in Co Cork. Albert was an Army services
staff sergeant major.

Patrick Sheehan took up residence in 1913.

He was succeeded by Emily M. Sheehan in 1932 and in 1933
Patrick Maher became the tenant. Mary J. Maher succeeded in
1951.

No 52 – Built by Benjamin Forde[240] (The Home of George Bennett & Family before they moved to Hill House)

1837 Number 48 - £15
1849 Number 56
1851 Number 52 – Valuation £13
1901 Census Number 46
1911 Census Number 55
2015 Number 15 Kilbrogan Hill East

Immediate Lessors
? Duke of Devonshire to Benjamin Forde
1836 Joseph Bennett
1851 Joseph Bennett

---

[240] Registry of Deeds. 1836 16 120

A lease executed on 15th August, 1836 between Benjamin Forde, Architect, and Joseph Bennett[241] applied to this house as well as No 49, 50 and 51. Joseph paid £754 10/- to Benjamin Forde for various properties including this house which was occupied by James Dixon.

Occupiers

In 1837 the occupier was James Dixon. He served as a member of the Market Jury in 1840 and was living on North Main Street at that time.[242]

Thomas Barter was resident in 1849.

William Sullivan was the occupier in 1851.

Joseph William Bennett, the first child of George Bennett and his wife Catherine Anne Scott Harrison was born at this property on 21st April 1855 at this property. George Bennett's name appeared on the first valuation record in 1856. William Sullivan became the next occupier and shortly afterwards Thomas G. Walker became the tenant. He was followed by Miss Stawell and following her residency up to 1861 Joseph Bennett was recorded as the occupier. The property then remained unoccupied for a time until sometime in the mid 1860s when Ellen Mathew became a resident.

By 1874 Mary Jane Fuller had become the occupier and she was followed in 1877 by John Seymour Theobald.

On 6th October 1882[243] John Seymour Theobald, a shopkeeper, of North Main Street, Bandon was declared a bankrupt.

Theobald was the only son of John Theobald of Spratton Hall, Northampton and his wife Ann Seymour. He married Persis Barter. They had at least one daughter Persis who married John Richard Belcher in New Zealand in 1896. The family moved from this house in 1882 to No 100a. Shortly afterwards he and his family moved to New Zealand and he died there aged 67 on 28th

---

[241] See Appendix. Biographies
[242] Lismore Papers
[243] Freeman's Journal of 25th October 1882

August, 1895.[244] The property was vacant for a while before Zacharius Harris moved in during 1883.

Alexander Harris was the next occupier. His name was recorded in the electoral register of 1884. The property was described as a house with offices, yard and garden at a rateable valuation of £13. He moved out in 1886.

Thomas Cooper, an accountant[245], took up residence in 1890. He was succeeded by Paul Buttimer in 1898, John Shinkwin shortly after followed by Catherine Shinkwin in 1900.

At the time of the 1901 census the occupier was Catherine Shinkwin, a widow living on interest from investments. She was living her with her mother, Mary Murphy, also a widow. They had a servant, Mary Carroll

Catherine Shinkwin, was still at the residence in 1911 and was described as a widow with no children. She was living with her mother, Mary Murphy who had had nine children, two boarders, William Daly, an employee of the Munster Bank and Ernest Phipps, a veterinary surgeon and a servant Kate Hickey.

William Thompson moved into the property in 1919 and he was succeeded by Deegan, RIC in 1922. James O'Mahony was the next occupier in 1923.

---

[244] Papers Past. New Zealand.
[245] Guys Directory of 1893

No 53 – At one time a Teacher Training School

1837 Number 49 – Valuation £20
1849 Number 57
1851 Number 53 – Valuation £13 5s
1901 Census Number 47
1911 Census Number 54
2015 Number 16 Kilbrogan Hill East

1837 Number 49 – Valuation £20
1849 Number 57
1851 Number 53 – Valuation £13 5s
1901 Census Number 47
1911 Census Number 54
2015 Number 16 Kilbrogan Hill East

Immediate Lessors

1851 The Duke of Devonshire
1897 Sir John Arnott

Occupiers

In 1837 the occupier was Mary Baldwin.

Robert Popham was resident in 1849.

The house was unoccupied at the time of the Griffiths Valuation.

By the time of the first valuation in 1856 the Hon and Rev Charles Brodrick Bernard was listed as the tenant and the building was used by the Church of Ireland as a teacher's training school.

In 1858 John Turbitt took up residence. On 15th October, 1859 repairs were made to the house as it had previously been let as a school house. The repairs cost £11.17.8. The annual rental was £13.[246] On 7th August 1860 he had a wall built for 9/-.

---

[246] Berwick's Accounts.

John Turbitt Esq of Bandon had a daughter Mary Anne who married on 13th February 1866 Mr William Wagner of Belfast, son of Richard Wagner Esq, Dunmanway, Co Cork. Mary Anne Turbitt was the granddaughter of Lieutenant Colonel Hugh Gore Edwards, Fintona, ex High Sheriff of Co Tyrone.

John Turbitt emigrated to America in 1868 and left his wife and children in 'embarrassed circumstances' in the house as they were unable to pay the rent. The Devonshire Estate reclaimed the property and recorded a loss of rent of £26 into the accounts.[247]

George Gabriel took up residence when the Turbitt family were evicted. George was given an allowance of £1 from his annual rent for not having possession of his house for a month after the letting was made presumably because the Turbitt family were still occupying the house. George Gabriel was an agent for the Royal and Star Insurance. An entry in the Lismore Papers recorded repairs to the property during his occupancy on 25th March 1868.[248] In 1866 his rent had been increased from £13 to £15 pa and his payments were annual.

The property was vacant in 1871

J. McConkey rented the stable from Mrs A.M. Spiller in 1873

William Anthony M. Spiller Esq became the occupier in 1872. He died aged 68 on 17th January 1874. Letters of Administration were granted on 22nd May, 1874 to his widow Esther Waring Spiller of Hertford House, Plumstead, Kent, the guardian of the grandchildren and legatees. He left effects under £100.

Anna Banfield succeeded William Spiller in 1874. Mrs A. Banfield's name appeared in the Guys Directory of 1893. Previously she had been living with her husband Thomas Banfield at Shinagh. Thomas died on 4th January, 1874. Letters of Administration were granted to Anna on 24th February, 1874 when she was living at Shinagh. Thomas Banfield left effects under £3000.

---

[247] Lismore Papers. MS 7058
[248] Lismore Papers. MS 7058

In the 1901 census Anna Banfield was described as a widow, aged 63, born in Bandon and living on income drawn from land. Her son, Thomas William Hill Banfield, aged 31, born in Bandon on 18th December, 1869 and baptised at Christ Church Kilbrogan, was living with her and was also living from income from land. Kate Desmond, a servant, was living with them. She was also born in Bandon.

At the time of the 1911 census, Thomas William Hill Banfield was living alone at the property on income derived from investments. He had a servant, Mary Burke, born in Co Kerry. Probate was granted in 1920 and Elizabeth A. Levis was the executrix.

The house became vacant in 1916

George[249] took up residence in1917. He was succeeded by John Heron in 1918. He lived for 34 years at the house and was succeeded in 1955 by Gertrude Heron.

---

[249] Surname not known

No 54
1837 Number 50 –
Valuation £20
1849 Number 58
1851 Number 54 –
Valuation £13 5s
1901 Census Number 48
1911 Census Number 53
2015 Number 17 Kilbrogan
Hill East

Immediate Lessors
1851 The Duke of Devonshire

Occupiers
In 1837 the occupier was Margaret Long.

Mrs Hawkes was resident in 1849.

The house was vacant at the time of the Griffiths Valuation in 1851.

By 1856 the Hon & Rev Charles Brodrick Bernard was listed as the tenant and shortly afterwards James Craig took up residence. He was replaced by David Craig in 1864.

David Craig was an Agent for Sir John Arnott. Following the death of Richard Hodson in 1915, he was responsible for collecting the ground rents, tolls etc for the estate along with Samuel Johnston of North Main Street and Daniel Crowley of The Shambles.

In 1884 John T. Johnston's name appeared on the electoral register as a Major in Her Majesty's Army who was occupying four rooms in the house which included a sitting room on the ground foor at the front, a bedroom and dressing room on the first floor in the front and a back room on the first floor at the rear. All were furnished. The house was rated to David Craig at £13 5s and the landlord, David Craig, was also residing at the property. David died on 18th December 1891. His will was proved by Rev Thomas Brown and Rev John James McClure of Duncane, Co Antrim, both Presbyterian ministers. He left effects of £1,699 12s 7d.

In 1893 James Melville Craig replaced David Craig in the valuation records.

At the time of the 1901 census, James Melville Craig was living at the property with his wife, Ellen John and a servant, Catherine Hegarty. There were no children recorded.

In the 1911 census James Melville Craig was still living at the house with his wife Ellen John, two sons Henry Stuart and Marshall Moore and a servant Mary Barry. His occupation was estate steward and he was born in Co Cork. He had four children but only two were still living.

James died on 29th July 1914 at Coolmain, Kilbrittain. Probate was granted at Cork to his widow, Ellen Craig. He left effects of £744 9s 7d.

Mrs Craig succeeded James Craig. The death of Ellen Craig on 16th January 1937 was recorded in the St Patrick's burial records.

No 55
1837 Number 51 – Valuation £15
1849 Number 59
1851 Number 55 – Valuation £10 10s
1901 Census Number 49
1911 Census Number 52
2015 Number 18 Kilbrogan Hill East

Immediate Lessors
1816 Hannah Baldwin from Duke of Devonshire[250] for 99 years
1851 Hannah Grey
1879 Emily Mayne
1905 Richard Wheeler Doherty

Hannah Baldwin entered into a lease with the Duke of Devonshire on 1st April 1816 for the lives of the lessee, Robert Popham and Regina Popham and for 99 years running concurrently at £5 5s. The site was described as a plot whereon an old house was standing in the occupation of Hannah Baldwin measuring 31'6" in breadth at the front and with a depth from front to back of 380'. It was bounded on the west by the street, on the east by a stream dividing Coolfadda from Knockbrogan, on the south by the holding of Benjamin Popham Esq and on the north by a dwelling house and premises of William Rogers.[251]

The lease of 6th June 1879 transferred by Francis Gray (sic) of 34 Dame Lane, Dublin, Trimming Manufacturer to Emily Mayne of Bandon, a spinster. The house was described as having a breadth of 31' 6" with a depth of 380'. The term was for the remainder of the 99 year lease which had commenced on 1st April 1816.

Occupiers
The original house on this site in 1816 was occupied by Hannah Baldwin (It may also have occupied part of the site of an adjoining property)

---

[250] Registry of Deeds 1879 27 214
[251] MS 6189, Lismore Papers

In 1837 the occupier was Susan Wright.

John Payne, a baker and grocer, was recorded as the resident in 1849. He was still in the property in 1851.[252]

By 1856 Frederick Mayne had become the occupier and he was succeeded by Miss Emily Mayne following his death in 1859.

Frederick Mayne was born in 1773 and died aged 86 on 25th December, 1859. He was buried at Christ Church, Kilbrogan. His daughters erected a plaque in his memory in Christ Church. In 1844 he was resident in Callatrim. His eldest daughter, Anna Julia Mayne, married George Hayes of Castle View in 1844 at Brinny Church of Ireland.

Miss Emily Mayne held the property until 1892. The next occupant was Charlotte Young and in 1901 the house was recorded as vacant so no details appeared in the census.

In 1903 William Dineen was the occupier.

William Dineen was still living at the premises during the time of the 1911 census. Also at the property were his wife, Julia, and two adult sons, William who was an unemployed commercial clerk and John who was a commercial clerk in an ironmongery business. William was 74 and was living on interest from personal investments.

In 1922 William was succeeded by John Dineen and by 1935 James Hayes had taken up residence. He was succeeded by Frances Hayes in 1951 and in 1953 the property became vacant. John Lordan became the occupier in 1954.

---

[252] Slater's Directory of 1846

No 56 – Public House – Now Chaplins (part of No 57 - Kilbrogan House - until 1844)

1837 Number 52 – Valuation £12
1851 Number 56 – Valuation £6 5
1901 Census Number 50
1911 Census Number 51
2015 Number 19 Kilbrogan Hill East

Immediate Lessor

1818 John Lawrence Hornibrook[253] (see also No 57)
1844 Richard Lawrence Hornibrook
1844 Michael McCarthy
1885 Allman Dowden & Co (formed in 1885 when Dowden & Co was dissolved)
1938 Beamish and Crawford

The original lease on this property also included Kilbrogan House (No 57). It was for 99 years from 25th March, 1818 for the lives of John Lawrence Hornibrook and his sons, Thomas and Matthew.

Richard Lawrence Hornibrook, of Firville, near Bandon, acquired the lease on 28th September 1844 on the death of his father John Lawrence Hornibrook of Ballynascarthy. His mother was Henrietta Cole Hornibrook.[254]

On 31st December 1844 Richard Lawrence Hornibrook assigned the lease to Michael McCarthy for 61 years to run from 29th September 1844 at an annual rent of £7 10s. The lease passed to Johanna Mahony and on 16th May 1885 she conveyed it to William Shaw of Beaumont, Bandon, MP and James Clugston Allman, brewers both trading as Allman Dowden and Co.[255]

---

[253] See Appendix. Short Biographies.
[254] Registry of Deeds. 1844 17 48 of 28th September 1844
[255] Registry of Deeds. 1885 23 29

In 1858 Nicholas Cole Bowen, aged 39 and upwards of Sunville, Co Cork obtained a judgement against Nicholas Cole Bowen Hornibrook. Nicholas Cole Bowen Hornibrook had disposing power of No 56 and No 57.[256] Nicholas Cole Bowen Hornibrook was a son of John Lawrence and his wife Henrietta (Cole Bowen). Nicholas was Henrietta's brother.

Occupiers
In 1837 the occupier was Michael McCarthy, a publican. He was still the occupier at the time of the Griffiths Valuation in 1856. In 1861 he was succeeded by Johanna Mahony. In about 1886 Simon Sheehan took over. He died on 2nd May, 1900.[257]

By the time of the 1901 census Julia Sheehan was living at the property as a widow and licensed vintner aged 63. Her son Michael was living with her. He was aged 25 and his occupation was assistant rate collector.

In the 1911 census Michael Sheehan was recorded as being in residence with his wife Lizzy and seven children, Julia Mary, aged 6, Margaret Anne, aged 5, Mary aged 4, Kathleen aged 3, Simon Jerome aged 12 and Christina. Michael's occupation was assistant rate collector. His mother Julia Sheehan was living with them. She was aged 75

Mrs Sheehan died on 23rd January, 1915.[258] The valuation records show that Michael took over from Julia in 1915.

In 1935 it became vacant and by 1938 Miss Margaret Coghlan had become the occupier. ? Dolay was recorded as the tenant in 1951 and was succeeded by Edward O'Driscoll in 1961.

---

[256] Registry of Deeds. 1858 37 39
[257] St Patrick's Burial Register.
[258] Ibid

No 57 – Kilbrogan House – (joined with No 56 prior to 1844 and the site of the Kilbrogan Rectory from at least 1766 until the early 1800s)

1775 Number 65 -
1837 Number 53 – Val: £55
1851 Number 57 – Val: £44 10s
1901 Census Number - 51
1911 Census Number – 50
2015 Number 20 Kilbrogan Hill East

Immediate Lessors

1775 John Lapp
1818 John Lawrence Hornibrook[259] from Duke of Devonshire
1856 Richard Lawrence Hornibrook of Firville
1893 Lease to George Thomas Jones
1896 Freehold from Duke of Devonshire to George Thomas Jones
1900 Richard Wheeler Doherty
(This property was never part of Sir John Arnott's holdings)
1922 Jessica Florence Heath (daughter of Richard Wheeler Doherty)
1967 Eugene T. Callanan

Occupiers

A large house, office and garden stood on the site of this property in 1775. It was the only house in the street at the time which had railings at the front of the building. The coach house was shared with the neighbouring properties (No 58 & No 59), the walls of which are still standing. The garden in 1775 incorporated the gardens of No 58 and 59 and the description referred to an orchard, a meadow field and an arable field.

From as early as 1766 the house was used as the Kilbrogan Glebe and was occupied by Rev Dr St John Browne, LLD, who was prebendary, rector and vicar of Kilbrogan and Murragh, rector of Killowen, chancellor of Ross and rector of Innishannon and

---

[259] See Appendix. Short Biographies.

Leighmoney[260]. He was the son of Edward Browne and a younger brother of Jemmett Browne, Bishop of Cork. In 1738 Rev Dr Brown married Amelia St George of Kinsale. He was married a second time to Mrs Elizabeth Hodder. He died in Bandon in 1796. He bequeathed £100 to Christ Church so that the interest could be paid to the poor of Kilbrogan.

Rev Dr Brown had a son, Rev Thomas Adderly Brown who became chancellor of Ross, a son Rev St John Browne, a scholar of Trinity College Cambridge and a son Sir St George Sackville Browne, KCB, Lieutenant General in the East India Service.

Rev John Kenny, LLB succeeded Rev Dr Brown in 1796. As the new glebe was not built until 1813, it is likely that he became the next occupier of the house. He died in 1814 and was buried in Ballymartle. His wife was Mary Herbert of Muckross House.[261]

The house was either completely rebuilt or substantially altered in 1818. John Lawrence Hornibrook entered into a lease for 99 years from 25th March, 1818 for the lives of John Lawrence Hornibrook and his sons Thomas and Matthew.

Adjoining property deeds imply that the occupier of the property in 1816 was William Rogers.

By 1837 the occupier was Lieutenant Colonel Charles Teulon of the 28th Regiment who fought at the Battle of Waterloo[262]. His brother John lived in the next door property (No 58) at that time.

Captain Richard Lane Esq was recorded as the occupier by 1849 and his name appeared again in the records of 1851. His mother, Elizabeth Parker Lane, was living with him when she died on 11th November 1854 aged 81.

Richard was born in 1803 and was the eldest son of Abraham and Elizabeth Parker Lane (formerly Dunscombe of Mount Desert). He died on 27th February 1884 and was buried at Christ Church, Kilbrogan along with his parents. His parents lived in Dublin for a

---

[260] Christ Church, Kilbrogan Records.
[261] The History of Bandon. George Bennett
[262] See Appendix. Biographies

period and in 1831 moved to 2 Devonshire Square, Bandon (now the Hamilton High School). Richard's father was a Burgess of Cork and Sheriff in 1798.

Richard entered Trinity in 1818 and progressed to the Kings Inn in 1821. He became a Captain. He lived at Kilbrogan House up to his death in 1884. He had a brother, Nicholas Dunscombe who practised as a barrister in Liverpool and died there in 1847. Another brother, Abraham B. Lane also studied Law and a sister Sarah married Rev Richard Thomas Meade in 1843. She was one of several other sisters.

In the electoral register of 1884 the property was described as a house with offices, yard and garden. It had a rateable valuation of £44 10s and Richard Lane's name still appeared on the register.

Following Richard Lane's death in 1884 the property passed to Miss Lane.

In 1889 James Hojel became the occupier. James Hojel was County Inspector of the Royal Irish Constabulary, Cork West Riding Force. He had previously served with the Co Fermanagh force. His predecessor as County Inspector was Arthur Curling who lived at No 2 Devonshire Square and remained in the residence following his retirement. (Arthur's predecessors at No 2 Devonshire Square were mostly County Inspectors so James Hojel broke with tradition by residing at Kilbrogan House). He died on 12th November 1891 aged 56. A monument was erected in his memory at Christ Church Kilbrogan by the officers and men of the Cork West Riding Force who had been under his command as well as by men of the County Fermanagh Force.

Alice Hojel, his wife, died on 8th July 1916 aged 83 and was buried with him. She moved out of Kilbrogan House following her husband's death.

Richard Clear[263] occupied the property for a year from 1891 to 1892 and was succeeded by George Thomas Jones, a land agent. On 22nd March, 1893 George Thomas Jones entered into a conveyance with John Lawrence Hornibrook of Charleville, Co

---

[263] See also No 49

Cork and Emma Emelia Hornibrook of No 2126 Arch Street, Philadelphia, USA, a widow, and there was a further conveyance dated 20th March, 1896 between George Thomas Jones and the Duke of Devonshire for the leasehold interest. George Jones sold his interest to Richard Wheeler Doherty for £900 on 16th March, 1900. That sale included the public house next door which was then occupied by the Sheehans.

In 1901 Patrick Joseph McCarthy became the new tenant. He was the son of a solicitor, also Patrick, from Co Limerick. Born in 1858, he was educated at the University and Diocesan Schools at Limerick and at Queen's College Cork. He became articled with J.C. and A. Blake, solicitors in Cork. He was admitted as a solicitor in 1879.

His practice in Bandon was on South Main Street. He was a member of the Bandon Town Commissioners and was chairman for several years. He married Lily, the daughter of Patrick Donegan, JP of Dublin on 11th September, 1894 and they had two sons and four daughters.

A note in the records at this time stated 'no improvements in buildings as reported except green house in garden. Not sufficient to cause increase in value.'

In the 1901 census Patrick Joseph MacCarthy, was described as a solicitor with his wife, Lily, his daughter Marie and two servants, Elizabeth Keating and Norah O'Neill.

Patrick Joseph MacCarthy was still resident in 1911 and was described as a solicitor who was living with his wife Lily M.J, daughter Kathleen, son Cornelius, a domestic servant Mary Flynn. The MacCarthy family moved to No 39 in 1916.

Joseph Brennan succeeded the MacCarthys. On 29th September, 1916 Joseph Brennan senior entered into a lease on the property with Richard Wheeler Doherty for fifty years to mature in 1966 subject to a yearly rent of £40. At the time of the marriage of his son Thomas Brennan to Josephine O'Shea, the daughter of Henry O'Shea of Oldcourt, on 11th October 1923, Joseph put the remaining lease of the property into trust for his remaining life and afterwards for the life of his son Thomas and his heirs.

The family had lived at Hill Terrace in 1887 when Joseph Brennan junior was born. Joseph junior entered the civil service and in 1922 he became the State's first Comptroller and Auditor General. In 1942 he became the first Governor of the Central Bank of Ireland. His signature appeared on the banknotes from 1928 until 1953.[264]

Joseph Brennan junior died on 30th May, 1948 and the remainder of the lease was sold to Dr Eugene Callanan on 6th December 1948. He lived at the property until his death on 3rd August, 1983. His wife, Kathleen Vera Callanan succeeded him and died shortly aftwards on 1st January, 1984.

[264] Bandon Historical Journal. No 16. History of our Currency, from the Pound to the Euro. Sean Connolly

No 58
1775 Number 66 – A slate house which was on the site of both No 58 and No 59
1837 Number 54 – Valuation £28
1851 Number 58 – Valuation £21 10s
1901 Census Number - 52
1911 Census Number – 49
2015 Number 21 Kilbrogan Hill East

Immediate Lessors
1775 John Lapp
1821 Thomas Biggs Esq
1851 Jacob Biggs Esq
1856 William J. Biggs

Occupiers
The slate roofed house which stood on the site of No 58 and No 59 in 1775 was occupied by Richard Gillman.

In 1837 the occupier was John Teulon Esq[265] who was still recorded as resident in 1851 at the time of the Griffiths Valuations.

John Teulon died in 1861 and was succeeded by his son George Beamish Teulon.

George Beamish Teulon was succeeded by A.S. Gore in 1882. His name appeared on the electoral register of 1884. The house was described as having offices, a yard and a garden and had a rateable valuation of £21 10s.

The property was vacant from 1886 until 1888 when Miss Limerick became resident for two years. She was succeeded by George Jones in 1890 and by Mary Jane Baldwin in 1895.

---

[265] See Appendix. Short Biographies

At the time of the 1901 census Mary Jane Baldwin was the occupier. She was living on her own aged 41 and had been born in Kinsale.

Michael Quinlan took up residence in 1905

In the 1911 census Michael was described as living with, his wife, Annie, six children and a servant, Mary Hallahan. Michael was a national school teacher, a daughter Bridget was also a national school teacher and a son John was a managing clerk. The rest of the family were scholars. Michael and his children were born in Co Cork and his wife was born in Kings County.

In 1924 the occupier became the Bank of Ireland. The Bank held the property until 1960.

No 59

1775 Number 66 – a slate house which was on the site of both No 58 and No 59
1837 Number 55 – Valuation £28
1849 Number 63
1851 Number 59 – Valuation £23
1901 Census Number - 53
1911 Census Number – 48
2015 Number 22 Kilbrogan Hill East

Immediate Lessors

1775 John Lapp
1821 Thomas Biggs Esq
1851 Jacob Biggs Esq

Occupiers

In 1837 the occupier was Isaac Biggs.

Mrs Elizabeth Meade was the occupier in 1849.

Mary Bradshaw was recorded as the occupier in 1851. However, as the death was recorded in Bandon in 1850 of Mary Bradshaw aged 75, the widow of Benjamin Bradshaw of Lower Baggot Street, Dublin, the records may not have been up-to-date.

By 1856 the occupier was Charles Peter Teulon.[266]

In 1884 the name of Charles Peter Teulon appeared on the electoral register. The property was described as a house with offices, yard and garden at a rateable valuation of £23.

Charles Peter Teulon died in Bandon in early 1892.

The property became the residence of William M. Newport in 1892.[267]

In the 1901 census William Newport was recorded as a bank accountant aged 51 and widower from Co Kilkenny who was living at the property with his four young children, Elizabeth aged 17, a son Francis aged 16, Robert aged 11 and Garnet aged 9 and a servant, Mary Nash aged 17.

William Newport moved out in 1903 and Richard Neville, a solicitor, became the new occupier.

In the 1911 census Richard Neville was recorded as a solicitor and coroner aged 50 married and living at the time with his daughter Ellen Mary, aged 9, Hannah Mary aged 8, Thomas Anthony aged 6, James aged 5, Gertrude aged 3 and Mary aged 1. The two domestic servants were Mary Riordan aged 18 and Hannah Duggan aged 17.

Richard Neville died on 9th March, 1927. He was succeeded by Mrs Mary Neville. The Representatives of Mrs Neville were registered as the tenants in 1952 and in 1954 Mary Collins resided at the property for one year until 1960.

---

[266] See Appendix. Biographies
[267] Guys Directory of 1893

No 60
1849 Number 64
1851 Number 60 – Valuation £6
1901 Census Number - 54
1911 Census Number – 47

Immediate Lessors
1851 Jeremiah Sexton
1856 Thomas Kingston Sullivan[268]
1884 The Duke of Devonshire

Occupiers
Michael Murphy was the occupier in 1849 and by 1851 Jeremiah Murphy was recorded as the tenant.

By 1856 the occupier was Eugene McCarthy. He was succeeded by Honora McCarthy and in 1860 Marmaduke Brangan and his family took up residence.

The Brangans had moved from an address in Kilbrogan Street. Marmaduke was an attorney's writing clerk and was recorded as such on many deeds relating to North Main Street. He was born on Castle Road, Bandon to Marmaduke and Mary. Marmaduke and his wife Mary had a son Marmaduke baptised on 12th July 1860 (born on Kilbrogan Street), Richard John born on North Main Street on 18th December 1861 and baptised at Christ Church on 26th December, a son John born on 7th March 1863 and baptised on 25th March, a daughter Margaret born on 17th April 1864 and baptised on 27th April, a son Marmaduke baptised on 11th May, 1865 and a daughter Mary Eliza baptised on 25th July 1866, a son Edward born in 1869. The Brangans moved from here to the town hall (No 80).

---

[268] See Appendix. Short Biographies.

In 1864 Thomas Strafford took up residence until 1868. John Reen became the occupier until 1870 when Daniel Desmond moved in. He was succeeded in 1872 by John Forde

John Forde died at his residence on 17th January, 1901 aged 68. His wife died on 4th September, 1922 aged 90. Both were buried at Christ Church, Kilbrogan.

Mary Forde took over from John Forde in 1902.

The 1901 census described Mary Forde aged 68, a widow as the occupier living with Annie E. Bruce aged 37 and also a widow and niece and Elizabeth A. Allen aged 36.

By 1905 Marmaduke Brangan had become the occupier.

The 1911 census records the occupier as Marmaduke Brangan (45), hardware clerk, with wife Elizabeth (43), son Thomas George (3), son Marmaduke (12) and daughter Mary Martha (1).

Marmaduke Brangan and family moved out in 1918 and Rita Boylan became the occupier. She was succeeded by Mary Boylan in 1922 and by Annie Boylan in 1936. In 1949 the occupier became Michael O'Neill. Some time afterwards the property was joined with Number 61.

No 61 – The Old House
1837 Number 56 – Valuation
£27
1851 Number 61 – Valuation
£22 (£13 in 1856)
1860-1864 Military Barracks
1864-1884 Private Residence
1884 – Police Barracks
1901 Census Number
1911 Census Number
1918 – The property reverted
to a house

Immediate Lessors
The date of the original lease from the Duke of Devonshire was
possibly the 1790s
George Cornwall
1851 Thomas Kingston Sullivan

Occupiers
In 1837 Zachariah Cornock Hawkes Esq was the occupier.[269] He
was a landlord who held various properties throughout the
County. He was also a freemason. By 1856 he was recorded as
living at Moneen House which is located near Crossmahon,
Bandon.

Zachariah was born in 1820, the son of John Hawkes and Mary
Cornock and he died on 27th March 1874 at Moneen House. (John
Hawkes junior of Bandon married Mary Cornick, the daughter of
Isaac Cornick Esq of Co Wexford in March 1789[270]).

Zachariah married Henrietta Margaret Long in 1840 and they had
John Hawkes (b 8/11/1841[271]), Zachariah Cornock (b
18/7/1843[272]) and Richard Henry (b 26/7/1844[273]) and Margaret
Louisa (b 26/6/1846). Margaret Louisa was born at North Main
Street which implied that they were resident at the premises until

---

[269] Slater's Directory of 1846
[270] Walkers Hibernian Magazine of 1789
[271] Christ Church, Kilbrogan. Baptism record
[272] Christ Church, Kilbrogan. Baptism record
[273] Christ Church, Kilbrogan. Baptism record

at least 1846. Zachariah's wife died in 1860. He was married again on 2nd June 1860 at Desertserges to Mary Anne Harris.

Thomas Kingston Sullivan was recorded as the tenant in 1849 though may have held the tenancy on behalf of the Tresilian family as he also had possession of the Retreat on the Dunmanway Road in 1849.[274] He lived at the Retreat until he died. His daughter Dorothy died at the age of three in 1849 which he implied that he was not resident at No 61.

Hezekiah O'Callaghan, an accountant and teller at the Provincial Bank from at least 1845[275], was the occupier at the time of the Griffiths Valuation of 1851. He appears to have succeeded Thomas and Jane in 1849. Hezekiah married Catherine Tresilian. Jane, the wife of Thomas Kingston Sullivan was a sister of Catherine, the wife of Hezekiah.

Hezekiah and Catherine moved from No 61 to No 1 when Hezekiah became Manager of the Provincial Bank.

By 1856 George Irwin had become the occupier. George and his wife Jane Maria had a daughter Sarah Elizabeth born on 11th September 1855 while they were resident on North Main Street.

His name was replaced by Thomas Kingston Sullivan in 1860 when the property became a militia barracks.

By 1864 'Militia Barracks' had been crossed out of the valuation record and the occupier became Frederick Delacour Cornwall who also had possession of No 63.

Captain Frederick Delacour Cornwall married Mary Fry, the daughter of Major Fry of the 63rd Regiment and his wife Eliza Amelia. Major Fry was living at No 81 from 1868 until he died on 11th June 1869.

Frederick was the son of William Cornwall who married Jane Delacour in 1807 and was grandson to George Cornwall who

---

[274] See Appendix. Biographies
[275] Southern Reporter, 12th June, 1845. He subscribed to 250 shares in the Cork and Bandon Railway and his position was described as accountant, Provincial Bank.

started the Cornwall brewery business in Bandon. Frederick grew up on Watergate Street where his father, William, ran the brewery with Frederick's uncle George until they both went bankrupt. The business passed to Henry Cornwall, another uncle of Frederick's and brother of William and Georgel.

Frederick and his wife Mary Fry had eight children, Florence Kate baptised on 27th June 1861, Ida Mary baptised on 20th July 1864, Richard Fry b 1865, Frederick William born 1867, Newenham Robert b 1869, Charles Ernest born 1871.

Frederick was recorded in the register of vestrymen at Christ Church, Kilbrogan in 1870. In 1869 Captain Frederick recorded this address as 'The Old House'[276]

The Cornwalls left the property in 1874 and moved to New Zealand where their names first appeared in records in 1875. They had two further children in New Zealand, Frances Mary and Eileen Kathleen.

The Cornwalls were succeeded by widow Stephenson who spent a year at the property. The property became vacant until 1877.

Henry MacDonnell occupied the property from 1877 until 1882 when he emigrated to England. On 27th February, 1882 an auction of his effects was held at the house which was known as "THE OLD HOUSE".

---

[276] Skibbereen Eagle. Christ Church Kilbrogan Vestry Report 3rd April 1869

KILBROGAN HILL, BANDON
IMPORTANT UNRESERVED AUCTION
On
TUESDAY NEXT, FEB 27th, 1862

THOS. McCABE has been favoured with
Instructions by Henry MacDonnell
Esq, on Removal to England, to Sell, by
UNRESERVED AUCTION, on above
date at Eleven o'Clock, at his Residence,
"THE OLD HOUSE" Kilbrogan Hill,
BANDON, all his Superior HOUSEHOLD
FURNITURE and EFFECTS, the Ap-
pointments of Drawing, Dining and Five
Bedrooms, Hall, Study, Pantry, Kitchen
&c., including nearly new richly carved
Walnut Suite, viz., Spring seated Lounger
Easy, Arm, and 6 small Chairs, in rich
brocaded sea-green damask; Brilliant toned
Cottage Piano, in rosewood case; Carved
and Inlaid Walnut Chiffonniere, marble
top, mirror back, and doors; beautifully
carved Ebonized Gilt Chimney Mirror,
Framed Engravings, New Brussels Carpet
and Rug, Cocoa Matting Tarpaulins, Win-
dow Hangings, Centre, Dining, Work and
Chess Tables; Dining, Arm, and Folding
Chairs; Massive Side board, Glass Book
Case, Chest Drawers, Chiffonniers, solid
mahogany nearly new Writing Table, Slope,
and 9 Drawers, in perfect order: Office
Chair, Iron Safe, Letter Copying Press,
Hat and Umbrella Stand, Hall Chairs,
Fowling Piece, Dinner Ware, China and
Glass, Plated Cruits, Butter Cooler, &c,
Enamelled Bedsteads, Cots, Prime Feather
Beds, Best Hair Mattresses, Dressing
Tables, Stands, Ware, Glasses, Chests
Drawers, &c. KITCHEN – Press, tables,
Chairs, Drainer, Utensils, American Stove
and Fittings, New Green-house (17 ft 3 In.
Long. 9 ft 5 in. wide, and 7 ft high glass
roof and front, large centre 5 Tier Flower
Stand, Choice Exotica, fine Stock Bees in
new bar-framed hive; Garden Net, Wheel-
barrows, Parambulator, Implements and a
great variety of other valuable property.
Carpenters Tools &c. See Posters.
THOMAS McCABE,
Auctioneer, Valuer, &c,
The Auction Mart, Bandon   (178)

In 1884 the building became a police barracks. It was newly roofed and part of 61 was added at the rear. This description applied to No 61 and 63.

In 1888 a note was added to the records stating that the police had returned. In 1898 another note appeared in the records stating that the constabulary had returned. Police Barracks was crossed out and Constabulary Barracks inserted. The references are for 61 and 62. Number 62 became No 63 in the records.

The building did not revert to a house until 1918 when M.C. Healy took up occupancy. He remained at the property until his death. His representatives succeeded him in 1939. Margaret Healy was the tenant in 1941. Mrs Jessica Heath was recorded as the tenant in 1945. Michael Mehigan held the tenancy in 1953 and in 1955 James McElligott became the occupier.

Michael O'Neill purchased the property in 1959 and consolidated 60 and 61.

No 62 – House, office, yard (No 62 and No 63 switch numbers in about 1900)

1849 Number 66
1856 Number 62
1901 census no 56
1911 census no 45
2015 Number 17 Kilbrogan Hill West

Immediate Lessor

Deeds imply that this property was leased for a time to George Cornwall, the brewer who died in 1825. The leasehold interest was sold to Richard Exham Esq, a solicitor, by auction in 1839.[277]

1851 Thomas Kingston Sullivan
1849 Next door were stores belonging to Thomas Kingston Sullivan.
1897 Sir John Arnott

Occupiers

At the time of the Griffiths valuation in 1851 the Constabulary Force was the tenant. The property was used as a police barracks.

By 1856 the occupiers were described as 'lodgers' and the valuation was £8. In about 1860 William Brewster moved in for a short time. John Goldsmith became the next occupier.

John Goldsmith was succeeded by Michael Bergin in 1868 and by Thomas Dixon in 1867. Samuel Cottrell moved to No 62 from No 33 in 1870 and spent just one year at this property. It is not known where he was resident between 1870 and 1874. In 1874 he took up residence in No 70 and remained at that property until 1880. Michael Bergin became the occupier for a short period.

Marmaduke Brangan took up residence in 1871.

---

[277] Southern Reporter. 19th January 1839

In 1893 John Brangan succeeded Marmaduke Brangan and the No was recorded as 63.

In the 1901 census John Brangan was described as aged 38, a drapers clerk, Church of Ireland, living with his wife, Sarah aged 39

John G Brangan was still in residence at the time of the 1911 census and was described as aged 48, a draper's assistant and as living with his wife Sarah aged 47.

In 1918 Mrs Brangan was recorded as the occupier and in 1922 the property passed to Elizabeth Brangan. Violet Shorten took on the property in 1928 in followed by David Wright in 1931, in 1934 James Lynch and in 1938 James Burke. He was succeeded by Mrs Ruth Harpur in 1939 and in 1949 James Burke became the occupier once again.

No 63 – A Store at the rear of No 61
1856 Delapidated Store

In 1860 the building was described as a militia store. The number becomes No 62 in the valuation records and by 1900 was grouped together with No 61.

No 64 – Kays Flowers
1837 Number 58 - £22
1849 Number 68
1851 Number 64 - £17 10s
1856 to 1884 – A barracks offices and yard
1901 Census Number - 57
1911 Census Number – 44
2015 Number 16 Kilbrogan Hill West

Immediate Lessors
1824 George Cornwall – 99 year lease (He died in 1825)
1839 Rev Thomas Waugh
1851 Rev Thomas Waugh
Hannah Hope Belcher (daughter of Rev Thomas)
1884 William Belcher, MD

Robert Tresilian Belcher became the sole assignee in bankruptcy of the estate and effects of George and William Cornwall, bankrupts, who had traded under the name of George and William Cornwall, brewers, malsters, dealers and chapmen. The premises had been demised by the Duke of Devonshire to their father, George Cornwall on 23rd January 1824 for 99 years at a yearly rent of four pounds payable half yearly.

On 15th January 1839 Robert Tresilian Belcher sold the premises to Rev Thomas Waugh[278], a preacher in the Wesleyan Church, for £160. The details of the lease recorded that the premises was on the west side of North Main Street and was 40' in width at the front and with a depth from front to rear of 320', bounded on the east by North Main Street and on the west by the lands of Coolfadda. Other holdings of George Cornwall Esq deceased bounded the property on the north and on the south, the property was held by George Kingston Esq deceased. The Cornwall interest in the holdings to the north of No 64 was purchased by Richard Exham Esq, solicitor.

---

[278] Rev Waugh lived at the Lodge, Bandon. He died at his residence on 6th May 1873 aged 88. In 1834 his address was the City of Limerick. (ROD 1834 14 266)

199

Reference is made in the deed to the passage on the north side of the premises which was described in the deed as 7' wide and which ran between the property and the premises owned by the bankrupt William Cornwall on the north side.

Thomas Kingston Sullivan was a party to the passage for the lives of John Popham of Bandon, Benjamin Popham and Bradshaw Popham, 2nd, 3rd and 4th sons of John Popham of Bandon deceased who were named in the original indenture and for the residue of the term of 99 years and lives, Thomas Kingston Sullivan and his heirs had a right of passage through the gateway.

Occupiers
In 1837 the occupier was Rev William Stewart

Mrs D Nash was recorded as the resident in 1849. There was a note attached to the valuation record to deduct the rent of the gateway

The occupier was John Sullivan at the time of the Griffiths Valuation in 1851.

By 1856 the premises was used as barracks offices and yard.

It continued to be a barracks until 1884 when it reverted to a house and Hannah Hope Belcher became the occupier. Hannah was the daughter of Rev Thomas Waugh who held the lease. She married Henry Belcher Esq at St Mary's Shandon on 1st May, 1828[279].

Alfred Leonard moved in during 1886. He had been living at No 73 from 1881 to 1886. His wife was Mary (Minnie) Kingston Sullivan, a daughter of William Connor Sullivan and a niece of Thomas Kingston Sullivan.

The Leonards were succeeded by Patrick Curley in 1894. He lived at the property for two years. In 1896 Jane Whiting moved in and spent one year in residence. Thomas Walsh succeeded her in 1897 and John Popham in 1898. John was in the property for three years and in 1901 it passed to William Hennis.

---

[279] Cork Constitution. 3rd May 1828

In the 1901 census William H. Hennis was described as aged 55, a private gentleman, living with wife Charlotte E aged 46, daughter, Francis I Hennis aged 13, daughter Charlotte E aged 12, son William H aged 4 and Jane Shorten, servant, aged 17

John H. Hennis took over from William in 1902 and in 1905 William James Lee moved in.

In the 1911 Census William James Lee was described as aged 46, a grocer, merchant, wife Emily Lee (39), daughter Iris Aline Lee (2) and servant Hannah O'Brien (20)

Thomas B Levis moved in during 1914. John Healy succeeded him in 1935. Patrick Staunton became the occupier in 1960.

No 65
1837 Number 59 - £13
1849 Number 69
1851 Number 65 - £7 15s
1901 Census Number - 58
1911 Census Number – 43
2015 Number 14 Kilbrogan Hill West

Immediate Lessors
George Kingston Esq
1851 The Duke of Devonshire

George Kingston Esq is recorded as the lessor of the property in a deed of 1840[280].

---

[280] ROD. 1830 14 286

Occupiers

In 1837 the occupier was Anne Sealy.

Miss Mary Cole Bowen was resident in 1849 and was still the occupier at the time of the Griffiths Valuation of 1851.[281]

By 1856 the occupier had become James Mahony. He was succeeded by William Peyton, a blacksmith, who moved to this address from No 15. On 16th March 1867 William Peyton died. His will was proved by Mary Peyton, widow and sole executrix. He left effects of under £20. The lease passed to Thomas Peyton. Ralph Peyton succeeded Thomas in 1871. Thomas Peyton was recorded as the tenant in 1876.

In 1883 Thomas Peyton was no longer at the property and no Peytons lived on North Main Street after that date.

The building was re-roofed in 1883 and was subsequently vacant for a short time. In 1884 Mary Eaton took up residence.

Francis Banfield became the next occupier in 1886. Francis remained in the property until 1892 when Mrs Gillman was recorded as the resident. John Walsh became the occupier in 1894

In the 1901 census John Walsh was described as aged 64, a draper, living with his daughter Margaret, governess, aged 28, son, William aged 24 (law clerk), daughter Mary (school teacher) aged 20, daughter Annie (milliner), aged 17, daughter Frances aged 11, mother in law, Mary White aged 81 and sister in law, Margaret White aged 48

William J. Walsh aged 34 was the occupier at the time of the 1911 census. A solicitor's managing clerk, he was living with his aunt Margaret M Walsh (38), sister Margaret M Walsh (38), sister Mary E Walsh (30) – school teacher, sister Annie A Walsh (27), sister Frances M Walsh (21) – book keeper and cousin Edward John Murphy (3)

---

[281] She may have been a daughter of Rev Nicholas Cole Bowen (see biographies)

The house occupier was recorded as the Representatives of William J. Walsh in 1952 and by Catherine Walsh in 1954.

No 66
1837 Number 60 – Valuation £15
1849 Number 70
1851 Number 66 – Valuation £10 5s
1901 census Number – 59
1911 Census Number – 42
2015 Number 13 Kilbrogan Hill West

1837 Number 60 – Valuation £15
1849 Number 70
1851 Number 66 – Valuation £10 5s
1901 census Number – 59
1911 Census Number – 42
2015 Number 13 Kilbrogan Hill West

Immediate Lessors
1820 Joseph Williams (from the Duke of Devonshire) – 41 years

The Lismore papers recorded that the original lease of 28th December, 1820 to Joseph Williams, Cotton Manufacturer, was surrendered on 23rd October, 1852 by Jane Anne Hayes who had assumed title from Joseph Williams. The property was described as being on the west side of North Main Street with Mr King's field at the rear. The lease was for the lives of Rev Richard B. Bernard and the Hon W.S. Bernard and 41 years at a rent of £7 19s. The plot was described as having a breadth at the front of 31' and a depth of 136'.

Occupiers
In 1837 the occupier was Richard Williams and he was still in residence in 1849. He was paying an annual rent of £7.

Janes Anne Hayes was the occupier in 1851. She surrendered the lease in 1852. By 1856 the occupier was George O'Connor. Miss Loane moved in during 1858.

In 1883 a new roof was put on to the house. Miss Giveen took up residence and was succeeded in 1886 by the Webbs. In 1888 Mrs Eaton became the new occupier and she remained in the premises until 1897.

In the census of 1901 Patrick Murphy (national teacher), aged 40 was the occupier and was living with his wife Margaret (36), Timothy J (14) son (book keeper), son John T aged 13 (cycle maker), daughter Margaret (10), daughter Kathleen (8), daughter Elizabeth (6), daughter Cecilia (4), son Patrick (2) and daughter Jane.

Patrick Murphy was succeeded by Bartholomew Murphy in 1906 and by William Murphy in 1911.

In the 1911 census Hanora Murphy (73) was resident with her daughter Mary Murphy (33) and son William Murphy (33) – commercial clerk, wine and spirit business.

Hanora Murphy was listed as the occupier in the valuation record of 1916. Mary Murphy took up residence in 1921 and by 1922 the house was vacant for a while before Charles Crowley moved in during 1923. The representatives of Charles Crowley were registered in 1960 and in 1961 Kathleen Crowley was recorded as the occupier.

No 67
1837 Number 61 - £20
1849 Number 71
1851 Number 67 - £15 15s
1901 Census Number- 60
1911 Census Number – 41
2015 Number 12 Kilbrogan Hill West

Immediate Lessors
The Representatives of Attiwell Roche
1858 George Roche
1884 Marmaduke Brangan

Occupiers
In 1837 the occupier was Henrietta Hornibrook.

William Gore Brett was registered as the occupier in 1849.

The property was unoccupied at the time of the Griffiths Valuation in 1851

In 1856 John Keys was the tenant before moving to No 71 where he remained until 1861 and after which he moved to No 43.

Rev Samuel Shaw moved in very shortly afterwards.

George Thomas Evans took up residence during 1858.

Rev Richard Hussey Loane became the occupier in 1860 and stayed at the house until 1864. (He had been resident at No 80 in 1851). On 6th August 1860 Rev Richard and his wife Jane had a son George Bradshaw Loane born on 9th July 1860 and baptised at Christ Church on 6th August. His occupation was recorded as curate of the parish.

Mrs E.M. Sweeney took up residence during 1864. She stayed for 19 years until 1883.

William Connor Sullivan JP became the occupier in 1883. His name appeared on the electoral register of 1884 as the occupier of the property which was described as a house with offices, yard and small garden at a rateable valuation of £20. At the same time he was also the occupier of a tannery and house on Watergate Street.[282]

In 1884 Denis O'Sullivan, an Inland Revenue Officer, was renting two rooms in the house; a sitting room in the front of the ground floor and a bedroom at the rear of the first floor.

William Connor Sullivan died two years later in 1886 at which time Major Johnson became the occupier. Three years afterwards, John D. Swan moved in and stayed for eight years. He was an accountant at the Provincial Bank at No 1.

Mr Swan's successor was Samuel Lovell who took up the tenancy in 1897.

Samuel Lovell was aged 45 at the time of the 1901 census and was described as an Officer of Inland Revenue residing with his wife Annie Lovell aged 35. The property was described as first class with seven windows at the front and eight rooms occupied by the family.

The Lovells spent eight years in the house and were succeeded in 1905 by David Rafferty. The next occupier was Mary A Cox in 1907 followed by Edward William Carrette in 1911. He was the Head Post Master.

By the time of the 1911 census, Michael Collins was the occupier. Aged 55, a stove clerk and ex sergent RIC, he was living in the house with wife Ellen (45), son Thomas J. (clerk)(23), son James (clerk) (20), daughter Helena (17), daughter Susan (seamstress) (16), son Michael C (15) (assistant at grocers shop), daughter Kate (13), son Cornelius (11), son Lawrence Edward (10), daughter Margaret A (8), daughter Bridget A (6), son Leo Anthony (5), son Joseph G (4) and Ita Gertrude Collins (2).

---

[282] See Appendix. Biographies

Michael Collins and family continued in occupation for many years. The representatives were registered as the tenant in 1950. In 1954 the tenant was Ita Collins and by 1959 the property had become vacant.

No 68 (69 is a garden and passage)
1837 Number 62 – Valuation £30
1849 Number 72
1851 Number 68 – Valuation £23
1901 Census Number - 61
1911 Census Number – 40
2015 Number 11 Kilbrogan Hill West

Immediate Lessors
1851 The Representatives of Attiwell Roche
1867 The Representatives of John Tresilian Belcher

John Tresilian Belcher died on 9th October, 1864 in Bandon. He was a solicitor. His sole executrix was Fanny Coleman Tresilian Belcher. He left effects of under £3000.

Occupiers
In 1837 the occupier was recorded as Robert Tresilian Belcher, a Justice of the Peace.

In the pre-valuation records of 1849, the year of Robert's death, he was still recorded as the occupier at an annual rent of £17. The house had fowl house, scullery, laundry and coal house. He was also recorded as the tenant of Number 73, a house with a gate.

Robert died in 1849 and was succeeded by his wife Alicia who was still recorded as the occupier in 1851.

Robert and Alicia's son, John Tresilian Belcher, had become the tenant by the time of the first valuation records in 1856, the year of his marriage to Fanny Coleman Rogers.

Fanny's father, Robert Rogers, served as a Lieutenant at the Battle of Waterloo with the 2nd Battalion of the 30th Foot. He was posted to County Cork in 1817 in anticipation of leaving active service. On 18th October 1817, he married Elizabeth Coleman at St Nicholas Church of Ireland in Cork. Elizabeth was the daughter of Patrick Coleman, a master builder of Bandon. She was one of eight children. Fanny spent the first twelve years of her life up to 1831 at No 2 Devonshire Square. The Rogers moved from Devonshire Square to Kilbrogan Street. In 1843 the family moved to Galway as her father, Robert, was appointed as a staff officer of pensions. In 1851 he moved to Amhertsburg, Ontario with some of the family. Fanny remained in Ireland

Fanny and John had six children; John Tresilan Belcher born on 28th June 1855, Fanny Elizabeth Tresilian born on 13th April 1857 and baptised at Christ Church on 5th May 1857, twins, Theresa Tresilian and William Henry Tresilian born on 4th January 1859, Alice Tresilian Pearson born on 30th November 1851, Robert Naylor Tresilian born on 3rd October 1853.

John senior died at this residence on 9th October, 1864 aged 38. The property passed to William Arthur Hendley. He lived at the property for three years until 1868.

In 1869 Captain Henry Lucas moved into the premises and was resident until 1876. His wife had a daughter on 15th September 1873 whilst they were living at this address. He was recorded in the register of vestrymen at Christ Church, Kilbrogan in 1870.

In 1876 Captain Lucas was succeeded by Thomas Rodwell. He was in residence until 1886 after which the house was vacant for two years. Thomas's name appeared in the electoral records of 1884. The property was described as a house with offices and a yard. The rateable valuation was £23. The garden and paddock were separately assessed at a rateable valuation of £4 5s.

Francis J. Levis became the occupier during 1888 and was in residence until 1891. George Levis succeeded him and was in residence until 1893.

William H. Yeates held the tenancy for a year between 1893 and 1894. He was succeeded by John R. Kerr who spent five years at the house before moving to No 71.

William Henderson, a veterinary surgeon, became the next occupier in 1899

In the 1901 census William Henderson was described as a, veterinary surgeon, aged 37, living with his wife Sarah aged 33, daughter Agnes Johnstone Henderson, aged 8, daughter Mary Adeline Henderson aged 6, son John William Henderson aged 3 and Emily Scott Henderson aged 2. They were Presbyterian. In addition, they had two servants Mary Cuddy, aged 21 and John O'Brien aged 15. The property was described as having nine windows at the front and thirteen rooms occupied by the family.

Major Hosford was recorded as the occupier for a short period.

In the 1911 Robert Tottenham was described as aged 45, a Major in the Indian Army living with his wife Hilda (31), daughter Mavis (11), daughter May (10), daughter Lynda (7), a visitor Rennee Parkinson and servants Kate Hennessy (20), and Abina Hennessy (18)

Timothy Coffey assumed the tenancy during 1913 and was in residence until 1924. He was a JP. William Murray succeeded him. His representatives were recorded in 1940 and in 1942 the tenant was registered as Mrs Bridget Murray. Mrs Ellen became the occupier in 1956.

No 69 – garden and passage

No 70
1837 Number 63 – Valuation
£14
1849 Number 73
1851 Number 70 – Valuation
£10
1901 Census Number - 62
1911 Census Number – 39
2015 Number 10 Kilbrogan Hill
West

Immediate lessors
1851 The Representatives of Attiwell Roche
1864 George Roche (eldest son of Attiwell)
1874 Thomas Kingston Sullivan

Occupiers
In 1837 the occupier was Elizabeth Jenkins.

Robert Belcher was the occupier in 1849. (See also No 68 as the family lived in both properties).

John Tresilian Belcher was the occupier in 1851.

At the time of the first valuation record in 1856 the Representative of Robert Tresilian Belcher was the occupier.

In 1864 the occupier was still listed as the Representatives of Robert Tresilian Belcher. Robert died on 18th October, 1849. Robert's widow, Alicia Tresilian Belcher, continued to live at the address following her husband's death until 1867.

An advertisement appeared in the newspaper of March 1867 to sell the contents of this house on Kilbrogan Hill on Friday, 22nd March 1867 at noon on the instruction of Mrs Belcher.

Items included a piano by Ralph Allison & son, tapestry, carpets, engravings, book cases, books, a new carriage for one or two horses, a thorough bred setter dog, donkey, but and harness, fancy pigeons as well as tables chairs, curtains, blinds, beds etc.

Following the sale of the contents of her house, Alicia moved to 11 Belgrave Street, Commercial Road, Stepney, London to live with her son, Robert who was a customs officer[283] and to be close to her daughter, Margaret's, family. Margaret married Stewart Tresilian, also a customs officer in London, on 2nd May, 1866.

John Stephenson moved into the premises in 1867 and had left by 1870. He was recorded in the register of vestrymen at Christ Church, Kilbrogan in 1870. He died on 9th July, 1874. His wife was a Miss Beamish of the family who owned Beamish and Crawford Brewery.

The house was vacant for a period in 1873. Samuel Cottrell became the next occupier and remained for six years from 1874 until 1880.

Thomas Cooper, an accountant, took up residence during 1880 and remained at the property until 1890 when he took up residence at No 52. He was succeeded at No 70 by Mrs Levis who lived at the house until 1895 when Rev Jeremiah Coughlan became the occupier.

In the 1901 census Jeremiah Coghlan was described as aged 43, a Roman Catholic curate living with Mary Coghlan, his mother, aged 76, Daniel Coghlan, a nephew aged 17 and Mary Magnihan, a domestic servant and house maid aged 26. The property was described as a second class house with four windows at the front and eight rooms occupied.

Michael Sullivan became the next occupier in 1903 and he was succeeded in 1906 by Albert Wyatt who spent four years at the house. In 1910 Andrew Ganly moved in. He was succeeded by William Creagh in 1911.

William Creagh was described in the 1911 census as a bank clerk (30), living with his wife Christina (30), a visitor Walter Purcell, a solicitor (26) and Mary Kate Dalton (28), servant

---

[283] UK Census of 1871

Mr Chappens became resident during 1917 and he was succeeded by Mrs J.B. Levis in 1918. Edward William Carrette followed in 1919 and was in residence until 1932[284] when Thomas Good became the occupier. He was succeeded by Elizabeth Good in 1934. Jane Bradfield became the next tenant in 1952 and in 1960 Mary K. Good was recorded as the occupier.

No 71
1837 Number 64 – Valuation £18
1849 Number 74
1851 Number 71 – Valuation £14 10s
1901 Census Number – 63
1911 Census Number – 38
2015 Number 9 Kilbrogan Hill West

Immediate Lessors
1851 The Representatives of Attiwell Roche (George Roche)
1856 John Keys
? George Roche
? Thomas Kingston Sullivan

Occupiers
In 1837 the occupier was Mary Hornibrook.

Rev Dominick Murphy was the occupier in 1849.

In 1851 Grace Beazley was recorded as the tenant. She was a widow and she took possession of the house on 25th March 1851 at a rent of £16 per annum. The house had been let previously to Rev William Johnson who had died. She was given the house in good

---

[284] Edward Carrette died on 12th April 1935 and his wife Jane died on 20th February 1914. They were buried at St Peters, Ballymodan.

order with blind rollers and was to be responsible for all taxes with the exception of the landlord's part of the poor rate. Her annual rental of the house was extended until 29th September 1852 on the provision that she gave notice of her departure by 1st July 1852 and if not, she would assume a yearly tenancy.

The next occupier was Robert Henry Howard and his wife Louisa. They had a daughter Mary Julia, born on 30th October 1856 and baptised at Christ Church Kilbrogan on 11th March, 1857. His occupation was recorded as gentleman.

Thomas Keys was the occupier in the 1850s and he was succeeded by Thomas Hamilton. Thomas and his wife Frances Mary had a son Frederick Miller Hamilton born on 19th May 1859 and baptised at Christ Church on 27th May. Thomas's occupation was recorded as Sub Inspector of the Constabulary.

David Jermyn succeeded the Hamiltons in 1861 and he remained in the house until 1886. David and his wife Anne had a daughter Anne born on 4th January 1863 and baptised at Christ Church on 25th January 1863. His occupation was recorded as school master of a Training Institution. Their daughter Elizabeth Jane was born on 26th August 1864 and baptised on 28th September.

David was recorded in the register of vestrymen at Christ Church, Kilbrogan in 1870. His name appeared on the electoral register of 1884 and the property was described as a house with offices, yard and a garden. It had a rateable valuation of £14 10s.

In 1890 Miss Norcot moved into the house and she was succeeded by Francis J. Levis in 1895. In 1898 John K. Kerr became the occupier.

John K. Kerr was described in the 1901 census as aged 40, a Presbyterian Civil Engineer who was living with wife Janet, Church of Ireland, aged 37 and son Robert, Presbyterian aged 10, daughter Mary aged 6, daughter Annie aged 3 and a governess Helena aged 24 and servant Minnie Crowley aged 25. The property was described as a first class house with eight windows at the front and eight rooms occupied.

Edwin Pope became the occupier in 1905[285] and was succeeded in 1910 by Frederick W. Vereker.

The 1911 census recorded Frederick Vereker as the occupier, aged 38, a civil engineer who was living with his wife Margaret aged 28 and a servant Norah Hawkes aged 23.

A newspaper advertisement of 1926 offered an exceptionally attractive and well appointed residence held free of rent forever to be sold by auction on 20th July 1926 with instructions from F.W. Vereker Esq.

[285] A burial of Susan Wood Pope aged 14 months of Kilbrogan HIll was recorded in St Peter's Ballymodan on 5th October 1903.

Kilbrogan Hill, Bandon
EXCEPTIONALLY ATTRACTIVE AND
WELL-APPOINTED
RESIDENCE
HELD FREE OF RENT

J.P. JEFFERS
Is favoured with instructions from F.
W. Vereker, Esq., to sell by auction
On Tuesday, 29th July, 1925, the interest
In this particularly desirable Residential
Property, held Free of Rent for ever.
The House is substantially built, and
in excellent order. The accommodation
Includes Drawing-Room, Dining and
Morning-Rooms, 4 Bedrooms, Bathroom
(H & C), Hot Press, Kitchen, Sculler
ies, Cool Larder, etc,: lit throughout with
Electric Light, and with all modern con-
veniences. The Premises are well designed with front and back staircases.
There is a well-enclosed Garden, nicely
stocked with Tomato House, Tool house
etc., an extensive Fowl Run, and a useful Yard, with side entrance.
The situation is exceptionally attractive, the windows and garden commanding fine views of the river and surrounding countryside. The Residence has for
many years been occupiedby the engin-
eers of the Railway Co., and is now being
sold owing to the amalgamation of the railway lines.
No Rent. No Landlord. Low Rates
Cards to View from Undersigned.
Sale on the Premises at 12 o'clock
Usual Deposit required. Particulars and
Conditions from
P.J. O'Driscoll, Sols. Bandon

Patrick Crowley became the occupier in 1930. The property became vacant in 1959 and in 1960 Eileen Stevens assumed the tenancy.

No 72
1837 Number 65 – Valuation £15
1849 Number 75
1851 Number 72 – Valuation £8 10s
1901 Census Number - 64
1911 Census Number – 37
2015 Number 8 Kilbrogan Hill West

Immediate Lessors
1851 The Representatives of Attiwell Roche
? Thomas Kingston Sullivan
? Sir John Arnott

Occupiers

In 1837 the occupier was William McCreight. He was the son of William McCreight. He had sister Ann who married John Revell Drury in 1836. William lived for a time at Ummera House on the banks of the Argideen River near Timoleague. He served as a member of the Timoleague Famine Relief Committee. His father in law was James Baldwin of Lisnagat (William married Mary Milner Baldwin of Lisnagat in 1836).[286]

David Scott, a Medical Doctor was the occupier from at least 1849 until 1856.

By 1856 the occupier was Maria Ormston and between 1856 and 1861 there were a number of residents. John Keyes succeeded Maria Ormston. John Morris became the next occupier and he was succeeded by Anthony G. Sedley who moved out in 1860.

William Cornwall spent one year at the property from 1860 to 1861. He was aged 69 at that time.

---

[286] Baldwins of Lisnagat by Alexandra Buhagiar

William married Jane Delacour in 1807 and had six children. He was the brother of Henry and George. His father was George Cornwall, who started the Cornwall brewery in the 1700s. His son Captain Frederick Delacour Cornwall and family were living at No 61 and 63 for ten years from 1864 until 1874 after which they moved to New Zealand.

In 1861 William Cornwall moved into No 73. Dennis Cummins succeeded him at No 72 and he remained in residence for eight years until 1869.

Edward Henry Alcock became the occupier in 1869. He was succeeded by Alexander Alcock and then by Jane Nash in 1870 who was, in turn, succeeded by Henry Cornwall Nash in 1874, a relative of William Cornwall who had lived in the house from 1860 to 1861

Henry Cornwall Nash was baptised on 24th March 1821 at Brinny Church of Ireland. He was the son of the miller and landowner, John Nash of Brinny House who had married Elizabeth Cornwall, the sister of George Cornwall of Bandon, the brewer and malster. Henry married Sara Elizabeth Johnson on 10th October, 1854 at Knockavilly Church of Ireland. She was the daughter of Rev William Johnson. Henry was recorded as a land commissioner and farmer of Glenview, Upton. Henry and his wife were reorded as the tenants in the 1880s. Sara died on 12th June 1896.

In the 1884 electoral records for the Borough of Bandon Bridge Henry Cornwall Nash of Glenview, Upton, was recorded as the 'occupier, inhabitant, householder or lodger' of this property which was described as having offices and a yard at a rateable valuation of £8 10s. Henry lived at Glenview and was most likely leasing this house for family members.

In 1895 Maria Anne Ormston became resident in the property and by 1900 she was joined by Mrs Coughlan. Maria Anne's parents were Richard and Elizabeth Tresilian. Richard was a wine and spirit merchant.

Maria Anne was one of a family of eight. Her brother, Stewart Richard, lived with his family at No 82 from shortly after his wedding in 1852 until he died in 1885.

In 1849 Maria Anne Tresilian married Dr Henry Ormston who was the brother of Catherine and Jane Hawkesby Ormston. Amongst their children they had Robert Henry who was born in 1856 and who became a doctor like his father. Robert died in 1896 of malarial fever.

Maria Anne Ormston was described in the 1901 census as aged 83, a widow, living on own interest with Dora Sullivan aged 86, her sister, also a widow. Also living in the house was Nora O'Brien aged 24, a servant. The property was described as second class with five windows at the front and seven rooms occupied.

Dora was the widow of William Connor Sullivan who she married in 1838. They lived for a period at Overton. William died in 1886 in Bandon. Dora and William had four children, Hester who married Rev William Livingston Leachman and emigrated to the US, Richard who became a doctor and emigrated to Australia, Minnie Kingston who married Major Alfred Richard Leonard and John who married Emily Rose Leonard.[287]

Maria Anne Ormston died in 1907 and was buried at Christ Church, Kilbrogan.

James Porter assumed the tenancy during 1905 and he was succeeded by John Jones in 1909.

In the 1911 census John Jones was described as aged 72, a builder who was living with his wife Margaret (70), a son John Jones (35) builder and Nora Jones, a daughter in law (28)

In 1915 John Jones's name appeared in the Cork and Munster Trade Directory as a builder and contractor.

The Jones continued to live at the house until 1946 when Mrs Nora Jones was recorded as the occupier. The Cork Diocesan Trustees took up the tenancy in 1960.

---

[287] See Appendix. Biographies

No 73
1837 Number 66 - £13
1849 Number 76
1851 Number 73 - £8 10s
1901 Census Number - 65
1911 Census Number – 36 –
divided into two
2015 Number 7 Kilbrogan Hill
West

Immediate Lessors
1851 The Representatives of
Attiwell Roche
1860s George Roche
? Thomas Kingston Sullivan
1890 The Duke of Devonshire
1897 Sir John Arnott

Occupiers
In 1837 the occupier was Susan Popham

The property was vacant in 1849.

Anne Hornibrook was recorded as the occupier in 1851.

William Cornwall became the occupier between 1854 and 1861.
He was the brother of George and Henry, brewers and malsters.
William and George became bankrupt in 1837.

In 1861 William moved to No 75. He was succeeded in No 73 by
Thomas Poole who was recorded as the occupier from 1861 until
1870.

William Fuller was listed as the occupier from 1870 to 1872 and it
then passed to Mary Jane Fuller who was resident from 1872 to
1874.

Francis Stephenson Hoyte was listed as the occupier in 1874. He
was a division officer in the Revenue Department.

In 1881 Alfred Leonard took up residence for five years. He was
an accountant. Alfred married Minnie, the second daughter of
William Connor Sullivan and his wife Dora (Tresilian), at Christ
Church, Kilbrogan on 25th November 1876. He was the son of
Major Leonard of the Royal Marines. Alfred was recorded on the
1884 electoral register. The property was described as a house
with offices, a yard and a small garden. It had a rateable valuation
of £8 10s.

William Connor Sullivan's family succeeded Alfred Leonard in
1886.[288] (William died in 1886) They remained in the house for
two years and were succeeded by Mrs Webb in 1888. William's
widow was living with her sister, Maria Anne, in No 72 at the time
of the 1901 census.

On 26th July 1865 Richard Webb, Gentleman, married Anne
Townsend at Dunderrow. Richard Webb may have been the land
agent for Samuel Beamish (see 1870 land holders register). In
1863 Rev R.F. Webb was rector of Dunderrow. He married the
youngest daughter of Samuel Beamish.

The Webbs were buried at Christ Church, Kilbrogan. The
inscription reads: In loving memory of Townsend Gun Webb who
died 21st May, 1892 aged 26 and of Samuel Beamish Webb who
died 28th February 1898 aged 30 years and of their mother Anne
Townsend Webb who died on 11th May 1914 and also of Gertrude
Hamilton Bryan who died on 19th February, 1902.

Anne Townsend Webb appears in the valuation record as the
occupier in 1900

In the 1901 census Anne was described as aged 68 and a widow
who living on private income. Born in Shropshire, she was living
with a female servant Catherine Dolan aged 60.

By the time of the 1911 census, the house appeared to be divided
into two. Annie Townsend Webb was aged 80 and was living with
her servant Eliza Berry aged 35. At the same time Elizabeth
Halburd, aged 46 was living at the property with her sister Frances
Halburd, aged 42, a professional nurse.

---

[288] See Appendix. Biographies

Anne Townsend Webb died in 1914 and after this Elizabeth Halburd was registered on her own in the valuation records.

Elizabeth R. Halburd died on 11th January 1942 aged 80 and is buried at Christ Church Kilbrogan. The headstone reads: Sacred to the memory of Anne, second daughter of John J. Halburd Esq of Bandon who died on 9th April, 1838 aged 19. The headstone also records the death of Frances Gillman who died on 28th June 1944 aged 82.

Mrs Francis Gillman became the occupier of the property in 1943. She died on 28th June 1944 aged 82. Patrick Murphy succeeded her in 1944. He was succeeded by James Murphy in 1961.

No 74
1837 Number 67 – Valuation £20
1851 Number 74 – Valuation £13 5s
1901 Census Number - 66
1911 Census Number – 35
2015 Number 6 Kilbrogan Hill West

Immediate Lessors
1851 The Representatives of Attiwell Roche
1860s George Roche
1874 George Fuller

Occupiers
In 1837 the occupier was Rev William Robert Molesworth. He was the elder son of Major Bysse Cole Molesworth, who was the fourth son of Robert, the second son of Bysse, seventh son of the first Viscount Molesworth. He was a vicar in Ardfield from 1842 to 1847. He died in 1866. His brother, Herbert Phillips Molesworth, was curate of Christ Church, Kilbrogan for nine years until his death from famine fever on 1st July 1847.

Attiwell Roche was recorded as the occupier in 1849.

By 1851 the occupier was Belinda Hornibrook. Joseph Bennett had become the occupier in 1856 and was shortly afterwards succeeded by Thomas Barter and then by William Barter. Henry Barter followed shortly afterwards and by 1861 Henry Arnold had taken up residence.

Henry Arnold moved out in 1864 and was succeeded by Thomas Carr who remained in the house until 1867. The next occupier was James Elliott.

Henry Arnold moved back into the property for a short time in 1874 and was succeeded by Bennett Hayes, a corn merchant of South Main Street[289] who in turn was succeeded by Mary Lynch in 1884.

In the 1901 census Mary Lynch was described as a house proprietor aged 60 who was living with her niece, Hannah Lynch, aged 21, Katie Lynch niece aged 19, Stephen Lynch, nephew aged 20, practicing chemistry, boarder Michael McSwiney aged 25, catholic clergyman and Richard Chute boarder aged 32, a bank official.

Mary Lynch was succeeded by her niece Katie Lynch in 1910

In the 1911 census, Katie Lynch was described as a housekeeper (29) with boarders Kate Connell, a lady aged 68, Mary O'Keeffe, a seamstress aged 29, William Ahern, a manager aged 30, Robert Buttermore, a doctor's clerk aged 30.

Katie remained at the property until Patrick Murphy moved in during 1950. Michael O'Carroll became the next occupier in 1962.

---

[289] Slater's Directory of 1870

No 75
1837 Number 68 –
Valuation £25
1849 Number 78
1851 Number 75 –
Valuation £18 10s
1901 Census Number - 67
1911 Census Number – 34
2015 Number 5 Kilbrogan
Hill West

Immediate Lessors
1851 The Representatives of Richard Williams
1880 George Fuller
1944 Edgar James Mills

Occupiers
In the 1837 census the occupier was Ann Gonne. In 1845 she
subscribed to 100 shares in the Cork and Bandon Railway. She
was described as a spinster of Bandon.[290]

Mrs Bradshaw was resident in 1849.

The house was unoccupied at the time of the Griffiths Valuation in
1851.

In the 1850s Rev John Egan[291] took up residence. He was licensed
as a curate of St Finbarre's in Cork in 1821 and in 1824 was
librarian and catechist at the cathedral. From 18th January 1850
until his death on 17th June, 1855 he was rector of Kilbrittain. He
was 75 at the time of his death. In his will he requested to be
buried in the vaults of Ballymodan church at a cost of no more
than £40. As he had no living relative at the time, he left his
effects to the two schools near Lucan for educating the children of
clergy.

---

[290] Southern Reporter. 12th June 1845
[291] Slater's Directory of Bandon, 1856 and Brady's Clerical & Parochial Records

Rev John Egan was succeeded by William McCreight. William died on 3rd September 1861 aged 61[292]. His wife Mary Baldwin McCreight died, aged 45, on 31st May, 1862.[293] (See No 39 and No 72 also).

William Cornwall became the next resident in 1861 (He had moved from No 73 which he had vacated for Thomas Poole in 1861). He died aged 73 on 24th July, 1865. William was a brother of George and Henry Cornwall, brewers and malsters of Watergate street who became bankrupt.

J. Rodwell, SJ succeeded William Cornwall. John Stephenson became resident in 1870. He died on 9th July 1874. In 1875 was replaced by David Hunter.

David Hunter remained in residence for four years until 1879 when Hester Anne Sullivan moved in. Hester was a daughter of William Connor Sullivan who married Dorothea Tresilian. She moved out in 1883 following her marriage to Rev William Livingston Leachman. They emigrated to the USA where William became a clergyman in the US Episcopal Church.

In 1884 William Connor Sullivan succeeded Hester Anne Sullivan.

The Sullivans no longer occupied the property in 1886 and the house was vacant until 1888 when John Parker Mills took up residence. He was a music teacher.[294] He played the organ at St Peter's Church of Ireland.

In the 1901 census James Parker Mills was described as aged 49, professor of music, living with wife Mary Diana Mills aged 35 and son Edgar Parker Mills aged 4, son Cecil James Mills aged 3 and servant Ellen Mahony aged 18

By the time of the 1911 census, James Parker Mills aged 59 was living with his wife Mary Diana (49) and son Edgar Parker (14) and son Cecil James (13)

---

[292] Christ Church, Kilbrogan Burial Record
[293] Christ Church, Kilbrogan Burial Record
[294] Guys Directory of 1893

James Parker Mills died on 5th June, 1931 aged 81. He was succeeded by his wife Mary Diana in 1934. She died on 6th April, 1942. Their son Canon Edgar Parker Mills, served for over fifty years at St Finbarre's Cathedral and he died aged 88 on 12th June 1984. All are buried at St Peter's, Ballymodan where James was organist for over sixty years.

Mary Diana Parker was succeeded by Garda Michael C. Tully in 1944. He was succeeded by Jeremiah Crowley in 1950 and by Kathleen O'Connor in 1953.

No 76
1837 Number 69 – Valuation £16
1849 Number 79
1851 Number 76 – Valuation £10 10s
1901 Census Number - 68
1911 Census Number – 33
2015 Number 4 Kilbrogan Hill West

Immediate Lessors
1851 The Representatives of Richard Williams
1879 George Fuller
1924 James Parker Mills
1950s The Parker Mills Estate

Occupiers
In 1837 the occupier was Anne Jenkins.

Mrs Hornibrook was recorded as the occupier in 1849.

The property was unoccupied at the time of the Griffiths Valuation in 1851.

By 1856 Anthony Guest had become the occupier and he was succeeded shortly afterwards by Rev Thomas Glasson Bennett and then by William Sillifant. In 1860 the occupier was recorded as Richard Wheeler Esq and his wife Alicia. Richard had grown up at the Wheeler home at Fort Prospect. He died on 21st February 1866. His successors were recorded as his representatives until 1870. Richard left effects under £600.

The property was vacant for two years before George Rye became the occupier in 1872. George Rye was succeeded by Thomas Boyle in 1875.

In 1884 Isaac Biggs assumed the tenancy. The rateable valuation at the time was £10 10s and Isaac was recorded as the occupier on the electoral role[295]. Isaac resided at the property until 1886 when the property remained vacant until 1888.

Thomas Coath moved in during 1888. He was employed as a Revenue Officer. A note in the valuation data of 1888 recorded that a passage at the side of the building was making the property difficult to value.

Thomas was followed by Joseph Brennan in 1892, Frances Crowley in 1897 and Josephine Calnan in 1901.

At the time of the 1901 census Josephine Calnan was described as aged 24 living with her sister, Kathleen Calnan aged 22 and sister, Bridget Calnan aged 20. Josephine was living on her own means

James O'Donoghue became the occupier 1907 and was succeeded three years later in 1910 by Patrick Sheehan.

Patrick Sheehan was described in the 1911 census as an accountant aged 33 who was living with his wife Emily, a teacher aged 30, a daughter Jane and a servant Bridget aged 20.

Kate Hayes became the occupier in 1914.

---

[295] Electoral Records. 1884

Francis E. Smith succeeded Kate Hayes in 1921 and lived at the property until Patrick Dwyer moved in during 1954.

No 77
1837 Number 70 – Valuation £18
1849 Number 80
1851 Number 77 – Valuation £14 10s
1901 Census Number - 69
1911 Census Number – 32
2015 Number 3 Kilbrogan Hill West

Immediate Lessors
1851 The Representatives of Richard Williams
1879 George Fuller
1924 James Parker Mills

Occupiers
In 1837 the occupier was Anne Penrose

Richard McManus was recorded as the tenant in 1849.

The occupier was Dorah Tresilian in 1851.

By 1856 Sarah Evanson resided at the property. She was succeeded by George Rawlins and then by James Bogue. James and his wife Elizabeth had a daughter Alison Janet Augusta born on 8th September 1858 and baptised on 27th September at Christ Church. His occupation was recorded as a gentleman.

The next occupant was Rochford Connor followed by Dennis Cummins in 1858. Rochford and his wife Mary had a son, William, born on 25th June 1858 and baptised on 7th July at Christ Church. Rochford was an excise officer.

By 1861 the property had become vacant.

Miss Scott moved in during 1863 and remained until 1867. She was succeeded by Henry Arnold. He was recorded in the register of vestrymen at Christ Church, Kilbrogan in 1870.

Between 1870 and 1874 a number of different people held the lease of the property namely William Christopher Dowden, George Lyons, George Clugston Allman followed by James Clugston Allman. William Christopher Dowden's name appears as the tenant in No 77 in 1872.

Thomas Cooper, an accountant, moved in during 1874 and remained in the property until 1880 at which time he transferred to No 77.

George Lamb and his nephew Devonshire Penrose Hawkes took up the tenancy in 1880. The latter was aged 29 and George Lamb was aged 54. The property became vacant in 1883. George and Devonshire and their family had moved to No 39.

Devonshire Penrose Hawkes was the son of Quayle Welstead Hawkes. He married Sara Popham Hosford on 1st August, 1878. She was the daughter of Joseph Hosford and Anna Maria Lamb who were married on 23rd February 1854 at Desertserges. In the 1901 census Devonshire Hawkes was living at Barryshall, Timoleague and he was recorded as a gentleman and farmer. George Lamb and his wife Annie were still living with them.

A note in the records states that the rear of the premises was 'all down'. The rent was reduced.

Frederick Reid spent two years at the property and was succeeded by William Porter in 1888. He lived in the house for four years.

In 1892 Henry Parker took up residence and was followed by Paul Buttimer in 1894.

Paul Buttimer was succeeded in 1897 by Patrick Crooks, a foreman and cooper who spent six years at the property with his family.

Patrick Crookes was described in the 1901 census as a foreman, cooper, aged 37, living with Ellen Crookes his wife aged 35 and daughter Catherine Crookes, aged 14, daughter Mary Crookes aged

12, son Patrick Crookes aged 9, daughter Bertha Crookes aged 7, son Robert Crookes aged 3 and daughter Ellen Crookes aged 11.

By 1903 Jane Popham had taken up residence and she was succeeded by James Murphy in 1905. He remained as the occupier until 1915.

James Joseph Murphy was the eldest son of Michael Joseph Murphy of Lough Neill House, Crookstown where James was born in June 1876. He was educated privately and at the Christian Brothers School, Cork. He took up employment with Joseph Brennan, Brewer's Agent and Secretary to the West Cork Bottling Company Ltd and worked for them for at least 18 years. In June 1906 he married Agnes, the third daughter of Michael Hanly of Castletownberehaven and had a daughter Eileen born 1907, Una born January 1909 and Kathleen born May 1910.

Mr. J. J. Murphy.

In the 1911 census James Joseph Murphy aged 35 was recorded as a commercial traveller living with his wife Agnes M aged 28, daughter Eileen M aged 3, daughter Lin J aged 3 and daughter Kathleen and a servant Bridget White aged 22.

Daniel Curran took up residence in 1915 and was succeeded by Cris Alcock in 1922.

In 1924 the occupier was Joseph Hyde. Ernest Lee became the next tenant in 1928 and in 1947 the entry was changed to The Representatives of Ernest Lee. Claire was recorded as the occupier in 1950 and she was succeeded by Patrick Donovan in 1952.

No 78 – The Brogan Inn and adjoining house

1837. Number 71 and 72 were combined. Valuation £35. The occupier was John Tresilian
1849 Thomas Kingston Sullivan (81). Solicitors Office
1849 Thomas Kingston Sullivan (82). House, coach houses, shed, granary
1901 Census Number 70 (house), 71 (public house) and 72 (house)
1911 Census Number 29 (public house), 30 (house) and 31 (house)

For many years this premises was comprised of two houses and one public house. By the time of the first census they were recorded as three separate properties.

The Griffith Valuation Record of 1851 listed the Immediate Lessor as Thomas Kingston Sullivan Esq and the occupier as William Gore Brett Esq.

When the valuation records commenced in 1856, the premises was divided into (a) a house, (b) a public house and (c) an office.

The part of the premises which was licensed was in the control of the Foley family for fifty three years from at least 1856 until 1909.

78a -No 70 in the 1901 census and No 30 in the 1911 census

In 1856 the immediate lessor of 78a was the representative of Robert Tresilian Belcher who had died in 1849. Thomas Kingston Sullivan was the occupier of the house and office at 78a from 1856 until 1866. He most likely used the building as an office as he resided at the Retreat on the Dunmanway Road.

Thomas K. Sullivan was succeeded by Patrick Foley for one year. In 1867 William Foley took over the house and Patrick had the public house at 78b. This arrangement continued until the death of Patrick in 1873.

From 1874 until 1879 William Foley's name was registered as the sole occupier of the house, pub and office.

By 1879 the two premises were divided once again. William O'Reilly moved into 78c (recorded as 78a in the valuation book). William Foley was still in residence in 78a and also ran the public house. The rateable valuation of William's portion of the property in 1884 was £19 and it was described as a house, offices, yard and garden.

Thomas Kingston Sullivan had become the immediate lessor in 1866. He took over from the representatives of Robert Tresilian Belcher and still had the lease in 1879.

In 1899 William Foley was recorded as a Miller and Merchant of North Main Street. In the same year he stood for election to the new county council. He stood against John Walsh of Shannon Lodge, Mineral Water Manufacturer and Brewer's Agent and was defeated.

HOUSE (78a) – No 30 (1901 census) and No 70 (1911 census)

In 1898 J. P. McCabe took on a house and yard from William Sullivan. Shortly afterwards he was succeeded by Mrs Bradish and by 1901 John Dennehy had taken up residence.

In the 1901 census John J. Dennehy was described as aged 23, a clerk to the county surveyor, living with his wife, Mary Jane Dennehy, aged 23. The house was recorded as having nine windows in front whereas the pub next door had just two.

There were a number of occupants between the two censuses.

Richard St George was in the house from 1903 until 1908.

John William Gillman, an insurance agent, moved in during 1908. John Gillman who was married to Frances was the son of Colonel Gillman. John died on 13th February 1917 aged 63 and was buried at Christ Church, Kilbrogan. Probate of his will was granted to Frances Gillman, his widow. He left effects of £485 2s 10d.

Thomas J. Murphy in 1911 and then Sergeant Dolan who was recorded in the census..

Philip Dolan was described in the census as aged 39, a sergeant in the RIC, was living with his wife Kathleen, aged 28, daughter Anne, aged 2 and a sister in law, Maria O'Sullivan aged 34 and a seamstress. The house was recorded in this census as having six windows.

The licensed premises - No 71 in the 1901 census and No 29 in the 1911 census

The immediate lessor in 1856 was Thomas Kingston Sullivan who was occupying 78a. From at least 1856 Patrick Foley was the occupier of a house, office and yard of 78b. He ran a public house and had the agency for Beamish & Crawford.[296]

An article in the Cork Examiner of 25th February, 1863 recorded that a number of men were drinking in the public house of Mr P. Foley, near Mr Sullivan's committee rooms. They commenced fighting amongst themselves and sticks, pokers and stones, constituted their weapons. In the row the door of the house was wrenched off and the windows broken in. One man pummelled another's head with the thick knobby head of a poker. Two men got their heads fearfully cut with stones and considering the freedom with which these weapons were used, it was surprising that the list of wounded was not greater. One fellow was observed with his pockets full of stones which he flung in through the doors and windows of the hotel. They did not even confine their attacks to those who were opposed to them but attacked the inoffensive. The Sub Sheriff whilst walking down the street was attacked by some of those drunken fellows who endeavoured to trip him up. One he floored and the rest were taken off by the police.

Patrick Foley died on 7th August, 1873 aged 75 and was buried in Kilmurry. William Foley was recorded as the single holder of the entire premises from 1874 until at least 1879. He was described in the 1881 street directory as a grocer and publican.

In the 1901 census William Foley was recorded as having the public house with a note that the owner lived elsewhere.

Mary Kearney succeeded William Foley in 1909 though he continued for many years as the immediate lessor.

In 1911 census Mary Kearney, aged 71, a vintner, was recorded as living in the premises with her daughter, Bessie Kearney, aged 46.

---

[296] Coughlans Directory of 1867

The Kearneys were succeeded by Patrick Hawkes in 1921. He was succeeded in 1962 by Kathleen O'Sullivan.

HOUSE – 1901 census (No 31), 1911 census (No 72)

Robert Coath lived in this part of the premises from 1879 to 1881. William O'Reilly succeeded him from 1882 until 1884. Oswald M. Massy became the next occupier in 1884. His name appeared on the electoral register of 1884 and the property as described as a house with a rateable valuation of £10.

Oswald Massy was succeeded by Thomas Forde in 1881. Thomas was recorded as the occupier on the electoral register of 1884. He remained in the house until 1895 when John Howard moved in for one year. John Murphy was the occupier in 1896 and in 1897 Mary Sullivan moved in.

In the 1901 census the house (Number 31) was described as having four windows at the front and was a private dwelling house.

In 1901 Mary H. Sullivan was recorded in the census as the occupier. Mary was aged 55, single and living on her own means with Anne Howe, aged 39, also living on her own means.

In 1911 Census (Number 72) Mary Sullivan was aged 66 and at this time was living on her own.

Mary was succeeded by Anna S. Howe who in turn was succeeded by R. Fitzgerald. The next occupier was F.W. Gliettsmann and he was then followed by Patrick Hawkes

SUGAR LANE
The lane originally ran from Kilbrogan Hill through the Shambles, across Allen Square and down to the river adjacent to the old Pumping Station.[297] The lane was peppered with weavers' cabins.

---

[297] Bandon Historical Journal. No 9. The Laneways of Bandon. Sean Connolly

THE SHAMBLES

The estimates for a new fifteen sided Shambles or meat market were submitted in 1816 and the building was completed in 1817 [298]. An earlier Shambles was recorded at Bridge Place (No 4). In 1785 The Corporation of Bandon Bridge felt that the absence of a meat market was very inconvenient for the inhabitants and as a result, the Provost at the time, William Connor Esq, had a market erected on a plot of ground already laid out for the purpose which adjoined the bridge (See Bridge Place – No 4). In return for building the meat shambles at his own expense, the corporation agreed that stalls would be offered to butchers and victuallers in and about the town of Bandon and that Connor would be entitled to set and receive the rents from the stalls. Furthermore, there would be enough space to accommodate the butchers who supplied the town with meat.[299]

The Shambles had 22 stalls which were rented to individual butchers and were solely for the sale of meat. A veterinary office and a market jury room were located in the house at the Allen Square side of the site which formed the main entrance to the market. It was in use up to 1846 when it was described as an ugly and unsightly nuisance. Access to the Shambles was via an arched

---

[298] Lismore Papers. MS 43,764/21
[299] Borough of Bandon Bridge Corporation Minutes of 28th July, 1785

entrance in a house on the western side of the building which faces Allen Square.[300]

BANDON SAVINGS BANK – Cavendish Row

BANDON SAVINGS BANK[301]

THE General Meeting of the Trustees, Managers
and Depositors, will be held at the Court-House
on TUESDAY next, the 25th Inst at Twelve o'Clock,
to receive the Report of the proceedings for the last year.
Clergymen of all persuasions are respectively invited to attend.   J.J. WHEELER
    Bandon, Jan. 20.   Secretary

The Bank was closed in February 1849 once all the depositors had been paid off with interest. The trustees paid the retiring officers a gratuity of half a year's salary.[302] The trustees and managers were unwilling to conform to the provisions of a new Act of Parliament in 1848 and therefore decided to unwind its affairs. It re-opened in February 1859.

---

[300] A History of Bandon. Paddy Connolly
[301] Southern Reporter, 22nd January, 1825
[302] Belfast Newsletter. 6th February, 1849

In 1889 the Savings Bank building was taken over by the Freemasons. They spent £22 13s 1d in suitably fitting the property for their needs. The new lodge room was officially opened on 9th April, 1890. In 1895 the Freemasons entered into a lease with the Duke of Devonshire for 31 years at a rent of £5 to expire on 25th March 1921. In 1912 the lease was renewed for 100 years with their landlord, Sir John Arnott who had purchased the freehold from the Duke of Devonshire. Further alterations and improvements were made in 1912 at a cost of £70.

On 11th August, 1922 the premises was ransacked and the lodge furnishings and wall displays were thrown from the windows and were burnt in the street. The Hall was subsequently refurbished and was opened on 14th October 1926.

The property remained the home of lodge 84 until 1991.[303]

No 79 – The Court House – The Grand Jury of County Cork

The Court House was built in 1802 by the Duke of Devonshire's Estate and it was leased to the County Grand Jury. It was re-constructed in 1841, 1886 and again in 1927 after it was partially burnt in 1922. It was once again refurbished in 1989.

[303] Two Hundred and Seventy Five Years of Freemasonry in Bandon. David J. Butler & Alwyn C. Williams

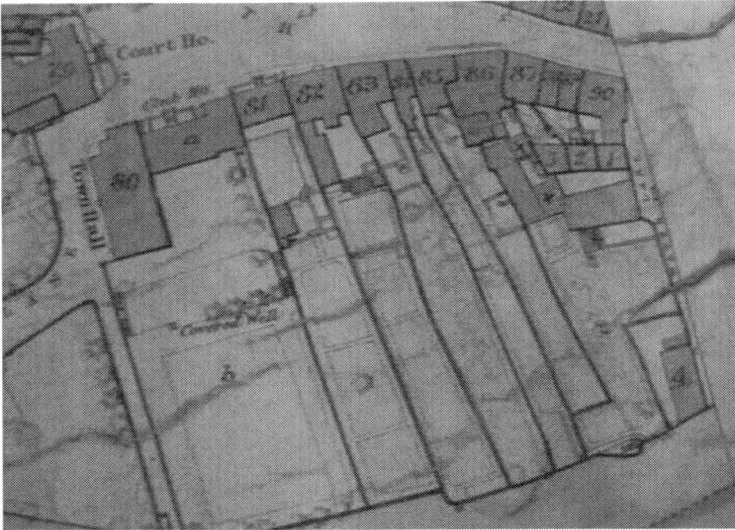

A view of the Mill from the footbridge. From the Lawrence
Collection
With permission of the National Library of Ireland

THE COOLFADDA MILLS (also known as THE BANDON MILLS)

On Lady Day 1752 Ralph Clear and Thomas Bourk entered into a lease for the mills and ten acres of land at Coolfadda with the fishing rights for 33 years at a rent of £90. They were forced to surrender the lease nine years later on 10th August, 1761. Richard Savage and John Harris, both of Bandon, subsequently took up the lease for the lives of John Harris, his wife Catherine Harris and Charles Savage, son of Richard Savage, one of the lessees. They were ejected and the property passed to the Biggs.[304]

On 24th January 1794 a vestry meeting was held at Christ Church for the purpose of levying from the inhabitants and landholders of the parish the sum of £491 7p as compensation to be paid to Messrs Jacob and Thomas Biggs for the losses and damages which they sustained on their mills and corn stores at Mill Place on 15th November 1792.

It was agreed by the minister, church wardens and the majority of parishioners that the sum be raised and that Messrs Robert Travers, Richard Gillman, John Wheeler, Lionel Becher, Thomas Lisson, William Banfield and Horatio McCarthy be appointed as assessors.

Collectors were nominated for the townlands in the parish. Thomas Clugston and Laurence Hornibrook had responsibility for the town of Bandon, Benjamin ? and William Moxly, Barretts Hill, Walter Rogers and John Crowly, Callatrim Street and the Cork Road, Daniel Carthy and William Farr as collectors for Watergate and the Cork Road which adjoined it (part of Knockbrogan), John Lovell and Thomas Joyce for Coolfadda and Shinagh, Lord Bandon was assigned the Park and Thomas Banfield, Carnlough. The other collectors were John Sullivan, the Bridge and William Rogers, Gurteen, John Northridge, Callatrim, Samuel Hornibrook, Little Silver and Mishells, Jonathan Hosford and Thomas Gash, Derrygarriffe and Lissabroeder, Maskelyne Alcock Esq and Joseph Hosford Derrymueta and Mallowgaton, John Baldwin, Lauragh and Timothy Lyon and Daniel Quinlan, Carhue. James Stanley, James White and Richard Mellefont, Derrycoole.

---

[304] MS 6176 Lismore Papers

Others mentioned were Rev Richard Townsend, John Wilson and John Wren.

William, Jacob and John Biggs entered into a new lease for the Coolfadda Mills with the Duke of Devonshire on 1st April 1816 at an annual rent of £131 18s 9d. The mill was described in the lease as being situated on the river along with a stretch of land of about 10 acres, the fishing rights and a plot ground which was situated at the court house and enclosed by a wall together with a small strap of land to the south of the said wall which had been in the possession of Arthur Beamish Bernard Esq and which plot had been made use of by the Duke of Devonshire as a storeyard. Also included was a store house. The mill was bounded on the east by the street and a public passage leading to the river and on the west side by the barrack yard and on the north by the wall which separated the back concerns of the intended new street (Cavendish St) from the mill premises.[305]

In 1838 the Biggs were exporting 7000 sacks of flour and 6600 barrels of wheat. Their carriage to Cork amounted to £725.

TO BE SOLD[306]
A LARGE Quantity of Prime Kiln Dried **WHEAT**,
in Lots, to suit Purchasers, of not less than **ONE HUNDRED BARRELLS – TERMS CASH**
Apply at the Office of the Bandon Mills

The mill was idle in 1844[307] and it was put up for sale in early 1847.

---

[305] MS 6189 Lismore Papers
[306] Newspaper Advertisement. 13th May, 1841
[307] W.A. Spiller. A Short Topographical and Statistical Account of the Bandon Union

---

[308]**BANDON MILLS &c.**

TO BE SOLD.

THE INTEREST in the **BANDON MILLS** and
FISHERY of the **BANDON RIVER**, attached –
House, Offices, Garden, and about 10 Acres of land adjoining, and about 4 1/2 Acres more at the South Side of
the River.

For Cards to view, Title, Terms, and all other particulars, apply to **EDWARD DOHERTY**, Solicitor,
68, South Main Street, Bandon

Following the death of Jacob Biggs in 1852, the Biggs sold their
leasehold interest to Edward Bell, a Scottish miller, who took up
residence at Floraville.

Shortly after Edward Bell assumed control of the mill, an attempt
was made by the courts to compel Mr Bell to fence in his weir and
prevent the obstruction of fish through the gap. The mills had at
that time had been transferred from the control of Messrs Biggs[309]
and were being extensively worked by Mr Bell. Thomas Kingston
Sullivan represented Mr Bell and the Duke's agent, Alexander
Swanston, was also present at the Bandon Court Sessions as the
Duke of Devonshire was the owner of both the fishery and the
freehold of the mill. Defendants also included Edward Bell's mill
wright, John Kidney, who was also a miller on his own account
and Patrick Foley, one of the millers at the site. At issue was a
board which was placed across the weir and which was obstructing
the passage of fish. The defendants claimed that if removed, the
mill would become slack thus injuring its working power.

A water bailiff, John Mahony, was called to give evidence that he
witnessed six salmon being removed from Mr Bell's net. The case
came up again in succeeding years including on 31st October, 1854
when Mr Bell excused himself to attend the funeral of his uncle Mr
Moss of Kilkenny who had died suddenly. In 1864 Edward's son,
John along with Mr Gould, one of the millers, appeared at the

---

[308] Newspaper Advertisement. 1847
[309] Cork Examiner. 1st April, 1853

Bandon Petty Sessions accused of using a device known as a gaff to catch fish on part of the river which was flowing through the mills and which was contrary to law. The water bailiff, Jeremiah, Coughlan, witnessed the men with two gaffs at the water which flowed between the mill wheel and the end of the tail race.

At a meeting which took place in the Court House in January 1860[310] to discuss matters arising in relation to the Cork and Bandon railway, Mr Bell remarked that the railway company had increased their charges to a very great degree. From time to time he sent 500 bags of flour by rail but he believed that the more traffic the railway received, the more they charged. It was also considered unjust that if a cargo of corn was shipped through Cork, the Corporation of Cork charged tolls on it.

For a period Edward Bell ran the mill with a partner, Mr McDonnell. Bell sold his lease in 1871 to Allman Dowden & Co and they subsequently modernised the premises. They erected a new water wheel in 1874[311] and after two years it was replaced by a steam engine with a set of turbine wheels.

William Christopher Dowden, William Shaw and James Clugston Allman were recorded as the occupiers of the mills and offices in 1884. The rateable valuation was £295.[312]

Sometime between 1884 and 1892 there was a note in the valuation records as follows: 'The whole concern is as good as ever it was as they buy American flour and retail it instead of grinding wheat themselves.'

In 1892 a note in the valuation records stated that the mill was at rest for twelve months.

The Coolfadda Mills were advertised for sale by Dowden & Co in 1899.

---

[310] Cork Examiner, 30th January 1860
[311] Valuation Record
[312] Electoral Register. 1884

COOLFADDA FLOUR MILLS,[313]
BANDON.
TO BE LET

The above Mills, commanding the full supply of water
of the Bandon River, and containing two turbines of 80
horse-power, and a steam engine of same capacity.
These Mills are eminently suited for any manufacture
requiring cheap motive power, and their position is
highly favourable for Flour Mills, Woollen Mills, or any
other branch of manufacture.—For particulars apply to
DOWDEN & CO,
COOLFADDA MILLS, BANDON, CO CORK   11305

It was still vacant in 1903 and the rates were reduced to £70.

By 1922 the mill was leased by the Bandon Mills and Electric
Lighting Co Ltd which was controlled by the Brennan Family. The
immediate lessor was Dr J.J. Welply who had taken over the rights
to the mill from William Christopher Dowden and James Clugston
Allman. A note in the valuation record of 1920 reads as follows:
'mill not fully equipped – No grinding done.' In 1922 it was
described as a corn mill with offices, garden and a flour store.

---

[313] Freeman's Journal, 12th August, 1899

[314]**THE OFFICE** of the **BANDON MILLS**, was
Burglariously entered on the night of the 8th Inst.
and some COPPER COIN stolen from thence. W.J. and J.
BIGGS (the Proprietors) will give the above Reward
on the Conviction of one or more of the party concerned.
TWENTY POUNDS will be paid for any private information, which may lead to a discovery.
We being desirous of having the perpetrators of the
above mentioned Burlarly brought to condign punishment will in addition to the above mentioned Reward
pay the Sums set opposite to our respective Names, to
such person or persons, who shall within **SIX CALEN-
DAR MONTHS**, from the date thereof, Prosecute to
Conviction the persons concerned in the above mentioned
Burglary and Robbery   Bandon, June 15, 1827

Name	Sum	Name	Sum
Bandon	£20.0.0	Michael England	£1.0.0
John Swete	£5.0.0	Thomas Bennett, jn	£1.0.0
Edward Doherty	£2.0.0	F. Hayes, MD	£1.0.0
John Wheeler, jn	£1.0.0	John Scott	£1.0.0
James Scott	£1.1.0	Denis Quinlan	£1.0.0
William Connor	£2.0.0	Edw. O'Connor	£1.0.0
Richard Tresilian	£1.0.0	Stewart Tresilian	£1.0.0
John Clerke	£2.0.0	Richard Wheeler	£2.0.0
John B. Williams	£1.0.0	Thomas Baker	£1.0.0
John & W. Sullivan	£1.0.0	Isaac Biggs	£5.0.0
William Sullivan	£2.0.0	J. Homan MD	£1.0.0
H. Belcher	£1.0.0	Thomas Gash	£1.0.0
John Hunter	£1.0.0	William Hunter	£1.0.0
Wm Kingston	£1.0.0	Andrew Moore	£1.0.0
Denis Falvey	£1.0.0	Robert Moore	£3.0.0
W. Kingston	£1.0.0	Edward Gillman	£3.0.0
John C. Swanton	£1.0.0	Geo & H. Cornwall	£5.0.0
Robert Fuller	£1.0.0	P.B. Sweeney	£3.0.0
John Shine	£1.0.0	Paul Williams	£1.0.0
Joseph Bennett	£1.1.0	John Tresilian	£1.0.0
Wm Jenkins	£1.0.0	F.B. Hingston	£1.0.0
John Wheeler	£2.0.0	Timothy Murphy	£1.0.0
Wm Shine	£1.0.0	John Lordon	£1.0.0
Mary Sullivan	£1.0.0	George Dowden	£1.0.0
Michael Galwey	£2.0.0	C. Dowden	£2.0.0
William Dowden	£1.0.0	R.N. Rogers	£1.1.0
Thomas Fuller	£2.0.0	George Knott	£2.0.0

---

[314] Southern Reporter, 23rd June, 1827

MILL PLACE – Floraville – also known as Mill House

Arthur Bernard leased 'The Great House and Meadow' located on this site for 41 years from Lady Day 1738 until 1779 at a rental of £15.

John Swete lived Floraville as early as the late 1700s. He was the son of Benjamin Swete of Pleasantfields who married his cousin Joyce Swete (She was also married to Jonas Travers).[315] Although he owned Ballinacurra House near Kinsale for a period until 1791, he appears to have always resided with his family at Floraville.

Another early reference to John Swete Esq as a resident of the property dates back to 1811 when he was described as a member of a Jury at the assizes for the County of Cork.[316]

John Swete was an active member of the Corporation of Bandon Bridge and served as a magistrate. He also acted as Agent for many years for the Earl of Bandon.

On 30th June, 1837 John's sister, Thamar Swete, died at Floraville aged 76 and was buried in Timoleague. She was the widow of Benjamin Swete of Bandon.

John Swete died on 22nd February, 1839 and was also buried in the Swete family vault in the Church of Ireland graveyard in Timoleague[317]. His wife Martha passed away on 13th May, 1839.[318]

On 31st October, 1839 one of his daughter's, Mrs Blood[319], held an auction of some of her father's effects at her house on North Main Street which was formerly the house of John Swete, Esq. The items included a handsome travelling carriage and harness, a quantity of gig and cart harness, furniture, carpets, rugs as well as

---

[315] See Appendix. Biographies
[316] Saunders's Newsletter of 7th September, 1811
[317] Freeman's Journal. 26th February, 1839
[318] Southern Reporter. 16th May 1839
[319] Described in the valuation records as a lunatic daughter who married secondly Mr Bowen

200 flour bags and a quantity of old timber and window sashes. The auction was conducted by John Fawsitt, an auctioneer.[320]

In the 1840s there are references to Adam Newman, junior as being the occupier. He was the son of Adam Newman of Dromore House, Mallow.

Jacob Biggs Esq lived at the property for a time following John Swete's death though it's not known if this was before or after Adam Newman. Jacob died in March 1852 aged 71.

Edward Bell, a Scot, took over the mill following the death of Jacob Biggs in 1852 and took up residence in Floraville.

Edward and his wife Margaret (Reed Davis) had several children born at Floraville namely Vernon James born 26th June 1852, Edward Thomas born 19th July 1854, James William born 6th May 1856, Evangeline Mary baptised on 30th April 1858, Fanny Louisa born on 12th December 1859, Beatrice Maud born on 10th December 1861, Thomas Reed Davis born on 2nd May 1863 and Francis Henry born on 20th November 1864 and who died aged 6 months on 14th April 1865.[321]

In 1871 Edward and his wife Margaret entered into a lease arrangement with William Christopher Dowden and George Lyons who were both millers and partners in trade. Messrs Dowden and Lyons granted an annuity of £250 to Edward and £125 to his wife Margaret. If Margaret survived her husband, she was to be paid twelve months after her husband's decease. The annuities were to be charged out of the Bandon Mill and ten acres which were formerly in the possession of Arthur Beamish Bernard.[322] The lease refers to the original lease of 1st October 1816 from the Duke of Devonshire to William, Jacob and John Biggs of the mills of Coolfadda, later named the Bandon Mills. The original lease commenced on 29th September 1816 and was for 99 years. Edward Bell's lease arrangement also required the consent of the executors of the estate of Henry Hassett of Woodlands, Margaret and John Hassett.

[320] Southern Reporter. 24th October, 1839
[321] Christ Church, Kilbrogan. Baptism Records
[322] ROD. 1871 17 122 and 123

William Christopher Dowden was recorded as the occupier of a house with offices and garden at Mill Place in 1884. The rateable valuation was £33.

In 1888 James Moriarty, the shop keeper and woollen merchant and his wife Frances (nee Shine) took up residence. James died in 1899 after which the name in the valuation record appeared as Mrs Frances Moriarty.[323] In the 1901 census she was described as aged 75, Church of Ireland, a widow, living on interest with a parlour maid servant Mary Ryan, aged 52 and a general servant, Annie McSweeney, aged 23. She died shortly afterwards in 1901.

Dr. J. J. Welply.

Shortly after the death of Mrs Frances Moriarty in 1901, Dr John Jagoe Welply became the occupier.

Dr Welply was occupying the property at the time of the 1911 census. He was the son of William Norwood Welply of Kilronan,

---

[323] Church & Parish Records of United Diocese of Cloyne & Ross. J.H. Cole

Co Cork. Born in 1851, he was educated privately and at Queen's College, Cork. He was engaged in medical practice in Bandon from 1879. He acted as medical officer of the Bandon Dispensary and Medical Officer of Health for the Bandon District. He married twice, firstly in 1880 to Ellen Jagoe, the daughter of John A. Jagoe of Westfield, Co Cork by whom he had one son and one daughter and secondly in 1910 to Jane, the daughter of George Crofts of Templehill and Concamore, Co Cork. His son, John Jagoe Welply, was born in Bandon in 1880 and was educated at St Faughanan's College, Rosscarbery and at the Bandon Grammar School. He married on 10th December 1904 Oriel Adelaide Cave, the only daughter of Arthur Oriel Singer Cave formerly of Rossbrin Manor, Co Cork.

The entry in the 1911 census recorded Dr Welply as aged 59, living with his wife Jane aged 53, a daughter Ellen Mary Elizabeth aged 26, a servant Ellen Hales, aged 40 and a servant Mary Anne Nash aged 28.

The Welplys continued to live at the property until 1937 when Mrs Ellen Mary E. Webster took up residence. She was succeeded in 1965 by Dr Brien Welply.

MILL LANE (also known for a period as Bell's Lane, after Edward Bell)

The lane ran from the site of the present Town Hall to the footbridge. A timber footbridge was built in 1853. It was replaced in 1908 with the present structure by John Buckley, a local builder.

No 80 – Present site of part of Town Hall.
1837 Number 73 –
Valuation £50
1849 Number 88
1851 Number 80 –
Valuation £38 5s

Immediate Lessors

1775 Arthur Bernard Esq of Palace Anne
1817 George Cornwall – 99 year lease
1829 Dr George Loane
1838 John O'Brien
1851 Rev Dominick Murphy and Timothy Mahony
1871 – New Lease for 99 years
1919 – Freehold purchased from Sir John Arnott

On 1ˢᵗ April 1817 the Duke of Devonshire conveyed the site to George Cornwall, the brewer and malster, of Watergate Street for a period of 99 years to run until 1916. The yearly rent was fixed at £16 payable on 25ᵗʰ March and 29ᵗʰ September. By the terms of the lease, George Cornwall was contracted to spend £1000 on a good and substantial dwelling house. The site was described as being a plot on which an old house had formerly stood. It measured 112' in breadth and had a depth of 296' and was bounded on the east by a holding of Timothy Murphy and on the west by the lane leading to the river.[324]

George Cornwall senior built a house on the site. He died in 1824 and by the terms of his will which was published on 3ʳᵈ February, 1825, he bequeathed the lease to his son George.

On 29ᵗʰ September 1829, George Cornwall junior conveyed the house and premises to George Loane, a doctor of medicine and surgeon, for 86 years at an annual rent of £50 10s 11p payable half yearly. George Loane was to surrender the house and premises at

---

[324] MS 6189. Lismore papers

the end of every five years. On 15th October, 1835 the rent was reduced to £45 2s 11p leaving a profit of £28 12s 2p.

George Cornwall junior was declared a bankrupt in 1837 which affected the lease which he had conveyed to George Loane.

Robert Tresilian Belcher, the assignee in the bankrupty of George Cornwall junior in 1837, gave notice of an auction to the highest bidder at the reduced yearly profit rent of £28 12s 10p. John O'Brien, a shop-keeper, purchased the lease for £430.[325]

Thirteen years later on 19th April 1851 John O'Brien assigned the lease to Rev Dominick Murphy, then a Parish Priest of Douglas Road, Cork and Timothy Mahony of Cork Esq.[326]

Rev Dominick Murphy and Timothy Mahony contracted with William Shaw of Beaumont, Co Cork, John Wheeler of Bandon, William Connor Sullivan of Overton in Bandon, Richard Lane Allman of Glenview near Bandon and Thomas Kingston Sullivan of The Retreat, Bandon as trustees on their own behalf and on behalf of other subscribers to the Bandon Town Hall. Rev Dominick and Timothy Mahony demised to sell to the trustees all their term and interest in the premises under the original deed of 1816 for the residue of the 99 years.

The site demised to the trustees was bounded on the west by a lane leading to a timber bridge across the river. On the east of the site was a holding formerly occupied by Timothy Murphy but by 1864 in the occupation of Thomas Clear.[327]

Occupiers
George Loane was the occupier in 1837. He had purchased the lease from George Cornwall in 1829. George was a medical doctor and surgeon who served in the 8th and 49th regiments. He married Sarah Elizabeth Bradshaw in 1826. They had six children, Anne Frances, Richard Hussey, Mary Webb, Sarah Bradshaw, Georgina Rowland and Rowland Walpole. George died in September 1837.

---

[325] Registry of Deeds. 1838 7 276
[326] Registry of Deeds. 1851 12 80 of 19th April 1851
[327] Registry of Deeds. 1864 21 9

Mrs Sarah Loane was the occupier in the valuation records of 1849.

Rev Richard Hussey Loane, a son of George and Sarah, was recorded as the tenant in 1851. It's likely that he moved from this house to No 67 shortly before 1860. However, there may have been a lag in updating the records as in 1859 Rev Richard Hussey Loane's address was Rushbrooke when he married Jane Green, the daughter of Samuel Green of Youghal and his wife Susan Green, the daughter of Roger Green. Susan's grandmother was Alice Allin who was a sister of James Allin who bequeathed the Allin Institute to the Protestants of Bandon in 1867.

Rev Richard Hussey Loane and Jane were married at Kilshannig. They had four children, Alice Susan, George Bradshaw (died young), George Green and John Samuel.

Marmaduke Brangan and his family moved from No 60 to a house in the town hall in 1864. They gave their address as the town hall in 1865 when their son Marmaduke was baptised. A portion of the building had been made into a dwelling and the town hall trustees received rental income from the house.

Caretakers included George McElroy, John Byrne, his widow, John Curran, Edward O'Riordan and Richard Long. Most of these lived on the premises.

The first moves towards creating a new town hall took place in 1861. A committee was formed to take over the lease of the property and to raise funds for its construction. Discussions were had as to whether to alter the existing building or to re-build. Tenders were sought for a re-build. Richard Brash of Cork was the architect and Henry Hunter of Bandon was recruited to erect the new building for £700.[328]

The proposed community building was to contain a news room, a library, an assembly room and a museum. There were to be lectures on literature and the sciences and their application to the arts and manufactures. The reading room was to be open to the public at the lowest possible charge.

---

[328] Bandon Historical Journal. No 9. Paddy Connolly

It was agreed that an AGM would take place each year on the first Monday of October. Membership arrangements were put in place so that the building would be financially viable. All the contributors of £2 annually would be able to vote, contributors of £5 to £20 would have two votes, those contributing £20-£50 three votes and a contributors of £50 or upwards would have four votes. No meeting would take place unless seven contributors were present.

On 15th August 1861 a list of subscribers to the town hall appeared in the Cork Constitution. Residents and immediate lessors of North Main Street who subscribed included William Christopher Dowden (£20), Thomas Kingston Sullivan (£50), Thomas Clear (£10), J. Teulon JP (£10), R. Hunter (£5), William Robinson (£3), William Connor Sullivan (£20), William Cornwall (£1)

Four mortgagees, The 4th Earl of Bandon, William Holland Kingston, Richard Wheeler Doherty and John Richard Wheeler Esq extended £400 to the trustees and the premises was used to secure the loan. Any complaints were to be appealed to the Duke's Irish Agent, Francis Currey. The witnesses to the deed were Samuel Cottrell, Marmaduke Brangan, Richard Forde, Alfred Leonard and Henry McDonnell. The Duke made a contribution of £100 towards the new building in 1862.[329]

A group spearheaded by Colonel William Smyth Bernard and William Shaw convinced the County Grand Jury to recommend the granting of a loan from the Irish Reproductive Fund which had under the control of the Lord Lieutenant of Ireland since 1822 and was intended for famine relief.

The town hall was formally opened by the 7th Duke of Devonshire at a banquet which took place on 6th October 1862. It was chaired by Captain Wheeler. The Duke stayed at the Kilbrogan Rectory which was, at the time, home to Rev Charles B. Bernard.

The new 99 year lease was agreed in 1862 but was revised in 1876 as it hadn't been fully executed. It was to run for 99 years from 1871 until 1970.

---

[329] Lismore Papers. MS 7053. 1861-1862

The trustees were William Shaw of Beaumont in Cork, MP, Richard Lane Allman of Allmans Distillery who resided at Woodlands JP, John Rawdon Berwick Esq (the Duke's Bandon Agent and a JP), William Christopher Dowden Esq and two brothers, William Connor Sullivan of Overton, a local Merchant and Thomas Kingston Sullivan, a solicitor. The annual rent was £10.

The Lawn Tennis Club was founded in 1884. It had two courts. A cricket pitch was also created.

Stewart Richard Tresilian acted as secretary for the coal fund committee and he was also part of the committee of the town hall. In the early 1900s his executors furnished accounts to the trustees of the town hall claiming an outstanding balance owed to his estate of £117.47.

For a period in the 1890s Richard Clear acted as the Honorable Secretary. He resigned his position in 1902.

A dispute arose in 1895 when it came to light that £400 had been borrowed from the coal fund to finance the establishment of the hall. The coal fund had been set up in the 1792 to provide coal to the poor regardless of religious denomination. A letter was sent to the surviving mortgagors requesting the repayment of the funds with interest. Interest had not been paid on the loan for many years. The letter was addressed to Captain J.R. Wheeler, JP, Bandon. He replied that he knew nothing about the mortgage and had never been a trustee.

The town hall derived its small income from the cricket ground, from the subscribers to the hall, from the billiard room and from a part of the property which was sub let. It appeared to be experiencing financial challenges in the early 1900s.

In 1902 the only surviving trustee, Richard Lane Allman, called a public meeting and Lord Bandon, Jeremiah J. McDaniel, Mathias Cummins Hickey and William Foley were appointed as trustees along with Allman. In 1919 they bought the freehold of the property from Sir John Arnott for £150. This was following a dispute about outstanding rent which had been owed to the Arnott Estate by the town hall.

In 1915 M.C. Hickey acted as Honorary Treasurer and W. Foley was the Honorary Secretary.

After 1967 the Hall fell into disuse. It wasn't until 1976 that a major refurbishment of the hall began with the assistance of the training council FAS. A revision of the trust was granted by the High Court and the trust is now managed by a limited company of trustees.

No 81
1837 Number 74 – Valuation £28
1849 Number 89
1851 Number 81 – Valuation £18 10s
1901 Census Number - 75
1911 Census Number - 23

Immediate Lessors
1816 Timothy Murphy (from the Duke of Devonshire)
1824 John Harley (from the Duke of Devonshire)
1843 Octavius O'Brien
1845 Thomas Kingston Sullivan

The original lease for this plot seems to have been entered into on 1st April 1816 between Timothy Murphy, a farmer and the Duke of Devonshire. He was forced to surrender the lease on 13th July, 1822.[330]

John Harley of Bandon, Gent, entered into a lease with the Duke of Devonshire in 1824 for the lives of Henry Harley, John Harley and Osborne Harley, the sons of the lessee and 99 years running concurrently. The plot was described as a messuage or tenement

---

[330] MS 43 215/5. Lismore papers

on the south side of North Main Street, 37'6" in breadth and bounded on the east by Dr Clerke's holding and on the west by the holdings of George Cornwall.[331]

On 5th June 1843 John Harley Esq of Clonroad near Ennis and Osborne Harley of the same address conveyed the lease to Octavius O'Brien, an attorney in Dublin.

On 20th March, 1845 Octavius O'Brien and John Harley Esq of Ennis conveyed this property and other holdings to Thomas Kingston Sullivan Esq for £700.[332]

Thomas Kingston Sullivan assigned the lease of this property to Jane Clerke on 13th February 1851.

Occupiers
Franklin Baldwin was recorded as the occupier in the tithe applotments which suggests that he was in residence long before 1837. Pigots Directory of 1824 recorded Franklin Baldwin, Attorney, of North Main Street. He was noted for his interest in sport and was a steward at the Bandon Steeple Chase which took place in April 1834.[333] He was assisted by Captain Adderley Beamish and Major Nugent of the 7th Dragoon Guards.

Franklin Kirby Baldwin was listed as the occupier in the records of 1837. His father was William Baldwin who married Mary Kirby, the daughter of Major Franklin Kirby, of Barnborough Grange, Yorkshire. They lived at Lisarda, Castle Baldwin and Mount Nelson, County Cork.[334]

Franklin was an attorney and coroner[335]. He was admitted as a freeman of the Corporation of Bandon Bridge in 1831.

---

[331] Registry of Deeds. 1843 9 288 of 5th June 1843

[332] Registry of Deeds. 1845 5 137

[333] Evening Heralrd. 11th April 1834

[334] www.winters-online.net/Baldwin-of-Cork

[335] Slater's Directory of 1846

> [336]TO THE NOBILITY, CLERGY AND FREE-
> HOLDERS OF THE COUNTY OF CORK
> MY LORDS AND GENTLEMEN.—Having ascer-
> tained that the office of CORONER of your County will
> shortly become vacant, I beg leave to offer myself to your
> notice, as a Candidate for it. The favour with which I
> have been honoured, wherever it has been in my power to
> make personal application, encourages me to hope for the
> same, where time and circumstances preclude my seeking
> your support in person. Should your general suffrages con-
> fer on me the situation which I solicit from you, I beg to
> assure you, that the being honoured with your choice will,
> of itself, endure the strict fulfillment of official duty on my
> part.—I am, my Lords and Gentlemen,
> Your very obedient Servant,
> Bandon, June 16, 1828.   **FRANKLIN BALDWIN**

He married Barbara Morris Evanson on 30th July 1822. They had ten children; William, Nathaniel, Franklin, Mary Harriet, Henry Clement, Alleyne, Susanna, Edward Beecher, Clement and Fanny Susanna. Franklin died in 1849. He was recorded as the occupier of the house up to the time of his death.

In 1842 a meeting was held in the court house to hear the report of a committee appointed to analyse the extension of navigation of the river to Bandon. Franklin was the chairman of the committee.

The occupier was Jane Clerke at the time of the Griffiths Valuation in 1851. Jane lived at the premises until she died on 22nd September, 1859. Letters of Administration were granted to her brother, Major General St John Augustus Clerke,[337] who was the sole surviving next of kin. She left effects under £400.

She leased the garden to her neighbour, Stewart Richard Tresilian. Jane Clerke entered into a lease with Thomas Kingston Sullivan on 29th September 1850 for her life at a yearly rent of £2. All taxes and assessments were to be paid by Thomas Kingston Sullivan.[338]

---

[336] Cork Constitution, 19th June 1828
[337] See Appendix. Biographies.
[338] Registry of Deeds. 1851 6 165 of 13th February 1851

In 1861 Thomas Clear moved to this property from No 6 where he had been living from 1856 until 1861. He was in the property until 1868, two years before he died.

Major Fry succeeded Thomas Clear in 1868 and lived in the property for a year. He died on 11th June 1869 aged 73. He served in the 63rd regiment and was buried at Christ Church, Kilbrogan. Major Fry had a daughter Mary who married Captain Frederick Delacour Cornwall. At the time she was living with her husband and family at No 61.

The next occupier was John Sullivan who moved in during 1870.

Two years later in 1872 Rev Thomas Neligan Kearney occupied the property. He was born in 1819 and was the son of John Kearney. He was rector of Kilbrittain from 1868 to 1872 when he resigned.

In 1873 Rev Thomas moved to Maidenhead in England where he became vicar of St Andrew and St Mary Magdalen. In 1880 he became vicar of Throwley in the diocese of Canterbury. He married in 1856, Martha Matilda, second daughter of Thomas Neligan, lieutenant of the 83rd Ft regiment and he had one daughter, Mary Alice Kearney. He died on 30th March 1884, aged 65.

In 1873 Rev Kearney was succeeded at No 81 by Richard Clear, the son of Thomas Clear who had lived in the property for a period until 1868. Richard lived in the property for six years until 1879. Richard lived at No 49 from 1898 until 1921. He was also resident for a short period at No 57 and spent some years at Janeville on Watergate Street.

In 1881 Rev John Lindsey Darling was recorded as the occupier. He was curate of Ballymodan Church of Ireland from 1876. Following the death of Rev Bleakley in 1878, he was appointed rector. During 1881 he became rector of Kinsale and remained there until 1895. Rev J.L. Darling was the eldest son of Richard Sisson Darling of Trinidad. He graduated from Trinity in 1877. He married in 1881 Mabella Roberta, daughter of Rev R.H. Maunsell Eyre of Innishannon. In 1895 he moved to the Mariners Church in Kingstown, Dublin.

In 1882 Miss Browne took up residence and stayed until 1886 when Albert B. Burns succeeded her. His successor was James Carey in 1893. In 1897 John Barry Deane was the resident.

In the 1901 census John Barry Deane was described as a solicitor, aged 38, living with Annette Maud Deane aged 26, an aunt Mary Elizabeth Smith and a maid servant, Kate O'Brien aged 27.

In the 1911 census John Barry Deane, aged 49, was described as a solicitor, living with his aunt, Mary Elizabeth Smith, a widow aged 54, and a domestic servant, Hannah Coughlan, aged 19. The rest of the family was recorded as being away.

John Barry Deane and family lived at the premises until 1923 when Catherine Hennessy became the tenant. Catherine continued to reside at the property until 1942. She was succeeded by William V. Tayler. Mrs Hannah M Tayler was the next occupier in 1945 and was still living in the property until 1852 when David Hegarty took up residence. In 1958 the property became vacant. Michael Hymes, a post master, became the next occupier in 1959.

No 82 – ODM Accountants

1837 Number 75 – Valuation £34
1849 Number 90
1851 Number 82 – Valuation £22 15s
1901 Census Number - 76
1911 Census Number - 22

Immediate Lessors
Details of Original Lease not known
1851 The Duke of Devonshire
Colonel Shadwell Clerke
1898 Sir John Arnott

Colonel Shadwell Clerke held the lease on this property at least from 1879 to 1887. Richard Wheeler Doherty administered the lease on the Colonel's behalf.[339]

Occupiers
The occupier was Margaret Hornibrook in 1837.

In 1849 Robert Travers Cole Bowen was recorded as the resident. He was a land agent. He was the son of Rev Nicholas Cole Bowen and Brianna Cole. Rev Nicholas was the fifth son of Henry Cole Bowen Esq of Bowens Court, Kildorrery. A sister of Robert's, Henrietta Cole married John Lawrence Hornibrook of Ballinascarthy.[340]

By 1856 Charles Allman[341], a corn merchant, had become the occupier and shortly afterwards he was succeeded by Stewart Richard Tresilian.

Charles Allman was the father of Stewart's wife, Matilda Rebecca Allman. He was a first cousin of Richard Lane Allman and James Clugston Allman who became the joint owners of Allman, Dowden & Co brewers. Richard and James were involved in Matilda's marriage settlement. The Allmans were Unitarians. George Allman who married Mary Clugston acquired 46 acres of land in Old Chapel and built a massive cotton mill, the remains of which are still visible.

Stewart Richard married Matilda Rebecca Allman in Bandon on 26th June 1852. Their family included Richard Stewart, Charles Allman, Sarah Wilson, Elizabeth Sarah born on 9th November 1858 at baptised at Christ Church on 30th November, Stewart born on 24th September 1860 and baptised at Christ Church on 31st October, George Allman Tresilian born on 15th September 1862 and Robert born on 11th August 1864 and baptised on 2nd September.

---

[339] Doherty Estate Papers held at the Cork Archives
[340] See Appendix. Short Biographies
[341] Slater's Directory of Bandon, 1856

Stewart Richard Tresilian was the son of Richard Tresilian, a wine and spirit merchant who married Elizabeth Popham in 1807 at Brinny. Stewart worked for a short time with his father as a wine and spirit merchant. He acted as a land agent. He was appointed as Clerk to the Bandon Board of Guardians in 1838. He was recorded in the register of vestrymen at Christ Church, Kilbrogan in 1870. He was also a member of the freemasons, an officer of the fishery conservators and Honorable Secretary of the Bandon Coal Fund.

Stewart Richard Tresilian paid a yearly rent of £22 paid half yearly in March and September. The rent included the poor rate and income tax. The rent was administered by Richard Wheeler Doherty.

Stewart's name appears in the electoral register of 1884. The property was described as a house with offices and garden at a rateable valuation of £22 15s. Stewart Richard died on 4th July, 1885. In 1887 John Jones became the occupier.

In the 1901 census John Jones was described as a collector of income tax and a land agent, aged 69, living with his son William Dawson Jones aged 40, a draper, daughter Rebecca Jane Jones aged 27, son Richard William Jones, an accountant aged 31, daughter in law Nannie Jones aged 33, grand-daughter Gladys Jones aged 10, grandson John Edmund Jones aged 8, grandson George Thomas Jones aged 7, grand-daughter Mildred Francis Jones aged 4, grand-daughter Catherine Doris Jones aged 2, Effie Jones aged 1, grand-daughter and Margaret O'Driscoll, a servant aged 29 and Ellen Galvin, the children's friend, aged 19.

In the 1911 census, John Jones was recorded as a land agent, head constable of the RIC and a widower. He was living with his son William Dawson, a draper aged 50, a son Richard Williams aged 42, a manager of a flour store, a son George Thomas, a retired land estate agent aged 46 who was married, a daughter in law Annie Jones aged 41, a grandson George Thomas aged 17, a grand daughter Mildred Frances aged 14, a grand daughter Kathleen Doris aged 12, a grand daughter Effie aged 11, a grand son Clarence William Whiteside aged 8 and a nurse and servant Ellen Galvin aged 28.

George Thomas Jones senior died aged 54 on 10th January 1919 and his burial took place at St Peter's, Ballymodan.

William Dawson Jones succeeded his father in 1925.

By 1935 Patrick O'Driscoll was residing at the property. William Hosford took up residency in 1936. Dr Eugene Callanan became the occupier in 1944 (He moved to No 56). Benjamin Shorten was the tenant in 1950, the representatives of Benjamin Shorten in 1952 and in 1953 Lionel P. Baldwin became the occupier.

1775 Map of part of Lower North Main Street

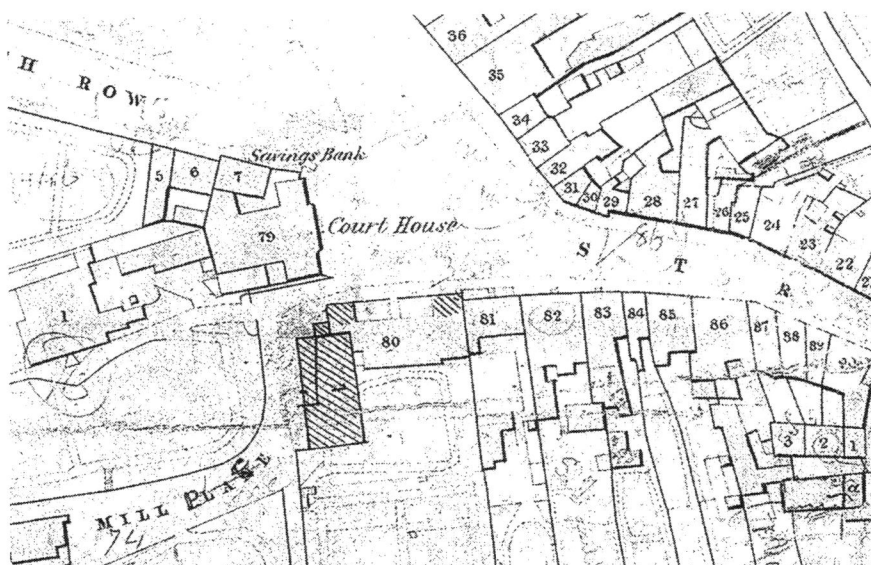

Early Griffiths Map of part of lower North Main Street

No 83 – A shop and dwelling house – 1600s timber frame. Formerly Forrester's Pottery Shop
1775 Number 42
1837 Number 76 – Valuation £18
1849 Number 91
1851 Number 83 – Valuation £15 10s
1901 Census Number - 77
1911 Census Number - 21

Immediate Lessors
1816 Rebecca Williams from the Duke of Devonshire. 41 years
1857 The Duke of Devonshire
1897 Sir John Arnott

Rebecca Williams entered into a lease with the Duke of Devonshire on 25th March 1816 for 41 years with expiry in 1857 at an annual rental of £9.13.10.[342]

Occupiers
In 1837 the occupier was recorded as Rebecca Williams. It is likely that they occupied the house from the commencement of the lease in 1816. In 1846 Anne and Rebecca Williams were jointly listed at the address.[343]

Miss Anne Williams was registered as the occupier in the early valuation records of 1849 and at the time of the Griffiths Valuation of 1851. Her occupation was described as gentry. In 1856 Anne and Rebecca Williams were recorded as being together at the property.[344]

Anne Williams was succeeded by Timothy Leary by 1861. He was in the property until 1868 and was paying a yearly rent of £15. He was classified as a weekly/monthly payer.

William Lynch became the occupier on 29th September 1867. He was registered in the Devonshire Estate accounts as a yearly tenant. The Devonshire Estate carried out repairs to the house in 1868. William's name appeared on the electoral register of 1884. The property was described as part of a house with offices, yard and a garden at a rateable valuation of £8.

William Lynch was succeeded in 1891 by John Shorten and in 1892 by Eliza Shorten

In 1874 the shop was leased by William Lynch to John Buckley. In 1879 William leased the shop to Jeremiah Donohue, to Walter Sinnott, a watch maker[345] in 1880 and to James Mills in 1882. James Mills name appeared on the electoral register of 1884 and his share of the property was a shop and room at a rateable valuation of £6.

---

[342] MS6185. Lismore Papers
[343] Slater's Directory of 1846
[344] Slater's Directory of 1856
[345] Slater's Directory of 1881

The shop was vacant for a while after 1886 until John Shorten moved into the house in 1892. He took on the shop as well as the house in 1891 and Eliza Shorten succeeded him in 1892.

The 1901 census recorded Eliza Shorten as a shop keeper, aged 48, living with her brother Wilson Shorten, RIC pensioner aged 55, a boarder Caroline Rice aged 17, a boarder, Anne Tanner aged 72 who was a retired farmer's daughter, a boarder Hanorah Collins a retired maid and Susan Saberry aged 74, a retired nurse and also a boarder.

By the time of the 1911 census Eliza Anne Shorten was aged 62 and was a dealer in oil, egg and sundries. She was living with Ellen Keohane, a boarder and superintendent in the hosiery factory aged 45, a room keeper Anne Maguire aged 75, a room keeper Eliza Jennings aged 72, a room keeper Hanorah Collins aged 71.

Eliza Shorten resided at the property until 1914 when M. McQuire became the occupier. Frances Bird became the next tenant in 1922 and also the immediate lessor taking over from Sir John Arnott. In 1927 Frances Atkins was listed as the tenant.

William Beare became the occupier in 1953 and in 1955 George Beare succeeded him.

In more recent years the Forrester Family operated a pottery business from this premises.

No 84
1837 Number 77 – Valuation £12
1851 Number 84 – Valuation £9 5s
1901 Census Number - 78
1911 Census Number - 20

Immediate Lessors
Earlier lease details not known
1851 Benjamin Forde
1869 Richard Wheeler Doherty as agent for Col Shadwell Clerke

Occupiers
In 1837 the occupier was William Topham and he was still resident in 1849 and in 1851. His occupation was recorded as shoe maker.[346]

John Topham had succeeded William by the time of the first valuation in 1856. He was a boot and shoe maker.[347] John Topham married Elizabeth Jane Harman. They had a daughter Rachel Alice Margaret on 25th November 1864, John Topham born on 8th March 1868 (he died in the same year) and Elizabeth Jane Topham born on 26th October, 1870.

Richard Wheeler Doherty administered the lease for Colonel Shadwell Clerke from at least 1869 until 1887. John Topham paid an annual rent of £8 on a half yearly basis. In 1883 the house was repaired at a cost of £30 and the rent was increased to £9.10 payable half yearly.

---

[346] Electoral Register of 1832
[347] Coughlan's Directory of 1867

John Topham died in 1883. In the electoral register of 1884 the property was described as a house with offices, yard and a garden at a rateable valuation of £9 5s. Mrs Elizabeth Jane Topham became the tenant following his death. She died in mid 1895 and Alice Topham was then registered as the occupier.

According to the 1901 census, Alice Topham was a dress maker, aged 34, living with her sister Margaret, aged 30 and Elizabeth aged 28. Alice died at the end of 1901 and was succeeded by Margaret.

The 1911 census recorded Margaret as aged 44. She died on 31st August 1931 and was buried at Christ Church Kilbrogan. Elizabeth Jane was living with Margaret. Elizabeth died on 14th April 1956 and was buried with Margaret. Robert Topham, aged 90, a cousin and retired boot maker was also living with them. He died on 30th November 1913 aged 93. His burial took place at St Peter's, Ballymodan.

R. Topham was still recorded as a boot and shoe maker in 1915.[348] Elizabeth succeeded Margaret and in 1958 the house was vacant for two years until 1960. Simon O'Dowd became the occupier in 1960. He operated a sweet shop.

---

[348] Cork and Munster Trade Directory. 1815

No 85 For a time the Bandon Commercial Club and more recently a Nursing Home
1837 Number 78 – Valuation £26
1851 Number 85 – Valuation £17 5s
1901 Census Number - 79
1911 Census Number - 19

Immediate Lessors
1851 Richard Dowden
1856 Richard Good
1860s Thomas Kingston Sullivan

Occupiers
In 1837 the occupier was John W. Lindsay.

Sarah Roche Gash was the occupier in 1849 and was still in the property in 1851. She was from Little Silver, Bandon.

By 1856 the property became vacant for a short while before Miss Stawell moved in. Her family were from Coolmain Castle in Kilbrittain.

Miss Stawell continued to reside at the property until 1887 when Catherine Stawell became the occupier. She remained at the house until she died on 18th February, 1900. The executor of Catherine's will was Alexander E.S. Heard, a resident magistrate. She left effects of £536 15s 7d

After the death of Catherine Stawell the property became vacant for a short while.

By the time of the 1901 census John West, a Naval Pensioner, aged 59 was residing at the property with his wife Maria West aged 39, Dora West aged 21 and Bertram McMarrow aged 5.

In 1902 the property became the premises of the Bandon Commercial Club. James Kingston was recorded as the secretary.

The property was described as a technical school in the valuation record.

The immediate lessor became John Brangan in 1905 followed by the representatives of Marmaduke Brangan in 1907.

There was no listing for the property in the 1911 census.

By 1930 the immediate lessor became John Buckley, Bridget Drummy (1931), Mary Donegan (1934). In 1949 the property became vacant. Daniel O'Brien became the tenant in 1960.

No 86 – a shop and dwelling house
1837 Number 79 – Valuation £35
1849 Number 94
1851 Number 86 – Valuation £27 10s
1901 Census Number - 80
1911 Census Number – 18

Immediate Lessors
1818 – Joseph John Wheeler (from Duke of Devonshire)

The lease was originally conveyed by the Duke of Devonshire to John Wheeler on 1st April 1818 and was surrendered in 1875[349]. (He was ejected). The lease was for the lives of Hon Rev Richard B. Bernard and Hon W.S. Bernard with 41 years running concurrently at a rent of £10 10s. The site was described as being a plot where an old house was standing already in the possession of J.J. Wheeler, in breadth 26' and in depth 83', bounded on the north by the street, on the south by the premises in possession of John Wheeler, on the west by the holdings of William Jenkins and

---

[349] Lismore Papers

on the east by the holding of Joseph Bullen with the free liberty of using the lane or passage from the meeting house lane to the premises. The terms of the lease required Joseph John Wheeler to expend £100 on repairs.

In the original lease of 1818 the site was described 'as east Mrs Jenkins and Preaching House Lane, south Bandon River and west by Mary Sullivan'.

The deed of 1857 recorded the breadth as 35' at the front and a depth of 315'. It was bounded on the north by the main street and on the south by the river, west by Mary Sullivan, widow. On the east was a holding of William Jenkins. The property was also partly bounded by Preaching House Lane (Water Lane). The house was mentioned in a Wheeler family deed of 1857.[350]

Occupiers
John Wheeler was most likely both the immediate lessor and occupier of this property from the date of the first lease in 1818. He was still recorded as the tenant in 1837 and in 1840.

Mrs Wheeler was the occupier in 1849. The property was described as large with stables, a fowl house and a mangle house.

The occupier was Anne Wheeler at the time of the Griffiths Valuation in 1851.

By 1856 John Wheeler was the occupier. He resided at the property until 1874 when Richard Wheeler succeeded him. John Wheeler was recorded in the register of vestrymen at Christ Church, Kilbrogan in 1870.

Prior to 1875 the property was described as a house, garden and yard. It was then divided into 86a and 86b. Walter Bullen became the tenant of the Duke of Devonshire. He converted part of the property into a shop with a stable, house and loft at a value of £22. In 1880 he added stables and became the lessor. The value was £20 and £2 for the stables.

Walter leased the office and yard to James Bradfield in 1874.

---

[350] Registry of Deeds. 1857 13 94

Walter was born in 1825. His parents were Henry Bullen (1793-1849) who married Abigail Sarah Whelply (1794-1855). Henry was a farmer at Lissapooka who moved to Castle Road and became a grocer, pawnbroker and auctioneer. Henry and Abigail had five other children. Walter's grandfather was Walter Bullen who married Sarah Bennett. They had a camflet manufacturing business and house in Blackpool, Cork.

Walter, a Methodist, married twice. His first wife was Jane Beamish Bullen, his second cousin and daughter of Joseph Bullen and Jane Beamish of Skibbereen. They married at Creagh on 26th October 1850 by licence. He was a shopkeeper in Skibbereen at the time. His wife died near Bandon in childbirth on 29th September 1855.

Walter married secondly Elizabeth Jane Ford, daughter of Rev Adam Rice Ford and Mary Bentley on 11th November 1856 in Youghal. He gave his occupation as draper of Bandon. They had eleven children, Henry Bentley (1857-1906), Caroline Amelia (1859-1914), John Whelpley (1860-1948), Selina Jane (1862-1937), Alfred Constantine (1864-1932), William Arthur (1866-1935), Annette Elizabeth (1868-1958), Walter Ernest (1870-1870), Joseph Edward (1869-1872), Augusta Maud (1871-1948) and Frederick Charles (1874-1940).

From 1857 until 1862 Walter was living at Roundhill in Bandon. By 1864 he was recorded at North Main Street (See No 23). He joined the Bandon Masons in 1869.

The Bullens moved to 6 North Mall, Cork in 1881. He died there on 23rd December 1897 aged 72 and he was buried at Christ Church, Kilbrogan. During his life he had undertaken careers as a chandler, grocer, auctioneer, insurance agent and tanner.

At the time of the 1901 census his widow was living at 5 Southern Road, Cork. She died on 14th July 1913.

Walter was succeeded in 1881 by Timothy O'Keeffe and Joseph Good

In 1882 John Richard Wheeler took up residence. (He had been renting the stables and office of No 87 in 1866). He served in the first Battalion of the Royal Regiment. In 1863 he married Penelope Biggs Wheeler, the daughter of John Wheeler, commander R.N. who married Harriet Biggs (daughter of Thomas Biggs). Their children John (b 1865), Richard Thomas (b 1868), Charlotte Mary (b 1870) and Thomas Arthur (b 1871) were all recorded as being born on North Main Street and were baptised at Christ Church Kilbrogan.

John's name appeared in the electoral register of 1884. The property was described as a house, shop, offices, yard and garden with a rateable valuation of £28. He also held land at Knockbrogan which had a rateable valuation of £11.

John Richard Wheeler was described as a Captain of the 2nd Regiment of Foot in the Guys Directory of 1886. In Slater's Directory of 1881 he was described as a Captain of the Royal Navy.

In the 1901 census John Richard Wheeler was recorded as a JP, aged 77, living on interest from money together with his son Thomas Arthur John Wheeler aged 29, a daughter Harriet M. Wheeler aged 34 and a servant and widow, Jane Wright aged 40.

John Richard Wheeler was succeeded by his son Thomas Arthur Wheeler in 1903 and by Rebecca Bradfield in 1904. She had moved from No 23 where she had been resident from 1903 to 1904 (See her biography under No 23). Her sister was Sarah who married Joseph Nagle.

In the 1911 census Joseph Nagle was living at the property. He was aged 50, an ex RIC pensioner and he was living with his wife Sarah Nagle aged 48, a daughter Rebecca Win Nagle aged 17, sister in law Rebecca Bradfield aged 42, boarder Barbara Hewitt Baldwin aged 72, boarder Henry Barrett aged 16, boarder Edward C. Daly aged 22 and a clerk in the Munster and Leinster Bank, a boarder Kirkwood McKibbin aged 27, a school master, Norah Crowley aged 30, a domestic servant and a boarder Truman Joseph Muggison aged 37, a mechanical engineer.

In 1915 Rebecca Bradfield was recorded as running a restaurant at the premises as well as accommodation for visitors and her charges were moderate.

The property was vacant in 1922 and in 1923 Jane O'Connell moved in. She was succeeded by John O'Connell in 1927. John Howard was the occupier in 1944. He was followed by Mrs Mary Cotter in 1946

No 87 – New build in 1840
1837 Number 80 – Valuation £14
1851 Number 87 – Valuation £16 15s
1901 Census Number - 81
1911 Census Number – 17

Immediate Lessors
1840 Robert Fuller (from Duke of Devonshire) – 99 years
1851 Robert Fuller Esq
1856 The Duke of Devonshire
1897 Sir John Arnott

Robert Fuller, a shopkeeper, entered into the lease with the Duke of Devonshire on 24th March 1840. He was contracted to spend £300 erecting one substantial messuage or tenement to a plan approved by the Duke of Devonshire. It was to measure 25' at the front and the depth of the plot was 80', bounded on the south by a lane leading to John Wheeler's premises. It was bounded on the west by John Wheeler's and on the east by Benjamin Forde's holdings.[351]

The lease was for the lives of George Fuller (15), Amelia Fuller (8), Eliza Fuller (3), the son and daughters of Robert and 99 years at a rent of £6 pa, payable half yearly. The lease stipulated that Robert Fuller was to build one house which was not to be divided into two

---

[351] MS 43 215/5. Lismore papers

without the permission of the Duke of Devonshire. No trade was to take place in the building without a licence. He was subsequently ejected for non payment of rent.[352]

Occupiers

In 1837 the occupier was Denis Murray.

Ralph Fuller was recorded as the occupier in 1849 and again in 1851 at the time of the Griffiths valuation.

By 1856 James Seymour had become the tenant. He was succeeded by Jonathan Tanner, a grocer. Mrs Tanner[353], also a grocer, took over in 1866 and at the same time John Richard Wheeler was recorded as the tenant of the stables and office.

In 1882 Sarah McCarthy became the occupier and in 1883 she rented the shop to John Burchill. The rateable valuation for the shop in 1884 was £5 and John W. Burchill was recorded as the occupier.[354]

Sarah McCarthy was succeeded by Mary Lane in 1888. Jeremiah Eaton became the occupier 1892 and Mary Reen took over in 1892.

John Burchill ceased to occupy the shop in 1892. It passed to Eliza Wilson, a dressmaker and milliner.[355]

By the time of the 1901 census the occupier of the house was still Mary Reen aged 40, a lodging house keeper. She was living with her brother, Charles McCarthy, baker, aged 23 and servant Anne Coveney aged 17. Also living at the property were Thomas Nolan, a boarder aged 23, a clerk boarder Jeremiah Murphy who was a carrier, aged 21, a boarder Robert Buttimore, who was a drapers clerk, aged 21, a boarder James J. Murphy, an accountant aged 27 and Timothy Murphy aged 19 also a boarder and a drapers clerk.

Mary Reen was also resident at the premises at the time of the 1911 census. She was described as a widow, aged 52 living with her

---

[352] Lismore Papers
[353] Slater's Directory of 1870
[354] Electoral Register. 1884
[355] Guy's Directory of 1893

brother Charles G. McCarthy who was aged 33 and single and a brother John J. McCarthy aged 43, single and a clothier.

Mary lived at the premises for 26 years. Her successor, John McCarthy, moved in during 1918 and he lived at the house for many years until his death. His representatives were registered in 1958.

No 88 – Shop – Built by Benjamin Forde in 1839[356]
1849 Number 96
1851 Number 88 – Valuation £8
1901 Census Number - 82
1911 Census Number – 16
No record of a house in 1837.

Immediate Lessors
1839 Benjamin Forde (from Duke of Devonshire)
1851 Benjamin Forde
1863 Richard Wheeler Doherty

The original lease between the Duke of Devonshire and Benjamin Forde was dated 31st December 1839. Forde subsequently built two houses (no 88 and no 89) bounded on the south by John Wheeler's lane and on the east by James White (no 90) and on the west by Dennis Murray (No 87). The lease was for the natural lives of John Popham aged 14, Benjamin Popham aged 12 and Bradshaw Popham aged 6, 2nd,3rd and 4th sons of John Popham of Bandon or 99 years from 25th March 1837 at a rent of £5 5s to be paid half yearly.[357]

---

[356] Registry of Deeds. 1856 2 176
[357] Registry of Deeds. 1856 2 176

Occupiers

R. Bourke was recorded as the occupier in 1849.

Honoria Murphy, a grocer, was the tenant in 1851.

By 1856 Richard Topham, a boot & shoe maker and leather dealer[358], had become the occupier. Richard and Robert Topham were recorded in the register of vestrymen at Christ Church, Kilbrogan in 1870.

Richard Topham who was born in 1793 died aged 83 in 1876. He was succeeded by Robert Topham, also a bootmaker.[359] His name appeared on the electoral register of 1884. The property was described as a house with offices and yard. It had a rateable valuation of £8.

Robert was living at the property at the time of the 1901 census and was described as aged 30, single and a boot maker. He was living on his own.

Daniel Jones became the occupier in 1906 and remained for four years until 1910 when the property was occupied by Thomas O'Keeffe. In 1915 the property became vacant and in 1916 John Callaghan moved in. He lived in the house until Michael Lynam moved in during 1922. Daniel succeeded Michael in 1925.

Curiously the 1911 census records the occupier as Thomas Stafford aged 78, a retired builder living with his wife Ellen aged 72 and Julia M. Stafford, their daughter aged 25. There is no mention of Thomas Stafford in the valuation records and Thomas O'Keeffe is not recorded as vacating the property until 1915.

Thomas O'Keeffe was recorded as the resident after the 1911 census until 1915 when the house became vacant. In 1916 Daniel Callaghan became the occupier and he was succeeded by Michael Lynam during 1925. He remained there until 1932 when John Keating took up residence. John was followed by David Webb in 1936 and for a while afterwards the property was vacant before John Nagle moved in during 1939.

---

[358] Slater's Directory of 1856
[359] Guy's Directory of 1893

No 89 – Shop and dwelling house – Built by Benjamin Forde in 1839[360]
1849 Number 97
1851 Number 89 – Valuation £8
1901 Census Number - 83
1911 Census Number - 15

No record of a house in 1837.

Immediate Lessors
1839 Benjamin Forde (from Duke of Devonshire)
1851 Benjamin Forde
1863 Richard Wheeler Doherty

The original lease of this house and No 88 was granted on 31st December 1839. Benjamin Forde built two houses on the site (No 88 and No 89).[361]

Occupiers
Catherine Massey was the occupier in 1849 and remained in the property until 1886. She was a milliner, dressmaker and haberdasher[362]

Catherine Massey remained in residence for many years until 1886. A succession of residents followed her.

By the time of the 1901 census the occupier was Hannah Reen, a dress maker aged 28 who was living with Ellen Reen aged 65, her mother, John O'Shea aged 30, a plumber and boarder, Elizabeth O'Shea aged 25, also a boarder, Kathleen O'Shea, a boarder, John

---

[360] Registry of Deeds. 1856 2 176
[361] See details for No 88
[362] Slater's Directory of Bandon, 1856

Punch aged 33, a plumber and boarder and Daniel Desmore aged 80, a blacksmith and boarder. The property was recorded as having five windows at the front.

Hannah was succeeded by John Punch in 1909. He was still the occupier at the time of the 1911 census and was described as aged 43, a plumber living with his with wife Hannah (38), son Vincent (5), daughter Nellie (1) and servant Katie Tobin (13)

John Punch moved out in 1914 and the house became vacant. In 1918 Thomas Tanner took up residence. He was succeeded in 1925 by John Keating. Michael Lynam was recorded as the tenant in 1936. He was followed by William Russell in 1941. William Scott was recorded as the occupier in 1951. It became vacant in 1955.

No 90 – A Licensed Premises – No longer standing
1837 Number 82 – Valuation £15
1849 Number 98
1851 Number 90 – Valuation £11 10s
1901 Census Number - 84
1911 Census Number – 14

Immediate Lessors
Date ? James White
1840 John Harley Esq
1843 Octavius O'Brien
1851 The Duke of Devonshire
1897 Sir John Arnott
1912 Allman Dowden & Co
1917 Sir John Arnott

On 26th March 1840 James White, a publican, assigned the dwelling to John Harley Esq of Clonroad, Ennis. It was 28'6 in breadth at the front and to the back adjoined Preaching House Lane, called Water Lane in 1840. The lease included all the houses at the back which were in the possession of Joseph Bullen. The houses were bounded on the north by a vacant space owned by John Wheeler for the remainder of the 41 years from 25th March 1816 subject to yearly rents as set out in the head lease and subject to a mortgage of £150 to be repaid with interest.

Occupiers

In 1837 the occupier was James White.

Maurice Scollard was the occupier in 1849. He was a publican[363]

In 1851 the occupier was Cornelius Callaghan, a publican

On 14th February 1854 Swanston, the Duke's Agent, took possession of the house from Mrs Wilson and let it to George Grandon, a local cattle dealer, from 25th March 1854 as a yearly tenant at £16 per annum. Mrs Wilson had paid rent up to 25th March 1854. John Wilson had been recorded as the occupier before Mrs Wilson.

In 1862 extensive repairs were carried out to the house. A new roof was applied, the chimneys were rebuilt, the walls were raised two feet and new windows were installed at a cost to the Devonshire Estate of £47 13s 3d.[364] George Grandon, a shop keeper[365], died on 10th May 1863 and his wife Julia succeeded him. Letters of Administration were granted at Cork to Julia, his widow on 18th April, 1864.

In 1866 Mrs Grandon was followed by John Hickey, a provision & spirit dealer[366]

In 1870 the Duke's Agent made a payment to John Hickey of £1 10s 0d for building a flight of stairs in his house.[367] He appeared on the electoral register of 1884 and the property was described as a house, offices and yard with a rateable valuation of £15.

John Hickey, a vintner,[368] resided at the property for 28 years until 1894 when Michael Walsh became the occupier.

In the 1901 census Michael Walsh was recorded as a publican aged 48 living with wife Cathrine Walsh aged 47, son James P. Walsh aged 15, Julia Walsh aged 14, Patrick Walsh aged 12, Ellen Walsh

---

[363] Electoral Register of 1832
[364] Lismore Papers. MS 7054
[365] Calendar of Wills. National Archives of Ireland
[366] Coughlan's Directory of 1867
[367] Lismore Papers. MS 7061. Bandon Accounts
[368] Guys Directory of 1893

aged 11, Cathrine Walsh aged 10 daughter, Michael J. Walsh son aged 8, Mary Walsh daughter aged 7, Stephen O'Driscoll , a labourer and relative aged 47 and Jeremiah McDonnell aged 8, a boarder, living on saved money

Michael Walsh's name was on the parchment which listed the committee members responsible for the erection of the Maid of Erin statue. He also acted as a Town Councillor.

Michael and his family were still in residence by the time of the 1911 census. He was recorded as aged 58 living with wife Kate (50), daughter Julia (23), son Patrick (22), daughter Mary (16) and son Michael John (17)

An obituary appeared for Michael Walsh in the Eagle dated 20th May 1911. He had passed away at his residence on North Main Street following a long illness leaving a widow and family. The funeral took place at St Patricks Church and he was buried at Kilmalooda graveyard. The officiating clergy were the Very Rev Canon Shinkwin and Rev R.J. Burts. Amongst the chief mourners were his wife, sons Patrick and Michael, his brother in law, Timothy O'Driscoll of Enniskeane and his daughters Julia, Nellie and Mary

In 1915 Mary Chambers took over the tenancy and in 1917 the property was occupied by Beamish and Crawford. Daniel Regan became the occupier in 1919.

Daniel was succeeded by Kathleen O'Regan in 1933 followed by William Scott in 1938. By 1959 the house was described in the valuation records as being in ruins.

Preaching House Lane/Water Lane

No 91. Also known as RIVERSIDE HOUSE – No longer standing. The site of a Methodist Chapel in Bandon which was built in 1789.

The Methodist Chapel

The Methodist Chapel on this site replaced the chapel which was built on the site of the Bridewell (No 48). It was erected in 1789 on a plot of waste ground directly in front of the church gate at Kilbrogan and adjoining what became the fish market. The Methodist congregation had been using a large room of a house on the site of the Bridewell before the new chapel was built.[369] The building was said to have been half the size of the new church and of similar design with a gallery around three sides. It had two separate doors for gentlemen and ladies.

The new church was opened for public worship on 7th May 1789 by Rev John Wesley when he was 86 years old. It was his last trip to Bandon. He stayed at the home of Mr Thomas Bennett of Shannon Street[370]. A small dwelling was erected at the back of the chapel for their minister.

When the lease expired, the Methodists were not offered a renewal but instead were put on a yearly rental. They considered that this

---

[369] The History of Bandon. George Bennett. See also No 48
[370] Thomas Bennett inherited the lease on the death of John Homan in 1828.

was harsh as they had paid for the erection of the buildings on the site.

It appears that the Devonshire Estate ear-marked the site for residential development without the knowledge or consent of the Methodists who were using the chapel and who had been confident that the lease would be renewed. On 6th October, 1820 James Scott wrote to William Curry, the Duke's Agent, expressing his dissatisfaction that the Duke was driving them out of a house which had been built for the worship of God and on which they had spent between £600 and £700.[371]

Scott felt that, whilst private interests were being liberally attended to, a place of worship was the only object of attack and he looked on it as an assault against Methodist principles and an attempt to make them suffer. According to Scott, the Methodists believed that everything was being done to accommodate others and that even 'Popish chapels' were liberally attended to and no attempt was made to disturb them. Furthermore, he considered that some of the Methodists ranked among some of the Duke's best and most improving tenants in the town during that period.

The agent replied that he was concerned at the harsh terms of Scott's letter and the improper manner in which he represented the respectable body of Methodists of the town. He added that a new site was to be offered to them as well as a handsome sum.

The Duke of Devonshire contributed £250 towards the cost of the construction of the new church next to the bridge which totalled £2160. The foundation stone was laid by Rev Thomas Waugh on 12th April, 1821. Trustees of the church included Thomas Bennett, senior and junior, George Harris, Henry Cornwall and John Wheeler Sullivan who all had property interests on North Main Street.

---

[371] MS 43 399/2 Lismore Papers

Riverside House

1837 Number 83 – Valuation £28
1851 Number 91 – Valuation £21 10s
1901 Census Number - 85
1911 Census Number – 13

Immediate Lessors
1824 Dr John Homan for lives of John Homan, Thomas Popham, the son and Regina Popham, the daughter of John Popham of Bandon for 99 years at a rent of £6.[372]
1828 Thomas Bennett and his heirs
1851 Rev Thomas Glasson Bennett
1950s The Trustees of the Legion of Mary Boys Club

A lease dated 1824 exists from the Duke of Devonshire to John Homan for the land with the requirement that John Homan should erect within one year a substantial dwelling laying out £400 and upwards. The house which was built but no longer exists was two storeys over basement. A large conservatory was added to the back of the hall. There was a coach house and a garden with green houses which ran down to the river.

Dr John Homan practised as a physician on South Main Street. On 30th August 1828, shortly before his death, he assigned the lease to Isaac Biggs and Henry Heazle, cotton manufacturers, in trust for Thomas Bennett and his heirs for an annuity of £80 to run for two years from 29th September paid to John Homan by Thomas Bennett. The property was 'bounded on the east by the fish market and on the west by Wheelers Lane.'

John Homan died intestate on 20th October, 1828 and the lease was assigned to Thomas. In his will of 27th April, 1841, Thomas Bennett left the property to his son, the Rev Thomas Glasson Bennett, then curate of Innishannon. He was a cousin of George Bennett.[373]

---

[372] Registry of Deeds. 1837 2 33
[373] See Appendix. Biographies.

Occupiers
The Tithe Applotments which pre-date the 1837 valuation record listed John Homan as the occupier. In Pigot's Directory of 1824 he was described as a Physician of South Main Street, the same year as the lease which was executed between Homan and the Duke of Devonshire.

In 1837 Edward Toole, a medical doctor, was the occupier. He may well have succeeded John Homan following his death in 1828. He was still the occupier in the pre-valuation record of 1849 and in the Griffiths valuation of 1851. Edward had a daughter, Ursula, who married William Adams Nash who was a soldier.

Edward was recorded in the register of vestrymen at Christ Church, Kilbrogan in 1870.

Edward Toole continued to occupy the house until 1882 after which it was vacant for a period. William Sullivan moved in during 1883 and in 1884 Herbert Baldwin became the occupier.

Herbert was succeeded by Dr William Fuller Bennett in 1889. He was a son of Rev Thomas Glasson Bennett and his wife Mary (Fuller)

In the 1901 census William Fuller Bennett was described as Surgeon, Lt Col, Retired, Medical Doctor, aged 57, who was living with his wife Alberta Annie Bennett, son Thomas George Bennett aged 16, son William De Courcy Bennett aged 14, daughter Violet Bertie May Bennett aged 13, son Percy Francis Lionel Garnet Bennett aged 11, daughter Florrie Muriel Frances Rose Bennett aged 10, Lizzie M Dwyer aged 19 a female servant and a housemaid, Kathleen F Dwyer, cook, aged 18 servant.

Surgeon Lieutenant Colonel William Fuller Bennett, Medical Doctor was the son of Rev Thomas Glasson Bennett. William was born on 9th May 1843 and was educated at Queen's College Cork and the Royal College of Surgeons, Dublin. He qualified as a medical doctor in 1858 and in 1869 he joined the staff of the Army Medical Service. He served in Singapore, Hong Kong and Ceylon. In 1873 he was in the Ashantee war under Colonel Wolseley (subsequently Lord Wolseley). He was then stationed in India where he served under Lord Roberts in the Kabul Kandahar campaign. Following this service, he spent two years at home before going to Egypt where he was stationed at Assouan.

William Fuller Bennett retired in 1888 with the rank of Surgeon Major and was subsequently promoted to Surgeon Lieutenant Colonel. He married in 1883 Annie Alberta (Bertie) Beamish, the daughter of George Beamish of Meelan House, Bandon. She was born in 1861 and died in 1937. They had three sons and two daughters:- Thomas George Herbert born 1884, William De Courcy born 1887, Violet Bertie May born in 1888, Francis Lionel Percy Garnet born 1889 and died 1959 and Florence Muriel Frances Rose born in 1891 and died in 1906.

Surg.-Lieut.-Col. W. F. Bennett, M.D.

William Bennett died aged 71. His funeral took place on 6th March 1915 at St Peter's, Ballymodan. Following his death, his family went to live in Bangor, Co Down. His son William De Courcy died on 17th January 1918. His address was the Bungalow, Bandon. He was a Major, ASC and he left his effects to his widow Christina Matilda Caldwell Bennett

At the time of the 1911 census William Fuller Bennett (67), was living at the property with his wife Alberta Annie (49), son Thomas George Herbert Bennett (26), daughter Violet Bertie May Bennett (23), son Francis Lionel Percy Garnet Bennett (21), visitor, Dora Eveline Hornibrook (31), servant Norah McCarty (34)

By 1921 the valuation record lists Mrs Dr Bennett as the occupier followed by Mrs A.F. Bennett in 1922. The Bennetts were succeeded in 1925 by David Gillman Scott.

David Gillman Scott had a son, Dr Harold Gillman Scott born 26th June 1914 and who died in the UK on 2nd February 1995. He became a doctor and married Ingeborg Hedwig Johanna. David Gillman Scott was born about 1870 and died in 1956.

The house was used as a Boys Club in the 1950s. After the house was demolished, the site became O'Donovan's Builders Yard.

No 92 – O'Neills Garage and now Patrick Horgan's Tyres. Former site of Fish Market.

Immediate Lessor
1816 George Harris – The lease was cancelled to create the Fish Market
1851 The Duke of Devonshire
1897 Sir John Arnott
1924 George Bateman

George Harris was a worsted manufacturer, wool comber and woollen draper[374]

Occupiers
The building was 'unoccupied' for many years.

Mary Lewis took over the property in 1920.

---

[374] See also No 100 and Appendix. Short Biographies

In the 1920s George Bateman set up a garage which is noted in the valuation record. He employed Tommy O'Neill who later acquired the garage. In turn, it passed to his sons, Dermot and Peter. George Bateman married Gladys Armitage, a widow – formerly Lee). George had a light plane which he kept at Laragh. He used to take paying passengers.[375] He lived at Red Top on the Dunmanway Road.

No 93 – Shop and dwelling house – No longer standing
1837 Number 84 – Valuation £14
1849 Number 101
1851 Number 93 – Valuation £11 10s
1901 Census Number - 86
1911 Census Number – 12

Immediate Lessors
1851 Benjamin Forde
1863 Richard Wheeler Doherty[376]

Occupiers
In 1837 Daniel McCarthy was the occupier. He was a shoe maker.

Richard Joyce was recorded as the occupier in 1849. Richard married Rebecca Stephens. They had at least two children, William John (b 1836) and Richard Thomas (b 1838).[377] Richard was a boot and shoe maker.[378] By the time of the Griffiths Valuation of 1851 Richard Joyce and Anne Brangan were both listed as the occupiers. Anne Brangan's sister, Rebecca Stephens married Richard Joyce and they were all living together for a period on South Main Street.

Anne Brangan was a grocer.[379] Anne Stephens married Richard Brangan at Christ Church, Kilbrogan on 24th April 1821. Her husband Richard died on 4th March 1831 aged 37 and was buried at St Peters Church, Ballymodan. They had at least four children,

---

[375] Bandon Historical Journal No 20. George Bateman of Bandon and his Tiger Moth (ca1932)
[376] Registry of Deeds. 1863 37 132
[377] Both baptisms were at St Peter's, Ballymodan.
[378] Slater's Directory of 1846
[379] Slater's Directory of 1856

Rebecca (b 1822), Edward (b 1824) recorded as a shoe maker of Boyle Street in the 1846 Ballymodan census, Richard (b 1829) and Anne (b 1830),

Following her husband's death in 1831, Anne and her family moved to North Main Street from South Main Street[380].

By 1868 Mrs Brangan was recorded as the sole occupier.

In 1870 William Robinson (1846-1884) became the occupier. He was formerly of Londonderry and was 38 when he died on 6th July 1884. He married Ellen Brangan in 1869 at the age of 23. His occupation was recorded as farmer in his will. He was succeeded by his widow, Ellen. The family was Presbyterian. William's name appeared on the electoral register of 1884. The property was described as a house with offices, a yard and a small garden at a rateable valuation of £11 10s.

The 1901 census describes Mrs Ellen Robinson aged 50, head of family, living with her daughter Anne Jane aged 28, an assistant in her mother's shop, son John Alexander aged 26, daughter Ellen Jensen aged 22, Mary L Robinson daughter aged 22, Frederick W. Jensen aged 1 grandson who was born in Denmark.

Ellen was still in the property at the time of the 1911 census, aged 60, a shop keeper and widower, living with her daughter Anne Jane (32), daughter Ellen (28), daughter Mary Louisa (24), nephew Freddie Robinson (10), farm servant Michael Brien (32)

In 1915 Mrs Robinson was recorded as a china dealer.[381]

Catherine Northridge succeeded Ellen in 1921. She lived at the property until John Coleman moved in during 1931. The house became vacant in 1962.

No 94 – Shop and dwelling house – No longer standing
1837 Number 85 – Valuation £10
1849 Number 102

---

[380] Ballymodan Census of 1834
[381] Cork and Munster Trade Directory. 1915

1851 Number 94 – Valuation £6 10s
1901 Census Number - 87
1911 Census Number – 11

Immediate Lessors
1851 Benjamin Forde
1863[382] Richard Wheeler Doherty
1933 The Representatives of Richard Wheeler Doherty
1950 Jessica Heath

Occupiers
In 1837 the occupier was Denis Rinn, a shoe maker.[383]

James Donovan was the occupier in 1849 and he was still registered at the property in 1851.

By 1856 Hannah Sullivan had taken up residence and was followed shortly afterwards by Frances Nunhall. James Leary was the next occupier. James was succeeded by Edward Grainger who in turn in 1864 was followed by Robert Baker, a wool comber. He remained in the premises until 1866 when he was succeeded by John Donovan. In 1869 George Turpin, a watch maker, moved in from No 12 on the opposite side of the road. His wife died in 1870.

George was recorded in the register of vestrymen at Christ Church, Kilbrogan in 1870.

In 1880 George moved to No 96 and John Coughlan took up residence and spent two years at the property before James Ryan took over in 1882. His name appeared on the electoral register of 1884 and the property was described as a house with offices and yard at a rateable valuation of £6 10s

Mrs Sweeney moved in during 1884 and by 1889 Ellen Sweeney was recorded as the occupier.

The 1901 census recorded the occupants as Norah Harding, a lodging house keeper aged 35 living with Alfred Harding, son, shop assistant aged 15 and Jessie Harding aged 11 daughter, John

---

[382] Registry of Deeds. 1863 37 132
[383] Elector list of 1832

Harding aged 9 son and Patrick Leary, tailor aged 34 boarder, and Ellen McSweeney aged 70 mother.

Constable Cronin occupied the property for a year in 1907 and was succeeded by Julia Hart in 1908. Edward O'Donovan became the occupier in 1911. He was listed in the 1911 census as aged 27, a hotel boots living with his wife Eileen aged 27 and a lodger Charles O'Callaghan aged 38 who was a harness maker.

Margaret O'Regan moved in during 1913. She was succeeded by Richard Lane in 1915, by Mary Lane 1918, by John Scannell in 1931 and by Timothy Lynch in 1935.

No 95 – A shop and dwelling house – No longer standing
1837 Number 86 – Valuation £10
1851 Number 95 – Valuation £6 10s
1901 Census Number - 88
1911 Census Number – 10

Immediate Lessors
1851 Benjamin Forde
1863 Richard Wheeler Doherty[384]

Occupiers
In 1837 the occupier was John Tanner, a baker and publican. He was still in residence in 1851.

John and his wife Catherine had a daughter Eliza born in 1844.

By 1856 Edward Olliffe had become the tenant and was shortly afterwards succeeded by Mary Falvey and then by Michael O'Mahony.

By 1860 James Norris had become the occupier. A local diary entry recorded that Jack Mahony's wife died at James Norris's on 10th June, 1875.

---

[384] Registry of Deeds 1863 37 132

James Norris operated an Eating House[385]. He remained in the property until 1886 when John Hoeford ? took up residence. He was succeeded in 1898 by John Reen.

In the 1901 census, John Reen, aged 36 and a posting car owner, was recorded as living with his wife, Lizzie, aged 32, son John aged 13, son Michael aged 11, son Robert aged 7, son Denis aged 5 and daughter Kathleen aged 3.

By the time of the 1911 the Reens were still in residence. Lizzie Reen (42), the house holder, married, was living with her son Robert (16), a winder at the hosiery factory, son Denis (14) a porter, daughter Kathleen (11) and daughter Hannah (9)

By 1935 Elizabeth Reen was listed in the valuation record as the occupier. The house became vacant in 1957 and by 1961 it was recorded as being in a dilapidated state.

No 96. No longer standing
1837 Number 87 – Valuation £14
1849 Number 104
1851 Number 96 – Valuation £8
1901 Census Number - 89
1911 Census Number - 9

Immediate Lessors
1851 Peter Good
1856 Benjamin Forde
1864 Richard Wheeler Doherty on behalf of Hon & Rev Charles Brodrick Bernard[386]
1950 Jessica Florence Heath

Occupiers
In 1837 the occupier was Henry Lane, a leather seller.[387]

William Buttimere was the occupier in 1849.

---

[385] Slater's Directory of 1881
[386] Registry of Deeds. 1863 37 132
[387] Slater's Directory of 1846

The occupier was Eliza Aldworth at the time of the Griffiths Valuations in 1851.

By 1856 the occupier was Peter Good. He was succeeded shortly afterwards by Anne Good and then by Abraham Buttimore.

In the 1860s George Wood became resident. George and his wife Mary Frances had a son George Henry, born on 4th May 1859 and baptised at Christ Church on 10th May. His occupation was recorded as gentleman and shopkeeper. Shortly afterwards William Glasson, a wool comber[388], took up residence.

George Turpin, boot and shoemaker,[389] became the tenant during 1880. He was previously at No 94.

His name appeared in the electoral register of 1884 and the property was described as a house with offices and yard at a rateable valuation of £8. George Turpin died on 31st December 1898 aged 74[390]. His burial took place at St Peter's, Ballymodan. Thomas Seymour, a boot maker, became the next occupier in 1897.

George was leasing the property from Hon Rev Charles Bernard. Richard Wheeler Doherty administered the rent on his behalf. This was for a period dating from April 1885 until 17th October 1889. The yearly rental was £14.8.0.

In the 1901 census Thomas Seymour was recorded as a boot maker aged 44 living with wife Mary Jane (43) and daughter Alice (15)

Thomas was still at the property by the time of the 1911 census. He was recorded as a boot maker (54), with Mary Jane (53), wife and Alice (23) daughter and William E Seymour – boot maker (52), a brother

Thomas Seymour was recorded as having a boot and shoe warehouse and wholesale and retail leather store in 1915.[391] Thomas was succeeded by Alice in 1950.

---

[388] Coughlan's Directory of 1867

[389] Guy's Directory of 1893

[390] A death of a George Turpin of Bandon is also recorded in 1886.

[391] Cork and Munster Trade Directory. 1915

No 97 – Formerly a licensed premises and bakery
1837 Number 88 – Valuation £22
1851 Number 97 – Valuation £14
1901 Census Number - 90
1911 Census Number – 8

Immediate Lessors
1851 Eliza Fuller
1906 Joseph Fuller
1931 Sir John Arnott

Occupiers
In 1837 the occupier was Robert Fuller.

John O Donoghue was recorded as the occupier in 1849. He was a baker and a publican and he remained in the property until 1856.

Shortly after 1856, William Grainger became the occupier. His tenancy expired on 29th September, 1860.[392] Thomas Forde, a spirit dealer, became the next resident.

---

[392] Lismore Papers. MS 7053 1861-1862

BANDON

**TO BE SOLD BY PUBLIC AUCTION ON
WEDNESDAY** Next, the 5th **OCTOBER**
in the Town Hall, Bandon, the House and Premises
with Gardens at rere, known as No. 88 North Main
Street, Bandon. They are situate in the best part
of the town and are at present let to Mr Thomas
Forde as a yearly tenant at £20 a year. There is a
good Licensed Spirit Business done on the Premises.
They are held for a term of 99 years, from the 25th
March, 1818, at the low yearly rent of £7 6s 9 3/4d
N.B.—The License is not the Property of the
vendor.
MR JOHN FAUCITT is instructed to Sell by
Public Auction in the Town Hall, Bandon, at the
hour of One o'Clock on Wednesday Next, the 6th
October, the above very desirable Premises.
For further particulars apply to the Auctioneer,
Bandon.
    **THE MUNSTER HOUSE AND LAND AGENCY
OFFICE
69, SOUTH MALL, CORK   (885)**

The advertisement for the property appeared in the Cork
Examiner in 1870.

Thomas Forde resided at the property until 1886 when Daniel
McSweeney became the occupier. He was succeeded in 1888 by
Thomas Mahony and in 1898 by David Flynn.

In the 1901 census David Flynn was recorded as a publican and
cycle agent aged 36, living with his wife Margaret (30) attending at
her shop and daughter Hannah.

In 1906 the occupier was listed as the Representatives of David
Flynn.

By the time of the 1911 census, Margaret Flynn (38), a publican and widow, was living with her daughter Josephine (10) and boarder John Fitzgerald aged 24 – an agent

In 1914 Stephen Hennessy took over and remained for a year when the property became vacant. He was recorded as a high class grocer, tea, wine and spirit merchant in 1915.[393] In 1917 Michael O'Driscoll took up residence.

In 1935 Denis Whooley became the occupier. He was a boot maker.

No 98 – Shop and dwelling house
1837 Number 89 – Valuation £16
1849 Number 106
1851 Number 98 – Valuation £12
1901 Census Number - 91
1911 Census Number – 7

Immediate Lessors
1851 Matthew Hunter
1900s The Hunter Estate

Occupiers
In 1837 the occupier was Thomas Montjoy, a watch maker.[394] He was recorded as living on North Main Street as early as 1824 possibly at this address and was probably the son of William Montjoy who married Elizabeth Patterson in 1793. Thomas and his wife Barbara had issue: Maria baptised at Kilbrogan on 22nd January 1824, William baptised on 26th August 1826, John

---

[393] Cork and Munster Trade Directory. 1915.
[394] Pigot's Directory of 1824

baptised on 9ᵗʰ November 1831, Jane baptised on 20ᵗʰ August 1834 and buried on 2ⁿᵈ October 1834 and Martha Anne baptised on 11ᵗʰ April 1838.

John Payne was the occupier in 1849.

The occupier was Eliza Fuller at the time of the Griffiths Valuation in 1851.

By 1856 the occupier was John Giles, a tallow chandler[395] (a soap and candle manufacturer). Mrs Giles succeeded John Giles in 1867. She had ceased occupancy in 1881. Henry O'Neill was the occupier in 1882, Miss Susan Bradfield in 1883. Her rental payments are documented in Alfred Hunter's cash book. She paid £20 per annum which included the house and premises. Her payments were quarterly.

Susan Bradfield was one of nine children of Richard and Mary Shorten Bradfield. Richard and Susan married in Desertserges on 18ᵗʰ January, 1845. Susan's father married twice. His first wife was Bridget Keeffe and his second wife Mary Shorten. Susan was baptised on 29ᵗʰ September, 1856 and she took on the shop on North Main Street in 1883 when she was 27. Shortly after this, Susan emigrated to Roxbury, near Boston, USA where she ran a grocery store.

William Syms, a tailor,[396] succeeded Susan Bradfield in 1884. He paid rent monthly and the poor rate was half. His name appeared on the electoral register of 1884. The property was described as a house with offices and a yard. It had a rateable valuation of £12.

William Syms was still at the premises by the time of the 1901 census. He was described as a master tailor aged 62 living with wife Sarah aged 58 and son Edward aged 32, a draper assistant (he died in Bandon in 1912) and son William aged 30, a tailor (he died aged 50 in 1924), and daughter Anne aged 26 and daughter Francis aged 22 and son Henry aged 15.

William Syms senior died in 1906.

[395] Slater's Directory of 1856
[396] Guys Directory of 1893

William was at the premises in 1911. Census and was listed as aged 40, a master tailor living with his wife Mary Ann (otherwise Fuller)[397], daughter Sarah Lelian and boarder William Thomason (42).

In 1915 William Syms was recorded as operating as a tailor.[398]

Mrs Mary Syms was listed as the occupier in 1925.

Her successor was Miss Lilian Syms who in turn was succeeded by Mary Syms in 1939 and by Lilian Buttimore (nee Syms) in 1944.

No 99 – Presently a Dental Practice
1837 Number 90 – Valuation £15
1849 Number 107
1851 Number 99 – Valuation £9
1901 Census Number - 92
1911 Census Number – 6

Immediate Lessors
1851 John Harris
1933 William O'Grady

Occupiers
In 1837 the occupier was Robert Clarke.

John Giles was recorded as the occupier in 1849 and he was still in the premises at the time of the Griffiths Valuation in 1851.

---

[397] William Syms married Mary Fuller on 9th July 1908
[398] Cork and Munster Trade Directory. 1915

John was the son of Robert Giles, a boot and shoe maker. In 1851 he married Sarah Allshire.

By 1856 John Giles had been succeeded by Mrs Nixon and shortly afterwards by Hannah Sullivan. By 1860 Samuel Salter had become the occupier and he remained at the property until 1870 when Joseph Allshire, a grocer[399] transferred to this premises from No 26.

The occupiers in the 1880s were listed as Joseph Allshire senior and Joseph Allshire junior. In the electoral records of 1884 Jason Allshire was recorded as an accountant. The premises was occupied by the family as landlords as both their residence and place of business and was rated with offices and yard at £10 to Joseph Allshire senior and Joseph Allshire junior. Their front sitting room was located on the second floor and the bedroom was at the rear of the same floor.

Margaret Grady took over from them in 1886. She was a provision merchant.[400] The Allshires were recorded at No 6 in 1896.

Margaret Grady was still at the property during the 1901 census. She was described as a shop keeper aged 45 living with son William aged 30, a cattle dealer, son Jeremiah aged 27, a cattle dealer son David aged 24, a cattle dealer daughter Mary aged 22, daughter Nellie aged 20 and son John aged 19, a cattle dealer

Margaret was succeeded as occupier in the 1912 valuation record by James Daly though he was listed as the occupier in the 1911 census return.

In 1911 James Daly (57), a farmer was living with his wife Ellen (45), daughter Teresa (15), daughter Eileen (14), son John James (12) and daughter Florence (6)

In 1932 John Daly succeeded James as the occupier. In 1942 Ellen Daly became the tenant[401]. Florence (Flossie) was recorded as the resident in 1959. She lived in the property with her sister Eileen.

---

[399] Slater's Directory of 1870
[400] Guys Directory of 1993

No 100 – A Shop and dwelling house
1837 Number 91 and 92 combined – Valuation £35
1851 Number 100 – Valuation £25 10s
1901 Census Number - 93
1911 Census Number – 5

Immediate Lessors
1860s John and George Harris
1897 Sir John Arnott
1938 William O'Grady

Occupiers
In 1837 the occupier was George Harris, a worsted manufacturer, wool comber and woollen draper.[402]

In 1839 George Harris senior assigned to his son George, also a shop keeper, the leases which he held and which were originally dated 1st April, 1817 and also 31st December 1824 which included all plate, linen, stock in trade subject to payment of a yearly rent and the sum of £150.[403] His son, William Harris was a witness and his address was Clonakilty.

The record for George Harris in 1849 stated that the premises included a potato house, a wool store, a car house, stables, a shop and a house

---

[401] A death of Ellen Daly on 16th October 1941 was recorded in the St Patrick's burial register. (nee O'Callaghan). A death of John Daly was recorded on 20th March 1946.
[402] See Appendix. Short Biographies. George Harris
[403] Registry of Deeds 1839 13 6 of 14th May 1839

The occupier was John Harris, a linen and woollen draper[404] at the time of the Griffiths Valuation in 1851.

In the 1860s brothers John and George Harris became the immediate lessors as well as the occupiers.

George Harris junior died on 22nd October, 1864 aged 46. In the same year the name on the lease changed to James Harris. The House was split in the 1860s into 100a and 100b.

In 1867 Charles Cooper, an apothecary and physician, moved into 100a. He was recorded in the register of vestrymen at Christ Church, Kilbrogan in 1870.

Andrew Murray was leasing an office at 100b in the 1860s. A note in the Lismore papers stated that in 1867 his rent was increased from £7 10s 0d to £ for the year. Andrew Stafford was leasing a workshop at 100c. Denis Leary took over 100b from Andrew Murray in 1876. A note in the valuation book reads as follows:- 'political agents wanted 3 rooms on top valued. Can't be done'

In 1882 John Seymour Theobald became the occupier of 100a (the house) with John Harris as the immediate lessor. Theobald had moved from No 52.

A notice appeared in the Freeman's Journal of 25th October, 1882 as follows:- Bankrupts – Adjudication. October 6th – John Seymour Theobald of North Main Street, Bandon, in the County of Cork, Shopkeeper. Shortly afterwards the family emigrated to New Zealand where he died.

In the electoral register of 1884 John Seymour Theobald and James Harris were described as the joint occupiers of the property which included a house, offices and yard and had a rateable valuation of £18 10s.

In 1884 James Harris took over from Charles Cooper and the Duke of Devonshire became the immediate lessor.

---

[404] Slater's Directory of Bandon, 1856

Following James Harris, there were a number of tenants in the house in quick succession. Daniel Leary became the occupier after James in 1886. He was succeeded by Patrick O'Leary in 1892 and by Ellen O'Leary in 1899.

In 1900 Isabella Turpin moved in. She was succeeded in 1901 by Annie Turpin, a dress maker.

Patrick O'Leary took over the work shops and office in 1892 from Daniel Leary and they were taken on by Isabella and then by Annie when they moved into the property.

The 1901 census described Annie Turpin as a dress maker aged 32, living with sister Jane Turpin aged 39, sister Isabella Turpin, milliner, aged 34, sister Sarah Turpin, dress maker aged 30 and Richard W Turpin aged 25 brother, accountant.

Annie Turpin was succeeded by James Murphy in 1909. William O'Grady followed him in 1913 in the valuation record though he was described as the occupier in the 1911 census.

In 1911 William O'Grady, aged 40, a cattle dealer, was living with his wife Lizzie, aged 29 and brother John (30) – cattle dealer, brother Jerry (35) – cattle dealer and mother Margaret O'Grady (60)

Mrs E O'Grady was recorded as a cattle dealer in 1915.[405] Part of the property was recorded as a workshop.

By 1938 the building becomes vacant and William was listed as the immediate lessor. John Atkins moved in during 1945. He ran a printing business. Kieran J. Kissane was recorded as the occupier in 1958.

---

[405] Cork and Munster Trade Directory. 1915

No 101
1901 Census Number – 94
1911 Census Number - 4

Immediate Lessors
1816 George Harris – 99 years
1826 Thomas Beamish
1833 Henry Cornwall
1851 William Connor Sullivan Esq
1927 The Scots Church
1977 David Craig

A lease dated 1st April, 1816 was entered into between the Duke of Devonshire and George Harris for his life and the lives of his sons, William and George and/or the survivor of them for 99 years at a yearly rent of £14 14s. An old house stood on the plot which was occupied by George Harris.[406] The site was described as being 43' in breadth and 115' in depth and was bounded on the north by the street, on the south by the river, on the east by J. Sullivan's holding and on the west by the holding of J. Wheeler Sullivan.

On 20th January 1826 George Harris, in consideration of £400, granted to Thomas Beamish the land, house and improvements for 100 years provided his estate should last subject to yearly rent and repayment of £400 plus interest at 6%. On 29th July 1833 Thomas Beamish assigned the lease to Henry Cornwall which included the land and two new houses. Henry later conveyed the lease to William Connor Sullivan.[407] In 1826 the plot was bounded on the

---

[406] See Appendix. Biographies
[407] Registry of Deeds. 1842 3 28

east by John Sullivan's holding and on the west by John Wheeler Sullivan's holding. The breadth of the plot was 50'[408]

Occupiers
William Morgan was the occupier in 1849 and was still at the premises in 1851. He was a wool comber.[409]

By 1856 James Roberts, a flour factor[410] had become the occupier.

In the 1860s Thomas Stafford was listed alongside James Roberts.

Thomas was a grocer and timber merchant and James Roberts was a chandler and flour dealer.

James Roberts was succeeded by John Buckley in 1877. Daniel Allen, a grocer[411], became the tenant in 1880 and by 1882 the property was vacant. In 1884 the Shines moved in. The name 'Shine' appeared on the electoral register of 1884 and the property was described as a house with offices and a yard at a rateable valuation of £13. Jeremiah was also recorded as being the occupier of a house in Castle Road which had offices, a yard and an orchard at a rateable valuation of £8. In 1885 Jeremiah Shine , a plumber, [412] was listed as the occupier.

The 1911 census was blank though the name of Jeremiah Shine still appeared in the valuation record as the occupier.

In 1915 Jerome Shine is recorded as a plumber.[413] In 1927 it was recorded as a shop. Jeremiah Shine died on 10th March 1928.

Bartholomew Shine took over from Jeremiah as the occupier. He died on 30th August, 1930. He was succeeded by Alfred Mason in 1933. William Eccles became the occupier in 1942.

[408] Registry of Deeds. 810 546 091
[409] Slater's Directory of 1856
[410] Slater's Directory of 1856
[411] Slater's Directory of 1881
[412] Guys Directory of 1893
[413] Cork and Munster Trade Directory. 1915

No 102
1901 Census Number - 95
1911 Census Number – 3

Immediate Lessors
1851 William Connor Sullivan Esq
1877 David Craig

Occupiers
Iin 1849 and in 1851 James Sullivan a flour factor[414] was recorded as the occupier. He was succeeded in 1860 by James Roberts, a chandler and flour dealer.

In the valuation record of 1877 Jeremiah Regan and Cornelius Regan were listed as the occupiers. In the electoral register of 1884 they were also jointly recorded as the occupiers and the property was described as a house, with offices and a yard at a rateable valuation of £11. Cornelius was a boot and shoe maker.[415] They were at the property until 1894 when Jeremiah Crowley became the resident. He was succeeded by Timothy O'Regan in 1897 and by Jerome Shine in 1900.

In the 1911 census Jerome Shine was described as a plumber, single, aged 48.

In 1930 The Scots Church Representative Body took over the immediate lease of the house, shop and yard from David Craig. At the same time Robert Reen took over as the occupier. The property was recorded as a shop (See also No 103).

---

[414] Slater's Directory of 1856
[415] Slater's Directory of 1881.

No 103
1849 Number 111
1901 Census Number - 96
1911 Census Number -2

Immediate Lessors
1851 William Connor Sullivan Esq
1938 The Scots Church Representative Body
1933 Rev Brown

Occupiers
Quinane was recorded as the occupier in 1849.

The occupier was James Roberts at the time of the Griffiths Valuation in 1851.

By 1856 Samuel Salter had become the occupier. He was succeeded in the early 1860s by John Donovan, a saddle and harness maker.

James Roberts, a flour dealer, took up residency in the late 1860s. David Grady became the next occupier in 1877. His name appeared on the electoral register of 1884 and the property was described as a house and yard with a rateable valuation of £7.

Mary Walsh took over from David Grady in 1886 and was still the occupier at the time of the 1901 census. She was described as a victualler, aged 40, living with her sister Ellen Walsh also a victualler aged 32, and John Francis Walsh aged 9, a nephew.

In 1910 Ellen Walsh was recorded as the occupier. In the 1991 census she was described as single, aged 38, living with her nephew John Walsh.

A note in the valuation record of 1936 stated 'at rear part of 3 Bridge Place'

Ellen Walsh was succeeded by Thomas Gabriel in 1933 and in 1938 by the British Legion Club who held it until at least 1940. William Riordan became the occupier. In 1944 M. O'Driscoll became the tenant. He was succeeded by Cornelius Holland in 1948. Michael Fitzgibbon became the tenant in 1957. This property now forms part of Reens Shop.

No 104 – A licensed premises for a period & presently the site of an undertakers and funeral home.
1901 Census Number - 97
1911 Census Number – 1

Immediate Lessors
1851 George French
1861 George French and George Gibson
1876 George French

Occupiers
Ellen Shorten was recorded as the occupier in both 1849 and in 1851.

By 1856 Andrew Murray had become the occupier.

In March 1868 Andrew Murray's rent was increased by the Devonshire Estate from £7 10 0 to £10 per annum.

In 1876 the number of the property was listed as 104 and 105 with a note stating that new buildings had been erected in 1872.

In 1883 Hanoria Doyle became the new tenant. She married Patrick Kelleher[416] and in 1885 his name appeared on the valuation register. The house was rated at £11. Patrick died on 8th April 1894.

Honora Keleher continued to occupy the premises following the death of Patrick and the building was listed as a licensed premises.

In 1901 Honora was listed as a licensed publican, aged 64, living with Mary Murphy, a bar maid, aged 17 and cousin and Kate Callaghan a servant aged 22.

In 1904 Julia Keane became the occupier and in 1907 the immediate lessor became Allman Dowden & Co (A company which was formed in 1885 when Dowden & Co was dissolved)

In the 1911 census Jeremiah Keane aged 54 was listed as an ex police pensioner living with his wife Julia (39), son John Patrick (17, son Jerh Jos (9), daughter Han Morin (6), son William (5), daughter Agnes (2), lodger Patrick desmond (21) a labourer, lodger Patrick Griffin (67), a farmer

The Keanes were succeeded by Timothy Hayes in 1914, by Daniel Buckley in 1915 and by Ellen O'Connell in 1918. She was succeeded by Bridget O'Donoghue in 1934. The house became vacant in 1932. Michael O'Reilly held the tenancy in 1944 and in 1949 it was described as dilapidated and being used as a furniture store.

No 105

1849 John Murphy – a saddling shop
The Griffith Valuation Record lists the Immediate Lessor as Ellen Shorten. The property was unoccupied. By 1856 the immediate lessor was Andrew Murray and by the 1860s the property was linked with 104 in the valuation records.

---

[416] Electoral Register for Bandon Bridge. 1884

A view of Bridge Place and the Allin Institute before it was burnt.
From the Lawrence Collection
With permission of the National Library of Ireland

BRIDGE PLACE – The properties were recorded as North Main Street in the 1901 and 1911 censuses

No 1
1856 – Number 1 Bridge Place

This was the site of the Vegetable Market for many years. There was a shed and a yard on the site. The property was classified as 'exempt' in valuation records.

The site was still recorded as a vegetable market with 'exempt' valuation status in 1910.

No 2 – Once a bakery. More recently a butcher. Known as Jordan's Corner

1775 Nothing on the site
1851 Number 2 Bridge Place
1901 Census – No 98. A Shop
1911 Census – No 104. A Butcher's Shop

Intermediate Lessor

1851 William Connor Sullivan
1856 William Connor Sullivan
1884 John McSweeny

Occupiers

The tenant at the time of the Griffiths Valuation in 1851 was Henry Lane.

The occupier in 1856 was Mrs Burchill. She was succeeded in the late 1850s by Samuel Burchill.

---

[417]CABBAGE PLANTS
ENFIELD MARKET, NONPAREIL, ATKINS MATCHLESS, THE EARLIEST OF ANY.

A LARGE QUANTITY of very Strong PLANTS, fit
For immediate Planting, very cheap, as the ground
They stand on is wanted.
Apply to Mr BURCHILL, North Main Street, Bandon
(2784)

Samuel remained as the tenant until he died on 23rd September 1865. Letters of Administration were granted at Cork to Sarah

---

[417] Cork Examiner, 21st September, 1857

Burchill, his widow and a legatee on 20th December and her address was given as Harbour Hill, Bandon. He left effects under £350.

The Burchills were succeeded by Robert Payne, a baker. He died on 9th August 1870 and his wife Rebecca was recorded as the occupier. Letters of Administration were granted to Rebecca, his widow on 22nd February 1871. He left under £300.[418]

An advertisement appeared in the Eagle of 1883 offering the property for sale:

TO BE SOLD
THE INTEREST in the Old-Established BAKERY, with DWELLING-HOUSE Bandon Place, Bandon. Apply to A.W. SMITH
(l49-tf)   On the Premises

 Timothy Mahony was recorded as the occupier from 1884 until 1887 after which there were a succession of tenants including Mrs Griffin, Thomas Seymour (1894) and Mary Anne Shanahan in 1898.

In 1901 the premises was described as a shop occupied by Mary Anne Shannon but the family were residing elsewhere. The building was recorded as having eight windows at the front of the premises.

John Fitzgerald became the occupier in 1906 and by 1908 Mary Fitzgerald had succeeded him.

In the 1911 census Mary Fitzgerald (27), single was living with her brother, John Fitzgerald (24), a butcher.

Mary was succeeded by Joseph Carey. Anthony Jordan became the next occupier in 1964.

---

[418] Calendar of Wills. National Archives of Ireland

No 3
1775 Nothing on the site
1837 – Number 2 Bridge Place
1851 – Number 3 Bridge Place
1901 Census - No 99 North
Main Street. A Licensed
Premises
1911 Census – No 103 North
Main Street. A Licensed
Premises

Intermediate Lessor
1816 John Sullivan to the Duke of Devonshire
1851 William Connor Sullivan
1856 William Connor Sullivan
1884 John McSweeny (a timber merchant of The Hill, Bandon)

The original lease was granted by the Duke of Devonshire to John Sullivan on 1st April, 1816[419]. He was a tanner who married Mary Kingston. They had at least William Connor Sullivan (1809-1886) who married Dorothea Tresilian in 1838, John Kingston Sullivan, Anne Sullivan (a spinster in 1833), Elizabeth Sullivan and Thomas Kingston Sullivan (1815-1902). Thomas was their youngest son. He married twice and had a very large family.[420]

The original lease recorded that the plot measured 34' at the front, the depth was 75' and it was bounded by a passage to the old shambles. (The old shambles was also recorded in a lease relating to No 4 Bridge Place). The lease was for three lives at an annual rent of £11. Another deed exists dated 6th February 1833 between John's eldest son, William Connor Sullivan, Mary Sullivan, his mother and widow, Anne Sullivan, John Kingston Sullivan, Elizabeth Sullivan and his youngest brother, Thomas Kingston Sullivan).

---

[419] Registry of Deeds. 1858 10 185
[420] See Appendix. Biographies

The original lease of 1817 for No 4 Bridge Place recorded that the plot was bounded by the property of John Sullivan who was a tanner.

Occupiers

William Connor Sullivan was recorded as the occupier in 1837 and he was still at the property in 1846.[421] Sometime between 1846 and 1851 William and his family had moved to another property though they still retained the lease. William entered into a mortgage for £4000 with the Bank of Ireland on 16th November, 1857. He surrendered the deeds of this property amongst others as security for the loan.

James Hamilton was recorded as the occupier in 1851 and the rateable value was £26.

Frederick Lyster was the tenant in 1856. His name appeared in the 1856 Slater's Directory as 'Station, Shannon Street' (possibly station-master of the railway). The rateable valuation was reduced to £23.

Matthew Lee succeeded Frederick Lyster in 1867. Lee family members inherited the property over the years and it is still in the same ownership today.

In 1884[422] Arthur Hitchmough, a clerk in the Provincial Bank of Ireland, was occupying two rooms of the house, one on the first floor at the front which was a sitting room and the second on the second floor which was used as a bedroom. The shop was located on the ground floor. The building was rated at £23 at the time. William James Lee, a shop assistant, was also living in the property at the same time. He had the use of two rooms, a sitting room on the first floor at the rear of the building and a bedroom on the second floor at the front. Both were furnished. The landlords were Richard, Susanna and Samuel Lee and they also resided at the premises. The rateable value was £23.

---

[421] Slater's Directory of 1846.
[422] Electoral Records of Bandon Bridge. 1884.

The valuation records show that the property passed from Matthew Lee to Susanna followed by Samuel and then Richard Lee. In 1901 the property became licensed.

Samuel succeeded Susanna and Richard in 1889.

In the 1901 census Samuel (45), a grocer, was living with his wife S. Emily, (35), and son Matthew Ernest (6), daughter Gladys Irene (3), son Samuel A. Roy, mother Susanna (70), brother William J.M. (36), visitors Phoebe M and G.L. Victor Drought and a servant Lizzie O'Brien (21)

The occupiers at the time of the 1911 census were recorded as Samuel Lee (55) along with his wife Emily (45), their son Matthew Ernest (16), daughter Gladys Irene (13), Samuel A. Roy (10) and a servant Kate Crowley (29).

In 1928 Samuel A. Roy succeeded Samuel Lee. A.H. Lee was recorded as the next tenant. Richard Lee became the next occupier in 1964.

No 4 The site of an old Shambles according to lease of 1817
1775 Nothing on the site
1817 – A plot of land
1837 – Number 1 Bridge Place
1851 – Number 4 Bridge Place
1901 Census – No 100 North Main Street
1911 Census – No 102 North Main Street

Intermediate Lessor
1817 William Sullivan from Duke of Devonshire – 99 years
1856 The Duke of Devonshire
1897 Sir John Arnott
? John Travers Jeffers

William Sullivan[423] was assigned the lease of a plot by the Duke of Devonshire on 1st April, 1817. The lease recorded that the plot was once the site of an old shambles. The lease was for the lives of Thomas Hornibrook Sullivan, John Sullivan and James Sullivan and 99 years at a rent of £8 8sp.a.[424] The site was described as measuring 33'6 in breadth and with a depth of 97' from front to rear.

William Sullivan built a house on the site. He may have lived in the house himself as the occupier in 1837 was recorded as William Sullivan Esq. At that time the estimated value of the property was £36. In his will he bequeathed the house to Thomas Hornibrook Sullivan[425] who, in turn, sold it to his brother Samuel for £200 in 1852. According to the lease, the house measured 32' at the front and it was bounded by John Sullivan's (No 3)

William's son, Thomas Hornibrook Sullivan Esq, was recorded as the occupier in the Griffiths valuation of 1851.

In 1852 Samuel Hornibrook Sullivan took up residence.

Samuel Sullivan died on 10th February 1890 after which the property passed out of the Sullivan family. His will was proved at Cork by Louisa Sullivan at the same address and a spinster, most likely another daughter. He left effects of £558 4s. She was the sole executrix of his will.

A number of tenants followed Samuel Sullivan in quick succession namely Edward Heard, Richard Heard, Arthur Smyth (1891), William Henderson (1893) and William Wilson in 1901. Part of the premises was used for a time in 1893 as meeting rooms for the Plymouth Brethern.

Richard Heard was still the occupier of part of the house in the early 1900s. A separate section was occupied by William Wilson who was succeded by Jessie Cronin (1902). Richard Heard was succeeded by 'Bright' in 1914.

---

[423] See Appendix. Short Biographies. William Sullivan
[424] Registry of Deeds. 1852 5 122 and MS 6189 Lismore Papers
[425] See Appendix. Short Biographies. Thomas & Samuel Hornibrook Sullivan

In the 1901 census Jessie Cronin, a presbyterian (43) and a widowed Nurse who had been born in England was living with her daughter Georgina (18), Flossie (12), Gladys (8) and boarders Oscar Needham (26), an ordnance survey official, his wife, N. Clare Needham (24) and Hannah O'Sullivan (23)

William Porter took up residence in 1903 followed by Richard Heard in 1907. Edward Heard was the immediate lessor.

Sarah Syms was living at the property at the time of the 1911 census. She was a widow, aged 69, living with her daughter Annie Syms, a shop assistant, aged 33. The house was recorded as having twelve windows.

Jasper Jeffers became the resident of the entire property in 1924. Jeffers was succeeded by the Trustees of the Christian Brethern in 1935. Julia Keane rented part of the building from the Trustees (recorded as offices and yard in the valuation records).

Hannah Keane succeeded Julia in part of the building. John O'Sullivan was recorded as the tenant in 1966. The property changed hands again in the 1970s and since that period has been converted into apartments.

KILBROGAN PLACE – These two houses were recorded as Kilbrogan Street in the valuation records.

No 1
1901 Census
1911 Census – 56 Kilbrogan St

Intermediate Lessor
Original lease details not known
1856 Benjamin Forde
1867 Richard Wheeler Doherty

Occupiers
In 1856 the occupier was recorded as Rev John Pratt. He was succeeded by William G Reid and was followed shortly afterwards by David Hunter. The premises included a house, office, yard and garden.

In 1864 Edward Doherty took up residence. In 1870 Edward Doherty was succeeded by Richard Wheeler Doherty. Dora Doherty became the occupier following Richard Wheeler Doherty's death in 1883. Peter Coulan succeeded Dora Doherty in 1886 and he was followed by Miss Popham in 1891. She lived at the premises until 1903 when Margaret Taylor was recorded as the occupier. Sir John Arnott ceased to be the immediate lessor in 1904.

Mercy Mary Cox (41), a widow, was living with her mother Mercy M. Wright (83) in Skibbereen at the time of the 1901 census. Both were recorded as tea and wine merchants. Her son John Charles Cox (14) was living with them as well as a servant, Mary Corcoran (25). By the time of the 1911 census Mercy (52) was living at Kilbrogan Place with her son Henry (30), a bank official who was born in England, his wife Lillian Maude (25), Phyllis Rudsey Maude Cox (2) and a servant Ellie Driscoll (20)

Mercy Mary Cox was succeeded as the occupier by James Percy Jeffers in 1915.

Katherine Jeffers was recorded as the occupier following James Percy Jeffers death in 1926. Kathleen Jeffers succeeded Katherine. Kathleen was followed by James McKenna in 1955.

No 2
1901 Census
1911 Census – 55 Kilbrogan St

Intermediate Lessor
1856 Benjamin Forde
1867 Richard Wheeler Doherty

Occupiers
In 1856 Regina Popham was the occupier of the premises which included a house, office, yard and garden. Sophia Hornibrook became the tenant in 1867. By 1870 J. Rodwell was recorded as the occupier and he was succeeded by John R. Wheeler. Robert Coath became resident in 1883 and he was followed by Thomas Menagh.

In 1893 George Levis assumed the tenancy. He was no longer the occupier by 1904.

Frederick Campbell Wallace DJ was living at this address at the time of the 1911 census. He was aged 45, born in Co Down and was a District Inspector of the RIC. His wife Ethel Jane (39) was born in England. They had three children and two were living with them at the time of the census, Percy William (11) and Mary Marguerita (8). They were both born in Co Mayo. Also in residence was a servant, Mary Ellen Hickey (18), born in County Cork.

Frederick Wallace was succeeded by Sarah Webster in 1914 and then by George C. Bateman in 1923.

John Dinneen became the next occupier in the 1930s and he was followed by William A. Dinneen. Richard Walsh took up the tenancy in 1956 and he was succeeded by Elizabeth Walsh in 1960.

THE ALLIN INSTITUTE and RAGGED SCHOOL

The building was bequeathed to the protestant community of Bandon by James Allin in 1867. Born in 1780, James was the son of John Allin, a wealthy merchant in Youghal. The original building which was 3 storeys high was burnt on the morning of 29th June, 1921. It was subsequently re-built as a two storey property and was re-opened on 29th June 1925. The billiard room at the side of the main building was added in the early 1900s. It survived the fire. The ragged school which was located in the original building operated until the mid 1890s.

JACK APPELBE'S CROSS

Graves "Jack" Appelbe of Kildarra died on 31st January 1903. His sister, Mrs Emily Axford was the wife of Walter Axford, a staff surgeon in the British Navy. She erected a celtic cross with the inscription "Lest we forget, Jack Applebe died January 31, 1903 aged 36, who had done his work and held his peace and had no fear to die." Emily Axford had not sought permission to erect the cross and when asked to remove it, took no action. It was removed by the rector, Rev Benjamin Fawcett, the church wardens and select vestry and placed in Church Lane. Jack Appelbe had also been incorrectly buried in a grave next to the Applebe family plot which was the burial place of Richard Hudson and family.

The discovery of the dismantled cross in Church Lane stirred up anger as it was said that the Church had removed it because they believed it to be "Romish, ritualistic and idolatrous"

On 18th January 1904 William Kearney requested the Bandon District Council to erect a monument in the form of a celtic cross on the site of the present Sean Hales statue. It stood on the site for many years.

SEAN HALES MONUMENT

Brigadier General Sean Hales, TD, was born in Ballinadee on 30th March, 1880. He served as a volunteer, soldier and statesman and was killed in Dublin on 7th December 1922. The monument was erected in his memory in recognition of his services to the cause of Irish Freedom.

Catherine FitzMaurice

CHAPTER 6

THE DEVONSHIRE ARMS HOTEL

Contributed by the late Patsy O'Shea, a direct descendant of the
Loane family who ran the hotel for many years

From the Lawrence Collection
With permission of the National Library of Ireland

In October 1822 Paul Williams of Coolfadda, architect, building
contractor and inn keeper, proudly opened the new Devonshire
Arms Hotel[426]. Paul Williams had previously been proprietor of
the King's Arms in Lower North Main Street (No 5 & 6) which he
took over from John Burchill in 1813. The rent for the King's Arms
is not known but Paul Williams paid an annual rent of £41 for the
Devonshire Arms.[427]

It had not been without some misgiving though that Paul Williams
had taken over the lease of the grand new premises. In December
1821, the Duke's agent reported that Williams was reluctant to

---

[426] There had previously been an hotel of the same name on South Main Street
[427] Bandon Historical Journal Issue No 8. Page 22

take up the lease and was asking for a rent 'holiday' for one to two years on other houses and for a loan to assist with additional furniture[428]. The loan was apparently granted and the venture went ahead. The rent was £40 pa and the lease commenced on 29th September 1822. In return for agreeing to the lease on the new hotel, he surrendered the lease on the former inn (No 6). Mr Currey, the Duke's Agent, agreed to advance Paul Williams £100 to purchase furniture for the new inn and he was to repay the loan over time with interest.

Clearly the hotel was developed under the auspices of the then Duke of Devonshire. Whilst the main building was begun in 1819, the Duke also funded the building of a public house next to the inn in 1823[429] when he paid 'Williams and Hickey' (probably Paul Williams and Edward Hickey) £200 for their work on this. Estate records indicate that the whole complex was finally completed in 1826. Paul Williams was to pay a rent of £12 pa for this separate building.

Williams had offered service to the nobility and gentry at the King's Arms but The Devonshire was an ambitious step up for the Bandon builder and was to become a feature of Bandon social society and the scene of numerous civic events in the following decades.

The quality of the Devonshire Arms Hotel was emphasized in Williams' advertisements of his new establishment:
'...extensive drawing rooms, commodious private apartments, sitting rooms, airy bedrooms ... with every out office necessary for an extensive hotel. Good Post Chaises, able horses and careful drivers ...[430]

There are many references to Paul Williams in the Corporation accounts of the time and in the papers of the landlord, the Duke of Devonshire. Clearly he was a significant contractor of the time, being involved in the building of roads and various redevelopment works. He also appears as a backer of Tory candidates in the parliamentary elections.

---

[428] Lismore Papers
[429] Bandon Historical Journal Issue no 3. Page 36
[430] Bandon Historical Journal Number 8. Page 27

The connection between the Devonshire Arms and the Loane family possibly began with a Paul Williams who married Parnell Loane in 1786. Parnell's parentage has not been proved but the forename of Parnell can be found in the Loane family as far back as 1581 in Essex. Whilst again no connection has been found between the Loanes of Essex and the Bandon Loanes, it is an interesting possibility.

No record of the births of the children of Paul and Parnell Williams has been located yet[431]. His daughter, Mary Williams, was recorded as the youngest daughter of Paul Williams on her marriage (as Mary Williams Dawson) to Abraham Loane in 1848. Abraham Loane was recorded as a widower, TCD graduate and the son of Thomas Loane, later records suggesting that this was the Thomas Loane who married Mary Collins in 1796. Mary married William Dawson, a Bandon Inn keeper in April 1840 at Frankfield Church, Cork. She was widowed very shortly afterwards and she married again.

Her sister Rebecca married William Dawson of Cork, a woollen draper.[432] They had a brother, Paul Williams. William Dawson held a half part share in a leases of a house on North Main Street in 1852. He was described as a woollen draper of the City of Dublin, previously of Bandon. He conveyed the share of the lease to George Gibson.[433]

---

[431] It appears that either Paul Williams married twice or that possibly there was a younger Paul Williams who was baptising children in the early 1800s. Another daughter of Paul and Mary Williams, Catherine, married George French, RN, in 1822. Bandon Historical Journal Issue No 8. Page 27. This may be the George French of Bandon who died in 1878 aged 89 years. A George French was also a witness at the marriage of Abraham Loane and Mary Williams Dawson in 1848. Ballymodan headstone inscriptions record Catherine French died at Haulbowling Island on July 1st, 1831 aged 30 years. Also her sister Hester Williams died March 20th, 1828 aged 19 years and Richard Williams died 9th September 1834 aged 33 years. It is possible that George French married another sister, Jane Williams, in Blackrock in 1834 – from Church Records.
[432] Registry of Deeds. 1840 16 224
[433] Registry of Deeds 1852 3 266 of 4th February 1852

Meanwhile at the Devonshire Arms, by the 1830s assemblies of Protestants were held in what was described as '...a large and well conducted inn and posting house, containing a spacious ballroom, in which also concerts and music meetings occasionally take place.[434]

Paul Williams senior died in 1840 and his daughters Rebecca Dawson and Mary Dawson were the adminstrators of his will. Their father had left various property interests including new dwelling houses which he had built on Bridge Street and a dwelling house and premises on North Main Street to the north of the Shambles and south of Edward Scott's holding as well as the lease of the hotel.

The importance of his hotel in the civic life of Bandon was already established and by 1840 the Liberator, Daniel O'Connell, was addressing large gatherings of townspeople at the Devonshire Arms. It seems somewhat astonishing that the Protestant burgesses of Bandon could greet, admire and agree with O'Connell, who was campaigning on Catholic emancipation – something which was remarked upon at the time.

Along with civic events, business was also conducted at the Devonshire. During the 1840s, meetings to discuss the formation of the Cork and Bandon Railway Company were held at the hotel, with the Company being incorporated in 1846 and the Railway being opened for traffic in 1851.

Upon the death of Paul Williams senior, there appeared to have been some dispute over who should take over the lease. His son, Paul Williams, had been in India where he was said to have 'acquired bad habits'. In a letter to the Duke, William Dawson expressed the view that 'Paul Williams is not competent to take over the Devonshire Arms and farms.' He suggested that Paul's sister take over the lease as 'she has run the hotel for two years'. It was decided that Paul Williams junior would receive an annuity to be charged against the houses in Bridge Street.[435]

---

[434] Lewis's Topographical Survey of Ireland 1837
[435] Lismore Papers

Mary Dawson was a woman of strong views evidently, as the landlady of the Devonshire Arms was recorded as refusing to provide one Lieutenant George Lockwood of the 8th Hussars with a separate room, on the grounds that the obligation to do that applied only to 'other ranks'.[436] A case was brought against Mary but was dismissed at the sessions hearing. The Army sought a legal opinion on this which seems to have upheld Mary's stance. This relationship with the military may have been the beginning of a double identity which seemed to follow the hotel through much of its existence.

By 1856 Abraham Loane, having married Mary Williams Dawson in 1848, was listed as the proprietor of the Devonshire in Slater's Directory of that year. A post nuptial settlement was recorded between Abraham and Mary. The Hon & Rev Charles Brodrick Bernard and Rev John Pratt were to act as the trustees. Abraham had agreed to settle for the use of his wife, Mary, the hotel, lands at Callatrim and £1101 in government bonds. The trustees were only willing to administer the bonds but not the properties.[437]

Some references imply that this is the Abraham who was also farming at Downdaniel, Kilpatrick but there is ambiguity here. There were in fact at least two Abraham Loanes of about the same age. The hotel proprietor died in 1879, his residence was given as the Devonshire Arms and the informant was Sarah Anne Loane (probably the daughter of William Loane of Lissabroder, Kilpatrick, and a niece of Abraham).

The second Abraham, more likely to be the farmer at Kilpatrick, died in 1876 aged 82 and the informant was John Loane of Watergate. It is likely that this informant was John Loane who was born in 1823, son of Abraham Loane and Margaret Crowley, Margaret having died in 1870. Family records imply that there was a constant presence at the Downdaniel/Kilpatrick farm.

The Devonshire Arms Hotel however, features prominently in the Lissabroder Loane family. William Loane, son of Thomas Loane and brother of Abraham, died there in 1866; at least one of William's daughters, Rebecca, lived there with her aunt Anne and

---

[436] UK National Archives Reference
[437] Registry of Deeds. 1854 25 210

married from there to David Forsyth in 1881. Another daughter of William's, Sarah Anne, was the informant on a number of deaths of those living at the hotel.

The establishment was clearly a leading part of the social life of the town – in 1867 it features in a large advertisement in Coghlan's Directory with a coat of arms and the motto 'Ca Vendo Tutis' – nearest translation appears to be 'Safe by being on one's guard', a rather peculiar motto for a hotel, or maybe not.

It was not unknown for people to become resident at the hotel in their later years. Colonel Teulon died at the Devonshire Arms Hotel on 16th January, 1873. He was buried at Upper Shandon, Cork.

Apparently Abraham and Mary Loane kept the hotel safe for over thirty years. Abraham Loane made several attempts to dispose of his interest in the Devonshire Arms in the 1870s and in 1878 was close to agreement with George French (who operated the Railway and Commercial Hotel in Shannon Street and whose mother was the sister of Mary Williams Dawson Loane). However, the Duke's agent disapproved of this 'private' arrangement as 'Mr Loane has never advertised the concern to be disposed of, or given the public an opportunity of knowing that so large an establishment was in the market'.[438] It transpired that Abraham did not have an agreement with George French – the furniture and plate had been valued at £338.17.1 and Abraham considered this to be too low.

In her later years, Mary left the protestant church and was received into the Catholic Church by Rev Canon McSwiney, then parish priest of Bandon.[439] When she died in 1878, the catholic clergy arrived to accompany her funeral to the family burial place. A dispute then arose and the two protestant clergy present locked the gates of the cemetery to prevent Father McSwiney from carrying out his intentions. The gate was unlocked by the sexton and the burial took place though 'a good deal of excitement prevailed, no breach of the peace occurred'[440]

---

[438] Lismore Papers
[439] New Zealand Tablet, 11th October 1877
[440] Ibid

Despite their apparent 'victory', the protestant clergy stated that they would take the matter further. Whether they did or not is not known. Mary was buried in the family plot at Christ Church. She lived through a period of great change in the town when the prosperity of the early 1800s was replaced by severe hardship as many trades were overtaken by mechanisation and competition. The 1840s would bring even further suffering and migration as the Great Famine took hold. Mary had to adjust the business to the changing economics of the time.

With the death of Mary Williams Loane in 1878 and her husband Abraham in 1879, the hotel passed to Abraham's sister Anne, a spinster and sole executrix of his will. She was described by the Duke's agent as 'a very old woman who is incompetent to manage it herself.[441] Anne Loane died in 1882 and was recorded as a hotel keeper residing at the Devonshire Arms, with the informant being David Forsyth. David Forsyth and Rebecca Loane were married in 1881; Rebecca was recorded as the daughter of William Loane and her residence was the Devonshire Arms Hotel.

A deed of agreement between Anne Loane, spinster, and David and Rebecca Forsyth in 1881 stated that the Devonshire Arms and the house next door were to go to her niece, Rebecca Forsyth and her husband David, along with two dwellings in Bridge Street leased for many years by the Duke of Devonshire to Thomas Loane – Anne Loane's father. The rents on these dwellings had been paid for some years earlier by Abraham Loane of the Devonshire Arms.[442]

Sadly Rebecca Loane Forsyth also died in 1882 and the Devonshire Arms was subsequently run by David Forsyth, born in 1855 in Glasgow, the son of John Forsyth, a book seller and publisher. This tenure, too, was not without controversy – the Duke's agent considered him totally unfit to run the hotel and some moves to eject Forsyth were initiated, clearly without effect. David Forsyth died in 1887 aged 32 years and the hotel was then run by his second wife, Margaret Mary Murphy, whom he married in 1882, later with the assistance of their two children – Michael John Forsyth and Marion Forsyth. The interest in the houses in

---

[441] Lismore Papers
[442] Lismore Papers

Bridge Street was disposed of by David Forsyth and Wilhelmina (Loane) Armstrong in 1882.[443]

A Dental Practitioner's Advertisement of 1883

> **DENTISTRY.**
>
> MR J.F. OLIVERE, Surgeon Dentist
> (late of Messrs J. CORBETT & SON
> of Cork) will attend Professionally at the
> DEVONSHIRE ARMS HOTEL, Bandon
> on the Third Monday of every month
> where he may be Consulted from Ten until
> Five; and on the following day, Tuesday
> at DONOVAN'S HOTEL, Clonakilty from
> Ten until Five. At BECHER ARMS
> HOTEL, SKIBBEREEN on the FIRST
> THURSDAY IN EVERY MONTH from
> Twelve until Five
> Town Address:-- 10 COOK ST. CORK
> (14)

Directories show that the Devonshire Arms was held by the Forsyth family until at least 1914 when Mrs M. Forsyth was listed as the proprietor. It is probable that this remained so until her death in 1919. In 1915 an advertisement for the hotel described it as situated in a pleasantly and healthy situation with spacious, well ventilated dormitories, hot and cold baths, good storage for motors, billiard and ball rooms; boots to attend all trains. Mrs Forsyth was the proprietor.

Later land records suggest that the hotel was then run by her son Michael Forsyth and later by her daughter, now Marion Healy. The land records show a somewhat confusing change of ownership pattern in the 20th century as the hotel seemed to see saw backwards and forwards between owners and lessees.

The Devonshire Arms had by now probably seen its grandest days. During the 1920s it was again about to see troops and political activity. The hotel housed a detachment of Black and Tans from 1920 to 1922, then became a Free State Army Barracks until 1924. Some sources say that Michael Collins left from the Devonshire to meet his death at Beal na nBlath. Later it was said that his escort

---

[443] Registry of Deeds

car was stolen from the hotel. Although the hotel probably resumed its role as a leading hostelry in the years between the wars, from 1940 until 1945, the hotel again saw military service, being used as a National Army Barracks.

But times had changed in Bandon and the old-style grandeur of the Devonshire was now somewhat out of place. In the 1960s a large dance hall was built at the rear of the hotel and again many social events were held in what became 'The Orchid'. The death knell for the 'grande dame of Bandon' was heard in 1971 when economics were said to have forced the owners to demolish the main building. A fire destroyed the Orchid dance hall in 1976 and by the 1980s the site had been cleared and no trace could be seen of the hotel which had been a leading venue for politicians, gentry and visitors to Bandon for over 150 years.

Today the Devonshire Arms Hotel is no more and the Loane family has scattered around the globe – there are known members in Canada, America, Australia, England and New Zealand, with several still in Ireland. The descendants of Paul Williams have not been traced by this author.

Now a new building stands on the site of the Devonshire Arms Hotel gazing out over the old Shambles. Some say parts are haunted and that would hardly be surprising given its colourful past. We can only wonder what Paul Williams would think of the development where his venture began in 1819. Possibly it is just the kind of project that his entrepreneurial spirit would have fostered.

DEVONSHIRE ARMS' HOTEL,
AND
POSTING ESTABLISHMENT, BANDON
OPEN and COVERED CARS always
Ready.
D. FORSYTH.
PROPRIETOR
(28-13183-13t)

Newspaper advertisement, February 1883

Appendix

Some Biographical Details relating to the Devonshire Estate

The 4th Duke of Devonshire, William Cavendish (b 1720-1764). Married Lady Charlotte Elizabeth Boyle, the daughter of Richard Boyle, 3rd Earl of Burlington. Inherited the Bandon Estate in addition to many other properties and holdings which belonged to Richard Boyle.

The 5th Duke of Devonshire, William Cavendish. (b 1748-1811). As eldest son, he inherited the Bandon Estate on his father's death.

The 6th Duke of Devonshire, William Cavendish (b 1790-1858). As eldest son, he inherited the Bandon Estate. He remained a bachelor. He invested a significant amount in Bandon and visited the town at least twice. He supported Catholic Emancipation. The title passed to the eldest son of the 3rd son of the 4th Duke.

The 7th Duke of Devonshire, William Cavendish (b 1808-1891). His younger son, Lord Frederick Charles Cavendish, was assassinated in the Phoenix Park in 1882 just after he was appointed Chief Secretary for Ireland.

The 8th Duke of Devonshire, Spencer Cavendish (b 1833-1908). He sold the Bandon Estates. Most of his holdings were conveyed to Sir John Arnott for the sum of £200,000.

Sir John Arnott (1814-1898). Born in Auchtermuchty, Fife, Scotland, he was the son of John Arnott and Elizabeth, the daughter of Alexander Paton. He arrived in Cork in 1837 to work at Grants of Patrick Street, Cork. He opened a drapery store in Cork which he later expanded across Ireland and Britain including Arnotts of Henry Street and Arnotts in Glasgow.

He was elected Lord Mayor of Cork three times in 1859, 1860 and 1861. He was a Justice of the Peace for Cork City and County and served as MP for Kinsale between 1859 and 1863. He was created a Knight Bachelor by the Lord Lieutenant of Ireland in 1859.

He married Mary, the daughter of John James McKinlay. They lived at Woodlands in the Parish of St Anne's, Shandon. He acquired the freehold of the majority of properties on North Main Street and Kilbrogan Hill in 1897.

Devonshire Lismore Agents

William Connor. Head Irish Agent from 1760 to 1792
Henry Bowman. Head Irish Agent from 1792 to 1797
Thomas Knowlton. Head Irish Agent from 1797 to 1816
W.A. Ashby. Head Irish Agent from 1816 to 1817
William S. Currey. Head Irish Agent from 1817 to 1839
Francis E. Currey. Head Irish Agent from 1839 to 1881
Chetwode H. Currey. Head Irish Agent from 1881 to 1883
Richard H. Power. Head Irish Agent from 1885 to 1895

Devonshire Bandon Agents

John Swanston (b 1785-1860). Born in High Laws, Berwickshire, Scotland, he moved to Bandon in 1819 to act as local agent reporting to Colonel William S. Currey who was based in Lismore. Prior to his move to Bandon, John had spent nine years at the Devonshire Estate Irish headquarters at Lismore acting as Bandon agent and reporting to Currey.

Alexander Swanston. Born in 1809 in the UK, he worked as his father's assistant in 1826 and took over from him in the late 1830s. In 1844 Alexander Swanston was Chairman of the Town Commissioners. In the same year he was recorded as earning £331 in his role as Bandon Agent. He held his position as the Bandon Agent until 1858. He became a Liberal Member of Parliament for Bandon Bridge from 1874 to 1880 and a merchant and had a country seat in Norwood, Surrey.

John Rawdon Berwick (b 1809-1889), the third son of the Rev Edward Berwick, Vicar of Leixlip. He was agent from 1858 to 1889. He never married.

Richard Edmund Hodson (b 1856-1915). He was the third son of Sir George Frederick John Hodson. He married Margaret Pemberton in 1892 and they had three sons. Whilst he was agent, the Devonshire Estate in Bandon was sold to Sir John Arnott. Hodson died on 8th July 1915 and was buried at Christ Church Kilbrogan.

Under the terms of the Wyndham Land Purchase Act of 1903 Hodson sold the farm holdings of the estate to the occupying farmers.

Devonshire Legal Agents for Bandon
Bandon did not have its local agent devoted to just Bandon affairs until 1812 when Thomas Seward was appointed as the Agent for East Cork and Benjamin Popham held the legal agency for Bandon and the local area.

Thomas Garde. Head Irish Legal Agent from 1770 to 1807 not based in Bandon

Benjamin Popham. Head Irish Legal Agent until 1812. Susequently Bandon Legal Agent. He was the second son of Robert Popham, malster, of Moss Grove and his wife, Martha. He was born in 1780 and was educated at Castlebar. He entered Kings Inn in 1796. From 1812 he became the legal agent for the Duke of Devonshire's Bandon Estate. From his office which was next to the Devonshire Square houses he supervised the erection of buildings such as the Shambles and the Devonshire Arms Hotel, he was responsible for the furnishing of dwellings and the registering of the freeholders until the arrival of Swanston in 1819 when he took over all but the legal work.

Benjamin lived at Coolfadda House from 1817 until his death in 1847. He took on a lease on North Main Street in 1822 and following his death in 1849, notice was served on Regina Popham of Bandon, Robert Popham of Mawbeg and Anna Maria and Elizabeth Regina Popham, daughters of Mawbeg. The Pophams were ejected. The property was on the east side of the street between the road and the stream, bounded on the north by Mrs Hannah Baldwin and on the south by William Jenkins.

Devonshire Bandon Stewards
David Craig
James Craig

Devonshire Bandon Bailiff
Jonathan Tanner

Short Biographies of some Immediate Lessors and Tenants recorded in the 1700s

William Baldwin married Mary Milner on 22nd October 1762 at Murragh. William leased 367 acres of land at Lisnagat from Thomas Baldwin for 995 years.[444] The Baldwins were one of the first settler families in Bandon.[445]

Arthur Bernard Esq was the brother of Judge Francis Bernard of Castle Bernard. Arthur married Anne Power, the daughter and co-heiress of Roger Power (Le Poer) of Mount Eglantine, Co Waterford. Arthur erected Palace Anne near Murragh in 1714. They had 14 children. His daughter Anne married William Connor. Arthur leased the site of the mill and Floraville in the 1700s.

Thomas Bryan was a clothier in Bandon in the early 1700s. He lived on North Street in a house which had been the property of Samuel Browne of Bandon, a cordwainer.

Thomas had moved to the City of London by 1737.[446] He acquired an 80 year lease on 8th April 1727 from John Love of a holding which was bounded on the east by Walter Travers, on the west by Francis Lisson and on the north by the churchyard. The yearly rental was £7. He assigned the lease in 1737 to John Stammers for £100.

William Bull, tanner, and his wife Hanna Hore were married in 1704[447]. They had a son William junior who married Sarah, daughter of Richard Ward, also a tanner on North Main Street. William and Sarah had at least two children Susanna and Elizabeth Bull (who married firstly Mr Vance and was widowed by 1756 and secondly John Oliffe, a woolcomber). William senior was

---

[444] Baldwins of Lisnagat. Alexandra Buhagiar
[445] George Bennett. The History of Bandon
[446] Registry of Deeds. 289 896 63877 of 1737
[447] Index to Marriage Licence Bonds, diocese of Cork and Ross

provost in 1720. By his will of 5th March, 1737, he had made his son the sole heir which included the house and tanyard.[448]

William Bull senior and Ralph Clear senior had acquired a lease on lands at Farranmareen in East Carbury which had been formerly in the possession of Thomas Ware who resided at Woodfort. In 1718 William Bull senior leased the lands to Joseph Hosford and Edward Duke Maneare at a yearly rent of £21. The lease included a holding on North Main Street. In 1725 William Bull released 196 acres to Richard Ward, his son in law, and to John Jones who in turn passed the lands in 1758 to Dr Joseph Ledbetter.[449]

Ralph Clear was a clothier in Bandon in the early 1700s and became provost in 1732[450]. He was descended from one of the first settler families in Bandon.[451] His eldest son and heir was also Ralph. In 1748 Ralph junior was in possession of a house, cabin and one acre in Kilbrogan as well as lands in Coolfadda and a house in the possession of Robert Doman which he mortgaged to Francis Banfield of Carhue for £125.[452] In 1752 Ralph entered into a lease with the Midleton Estate which included several houses in Irishtown and nineteen acres to hold for the lives of Richard Clear, his second son, Thomas Ward and William Ward at an annual rent of £78 6s. By the terms of the will of his father, Ralph also inherited lands at Ardbrack, Kinsale for the term of his natural life only. On 3rd May 1759 Ralph junior demised the holdings to John Moxley of the city of Cork for 99 years.[453]

Ralph Clear was the ancestor of the Clears who resided in North Main Street in the 1800s.

Daniel Connor was the son of Cornelius O'Connor who married Joane Splane in 1670. He was a receiver of rents for Boyle's Bandon Estate. provost in 1706, 1722, 1735, 1743, 1748 and 1750. He had seven children including Daniel (died 1733), George who married Elizabeth Southwell and who settled at Ballybricken, Monkstown, Cork, Mary who married Rev Bartholomew Thomas

---

[448] Registry of Deeds. 192 264 132217 and 92 391 65070 of 1738
[449] Registry of Deeds. 192 264 132217 of 31st May 1758
[450] Registry of Deeds. 183 123005. 6th July 1756
[451] George Bennett. The History of Bandon
[452] Registry of Deeds. 196 517 103927 of 1748
[453] Registry of Deeds 196 602 132049 of 1759

of Everton, Carlow, William who married Anne Bernard in 1721, Jane who married John Lapp, Elizabeth who married Richard Gumbleton and Sarah who married Mr Wade.

William Connor senior married Anne Bernard, the daughter of Arthur Bernard of Palace Anne and granddaughter of Judge Francis Bernard of Castle Bernard. They had sons Roger (eldest son and heir), Daniel (b 1723), Cornelius, Arthur and William (b 1731). William became the Devonshire Agent for the Bandon Estate in 1739. He was appointed Head Agent in 1748 and acted as the Earl of Cork and Burlington's attorney from 21st March 1753.

William Connor junior became agent for the Devonshire Estate and was forced to resign in 1792.

Abraham Davies was a miller whose will was proved in 1727. He was a miller.[454] The surname was on the list of first settlers in Bandon.

Rev Solomon Foley was born in 1663 in Clonmel, Co Tipperary and was a younger brother of Samuel Foley, the Bishop of Down[455]. Solomon entered TCD at the age of sixteen. Abraham Watkins leased No 115 and No 116 (map 1717) to Rev Solomon Foley, the son of Rev Solomon Foley, armiger. On 24th May 1716 Abraham Watkins transferred to Rev Solomon his lease of the tract of land between the church yard and Water Gate (see entry for Abraham Watkins).[456] However, the map of 1717 still records Herbert Love as the immediate lessor so may not have been up to date.

In 1694 he became rector of Kilmeen and vicar of Drinagh and prebendary of Kilnaglory and in 1698 he became rector of Ardnegihy and Killcully. By 1704 he was recorded as prebendary, rector and vicar of Kilbrogan.

Rev Solomon and his wife Margaret had a daughter who married James Jackson, possibly the person who was provost of Bandon in

---

[454] Registry of Deeds. 93 120 65071 1738
[455] Brady. Clerical and Parochial Records
[456] Registry of Deeds. 16 7730 24th May 1716

1716 and again in 1730-1731.[457] James and his wife had a daughter Susannah Jackson. James Jackson's brother, William, was vicar of Christ Church, Kilbrogan.

Rev Solomon's daughter Susanna married his curate Rev Robert McClellan of Bandon Bridge in 1736. Rev Robert was priested in Cork in 1737. He was a step brother of Rev Paul Limrick of Schull whose daughter Bridget married Benjamin Sullivan, formerly Clerk of the Crown for Cork[458]. Rev Robert McClellan died in 1761.

Rev Solomon's wife, Margaret, predeceased him on 28th March 1731 and Rev Solomon was buried on 26th February 1738. In his will he directed that he should be buried in the chancel of Christ Church near his deceased wife Margaret.

The bell of Christ Church was installed during Rev Foley's occupancy. It was cast by an Italian bell founder and bore the inscription "Edward Spillane and James Moxley, S.N. Church wardens. 1734."

They also had the following children, Jane buried 12th July, 1708, Amy buried 26th September 1709, George buried 15th August, 1710, Robert buried 30th April, 1712 and Solomon buried 22nd April 1725.[459]

Richard Hammett, clothier, married Elizabeth Daniel (her mother Mary was widowed by 1767). They had at least a son Richard and a daughter Cathren baptised in 1753 at Christ Church. Her sponsors were John Gillman, George Hammett, Mary Browne and Elizabeth Bull. A will was proved in 1785 of Richard Hammett, the elder, woolcomber of Bandon.

John Hammett married Sarah Bayly. They had triplets born in 1755, Richard, Elizabeth and Alicia. Their sponsors were Richard senior and junior (See previous entry), Alicia Bayly, Hanah Bayly, Mary Browne and John Gillman.

[457] The History of Bandon. George Bennett
[458] Registry of Deeds. 86 170 59831 1736. Marriage Settlement
[459] Ibid

Anthony Harris of Bandon married Miss Susanna Wrixon at Ballinadee[460] on 21st September 1771. A deed of 1782 refers to Anthony Harris of Rock Castle (Ballinadee), Cork, Thomas Quin and Thomas Barter of Bandon.

Thomas Holland, a linen merchant, grocer, spirit dealer and stamp distributor. He was recorded as both an occupier and immediate lessor in 1775. He married Elizabeth Fuller. They had at least Ann, baptised 1761, Margaret baptised 1763, Thomas baptised 1764, John baptised 1765 and Hester baptised 1767[461]. Hester married George Kingston Esq.

At the time of his marriage to Elizabeth Fuller, a widow, Thomas held numerous leases which were recorded in the marriage settlement
- Land and tenement adjoining Edward Nash, a blacksmith, in Coolfadda (original lease was for 121 years)
- Small plot in Sugar Lane called Morgan Walsh's tenement for the lives of D. Gibson, William Snow junior, Thomas Lucas, the eldest son of Jasper of Rickfordstown for 21 years
- A house on North Street where John Austin, the gunsmith, lived. The lease was from James Kingston of Ballycatteen for 65 years from 25th March 1739
- A tenement where John Harris lived on North Street by lease dated 25th March 1741 from James Kingston of Ballycatteen for 63 years
- Cabbins on Sugar Lane held by Julian Holland. Lease from Francis Bernard for 31 years from 25th March, 1752
- A farm at Cloghonabodg in possession of Thomas Seaberry, the elder, under lease from John Loan for lives
- Lands at Coolfadda of 6 aces for 39 years from Mr Hammett.
- A house formerly in possession of Thomas Wheeler by original lease from Mr Hammett for 51 years from 1st May 1718
- Two houses in the tenancy of George Bennett and David Rains.
- A house on Sugar Lane held by lease under William Giles

---

[460] O'Kief, Coshe, Mang
[461] Baptisms from Christ Church Kilbrogan church records.

- Legoes holding in Sugar Lane held by Stephen Moxley and his under tenants and adjoining holdings held under leaze from Francis Bernard

CHANCERY.

Wm. Hargrave, and Mary Hargrave, otherwise Snowe, his Wife, Executrix of William Snowe, deceased. **Plaintiffs.**

Ann Holland, Elizabeth Holland, Spinsters, William Holland Kingston, and others, **Defendants.**

PURSUANT to the Decree of her Majesty's High Court of Chancery, in Ireland, made in this Cause, bearing date the 1st day of May, 1338, I hereby require all Persons having Debts, Charges, or Incumbrances, affecting the real and Freehold Estates of Thomas Holland, deceased, in the Pleadings in this Cause mentioned, prior to or cotemporaneous with the Plaintiff's demand; and also all Creditors and Legatees of the said Thomas Holland, to come in before me, at my Chambers, on the Inns-quay, Dublin, on or before the 22d day of October next, and prove their respective demands, otherwise they will be precluded all benefit arising from the said Decree.—Dated this 19th day of September, 1838.

For Mr. TOWNSEND.

THOMAS GOOLD.

Thomas Grier, Solicitor for the Plaintiffs, 26, Upper Dominick-street.

Dennis Kelly, a 'tyler', and his wife Katherin held the lease on the tenement called Roche's and Clarke's (see map of 1775 and Numbers 55 to 59 in index of 1715). In 1748 they assigned the lease to Joseph Holland, a clothier for two lives and 21 years in reversion.[462]

John Lapp[463] lived in Bandon. In 1720 he married Jane Connor[464], the daughter of Daniel and Margaret and sister of William (see entry for Connor Family). He had a daughter Jane who married Robert Dring in 1718 (the son of Simon Dring and Temperance Morris). A deed of 1726 records John Lapp as a

---

[462] Registry of Deeds 136 70 90546
[463] National Library of Ireland. MS 811
[464] Marriage Licence Bond.

merchant of Bandon. John and Jane also had a son John who married Ann Falkiner (Falconer) in 1747. She was the daughter of Ruth Riggs who married Caleb Falkiner in 1707.[465] Her brother Riggs Falkiner was MP for Clonakilty from 1768-1776. He was created a Baronet on 24th August 1778 and he lived at Anne Mount. The Falkiners settled in Ireland in the 1650s and were from Brigard, Leeds. The Lapps were on the list of the first settlers in Bandon.

Dr Joseph Ledbetter, son of Thomas, was born in Bandon in 1706[466]. He entered Trinity on 10th June, 1721 and became a Doctor of 'physick'. He had a son Thomas born in 1736[467].

Susanna Ledbetter was described in her will as of the City of Cork and widow of Joseph, Medical Doctor, deceased. She left bequests in her will to Colonel James Barker of Bandon and Jonathan Clerk also of Bandon which included interest in lands at Corleagh near Palace Anne. She directed that income from the rents were to be paid to her nieces, Sarah Bermingham and Ann Ballard, the wife of John Ballard of the City of Cork and she bequeathed lands in Coolfadda to her nephew William Broughton and his wife Lydia.[468] Joseph had pre-deceased her in 1788[469] and was buried at Christ Church, Kilbrogan. Rev John Moore, the rector of Innishannon from 1702-1838, married Anna Maria Folliott. A daughter married Dr Joseph Ledbetter as Dr Joseph is referred to as 'son-in-law' in the will of Rev Moore dated 1748.[470] A Joseph Ledbetter of Bandon, Medical Doctor married Miss McClellan in 1761.[471]

Thomas Legg. On 28th February 1729 Thomas Legg senior, a tanner, granted the lease of No 65 (see 1717 street index) to Thomas Legg junior, for £31. In 1738 Thomas Legg junior assigned the lease to Richard Hammett, a clothier.[472] By 1740 the interests of Thomas Legg junior were seized by the High Sheriff of

---

[465] Ibid

[466] Alumni Dublinenses (TCD)

[467] Devonshire Lease of 1752 records his only son as 16

[468] Registry of Deeds. 723 494205 28th January 1818

[469] Ireland Diocesan and Prerogative Wills & Administrations Index 1595-1858

[470] Brady's. Clerical and Parochial Records. Vol 1

[471] Faulkners Journal of 19th September 1761

[472] Registry of Deeds. 89 305 63336

Co Cork as he had an outstanding debt of £62 18/. It was assigned to Francis Adams of Cork.[473]

Major Herbert Love Esq resided in the parish of Murragh[474]. His family settled in Ireland at the time of Cromwell and were granted estates in County Cork and elsewhere. He was the son of Major John Love of Kinsale Fort, one of the 'Forty Nine Officers' who died in 1670. Major John Love's wife Jane was the sole executrix to the will of her husband and the witnesses were the Earl of Barrymore, Sir Richard Gethin and Robert Southwell. John Love was buried in Ringrone church yard.

Major Herbert was John's eldest son. John also had sons Barry and John and two daughters Jane and Mary. Herbert married Judith, the daughter of Colonel Randolph Clayton of Mallow. Judith's mother was the eldest daughter of Sir Philip Percival. Herbert and Judith had three sons, John, Herbert and Barry and three daughters, Katherine who married Walter Travers Esq, Elizabeth and Judith. Herbert died in 1725 and was buried in Ringrone along with his father, brothers and sisters. His will referred to property in Cork and Tralee. His eldest son John was his executor.[475]

A large tract of land between Water Gate and the Church Yard was acquired by Major Herbert from Abraham Watkins under the terms of a lease dated 27th January 1698. It became known as Love's holdings (See map of 1775). The land was part of a total of 564 acres which he leased for 99 years. On 24th May 1716 transferred the tract of land between Water Gate and the Church Yard to Rev Solomon Foley for £150 as well as an annual rental of £60 for the first four years and £70 thereafter.[476]

Elizabeth Love who married Rev Benezar Mordock, rector of Kilshannig was a daughter of Major Herbert. (Rev James Hingston married Rev Benezar and Elizabeth's daughter Katherine in 1741). They had a son John Hingston who became curate of Kilbrogan in 1762. John Hingston married Alicia Bernard in 1782. She was the second daughter of Arthur Bernard

[473] Registry of Deeds 100 478 71307
[474] Clerical and Parochial Records. William Maziere Brady
[475] Grove White Notes
[476] Registry of Deeds. 16 7730 of 24th May 1716.

Esq of Palace Anne by his wife Mary Adderley). They also had a son James who became vicar general of Cloyne, a son William and a son Benezar who served in America during the War of Independence.

John Love inherited Herbert's holdings. His address in 1727 was Litterdella, Cork.[477] John was married three times, firstly to Mary Tresilian by whom he had a daughter Mary who married Patterson Esq and whom he cut off because she married contrary to his express command, secondly to Ann, the daughter of George Ward Esq of Great Yarmouth by whom he had a daughter Elizabeth and thirdly to Sarah Casaubon by whom he had his son and heir, William and also Judith and Catherine who married in 1758 John Vincent Esq, the son of the mayor of Limerick.

He leased the North Main Street holding to Thomas Bryan of Bandon, a clothier. Thomas Bryan had moved to the City of London by 1737.[478] The plot of land which he had leased in 1727 for 80 years from John Love was recorded as being bounded on the east by Walter Travers (the husband of John Love's sister Katherine), on the west by Francis Lisson, on the north by the church yard and on the south by North Main Street. Thomas Bryan had a mortgage of £100 for the holding from Russell Wood in Cork. He assigned the lease to Jn Stammers of Bandon, a merchant, who in turn paid the £100 to Russell Wood.

John Love's will was dated 29th December 1750 and was made at Bath. The will referred to property in St Mary's Shandon, Tralee and to Castle Saffron. His son and heir was William Love Esq of Castle Saffron and Ballea, Co Cork.[479]

James Rice was an innkeeper who was recorded on the 1717 map as being resident in a large, two storey house with stables and garden. It was located between the church yard and Water Gate and could have been where Burchills had their inn in the late 1700s (No 6). The site was assigned by Abraham Watkins to Herbert Love in 1698 and by Herbert Love to Rev Solomon Foley in 1716. James Rice died in 1732. He was the father of Hannah

---

[477] Registry of Deeds. 55 208 36596 of 12th January 1727
[478] Registry of Deeds. 89 896 63877
[479] Grove White Notes

who married William Bass, also an innkeeper. His widow was Elizabeth Rice. A marriage of James Rice to Elizabeth Travers took place in 1720.[480]

James Rice had a house on North Main Street at the time of his death which was lived in by John Ward. He bequeathed it to Hannah and she mortgaged the property to Daniel Connor for £50.[481]

Rev William Robinson was the son of Rev Thomas Robinson of St Michaels, Kirkham, Lancashire. He married Anne Moorcroft and they had a number of sons including William and Thomas, who married Dorothy, daughter of Samuel Townsend of Firmount in the parish of Donoughmore, Co Cork. He became rector and vicar of Christ Church in 1739 and he died in Bandon in 1746. His son William married Rebecca Payne and they lived near Bandon. Their son James married Mary Lovell on 1st May 1806 at Christ Church. James became an inn keeper (No 5). His son William ran the operation as a wine and spirit store.

Andrew Roche was a cooper. One of his holdings became known as Clarke's and Roche's tenement (see map of 1775). In 1720 he took on a lease from the Boyle Estate for Webb's tenement which was then in possession of Abraham Beare. (Webb's tenement was next to Clarke's and Roche's on the west side of the street). The lease was for the lives of Richard Clarke, a shoemaker, Daniel Deason, son of Jervis Deason deceased and Hannah Luskin, the daughter of John Luskin of Ballymountain. Andrew Roche's will was proved in 1759.

Captain William Snowe was an agent to Henry Boyle, 1st Baron Carleton at Castlemartyr, Co Cork. He then served as agent for the Earl of Cork and Burlington's Estate in Bandon between ca 1711 and 1720.[482] William, senior's, wife died in 1731.

William Snowe junior of Cork, an Ensign, married by licence Mary Holland, the daughter of Thomas Holland[483], the merchant on 9th January 1770 at Christ Church, Kilbrogan. They had Salisbury

---

[480] Index to Marriage Licence Bonds. Diocese of Cork and Ross.
[481] Registry of Deeds 74 52250 of 12th December 1733.
[482] NLI. Lismore Papers
[483] Thomas Holland lived in a house on the site of the Provincial Bank (No 1)

Snowe born 10th April, 1777 and William Haviland born 9th May 1778. William married Christiana Sophia Ponnoll in Antony, Cornwall on 13th July 1803. He died in Chatham, Kent on 6th June 1831. The executors for William Snowe were William Hargrave and Mary Hargrave, otherwise Snowe. (see entry for Thomas Holland (1775)

Richard Ward, a tanner, had a daughter Sarah who married William Bull, also a tanner (see William Bull). Richard entered into some property transactions with John Jones who was a provost.

Abraham Watkins Esq by the terms of a lease dated 27th January 1698 demised to Herbert Love for 99 years the townlands which included Doverstown and Cappocknorlane and which amounted to 564 acres and which were situated in the Barony of Kinalmeaky. The lease included land and premises in North Street occupied in 1717 by Daniel Sullivan, James Rice and Timothy Sullivan.[484] George Bennett in his History of Bandon refers to Captain John Watkins, the son of Lieutenant Daniel Watkins who was made a freeman of the Bandon Corporation in 1652 and who was provost in 1672, 1681, 1682. He was also on the list of 1649 officers and possibly could have been the father of Abraham.

Abraham's will was dated 1715 and his residence was given as Cork City[485]. He predeceased his wife Mary who was recorded as a resident in Cork City in 1724. He left her a half plowland in Kilmacsimon to be sold by her for payments of debts and to raise funds for his children. He also left her a house and grounds 'outside North Gate' called the Potters Field and 'George House' which was within North Gate. He left £100 to his daughter Mary after settlement of debts and he bequeathed George House to her following his wife's decease but stipulated that if she married Derby Cartie, the fiddler, she would not inherit one penny and she would not inherit the house and lands. He also left his daughter Sarah Watkins £100 as well as £5 per annum following her mother's death and he left his daughter Amy £100 and £4 per annum to be paid out of the income from the house and lands.

---

[484] Registry of Deeds. 16 7730 1716
[485] Registry of Deeds. 24 13174 of 1715

Mary Watkins held the lease on No 115 and 116 of the map of 1717 and on 4th June 1724 she assigned the lease to John Travers. The house was described as having a slate roof and formerly in possession of Rev Solomon Foley. John Travers was still living at the house in 1775 (No 37). The house was located on the site of the house known as North Gate today (see entries for No 43 and No 44). Presumably the house was 'George House' as no other house was referred to in the will of Mary's husband, Abraham.

Abraham's wife Mary died in 1735. The sole executor of her will was Thomas Walker of the City of Cork, Gent. She still had George House which she had leased to John Travers for 41 years at £10pa. John Travers had died by 1735 and the house was occupied by his widow, Jane Travers. Anna Swete purchased the holding from Thomas Walker for £100.[486]

In 1740 Ann Chandler, a widow, who was living in Cork City was receiving the yearly rent from Potters Field and the George House. George Hawkins married Margaret who was the daughter of Ann Chandler and as part of a marriage settlement, George was granted the annuity. In 1741 George conveyed the annuity to Daniel Connor for £46.[487]

Watkins appeared as a surname on the list of the first settlers in Bandon.

Stephen Winthrop was the son of William Winthrop (born Bandon 1705) and Alicia Wrixon. Alicia's family were from Woodpark near Mallow. Stephen was born in 1738 in Bandon. His siblings were Benjamin, William, Mary, Bridget who married William Maunsell, son of William Maunsell and Alice Norcott, Sarah, Frances. The Winthrops were quakers.

Dissenting Meeting House was the address of James Clugston according to his will which was proved in 1780.

---

[486] Registry of Deeds. 79 57040 10th June 1735
[487] Registry of Deeds. 104 346 73295 of 1741

Short Biographies of some Immediate Lessors and Tenants recorded in the 1800s

William Belcher, MD was born in 1799. He was the second son of William who married Margaret Tresilian. William married Anna Waring. They had five children, Hester Waring (born 1830) who married August Spiller, Dora Porter (born 1832), John Waring (1837-1903), William (born 1834) who married Edith Bonham and Robert Tresilian (See House No 68).

William was actively involved in the freemasons. He served as treasurer and secretary of Lodge 84. His father, William, and two younger brothers, Henry and John were all medical professionals.

William died in 1837 and was buried at Christ Church, Kilbrogan.

Robert Tresilian Belcher was the eldest son of William, a Medical Doctor, who married Margaret Tresilian on 31st May 1792. Robert married his cousin, Alicia Tresilian, by licence in 1823. She was the only daughter of Margaret Eliza (otherwise Dillon of Belfast) and John Tresilian, an attorney. Alicia's parents had married in January 1797.

Robert and Alicia had five children; William born in 1824, John Tresilian born in 1826 (he qualified as a lawyer in 1842 and in 1856 he married Fanny Coleman Rogers), Thomas Dillon born in 1828 (he qualified as a lawyer in 1846), Robert, birth date unknown[488] and Margaret Eliza born in 1831 (she married her cousin Stewart Stewart Tresilian as his second wife in 1866 and went to live in England).

Robert Tresilian Belcher became a Lieutenant in the 32nd Regiment and was commended for his gallant conduct at the Battle of Waterloo. He returned to Bandon sometime before 1823 when he married Alicia. On December 1824 he was proposed and elected as a freeman of the town. He became a common council member on 27th February 1826 in place of Francis Sweeny. On 4th November, 1831 Robert along with the Right Honorable Francis

[488] Robert T. Belcher Esq, Lieutenant Royal Cork Artillery married Emelie Gertrude Mayne, 5th daughter of Frederick Mayne Esq of Callatrim House at Chirst Church on 14th October 1862 (Cork Examiner)

Bernard Esq, were elected free burgesses of the Borough of Bandon Bridge in place of Rev Somers Payne and Benjamin Swete.

Robert was elected provost of the Borough for the ensuing year on 24th June, 1836. He served as a Justice of the Peace. He was an active freemason who served as Worshipful Master from 1833-1835 of Lodge 84. He had also been affiliated with Lodge 20. He served as a Local Director of the Provincial Bank of Ireland (No 1) and as Treasurer of the Bandon Savings Bank on Cavendish Row (the building subsequently became the Freemason's Hall).

Following the bankruptcy of George and William Cornwall, brewers and malsters in 1837, Robert became the sole assignee of their estate. He was responsible for selling the remaining leases of their numerous holdings which included a number of properties on North Main Street.

Robert was actively involved in the creation of the Cork and Bandon railway and was present at the first meeting to discuss the construction of the railway which took place at the Devonshire Arms Hotel on25th September, 1833. He was elected as one of the committee of nine people to work on the proposal. The first sod was turned in 1845.

Robert died in 1849 and probate of his will was granted on 29th December 1849. He was succeeded by his wife Alicia who was still recorded as the occupier of No 68 in 1851.

Letters of administration of the estate of Robert Tresilian Belcher were granted to Robert's son, Robert Tresilian Belcher of 11 Belgrave Street, Commercial Road, Stephney, London, a Customs House officer. Alice had left the estate unadministered following the death of her husband and the effects were recorded as of no value.

Thomas Bennett of Castle Road, Bandon (1757-1845) who married Ann Hughes was a pawnbroker[489] and was a son of George Bennett, the clothier and shopkeeper who lived on Castle road. Thomas had a younger brother Joseph who also became a pawnbroker and who was the father of George Bennett, the

---

[489] ROD 758 456 515191

historian. Thomas was a devout member of the Methodist Church for more than 70 years. He entertained Charles Wesley on at least one of his visits to Bandon.[490] Father and son were both named Thomas and were the trustees and executors of the will of George Bennett, a clothier and shopkeeper of Castle Street. His father, the clothier, George left two houses to his son and grandson; a house on Castle Street which had formerly been in the possession of Thomas Fuller and a house near the Bridewell river which was in the occupation of Daniel Callahan.

On 21st April, 1819 Thomas purchased the lease of a property known as Bruce's Holding from Walter Tanner, a police constable who was the son and heir of Walter Tanner, a farmer in Gaggin.[491]

Thomas and his son Thomas entered into a mortgage with Giles Varian Sullivan, a cotton manufacturer and son of John Sullivan Esq, on 14th January 1828. In return for a payment of £300, Giles Sullivan farm let to them lands of East Curravoidy, Knockanagee and Ballynoe which had been held by original lease dated 1783 from Rev Dr St John Browne to John Sullivan. The land included 258 acres as well as a house on South Main Street.[492]

Thomas's son Thomas married Mary Glasson at Christ Church, Kilbrogan on 24th April, 1803. As the eldest son of a freeman, he was made a freeman of the Corporation of Bandon Bridge. In 1839 they were living in Shannon Street. Thomas and Mary had sons William, shop keeper of Bandon (the eldest son and freeman of Bandon) and Rev Thomas Glasson Bennett (see next entry).

Rev Thomas Glasson Bennett, MA, was born in Bandon and was the son of Thomas who married Mary Glasson. In 1840 Rev Thomas married Mary Elizabeth Fuller in Bandon. She was the eldest daughter of Thomas Fuller of Bandon and sister of George Fuller, Barrister at Law. George Fuller had at least two children, George of 37 Godolph Road, Shepherds Bush, London who married Charlotte Matilda and Thomas Fuller, a solicitor. (George Bennett suggests in his 'History of Bandon' that the Fullers were

---

[490] www.flyingphotons.com
[491] ROD 739 564 503900
[492] ROD 831 194 558729

descended from Ralph Fuller, one of the original colonists of Bandon).

He graduated with a BA from Trinity in 1833 and an MA in 1838. He was ordained Deacon in 1839 by the Bishop of Down and was priested in 1840 by the Bishop of Tuam. He served as curate of Templenacarrigy, Cloyne from 1839-1841 and was curate of Innishannon from 1841 to 1850, of Ballinadee from 1850 to 1857 and of Murragh from 1857 to 1866 before he moved to Kilmacabea.

Rev Thomas and Elizabeth had six sons and two daughters including Thomas George, baptised in Ballymodan, Bandon on 26th May 1841, William Fuller Bennett born 1844 (see No 91), Richard Bennett born 1845 who married Mary Emily Nash, Elizabeth Fuller born on 16th October 1846[493], Joseph John Bennett born on 9th November 1848[494] and Charles Henry Bennett who was born on 11th February 1853 in Ballinadee and who married Priscilla Rebecca Nash and Theodore Octavius Bennett born 1855 who married Ina Nash.

Rev Thomas resigned the parish of Kilmacabea in 1878 due to ill health and he died on the 18th March 1880 aged 68 at Patrick Street, Cork. The union of parishes of Kilmacabea included the parishes of Kilmacabea, Kilfaughnabeg and Myross all located near Leap. His widow, Mary, was one of the executors of his will which was proved at Cork on 26th April 1880. He left effects of under £100.

Joseph and Mary Bennett lived for a time at No 12 Castle Street, Bandon. Joseph, the younger son of George Bennett, a clothier, was a wealthy pawnbroker and merchant. He had a brother, Thomas (See previous entries) and a sister Dora who married William Kingston, the pawn broker[495]. Another daughter may have married James Scott as he is mentioned in several deeds. Joseph was the father of George Bennett who was born on 31st October, 1824 and who emigrated to Bandon, Oregon. In 1842 Joseph purchased a block of land in Dunworly from William

---

[493] Baptised at Christ Church, Innishannon

[494] Ibid

[495] Registry of Deeds. 1820 760 516188. Thomas Bennett, senior & junior were witnesses to the deed

Tresilian for the sum of £460. George inherited this land from his father.

George Bennett

George Bennett was born on 31st October, 1824. His grandfather was also George, a clothier, and his father was Joseph who married Mary. George attended the Bandon Grammar School before entering Trinity on 7th November, 1842. He graduated in 1847. In 1853 George married Catherine Anne Scott Harrison. Their first child, Joseph William was born on 21st April 1855 at No 52.

On 29th August, 1855 George Bennett signed a yearly lease with the Duke of Devonshire's agent, Swanston, for Barrett's Hill House (known as Hill House) and land at a yearly rent of £42 to commence from 29th September 1855 with the condition that he repaired the property. His other children were born at Hill House; George Augustine on 22nd July 1856, Alfred Constantine on 22nd August, 1857 and their only daughter Victoria Mary Catherine on 24th July 1860 (she died on 22nd April 1861)

George Bennett was actively involved in town and church affairs. He served for a time as a church warden and as a member of the select vestry. He was Honorable Secretary of the Masonic Lodge 84. He was also a poor law guardian for the electoral division of Kilbrogan. He wrote his first History of Bandon in 1860/1861.

On 21st February, 1873 a notice appeared in the Skibbereen Eagle offering the interest in Hill House and lands and shortly thereafter a public auction of his furniture took place.

On 26th May 1873 George Bennett, at that time aged 49, and his two sons Joseph William, aged 18 and George Augustine, aged 17 together with George Sealy of Bandon set off for Oregon, USA to join a school friend, Henry Hewitt Baldwin who had grown up in the Kingston Buildings and who left school at a young age and made his fortune in the US. George left his wife Catherine (Kate) and youngest son Alfred Constantine behind. Alfred entered Queen's College Cork in 1874 and graduated as a medical doctor. Catherine lived for a time in Cork City. In 1901 she was was living at No 50 North Main Street.

George Bennett died in Oregon on 18th October, 1900 and his wife Catherine died in Bandon on 12th August, 1904. The Bennett family vault is at Christ Church, Kilbrogan.

Rev Nicholas Cole Bowen was the son of Henry Cole Bowen of Bowen's Court and was ordained priest at Cloyne on 6th July, 1806. He married Bryanna Travers, the daughter of Robert Travers, on 23rd February, 1795 at Christ Church, Kilbrogan.

On 28th March, 1816 he became rector of Ballyfeard which was a small parish which was located twelve miles from Bandon. In 1831 the parish had a protestant population of just 78. In the mid 1830s Rev Nicholas was suffering from ill health and moved to Bandon to be close to medical assistance. He died in 1837.

Rev Nicholas and Bryanna had several daughters including Henrietta who married John Lawrence Hornibrook (see that entry) and four sons: Henry Cole of Dunderrow who married Elizabeth, the daughter of William Landers Esq of Kinsale, Robert Travers Cole who was baptised at Christ Church, Kilbrogan in 1801, Nicholas Cole who died aged 54 at Sunville near Bandon. A law suit took place between Nicholas Cole and Nicholas Cole Bowen Hornibrook, the son of his sister Henrietta which affected properties No 56 and No 57 on North Main Street. The fourth son was John.

Thomas Clear was born in December 1818 and died on 8th November, 1870. He was the son of Richard Clear who married Jane Lovell in 1810 and he had two brothers, Richard born in 1811, William born in 1815 and a sister Elizabeth born in 1817. He was a committed Methodist and his family erected a plaque in the Methodist Church in his memory which has survived. His son Richard was the executor of his will. Thomas left effects of under £7000

Thomas married Mary Robinson. She died on 26th March, 1859 aged 45. They had two children, Mary Jane (1843-1860) and Richard (1846-1917).

Thomas and Mary's son, Richard, lived in this house from 1873 until 1879. Their daughter, Mary Jane, died on 18th June 1858 at the age of 16. In 1846 Thomas Clear was recorded as living on the Old Cork Road and his occupation was a grocer and flour factor.

Dr Jonathan Clerke (1764-1838), a medical doctor, married Elizabeth Shadwell (1768-1842) by licence on 18th July 1788. They had:
- Sir Thomas Henry Shadwell Clerke (eldest son) born 1792. Educated Royal Military College, Great Marlow. Appointed Ensign 1808. He served in the Peninsular

Campaigns. He died on 19th April 1849 at Brompton Grove, England.

- Joseph Ledbetter. Died as an infant in 1793
- General St John Augustus Clerke who married Louisa Waring. They had at least six children including Henrietta Jane, Augustus Jonathan, Elizabeth Mary, Holt Waring, Shadwell Henry and Louisa Frances St John. He was a member of the freemasons and the Friendly Brothers. He was living at Overton in 1831. He resigned as a common council man in 1833.
- William Clerke
- Louisa Sarah, the youngest daughter. She married William Holland Kingston who was the brother of Sir George Strickland Kingston. She died in Sydney, New South Wales in 1839. Her husband returned to Bandon sometime afterwards and he is buried in the Clerk family grave at Christ Church.
- Jane. She died on 22nd September 1859 whilst living on North Main Street. (See No 81)

George Cornwall Esq (b 1754- 1825) was a successful brewer and malster. He founded the Watergate Brewery. His father died at Parkview (Ardnacarrig) in 1784. George held property in Tipperary as well as Bandon. He married Elizabeth Lee, the daughter of Henry Lee of Barna, Co Tipperary. They had at least five children, Mary Elizabeth b 1782 and who married Edward Gillman, Elizabeth b 1784 and who married John Nash of Brinny, George b 1785, Evan who died as an infant, William who married Jane Delacour and Henry. His sons George, William and Henry all worked at the brewery. George is buried in the family vault at Christ Church, Kilbrogan.

Richard Wheeler Doherty Esq, JP (1818-1883) was a Bandon law and business agent who lived at Oak Villa in Bandon. He was the son of Edward, a solicitor and his wife Sarah (Wheeler) whom he married on 31st December 1812. He had brothers Edward James, Richard Wheeler (b 1817) and John and sisters, Maria Wheeler (1819-1895), Sarah Mary, Harriet, Martha Wheeler and Mary. Richard married Martha Wheeler at Christ Church, Innishannon on 19th April 1849. Martha was a daughter of Richard Wheeler, a merchant.

He was admitted as a solicitor in 1842. A prominent member of the Conservative Body, he became their law agent in Bandon in 1832. He also served as a Justice of the Peace. He succeeded his father as law agent in 1877. He acted as agent for a number of people including the Earl of Bandon and the Bishop of Tuam.

Richard's eldest son, Edward Doherty Esq died at Oak Villa on Tuesday, 18th May 1880 aged 24.

His son Richard Wheeler, also a solicitor and land agent, married in March 1881 Elizabeth Anna Maria Biggs. They had Richard Edward Ernest Biggs Doherty (b 1882 and died South Africa 1918) and Jessica Florence b 1883 who married in Penzance in 1910 Frank Gascoigne Heath.

Richard died on 10th May 1883 and his will was proved by his son Richard Wheeler, solicitor and land agent of Oak Villa, Bandon. Richard left effects of £8,170 16s 7d.

The family are buried in a vault in the graveyard at St Peters. He was recorded as church warden and was a regular worshipper at St Peter's.

Richard Wheeler Doherty junior died on 12th June 1922 at Braeside, King's Road, Penzance, Cornwall. The administration of his estate was granted to his widow, Elizabeth Anne, to his daughter, Jessica Florence Heath who was living at Menwinnion, St Buryan, Cornwall and to her husband Frank Gascoigne Heath. He bequeathed the estate to his wife for her life which included his house properties in the parishes of Ballymodan and Kilbrogan. His wife was to have an annuity of £250 pa paid quarterly and she was to hold in trust all the property for their daughter and her heirs. Elizabeth Anne Doherty died on 19th October, 1939.

William Christopher Dowden's ancestors were originally protestant Presbyterian dissenters from near Taunton, Somerset who settled in Bandon in 1620. The original spelling of the family surname was Dowding. The family became successful Bandon linen manufacturers. William was the son of Christopher Dowden (1761-1832) and Mary (1768-1858). He became a principal in Allman Dowden and Co, corn millers and brewers. He died in 1887 and did not appear to have married.

Rev Benjamin Christmas Fawcett became rector of Christ Church, Kilbrogan following the death of Rev Eccles on 16th February 1880. From 1860 to 1871 he had acted as curate of Ballymodan. He married Miss Hewitt of Dublin and had several children. His daughter Eveline married Rev E. A. Golding of Ballinadee.

Rev Richard Henry Fawcett was the eldest son of Benjamin. He became curate of Kilbrogan in 1903 and resided at Killowen Glebe. He married a Miss Gaussen of Dublin.

Benjamin Forde, a slater and builder. His sons were Benjamin who became an architect and lived at Summer Cove, Kinsale, Frederick and George Meade Forde.

His daughter Anne Forde married John Dawson, the son of Richard Dawson and Susanna Good of Templemartin. John and Anne's son, John Wesley Dawson, was born in a house on North Main Street in 1843. They had a total of six sons and four daughters.

Forde was a prolific builder on North Main Street. Benjamin Forde junior was recorded as borrowing £1000 from Thomazine Cochrane of Lochcar, a widow for which he mortgaged several of his holdings on North Main Street which he had inherited from his father. This included leases from the Duke of Devonshire to his father which were originally dated, 1st April 1816, 31st December 1824, and 31st December 1839.[496] Benjamin died on 6th October, 1864 at Summer Cove. Prior to that he had been living at Crosses House in the City of Cork. His will was proved at Cork on 4th march, 1865 by his widow, one of the executors. He left effects of under £100.

George Williams French (1824-1900) operated French's Hotel in Bandon. His sons were Dr Albert Richard French and Joseph French. George died on 30th January 1900 aged 76. His address at the time of his death was Shannon Street (Now Oliver Plunkett Street), Bandon. His father, George French, formerly of Chatham

---

[496] Registry of Deeds. 1856 4 230 of 11th February 1856

and then of Bandon died on 22nd October, 1878. His son was his executor and he left effects under £600.[497]

George Fuller Esq of Rock House, Ballinadee, Bandon was the eldest son of Robert Fuller Esq, Newcastle House, Blarney. He married Annie Beamish, the eldest daughter of Samuel Hornibrook Sullivan Esq of Bridge Place, Bandon on 19th November 1868 at St Pauls Church[498]. George Fuller was living at Mossgrove House Bandon in 1883.

George Harris of Bandon was a successful linen and woollen draper and worsted manufacturer with a premises on North Main Street[499]. He entered into several leases with the Duke of Devonshire in 1816 and 1817. One lease was cancelled to create the fish market and another was purchased by Rev Charles B. Bernard to create steps leading up through the graveyard to Christ Church, Kilbrogan[500]. George married Sarah Sullivan on 15th June 1813 at Christ Church, Kilbrogan. Sarah had a brother Joseph who, at the time of the 1834 census, lived in Kilbrogan but dined with them at their home on South Main Street.

George and Sarah had several children all baptised at Ballymodan: Anne baptised 24th March, 1814, George baptised 25th September, 1816, John baptised 26th July 1818, Susanna baptised 2nd July 1820, William Richey baptised 31st March, 1822, Samuel baptised 23rd May 1824, Sally baptised 5th March 1826, Catherine Emily baptised 5th April 1828 and James baptised 24th January 1830. They were living on South Main Street at the time of the 1834 and 1846 Ballymodan protestant censuses.

William moved to live in Clonakilty.

George's eldest daughter Anne, married Mr Francis Scott at Ballymodan church on 28th July, 1840.[501] Francis and Anne had a son George Harris Scott born on 25th October, 1842 and baptised at the Methodist Church.

---

[497] Calendar of Wills. National Archives of Ireland.
[498] Cork Examiner of 20th November, 1868
[499] Slater's Directory of 1846
[500] Lease of 12th August, 1858
[501] Southern Reporter, 1st August, 1840

On 6th January 1853 their son John married Alice Sullivan, the daughter of John Wheeler Sullivan at Ballymodan.

Richard Dowden and George Harris of Bandon were referred to as very respectable woollen houses of old standing in a letter to the editor of the Dublin Morning Register of 8th December 1840.

George assigned his leases on North Main Street to his son, George, in 1839.

George's wife Sarah predeceased her husband on 7th September 1848. She was born on 1st May, 1792. George was 92 when he died on 24th June, 1856. Both are buried in the same plot at Christ Church, Kilbrogan.

George Harris junior was baptised at Ballymodan on 25th September, 1816. In 1840 his wholesale warehouse was located at 25 South Main Street. He advertised for sale grey and black calicos, jeans and every pattern of stout checks.[502] He also advertised as the agent for Allingham's Rotterdam Corn and Bunion solvent. In 1846 he was recorded as trading on South Main Street and at the same time his father was trading on North Main Street. He died on 22nd October, 1864. He had a son George, a Sunday school superintendent who emigrated to Philadelphia, USA in 1849 and was recorded as living there in a lease dated 1858.[503]

Lawrence Hornibrook of Bandon was a brother of Thomas Hornibrook (see below) and son of John Hornibrook, a successful tanner. Lawrence married Margaret Wood in 1777. They had at least one son, John Lawrence Hornibrook baptised on 6th February 1791 at Ballymodan and a daughter Jane baptised at Christ Church Kilbrogan on 7th August 1785, Lawrence died on 16th October, 1801.[504] Lawrence predeceased his siblings and his family did not inherit the lands of Dunkereen, Corran etc which were part of his father's estate.

---

[502] Southern Reporter, 1st April, 1841
[503] Lease dated 12th August 1858 between George Harris and Rev Charles B Bernard, Rector and Messrs John Keys & Stewart Tresilian, church wardens
[504] Registry of Deeds. 718 491 128 and Christ Church, Kilbrogan Death Register

John Lawrence Hornibrook was the son of Lawrence and was baptised at St Peter's Ballymodan on 6th February 1791[505]. He was living in Ballinascarthy near Bandon at the time of his death in 1844. He married Henrietta Cole Bowen, the second daughter of Rev Nicholas Cole Bowen, rector of Ballyfeard on 13th July 1820 in Bandon. Henrietta was a sister of Robert Travers Cole Bowen who lived for a period at No 82. Robert and Henrietta were grandchildren of Henry Cole Bowen of Bowens Court near Kildorrery in North Cork. Henrietta died in 1864.

John died in 1844 and left a widow, Henrietta Cole Hornibrook who was the administrator of his estate and passed holdings in North Main Street to their eldest son **Richard Lawrence Hornibrook** who lived at Firville, near Bandon.[506] A Thomas and Matthew Hornibrook were also referred to in the deed (Matthew was most likely the son of Thomas and his wife Mary Jane Belesaigne and therefore a first cousin of John Lawrence). The properties included No 56 and No 57 (Kilbrogan House).

John and Henrietta had offspring including Richard Lawrence who lived at Firville, Nicholas Cole Bowen who was born in 1831 at Springfield and who married Emma Emelia Bates at St Peters, Cork on 1st August, 1857. He died in 1866. She was living in the US in the 1890s but may have died in the UK, John Henry Cole Bowen (b 1834) who married Jane Cecil Baylee and who died on 1st March 1888, Mary, their youngest daughter who in 1865 married Thomas Lithgow, a commercial traveller, in Liverpool.

The estate of Richard Lawrence, the eldest son, appears to have passed to his brother, Nicholas Cole Bowen's widow, Emma and their son John Lawrence Hornibrook who had an address in 1893 in Charleville, Co Cork. Emma Emelia Hornibrook's address in 1893 was No 2126 Arch Street, Philadelphia, USA. She was described as a widow at that time.[507]

Thomas Hornibrook of Bandon was a tanner and was the son of John Hornibrook who owned the lands at Dunkereen. Thomas's eldest daughter, Jane Hornibrook married William

---

[505] Ballymodan. Baptisms
[506] Registry of Deeds. 1844 17 48 of 28th September, 1844
[507] Reference in a property deed of North Main Street.

Sullivan of Bandon on 2nd August, 1804.[508] By 1817 Thomas was the only surviving brother of the late John Hornibrook of Bandon and his widow Anne. His brother Lawrence had died in 1801 (See previous biographies). Thomas also had a sister Jane who married Philip Peterson Bickford of Kinsale at Christ Church, Kilbrogan on 25th October 1799 (they had a daughter Anne Hornibrook Bickford who was resident for a period at No 50 until her death in 1874), a sister Anne and a sister Mary who were both spinsters in 1817. In return for a payment of £600 made by Thomas to each of them, Jane and her husband Philip and Mary and Anne gave up their claims to the lands of Dunkereen as well as all other goods and chattels which had belonged to their father John.[509]

Thomas held the Bolting Mill in Ballinadee which he offered for lease on 29th September, 1825 along with the bolting mill of Corran which was situated near Killeady Hill and two farms of 50 acres each at Corran and 150 acres of land at Dunkereen.[510]

In 1834 he granted to John Thomas Hornibrook, Rev Thomas Waugh and John Hornibrook junior the fee simple and freehold of the lands of Corran in East Muskerry, the lands of Dunkereen which were upwards of 450 acres which he was holding for 99 years and also part of the lands of Dunkereen called Clash also for 99 years, the lands of Ballydonahy and Lisheedy in the Barony of Kinalea which he held under William Henry Herrick Esq for 3 lives and the lands of Crosses held under Edward Hale Adderly Esq for one life in Kinalea and two houses and gardens in the Barony of Kinalmeaky and a walled in garden, offices and school house in Kinalmeaky which he had purchased from Daniel Daly deceased, Cornelius Keahilly and Elenor Keahilly and the lands of Clongones which he purchased from Simon Farthing Davis Esq. He made over the bolting mill, house (Annsville) and grounds in Ballinadee together with 104 acres to his son Mathew Belesaigne Hornibrook and his heirs as well as a dwelling house in North Main Street.[511]

The lands of Corran were put up for auction in the Court of the Commissioners for the Sale of Incumbered Estates on 24th June, 1853 and were described as the Estate of William Barter

[508] Registry of Deeds. 567 18 377940 Marriage Settlement
[509] Registry of Deeds. 718 491128
[510] Cork Constitution. 29th September 1825
[511] Registry of Deeds. 1834 14 266

Hornibrook, John Thomas Hornibrook, Rev Thomas Waugh and John Hornibrook junior. The petitioner was William Barter Hornibrook, a brother of John Thomas.

John Thomas Hornibrook was born in 1786 at Springfield, Co Cork and he died in Bandon on 13th October 1876 aged 90. His will was proved at Cork by his widow, Ellen Hornibrook and by Thomas Hornibrook Esq of Kinsale[512]. He left effects under £4000. John's father, Thomas, acquired the rights to the house and lands of Rockfort from Richard Lane, the Cork Clothier and miller at Rockfort who was listed as a bankrupt by 1815.

In April 1821 Thomas assigned the lands and property to his son John Thomas. John Thomas was the only son of Thomas Hornibrook of Springfield, Co Cork. He had a sister called Ann who predeceased him.

John Thomas married Elenor (Ellen) Wiseman, the daughter of John Wiseman of Garryhankard, Co Cork who was born in 1796 at Annesville, Ballinadee, Cork. They married on 2nd January 1821 in Brinny Church of Ireland. The occupation of John Thomas was described as a tanner and a gentleman. He owned the Rockfort Mill near Rockfort House which he inherited from his father and at the time of his marriage was living at that address possibly until 1828 when he advertised it for lease after which time his address was Beechmount. The advertisement, dated 2nd February 1828, offered a house, offices, garden and orchard together with any quantity of land from 5 to 84 acres within one mile of Innishannon and three of Bandon to be let from 25th March, 1828. He gave his address in the advertisement as Beechmount.

At the same time he advertised a dwelling house in the North Main Street of Bandon with good offices and a garden and 'with every accommodation for a respectable family for which immediate possession can be given.'[513]

In 1834 John Thomas and his family were living at Beechmount.[514]

---

[512] Calendar of Wills. National Archives of Ireland.
[513] Cork Constitution. 2nd February 1828
[514] ROD 1834 14 266

John Thomas had two sons and four daughters:-

Thomas born on 30th November 1821 at Rockfort House immigrated to New Zealand where he lived for about thirteen years. He died at Heidelberg, Victoria, Australia in 1889. Thomas married Helen Neale Welsh of Youghal on 31st March 1846 at Knockavilly Church of Ireland. Helen was the youngest daughter of Henry Pierce Welsh Esq, Solicitor of Heathfield, Youghal. At the time of his marriage, Thomas was residing at Beechmount near Brinny. His wife, Helen, was living at the time in the Kingston Buildings in Bandon. They had three children, John Thomas born 13th Sept 1847 and baptised in Brinny Church of Ireland on 19th September, 1848, Henry Pierce born 5th February, 1850 at Annes Villa and baptised at Brinny on 5th February 1850 and Charlotte Anne born 8th July 1851 and baptised at Brinny on 15th July 1851. Thomas married a second time in Australia to Emma Sarah Day who was born in Wandsworth, Surrey on 6th December 1830.

John Wiseman was born on 20th February 1827 at Rockfort House. He immigrated in about 1857 to Australia. He married Annabella Manning from Portadown, Ireland in 1859 at Sandhurst, near Bendigo in Victoria, Australia. They had six children. He died on 1st November 1901 in Sandford, Victoria, Australia.

Frances Anne Hornibrook married George Beamish. She was born on 23rd April, 1825 in Rockfort and died on 20th February 1892 in Meelin House, Bandon. Her husband, George, was born in Ballymountain House in March 1812. They were married on 20th August 1857 in Knockavilly Church of Ireland. They first lived as a married couple in the Kingston Buildings where their first son was born in 1858. They had four other children, Ellen Wiseman born 1860, Alberta Annie born 1861, Maria Frances born 1862 and Mary Georgina born 3rd June 1866.

Mary Jane was born on 28th October 1828 and died in Brinny on 28th November 1877. She married Rev James Stevenson, the rector of Brinny.

Margaret Wiseman was baptised on 16th April 1833 at Brinny, the third daughter of John Thomas Hornibrook. On 1st March 1859 she married Alexander Latimer Waring. She died on 14th April 1963 having had just one son, Frederick William Latimer Waring and a daughter Ellen Amelia who was born in March 1862 in Shropshire

Ellen Victoria was born on 22nd February 1840. She married William Price Pearde of Innishannon on 29th January, 1863 at Dunkereen House, the home of Ellen's father, John Thomas. She died on 9th October 1889 at Kilbrogan Hill, Bandon. William was the son of Henry Pearde. They had nine children. She is buried at Christ Church, Kilbrogan alongside two daughters, Kathleen Elinor and Edith Ethel.

Two different William Jenkins were recorded as holding leases on the street.

William Jenkins practised as a medical doctor in Bandon for twenty years and lived on North Main Street. He was the son of William Jenkins Esq of Mishells House who was a Barrister at Law and Deputy Recorder of Cork by Catherine, daughter of Robert Tresilian, a Medical Doctor of Bandon. [515] William junior died on 26th February, 1823. His widow Anne lived with her daughters on North Main Street following his death. She exchanged several letters with the Agent of the Duke of Devonshire complaining about the very poor condition of her house. She hired an architect to advise her. A daughter Mary married Rev Richard Hayes in July 1833.[516] William's widow, Anne, died on 11th August, 1847 in Bandon.[517]

William Jenkins, the watch maker, had a son also named William.[518] William and his wife Catherine had at least four other children namely Robert born on 7th April 1813, Henry baptised on 28th April 1820, George baptised on 28th January 1823 and Mary Anne baptised on 4th November 1826.

Newth Jenkins, a watch maker, served on the vestry of Christ Church and was made a freeman of the City of Cork on 29th September, 1769. He opened a watch making shop in Cork opposite the Cork Arms in the spring of 1763 and had moved to Bandon by 1787. He married Miss Mary Hewett on 9th December

---

[515] The Constitution (Cork Morning Post). 1823
[516] Brady. The Clergy of Cork, Cloyne and Ross. Biography of Rev Richard Hayes
[517] Dublin Evening Mail, 27th August, 1847
[518] MS 43 159/8 lease. Lismore papers

1772 and had at least a daughter Anne who married Corliss Baldwin in 1810 at Templemartin Church of Ireland. In 1817 Newth was leasing a property on North Main Street to Elizabeth Alcock. He died on 15th April, 1821.[519]

George Kingston Esq married Hester Holland in 1798. Hester was the daughter of Thomas Holland and his wife Elizabeth Fuller[520].

In 1802 George Kingston was responsible for the construction of the 16 apartment building on Hill Terrace on the site of a timberyard which was formerly held by John Kingston under the Corporation of Bandon. The Kingston Buildings passed to his daughter Mary Catherine and her husband, Thomas Sherlock, in 1852. He held a number of the leases on North Main Street.

There were two William Kingstons who held leases on North Main Street and who do not appear to have been closely related:-

William Kingston, a pawnbroker. He married Dora Bennett, the daughter of George Bennett, the clothier and sister of George Bennett's father, Joseph. On 7th February, 1854 at Christ Church, Innishannon, William Kingston, the son of William, married Ellen Vickery, the daughter of George, a merchant of Innishannon. The witnesses to the wedding were Robert Edwards, George Bennett and Joseph Stanley.

William Holland Kingston, eldest son of George and Hester (See above). He was baptised on 1st June 1799. In 1823 he was elected a freeman of the Borough

---

[519] Christ Church, Kilbrogan. Burial Register

[520] See Thomas Holland's biography as an immediate lessor of 1775

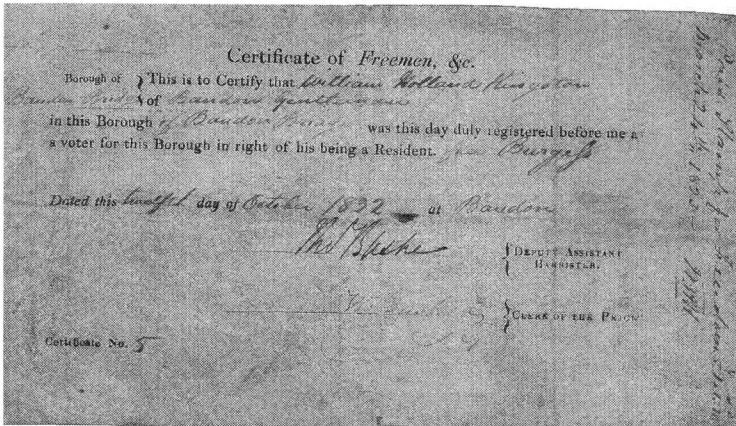

On 29th April 1829 he became a common council man and on 2nd September 1830 he was elected a Free Burgess in place of Rev Thomas Meade.

> [521]CORPORATION OF BANDON --- At a Meeting of the Corporation of Bandon, held at the Town Clerk's Office on Thursday last, the 16th inst. WM. HOLLAND KINGSTON, Esq was unanimously elected a member of the Common Council, in place of the late THOS. QUIN, Esq deceased. And MR WM. HUNTER, of the North Main Street, Bandon, Was at same time admitted a Freeman.

He married Louisa Sarah Clerke in Christ Church Kilbrogan on 24th April 1834. She was the youngest daughter of Jonathan Clerke, Esq, MD who lived on North Main Street and who was buried at Christ Church.

In 1836 William entered a petition in the House of Commons that a clause be introduced into the Grand Juries (Ireland) Bill to repay certain sums expended by his father on the roads in the County.

William Holland Kingston became bankrupt in 1837[522]. He was indebted to Hester Waring for £200 and to secure the debt he conveyed some of his leases of North Main Street which he had

[521] Southern Reporter, 23rd April, 1829
[522] Registry of Deeds. 1837 21 57

inherited from his father, George Kingston, as the eldest son. He left for New South Wales with his wife Louisa Sarah Clerke who died shortly afterwards in Australia. He returned following his wife's death and became resident in Dublin in the 1850s.[523]

His lands of East Gully between the town and Castle Bernard were put up for auction as part of the Incumbered Estates Court on 2nd March 1851.

On 8th May, 1856 Eliza Johnson secured a judgment against William for £89 9s as he had disposing power of properties in North Main Street which were occupied by the Provincial Bank of Ireland and its manager at the time, Hezekiah O'Callaghan.[524]

The Bank of Ireland sought immediate payment of £4000 in 1865. William had paid over the sum and requested various title deeds as security. He died in Bandon in 1881.

James Moriarty was the son of Cornelius Moriarty, also a shop keeper. On 28th September, 1848 James married Frances Shine, the daughter of John Shine, an accountant at Christ Church, Innishannon. James took over the woollen drapery business of the clothier, Stewart Tresilian in South Main Street on 15th March, 1845 following Stewart's death. James assigned the lease of No 1 Bank House to Thomas Banfield of Shinagh. James died on 31st Octoner, 1889 aged 77 years whilst living at Floraville. His wife Frances continued to reside at the property following his death and was still living there at the time of the 1901 census along with two servants. She died on 14th July, 1901 aged 77 years. Both are buried in the Moriarty family grave at St Peter's, Ballymodan.

Attiwell Roche was living on Cavendish Quay in 1846[525] and was described as a very old man. He had been a cabinet maker.[526] His grandfather, George Roche, had leased Stammers tenement before Attiwell took on the lease in 1783. A marriage wass recorded in 1785 of Attiwell Roche to Rebecca Davies.[527] He was listed in the tithe applotments as holding land at Cripplehill, Kilbrittain. He

---

[523] Registry of Deeds 1856 8 52 of 10th March 1856
[524] Registry of Deeds. 1856 17 135
[525] Ballymodan Protestant Census of 1846
[526] Devonshire leases 1700s
[527] Kinsale Council Book.

wass buried with his family in St Peter's graveyard, Ballymodan. The inscription reads:- 'The Burial Place of Attiwell Roche and Family. Here lieth the remains of Dora the affectionate wife of Geo. Roche. She died September 10th 1836 aged 34 years.'

His son, George Roche, inherited his estate. He was a mill wright at Mr Sweeny's mill and also the owner of a public house. He was married to Mary and had two daughters, Mary and Martha and and an only son James who became an Excise Officer in the UK. George and his family were living on Castle Road in the Ballymodan Protestant census of 1846. For a time Attiwell was the immediate lessor of Nos 67, 68, 70, 71, 72, 73, 74 on the west side of Kilbrogan Hill. George died on 14th February, 1868 whilst living on South Main Street. His will was proved by Mary, his widow and Martha Roche, his spinster daughter. He left effects under £200.[528] In a directory of 1867 he was recorded as a flour dealer of 64 South Main Street.[529]

William Sullivan Esq was a tanner of North Main Street[530]. He married Jane Hornibrook in Brinny on 4th August, 1804. She was the eldest daughter of Thomas Hornibrook (See his entry above). They had at least two sons, Samuel Hornibrook Sullivan and Thomas Hornibrook Sullivan. (See also No 4 Bridge Place). William died on 18th December, 1836 aged 64[531]. A notice in the Southern Reporter of 28th March, 1837 requested all those who were indebted to Mr William Sullivan at the time of his death to furnish their accounts to Mr Thomas Hornibrook of 71 North Main Street (now No 78, The Brogan Inn) on or before 23rd April, 1837.

Thomas Hornibrook Sullivan, son of William Sullivan Esq tanner, was born in 1806. He was a brother of Samuel Hornibrook Sullivan. Thomas married Anne Varian Sullivan[532], the daughter of the late John Sullivan Esq of Bandon on 2nd June 1836. They had a daughter Mary Hornibrook Sullivan who was born in January, 1845 and who died in Bandon in 1918.[533] Thomas subscribed to 1000 shares in the Cork and Bandon Railway in

---

[528] Calendar of Wills. National Archives of Ireland.
[529] Coghlan's Directory of 1867
[530] Pigots Directory of 1824.
[531] Christ Church, Kilbrogan. Burial Register
[532] Anne had at least one brother Giles Varian Sullivan
[533] Limerick Reporter. 31st January 1845

1845.[534] Thomas died on 5th August, 1874 aged 68 at No 51 North Main Street[535].

Samuel Hornibrook Sullivan, a tanner, son of William Sullivan Esq, married Catherine Beamish in Christ Church, Innishannon on 16th June, 1837. They had at least two children, Jane Hornibrook (b 1839) who married Charles Cooper on 11th October, 1866 and Anne Beamish (b 1841) who married George Fuller Esq of Rock House, the eldest son of Robert Fuller Esq deceased on 19th November 1868 at St Pauls Church, Cork[536]. Samuel died on 10th February, 1890 and his will was proved at Cork by Louisa Sullivan, a spinster, most likely another daughter. He left effects of £558 4s. She was the sole executrix of his will.

Thomas Kingston Sullivan Esq was a son of John Sullivan, a tanner, who married Mary Kingston. He married firstly Jane Tresilian in 1839 and had four children, John born in 1841, Josias Tresilian born in 1844, Dorothy born in 1845 and Matilda E. born in 1849. Jane died before 1860. He married secondly Mary Aphrasia Elizabeth Langford. They had twelve children. He qualified as an attorney and built up sizeable land holdings. He had a brother William Connor Sullivan. His grand-daughter, Anne Winifred Sullivan, became the second Duchess of Westminster when she married Hugh Richard Grosvenor on 7th February, 1947. He lived at the Retreat in Bandon until he died in 1902.

William Connor Sullivan Esq was a brother to Thomas Kingston Sullivan and son of John Sullivan, Tanner. He married Dorothea Tresilian in 1838 and had four children. He lived for a time at Overton, Bandon. In 1845 he purchased 1000 shares in the Cork and Bandon Railway.[537]

In 1853 Seward Large of Liverpool, a merchant, filed a lawsuit against Sullivan for £187 requesting that he dispose of property interests in North Main Street to satisfy the claim.[538] He became a bankrupt.

---

[534] Southern Reporter. 12th June 1845
[535] Christ Church, Kilbrogan. Burial Register
[536] Cork Examiner, 20th November, 1868
[537] Southern Reporter. 12th June 1845
[538] Registry of Deeds. 1853 19 59 of 1st July 1853

In the electoral records of 1884 he was recorded as the occupier of a tannery with offices and yard in Watergate Street (rateable valuation of £5 15s), a house and yard in Watergate Street (rateable valuation of £4 5s) and a house, offices, yard and small garden on North Main Street (rateable valuation of £20). He died on 6th November 1886. Letters of Administration were granted to Dora, his widow. He left effects under £10.[539]

John Swete Esq lived at Floraville. He was the son of Benjamin Swete of Pleasantfields who married his cousin Joyce Swete (She was also married to Jonas Travers). He was also a descendant of Captain John Swete of Mohonagha, Skibbereen who married Jane Abbott. John Swete's father, Benjamin, was a magistrate and high sheriff of Cork and was purported to have inherited £30,000 from a cousin, also Benjamin, who was a paymaster for the Duke of Marlborough. John was educated at a school at Hammons Marsh in Cork City. He lived with his schoolmaster, Jas. Cart.

On 24th February 1781 John Swete married firstly Martha Heard, the daughter of Bickford Heard and Susanna Maunsell[540]. He was elected a Freeman of the Corporation of Bandon Bridge on 15th June 1807 and on 24th June 1811 was elected a Common Council Man in place of Lord Bernard who had been promoted to a Free Burgess. John Swete took the place of Horatio Townsend as a Free Burgess on 13th March 1815. On 24th June 1824 he was first elected Provost for 1825. He elected Benjamin Swete of Greenville as his special Freeman on 16th December 1824. He served as Provost in the years 1827, 1829, 1831 and 1833. He also acted as Agent for the Earl of Bandon from at least 1822 until his death in 1839 and he served for many years as a magistrate.

John's eldest son was Rev Benjamin Swete who was born on 25th October, 1782 in Cork. He became prebendary of Kinsale and rector of Timoleague. He was buried in Ballymodan Church yard on 18th November, 1849.

---

[539] Calendar of Wills. National Archives of Ireland.
[540] Bickford and Susanna married in 1745. Cork Marriage Licence Bonds.

On 2nd December, 1823 John Swete Esq of Floraville's daughter, Eleanor, was married by Rev Benjamin Swete at St Nicholas Church to George White Esq of Douglas.[541] A second daughter, Anne Swete died on 6th March, 1845 at South Terrace, Cork.[542] On 30th June, 1837 John's sister, Thamar Swete, died at Floraville aged 76. She was the widow of Benjamin Swete of Bandon. She was buried in Timoleague.

John Swete died on 22nd February, 1839 and was also buried in the Church of Ireland graveyard in Timoleague[543]. John's father, Benjamin, both his grandparents and an uncle were also buried in the family vault in Timoleague.[544] John's father requested in his will that the vault be raised by four feet above the surface and that it be covered with a marble stone with his name, date and the coat of arms.

John's wife Martha passed away on 13th May, 1839.[545]

The Teulons were a French family who came to Ireland in the 1700s as Huguenot refugees following the revocation of the Edict of Nantes. They established themselves in Cork City and became noted silver and goldsmiths. John Teulon Esq married Mary Wood. He died in Bandon on 18th November, 1828 aged 81.[546] His children included John who lived at No 58, Charles who was a Lieutenant Colonel in the 28th Regiment and who lived for a time at No 57, his son Peter who was a Lieutenant Colonel of the 12th Madras Native Infantry, George who was a Lieutenant Colonel in Her Majesty's 35th Regiment, Thomas, Lewis who died young, Richard who was a medical doctor, Maria who married John Beamish, Frances and Catherine Maria.

John Teulon was born in Bandon in 1790. He was the eldest son of John who married Mary Wood, the daughter of Rev George Wood who was headmaster of the Bandon school in 1775 and was curate of Kilbrogan in 1761 (his wife was Jane Beamish of Kilmalooda). He was a Justice of the Peace and he married

---

[541] Dublin Correspondent. 4th December, 1823
[542] Statesman & Dublin Christian Record. 11th March, 1845
[543] Freeman's Journal. 26th February, 1839
[544] Abstract from will of Benjamin Swete of Pleasantfields.
[545] Southern Reporter. 16th May 1839
[546] Cork Constitution of November 1828

Catherine Morris Beamish in 1807. She was born in 1790 at Beaumont House, Co Cork and was the daughter of George Beamish of Clohine and Catherine Baldwin. John died on 2nd March 1861 in Bandon. UK probate was granted on 8th April, 1861. He left under £16,000.

John and Mary also had sons, Charles (see Lieutenant Colonel Charles below), Peter who was Lieutenant Colonel in the 12th madras Native Infantry and was commandant at Delhi, George who was a Lieutenant Colonel in her Majesty's 35th Regiment; Thomas, A.B., Dublin and who died in France; Lewis who died young; Richard, a Medical Doctor; Maria who married John Beamish, a Medical Doctor and Frances who died unmarried.547

John and Catherine had at least four sons, John who was born in 1812, Charles Peter, a barrister who was resident for a time in No 59, George Beamish, a JP and Thomas, a Major in the 35th Regiment. They also had at least one daughter, Catherine Maria.

Lieutenant Colonel Charles Teulon of the 28th Regiment. Fought at the Penninsula and at the Battle of Waterloo where his regiment suffered severely548. He lived at No 57. He died at the Devonshire Arms in 1873.

George Beamish Teulon was the son of John and Catherine. He was born in 1813. He was a Justice of the Peace in Bandon. In 1870 he was recorded in the register of vestrymen at Christ Church, Kilbrogan. In 1871 he was recorded as owning 2,714 acres of land. He died at Glenwood, Kilworth, Fermoy in June 1883 leaving a personal estate of over £15,300. His executor was his wife Dorcas Jane Teulon.

Following her husband's death, Dorcas Jane lived at both Glenwood, Fermoy and 14 Albert Mansions, Albert Road, Battersea, London where she died on 12th February, 1896 leaving an estate of over £36,000. The executors of her will were Townley B.B. Ball Esq and William F. St Leger, both of Fermoy and George C. Ball Greene of 53 Raglan Road, Dublin

---

547 George Bennett. The History of Bandon
548 George Bennett. The History of Bandon

Glenwood in Fermoy, a three bay, two storey house, passed to
Alfred Edward Fleury who was the husband of George's brother's
daughter, Anna. The Fleurys were another Huguenot family.

Charles Peter Teulon was a brother of George Beamish and son
of John and Catherine. He was born in 1815. He became a Justice
of the Peace and was on the register of vestrymen of Christ
Church, Kilbrogan in 1870. He lived for some time at No 59 and
was married to Anne. They had a daughter Anna Maria who was
baptised on 25th February 1856 at Christ Church, Kilbrogan. She
married Alfred Edward Fleury of Glenwood, Kilworth in 1877.
Their son Charles Alfred Teulon, Major Inniskilling Dragoons,
married Norah Emily, the daughter of Col McM. Bolster, RAMC.
Major Charles Alfred Teulon changed his surname to Teulon as a
requirement in order to inherit by the terms of the will of George
Beamish Teulon. In 1905 the Chief Herald of Ireland granted the
Arms of Teulon to Charles Alfred Fleury and recorded that his
surname be changed from Fleury to Teulon.549

Charles Peter Teulon died in Bandon in early 1892. His
beneficiaries were his daughter Anna Maria Fleury and her
husband Alfred Edward Fleury who lived at Glenwood. He left
effects valued at £14,421 14s 4d.

John Wheeler was a Commander of the Royal Navy. He
married Harriet Biggs, the daughter of Thomas Biggs Esq on 2nd
February, 1826 at Lower Shandon Church, Cork. Her father was
deceased at the time of their marriage.550 She died on 5th July
1849 aged 53. They had Rebecca Biggs Wheeler, born 1837 who
died on 19th October, 1853, aged 16, Martha Harriet, born 1835
and died aged 27 in November 1862. In 1866 he was chairman of
the Bandon Board of Guardians.

John Wheeler was demised a lease by the Duke of Devonshire on
1st April 1818. The plot was bounded on the north by North Main
Street and on the south by the river, on the west by Mary Sullivan,
a widow and on the east by William Jenkins and partly by
Preaching House Lane (Water Lane). The site was involved in a
marriage settlement between Thomas Hungerford Orpen, Medical

549 MS111. National Library of Ireland. Confirmation of Arms
550 Southern Reporter. 2nd February 1826

Doctor and son of Samuel Orpen and his wife Sophia Hungerford and his wife Margaret Augusta dated 1836. (See also No 81)

John Wheeler died on 6th May, 1873 and his will was proved by James Lane, Cork, Solicitor and John Richard Wheeler Esq of Bandon. He left effects under £1000.

John Richard Wheeler, JP of Bandon died on 9th October, 1901 and probate was granted to Thomas A.J. Wheeler and Frederick W. Wheeler Esquires. He left effects under £1017 8s 8d.

SOME ORIGINAL DEVONSHIRE ESTATE LEASES FOR NORTH MAIN STREET/KILBROGAN HILL

The records in the table have been compiled from documents in the Lismore Estate collection at the National Library of Ireland and from the books held at the Registry of Deeds. Without access to the individual title deeds of the properties, it has not been possible to confirm the original date of the leases of many of the houses. In the early 1800s the Devonshire Estate did not deposit copies of their leases with the Registry of Deeds as it was not a legal requirement. When the leases were sold from one intermediate lessor to another, they were often registered and in many cases these deeds referred to the original lease.

The table gives an interesting overview not only of the original date of the majority of the leases but also of the occupations of the lessees and in some cases the lives covered by the term of the lease. There are also several instances where multiple houses were built on one plot. Furthermore, there was a far wider disbursement of leases than in the 1700s with a larger array of occupations. Far fewer were landed gentry and most lived in or close to Bandon. Many maturing long term leases in the late 1700s and early 1800s may have been rolled over on an annual basis until at least 1816 which helps to explain why so many term leases were agreed from that time onwards. Following the Duke's visit to Bandon in 1812, it seems that he started drawing up plans for a substantial upgrading of the street.

Date	No	Term		Surname	Occupation	Other
10/2/1770			J.	Elliott	Watch maker	
25/3/1816	30 -32	41 yrs	D	Bushe		
25/3/1816				Biggs[551]	Merchants	Coolfadda Mills
25/3/1816		99 yrs	H	Baldwin		
25/3/1816	24		Miss es	Jenkins	Gentry	Lease surrendered

---

[551] William, Jacob and John

						19/4/1852
25/3/1816			J	Bullen	Shopkeeper	Evicted 1848
25/3/1816			T	Murphy	Shopkeeper	
25/3/1816	92		G	Harris	Worsted manufacturer	Cancelled to create fish mkt
25/3/1816	23		W	Shine	Shoe maker	Expired on death in 1850s
25/3/1816	27-28	41 yrs	R	Gash	Shopkeeper	
25/3/1816	35	99 yrs	W	Kingston	Pawn Broker	WK built hse
25/3/1816		61 yrs	G	Kingston		
25/3/1816	83	41 yrs	R	Williams		
25/3/1816	101	3 lives[552]	G	Harris	Worsted Manufacturer	
25/3/1816		99 yrs	W	Jenkins	Watch Maker	WJ built 3 hses
25/3/1816		99 yrs	P	Connell	Shop keeper	
25/3/1816		99 yrs	W.	Jenkins		
25/3/1816	4	99 yrs	J	Clerk	Doctor	JC built hse
25/3/1816		99 yrs	T	Lovell		2 leases
25/3/1816	3 BP	61 yrs	J	Sullivan		Bridge Place.
25/3/1816	5		P	Williams	Builder, Inn Keeper	
25/3/1816	41-42	99/2 lives	C	Hagarty	Rope maker	CH built 2 hses
25/3/1816		99yr/3 lives[553]	B	Forde	Slater	
25/3/1816	1-2		G	Kingston	Merchant	
25/3/1816		61yr/2 lives	G	Cornwall	Brewer	
25/3/1816			G	Kingston	Merchant	Site of P.O
25/3/1816	38-40	99 yrs	W	Jenkins		
25/3/1816		61 yrs	G	Kingston	Merchant	
25/3/1816	33	99 yrs	J.D.	Shorten	Shop keeper	JDS built hse
25/3/1817			J	Baldwin		
25/3/1817		61 yrs	J.	Tresilian		Inherited by Robert T. Belcher
25/3/1817		99 yrs	A.	Bull		
25/3/1817			A	Roche		
25/3/1817			E	Hayes		
25/3/1817			J	Collins		Ejected
25/3/1817	14		W	Sloane	Cordwainer	Expired on death
25/3/1817			J	Gosnell		Expired 1863
25/3/1817	17	41 yrs	W	Hunter		surrendered
25/3/1817	25-26	2 lives[554]	S	Sullivan	Shop keeper. Ejected before 1831	Richard Cole built hse
25/3/1817		99 yrs/ 3	W.C.	Sullivan	Tanner	Bridge Place

[552] Lives of George (lessor) & sons William and George
[553] Lives of Benjamin Forde (lessee), Benjamin, jr, & George, sons
[554] Lives of Samuel & John, sons of Samuel, the lessee

		lives[555]				
25/3/1817			G	Harris	Worsted Manufacturer	
25/3/1817		99 yrs/3 lives	R	Burchill		RB built hse
125/3/1817		2 lives/ 99 yrs	G	Cornwall	Brewer	GC built hse
25/3/1818			T	Gash		
25/3/1818		99 yrs	G	Harris		
25/3/1818		99 yrs	T	Hornibrook		
25/3/1818	57	99 yrs	J	Hornibrook		
25/3/1818		99 yrs	T	Murphy		
25/3/1818			J	Williams		
25/3/1818	86		J	Wheeler		Surrendered 1875
25/3/1819		99 yrs	T	Murphy		
8/12/1820	70 /71		Rev E	King	Clergyman	
25/3/1820		41 yrs	J	Williams		
25/3/1821		41 yrs	D	Carthy		
25/3/1821		99 yrs	G	Cornwall	Brewer	
25/9/1822		61 yrs	B.	Popham	Dukes Agent	ejected
25/3/1823		99 yrs	J	Hunter		
25/3/1824		99 yrs	I	Biggs		
23/1/1824	64	64 yrs	G	Cornwall	Brewer	
25/3/1824		99 yrs	J	Harley		
25/3/1824		61 yrs	A	Roche		
1/12/1824	91	99/3 lives[556]	J	Homan	Doctor	Riverside Hse
1/12/1824		99 yr/3 lives	B	Forde	Slater	
31/12/1824	20 -21	99yr/ 3 lives[557]	B	Forde	Slater	BF built 2 hses
31/12/1824		99yr/3 lives[558]	B	Forde	Slater	
31/12/1825	7	3 lives[559] /99 yrs	J	Swete	Gent	
25/3/1825		99 yrs	Rich ard	Williams		

[555] Lives of Thomas Hornibrook Sullivan, John, Sullivan & James Sullivan
[556] Lives of John Homan (lessee), Thomas and Regina Popham, children of John Popham of Bandon
[557] Lives of Benjamin Forde (lessee), Henry Belcher & John Belcher & life of longest liver
[558] Lives of Benjamin Forde (Lessee), Henry & John Belcher, sons of William Belcher, Apothecary
[559] Lives of William, Henry & John, sons of William Belcher

25/3/1825		41 yrs	Isaac	Biggs		
1826			D	Callahan		Expired 1845
25/3/1826		41 yrs	W	Sloane		
25/3/1826		99 yrs	G	Roche		
25/3/1826		99 yrs	A	Roche		
25/3/1827		99 yrs	J	Hunter		
25/3/1829		61 yrs	B	Forde	Slater	BF built 2 hses
1/12/1830			B	Forde		
31/12/1834		99 yr/3 lives	J	Harley	Gent	
5/7/1836			G	Roche		
31/12/1839		99 yr/3 lives[560]	B	Forde	Slater	BF built 2 hses
31/12/1839		99 yr/3 lives[561]	B	Forde	Slater	
1840		3 lives[562]	R	Fuller		Ejected 1840
1854			G	Grandon		
29/9/1867		41 yrs	W	Bullen	Merchant/Shopkeeper	

[560] Livs of John Popham (14), Benjamin Popham (12), Bradshaw Popham (6), 2nd, 3rd sons of John Popham of Bandon
[561] Lives of Benjamin (14), Frederick (11), George Meade (60, 1st, 2nd, 3rd sons of Benjamin Forde
[562] George (15), Amelia (8), Eliza (3) Fuller

SOME RESIDENTS OF NORTH MAIN STREET IN 1824[563]

Resident	Occupation	House if known
Franklin Baldwin	Attorney	No 81
Hewitt Baldwin Esq[564]	Gentry	
William & Mrs Barry, Academy	Academy	
Captain Robert Tresilian Belcher	Gentry	
Isaac Biggs	Gentry	
William, Jacob and John Biggs	Corn Merchants	Mill Lane
John P. Blair Esq	Gentry	
John Bullen	Leather Seller	
Joseph Bullen	Dyer	Possibly Water Lane
Robert Burchill	Publican	
Daniel Cahalane	Publican	
John Cahalane	Publican	
Eliza Clerke	Earthenware Dealer	No 9
Dr J. Clerke	Physician	No 4
John Cotter	Saddler & Harness Maker	
James Dawson	Boot & Shoemaker	
Mrs Donovan		
Nathaniel Evanson Esq	Magistrate	
Cornelius Hagarty	Roper Maker	No 41?

[563] Pigots Directory of 1824
[564] Hewitt Baldwin Esq was made a freeman of Bandon Bridge in 1826.

Cornelius Hagarty	Publican	
Thomas Hales	Publican	
William Hamilton	Timber Merchant	
George Harris	Linen & Woollen Draper, Cotton Manufacturers	No 100
Mary Hayes	Earthenware Dealer	
Thomas Hornibrook Esq	Gentry	No 57
William Hunter	Grocer	No 5
Mary Hussey	Wool Card Maker	
Mrs Jenkins		Widow of Dr William Jenkins
Rev Edward King	Clergyman	
William Kingston	Tallow Chandler & Tobacconist & manufacturer	No 35
Jane McIntosh	Grocer	
Thomas Montjoy	Watchmaker	No 98?
Timothy Murphy	Tanner	
John Popham Esq	Gentry	
Denis Ring, boot and shoe maker	Boot & Shoemaker	
O.M. Roche, Esq	Gentry	
John Scannell	Publican	
Julia Scannell	Publican	
Edward Scott	Flour Factor	
James Scott	Cotton Manufacturer & Stuffs	
John Scott	Coal Dealer	
Samuel Seymour	Brazier	
William Sheltis	Baker	

William Shine	Boot & Shoemaker	No 23
John Sullivan	Tanner	Junction of Watergate St
M. Sullivan	Tallow Chandler & Tobacconist	
William Sullivan	Tanner	
John Tobin	Publican	
John Tresilian	Attorney	
John Whiting	Tallow Chandler & Tobacconist	
John Williams	Grocer	
Paul Williams	Builder	No 6
Richard Williams	Pawn Broker	

An Advertisement of 28th August 1834

TO BE LET

From the 29th of September next
THE DWELLING HOUSE, extensive Out-
offices, Garden and Two Fields adjoining, lately in the
possession of Captain Vignolles, situate in the North Main Street,
Bandon.
Application to be made to WILLIAM HUNTER, Watergate
Brewery, Bandon   Aug 28

A early list of parishioners of Christ Church, Kilbrogan who served as church wardens

1789 Richard Gillman Esq and Newth Jenkins[565]
1790 Frances Fielding and Samuel Hornibrook
1791 Robert Travers and Richard Gillman
1792 Thomas Gash and William Chambes
1793 William Chambers and Joseph Stanley
1794 John Hosford of Mishels and George Giles
1795 Richard Donovan and William Moxley
1796 William Keyms and Richard Clear
1797 Francis Hutchins and William Stanley of Carhue
1798 James Sweeny and John Wright of Kilbeg
1799 Francis Travers and Thomas Clugston
1800 Ralph Hodges and George Northridge
1801 John Wheeler and Paul Williams
1802 William Banfield and Richard Gash
1803 William Lovell and John Williams
1804 George Harris and Thomas Lovell
1805 William Young and John Bennett
1806 William Moran and Sampson Sweeny
1807 William Banfield and John Sullivan
1808 William Sullivan and William Jenkins
1809 John Scott and James Douglas
1810 Francis Beek and Maskelyne Alcock Esq of Rough Grove
1811 Francis Beek and Maskelyne Alcock Esq
1812 William Connor and Thomas Porter
1813 William Shine and James Stanley
1814 Joseph Bullen and John Williams
1815 John Hornibrook and ?
1816 George Cooper of Callatrim and William Kingston
1817 William Bull and James Dawson
1818 John Popham – second entry crossed out
1819 John Hornibrook and William Hunter
1820 Benjamin Ford and Richard Bradfield
1821 William Gash and Richard Williams
1822 Thomas Bales? and Thomas Poole?
1823 Samuel Hornibrook and John Wright

---

[565] Newth Jenkins, a watchmaker, was made a freeman of the City of Cork on 29th September, 1769

1824 John Baldwin and William Sloan
1825 William Smith and Samuel Foulks?
1826 George and Henry Cornwall
1827 Thomas Gash and Robert Fuller
1828 William Lovell and Samuel Hosford
1829 Thomas Montjoy and William Stanley of Carhue
1830 Jonas Bernard and Thomas Barter
1831 Thomas Bullen and Benjamin Thompson
1832 Benjamin Forde and Laurence Lovell
1833 John Otley and William Connor Sullivan
1834 Richard Long and Denis Rinn?
1835 James Sweeny and James Halburd
1836 Robert Tresilian Belcher and John Halburd?
1837 John Lovell and Abraham Stanley
1838 Nicholas Haines and Joseph Nash
1839 Thomas Hornibrook Sullivan and William Penrose

A List of the Proprietors of Pews in Christ Church in 1788

No 1 In the chancel. The property of John Wright of Glandore
No 2 Maskelyne Alcock Esq[566]
No 3 The Provost of Bandon for the time being
No 4 The Duke of Devonshire
No 5 Mrs Alcock, senior
No 6 Mrs Elizabeth Barry
No 7 William Rogers and William Lisson
No 8 Henry Abbott
No 9 William Sloane
No 10 John Sullivan, John Hodges and Joseph Williams
No 11 ? Dudley, ? Leonard, James Glasson
No 12 John Burchill
No 13 Richard Gash
No 14 Susanna Bull and Emanuel Hutchins
No 15 William Jenkins
No 16 Thomas Williams
No 17 William Moxley and Jane and Anne Oliffe[567]
No 18 Robert ? and George Thomas
No 19 Samuel Baldwin and Henry Hudson
No 20 John ?
No 21 J. Stanley of West Carhue
No 22 Sold to Frances Beck
No 23 Widow Clear, Richard H? and Richard Williams
No 24 George Heazle
No 25 William Keyms, senior
No 26 John Lovell
No 27 Robert Lisson
No 28 Thomas Burke
No 29 Lawrence Hornibrook
No 30 Benjamin Hales and Paul Williams
No 31 The officiating clergyman and family
No 32 The Widow Burke
No 33 George Norris, William Young
No 34 Thomas Lovell

---

[566] Of Rough Grove
[567] In 1793 William Moxley married Jane Oliffe at Ballymodan

No 35 Thomas and William Joyce
No 36 The Countess of Bandon
No 37 Richard Clear
No 38 John Bennett
No 39 George Hammett
No 40 Anne Hornibrook and John Hornibrook
No 41 Mrs Elizabeth Holland and Isaac Jones Esq
No 42 George Giles
No 43 Mrs Callehan
No 44 Major Campbell

Galleries
No 1 Rev William Sullivan – 1806
No 2 William Chambers
No 3 Edward Cotter Esq *(an attorney at law)*
No 4 Transferred to William Shine
No 5 Benjamin Shorten, senior
No 6 John Connor Esq – given to George Cooper Esq
No 7 George Cornwall Esq *(a brewer)*
No 8 Francis Fielding
No 9 Rev Charles Hewett
No 10 Newth Jenkins *(a watch and clock maker)*
No 11 James Fielding *(a linen draper)*
No 12 William Banfield

A note was added as follows: 'Thomas Banfield was assigned the seat No 1 from John Wright of Glandore Esq'

A list of Proprietors of Pews in Christ Church Kilbrogan in 1822

A change to the numbering of the pews took place in 1822.

No 1 Dr Clerke
No 2 John Tresilian. 1829 Miss Penrose
No 3 William Giles. 1829 Thomas Montjoy
No 4 Mrs Sealy.   1829 John Tresilian and Robert T. Belcher
No 5 Thomas Hornibrook. 1829 Henry Cornwall Esq
No 6 George Hammett
No 7 Richard Bradfield
No 8 George Harris
No 9 Earl of Bandon. 1829 Lady Bernard
No 10 William Joyce and brothers
No 11 Thomas Lovell
No 12 Joseph Dawson
No 13 Earl of Bandon. 1829 Hannah Blood
No 14 Officiating clergy
No 15 John Wheeler
No 16 Thomas Hales & Paul Williams. 1829 Paul Williams alone
No 17 John Hornibrook. 1829 James Dawson
No 18 Poor. 1829 Anne Forde
No 19 John Lovell & William Connor. 1829 James Craig
No 20 Robert Burchill. 1829 Free
No 21 George Heazle. 1829 Free
No 22 Richard Williams. 1829 Free
No 23 Poor. 1829 Free
No 24 George Forde 1829 Free
No 25 David Bush & John Norris. 1829 William Brooks, John Palmer
No 26 Widow Moxly. 1829 Richard Williams
No 27 John Williams. 1829 David Bush and James Norris
No 28 The Jenkins Family
No 29 John Wright and Widow Bull
No 30 Captain Miller
No 31 William Topham. 1829 Rev John Browne
No 32 Ralph Clear & Widow Dudley. 1829 Francis Clear &Widow Dudley
No 33 Widow Hurley, Richard Williams & Samuel Sullivan. 1829 Samuel Sullivan & Abraham Loane
No 34 Strangers
No 35 William Sloane

No 36 Widow Turner and William Hornibrook
No 37 George Burtles
No 38 Maskelyne Alcock
No 39 Duke of Devonshire
No 40 Maskelyne Alcock
No 41 Charles Murray

Galleries
No 1 Childrens Gallery
No 2 Childrens Gallery
No 3 William Jenkins
No 4 William Sullivan
No 5 Rev William Sullivan
No 6 James Stanley
No 7 George Cornwall
No 8 Dr Jenkins
No 9 Joseph Bullen
No 10 William Shine
No 11 William Banfield
No 13 William Hunter
No 14 John Shine
No 15 Benjamin Forde
No 16 George Cooper
No 17 Mrs Sullivan
No 18 John Scott
No 19 Charles Hewett
No 20 Mrs Baldwin
No 21 John Harley
No 22 Jas. Baldwin, Jonas Bernard
No 23 Benjamin Popham
No 24 William Kingston
No 25 William Connor
No 26 Dr Belcher
No 27 John Sullivan
No 28 Childrens Gallery
No 29 Childrens Gallery
A note in the vestry minutes dated 5th May 1834 stated that pew
No 5, the property of the late Thomas Hornibrook Esq was
registered in the name of Benjamin Thompson, he having
purchased it from the heirs of Thomas Hornibrook

On 6th July 1833 William Jenkins sold his seat in the south gallery
No 3 to John Lovell.

Bibliography

Barry, John. *The Duke of Devonshire's Irish Estates 1794-97* Analecta Hibernica 22 (1960)

Barnard, Toby. *A New Anatomy of Ireland. The Irish Protestants, 1649-1770*

Bennett, George. *The History of Bandon and the Principal Towns in the West Riding of County Cork (Cork 1869)*

Brady, William Maziere. *Clerical and Parochial Records of Cork, Cloyne and Ross (1863)*

Butler, David J & Williams, Alwyn C. *Two Hundred & Seventy Five Years of Freemasonry in Bandon. (2013)*

Cole, John Harding. *Church and Parish Records of Cork, Cloyne and Ross. (1903)*

Dickson, David. *Old World Colony. Cork and South Munster 1630-1830.*

Donnelly James. *Nineteenth Century Cork: Its Land and People (1975)*

Dooley, Terence. *The Big Houses and Landed Estates of Ireland*

Grove White, Colonel James. *Historical and Topographical Notes etc. on Buttevant, Doneraile, Mallow and places in their vicinity. (1906-1915)*

Hodges, Rev Richard T. *Cork and County Cork in the Twentieth Century (1911)*

Kelly, Cornelius. *The Grand Tour of Cork*

Lewis's Cork. *A Topographical Dictionary of the Parishes, Towns and Villages of Cork City and County*

McCulloch, John Ramsay. *A Dictionary, Geographical, Statistical and Historical of the various countries, places and principal natural objects in the world. (1852)*

O'Flanagan, Patrick. *Irish Historic Towns Atlas. Bandon. Royal Irish Academy*

Prentice, Sidney A. and Mildred M. *Bear and Forbear.*

Proudfoot, Lindsay. *The Management of a Great Estate. Patronage, Income and Expenditure in the Duke of Devonshire's Irish Property c1816 to 1891. Irish Economic and Social History, xiii (1986) pp32-55*

Proudfood, Lindsay. *Urban Patronage and Social Authority. The Management of the Duke of Devonshire's Towns in Ireland 1764-1891 (Washington DC, 1995)*

Proudfoot, Lindsay. *Landlord Motivation and Urban Improvement on the Duke of Devonshire's Irish Esates c1792-1832. Irish Economic and Social History, xviii (1991), pp 5-23*
Spillar, W. *A Short Topographical and Statistical Account of the Bandon Union.*
The Council Book of the Borough of Bandon Bridge 1765-1840

Directories
Lucas Directory. 1787
Pigot's Directory. 1824
Slater's Directories. 1846, 1856, 1870, 1881
Coghlan's General Directory. 1867
Guy's Directories. 1875, 1883, 1886 1893, 1914
Kelly's Directory of Leather Traders. 1915
Bandon Historical Journals
Cork Historical and Archaeological Society Journals

Manuscripts and Collections
Registry of Deeds
Numerous Deeds

National Library of Ireland
Lismore Estate Papers.
Pedigrees

Cork Archives
Doherty Estate Papers

Irish Genealogical Research Society
Pedigrees

Society of Genealogists, London
Pedigrees

Representative Church Body
Church of Ireland Registers and Vestry Minutes

National Archives of Ireland
Pre-Valuation Records

Valuation Office
Valuation Records

INDEX OF NAMES

Bogue, James, 227
Bonham, Edith, 347
Bourk, Thomas, 239
Bourke, R., 275
Bowen, Henrietta Cole, 259, 353, 359
Bowen, Henry Cole, 352, 353, 359
Bowen, John Henry Cole, 359
Bowen, Miss Mary Cole, 202
Bowen, Mrs, 65, 68
Bowen, Nicholas Cole, 181, 353
Bowen, Rev Nicholas Cole, 259, 352
Bowen, Robert, 353
Bowen, Robert Travers Cole, 259
Bowman, Henry, 10
Boylan, Annie, 191
Boylan, Mary, 191
Boylan, Rita, 191
Boyle, Thomas, 226
Bradfield, James, 269
Bradfield, Mary Shorten, 295
Bradfield, Rebecca, 105, 271
Bradfield, Richard, 295
Bradfield, Susan, 295
Bradfield, Thomas, 84
Bradish, Mrs, 232
Bradshaw, Benjamin, 189
Bradshaw, Mary, 189
Bradshaw, Mrs, 223
Bradshaw, Sarah Elizabeth, 250
Brady, Richard Cole, 73, 74, 77, 78, 80
Brangan, Elizabeth, 191, 198
Brangan, John, 190, 198, 268
Brangan, John G., 198
Brangan, Margaret, 190
Brangan, Marmaduke, 190, 191, 197, 205, 251, 268
Brangan, Mary Martha, 191
Brangan, Richard John, 190
Brangan, Sarah, 198
Brangan, Thomas George, 191
Brash, Richard, 251
Breck, Dora, 156
Brennan, Joseph, 185, 226, 243
Brennan, Joseph, junior, 186
Brennan, Peter, 143
Brennan, Thomas, 185
Brett, Alexander, 164
Brett, Charles Tyndall Gore, 164
Brett, Charlotte Catherine, 164
Brett, Francis Hingston, 164

Brett, Hannah Tyndall Gore, 164
Brett, John Septimus, 164
Brett, Pilkington Jessop, 164
Brett, William Gore, 162, 164, 205, 231
Brewster, William, 197
Brien, Mary, 145
Brien, Michael, 287
Brookes, William Thomas, 78
Brophy, Robert J., 107
Brown, Rev, 304
Brown, Rev Thomas, 103, 106
Brown, Rev Thomas Adderly, 183
Browne, Edward, 183
Browne, Jemmett, 183
Browne, Miss, 258
Browne, Rev Dr St John, 90, 91, 182, 349
Bruce, Annie E., 191
Bryan, Thomas, 335, 343
Buckley, Daniel, 114, 306
Buckley, Ellen, 114
Buckley, John, 114, 248, 263, 268
Buckley, John , Senior, 112
Buckley, John, junior, 110
Buckley, John, Senior, 110
Buckley, Sean, 114
Buckley, Thomas, 113, 115
Bull, Ellen, 134
Bull, William, 335, 345
Bullen, Henry, 270
Bullen, Jane Beamish, 270
Bullen, Joseph, 21, 277
Bullen, Walter, 103, 104, 269
Burchill, John, 61, 273, 321
Burchill, Rachel, 112
Burchill, Samuel, 308
Burchill, Sarah, 309
Burchill, Solomon, 25
Burke, Catherine, 162
Burke, Henry, 162
Burke, James, 198
Burke, John, 50
Burke, Mary, 175
Burns, Albert B., 258
Bushe, David, 21, 119, 121, 122
Bushe, Jane, 121
Bushe, Thomas, 119, 120, 121, 122
Buttermore, Robert, 222
Buttimer, Paul, 172, 228
Buttimere, William, 290
Buttimore, Abraham, 291

Lordan, James, 98
Lordan, Mary, 98
Lordan, Minnie, 59
Love, Major Herbert Esq, 25, 88,
    342
Lovell, Annie, 206
Lovell, Elizabeth, 51, 53
Lovell, Jane, 53
Lovell, John, 51, 52, 53, 92
Lovell, Mary, 57, 61
Lovell, Samuel, 206
Lovell, Thomas, 56
Lovell, Thomas Esq, 56
Lovell, William, 19, 51, 52, 53, 57, 61
Lovell, William Esq, 56, 60, 72
Lovett, Rev Verney, 92
Lucas, Captain Henry, 208
Lucas, Henry, 164
Lucas, Thomas, 65
Lynam, Michael, 275
Lynch, Anne, 102
Lynch, Bridget, 102
Lynch, Cornelius, 126
Lynch, D, Reps of, 119
Lynch, Dennis, 114
Lynch, Hannah, 222
Lynch, Humphrey, 145
Lynch, James, 198
Lynch, Jeremiah, 102
Lynch, John, 102
Lynch, Julia, 102
Lynch, Katie, 222
Lynch, Mary, 102, 222
Lynch, Stephen, 222
Lynch, Timothy, 289
Lyons, Frank, 83
Lyons, George, 150, 228, 246
Lyons, John, 63
Lyster, Frederick, 311
MacCarthy, Catherine, 145
MacCarthy, Margaret M., 150
MacEnerny, Maurice Francis, 158
Macklin, Joseph, 96
Magnihan, Mary, 211
Magrath, Dr, 147
Maguire, Anne, 264
Maher, P., 170
Mahoney, Jeremiah, 50
Mahony, Bartholomew, 110
Mahony, Ellen, 224
Mahony, Hannah, 111
Mahony, Jack, 289

Mahony, James, 100, 202
Mahony, Johanna, 180, 181
Mahony, Mary, 48, 111
Mahony, Thomas, 293
Mahony, Timothy, 249, 250, 309
Manning, Kate, 83
Marshall, Johanna, 80
Mason, Alfred, 302
Massey, Catherine, 276
Massy, Oswald M., 234
Mathew, Ellen, 169, 171
Maunsell, Susanna, 369
Maunsell, William, 346
Mayne, Anna Julia, 179
Mayne, Emily, 178
Mayne, Frederick, 179
Mayne, Miss E., 179
McCabe, J.P., 232
McCarthy, Amelia, 150
McCarthy, Annie, 102
McCarthy, Catherine, 146
McCarthy, Charles, 86, 147, 273
McCarthy, Charles G., 274
McCarthy, Cornelius, 76, 185
McCarthy, Daniel, 286
McCarthy, Denis, 159
McCarthy, Eugene, 190
McCarthy, G, 83
McCarthy, Hannah, 100
McCarthy, Honora, 190
McCarthy, James, 100
McCarthy, Johanna, 165
McCarthy, John J., 274
McCarthy, Kathleen, 185
McCarthy, Lily, 185
McCarthy, Margaret M., 150
McCarthy, Marie, 185
McCarthy, Michael, 180
McCarthy, Miss, 149
McCarthy, P.J., 144
McCarthy, Patrick, 104, 185
McCarthy, Rev Denis, 147
McCarthy, Sarah, 104, 105, 141, 145,
    146, 147, 273
McCarthy, Thomas, 100
McCarthy, Widow, 150
McClellan, Rev Robert, 89, 338
McClelland, Mary E., 141
McConkey, J., 174
McConnell, Henry, 194
McCreight, Mary Baldwin, 224
McCreight, Valentine, 143

13966593R00232

Printed in Great Britain
by Amazon.co.uk, Ltd.,
Marston Gate.